THE PIONEER:

OR,

CALIFORNIA MONTHLY MAGAZINE,

EDITED BY F. C. EWER.

VOL. III. JAN. TO JUNE, 1855.

SAN FRANCISCO, CAL.:
PUBLISHED BY LE COUNT AND STRONG.
Monson & Valentine, Steam Book & Job Printers, 127 Sansome St.
1855.

AMS PRESS, INC.
NEW YORK
1966

AMS PRESS, INC.
New York, N.Y. 10003
1966

Manufactured in the United States of America

CONTENTS OF VOLUME III.

ORIGINAL PROSE ARTICLES.

Page.

Annie Seabrook. By EDWARD POLLOCK............................. 129
A Pair of Myths. By CAXTON...................................... 321
A California Lady's Opinion of Fanny Fern........................... 363
California in 1852. By SHIRLEY. Letter Twelve...................... 80
    "   "   "   "   "   Thirteen..................... 145
    "   "   "   "   "   Fourteen 216
    "   "   "   "   "   Fifteen...................... 305
    "   "   "   "   "   Sixteen and Seventeen.......... 354
Chinese Letters. Translated by QUELP............................. 161
Epitome of theTragedy of Faust. By JOHN S. HITTELL.................. 204
Finance.. 16
Facts—Not Fiction. By MRS. S. A. DOWNER.......................... 332
Going—Gone. By J. P. ANTHONY................................... 24
Hints on the Moral Influence of the Commercial Spirit of the Age. By W. A.
    SCOTT, D. D... 150
Law Review—Abstract Decisions of Supreme Court,.................... 42
    "   "   "   "   "   "   232
My Grandmother's Kitchen. By J. SWETT,........................... 35
Monthly Summary of Events from November 8, to December 1,............ 45
    "   "   "   " December 2, to December 28,........... 110
    "   "   "   " December 29, to February 13,........... 169
    "   "   "   " February 14, to March 8,.............. 237
    "   "   "   " March 9, to May 24,................. 368
Our Streets: The Chinese—The Candy Man. By J. P. ANTHONY,......... 75
Old Harvard. By OUTIS,... 300
Pacific Souvenirs. By J. N. APPLETON,.............................. 249
Republication of "The Eventful Nights of August 20th and 21st," Etc. By
    F. C. EWER,.. 257
Rest. By OLIVER OUTCAST,... 87
State Rights. By B. S. BROOKS,.................................... 1
Scientific: Fossil Remains,... 39
    "   The Coast Survey of the United States,...................... 99
    "   Meteors and Metoric Showers,............................ 167
    "   Geological Formation of the Great Cave in Calaveras,........... 236
Somewhat of the History and Geology of the Mines,.................... 311
The Poems of Alfred Tennyson. By CHARLES E. HAVENS,............... 28
The Nature and Influence of Poetry. By CHARLES E. HAVENS,........... 65
The Seasons in California. By A. H. B.,............................. 96
The Great Order of the Cave. By F. C. EWER,........................ 194
The Strange House of Dolgelly. By J. P. ANTHONY,................... 221
The War in Europe,.. 291
The Halls of the Past,.. 329
The old School-House. By J. SWETT,............................... 361

ORIGINAL POEMS.

                                                                             Page.
Boat Song.   By G.,.. 220
California.   By Mrs. L. H. Sigourney,................................ 23
Dreamy Reverie.   By J. Swett,.. 290
Elegy upon the Death of a Beloved Father.   By Fred. Crichton,......... 38
Ella Robb,.. 74
Faith.   By R. W. F.,... 85
Home Pictures.   By J. Sweet,.. 360
Invocation at Midnight.   By Edward Pollock,........................... 149
Lines on Hearing a Bell Tolling the Midnight Hour.   By D. M. J........... 15
Love,... 79
Life.   By G.,.. 144
Lines Suggested by the View from Telegraph Hill.   By J. P. Anthony..... 230
Musicians Going to California.   By Mrs. L. H. Sigourney,............... 95
My Love is an Angel.   By J. A. Nunes,....................................... 313
Off Cape Horn.   By Lawrie,... 290
Ode to Imagination.   By C. E. Havens,...................................... 353
Song of a Chrysalis.   By G.,.. 304
The Absent One.   By Mrs. E. V. P.,.. 23
To My Mother.   By W. C. P.,... 27
These be Thy Gods, O Israel.   By Luof...................................... 84
The Soul Unto Herself.   By F. C. Ewer...................................... 85
The Child and Flower.   By J. P. Anthony................................... 160
The Two Serenades.. 166
To Sallie.   By G.. 203
The Pagan Chalice.. 231
The Golden Gate.   By Caxton.. 299
To Minnie Spear.   By Shortfellow.. 310
The Poet's Life.   By J. Swett.. 328
The Mist of the Morning... 331
The Mariner.   By Samuel Webb.. 348
The Hills of Contra Costa.   By Caxton...................................... 367

—

EDITOR'S TABLE.

Gossip with Readers and Correspondents............57, 115, 182, 250, 316, 375
Musical and Theatrical, from Nov. 25, to Dec. 20.......................... 51
    "   "   " Dec. 21, to Mar. 20........................ 243
    "   "   " Mar. 21, to April 23....................... 314
    "   "   " April 24, to May 27........................ 374
Official Report of Prof. John Phœnix, A. M............................... 173
The Crime of Delay.   By Oliver Outcast................................... 240
The Lily of the Valley.   By S. C. Massett................................ 48
The Knickerbocker Gallery... 114

THE PIONEER.

VOL. III.]   JANUARY, 1855.   [No. 1.

STATE RIGHTS.

BY B. S. B.

THE unanimous opinion of the Supreme Court of California, delivered by Heydenfeldt, J., during the October Term of 1854, in the case
of Geo. Gordon, Appellant, *vs.* J. W. Johnson, Sheriff, Respondent,
is of so extraordinary a character, and involves possible results of so
serious a nature, as to be well calculated to stir the apprehension, and
awaken our citizens to a calm, thoughtful consideration of the relative
powers of the State and Federal Courts.

The defendant, upon the allegation that he is an alien, moved the
Court below to transfer the case to the District Court of the United
States, which was refused, and the refusal was assigned as error. With
this question an application was, also, considered, which had been
made in the case of Eldridge *vs.* Crowell, for a writ of error to this
Court from the Supreme Court of the United States, which was refused from the bench.

The conclusions arrived at by our Supreme Court were as follows,
viz:

1. That no cause can be transferred from a State Court to any
Court of the United States.

2. That neither a Writ of Error nor Appeal lies, to take a case
from a State Court to the Supreme Court of the United States.

In coming to this conclusion, the Court "state as axiomatic, that
the States are original sovereigns, with all powers of sovereignty not
expressly delegated by the Federal compact; that the Federal Government is a government of none but expressly delegated powers; and
that each is absolute and beyond the control or interference of the
other, within the sphere of its respective powers."

Starting upon such premises as "axioms," it is not at all surprising, that the Supreme Court should arrive at the above mentioned conclusions. But we cannot consider their propositions as axiomatic. The last statement, claimed to be an axiom is, if we understand it, the very question in dispute : "that each is *absolute and beyond* the control or interference of the other within the sphere of its respective powers. Is not that the question ? Whether the State within the sphere of its judicial power *is* absolute and beyond the control or interference of the Judiciary of the General Government ? But whether it is or is not, clearly a position upon which Hamilton, Story and Marshall have spent so much argument, and which the Supreme Court of the United States have unanimously decided to be erroneous, cannot be considered as axiomatic in any sense.

What is meant precisely by the States being "original sovereigns," is somewhat obscure. If by that term is meant the several State Governments, it certainly is not true. It is the people, who are the original sovereign. Nor is it true, that all powers of sovereignty, not expressly delegated by the Federal compact, remain in the State Governments. All power originally resides in the original sovereign, *the people ;* and they are still possessed of all the power they have not delegated. Part of this power is delegated to the General Government, part of it to the State Government, and the residue is still in the people. The General Government does not derive its power, as the Confederation did, from the *States;* it derives it from *the people,*—from the same source that the State Governments derive their powers,— and is, therefore, not a government of simply delegated powers, in the sense of an attorney or ordinary trustee; it is a government of delegated powers, in the sense that all governments are, which derive their powers from the people, and not by divine right. The true position is more properly stated by Justice Story, in the case of Martin *vs.* Hunter's Lessees, before the Supreme Court of the United States, 1 Wheaton's Rep., p. 324: "The Constitution of the United States was ordained and established, not by the States in their sovereign capacities, but emphatically, as the preamble of the Constitution declares, "by the people of the United States." There can be no doubt that it was competent to the people to invest the General Government with all the powers which they might deem proper and necessary; to extend or restrain these powers according to their own good pleasure, and to give them a paramount and supreme authority. As little doubt can there be, that the people had a right to prohibit to the States the exercise of any powers which were, in their judgment, incompatible with the objects of the general compact; to make the powers of the State Governments, in given cases, subordinate to those of the nation, or to reserve to themselves those sovereign authorities, which they might not choose to delegate to either. The Constitution was not, therefore, necessarily carved out of existing State sovereignties, nor a surrender of powers already existing in State institutions; for the powers of the States depend upon their own Constitutions, and the people of every State had the right to modify and restrain them according to their own views of policy or principle. On the other hand, it is perfectly clear, that the sovereign powers, vested in the State Governments by their respective Constitutions, remain unaltered and unimpaired, except so far as they were granted to the Government of the United States.

These deductions do not rest upon general reasoning, plain and obvious as they may seem to be. They have been positively recognized by one of the articles in amendment of the Constitution, which declares, that ' the powers not delegated to the United States by the Constitution, nor prohibited by it to the States, are reserved to the *States*, respectively, or *to the people.*'

The Government then of the United States can claim no powers which are not granted to it by the Constitution; and the powers actually granted must be such as are expressly given, or given by necessary implication. On the other hand, this instrument, like every other grant, is to have a reasonable construction, according to the import of its terms; and where a power is expressly given in general terms, it is not to be restrained to particular cases, unless that construction grow out of the context expressly or by necessary implication. The words are to be taken in their natural and obvious sense, and not in a sense unreasonably restricted or enlarged."

This appears to us a much more fair and proper statement of the case than that given by Justice Heydenfeldt. But, however this may be, the propositions laid down by the latter as the bases of his reasoning are certainly not axiomatic.

The learned Judge starts out with the assertion, that "at an early period, Hamilton, in the *Federalist*, and afterwards Story and Johnson, in the case of Martin's Heirs *vs.* Hunter's Lessees, have given us the argument in favor of the extent of power claimed for the Federal Judiciary. This was followed by the same reasoning in Story's Commentaries on the Constitution. On the other side of the question, we have, in the case above stated, the exposition of the Supreme Court of Virginia, and the argument of Mr. Calhoun, in his discourse on the Constitution and Government of the United States. We have read carefully on both sides, and, *convinced as we are by the reasoning of the latter, we are forced to the adoption of his conclusions.*"

If this were a statement of all the authority on either side, it would still seem somewhat remarkable, that any Court would find greater authority or force in the reasoning even of John C. Calhoun, than in the unanimous decision of the Supreme Court of the United States. But a more critical examination of the weight of the authorities, and of their number, will make the conclusion of our Supreme Court appear the more extraordinary.

In the first place, Hamilton was one of the framers and advocates of the instrument itself, and stood not alone in his exposition of its meaning. Upon this subject Justice Story says, 1 Wheaton, 351,

" It is an historical fact, that this exposition of the Constitution, extending its appellate power to State Courts, was, *previous to its adoption, uniformly and publicly avowed by its friends, and admitted by its enemies,* as the basis of their respective reasonings, both in and out of

the State Conventions. It is an historical fact, that at the time when
the Judiciary act was submitted to the deliberations of the first Congress, composed, as it was, not only of men of great learning and
ability, but of men *who had acted a principal part in framing, supporting or opposing that Constitution, the same exposition was explicitly
declared and admitted by the friends and by the opponents of that system.* It is an historical fact, that the Supreme Court of the United
States have, from time to time, sustained this appellate jurisdiction in
a great variety of cases, brought from the tribunals of many of the
most important States in the Union, and that *no State tribunal has
ever breathed a judicial doubt on the subject, or declined to obey the man-
date of the Supreme Court, until the present occasion.*"

Mr. Pinkney, *arguendo*, in the case of Cohens *vs.* Virginia, in the
Supreme Court of the United States, 6 Wheaton, 351, says,—

"The Judiciary Act of 1789, c. 20, contains *a cotemporaneous construction* in this respect of great weight, considering who were the
authors of that act; and which has been since confirmed by the repeated decisions of this Court, constantly exercising the jurisdiction in
question. This legislative and judicial exposition has been acquiesced
in, since no attempt has ever been made to repeal the law upon the
grounds of its repugnancy to the Constitution. *Transiit in rem judi-
catam.* But even before the Constitution was adopted, and whilst it
was submitted to public discussion, this interpretation was given to it
by its friends, who were anxious to avoid every objection which could
render it obnoxious to State jealousy. But they well knew that this
interpretation was unavoidable, and the authors of the celebrated letters of Publius, or the *Federalist*, have stated it in explicit terms."

Chief Justice Marshall, in the same case, holds the following language, viz :—

"Great weight has always been attached, and very rightly attached,
to contemporaneous exposition. No question, it is believed, has arisen,
to which this principle applies more unequivocally than to that now
under consideration. The opinion of the *Federalist* has always been
considered as of great authority. It is a complete commentary on our
Constitution, and is appealed to by all parties in the questions to
which that instrument has given birth. Its intrinsic merit entitled it
to this high rank, and the part two of its authors performed in framing the Constitution, puts it very much in their power to explain the
views with which it was framed. These essays, having been published
while the Constitution was before the nation for adoption or rejection,
and having been written in answer to objections founded entirely on
the extent of its powers and on its diminution of State sovereignty,
are entitled to the more consideration, where they frankly avow that
the power objected to is given, and defend it. In discussing the
extent of the judicial power, the *Federalist* says, ' Here another question occurs: What relation would subsist between the National and
State Courts in these instances of concurrent jurisdiction ? I answer,
that *an appeal would certainly lie from the latter to the Supreme Court
of the United States.* The Constitution in direct terms gives an appellate jurisdiction to the Supreme Court in all the enumerated cases of

federal cognizance in which it is not to have an original one, without a single expression to confine its operation to the inferior Federal Courts. The *objects* of appeal, not the *tribunals* from which it is to be made, are alone contemplated. From this circumstance, and from the reason of the thing, it ought to be construed to extend to the State tribunals. Either this must be the case, or the local Courts must be excluded from a concurrent jurisdiction in matters of national concern; else the judicial authority of the Union may be eluded at the pleasure of every plaintiff or prosecutor. Neither of these consequences ought, without evident necessity, to be involved. The latter would be entirely inadmissible, as it would defeat some of the most important and avowed purposes of the proposed government, and would essentially embarrass its measures. Nor do I perceive any foundation for such a supposition. Agreeably to the remark already made, the National and State systems are to be regarded as *one whole*. The Courts of the latter will of course be natural auxiliaries to the execution of the laws of the Union, and an appeal from them will as naturally lie to that tribunal, which is destined to unite and assimilate the principles of natural justice and the rules of national decision. The evident aim of the plan of the National Convention is, that all the causes of the specified classes shall, for weighty public reasons, receive their original or final determination in the Courts of the Union. To confine, therefore, the general expressions, which give appellate jurisdiction to the Supreme Court, to appeals from the subordinate Federal Courts, instead of allowing their extension to the State Courts, would be to abridge the latitude of the terms in subversion of the intent, contrary to every sound rule of interpretation.'

A contemporaneous exposition of the Constitution, certainly of not less authority than that which has been just cited, is the judiciary act itself. We know that in the Congress which passed this act, were many eminent members of the Convention which formed the Constitution. Not a single individual, so far as is known, supposed that part of the act, which gives the Supreme Court appellate jurisdiction over the judgments of the State Courts in the cases therein specified, to be unauthorized by the Constitution.

While on this part of the argument, it may be also material to observe, that the uniform decisions of this Court on the point now under consideration have been assented to, with a single exception, by the Courts of every State in the Union, whose judgments have been revised. It has been the unwelcome duty of this tribunal to reverse the judgments of many State Courts, in cases in which the strongest State feelings were engaged. Judges, whose talents and character would grace any bench, to whom a disposition to submit to jurisdiction that is usurped, or to surrender their legitimate powers will certainly not be imputed, have yielded without hesitation to the authority by which their judgments were reversed, while they, perhaps, disapproved the judgment of reversal.

This concurrence of statesmen, of legislators and of judges in the same construction of the Constitution may justly inspire some confidence in that construction."

Thus says Chief Justice Marshall, in delivering the unanimous opinion of the Supreme Court of the United States in the case of Cohens *vs.* Virginia, decided in 1821.

It will be perceived, that this argument does not rest upon the weight of the reasoning of Hamilton, but on the *fact* that this construction and explanation of the Constitution was thus publicly avowed by its friends before it was adopted; and it was under this explanation, and with this understanding, that the people and the States adopted that Constitution.

The authorities, then, in support of this appellate jurisdiction, may be stated thus:

1. That this was the opinion of those who framed the instrument, as avowed in their organ of unquestioned authority, the *Federalist*, by themselves.

2. That this was the interpretation laid before the people at the time they were deliberating upon its adoption, and was the understanding with which they adopted it.

3. The contemporaneous exposition given to it by the Congress of 1789, which included among its members a large number of those who assisted in framing the instrument.

4. The uniform acquiescence of all the State tribunals, with the exception of the two solitary cases coming from the State of Virginia, which were reversed by the Supreme Court of the United States, covering a period of 65 years.

5. The elaborate opinion of Justice Story, in the case of Martin *vs.* Hunter's Lessees, 1 Wheaton, 323, delivered in the Supreme Court of the United States, March 20, 1816, and unanimously concurred in by Chief Justice John Marshall, and Justices Washington, William Johnson, Brockholst Livingston, Thomas Todd, and Duvall.

6. The elaborate opinion of Chief Justice John Marshall, in the case of Cohens *vs.* Virginia, 6 Wheaton, 375, delivered in the Supreme Court of the United States, March 3, 1820, and unanimously concurred in by the whole Court, consisting of the same members as in the former case.

Such a weight of authority ought to set the question *forever and finally at rest.* What authorities, then, have the Supreme Court of this State, to sustain them in the decision which they have made? As they state them in their opinion, they are—

1. The decision of the Supreme Court of Virginia in the case of Martin *vs.* Hunter's Lessees, which was reversed by the Supreme Court of the United States, and completely refuted.

2. The argument of John C. Calhoun, in his discourse on the Government and Constitution of the United States.

The authority of the first decision of the Supreme Court of Virginia ought not to be placed in comparison with that of the Supreme Court of the United States. As to the reasoning of that Court, it would be an idle waste of words to attempt any examination of it, after the thorough examination and refutation which it has received from the Supreme Court of the United States.

But there is an historical fact which ought to be mentioned in connection with this decision. In 1809, the State of Pennsylvania proposed an amendment to the Constitution of the United States, by the appointment of an impartial tribunal to decide disputes between the Federal and State Judiciaries. In the Senate of the Commonwealth of Virginia it was referred to a committee, who (Jan. 26, 1810,) reported unanimously against it; their report was unanimously agreed to by the Senate; and they resolved "that a tribunal is already provided by the Constitution of the United States to wit: The Supreme Court, more eminently qualified from their habits and duties, from the mode of their selection, and from the terms of their offices, than any other tribunal which could be created. The members of the Supreme Court are selected from those in the United States who are most celebrated for virtue and learning, not at the will of a single individual, but by the concurrent wishes of the President and Senate of the United States. They will, therefore, have no local prejudices and partialities. The duties they have to perform, lead them necessarily to the most enlarged and accurate acquaintance with the jurisdiction of the Federal and several State Courts, together with the admirable symmetry of our government. The tenure of their offices enables them to pronounce the sound and correct opinions they may have formed, without fear, favor or partiality. The amendment proposed by Pennsylvania seems to be founded upon the idea, that the Federal Judiciary will, from a lust of power, enlarge their jurisdiction to the total annihilation of the jurisdiction of the State Courts : that they will exercise their will instead of the law and Constitution. This argument, if it proves anything, would operate more strongly against the tribunal proposed to be created, which promises so little, than against the Supreme Court, which, for the reasons above given, have every thing connected with their appointment calculated to insure confidence. * * * * The creation of a tribunal such as is proposed * * * * * would tend rather to invite than prevent a collision between the Federal and State Courts. It might, also, become, in process of time, a serious and dangerous embarrassment to the operations of the General Government." The House unanimously concurred.

These resolutions were passed in the same year that the writ of error in the case of Martin *vs.* Hunter's Lessees, was granted by the Court of Appeals, to remove the case to the Supreme Court of the United States, and shows very clearly, that neither the Legislature nor the Judiciary of that State entertained any such opinions, as were afterwards promulgated by the Court of Appeals, when the case came back to them. A judgment rendered under such circumstances is entitled to very little weight as an authority.

We do not wish to detract from the eminent position of John C. Calhoun as a patriot or statesman. But on a question of judicial construction, his course savored too strongly of the partizan for his State, to entitle his opinion to that weight and consideration due to the unanimous opinion of the Supreme Federal Court.

Where, then, are the authorities which the Supreme Court cites to sustain its decision in the case under discussion ? a decision which astonished the bar and the bench, and fills the mind of every good citizen with apprehension. For, in such a rule, we see ourselves deprived of every means of enforcing those provisions of the Constitution of the United States, which are intended for the protection of the rights of the few against the power of the majority.

Upon this subject Chief Justice Marshall expresses our views exactly: " The questions presented to the Court by the two first points made at the bar, are of great magnitude. and may be truly said vitally to affect the Union. They exclude the inquiry, whether the Constitution and laws of the United States have been violated by the judgment, which the plaintiffs in error seek to review, and maintain that, admitting such violation, it is not in the power of the government to apply a corrective. They maintain, that the nation does not possess a department capable of restraining peaceably, and by authority of law, any attempts which may be made by a part against the legitimate powers of the whole, and that the government is reduced to the alternative of submitting to such attempts, or of resisting them by force. They maintain, that the Constitution of the United States has provided no tribunal for the final construction of itself, or of the laws or treaties of the nation, but that this power may be exercised, in the last resort, by the Courts of every State in the Union. That the Constitution, laws and treaties may receive as many constructions as there are States, and that this is not a mischief, or, if a mischief, is irremediable. There, abstract propositions are to be determined; for he who demands decision without permitting inquiry, affirms that the decision he asks does not depend upon inquiry."

Having thus examined the weight of authority, we will look a moment at the reasoning of the Court. Judge Heydenfeldt says,—

" We have considered the suggestion that the power claimed has been acquiesced in by most, if not all the other States, and, generally, without any attempt to question or resist it; but we see no sufficient reason in this fact, for the surrender of a power which belongs to the sovereignty we represent, involving an assumption of power by another jurisdiction in derogation of that sovereignty."

We were not present at the argument of this cause, but we do not believe there is any lawyer at the bar of this State, who is fool enough to advance any such *fact* as a reason or justification for a surrender of any sovereign attribute. It is a falsification of the argument. The fact of this universal concurrence on the part of all the States, from the adoption of the Constitution to the present time, in one interpretation of the Constitution, is strong, if not conclusive evidence to any reasonable mind, that such is the proper construction. It is not advanced as a reason for the surrender of a power, but to show that no such power, in fact, exists. But further—

" We think, too, that the acquiescence in this usurpation of the Federal Tribunal, under an Act of Congress, not warranted by the Constitution, is not so much owing to a conviction of its propriety, as it is to the high character of the Court and the general correctness of its decisions."

This cannot be, because this construction of the Constitution was given first by the Congress who passed the law immediately upon the adoption of the Constitution; and, secondly, because the State Judiciary gave this construction to the Constitution, by allowing numerous writs of error to the Supreme Court of the United States, before that Court had taken any action under the law.

"Looking at both from a common point of view, it would seem singular how either one could stretch its arm in restraint upon the other, except in the event of a palpable usurpation, [Who is to judge of this usurpation?] and yet this is certainly attempted by the Judiciary Act of 1789. The governments of both original and delegated powers [neither of them possess any other than delegated powers,] bear the resemblance, in their practical organization, of having their powers distributed into executive, legislative and judicial departments. If the act in question had given power to the executive of the United States to control or revise the conduct of the State executive, or to Congress the power of assent or dissent to the acts of a State Legislature, there would have been but one voice in denouncing it; because the practical effect would have been more apparent. Yet, in fact, the control attempted to be given to the Federal Court over the State Courts, is of just the same importance, and as much in violation of the sovereignty of the States. ' Because,' says Mr. Calhoun, ' as the laws and acts of the government and its departments can, if opposed, reach the people individually only through the Courts, to whatever extent the Judiciary of the United States is made paramount to that of the individual States, to the same extent will the legislative and executive departments of the Federal Government; and thus the entire government itself will be made paramount to the legislative and executive departments, and the entire governments of the individual States.' And, again, ' If the State Courts stand in the relation of inferiors to the Supreme Court of the United States, what reason can possibly be assigned why the other departments of the State Governments, the legislative and executive, shall not stand in the same relation to the corresponding department of the Federal Government?' "

Now the Constitution of the United States is paramount to that of the States. The powers granted thereby are paramount; and, where the one conflicts with the other, the State Constitution yields. We cannot well see how the legislative powers can conflict. The Executive may, and we are under the impression that they have conflicted on several occasions. General Jackson, on one very celebrated occasion, employed the Executive power of the Union to coerce the Executive power of a Sovereign State, and we never heard the propriety of the act questioned out of that State. Granting this result, the simple answer to it is, that "The people wills it;"—the Sovereign thus decrees.

The fallacy of this reasoning is in the assumption of the false premise,—that the State Governments are Sovereigns, while the General Government is a joint attorney of all the States. Whereas, in fact, each State Government is an attorney of the people within its bounds, and the General Government is the Attorney-General of all the people in their collective capacity ; and they have willed and decreed that their said Attorney-General shall have a certain paramount authority over their several separate attorneys.

Chief Justice Marshall says : "This objection is sustained chiefly by arguments drawn from the supposed total separation of the judiciary of a State from that of the Union, and their entire independence of each other. The argument considers the Federal Judiciary as completely foreign to that of a State, and as being no more connected with it in any respect whatever, than the Court of a foreign State. If this hypothesis be just, the argument founded on it is equally so, but if the hypothesis be not supported by the Constitution, the argument fails with it.

This hypothesis is not founded on any words in the Constitution which might seem to countenance it, but on the unreasonableness of giving a contrary construction to words which seem to require it, and in the incompatibility of the application of the appellate jurisdiction to the judgments of State Courts with that Constitutional relation, which subsists between the Governments of those States which compose it.

Let this unreasonableness, this total incompatability, be examined.

That the United States form, for many and for most important purposes, *a single nation*, has not yet been denied. In war, we are one people. In making peace, we are one people. In all commercial regulations, we are one and the same people. In many other respects the American people are one ; and the government which is alone capable of controlling and managing their interests in all these respects, is the Goverment of the Union. It is their Government, and, in that character, they have no other. America has chosen to be, in many respects and to many purposes, a nation ; and for all these purposes her Government is complete, to all these objects it is competent. *The people* have declared that, in the exercise of all powers given for these objects, *it is supreme* It can, then, in effecting these objects, legitimately control all individuals or goverments within the American Territory. The Constitution and laws of a State, so far as they are repugnant to the Constitution and laws of the United State, are absolutely void. These States are constituent parts of the United States. They are members of one great empire—for some purposes sovereign, for some purposes subordinate.

In a Government so constituted, is it unreasonable that the judicial power should be competent to give efficacy to the Constitutional laws of the Legislature ? That department can decide upon the validity of the Constitution or law of a State, if it be repugnant to the Constitution or a law of the United States. Is it unreasonable that it should also be empowered to decide on the judgment of a State tribunal, enforcing such unconstitutional law ? Is it so very unreasonable as to furnish a justification for controlling the words of the Constitution ?

We think it is not. We think that in a government, acknowledgedly supreme with respect to objects of vital interest to the nation, there is nothing inconsistent with sound reason, nothing incompatible with the nature of government, in making all its departments supreme so far as respects these objects, and so far as is necessary to their attainment. The exercise of the appellate power over these judgments of the State tribunals which may contravene the Constitution or laws of the United States is, we believe, essential to the attainment of these objects.

The propriety of intrusting the construction of the Constitution and laws made in pursuance thereof, to the judiciary of the Union, has not, we believe, as yet been drawn into question. It seems to be a corollary from this political axoim, that the Federal Courts should either possess exclusive jurisdiction in such cases, or a power to revise the judgment rendered in them by the State tribunals. If the Federal and State Courts have concurrent jurisdiction in all cases arising under the Constitution, laws and treaties of the United States, and if a case of this discription brought in a State Court, cannot be removed before judgment, nor revised after judgment, then the construction of the Constitution, laws and treaties of the United States is not confided particularly to their judicial department, but is confided equally to that department and to the State Courts, however they may be constituted. 'Thirteen independent Courts,' says a very celebrated statesman, (and we have now more than twenty such Courts), 'of final jurisdiction over the same causes, arising under the same laws, is a hydra in government, from which nothing but contradiction and confusion can proceed.'

The requisitions of Congress, under the confederation, were as constitutionally obligatory, as the laws enacted by the present Congress. That they were habitually disregarded is a fact of universal notoriety.

With the knowledge of this fact and under its full pressure, a Convention was assembled to change the system. Is it so improbable, that they should confer on the judicial department the power of construing the Constitution and laws of the Union, in every case, in the last resort, and of preserving them from all violation from every quarter, so far as judicial decisions can preserve them, that this improbability should essentially affect the construction of the new system?"

"—— The judicial power of every well constituted government must be co-extensive with the legislative, and must be capable of deciding every judicial question which grows out of the Constitution and laws. If any proposition may be considered as a political axiom, this we think may be so considered."

So much for the probability or propriety of the existence of the power. Let us return to the opinion. Judge Hydenfeldt continues—

"But the question which naturally arises is, whence is this claim of power derived? In the authority to establish a Supreme Court and inferior Courts the Constitution gives appellate jurisdiction to the former, not a word is said in reference to the State Courts. The Supreme Court and inferior Courts to be established by Congress, are alone mentioned. They bear a certain relation to each other, and that relation only is explained in the grant of appellate power to the Supreme Court. It would be curious if any other construction could be justly held, because in the arrangement of powers between the grantors and grantee of sovereignty, it might be readily, and was doubtless supposed, that conflicts of opinion would arise as to the extent of the delegated authority."

We would remark in passing, that the power is not given by the Constitution to Congress to create a Supreme Court, but it creates that Court itself. Congress is not required to establish inferior Courts, but they may: "The judicial power *shall be* vested in *one Supreme* Court, and in such inferior Courts as Congress *may* from time to time ordain and establish." But this power *shall be vested*, and it *shall* extend to the cases enumerated in art. iii., sec. 2. There shall be a Supreme Court, it shall have original jurisdiction in certain cases, and in others the power can only be executed as appellate.

"It would not have been strange, if the States had expressly reserved to themselves, in case of conflict, the power of deciding the extent of the grant; but it would be an inexplicable anomaly for sovereigns to delegate to another certain of their most important rights of sovereignty, and, at the same time, confer upon the government of delegated powers the right to decide for both parties in every case of dispute."

If it would be improper for the Supreme Court of the United States to decide whether the Constitution from which it derived its existence was violated, it would be equally improper for the Supreme Court of this State to decide upon a violation of the State Constitution from which it derives its existence. Here is again that same confusion of sovereignties and governments. Do the Supreme Court mean that a Supreme Court cannot decide upon its own jurisdiction? What tribunal is to decide upon the jurisdiction of your own Court in those matters, which do not touch upon the present question? Does your Court exercise anything but delegated powers? You get your powers from the same source as the Supreme Court of the United States—from *the people ;* and you must, each of you, within your respective limits, decide upon the extent of the delegated power.

"The third article of the Constitution of the United States declares, that ' this Constitution and the laws of the United States which shall be made in pursuance thereof—and all treaties made, and which shall be made under the authority of the United States, shall be the supreme law of the land; and the Judges in every State shall be bound thereby, anything in the Constitution or laws of any State; to the contrary, notwithstanding.' This is a part of the compact, and by it the Judges of the State Courts are unquestionably bound. But wherefore was there any necessity for the stipulation, if in every question requiring a construction of the Constitution, laws and treaties, the Federal Judiciary had appellate control over that of the States."

The answer is very simple. The first part of the article is to place beyond question the paramount authority of the supreme legislature— to assert its supremacy—the very thing which our Court argues so

hard to show that it is not, and to give a rule of construction. Giving the Supreme Court appellate jurisdiction over the State Courts,
does not necessarily give the laws and Constitution a paramount
authority. And the last clause was intended to declare that Constitution and laws of higher authority even with State Judges;—so that
if the Supreme Court of a State should contumaciously refuse to obey
the Supreme Court of the United States, and submit to its authority,
the Judges of inferior tribunals throughout the State might, by the
oath which they have taken to support that Constitution, be compelled
to obey that higher law, and to disregard the commands and decisions
of their immediate superior.

"The basis for the claim of appellate power to the Supreme Court
of the United States, over the State Courts, is the assertion, that the
judicial power of the United States is exclusive."

Judge Heydenfeldt thus states the argument of his adversary, and
then proceeds to demolish it. We have read with great attention the
arguments on this subject, and cannot find any such pretense set up
by any one, except by Justice Johnson in his separate opinion. He
agreed with his brethren in the conclusion arrived at, that the Supreme Court had the appellate power in the cases enumerated in the
Constitution ; but he did not arrive at his conclusion by exactly the
same train of reasoning as the other Judges, and, therefore, he gave
a separate opinion. In this, after arriving at the result that this
revisory power exists, he expresses *a doubt* whether the power of the
United States Court is not exclusive ;—a *doubt*, merely, but finally
comes to the conclusion that it is not. The remainder of the Court,
and the whole of the Court in the subsequent case, in 6 Wheaton,
make no such argument ; nor did any of the counsel ; nor did any
member of the Congress who passed the law ; nor did any one of the
writers in the *Federalist*, the "able commentators" alluded to by
Judge Heydenfeldt. On the contrary, the basis of the revisory
power is placed by each and every one of them principally, on the
paramount authority of the Supreme Government, the jurisdiction
granted by the Constitution over certain *cases* and *subjects*, without
any restriction to any Courts, and the necessity of the case. Story
argues that the *exclusive jurisdiction* must be vested in the inferior
Federal Courts ; and the revisory power over the State Courts extends precisely to those cases in which the jurisdiction is not exclusive. And Marshall says, "That the Constitution and laws of the
United States are involved in a case, and makes a part of it, may
appear in the progress of a cause in which the Courts of the Union,
but for that circumstance, would have no jurisdiction, and which of
consequence could not originate in the Supreme Court. In such a
case the jurisdiction can be exercised only in its appellate form. To
deny its exercise in this form, is to deny its existence, and would be
to construe a clause dividing the power of the Supreme Court, in such
a manner as, in a considerable degree, to defeat the power itself. All
must perceive that this construction can be gratified only where it is
absolutely necessary. We do not think the article under consideration presents that necessity."

Here is no pretence of exclusive jurisdiction. On the contrary, there is an express recognition of concurrent jurisdiction. Having demolished this man of straw, the learned Judge proceeds to dispose of the objection, of the want of uniformity of decisions which would result, and the conflict of jurisdiction, both of which, he says, are incident to the judicial systems of every civilized people—a proposition which we respectfully submit, is absurd. He instances the solitary case of the conflict between the Court of Chancery and the Common Law Courts (and he might have added the Admiralty Courts) in England ; a matter which resulted from their want of a written Constitution, and was no more incident to their judicial system, than it was to the solar system. The conflict arose because there was no Constitution to which to resort, to determine their respective pretensions. But that was long ago settled, and there is no longer any conflict. It was accidental, not incidental. It was because both claimed to be sovereign and independant. The one was supposed to have the king in person, and the other claimed to have his conscience in keeping. This is the solitary instance cited, to show that conflicts of jurisdiction are necessarily incident to all judicial systems, and the only course is to let them fight it out.

With equal brevity and satisfaction the other difficulty is disposed of :

"As to the uniformity of decision, no sound reasoner will pretend that it is attainable."

Why not ? But if it is not, shall we, because we cannot attain absolute perfection, fly as far as possible the other way ? Because we cannot attain absolute uniformity, must we have decisions as various and discordant as possible ? But let us see why the law laid down by *one* Supreme Court, will not produce uniformity.

"Every State of the Union has her own Court. We know that the decisions of State Courts are various, and, upon important questions, differ widely from one another. This want of uniformity in reference to subjects within the exclusive jurisdiction of the State Courts is certainly not less hurtful or inconvenient, than it would be in regard to those matters in which the Courts of the United States have concurrent jurisdiction."

You might with equal propriety say that the law in different States are different. What has that to do with the matter ? The existence of a single Supreme Court in each State, secures a uniform interpretation of the laws and Constitution of that State, which is all that is desirable. Different laws and different interpretations of those laws may exist in different States, and we do not perceive that any very geat evil results from that. But what utter confusion would exist, if we had no Supreme Court in this State, and each District Court was left to interpret the laws in its own way.

"But even in regard to the latter, the act of 1789 fails to secure uniformity. The appeal is only allowed where the decision of the State Court is adverse to the law of Congress or treaty, etc. If, therefore, the State affirms the validity of a law of Congress and another State declares it void, if the Supreme Court of the United States sustains the latter, the rule will be different in two States."

This is not so. Until the Constitutionality of an act of Congress is questioned, there is but one rule, and that is in favor of the law. If it is declared unconstitutional, and the Supreme Court sustains that decision, then there is but one rule, and that is against the validity of the law. Until the decision of the Supreme Court there may be conflicting decisions, as there may be between our District Courts; but is that any reason why there should not be one Supreme Court to decide the conflict?

We have shown that the weight of authority is all on one side, and that against the decision of the Supreme Court of our State. We have also endeavored to show that the reasoning of our Supreme Court is utterly fallacious, and fails to present even a plausible reason for questioning a rule, which, from repeated adjudications, ought to be considered forever and finally disposed of. We shall not attempt to present even a summary of the reasoning on the other side, as our limits forbid.

The report of the case of Martin *vs.* Hunter's Lessees, 1 Wheaton, 304, covers seventy-four pages; and the report of the case of Cohens *vs.* Virginia, 6 Wheaton, 264, covers one hundred and eighty-four pages; and the arguments brought forward in these two cases, in support of the jurisdiction claimed, are absolutely unanswerable. To give even an abstract of the reasoning would extend this article beyond reasonable limits; and as these reports are easily accessible to every one, it is sufficient to refer to them. We might refer, also, to hundreds of cases in the State Reports, and to those of the Union, where the jurisdiction is sanctioned and upheld. But it is only our purpose to examine this opinion; to show that its reasoning is based upon false premises; that it misstates the grounds and arguments of the other side, and the weight of authority; and that all the arguments brought forward in support of the decision are fallacies.

LINES ON HEARING A BELL TOLLING THE MIDNIGHT HOUR.

BY D. M. J.

—

Hark! the midnight hour is tolling,—
  Tolling sadly on the ear,
Ushering, as it does, the morrow;
  And thus onward through the year.

Listen now! how sad 't is stealing,
  As the last chime draweth nigh;
To our hearts the truth revealing,
  That, like Time, we 're born to die.

Now, afar, we hear, receding,
  Its last echos on the blast,
'T is a day like those preceding,
  Numbered now among the past.

We may stop that bell from tolling
  Forth the hours that pass away;
But we cannot stop the rolling
  Of old Time, a single day.

FINANCE.

ANONYMOUS.

THE keenest men in all creation are our financiers. Finance is a grindstone, which brings a yankee blade to a wire edge; and, especially in this golden State of California, does it sharpen faculties to a razor-like keenness. Indeed, the times we have passed through, and are now passing through, would rub the green off most people, however verdant by nature. In almost every class or profession there is some particular point of honor—some raw place which makes the sensitive point of attack; in the banking fraternity this is the verdant;— the deadly affront is " to be come over "—to be humbugged. Fortified behind their money-bags, they are free from the necessities of life and unapproached by the public sympathies; and, therefore, the shafts of ridicule reach them through their plates of gold, unsoftened and unassuaged by any feelings of kindness or compassion. Above all want—representing only the creditor side of the Ledger, they are singularly prone to plume themselves upon their elevation—above the reach of being taken in. And when such a mishap does befall them, it is followed by a general explosion of laughter. To avoid this, the victim is forced to a very prudent silence, he does such acts of "good" nature " by stealth and blushes to find them fame;" he is so modest of parading his good nature as to be extremely solicitous to conceal the fact, preferring to smart in silence, rather than writhe in the double pangs of loss of money and reputation for keenness, and amidst the jests and derisions of the commons, whose lively sense of wit is refreshed with these exhibitions, as at a bear-baiting or a bull-fight. Such fancy scrip, however current in the saloons, is a good deal below par in the back parlor of the operator, who has thus unwittingly become the *operatee;* and even discomposes his Anaconda digestion, when disposing of a fat contractor at the rate of five per cent. per month, cooked up in a running mortgage on a Peter Smith title.

The " Oily Gammon " of Finance was the late Henry Meiggs. He brought financiering up to the standard of a regular scientific system of swindling. He aspired to no less a distinction than to be the Monroe Edwards of California; indeed, if we could accredit the spiritual theory, we would be apt to believe that Meiggs was all the time *en rapport* with the spirit of the lamented Edwards, who was his familiar, as Bacon and Swedenborg are of Judge Edmonds. Other men may have done a larger business than the lamented Henry, though this is not certain; they may have had more brilliant dashes; done more splendid larcenies in a sudden heat; but Meiggs was more systematic and continuous; more constantly on the stretch—more universal and more loyal to the felonious idea. Meiggs was a universalist in his creed of diabolic financiering. He devoured all of every sort—"from snowy white to sooty"—from the great banker to the small washerwoman. He was a shark that swallowed, indiscriminately, salmon and shrimp. He kept it going all the time, by day and by night, and at all times

of the night.   He was eternally mortgaging, forging, swindling under
false pretences, hypothecating.   He seldom did any thing under the
grade of felony; he never dared any danger below the dignity of the
penitentiary.   If he had been convicted for all his peccadilloes, the
State would have been entitled to, at least, a thousand years of his
life; and if his sins had been visited on his children, they would, in the
three generations have been able to colonize a new Botany Bay.   If
he had lived in the State Prison for fifty years, still he would have
swindled the State more largely than any body else; and fifty years
would have been hardly a larger dividend than he made the Lumber
Company declare on its stock.

His manners certainly were captivating in the extreme; for the address that takes in a Banker, unquestionably is, in the highest degree,
prepossessing.   Meiggs had much of the bland—the gentle—the *suavi-
ter in modo :*—but all these amenities are wasted in the banking-house:
his voice was silvery—but the Bankers don't care for that metal in
the voice, if it is in the purse.   He was very plausible, but the Banker
begins to be suspicious when every thing looks *too* specious.   Meiggs was
a High-Church Episcopalian; but the Bankers, remembering who it was
that drove some of their ancient and worthy craft from the temple, and
who it was, that, carrying the bag, made that ignominious contract for
the thirty pieces, have usually kept at a respectful distance from a religion which brings up these reminiscences, and which, moreover, indulges
in predictions and objurgations touching extortioners, usury and other
the like subjects, in no high degree complimentary to the profession.

If Meiggs had confined himself to the Bankers, probably no very
violent outcry would have followed his exploits.   The Commons, possibly, would have held, most unjustly, that he only "from the robber
rent his prey;" and would not have felt much more indignant than
a Cuban would feel at some fellow's breaking the screw off the *garote.*
But Meiggs carried the thing too far when he bilked his washerwoman.
We have lived in California several years, and, therefore, do not consider ourselves competent to pass upon moral questions.   We certainly
disclaim ethical prejudices and superstitions; but, as the Yankee said on
the Isthmus, when he saw a native hung by the guard, on a wager of
his life played for with cards—we *do* think that *was* irregular.

Well, Meiggs left.   We take that to be a fixed fact; and we like to
be certain of something, as the Hon. Mr. Harris, of Mississippi, said
of Col. Johnson's killing Tecumseh; though we have our own opinion
of *that*—but, no matter;—so we repeat—for when we do get hold of a
fact, in San Francisco, we like to make the most of it—the *scrip*tural
Meiggs left—*ita scripta est :* and divers bulls and bears, like Lord Ullin,
when his daughter took to the water, " were left lamenting."

Having rigged himself out, and fitted himself up in his own galleon
in true Cleopatra and Anthony style, he trusted Cæsar and his fortunes to the waves; and, though he had not put himself to the pains of
bidding formal adieu, nor even given a circular valedictory, signing
himself, as well he might, the public's much indebted servant, it was
soon noised abroad that he had gone.   He took no ship-papers from

the Custom-House ; he needed none ; he wished to break the monotony
of his reflections by forging them ; indeed, we suspect, by this time, he
has forged enough for the whole merchant service, besides having
"enough over" for the Russian fleet. Where he is gone, he did not
leave word. We are inclined to believe he has gone to Petropoloski, as the safest place he could find; and we should not be surprised if he was the Yankee who tolled the Allies up to where they
were so well peppered, as he had a great genius for getting his friends
into difficulties, probably looking, too, to a speculation in brass buttons—a metal which he had always put to good account. But, speaking of Meiggs, we get to imitating him and wander off ; so must pull
up.

Mr. Joseph Jones, was a fore-sighted and fore-handed man ; he
was as sharp as if he had received his early education in Thread-
Needle Street and graduated in Wall Street. All Jewry could not
teach him any thing of the mysteries of finance ; for, beside the
best Atlantic training, he had the rare advantage denied to the Hebrew Patriarch and Prophets of Discount and Deposit—of having
taken the higher degrees—the Royal Arch Chapter degrees in California,—when California was—something. He had borne the experiences of finance in California, from '49 on, with an easy greatness that
must have surprised himself. He could keep the run of the financial
cards like a Faro *habitué*, moving the beans along the wire as a card
turned up; and could calculate a failure to a day. Nothing fooled
him; all the airs and fussy pretensions of men ruffling it out against a
losing game, and putting on big appearances in the face of bankruptcy,
only excited a grim smile as he saw through them like glass. He
valued himself on securities; he liked security, as Falstaff hated it.
He was learned in the science of hypothecation; he was pretty strong
on mortgages; well posted on real estate, especially water-lots; knew
the omnipresent Peter and the Alcalde Grants ; but he was *profound* on scrip. If he did profess to know any thing—if he had a
human weakness, it was his pride of knowledge of scrip. He loved
scrip; it looked well—was easily counted;—it could be turned, like a
hot cake, from brown to browner; if it rose, it was so much made on
the old stock;—if it fell, it furnished so much more profit on the new.
He delighted to speak of it. He named it often to praise; "out of
the abundance of the heart, the mouth speaketh." He was fond of
saying "It was something tangible;" there was no question of titles,—
no decisions of Supreme Courts could touch it; no juries could ignore
it. It was like benevolence, it embraced every body; it was like law,
it was a universal bond; it was like charity, it covered a host of *failings*, and like charity, he wished it to begin at home ;—he liked the
prudent, modest, safe way it did business—appreciating itself at only
half of its value—a charming and rare quality in California, and
standing at the back of its friend, a promissory note, willing to be
sacrificed by that terrible Dragon, "Five Per Cent.," yet claiming only
to be good for half it called for. But we must drop the metaphor;—
Mr. Jones could well afford to be partial to scrip ; for scrip had

done a great deal for him. To his knowledge of the article he was indebted for a flourishing business and high position in the eminent house of which he was the direction; a distinction the greater, inasmuch, as it was unsolicited, and he, for such a position, rather a young man.

It was a source of very just gratification, therefore, that he saw the business under his charge growing larger and more profitable, and in two or three turns placing affairs, before in rather a ticklish condition, on a firm basis.

We can readily excuse his delight in seeing the scrip come in, and loans daily negociated at a rate which promised rich results to the operator ; in seeing a promissory note fortified behind a Controller's Warrant double its size, like a little drummer behind a tall grenadier ; there was a show of strength and a sweet satisfaction in seeing a promissory nicely folded in a rich slip of scrip—which conveyed the idea of the honeycomb in Samson's lion—and then as the clock ticked on, to know that *Time*, the *Edax rerum.*, joining partnership with the 3*s* and 5*s per centum* was slowly and surely consuming the reams of scrip, like metals in a powerful solvent, was enough to make a dyspeptic smile with a serene and pious complacency.

Mr Jones, soon took the measure of Mr. Meiggs—as he thought. He knew that Mr. Meiggs's business was very complicated. He had branched off—pressed—parrelleed—coppered on the ace—piled up transversely across the table, and run the checks into the pot, until the Devil or any *other* financier could not keep the run of his own game. He knew that breaking with such a man was only a question of time ; and, seeing a good deal of Meiggs's paper in the Bank, started to work immediately to get it out of the house ; in which effort he succeeded remarkably well. In vain Mr. Meiggs sought to borrow—the house never had anything to lend; in vain were good notes, well indorsed, offered—Mr. Meiggs found the Bank always closed to him ; in vain Mr. Meiggs offered real estate,—nothing could be done.

At last, Mr. Meiggs desired an explanation: " How is it, Mr. Jones," said he, " that before you came into this house, I could get whatever money I wanted, and now I can get none, it matters not what security or names I offer ?

Mr. Jones was a candid man—as a gentleman on the creditor side of the Ledger can afford to be, when nothing is to be made by being otherwise. Mr. Jones replied: " Why, *in candor*," (for whenever a man is going to say a disagreeable thing by a sort of cheating, he compensates *himself for the other man's feelings*, by making a claim to candor), " Mr. Meiggs, since you ask the question, I will tell you frankly. We did not wish to let you have the money because we thought you were going to break; and, as to indorsers, whenever you go down, you will carry every body on your paper with you; and as to mortgages, we don't care about doing any thing on them until titles are better settled! "

" But," said Mr. Meiggs, " if those things don't suit you, I can give you scrip."

The word scrip seemed to carry a charm to the ears of Mr. Jones.

It had a beautiful sound to him, quite drowning the music of "Lilly Dale" which the hand-organ was grinding out. He drew his chair closer to Meiggs; his manner fell from the judicial to the familiar; his face relaxed and his voice grew cozy and gentle, from firm and magisterial. "You said, Meiggs, you had scrip; why did'nt you mention that before? What sort of scrip?"

MEIGGS.—"Yes—scrip—I said scrip—city scrip—warrants—almost all kinds."

JONES.—"Why, if you speak of scrip, Meiggs, you begin to talk sensible. That's just what I want. How much money do you want? When do you want it? We can let you have just as much money as you want on scrip."

MEIGGS.—"Why, Mr. Jones, I only want about $15,000, and I want it to-morrow."

JONES.—"But can't you take more? $15,000 is not much money; and could'nt you take it now? We can let you have from $50,000 to $100,000 at five and a half; possibly at five; and I would like to close it now, and have the thing all fixed up at once. For, you know,—Never postpone until to-morrow, etc.—and I like to do business on business principles."

Mr. Meiggs agreed in the general principle; but thought probably there was an exception to the anti-procrastinating maxim, in the case of money at high interest, got before the borrower had any use for it;—which suggestion seemed, like Mr. Meiggs himself, to be quite plausible.

So the consummation of the arrangement was postponed until the following day.

The morning came, and so did Meiggs. He produced the documents. They were received by Mr. Jones, a good humored smile of recognition illuminating his countenance. He turned the papers over one by one. They were countersigned by the Treasurer, but wanted the signature of the Mayor. Mr. Jones called Mr. Meiggs's attention to the fact, and remarked that he prided himself on doing banking on business principles; that, as they were just commencing important, and, he hoped, mutually profitable operations, it was very important to start right; and, therefore, he suggested that the documents should be perfected before they proceeded further. Mr. Meiggs replied that the thing was all understood; that the Mayor would sign the papers at any time. He had been too busy to do it before; but it was all right.

Mr. Jones, turning to the desk, hastily wrote a line to the Mayor, inquiring if the scrip was all right; and, if it were a good security; and, slyly slipping the note and one of the warrants into the hands of a page, sent him off to the Mayor—keeping Mr. Meiggs amused in the meantime, by a little financial gossip, illustrating, to the great amusement of Mr. Meiggs, the aphorism that California was a bad country for a one-eyed man, by an account of some shrewd operator being taken in by an adventurous professor in the financial art.

The page returned with the tidings that the paper was all right; and the operation was closed by the passing over to Mr. Meiggs of

$15,000 for $30,000 in scrip. It occurred to Mr. Meiggs, as he was about leaving, that his friends, Messrs. McGree & McGray, had got him to indorse a note for $5,000, which would be due the next day; and he generously proffered to take it up with scrip—which he was suffered to do, and then the parties separated with mutual congratulations and expressions of regard.

After Mr. Meiggs left the house, Mr. Jones turned to Mr. Bell, who was the assistant in the house, with some exultation; and, after remarking how pleasant it was to do business on business principles, added that scrip was a thing he understood. "Now," said he, "Meiggs may break as soon as he pleases;—he may run off, but, (shaking the documents in his hand, and making an emphatic gesture), here is the scrip; here is something tangible; here is the real stuff and no mistake; this is security; we can go to bed on this; it is scrip when we go to bed—and scrip when we wake up."

The next morning after this interview, Mr. Bell suggested that the clerks had gathered a small savings-bank fund, and that it would only be generous to let them come in for a share of this Meiggs investment; as it was the only five per cent. stock held, that they should have a showing; it would encourage the young men to persevere in a laudable course of economy and thrift; it would show them, by lively example, what men might make of themselves by integrity, fidelity and industry, in the banking line. But Mr. Jones would not hear to it. He admitted the benefit of the moral example; but, then, they had duties to perform; they ought not to give away the cream of the business; scrip was something tangible; it was like conscience, it ought not to be lightly parted with; it was like generosity, it should be jealously watched over; it was like a house, it ought not to be split up and divided; and so Mr. Jones, for these and other good reasons, put his peremptory veto on the proposition.

The scene shifts. Meiggs took to the sea. His departure created a sensation even in San Francisco; a sensation only equaled by that produced by the ringing of the bell of the Vigilance Committee, or the passage of the Beach and Water Lot Bill. And now Mr. Frederick Simmonds, hearing of Mr. Meiggs's departure, and fearing it might injure his friends, the Bankers, stepped up to Mr. Jones, and putting his hand to his mouth, whispered—"Jones—Meiggs has run off; is all right?" Mr. Jones's countenance lit up with a smile expressing humor, keenness and self-complacency; he whispered back—"All—slick—as—a—gouge;" and, then, as if a little excited at the reflection of the way he had got Meiggs, continued—"Simmonds—if I *do* pride myself upon anything I ever did, it is this matter with Meiggs."

That same evening, just after dinner, Mr. Jones was sitting in the back-room of the Banking-House. He had been enjoying a comfortable meal, and was now leaning back, with his feet upon a chair, smoking, the smoke gently rising, as he held the cigar lightly between his lips, at an angle of thirty-nine degrees; he was evidently in a happy mood; profound tranquility possessed him; a bland serenity of soul, unbroken by a ripple of passion, or a thought of evil was his; this state

of mind, if not a virtue, is the best reward of it; if a selfish complacency, it leans to the side of benevolence or an intense good nature.
Mr. Jones was thinking of Meiggs and of the list of killed and wounded the next morning's bulletin would show, of his fraternity; and
felicitating himself upon his own happy escape. He was a fine-looking
fellow, and as he lay stretched out in an atmosphere of complacent enjoyment, was no bad representation of Virtue crowned by Victory,
yet modestly disclaiming or unostentatiously enjoying glory. We wish
his portrait had then been taken!

Alas! Alack-a-day! Ah us! We begin to wish we had not started
this scribbling; for our nerves are weak, our sympathies strong, our
benevolence unbounded as Meiggs's larcenies; and more, even, than
for the fair Cyprians, who, next to the Bankers, most suffered by this
inhuman monster, our compassionate nature mourns for shorn Israel.
Our pen chokes as we go on—but we suppress our sighs and proceed.

A customer came into the Banking-Room; Mr. Jones and Mr. Bell
were present; Mr. Jones arose and offered him a chair. After some
other words, he remarked that Mr. Meiggs had written a very singular letter back, saying that he was ruined in character, and other
things, leaving the inference that he had carried finance beyond swindling into felony; for even *that* can be done in California. Mr. Jones
looked at Mr. Bell; Mr. Bell looked at Mr. Jones; Mr. Jones felt
drawn towards the safe in which the warrants were, as strongly as if
he were a magnet. The gentleman left. Again Mr. Jones looked at
Mr. Bell; Mr. Bell looked at Mr. Jones; something must be said; Mr.
Bell ventured to say he supposed there was no doubt the warrants
were genuine; Mr. Jones replied a little tremulously—"There was no
doubt." Mr. Jones looked though as if something ailed him; his countenance was not so pleasant—a faint expression like sea-sickness came
over it—his swallow was a little choked; his cravat fitted him a little
too tight. He looked again at the warrants, as earnestly as a poker-
player at four aces, the third time, on a big bet;—there might be some
mistake. He went up to see Shark; Shark took the scrip to examine
by the Register. They did not fit.—There was no doubt; it was a
forgery; Mr. Jones was sold. Why go on? The scene grows tragic.
Something Mr. Jones had eaten the day before disagreed with him.
He did not feel well. A prudent regard for his health confined him
to his room for several days; and such was the strength of his mind
that he rejected the condolences of his numerous friends.

When he returned to the Banking-House, Mr. Bell, by way of saying something to amuse the mind of Mr. Jones, ventured to speak
about Meiggs's scrip—its tangibility—doing business on banking principles—Mr. Jones's understanding scrip—the disappointment of the
clerks in not being let in to the cream of the business and the like;
but Mr. Jones drew up his tall form with a most commanding dignity
and declared that if the important and solemn business of the house
were interrupted by ill-timed levities, he should quit the establishment;
from which we infer, that, probably in consequence of his dangerous
sickness, and the serious thoughts which such a state naturally induces
in the mind of a banker, Mr. Jones did not relish Mr. Bell's plea-
santries.

CALIFORNIA.

BY L. H. SIGOURNEY.

LAND of Gold! New England greets thee,
  O'er the mountain and the main;
With a sister's smile she meets thee,
  Youngest of our household train.

Many a form her bosom cherish'd
  Dwells beneath thy sunny sky,—
And their fond memorials brighten
  Every link of sympathy.

She, mid rocks and storms was cradled,
  Mid the threat of angry foes,
Then, in sudden, dreamlike splendor,
  Pallas-born, to vigor rose.

Children of one common country,
  Firm in Union let us stand,—
With combined endeavor, earning
  Glory for our Native Land.

Climes of gold, and climes of iron,
  Climes that reap the bearded wheat,
Climes that rear the snowy cotton
  Pour their treasures at her feet;

While with tender exultation,
  She who marks their filial part,
Like the mother of the Gracchi,
  Hoards her jewels in her heart.

HARTFORD, Conn., November, 1854.

THE ABSENT ONE.

BY MRS. E. V. P.

Do we miss thee at home? do we miss thee at home?—
While thou from thy loved ones in sorrow dost roam.
Yes! our fire-side circle is lonely and sad,
For we miss thy dear voice, that alone made us glad.

We miss thee, dear one, in our walks and our rides:
Each day seems to lengthen, though swiftly it glides;
And moments, and hours, we count with our tears,
And weeks seem to double, and months grow to years.

I miss thee at meal time, thy plate is removed,
(And also another's, whom fondly we loved);
I miss the fond smile that welcomed me there,
And the heart never weary my pleasures to share.

I miss thee at eve, when the moon in her pride,
All regal in splendor, glides on with the tide;
When the stars, growing pale, seem to fade from the sky;
'T is then that I miss thee, and wish thou were by.

When Nature hath sunk to a quiet repose,
And slumber hath hushed all my griefs and my woes,—
When silence comes down like a spirit of dreams,
And broods o'er the mountains, the vales and the streams;

Ah! then, in my sleep, how I bask in thy smile!
And my heart leaps with gladness and joy for the while;
But when gray morn awakes me, thy image is gone,
And I pray for thy presence in tears and alone.

"GOING, GONE."

BY J. P. ANTHONY.

AMIDST the panorama of moving humanity, and the shifting features of the busy thoroughfares of San Francisco, the Auctioneer presents himself prominently to our notice. His "Going, gone," the roll of his voice like the beating of a tattoo—his *staccato* exclamations arrest our attention as we pass along, and we walk into his sanctum ; for there is a vigor and earnestness in the tones of his voice, importing momentous matter, which we find it impossible to withstand. And.what is the argument ? Not a matter of life and death, nor yet affecting the well-being of the commonwealth, but the price, perchance, of a very pretty lot of pants, and the auctioneer, observing our advent, forthwith sets his gaze upon us with an expression, as much as to say—" *You* surely have more sense than to see them knocked down at a price so preposterously low."

The sentences of our auctioneer are stereotyped on his brain, and he deals them out with a vigor and rapidity that must challenge admiration. You will never find him out in his part ; he is ever ready on receiving his cue, the bids of his customers, whilst his oratorical efforts fall upon the tympanums of his hearers with the strength and regularity of a railway engine getting away. Our auctioneer is unquestionably a man of nerve ; the mastery over his features, which he so frequently displays, is positively prodigious. Fifty, a hundred dollars under the true value, shall he knock you down lots of his goods, and, beyond the declaration that it is particularly *shamefully* ruinous, he exhibits no further sign of his sufferings,—doubtless passing, like Hamlet's, all outward show—puts up another lot, and his "Going, gone," is again heard, vigorous as ever.

But, at times, our auctioneer is surrounded by a crowd, who, one and all, are so singularly obtuse, as not to percieve that he is actually, as he felicitously expresses it, "throwing goods away," and who, in spite of his best stereotyped rhetoric, will not raise their sweet voices in responsive bidding. At such a time it is that we are presented with a revelation of the genius—the divine fire that is within him,—the master strokes that elevate the profession, and make him truly great. Our auctioneer will pause, apparently astounded, dumb-founded—surveying the company with a look of positive amazement, and then, suiting the action to the word, in a manner that the royal student of Elsinore would have pronounced faultless, ejaculate the stock sentence for the occasion, " You are surely asleep; when are you going to wake up ? " Our auctioneer, it will be observed, taxes not the crowd with being actually demented, downright insane ; no,—he contents himself with intimating, only, that they are, one and all, at the antipodes of "wide-awakeism," and most just and proper the charge in all verity,—that is, presuming to be the truth, the whole truth, and nothing but the truth, his asseveration that they are letting slip an opportunity of purchasing twice twenty-five per cent. under value.

And we see no reason why **Mr.** Going Gone should not have as much reverence for veracity as any amongst us.

We are inclined to think that our auctioneer is a believer in spiritual manifestations, and that he is particularly favored in receiving communications. Nay, we have reason to believe that, when plying his vocation, he is ever surrounded by members of the invisible community; and, would he but confess it, very useful auxiliaries, we opine, they are. That he appreciates their services is clear, for to them he knocks down some of his greatest bargains. Failing to discover the individual whose bid is always ready when wanted, we have sometimes thought that our auctioneer had an attendant, who, possessing the ring of Gyges, turned the stone towards his body when required, becoming, forthwith, conveniently invisible.

Would you imagine, reader, that Mr. Going Gone has a soul above buttons, that he is a man of the finest sentiment, of the most exquisite sensibility? It is even so. Over yon collection of furniture, the household gods of a broken family, sent in by an unfortunate widow, think you, whilst chronicling them in his catalogue for to-morrow's sale, a sigh does not escape him? Does he not think of the pale-faced, melancholy one, who, in her somber weeds, yesterday had an interview with him relative to the sale of her little property? Think you not the items to him tell their mournful story? Here is a rocking chair; and as our Going Gone marks it down, " No. 5, a handsome, &c., &c.," be assured that he pauses in his task, whilst imagination pictures to his mind's-eye the wife, the mother, and on her knee the young prattler, who in that rocking chair shall prattle never more. Think you not he beholds the once sanguine father, who, with bright visions of a sunny future, had sought a new home on the shores of the Pacific, his footsteps dogged by misfortune, the *avant courier* of that broken spirit, and death, which have brought that rocking chair to the store of " Going, Gone ?" Here is the piano, the paintings, the books; what evenings never to return—quiet, homely, happy evenings they speak of to our auctioneer, as he proceeds to number them with his best descriptive commentaries! Nay, perhaps, he is familiar with the history of the family who consigned them to be converted, by the alchemy of his voice, into dollars; and, as he heads his advertisement with the announcement of " The property of a gentleman leaving the country," or " a lady giving up housekeeping," think not, reader, that his imagination never soars away from the one thought,—how many dollars will he realize from the sale. Our auctioneer has but little ostentation about him. He may be paid to be an actor, whose sterling merits need not the adjuncts of the flaring footlights, the tinseled dress, and the scenic back-ground. The overture to his performance is given by a single bellman; his stage may be said to be the open street; his audience any body who may choose to enter his theater of well filled boxes. His emblem is a blood-red flag, which flutters in the breeze some hour or two ere he mounts the tub— rostrum we should have written;—yet is it a question whether a banner, displaying the figure of Mercury, would not be far more appropriate, for as well as the messenger of Jupiter, was he not the God of oratory, of merchandise, and of—no, we will not write the rest. Ye Grecians fill up the hiatus.

The night Auctioneers and Cheap Johns are not to be included in the same category as our Going, Gone. They are a distinct species, to be found chiefly in Commercial Street and Long Wharf thoroughfares, which, probably, suggest to most of us thoughts of the Exodus and The Vicar of Wakefield. Here the most casual observer may see, every night, the descendants of Abraham with their unchanging social development, striking pictures framed in suits of clothes—as to us they seem, peering from their doorways with multitudinous pants and jackets dangling around them. Here, also, any night might be seen poor Moses buying of Jenkinson over again, and probably there are more Jenkinsons in our wonderful city than in any other gathering place of humanity in this sublunary sphere. Where in the wide world, we should like to know, can gold watches be sold as they are nightly sold here for a tenth of their value—ay, and the vendors growing fat thereon? Science sublime! Alchemy most wonderful!

Jenkinson sold Moses the spectacles, and his descendants flourish in disposing of gold watches in California.

> "If not a sous in thy lank purse appear,
>   Go, mount the rostrum, and turn auctioneer."

So wrote Juvenal, and we conclude as little or no capital was required, the ancestors of our Cheap Johns in his days flourished. Beneath the gleam of their bright lamps, the iron hardware of our Long Wharf gentry glitters brightly enough, which cannot, however, be said of their wit—that commodity being of the dullest and most meager character. And yet, withal, they succeed in drawing crowds, nightly, around them—a proof, perhaps, of the paucity of suitable cheap amusements for the mass of our population. The only one of the fraternity, who possessed aught like originality, has recently departed from the scene which he graced for long, and if we may judge from the numbers that were wont nightly to assemble before his stand, with a respectable pile did he make his final bow to the public. Anecdote and snatches of song enlivened his commercial transactions, but amidst the loud guffaws which these contributions elicited, was ever to be heard the chink of incoming dollars.

Another, who has also retired from the busy scene, animated the night by alternating the beating of a huge gong, with his own stentorian voice, which, without exaggeration, might be heard half a mile off, inviting the public to walk in, and occasionally bellowing forth, "Room for one more." The rush that the latter announcement intimated, it is scarcely necessary to say, existed only in his fertile imagination;—the cry of "Room for one more," going forth, not unfrequently, when our night Auctioneer was alone in his glory.

Milk and water copies, however, are they all, compared to the original Cheap John,—of whom an excellent portrayal was some time since presented at one of our theaters, under the Baker management, in Buckstone's melo-drama of the "Flower of the Forest;"—and we would recommend the fraternity of Long Wharf, when that piece is again presented, to attend, that they may learn how degenerate a race they have become, when compared to their progenitors, who bivouaced in the green lanes, and did their spiriting in the country towns of Old England.

Let us here leave the Auctioneers and the Cheap Johns to the tritons and minnows, alike wishing all prosperity. And when to mount the rostrum no more, their part, high or humble, in the great hurly-burly, shall be played out, may their last " Going, Gone," be all gentleness and peace!

TO MY MOTHER.

BY WM. C. P.

When Nature's feeble strength compels
    The mortal frame to rest,
And silently the dew-drop tells
    The bird to seek his nest,
At such a time, ere sweetest sleep
    Assumes its influence mild,
Thine eye appears, a watch to keep
    Around thy absent child.

And then, methinks, thy voice so sweet,
    In accents mild and clear,
With gentle chidings seems to greet
    My ever listening ear.
" My son! before you dare to sleep,
    Think o'er the day that's gone;—
No deed, no secret can you keep
    From God's eternal Son.

" Think o'er the day that's past and gone;
    Each action scrutinize;
For God doth keep for every one,
    A record in the skies.
Invoke your heavenly Father's care,
    To keep you through the night;
And to His throne again repair
    When breaks the morning light.

" Remember still, though years have flown,
    The lessons I have taught;
And prove, though you're to manhood grown,
    You have forgotten naught;
Did I but think thou hadst forgot
    The power of God to save,
'Twould bring my gray and silken locks
    With sorrow to the grave."

Mother! chide on; I will not dare
    To act against thy will;
Though age may fast upon me wear,
    Thou art my mother still!
Although compelled on earth to part—
    No more thy voice to hear—
Thy lessons to my childish heart
    Are still engraven there.

Mother! weep not; thy orphan child
    Remembers still the care
Which taught my heart, so young, so wild,
    To seek my God in prayer.
And though we never more shall meet,
    On spacious earth's domain;
In heaven we will each other greet,
    And never part again.

THE POEMS OF ALFRED TENNYSON.

BY C. E. HAVENS.

THE poet and poetess, whose writings best express the philosophic subtility which is so characteristic of a certain class of minds peculiar to our age, are Alfred Tennyson, and Elizabeth Barrett Browning. In the writings of both, it is easy to trace a refined Transcendentalism, which is not, indeed, entirely identified with the creed of those who profess to be teachers of this philosophy, but which so far coincides with it, as to leave no reasonable doubt as to what class of minds we must look to find a cause for this phenomenon in their poetry.

The false philosophies of the age, in the Satanic disguises of specious pretensions, and subtle sophistry, have perverted the intellectual truthfulness and power of many thinking minds, to a lamentable extent, and have tempted them to debase the genuine coin of genius with an alloy, which must destroy its currency, when the fact becomes fully and popularly known.

When Mr. Tennyson says, in his " In Memoriam,"—

> " There lives more faith in honest doubt,
> Believe me, than in half the creeds."

he merely repeats what has been said a hundred times before, by men who possessed none of his genius and not one quarter of his sense. It is nothing more or less than a repetition of the philosophic *slang* of the times ; and we must confess we were both surprised and pained on finding Mr. Tennyson so far the dupe of the author of " The Vestiges of Creation," as to pen the following lines :

> " They say,
> The solid earth whereon we tread
>
> In tracts of fluent heat began,
>   And grew to seeming random forms,
>   The seeming prey of cyclic storms,
> Till at the last arose the man,
>
> Who throve and branched from clime to clime,
>   The herald of a higher race,
>   And of himself in higher place,
> If so he type this work of time
>
> Within himself, from more to more ;
>   And, crowned with attributes of woe
>   Like glories, move his course, and show
> That life is not as idle ore,
>
> But iron dug from central gloom,
>   And heated hot with burning fears ;
>   And dipped in baths of hissing tears,
> And battered with the shocks of doom
>
> To shape and use. *Arise and fly*
>   *The reeling Faun, the sensual feast ;*
>   *Move upward, working out the beast,*
> *And let the ape and tiger die.*"[*]

[*] " In Memoriam," p. 188.

And again, in "The Princess," we find the same idea repeated:

> "This world was once a fluid haze of light,
>   Till toward the center set the starry tides
>   And eddied into suns, that wheeling cast
>   The planets: then the monster, then the man."

We can hardly believe Mr. Tennyson puts faith in any such nonsense as this, especially after the theory has been disclaimed and ridiculed by the highest living scientific authorities. We are satisfied, however, with merely pointing out this bad philosophy which disfigures so much of our finest modern poetry.

In attempting an analysis of our author's poetry, the first thing that arrests the attention, is the melody of words,—the musical simplicity of style. With the exception of Milton and Coleridge, he is surpassed by no other English author in this respect. The first stanza of the first poem is an illustration at hand.

> "Where Claribel low-lieth
>   The breezes pause and die,
>   Letting the rose-leaves fall:
> But the solemn oak-tree sigheth,
>   Thick-leaves, ambrosial,
>   With an ancient melody
>   Of an inward agony,
>   Where Claribel low-lieth."

We know of nothing in Milton's "Lycidas," more musical than the following from the "Lotos-Eaters":

> "Why are we weighed upon with heaviness,
>   And utterly consumed with sharp distress,
>   While all things else have rest from weariness?
>   All things have rest: why should we toil alone?
>   We only toil, who are the first of things,
>   And make perpetual moan,
>   Still from one sorrow to another thrown:
>   Nor ever fold our wings,
>   And cease from wanderings,
>   Nor steep our brows in slumber's holy balm;
>   Nor hearken what the inner spirit sings,
>   'There is no joy but calm!'
>   Why should we only toil, the roof and crown of things?"

"The effects of poetry," observes Madame de Stael, "depend still more on the melody of words, than on the ideas which they serve to express." The former appeals to the senses; the latter to the intellect; and we venture to say that the power of poetry over our *emotional* nature will be in proportion to the perfection of melodious expression.

Tennyson's versification is faultless. The delicacy of his ear does not allow a single verbal discord to pass unchallenged, and all the resources of the English language appear to have been laid under contribution by him in the selection of forcible and harmonious words.

It is evident also that Tennyson's genius is eminently constructive. He is a pains-taking artist of refined taste, in love with his profession, and in all probability as fastidious as Gray in the finish of his poetical productions. Rhyme is an ornament, and is not a necessity of his Muse. The exquisite melody of "The Lotos-Eaters," is equaled in his "Œnone" and "Morte d' Arthur," where he exhibits a great knowledge of musical effect in the subdivision of his sentences.

The *inventive* faculty, which Southey, of all modern poets possessed in the largest measure, is almost entirely wanting in Tennyson. We could hardly conceive the possibility of his writing a continuous epic. His genius delights in short flights. He rises like the lark into the Heavens, floods the blue concave with melody, and descends again to his lowly nest. In "The Princess," he has atoned for a deficiency of plot, by strewing songs and idyls along our pathway, and presenting a variety of separate pictures, abounding in a gorgeous description of details.

In common with Smith and Bailey, his poems abound in striking expressions; but his superiority over the former becomes abundantly evident, when, leaving details out of view, we base our judgment upon the general effect. The "smart sayings" of the Smith tribe are connected together by a series of inanities and sounding verbiage, which might better be written in prose, or not written at all. No "pillared marbles rare," or "generous arches," are built into or thrown over the blank interstices! The genius of these moderns is spasmodic to a frightful degree.

The poetry of Mr. Tennyson abounds in one grand defect; in the constant use of similes, instead of metaphors. There are too many comparisons and "likes." Genuine poetry is metaphorical. The ideas and images are parts of a symmetrical growth, and cannot be disjoined without violence done to the one or the other. They are thrown out simultaneously from the mind of the poet, and involve each other in the expression. They are fused in the alembic of the soul. A man of mere taste and sensibility would, in writing a poem, make use of similes. Having expressed an idea, he would next employ his taste and talent in finding a suitable illustration, and he would connect the two together by the word "like." Such poetry may be very choice in its language, and very beautiful in its sentiments; but it will also be sadly wanting in enthusiasm and life.

We would not be understood as affirming that our author never makes use of metaphorical language; on the contrary, the following quotations sufficiently refute the falsity of such an assertion:

> "Not like that Arthur who, with lance in rest,
> From spur to plume a *star of tournament*,
> Shot through the lists at Camelot, and charged
> Before the eyes of ladies and of kings."
>
> Vol. 1, p. 224.

> ——"quoted odes, and jewels five-words-long,
> That on the *stretched fore-finger of all Time*
> Sparkle forever."
>
> Vol. 2, p. 184.

> "Nor dare she trust a larger lay,
> But rather loosens from the lip
> *Short swallow-flights of song, that dip*
> *Their wings in tears, and skim away.*"
>
> "In Memoriam," p. 76.

> " Be near me when I fade away,
>   To point the term of human strife,
>   *And on the low, dark verge of life,*
>   *The twilight of eternal day.*"

" In Memoriam," p. 18.

> " And all the bugle breezes blew
>   Reveillée to the breaking morn."

" In Memoriam," p. 99.

Nor can we refrain from quoting the following beautiful similes :

> ———" yonder cloud

> That rises upward always higher,
>   And onward drags a laboring breast,
>   And topples round the dreary west,
>   *A looming bastion fringed with fire.*"

" In Memoriam," p. 31.

> " No longer caring to embalm
>   In dying songs a dead regret,
>   But like a statue, solid-set,
>   And moulded in colossal calm."

" In Memoriam," p. 209.

> " The gemmy bridle glittered free,
>   Like to some branch of stars we see
>   Hung in the golden galaxy."

" Lady of Shalott."

It will be noticed how, in all these quotations, the art of alliteration is made to produce a musical effect.

Mr. Tennyson has been a close observer of the peculiar scenery with which he has been surrounded, and its influence upon him is easily detected in his poetry. His faithful descriptions of nature have all the truthfulness of the Dutch school, idealized by a powerful imagination. His imagination abundantly saves him from the charge of being merely an imitative poet. One touch of his magic pen summons Nature before you, dressed out in its holyday garb, and glowing with ideal beauty. He loves Nature with a poet's heart. Whether he is describing the "*sullen*" yew standing in its "thousand years of gloom," the "towering sycamore" with all its "breadth and highth of foliage," the "whitening" willows, the "quivering aspens," the "*tangled* watercourses, *shot over with purple and green and yellow*," the "brook that loves to purl o'er matted cress and ribbed sand, or dimple in the dark of rushy coves," the "ridged wolds," or the "landscape *winking* through the heat," we detect the same close observation, the same wonderful power of description, the same overflowing heart worshiping at the footstool of its enthroned ideal, the same *unique* and remarkable faculty of entering at once into the *spirit* of Nature, and by one master-touch, embodying the essence in language sure of Immortality.

The sacredness of the subject hardly redeemed Mr. Tennyson from profanity in the use of the following lines :

> " But brooding on the dear one dead,
>   And all he said of things divine,
>   (*And dear as sacramental wine*
>   *To dying lips is all he said*)."

And we thought it an instance of bad taste in our author to say,

> "That not one life shall be destroyed,
> *Or cast as rubbish to the void,*
> When God hath made *the pile* complete."

The picture of Mariana's loneliness in the moated Grange, cannot be too highly commended. Every accessory that can highten the image of desolation is wrought up with inimitable skill. The "crusted flower-pots," the "rusted nails," the "weeds," the "flitting bats," in a twilight sky, the "glooming flats," the "shadow of the poplar" that falls across her bed, the creaking hinges and mouldering wainscots, the ticking clock and "thick-moated" sunbeams, are all combined to intensify the picture of vague hope and utter desolation.

We read the following poem over, lately, on one of those sweet, calm October days, when the landscape is lapped in haze and delightful warmth, the upland glowing in golden beauty, the beach and maple tinged with orange and scarlet, and no words can do justice to the poetic genius which has conveyed to us in such harmonious language the spirit of the scene:

> "Calm is the morn, without a sound,
> Calm as to suit a calmer grief;
> And only through the faded leaf
> The chestnut pattering to the ground:
>
> Calm and deep peace on this high wold,
> And on these dews that drench the furze,
> And all the silvery gossamers
> That twinkle into green and gold:
>
> Calm and still light on yon great plain,
> That sweeps, with all its autumn bowers,
> And crowded farms, and lessening towers,
> To mingle with the bounding main:
>
> Calm and deep peace in this wide air,
> These leaves that redden to the fall;
> And in my heart, if calm at all,
> If any calm, a calm despair:
>
> Calm on the seas, a silver sleep,
> And waves that sway themselves in rest,
> And dead calm in that noble breast
> Which heaves but with the heaving deep."

The beauties of Tennyson are not surface beauties. He gives the *spirit* of a scene as it strikes the soul, not the *form* as it strikes the eye. He cannot be appreciated without study and a prolonged acquaintance. He writes for the refined and educated; for men and women the *boudoir* and drawing-room. He must stand as the representative of the *aristocracy* of intellect in the *republic* of letters. This fact must forever keep his writings from a wide and extended celebrity. But to those who have once looked in upon his noble soul, through the transparent medium of his works, and made themselves acquainted with the movements of his extraordinary intellect, he must become valued and loved in a degree, that no other modern poet, with

the exception of Wordsworth, is able to command.   Much as he delights in the past, his sympathies are strongly on the side of progress,
spiritual elevation, and a higher state of humanity.   He is a man of
the times.

> "Ah! when shall all men's good
> Be each man's rule, and universal peace
> Lie like a shaft of light across the land,
> And like a lane of beams athwart the sea,
> Through all the circle of the golden year."

His faith in humanity is strong.   He believes that

> "—— through the ages one increasing purpose runs,
> And the thoughts of men are widened with the process of the suns."

and looks forward to a more perfect union and harmony of the sexes,
that shall bring the statelier Eden back to men.

> " *Then* reign the world's great bridals, chaste and calm,
> *Then* springs the crowning race of humankind."

Nevertheless, he acknowledges, that the age of struggles must pre-
cede the age of peace,

> ——"that which we are, we are;
> One equal temper of heroic hearts,
> Made weak by time and fate, but strong in will
> To strive, to seek, to find, and *not* to yield."

In scenes of pathos, Tennyson excels.   We are not sure that *tenderness* is not the prevailing characteristic of his poems.   Surely
nothing can be more affecting than the touching simplicity of the
"May Queen," and "New Year's Eve," and the following scene from
"The Princess," where the proud woman is humbled, is the very
quintessence of moving sensibility:

> "Pale was the perfect face;
> The bosom with long sighs labored; and meek
> Seemed the full lips, and mild the luminous eyes,
> And the voice trembled, and the hand.   She said,
> Brokenly, that she knew it, she had failed
> In sweet humility; had failed in all;
> That all her labor was but as a block
> Left in the quarry; but she still were loth,
> She still were loth to yield herself to one,
> That wholly scorned to help their equal rights
> Against the sons of men, and barbarous laws.
> She prayed me not to judge their cause from her
> That wronged it, sought far less for truth than power
> In knowledge: something wild within her breast,
> A greater than all knowledge, beat her down.
> *   *   *   *   *   *
> ——Her voice
> Choked, and her forehead sank upon her hands,
> And her great heart through all the faultful past
> Went sorrowing in a pause I dared not break."

In common with the best English poets, after Shakespeare, our
author is possessed of a fund of genuine humor.   True, it is confined
to a few exhibitions, but these sufficiently indorse its currency.   *Am-*

phion reminds us of our Yankee Lowell and Saxe, and *Will Water-proof's Lyrical Monologue* smacks of the good old times of Oliver Goldsmith. We think that Tennyson is deficient in spontaneity. No agitation accompanies his conceptions. He is not lifted on the wings of imagination from off his feet. He does not lose sight of the solid earth whereon we tread. His spirit is not whirled on the storm Euroclydon of impassioned ecstasy, or cradled in the dreams of an heroic trance. His eye is ever turned inward upon his own soul. His intellectual plummet sounds the depths of personal experience. He sits in solitude and silence to watch the fleeting impressions of the hour, to catch the far-off whispers of the spirit-land. His poetry does not resemble the living plant, crowned with the flower of impassioned genius, and redolent of incense ; it rather reminds us of a delicate mosaic, wrought up by infinite pains to some artistic and beautiful design.

But we must bring this criticism to a close. When we first took up our pen, we feared lest the excessive admiration we entertained for the poet and the man, should blind us to his faults and make us too indulgent of his errors. We hope we have not spoken in any case too harshly. Surely it is an honorable task to point out the faults of those whom we love and esteem ; and in this case, the man who has so well shown his affection for others, must be deserving of our best and highest regards.

Since Spencer wrote, English literature does not furnish a record of grief, so eloquent, as that which Alfred Tennyson has planted on the tomb of " Arthur Henry Hallam." The intellect and the heart met over that mausoleum, and the grave of the dead witnessed the epithalamium of love and sorrow. The stroke of Omnipotence which laid Arthur Hallam low on the shores of the Danube, almost crushed the heart of another that beat upon the banks of the Severn. But though the spirit of Tennyson could not fully comprehend the mystery of that dispensation which took from him the half of life, he turned it to wise and noble ends ; and the event which dictated the following lines, constituted the greatest epoch of his experience :

> " Break, break, break,
>   On thy cold gray stones, oh sea!
> And I would that my tongue could utter
>   The thoughts that arise in me.
>
> O well for the fisherman's boy,
>   That he shouts with his sister at play !
> O well for the sailor lad,
>   That he sings in his boat on the bay !
>
> And the stately ships go on
>   To the haven under the hill ;
> But, oh for the touch of a vanished hand,
>   And the sound of a voice that is still !
>
> Break, break, break,
>   At the foot of thy crags, oh sea !
> But the tender grace of a day that is dead
>   Will never come back to me."

MY GRANDMOTHER'S KITCHEN.

–

BY J. SWETT.

–

MANY years have gilded away since I last trod the nicely scoured floor of my aged grandmother's kitchen, and strangers now gather around its sacred hearthstone ; yet I well remember the old fashioned room, and, though far away from the old homestead, pleasant memories come floating through the mist of years ; and often, as to-night, in the stillness of my chamber, I am living over again the days when I reveled in my grandmother's antiquated hall.

Are there not *many* in whose minds the return of the holidays calls up home scenes, which, like old paintings in a picture gallery, have grown dim and dusty through the lapse of years ? The old farm-house in which my grandfather lived, was one of those magnificent two-storied shingle palaces found scattered all over New England ;— erected when timber was abundant and sturdy settlers seemed disposed to use as much of it as possible.

Its unpainted walls were black and weather-beaten ; warped clap-boards, which had loosened their rusty nails when the winds howled round the house, clattered mournfully against one another ; the roof was overgrown with green moss, which drew a precarious subsistence from the decaying shingles ; huge chamber windows were filled with boards instead of glass, and the whole air of the old building was that of some giant-framed old settler, with a face bronzed and hardened by exposure, and a muscular form clad in a plain, homespun suit of tow and linen. Though the storms of half a century had rocked the frame-work of the old house, its timbers were staunch and sound, and, like an old aristocrat, it looked down in contempt on the thin, white walls of the jaunty little modern cottages, springing up like mushrooms in the neighboring village.

But when its large rooms, in long winter evenings, were warmed by blazing fires in huge fire-places, the interior of the old farm-house brightened up, put on a cheerful smile, and stood the representative of New England character ;—cold, rough and uninviting to the eye of strangers, but concealing a central fire of deep feeling and true sympathy.

The kitchen, which would have contained a dozen California cooking cells, extended two-thirds the length of the house, and, being of proportionate width and hight, in addition to ordinary uses served as a grand hall for dances, apple-bees, quiltings and huskings.

The fire-place, which could conveniently swallow half a cord of wood at a mouthful, had a monster oven on one side, and on the other, a small seat, where, if the fire was not too hot, one could sit and study the stars twinkling over the top of the chimney.

The brick-work just over the fire-place, upon which my grandmother used to sharpen dull case-knives, with a skill absolutely marvelous—was worn quite smooth ; and higher up, close to the plastering, were four curious little recesses, sunk into the solid masonry, into which I could just peer by, standing on tip-toe in one of the high kitchen chairs.

They gave rise to much speculation in my youthful mind, and it was quite an epoch in my childish existence, when my curiosity was fully satisfied by ascertaining their use and contents.

My grandfather's cider-mug, pipe, tobacco and iron tobacco-box were deposited in one; in another, my grandmother's silver-bowed spectacles, in a red morocco case, her tin snuff-box, with a very curious lid, a plethoric little three-cornered pin-cushion, filled with pins and darning needles, a tin case of knitting-needles, and sometimes her knitting-work and a big ball of stocking-yarn; the third was ornamented with four copies of "Dudley Leavitt's Almanac,"—blackened by smoke, worn by much turning, and tied together at the corners by a waxed end,—an old pocket Bible in fine print, a Methodist Hymn Book, and a well-thumbed volume of "Pilgrim's Progress," with a startling frontispiece of Apollyon and Christian engaged in terrible conflict; and the last was usually found to contain a bunch of matches, some iron candlesticks, and four smooth-faced flat-irons.

Upon the hearth-stone of native undressed granite—worn smooth by long use—stood a sturdy pair of wrought andirons, grim and black, looking sullenly at the sooty back of the fire-place.

Above these swung a huge crane, hung all over with crooked hooks of various sizes, from the largest of which was suspended a monster tea-kettle of cast-iron, which, when tortured and roasted by a blazing fire, always manifested its agony by mournfully singing, or getting into a blustering passion and blowing off its heavy cover.

Yet, in spite of its asthmatic habits, the old black kettle always did its duty, and supplied my grandmother's little pet earthen tea-pot with a liberal daily allowance of hot water from its iron snout.

At one end of the kitchen was a long row of "dressers," with the lower shelves filled with milk pans of heavy earthenware or bright tin, while, on the upper were regularly ranged rows of pewter plates.

Two heavy platters, broad as the disc of the sun or the shield of Achilles, were flanked on either side by a host of little round pewter satellites, which, when scoured up by my grandmother's busy hands, shone like massive silver, and seemed a system of brilliant little full moons.

My grandmother regards these with peculiar affection, for they were the pride of her wedding dowry.

On the uppermost shelf was conspicuously arranged her China tea-set, with its diminutive plates, flat saucers and Lilliputian cups, on which were printed funny little Utopian landscapes.

When the old fire-place was filled with a bountiful supply of dry rock-maple, and huge pitch-pine knots as an extra stimulus, and the flame went warring up the great throat of the chimney like a volcanic fire, a kindred little mimic fire danced about the dressers, and blazed from the resplendent faces of the king and queen of platters.

Close by the dresser in a corner of the kitchen, stood the old-fashioned eight-day clock, holding up its aristocratic head, and looking down with sovereign contempt, whenever the parlor door was opened, on a little insignificant Yankee wooden time-piece, which modern innovation had placed on the parlor mantel.

How I loved to peep into that old clock, to watch the swinging of its great brass pendulum; or, standing in a chair, to peer into the mysterious little window in its head, where could be dimly seen a confused mass of wheels and pivots.   This old clock was one of the family. It had ticked away the happiest years of my worthy grandparents. Its *calculating* face had seen my grandmother change from a beautiful bride to a wrinkled and kind hearted old lady; it had seen my grandfather transferred from a sturdy young farmer, exulting in his strength, to an old man in the " lean and slippered pantaloon;" it had watched over a large family of sons and daughters, trained up to habits of industry, frugality and economy, and had seen them, one by one, go forth into the world; it had seen many a " parring bee," and ticked away the small hours of many a husking feast; it ticked away the dying moments of both my grandparents, and for aught that I know, is fagging on as when I last saw it, unconcerned and unmoved as if nothing ever happened to the family circle, that once loved and cherished it.   Close by the clock, always stood a great rocking-chair with a high perpendicular back, one wooden arm curiously turned, a leathern string in place of the other, and a great leathern cushion, which had once been used as a " pillion," in days when my grandmother and father used to ride together to church on Sunday.

Near the rocking-chair stood a little round light-stand, covered with a white linen cloth, on which lay the " old family bible," whose time-colored leaves I so often turned, to look at the " Family Record," read chapters full of old-fashioned *s's*, so much like *f's*, that I could detect no difference, and hunt for pictures of Moses, the Creation and Deluge.   Over the entry door hung an old " Queen's Arm," laid up in ordinary, except on the Fourth of July.   I regarded that old musket with peculiar veneration; for it had seen some service in its day, and was carried on my grandfather's shoulder in some hard fought battles of the Revolution.   Its stock was heavy and clumsy, like those clubbed with effect on old Bunker's Hill, and the rust-eaten barrel had a muzzle like a six pounder.   But it was a stauch old " Revolutioner," and I looked up to it with pride, and felt my young heart beat, as my grandfather would tell me of his battles and sufferings in the " Times that tried men's souls."   It was a dear old relic, which taught me the first lessons of patriotism; but the " old arm" eventually fell into the hands of Vandals, and I know not now where it is. At the window, which opened on the garden, stood the tea-table, on which my grandmother used to spread a cloth, white as the driven snow, and place her blue tea-set with curious little cups and saucers, on which was painted—if memory serves me right—a rural scene of a Chinese bridge and cottage, a Yankee girl seated on a three-legged stool milking a horned cow, and a back ground of palm-trees, lions and flocks of sheep.

But such delicious sage tea as my grandmother poured out into those queer cups! I remember the flavor to this day! and the delectable little cup custards—I shall never forget them!

My dear old grandmother, she little thought, while sweetening those cups of tea, she was sweetening the whole life of her little pet, to whose lips the bitter chalice was destined to be often pressed.

And, now, far away from the old kitchen, far distant from the friends of New England, the family circle is broken—ah! *nevermore* to meet to earth, those early memories come back to me like ministering angels.

ELEGY UPON THE DEATH OF A BELOVED FATHER.

—

BY FREDERICK CRICHTON.

—

> ALL this still legible in memory's page,
> And still to be so to my latest age,
> Adds joy to duty—makes me glad to pay
> Such honor to thee as my numbers may;
> Perhaps a frail memorial—but sincere;—
> Not scorned in Heaven, tho' little noticed here.—COWPER.

Father, farewell! no more on earth
  Thy form shall meet our view;
In vain, in homage to thy worth,
  Our tears thy grave bedew;
No more thy presence glads our sight—
No more thy words our ears delight;
Quenched is thy spirit's gentle light—
  Stilled is thine heart, so true.

No more shall anguish thrill thy breast,
  Nor sorrow cloud thy brow;
No torturing pain disturbs thy rest—
  Calm are thy slumbers now.
Full long, life's burden thou didst bear—
Full long its bitterest trials share;
Yet still, mid all thy woes and care,
  A patient sufferer thou!

Thy steadfast love our hearts must tell,
  For words are all too weak,
Deep in our memories e'er will dwell
  Feelings we cannot speak.
The love of friends, the world may know,
But thine was such as passeth show;
It warmed thine heart with inward glow,
  And brightened on thy cheek.

Again we mingle in the crowd—
  The rush, the throng of life,
While thou liest peaceful in thy shroud,
  Deaf to its cares and strife;
Yet ever mid the wild turmoil
That round us keeps perpetual coil,
Thy memory shall cheer our toil—
  Soothe pains 'neath which we writhe.

Green be the turf above thy head;
  There may the spring-flowers bloom,
And all their balmiest odors shed
  Around thy lowly tomb.
There may the early lambkins play,
The sky-lark carol all the day,
And nightingale, with sweetest lay,
  Enchant the evening's gloom.

Father in Heaven; who hear'st the prayer
  Of every child of thine—
Give us thy grace our lot to bear,
  Nor at our loss repine.
Give us the hope again to meet
The lost, the loved in Heaven to greet—
And, strengthened by that hope so sweet,
  We to thy will resign.

SCIENTIFIC.

[OUR readers are aware that, prior to the great exodus for California, much of the interior, and almost the entire western portions of our continent were comparatively unvisited by scientific research. The meteorology, the geology, the fossil remains, the ruins of cities and other evidences of a great and intelligent people who exist no more, the climatology, and even the geography of this section of the world, remained, as it were, sealed books. Within the last eighteen months, however, many interesting and valuable fragments of scientific information have made their way into light, through the medium of the dailies and weeklies of California. It is our intention to devote a few pages each month to the compilation of these various notices, accounts and descriptions of archæological and geological facts, and natural phenomena, in the hope that, by thus gathering the fragments, (almost useless in their present state), and presenting them in a connected, and, as far as possible, systematic form, we shall be able to supply a want which must have been long felt, not only by the scientific men of California, but by those of our readers in general, who are desirous of being, to say the least, not altogether uninformed when the archæological, the geological history, and, in general, the past condition of their adopted soil, shall be the theme of conversation.—ED. PIONEER.]

FOSSIL REMAINS.

No better preface to this chapter of the scientific department could be made, than that furnished by the remarks of Dr. W. O. Ayers, in his report of the meeting of the California Academy of Natural Sciences, Oct. 30, 1854.

"In many instances," says he, "and at various points within the State, during the last five years, fossil bones have been brought to light, in mining operations, in digging wells, etc. A few of these are still in existence, though by far the greater portion, so far as we can learn, are hopelessly lost.

It is most earnestly to be desired that those who have now in their possession any such fossils, or who may in future make discoveries of them, will preserve them with great care, and take measures for their proper study and investigation.

The subscriber will be very glad to receive fossil remains, from any and every portion of the State, and will endeavor to make them subserve the true ends of science. It may be remarked that a public collection is much more suitable for the preservation of objects of such interest, than any other can be, as it renders them more generally available. And any specimens that may be sent, as here requested, unless the donors direct otherwise, will be deposited (in the name of the donor) with the California Academy of Natural Sciences. Specimens, of which the owners may wish to retain possession, will be returned with care, as soon as accurate examinations and drawings can be made of them.

It is scarcely possible to over-estimate the value of a careful study of remains, such as those here mentioned, more particularly in a region where geological results bear so vitally on the interests of the community, as they do in California. The same cataclysm that buried the elephant and his brother monsters, and swept away the palm groves and luxuriant forests in which they had sported, brought the gold where it now lies, within our reach.

Every item of information concerning specimens, which may be forwarded, as to the depth at which they are found, the rock, clay or sand in which they lay, etc., will add much to their value. Even fragments of bones are worthy of preservation, since a very small piece will often reveal the character of the entire skeleton, and, of course, of the animal which it once supported."

In confirmation of the justness of the position assumed by Dr. Ayres, at the close of the above remarks, the reader need only to be referred to the researches of the celebrated George Curvier, of whom and his studies and labors in comparative and fossil anatomy, Jules Janin thus enthusiastically speaks:

"He was one entire science in himself,—I had almost said, he was every science; he was in every respect, of the family of Gallileo and Newton, of those men who at a single bound, attain the limits of the world. It was in the saloons of comparative anatomy, in the midst of their long series of skeletons, and in comparing modern fragments of bone, with these old worm-eaten bones of dead bodies which come to us from the deluge like so many fabulous vestiges of another universe, that George Cuvier was astonished by the startling discovery, that the greater part of those fossil bones had no analogies among those of living beings. Without doubt, those animals, of whom he did know even the name, had lived upon the earth; without doubt they had had their passions, their instincts, their utility, their loves. It was most certain that here were their bones; here was the head of this one; there, the thigh bone of that one; one had left in the slime of the globe this broken tooth; another that curved horn, and now this is all that remains of them; not an entire individual of their extinct families is preserved. Nor can they be identified with a single one of those names which are met with in Herodotus and the Bible. He set himself to work then to reanimate their mouldering dust, to renew their vanished forms, to restore to these petrifactions the names which they bore, when they roamed in the woods, when they swam in the sea, when they gazed face to face upon the sun. Surely it was one of those tasks, the very thought of which makes one shudder. What then? you are unable to tell the names of the dead bodies interred beneath the pyramids of Egypt, even when the name of the deceased is written upon the eternal stone, and do you dare to speak assuredly of what is the name of an animal, which had already become stone before the Pyramid of Cheops was founded? Nevertheless, this did Cuvier do. He has given names—as well as that God who made them—to those long vanished animals of the globe which the earth had engulphed in her bowels."

Thus, by observing certain differences between fossil bones and those of species still living, this celebrated naturalist was led to the discovery of numerous extinct animals, and even, in some instances, to the successful construction of their skeletons, many of which, as the mastodon and megatherium, were of immense size!

But, perhaps the most remarkable instance of a single bone, serving as a register or index to the formation of an entire animal, and the discovery of an extinct and hitherto unknown species, is that of the celebrated New Zealand bird, whose skeleton is exhibited in the Museum of the Royal College of Surgeons, London. The causes which led to its discovery, and the manner in which it was obtained, are thus related by Mr. S. Warren, in his entertaining book entitled "Intellectual and Moral Development of the Present Age:"

"It must first be premised, that Cuvier had said, that, in order to deduce from a single fragment of its structure the entire animal, it was necessary to have a tooth, or an entire articulated extremity. In his time the comparison was limited to the external configuration of bone. The study of the internal structure had not proceeded so far.

In the year 1839, Professor Owen was writing alone in his study, when a shabbily dressed man made his appearance, announcing that he had got a great curiosity, which he had brought from New Zealand, and wished to dispose of to him. Any one in London can now see the article in question, for it is deposited in the Museum of the College of Surgeons in Lincolns Inn Fields. It has the appearance of an old marrow bone, about six inches in length, and rather more than two inches in thickness, with both extremities broken off; and Professor Owen considered that to whatever animal it might have belonged, the fragment must have lain in the earth for centuries. At first he considered this same marrow bone to have belonged to an ox,—at all events to a quadruped, for the wall or rim of the bone was six times as thick as the bone of any bird, even the ostrich. He compared it with the bones in the skeleton of an ox, a horse, a camel, and every quadraped apparently possessing a bone of that size and configuration, but it corresponded with none. On this he very narrowly examined the surface of the bony rim, and at length became satisfied that this monstrous fragment must have belonged to a bird; to one at least as large as an ostrich, but of a totally different species, and, consequently, one never heard of, as an ostrich was by far the biggest bird known. From the difference in the strength of the bone, the ostrich being unable to fly, so must have been unable this unknown bird; and so our anatomist came to the conclusion that this old, shapeless bone indicated the former existence in New Zealand of some hugh bird, at least as great as the ostrich, but of a far heavier and more sluggish kind. Professor Owen was confident of the validity of his conclusions, but could communicate that confidence to no one else. And, notwithstanding attempts to dissuade him from committing his views to the public, he printed his deductions in the transactions of the Zoological Society for the year 1839, where, fortunately, they remain on record as conclusive evidence of the fact of his having then made this guess, so to speak, in the dark. He caused the bone, however, to be engraved; and, having sent one hundred copies of the engraving to New Zealand, in the hopes of their being distributed, and leading to interesting results, he patiently waited for three years; namely, till the year 1842, when he received intelligence from Dr. Buckland, at Oxford, that a great box, just arrived from New Zealand, consigned to himself, was on its way, unopened, to Professor Owen; who found it filled with bones possibly of a bird, one of which was three feet in length, and much more than double the size of any bone in the ostrich. And out of the contents of this box the professor was positively enabled to articulate almost the entire skeleton of a huge wingless bird, between ten and eleven feet in hight, its bony structure in strict conformity with the fragment in question; and that skeleton may be at any time seen at the Museum of the College of Surgeons, towering over, and nearly twice the hight of the skeleton of an ostrich; and at its feet is lying the old bone from which alone consummate anatomical science had deduced such an astounding reality; the existence of an enormous extinct creature of the bird kind, in an island where previously no bird had been known to exist larger than a pheasant or a common fowl."

A writer whose communication appears in the *Art Magazine* of January 1854, in relating the same story, says:

"That Professor Owen made a drawing of the skeleton of the bird, which he had deduced from the wonderful bone. And when the box arrived at his destination, the bones were put together on wires and *found the very skeleton which he had depicted.* Some of the vertebræ of the neck are yet wanting; but a wire represents the length to which they should extend. Let us hope, as gold hunting has now commenced in New Zealand, that some nugget-hunter will turn up, among his more ignoble treasure, those missing bones, and thus enable the worthy anatomist to complete his bird."

As german to this subject we insert an extract from the *San Francisco Herald* of Nov. 24, quoted from the *Calaveras Chronicle,* in which the writer endeavors to prove the existence of tertiary deposits in California:

"It is considered to be of consequence to be acquainted with the ages of our auriferous deposit, and more especially of the older ones, with a view to the discovery of new *placeres* by geological signs, or characteristic outward features. Notwithstanding the importance of organic remains as a test of age, from the paucity of these criteria in the auriferous formations, and the peculiar circumstances commonly attending the finding thereof, they are dubiously patent to the subject. It has often been urged by many, and by geologists of distinguished position, that there are no tertiary auriferous deposits in California. This assertion is gratuitous, and unsupported by any kind of evidence, even of a negative nature.

Organic remains, of presumed tertiary date, are found overlaying auriferous strata. Professor Trask has exhibited the fact of the existence of late tertiary strata near Murphy's—this formation extends westward beyond the head waters of the San Antonio, far up towards the Sierra Nevada. The reader will also be aware of the notation, by that gentleman, of an auriferous conglomerate formation of great extent in the northern part of the State, which he calls the 'Blue Range,' of a yet more ancient origin than that at Murphy's.

For curiosity's sake, a few examples are given of organic and other remains, found within the personal knowledge of the writer, in Calaveras county.

At Volcano, a perfectly preserved hyena's tooth, sixty feet from the surface, in a large land slip.

At Calaveritas, large stone mortars, from two to three feet in diameter, with their pestles, in the ancient bed of the river.

At Yankee, part of a bullock's horn, transformed into a magnesian concretion, with the silicified trunk of a pine, two feet in diameter, within a deposit from eight to ten feet deep, post-diluvial.

At Vallecito, human skulls, in post-diluvial strata, upwards of fifty feet deep.

At San Andreas, specimens of impressions of twenty-eight different kinds of trees, shrubs, etc., in drift, all of existing species, in the same vicinity, amongst which, were the live oak, scented willow, elm, mansenita, a kind of whortle, soap plant, absynthe, sun-flower, grapes, etc., within the debris of trachytic lava and boulders, at twenty-six feet below the surface, in an ancient water course. (These were found by the writer.)

At Moquelumne Hill, obsidian, large spear heads, (in '49) in Red Flat Gulch; and drifted wood in diluvian, ninety feet below the surface, near Stockton Hill—by the writer.

Near Murphy's, mammoth bones, forty feet below the surface—tertiary.

At Columbia, (Stanislaus) mammoth bones, in an osseous state, at a depth of thirty-five feet. The latter crumbled to dust upon exposure to the air; they consisted of the fragments of the thigh, and other bones of a huge animal; one of them was about eighteen inches long, and upwards of four inches in diameter—tertiary.

In the absence of reliable data, to be obtained from the observation of organic remains, satisfactory results may generally be arrived at, from an examination of the rocks themselves. The presence of these remains may be a criterion of age, but they may not indicate the presence or absence of auriferous earth, which to the practical miner is the main object.

It may be generally assumed, as an axiom, that the whole of the boulder and conglomerate formations, immediately derived from the wreck of the great quartz leads, are auriferous in some degree. It is presumed, also, that concentrated deposits near the original matrix are naturally the richest; and those concentrated from current influence—accidentally so—abundant examples exist. Of the former, we have an instance at French Hill; of the latter in the gulches adjoining.

An attempt at general classification of the ancient auriferous stratifications being made according to great quartz groups, in a transverse direction across the mining districts, we note:

The Boulder Formations, derivable from the oldest or Eastern Group.—These are comparatively poor in auriferous yield, because of the hardness of the matrix and the containing rock, the lesser degree of active disturbance to which they have been subject, and consequently the smaller amount of detrition.

The Middle Group Boulder Deposit.—These are more extensive and richer than the former, from consequences directly contrary, added to the fact that the range of quartz leads under this classification are more numerous, and are accompanied by the fuller presence of chemical decomponents, that only require an affinitive action from atmospheric influences, to aid greatly towards a denuding force; and,

The Western Conglomerates.—The quartz formations over which these are found, are more ramified, and yet more easily denuded than the former; the placer accumulations are, therefore, less concentrated in richness, but more generally diffused; the boulders are generally very much smaller, and (not as a consequence) the gold finer.

These divisions follow irregular lines from north to south. The first group terminates westward, on a line near Independence and McLinney's; the boulders are highly quartzose, but contain little pure quartz. The second terminates westward near Chile Hill and Vallecito, and is associated with huge boulders of quartz, and concentrated accumulations of gold on the bed rock. The western extends thence as far westward as placers have been found in the foot hills, and contains fine gold, very generally diffused in finer conglomerates and gravel."

LAW REVIEW.

ABSTRACT OF THE DECISIONS OF THE SUPREME COURT.

BELOW will be found an abstract of the decisions of the Supreme Court, delivered during the July Term, 1854. The abstract was prepared by E. B. CROCKER, Esq., and was first published in the Sacramento *Democratic State Journal :*

CAVENDER *vs.* GUILD.—Action on a foreign judgment. The limitation act of 1852 only alters a portion of Sec. 17, of the act of April 22, 1850, but does not change that part of the statute under which this suit was brought. The act of 1850 being unchanged, the limitation on foreign judgments is five years.

The interest laws of Missouri must be proved, like any other fact, and cannot be judicially taken notice of by the Court. The judgment presented does not call for interest, and without proof that the laws of Missouri allowed interest on judgments, none can be allowed.

EARL *vs.* BESSE.—To make property the wife's separate estate, it must have been conveyed to her before marriage, or if afterwards, it must have been by gift. Although the District Judge stated that the leased premises were the property of the wife, acquired by gift from her father during marriage, yet, as the evidence shows no proof of that fact, and as it is not his province, in a jury trial, to pronounce upon the facts, no weight can be given to it.

PIXLEY *vs.* ROWE.—Judgment reversed, because the Court failed to find the issues of law and fact separately.

YOUNGS *vs.* BELL.—Under the practice act, a party is not required to deny the genuineness of an indorsement under oath; and the District Court erred in admitting the notes in evidence without proof of their indorsement. When the answer sets up several distinct defenses, the party is not concluded by one plea, so long as he had others which went to the whole action.

HAWLEY *vs.* DALMAS.—The affidavit for an attachment ought to state the ground in positive terms—a description in the alternative has always been held insufficient.

ROSS *vs.* POWELL.—Our statute requires the action to be presented in the name of the real party in interest. One described in an instrument as the Attorney in fact of another, is not a trustee, and is not a necessary party to represent the principal. The wife was not a necessary party. Her joining in the mortgage was unnecessary to make it valid, unless it were her separate estate. If it be her separate estate, her rights are unaffected by the decree of foreclosure. The plaintiff's husband was joined in the suit with her. On motion of defendant, his name was stricken out. Defendant cannot now assign as error his non-joinder. When there is a defect in the complaint which is not pointed out by the demurrer, it must be considered as waived. When, upon any objection, we can plainly discover from the record that no injustice has been done, we will not reverse the judgment.

STEARNS *vs.* MARTIN.—All evidence in relation to a joint contract should be excluded where the pleadings set up a several contract alone.

RAY *vs.* PATTEN.—A foreign judgment is not "a contract, obligation, or liability for the payment of money founded on an instrument of writing executed out of this State," within the meaning of the statute of limitations.

CORWIN *vs.* PATCH.—When the answer contains no good defense, and the plaintiff submitted the case on the pleadings alone, the District Court properly excluded all evidence on the part of the defendant, and directed jury to find for the plaintiff.

EQUY *vs.* BUCHANAN.—There is no statement of the case or bill of exceptions, and consequently nothing in the record to impeach the judgment.

FOWLER *vs.* SMITH.—To enable defendant to prove that the notes sued on were given for a lot to which plaintiff had no title, the answer ought to aver paramount title in another person specifically waived, and offer to redeliver the possession, and account for the rents and profits.

An agreement to take a less amount in payment of a debt due, if made without consideration, is *nudum partum.* The defendant totally neglected to comply with his stipulations necessary to entitle him to the benefit of plaintiff's offer.

HARLEY *vs.* YOUNG.—The statement was served more than twenty days after judgment—the case must, therefore, rest upon the judgment roll. The statement should, in all cases, be signed by the Judge, except when agreed to by the parties or their attorneys.

DEMPSEY *vs.* MORAN.—A purchaser at Sheriff's sale, is not invested with title until six months after the sale, the time allowed for redemption. Ejectment, therefore, will not lie until the expiration of that time, as then the defendant may peaceably surrender the possession.

THE PEOPLE *vs.* KOHLE.—After twelve jurors in a criminal case had been called and accepted, the prisoner, having still ten peremptory challenges, has a right to challenge a juror at any time before the jury are sworn. He has a right to exhaust his challenges at any time before the jury are sworn.

THE PEOPLE *vs.* THOMPSON.—The affidavit for a continuance in a crimnal case should show that the testimony is not cumulative, and cannot be proved by others; that the application is not made for delay, and the character of the diligence used in trying to obtain the witness. The allegation that the party has used all the diligence in his power is not sufficient, it should appear what diligence was used—and this is very important in this country, where there are so many changes.

A plea of not guilty may be entered by the attorney in the absence of the prisoner, but not a plea of guilty. It was no error in the Court to fix the time for execution, beyond the time fixed by law; and it was competent for the Court at any time before final judgment signed, to amend its judgment, and fix the time within the period fixed by statute.

RITCHIE *vs.* PEACHY.—The statute respecting arbitration is but a re-affirmance of the common law, and gives a party no higher rights than he might have asserted in a court of equity in case of a mistake, fraud or accident. The misconduct contemplated by the statute, applies to improper conduct in fact, such as that of a witness or juror, as contradistinguished from a mere error of judgment. The case of Muldrow *vs.* Norris, 2 Cal. 14, lays down the proper rules on the subject of arbitrations.

SMITH *vs.* STILLMAN.—Consent of parties will not confer jurisdiction on a Court; but when a Court has once obtained jurisdiction, the form of action may be changed or modified; and all objections from questions of mere form or practice may be waived by consent of parties.

By the act of 1851, the Superior Court of San Francisco was continued, but the number of Judges was diminished. The Legislature has the right to abolish an office; but while the office is continued, the officer has a vested right in it, during the time for which he is appointed. The appointment to office, and its acceptance, is a contract, and neither party has the right to violate its binding efficacy. An officer cannot be legislated out of his right, and another provided to take his place.

REDMAN *vs.* BELLOMY.—The plaintiff claims under a Sheriff's sale, on an execution upon a decree of foreclosure of a mortgage, given by the defendant. Defendant is therefore estopped from setting up the defense attempted in this case.

ARMSTRONG *vs.* RAY.—By the award, the defendant was to leave the premises on the 9th. Plaintiff served notice to quit on the third, and commenced suit on the tenth. Under the award, plaintiff had no right to give notice to quit until the tenth; and then by the forcible entry act, defendant had six days in which to remove, before plaintiff's right of action accrued. The suit was, therefore, prematurely brought.

MOODY *vs.* MCDONALD.—There is nothing in the award suggestive of an appeal. Judgment affirmed with damages.

ALLEN *vs.* PHILIPS.—Error must be clearly manifest and will not be implied.

TREADWELL *vs.* WELLS.—Newspapers were admitted in evidence to prove notice of a dissolution of partnership. It was proven that one of the papers was taken by plaintiffs, and left at their place of business for several weeks. *Held,* that other papers were admissible, to show the publicity of the notice, and raise the presumption of actual notice to plaintiff.

The Court has no right to charge the jury with respect to matters of fact; and, therefore, correctly refused to give instructions of that kind.

WAN & Co. *vs.* CANNEY.—The statute does not require written complaints in actions before a justice of the peace; and the mere filing of an account is sufficient—and it is not error that the names of the plaintiffs composing the firm of Wan & Co. were not set out in the pleadings. The County Court, if deemed necessary, should have allowed the plaintiff to amend instead of dismissing the case.

CAHOON & LENT *vs.* LEVY—NATHAN (garnishee).—The answer of the garnishee does not disclose any lien upon the building, having priority of claim upon the fund in his hands. Judgment should have been entered in conformity with the liability of the garnishee upon his answer.

RICH *vs.* RUSSELL.—Counts in tort ought not to be joined with counts in contract.

If the plaintiff's object was to waive the torts and sue in contract, he ought to have so expressed in his pleadings.

GARCIA *vs.* SATRUSTIGUE.—When the statement of the case has not been made in conformity with the statute, it is no part of the record, and the case must rest on the judgment roll.

The declaration does not allege a delivery of the bond sued on. Advantage of this might have been taken by demurrer, but the defect is cured by the verdict, no demurrer having been filed.

KRITZNER *vs.* WARNER.—The contract declared on was joint, and if Warner was not a party to it, he could not be liable. The reception of money by him on the work done, would not fix his liability. It would be a mere circumstance to be left to the jury, tending to show that he may have been a party to the contract.

RIDDLE *vs.* BLAKE.—To rescind a contract upon the ground that the plaintiff could not perform because he had no title to the land, the answer should aver, and it should be proved, that there was an outstanding paramount title in another.

FITZGERALD *vs.* URTON.—The act giving jurisdiction to County Courts in cases of nuisance, does not take away the jurisdiction of the District Court, by the Constitution, over such cases.

BEQUETTE *vs.* CAULFIELD.—Possession is evidence of title, and gives a right of action against a mere trespasser, even where title may be shown to exist in another.

When a party can show nothing but a prior possession, it may be shown. that he voluntarily abandoned his possession without the purpose of returning, and his right will fail.

MOWRY *vs.* STARBUCK.—The time fixed by the Statute for the return of a jury by the Sheriff, is directory, and not mandatory.

It rests in the sound discretion of the Court to allow further evidence to be introduced by either or both parties, after the testimony has been closed.

In an action for work and labor, it is competent to show that the original contract plan had been changed at request of defendants, and the value of the extra work performed.

It is error to allow a party to read from a paper not in evidence, but as no harm could arise from it in this case, the verdict will not be disturbed.

WATSON *vs.* McCLOY.—Where the Court below has granted a new trial upon a review of the facts alone, this Court will not disturb it.

ROWE *vs.* KOHLE & WIFE.—Our statute does not change the common law, upon the relation of husband and wife, except in the particular cases expressly provided by the statute. A *feme covert* cannot contract under the laws of this State, so as to render her liable in a suit at law.

There are cases laid down in the books, in which a woman may bind herself and her separate property. In such cases a Court of Equity would enforce the contract. If this action was intended for a proceeding in Chancery, there are no equities disclosed in the bill. If the plaintiffs have any rights, they must maintain them in another suit.

FRUIT *vs.* PHELPS.—Plaintiff sold to defendant a contract for the sale and delivery of certain lumber, the plaintiff to perform his part of the contract. The lumber was to be delivered alongside of any ship plaintiff should designate, at any time after six months, upon three days' notice.

Held, it was not necessary to give this notice in writing, the contract not requiring it. The plaintiff should have been ready to pay for the lumber whenever it was ready for delivery, and the fact that he was absent in a remote region is no excuse for not paying.

It was not necessary for the defendant to prove that plaintiff was not ready to pay. The fact that he did not pay, and that the delivery was refused in consequence, was sufficient to sustain the defense, and relieved defendant from paying for the contract.

STURGIS *vs.* BARRY.—A motion for judgment against bail is similar to a *scire facias,* to which the defendant may interpose any proper plea by way of defense.

RAMIREZ *vs.* McCORMICK.—Plaintiff in a lease of a cellar reserved eight feet in width at one end of the building, from which the cellar which he retained can be reached, and there was no express stipulation that he was to have a right to enter through the premises of the defendant. *Held,* that the reservation of a right to use the cellar, did not imply a right to pass over the defendant's premises to reach the cellar, when he also reserved the eight feet of ground by which he would enjoy its use.

THE PEOPLE *vs.* STEWART.—The indictment for murder will not be set aside, on the ground that the Grand Jury found the bill solely on the depositions of witnesses, taken by the committing magistrate, the witnesses being in the county. The Grand Jury under the statute have the right to use such depositions.

The District Court, under the statute, may summon a trial jury under an order at any time, when necessary, during the term.

It is contended that it does not appear from the record that the prisoner was present at the trial and at the rendition of the verdict. If he was really absent, he should have shown that fact clearly, and there is enough in the language of the Judge when passing sentence, to raise the presumption that he was present at said time.

VERMEULE *vs.* SHAW.—The statement in the case is not certified by the Judge, nor agreed upon by the parties; it is therefore no part of the record, and is excluded from our consideration.

The judgment was entered on the 11th, and the Judge wrote his findings of fact and conclusions of law, but did not file it until next day. *Held,* sufficient.

Murray C. J. dissenting.

STOUGHTON *vs.* SWAN.—Notice to an indorser of the dishonor of a note or bill, is sufficient if it appear or can reasonably be inferred from the notice, that the bill or note has been duly presented for payment, and dishonored. The "protested" has a definite and legal signification, and is sufficient in a notice.

VINES *vs.* WHITTON.—The County Surveyor Act is explicit in including as evidence the surveys of any other than the County Surveyor, except where it may be necessary to rebut or explain the official survey.

It is the object of the act, whenever a re-survey is necessary that it shall be performed by the County Surveyor, and a record kept of it in his office.

MONTHLY SUMMARY OF EVENTS.

—

" With news the time 's in labor and brings forth
Each minute some."

—

November 8.   The official returns of the late election were published in the papers and showed the total vote of the State to be 84,604. . . . A fatal duel occurred near Oakland, between Col. D. J. Woodlief and Achilles Kewen, Esq., in which the former lost his life.   The distance was forty paces, and the weapons, Mississippi rifles.   Col. Woodlief fell dead at the first discharge.   Mr. Kewen, who was the challenged party received no injury.

November 9.   Several persons charged with illegally blockading Leidesdorff street with fish and fruit stands, were fined $50 each by the Recorder. . . . A diminutive daily paper, ten by twelve inches in size, entitled *Town Talk*, made its first appearance. . . . The Nic. S. S. Cortes left for San Juan carrying away treasure to the value of $873,280, and among her passengers Hon. J. B. Weller and lady, Hon. J. A. McDougall and Winslow S. Pierce, late State Comptroller. . . . A prize fight fight took place at Grass Valley between Con. Fitzgerald and Hugh Kelly.   4,000 people attended as spectators.   At the seventh round, the latter went down, when the ropes were cut and the spectators rushing in put an end to the disgraceful proceedings.

November 10.   The new Public School House of district No. 4, situated on Union street, between Kearny and Broadway streets, was dedicated with appropriate ceremonies.   Mayor Webb presided.   Prayers were offered by Rev. Messrs. Bryarly and Cutler.   Several original songs, written by Messrs. J. Truett and E. Grady were sung, and speeches creditable both to themselves and the occasion, were delivered by His Honor Mayor Webb, Messrs. Cutler, Moore and Billings.

November 11.   The Pennsylvania Fire Company, No. 12, tried their new engine.   It threw a stream of water 179 feet through 350 feet of hose and a seven-eighth nozzle. . . . The first sale of fifty-vara lots west of Larkin street, was made by Messrs. Wainright, Randall & Co. . . . The U. S. Steam Frigate Susquehanna, Commander Franklin Buchanan, arrived, eleven days from Honolulu.

November 12.   The third anniversary meeting of the City Tract Society was held in the First Congregational Church. . . . Wheeler, the pedestrian, completed the great feat of walking one hundred consecutive hours.

November 13.   The St. Francis Hook & Ladder Company, No. 1, housed their new truck, which had been built at an expense of $4,500, by Messrs. J. Berry & Co., of this city.   The occasion was celebrated by a procession of the members of the company and friends, through the streets, and a festival at their house. . . . The P. M. S. S. Golden Gate, arrived, eleven days and sixteen hours from Panama.   She brought news of the wreck of the steamship Artic, of the Collins line, by which 300 lives were lost.

November 14.   Mrs. P. Dillon presented the Lafayette Hook & Ladder Company, No. 2, a handsome gold embroidered silk banner, made in France, which the Company acknowledged by a vote of thanks. . . . The Italian Opera Company made its first appearance in "Ernani."   Madame Barili Thorn, assisted by Signora Becherini, Signs. Leonardi, Lanzoni, Scola and Laglaise, performing the principal parts.   Barili was enthusiastically received, and the representation was highly successful. . . . The twelfth quarterly report of the Public Schools, published in the *Herald*, showed the number of scholars during the present year to be 3,780, and an increase over that of the past year of 571 boys and 479 girls; making a total of 1050.

November 15.   Judge Norton of the Twelfth Judicial District Court, in the case of Hood *vs.* Fish & Williams, made an important decision against the validity of tax titles. . . . In the case of Leonard *vs.* Darlington, in the Fourth Judicial District Court, involving the question of the southern boundary of the city, the jury found a verdict sustaining the decision of the U. S. Land Commissioners. . . . The Mercantile Library Association had a benefit at the Metropolitan Theater. . . . The drawing of Duncan's great Art-Union Raffle took place at the Metropolitan Theater. The first prize, the Napoleon drawings or a gold ingot worth $5,000, was won by Capt. Warren of the sloop Roman. . . . A new paper published at Sacramento and entitled *The California Statesman* made its first appearance.

November 16.   Judge Freelon of the Court of Sessions decided that no trial for Crime or Misdemeanor could be valid unless made by a jury. . . . The New Steamer Eclipse was launched from the foot of Third street—she is the largest Steamer ever launched in California, being 235 feet long, 33 feet beam, 8 feet hold.   She was built in New Albany, Indiana taken to pieces, brought hither and again put together—she has six boilers, and two high-pressure engines of 800 horse power, cost $200,000 and is intended for the Sacramento trade. . . . The P. M. S. S. Golden Gate left, carrying treasure to the value of $1,675,318.

November 17.   Gen. Vallejo gave additional testimony before the U. S. Land Commission, which altered somewhat the direction of the Southern Boundary of the City, bringing it further to the North than was hitherto supposed.   Mons. and Madame Monplaisir had a benefit at the "People's Theater." . . . In the case of Lewis *vs.* Gordon & Stien being an action brought before the Twelfth District Court to recover damages for injuries sustained by the explosion of the Steamboat Secretary, the jury brought in a verdict against the defendants and awarding plaintiff $2,000. . . . The French Frigate Eurydice left the harbor, destination unknown.

November 19.   Mons. Espinosa had a benefit at the Metropolitan Theater, on which occasion the Pantomime of "Jocko" was produced. . . . The French Admiral Ship La Forte set sail for Mazatlan.

November 20.   The Nicaragua Company's S. S. Sierra Nevada arrived 12 days from San Juan, bringing news that contradicted the report that Sebastapol was taken—and of the discovery of the remains of Sir John Franklin and his party near Fox River.   They were supposed to have died of starvation while on their way overland to the Hudson Bay Co's settlements. . . . The Common Council adopted a resolution requiring the City Assessor to proceed forthwith and make an assessment of all the taxable property within the City, a requirement rendered necessary, because the Council had hitherto adopted the assessments made by the County Assessors, a course of procedure which, by the ruling of Judge Norton, in a case brought before him to test the validity of a tax title, was declared to be illegal. . . . The New World and Queen City, while on the passage from Sacramento, came in collision, inflicting some damage to the latter.

November 21.   Christy's Minstrels, who have been performing for some time past to crowded houses, gave a farewell concert preparatory to a tour in the interior. . . . Manuel Sanchez was arrested for shooting at a man named Juan Ringaud while wheeling a barrow across his rancho. . . . The U. S. Steam Frigate Mississippi, Capt. S. S. Lee, arrived in eleven days from Honolulu. . . . The proprietors of many of the drinking saloons of the City held a meeting for the purpose of considering the propriety of abolishing the "Free Lunches." . . . In the Court of Sessions, George Crow was sentenced to one year in the State Prison for stealing $600.

November 20.   In the matter of the Stands on Leidesdorff street, it was agreed by the parties, in the suits, to submit one case to a jury, and that the decision of that case should be final for all the others. . . . The proprietors of the drinking Saloons had another meeting upon the question of abolishing Free Lunches, but could come to no conclusion. . . . A number of trees were planted in Portsmouth Square.   The Russian Flag was run up, and a salute of twenty-one guns were fired on board the American ship Zenobia, in honor of the achievement at Petropoloski and the failure at Sebastapol, and a salute of seven guns as a token of respect to the Russian Consul Kostromitinoff, by whose direction the commemoration was made. . . . The Courts adjourned in token of respect to the memory of Ambrose Gorham, Esq., late Associate Justice of the Court of Sessions, who died the day previous. . . . A number of dogs, which infested Clay street near Kearny, were poisoned by some unknown hand, their dying agonies attracted a large number of spectators.

November 23. Appointed by the Governor to be observed as a day of Prayer and Thanksgiving. The Banking-Houses and principal places of business were closed. Religious services were performed in the Churches. The City Guards and San Francisco Blues paraded, and the day was passed by every one as it best suited his humor. . . . Three little children were found on Jackson street Wharf weeping bitterly, one was nine, one seven, and the other five years of age; they gave but an unsatisfactory account of themselves, but were kindly cared for by the proprietor of the "Bunch of Grapes."

November 24. A man named Henry H. Monroe was executed at Martinez, for the murder of James M. Gordon. . . . The case of the contested Election of Alderman Hyde, in the First Ward, was decided in favor of the incumbent, and a resolution was passed declaring Alderman Hyde entitled to his seat. . . . The Steamship Uncle Sam left, carrying treasure to the amount of $855,752, By a statement in the Herald, it appeared that there had been shipped from the State, during the month of November, $5,276,562 59. . . . Lee & Marshall's Circus commenced performing on the vacant lot, on Jackson street near the International Hotel.

November 25. A Writ of Habeas Corpus was issued from the Twelfth District Court, on behalf of John Lynkeus Nystrom and Johan Reubold Blom, Russian prisoners of war, on board the prize ship Sitka, on the ground that they were illegally restrained of their liberty, because they had been taken from a place within the possessions of Great Britain, brought to and held in custody in a place within the jurisdiction of the State of California. . . . Madame Anna Bishop had a benefit at the Metropolitan, on which occasion she appeared as Fra Diavolo, in the opera of that name, and was assisted by Mrs. Sinclair, as a vocalist in the character of Zerlina. . . . Commander Buchanan, of the U. S. Steam Frigate Susquehanna, was brought before the Recorder on a charge of maliciously and wilfully imprisoning one of his seaman named Joseph S. Chapman. The Recorder dismissed the case on the ground that the Court had no jurisdiction in the matter, inasmuch as it was proven that the alleged false imprisonment was by order of a superior officer. . . . A meeting of the Bar was held for the purpose of taking into consideration a resolution adopted by the Board of Assistant Aldermen, for the removal of the Law Library from the City Hall; a committee of five was appointed to take charge of the subject and report at some future meeting. . . . A number of trees, among which are the Green Bay Redwood and Mansenita, were set out in the triangular plats of Portsmouth Square. . . . The paving of Montgomery street from California to Clay street was completed and opened to travel. . . . U. S. Revenue Cutter, W. L. Marcy, Capt. Cornell, arrived from Monterey and a cruise.

November 26. A race came off on the Union Course, between the celebrated pacers, Joe Wilson, Daniel Webster and Lady Mac, mile heats, best three in five, in harness, for a purse of $250, which was won by Joe Wilson in 2.31. . . . Mr. William Wheeler, known as the "Western Walker," completed the task of walhing one hundred and one consecutive hours. . . . The pilot boat Dancing Feather," Capt. Fowler, arrived from the wreck of the Yankee Blade with four boxes containing treasure to the value of $68,000, which had been recovered from that ill-fated vessel. . . . Right Rev. Bishop Kip confirmed twenty-one persons as members of the Protestant Episcopal Church. . . . Rolla Powers, charged with the murder of Daniel Hoover, in September 1853, and arrested a short time since as he was about leaving for the Atlantic States, was acquitted by a jury summoned to try the case in El Dorado County. . . . The Russian prize ship Sitka sailed out of the harbor, carrying with her the Russian prisoners, in defiance of the writ of *Habeas Corpus* which had been served upon her.

November 27. The Board of Aldermen passed an ordinance creating a Police Fund of $1,000 for contingent expenses in arresting persons at large, charged with crime. . . . The Fifth Anniversary meeting of the San Francisco Bible Society was held at the First Congregational Church—Rev. S. H. Willey presiding. Rev. F. Buel read a report, from which it appeared that during the past year there had been issued by the society, in the English language, 2,360 Bibles and 2,865 Testaments; and in foreign languages, 312 Bibles and 275 Testaments; making a total issue of 5,812. . . . A report of the Chief Engineer, published in the *Alta*, showed the expenses of the Fire Department during the past year to have been $153,559 21. There are 55 cisterns, estimated to contain 1,742,000 gallons of water. The engines belonging to the city are Empire, No. 1; Howard, No. 3; Knickerbocker, No. 5; Pacific, No. 8; Vigilant, No. 9; Crescent, No. 10; and Columbia, No. 11. Hook & Ladder Companies—St. Francis, No. 1, and Lafayette, No. 2. Belonging to companies were Manhattan, No. 2; California, No. 4; Monumental, No. 6; Pennsylvania, No. 12, and Volunteer, No. 7. Owned by F. W. Macondray, Esq., Sansome Hook & Ladder, No. 3. Making a total of twelve fire engines in good order and ready for active service. . . . A man named W. H. Carlton was brought before Recorder Waller on a charge of having murdered a man named Epes, at Sanaii, Navigator's Island, as set forth in an affidavit of W. Harris, taken before V. P. Chapin, Presiding Judge of the Court of foreign residents at Samoa, and certified to by the U. S. Commercial Agent. But the Recorder, deciding that the matter did not come under his jurisdiction, on the grounds that both parties were subjects of Great Britain, dismissed the prisoner.

November 28. Hon. C. K. Garrison, late Mayor of the city, was honored with a complimentary dinner and a presentation of solid gold plate, as a testimonial of regard for his private worth and social qualities, by a number of his fellow-citizens.

November 29. A man named Whitfield was arrested for shooting another named Ellison, during an affray in a sailor boarding-house on Chambers street. . . . Mr. and Mrs. Barney Williams commenced a short engagement at the Metropolitan. . . . J. F. Morse, for stealing a watch, was sentenced to five years imprisonment in the State Prison, and his accomplice, Dunn, to one year. . . . A large lump of gold, weighing 160½ pounds was said to have been brought to the city and deposited at Adams & Co.'s Express Office. . . . A fire occurred at Nevada which consumed property to the value of $14,000.

November 30. A fire broke out in the Pacific Brewery, corner of Second and Jessie street, and consumed property to the value of $35,000. A little boy, the son of Mr. Charles Carter, was burned to death. . . . An indignation meeting of the electors of the First Ward, opposed to J. T. Hyde holding his seat as Alderman, was held at Chanorteau's building, corner of Pacific and Battery streets. A number of resolutions were passed, denying Mr. Hyde's claim to American citizenship, protesting against the mode of his election and the course of those Aldermen who decided in favor of its legality, and approving of that of those who did not. A committee was appointed to wait upon the gentleman with a copy of the resolutions and request him to resign. . . . A statement in the *Herald* showed that the value of real estate in the County of San Francisco, upon which State and County Taxes were levied, was $35,796,475, and the said taxes amounted to $610,330 74.

December 1. The P. M. S. S. Sonora left for Panama, carrying treasure to the value of $1,851,375 56. . . . The P. M. S. S. Stephens arrived, fourteen days from Panama bringing the mails and a large number of passengers. . . . A second indignation meeting of the First Ward electors was held at the corner of Pacific and Battery streets, which, after several indignant speeches, adjourned in procession to the City Hall, where they gave three groans for the offensive Alderman. . . . At a meeting of the members of the Bar, to consider the propriety of transferring the possession of the Law Library to an association of the profession, the committee reported that Mr. Olds had offered to sell the same for $17,000 ; and that the only practicable method of effecting the object of the meeting was to form a corporation under the statute, the members of which should pay $100 initiation fee, or $250 for life membership, thereupon become stockholders. The money so raised to be used in the purchase of the Library, and should be subject to a monthly tax to defray its expenses. The report was accepted and a committee appointed to obtain subscribers to the proposed association. . . . In the case of F. Argenti *vs.* The City of San Francisco, brought for trial before the Superior Court and involving the affair of the Harding Constable Sale of City Property, Judge Satterlee intimated that, though not interested in the case itself, he was in some questions involved in it, and that he would prefer to have it transferred to another Court. It was, by agreement of counsel, transferred to that of the Twelfth District.

EDITOR'S TABLE.

"THE LILY OF THE VALLEY."

—

[There is much of true feeling in the following beautiful sketch, to which we invite the attention of our readers.]

IN the month of May, 1853, I passed a very pleasant week at Geneva, Switzerland, tarrying two days in one of the little villages near the banks of Lake Leman; and you shall know how agreeably my time was spent, and of my meeting with "*The Lily of the Valley.*"

The reader is aware, that, in some parts of Northern Europe, the English language is spoken; indeed, in many of the Swiss Hotels, it is quite common. I was in one instance, however, fortunate enough to meet with a family who talked good old Saxon, the head of which was the host of the pretty little village Inn at which I rested. Here, as in other lands, the children have their "May Day Festival"; and, though I was not quite in time to witness their merry-making, I was in time to inhale the fragrance of the flowers—in time to tell you of the exquisite beauty, even though withered on the stem, of "The Lily of the Valley." What a lovely day it was—as, looking from the window of my Hotel, I watched the bright sun-beams, as they danced and sparkled on the clear blue waters of Lake Leman! The breeze was crisping the waves, so that they danced and gently tossed about the tiny boats, with milk white sails, that glided on its surface.

A very compact little vessel was hired for a moderate price, and, as she fluttered her wings to the wind, I seemed fairly to revel in the quintessence of quiet and repose. The first summer rain had lately fallen, and the valleys, hills and dales, refreshed by the showers, seemed to send up a song of thankfulness to Heaven, while the trees, filled with blossoms—some just putting forth their leaves, looked so green and lovely; and, as far as the eye could reach, it was one vast panorama of matchless beauty. On nearing a little village, the name of which I have forgotten, not very distant from the far-famed Zurich, whose waters have been immortalized in story and song, I observed, as I thought, an unusual gaiety and liveliness among the people, and was about remarking to my companion, that I imagined it was some *fête* day, when he informed me we had just arrived in time to see the *last* of the Swiss "May Festival." Children's sports are to me always interesting, and so away we went, through innumerable groupings of lads and lassies, and vineyards, bowers and gardens of surpassing beauty, the air seemingly laden with the perfumes of a thousand exotics, when, suddenly, in the distance, the well-known "May Pole" was seen. But the dance had ceased;—the little twinkling feet that so lately had trodden on the spring blossoms, had disappeared;—but, the "Lily of the Valley" was there, and its fragrance was sweet beyond description.

A little blue-eyed girl, of some seven summers, had just plucked the flower, and, placing it in her bosom, began to cry. This attracted my attention, and I went to her, and asked her to tell me the cause of her grief. She said that her little sister, whom they used to call the "Lilly of the Valley," had been taken from them, and she was going to send this flower with her to Heaven, to be planted there! I need not say I became much interested, and followed the little stranger for some distance; but, in the throng of children, I soon lost her.

The little ones that, on my arrival, were grouped together in the very hight of glee and excitement, as I fancied, were speaking in subdued tones, while the peasants, looked sad and gloomy.

Musingly I strolled to the Inn of the village, where I learned the cause of the ceasing of the festivities. Here, also, had they a "May Queen"; one they were wont to call the "Lily of the Valley." For three summers had she reigned over her little flowery band, when suddenly she was called away to bloom in the fields of light above.

But listen to the story as they told it to me:—

The sun never beamed more gloriously than upon the May-morn about which I am writing;—the last crowning of the "Lilly of the Valley," and though its little head was bent in sickness, the genial sunshine, it was thought, would revive, and the merry-making and excitement prove beneficial, rather than injurious. And so they placed her upon her floral throne.

The shoutings of a hundred tender voices went up; processions were formed, and garlands, wreathed by little hands, were tossed into the air. All eyes were turned towards the throne of roses, and her crown of pure white lilies, that she loved to wear, was placed upon her brow. She looked so lovely there, in her dress of buds and blossoms;—but she was *very pale*, and her eye looked up to Heaven! Could she have heard them calling her away? She smiled so sweetly, she could not be in pain;—and then she tried to raise herself, but the exertion was too much for her, and just waiving her little hand,

> "She fell, in her Saint-like beauty,
> Asleep by the Gates of Light!"

The color returned not to her cheek, and thus this tender floweret, in the very hight of its May Day glory, was taken to be transplanted into the heavenly nursery!

The May Day dance was over. Garlands and wreaths of flowers dropped from slender hands, that in their glee had held them—and tears flowed like rain; and, where so lately smiles, laughter, and the joyous strains of music floated in the air, sobbings now were heard, and rejoicings were at an end.

I thought it was a glorious way to die,—ere the young heart had grown familiar with the paths of sin. While e'en the spring flowers budded, bloomed and blossomed on her very breast—while the shoutings of innocent voices greeted her—her spirit passed silently away.

This is the story that they told me; and now I will tell you, my reader, *what I saw:*

On the night of the day that I arrived, the funeral of the little " May Queen" took place. Never before did I feel so strongly the impressiveness, nay, the *beauty* of Death, divested, as it seemed to be, of all its gloom and terror.

There was no coffin—no pall—no raven plumings—none of the trappings and somber liveries of the grave, seen there;—but, upon two pieces of *cedar wood,* bound tightly together with boughs of evergreen and myrtle, forming a sort of trellis-work, the body was placed, dressed in a garment of plain white, with a single flower—the "Lily of the Valley"—resting on the breast. The scene was most imposing. It was night; but the moon shone full upon that lovely face; it was so light—so very light—it did not look like *Death.*—And, then, it seemed to smile, as though a pleasant dream was her's;—or, perhaps, she was talking to the angels. And, then, each of the children kissed those little lips, so still now, and cold, and their hearts seemed breaking. I could hear their sobbings;—and they called her "Lily;"—and they seemed to think *that she could hear them!* and one said, she knew she smiled when they called her,—but now she had gone to God to be a Queen among his little angels! She was so very beautiful! And then they sang a hymn; and its distant echo among the hills made me think that it was answered by cherub voices;—it was so distinct, so very clear, that it startled me:—and, then, I saw them turn away and weep, for the "Lily of the Valley " had passed from their sight for ever!

JAMES PIPES, of Pipesville.

San Francisco, December 15, 1854.

[It is scarcely necessary to say that the above touching recital is from the pen of our esteemed friend, Stephen C. Massett.]

—

MUSICAL AND THEATRICAL.

Record of the Month, from Nov. 25, to Dec. 20.—We can at last chronicle the reinstatement of "The Legitimate" upon the San Francisco boards. The struggle between the Drama on one side, and the Opera and Ballet on the other, commenced a year ago. The former had held almost entire sway in California, ever since the first green curtain was spread; but, aided by the Roussets, Madame Thillon, the Monplaisirs and Bishop, the latter eventually won the field, and from April to December last, Shakespeare with all his laurels on his brow, was banished by their own suffrages, from the presence of the people. It is not without a feeling of pride, that we announce a change in public feeling. Rossini, it is true, appeals to our tastes. But while these should be cultivated, it must be remembered that Shakespeare appeals to our intellect. However softening in its effects,—however purifying and elevating may be Music, there is something ennobling in the Drama; and, while we rejoice in the patronage which the Opera has received among us, displaying the fact, as it does, that there is musical appreciation in San Francisco, we cannot but inwardly congratulate ourselves upon the fact that the Legitimate is not lost to us for another twelvemonth.

On the fourth *ultimo* the New American Theater opened. Although the houses were at first but thinly attended, the appearance of Stark the tragedian, whose engagement commenced on the eleventh, saved the management from a failure, by securing well-filled, and, at times, crowded benches. The Legitimate may therefore be considered as once again fairly in the field, and, with sock and buskin, and dagger, disputing possession with the baton, trills and *roulades.* The headquarters of the Opera during the past month have been at the Metropolitan, and the headquarters of Tragedy at the American.

Christy's Minstrels after performing in the Interior, returned to San Francisco. A portion of the troupe have left for New York, while the remainder have joined Backus's, who are still performing to good houses at the San Francisco Theater.

THE AMERICAN.—We are forced to say, with regard to the interior of this new structure, that it does not bear evidences of an educated taste. It is spacious, its general effect is brilliant, and we suppose it will seat as large an audience as the Metropolitan. But there is a want of harmony in its internal architecture. The proscenium seems to be a mixture of the Grecian and the Oriental. It is neither the one thing nor the other. From the stage to the ceiling, its general effect is fine; but those pendant nondescripts, that project from the ceiling over the foot-lights, cannot but be regarded as in bad taste. They are clumsily executed in themselves, and in addition, are entirely out of place. The act drop is only less objectionable than that at the Metropolitan. It is a sad hodge-podge, made up of a representation of the Golden Gate, a far suggestion of a clipper ship, a steamship, such as we venture to say has not its counterpart upon the surface of the Pacific, Atlantic, Indian or Frozen oceans, two pillars, and between them a melancholy Washington upon a pedestal. The *Wide West* facetiously remarks, that the cannon at Washington's feet was unfortunately located by the painter upon one of his little toes; which, it must be admitted, sufficiently accounts for his lugubrious cast of countenance. We join in its recommendation that the piece of ordnance be speedily rolled off. In short, the entire painting *means* nothing. But there it is, and, if we are to judge anything from the past, there it will be, with its fellow at the Metropolitan, for the next two years,—a species of chronic intermittent eye-sore, visiting the community five times nightly. The stage is lighted by gas from above; and the effect of the burners, counteracting as they do the unnatural lights and shades produced upon the face by the foot-lights, is far preferable to the effect of lamps at the wings. The seats are comfortable and well arranged for vision, and, in general, the auditory has an agreeable and sociable air.

MR. STARK.—In common with the numerous friends of this excellent actor, we welcome him to the foot-lights once more. His engagement is to last two weeks, and up to the present time of writing, sterling tragedies and dramas have been produced,—Messrs. Stark and Neafie alternating in the principal characters. Of Mr. Neafie we have already spoken, and have seen no cause to change our opinion regarding his abilities. Unfortunately, Mr. Stark's engagement occurred at a time when other duties precluded the possibility of our witnessing him, except in two characters, viz: Hamlet and Iago. The latter we have always considered as one of his best parts, the former as one of his worst. But since his return from Australia, we can predicate little upon a memory of his performances prior to his departure for our sister Dorado.

Mr. Stark is a tragedian. In comedy, he succeeds well, but not excellently. His Ruy Gomez is, or at least was, rather too stiff and artistic. His Falstaff is amusing, of course, but it must be admitted that he fails to bring out prominently, a deal of the humor of the character. Place Mr. S., however, in tragedy—in the highest walks of tragedy, and he is at home. In comedy, he exhibits talent, merely; in tragedy, genius. But even in tragedy, it is proper to state, that those who expect to find him a finished actor, will be disappointed. For to such as have watched him carefully, during the past four or five years,—confident of the genius that is in him,—certain of the crown that awaits him—jealous of his faults, and anxious for his triumph, one fact cannot but have manifested itself prominently. He has never ceased to improve. He is an incessant student. Not satisfied with the applause of to-day and of his friends, he has seemed ever to strive after an ideal of his own, which his admirers wot not of. At every engagement he has manifested real advancement; and the steps of his improvement have been rapid and brilliant. When he first arrived among us, he was of the Macready school. He had much to overcome before being proficient even as a follower of that sterling actor. His countenance was inexpressive. This misfortune he completely conquered; so much so, that in different characters he does not look like the same man. His voice was inflexible and would not obey the commands of his mind. By constant practice it deepened and at last yielded readily to his will, capable of " denoting truly," the shades of almost every passion. In many other respects—in reading—in ease upon the stage—in the conception of character—his improvement was so marked and gratifying, that there were many, who ranked him with Forrest and the brightest stars. But through all, he still remained of the Macready school. He went to New York. But Forrest was the great favorite, and so absorbed the public attention, that it was useless for a new light to attempt to shed its beams. To change the phrase a little, men turned from the rising to the mid-day sun. He came back to California, and his friends, who had no thought except to find him the same actor he was before, saw cause to applaud still further improvement in him. Yet the tone and action of Macready were about him. But, if he was a follower of Macready, he was a worthy and brilliant follower—for he had carried the style to a pitch of perfection, which justly entitled him to rank as at least the second American tragedian. He visited Australia. He reared a fortune and returned, in condition, so far as pecuniary matters were concerned, to snap his fingers in the face of any management under the sun. He returned; when lo, again, while his admirers had no thought, but that he had meanwhile remained simply as he was before, an excellent actor, they found in him another change. They had chalked out a course for him, but genius knew its own way, and, regardless of all, took it. Those who had admired him of old, visited the Metropolitan during his first engagement after his return, and almost invariably were disappointed in him. He had changed; and, most asserted, that he had retrograded. But judicious after-thought gave cause for rejoicing. For, having reached the limits of the Macready school, he had sprung nimbly away into *a fresh style ;* and those of his friends, to whom the fact that he was a follower of Macready, was the only unanswerable argument against him, may congratulate themselves that, however he may have appeared during his engagement at the Metropolitan, his course of improvement has not been checked. Although he may not be so far advanced in the style which he has recently adopted, it cannot be denied that the style itself is far preferable to that in which he was before accustomed to perform. From the stilted manner of the olden time, rendered dear, it is true by the genius of many of the brightest ornaments of the stage, he has passed at one leap into the preferable style of nature.

If we can judge anything by his Iago and Hamlet, we can think of no school in which to rank him. There was nature and spontaneity about the impersonations of the elder Booth; there is nature and spontaneity about those of Mr. Stark, but we cannot but think that the latter is rising into a peculiar,—a most excellent style of his own; and we hail the change—nay, the *real*, although, perhaps, to some, not visible *improvement*, with gladness. He is an admirable actor even now. With the exception of the Elder Booth, his superior has not been in California. But in his faculty for improvement, in his youth, in his love for his profession, in his unremitting labor, in his genius, in his consciousness (whatever others may say of him) that there are higher rounds in his ladder, which he can yet reach—we have an earnest of a future, more brilliant even than his present; of a proud distinction, indeed, when maturity shall sit upon him as a crown.

It was one of the most unfortunate steps that Mr. Neafie ever took, when he brought himself into contrast with Mr. Stark. In the one, we find the physical actor; in the other, the intellectual. In the one, we find a resort to stock positions and attitudes which have belonged to the stage from time immemorial; in the other, a freedom which has stepped lightly away from such stale and easily caught mannerisms. In the one, we find cold, heartless representations, which have been shaped with the anvil and hammer of long experience upon the stage; in the other, impersonations warm and fresh, coming from within and appealing to the mind, the heart and the soul. In the one, we see Neafie; in the other, the character presented. Here we see the out-Heroding of Herod; there a temperance begotten in the very torrent, tempest and whirlwind of passion. While in general the applause rumbles around and descends from gallery, for the one—for the other, we witness rapt, earnest and long-continued attention in silence, or are startled by quick claps from the parquette and dress circles.

We cannot better describe Mr. Stark's performance in Hamlet and Iago, than by saying that he must have studied Hamlet's address to the players, with a view to a strict compliance therewith. His readings were pure and accurate—his action graceful, and his conception excellent. We only regret that in many passages the tones of his voice were so faint that most of his beauties were lost to those who occupied seats in that portion of the house furthest from the stage. We trust this hint—and it is more important than the space it occupies might indicate—will be considered by him, and that he will reform the fault altogether. We have enlarged so frequently upon the characters of Hamlet and Iago on other occasions, that, even did our space warrant, we have not the heart to particularize here. We have limited ourselves to an attempt to speak of Mr. Stark in general terms and in a spirit of fairness and candor; and we trust to have an early opportunity to allude more particularly to his impersonations.

THE OPERA.—Since our last notice, we have been favored with a continuance of the representations of the Italian Troupe, who have presented a number of Operas which had not been before exhibited in this City. The present engagement closed on Monday evening, December 18. We regret to learn that the company are not so well pleased with their success as they anticipated.

There is little about the troupe to create a *furore* in their favor. It does not include any great star. Taken as a whole, it is, perhaps, the best that has visited us, simply, because it is more complete. But a fair estimate of the individual merits of its several members would not place any of them in the highest rank.

Signora Barili, as *soprano*, stands at the head of the troupe. But she cannot, as an *artiste*, be placed at the head of her profession. She has grown steadily in favor with the audience, and can boast a large circle of warm admirers and friends. Since her arrival, her voice has greatly improved in tone and power, though we believe that we have not yet heard it in its perfection. She has been more or less troubled with the hoarseness which attacks all strangers on their arrival, and it has only been a rare occurrence, that we have been permitted to enjoy the purity of her voice unaffected by this obstruction. Yet even when at its best, there has been a lack of power. Nor is this all. With purity in tone, great compass and much flexibility and smoothness, it lacks sympathy. It excites admiration, but not feeling. Signorina Bedei appears to us to present rather promise of future excellence, than claims to present distinction. Her voice possesses still less power than that of Barili. Her execution is correct and smooth, but it lacks force and brilliancy. Her action is inferior to her singing. Her walk is not graceful. Her positions lack dignity, and her gestures can scarcely be dignified with that name. The movements of her arms seem rather to accompany the music, than to express emotion or passion. We have regarded these as the faults of a *débutante*, which time, study, and familiarity with her position, would remove. Of Signor Scola we have already spoken. The tenor sustains, generally, the principle *rôle* in the Opera after the *soprano*, and he should be, at least, equal to any artist in the troupe. Such Signor Scola, by general consent, is not. Lanzoni possesses a magnificent voice, of considerable power and compass. His execution is generally accurate and tasteful. The *fiorituri* are introduced with taste, and always executed with care and smoothness. He dresses and looks his character well, and while always showing sufficient energy and dignity, does not over-act his part. Leonardi we need not criticise! an excellent *basso*, yet with some very prominent faults. Individually, then, the present company present no claims to *extraordinary* success; but if they were willing to be satisfied with a moderate success, they might continue their career here with increasing popularity, and with the assurance of a fair remuneration. We shall regret their departure exceedingly.

The Opera of "Nabuco" is similar in character to most of Verdi's Operas; intricate concerted pieces of great artistic skill, and brilliant instrumentation, with a lack of beauty and melody. It was placed upon the stage with great completeness; much of the music had been rendered familiar to the public ear by the Opera of "Judith," which was mostly compiled from "Nabuco;" and with many this diminished the attraction. But music of this character is never so beautiful, as in its proper place in the Opera for which it is written. It was generally well peformed. Signorina Bedei made her *début* in this Opera, and was well received. The opening *aria* in the second act was beautifully executed, and elicited a very unanimous *encore;* the duett with Scola in the same act, was sung with great spirit; but the *scena* with Nabuco (Lanzoni,) in the third act, although accurately rendered, was given with too little spirit. Mrs. Voorhies surprised all, and in the last act elicited very warm applause. The choruses were the best part of this Opera, and the triumphant march, played by the military band upon the stage, and the funeral march behind the scenes, had a grand effect. The part of Nabuco, presented by Lanzoni, was, however, the feature of the Opera. In the last scene of the second act, when the king loses his throne and his reason—in the *aria* and prayer in the fourth act and in the last scene and *finale* of the fourth act, he was truly admirable.

"Maria de Rohan" is one of the many Operas of Donizetti, which is seldom performed. No composer has written so many Operas; many of them, indeed, have scarcely survived their first representation, while others maintain their position with the best of the great musical works. For some reason, best known to the company, a portion of the Opera was omitted. This left the development of the plot somewhat obscure. The overture is excellent, and was brilliantly executed. The choruses, generally, are not remarkable, but the *finale* of the first act is very spirited and beautiful. Our old favorite, Herr Mengis, appeared before the public again in this Opera, after a long repose, and was warmly welcomed. His voice preserves its quality quite well. The rendering of the *solo aria* in the first act was smooth and graceful. His action, at times, was too violent, insomuch, that disapprobation was manifested by the audience during his singing in the last act. The *aria* in the fifth scene of the first act, is the gem of the Opera. Kate Hayes had rendered it familiar to our ears, but this did not detract from the pleasure with which it was received. Its execution was warmly applauded. The *piano* passages were rendered with great delicacy and grace, and the whole *aria* was executed with accuracy and smoothness.

Mrs. Voorhies appeared in this Opera. The *recitative* was sung badly, but the *aria* in the fifth scene of the first act was much better. Mrs. V. dresses with great taste, her carriage is graceful, and she is not inferior, as an actress, to any member of the troupe.

"Il Barbiere di Seviglia" has probably been played more times than any Opera of Rossini. Most of his Operas are master pieces. Some of them, however, have been failures; but the "Barber" is as great a favorite as any, although as a musical composition it is inferior to many other productions of this great master. He will write no more; but what he has written will live when many later works, now favorites on the boards, are forgotten. Scola was better received in the part of Il Conte, than in any he has yet presented, but seemed to us a failure. Signora Barili rendered the music of her part generally well, but the grand *aria*, "Una voce poco fa," has been sung here so much better before, that we were disappointed. The grand *finale* of the Opera was rendered with great spirit.

After the Opera, we had two evenings of operatic "*pot pourri*," which went off rather tamely. There was a lack of spirit in the company, and the music was rendered generally in a very slip-shod manner.

We would remark before closing, that, in giving a list of members of the troupe, last month, we inadvertently alluded to Mrs. Voorhies as "Seconda Donna," instead of "Contralto." The mistake arose from the fact, that we found a list of the troupe in one of the daily papers, and, having cut it out, wafered the extract, as it was, into one of the pages of our manuscript.

—

THE BALL OF THE PIONEERS.

THE ANNUAL BALL OF THE CALIFORNIA PIONEERS.—The Society of California Pioneers, in accordance with their custom, give their Annual Ball on the eighth of January. We have no doubt THE PIONEERS will so sustain their reputation that their graceful entertainment will be *the* ball of the season. The names of those gentlemen who have been selected as the Committee on Invitations, is sufficient guarantee that the affair will be brilliant and acceptable to the first society of our city, who—if we are to judge anything from the past—will adorn Musical Hall with their presence.

—

GOSSIP WITH READERS AND CORRESPONDENTS.

WE cannot better open our Gossip, than by calling the attention of our readers to the following touching sketch, which has been placed in our hands by the author of "Europe in a Hurry."

THE DYING MINSTREL.

BY GEO. WILKES.

POOR TOM BRIGGS! How well I recollect him as he used to enter between the first and second divisions of the performance, with his banjo on his shoulder, and his cheerful—"Good eve'nin' white folks!"

Black as he made himself, Tom Briggs could not help being handsome, while the special set of his red vest and the exquisite trim of his lower outline helped largely towards his title as the "Darky Apollo."

There are some persons so resolutely handsome that no paint will disfigure them, no garb entirely disguise, and of this sort was poor Tom Briggs. Wisely appreciating his good gifts, he preferred the silent favor they insured in the minds of an audience, to the clack which is the reward of preposterous exaggeration. He was the dandy nigger; clean as a race-horse, fine as a star, and when his finger struck the banjo, you felt that he was filled with the spirit of an artist. Altogether, Tom Briggs was an extraordinary person, and had he chosen a less humble instrument, and subjected his taste to the tutelage of science, he would have achieved an elevated and refined renown. As it was, he distanced rivalry, elevated the banjo to the rank of the guitar, and rendered his performance not only the feature of a concert, but a by-word of surprise. This makes him a character worth notice. Whenever any one played to ears which had once heard him, the comment inevitably was—"Ah, but you should have heard Tom Briggs!" This was fame; and Tom Briggs felt its inspiring influence, and day by day he played more famously because of it.

Success develops genius. Those who cannot win it stop on the near side of Jordan; and there they must remain till it gives them strengh to get beyond. But Tom Briggs took one jump to the right side of Happy Valley, and leaving competition in the rear, made it useful to him in the way of contrast. Every one conceded the superiority of Tom Briggs! All minstrel managers endeavored to secure him, and it is the misfortune of us here that he was forced to leave the band for the cemetery in the first week of his arrival on these shores.

But Tom Briggs had other merits than attached to his pursuits. He possessed a kind and gentle spirit, he was shy, modest and reserved, and free from the hard habits which characterise many of his class. He had a great notion, too, of being a gentleman, and instead of hanging about taverns and passing his time in vulgar pleasures, he devoted himself to elegant attire, good company and that laborious practice, which is the mother of improvement.

Nevertheless, Tom Briggs pursued these inclinations without offense to his professional associates. With all his niceness of dress and manner there was no exceptional vanity in his bearing; nothing about him which the most jealous critic could style "airish." He had an inborn gentility which oozed out of him as it were, gracefully, and you could feel no more objection to it, than to the just pride of a handsome girl who only evinces an amiable desire to be fine. Elegance was his "natural gait," and I verily believe his comrades took as much pride as himself in his straw kids; and perhaps felt that they were in some way associated with the dignity of the band. Certain it is, that his unassuming excellence had made a deep impression on their minds, and when he was lowered out of sight, many a tear dropped silently into the fresh sand that laid ready to be heaped into his grave!

The evening performance that succeeded this ceremony, was a doleful one. "For my part," said Horn, "I scarcely knew what I was about. Tom and I had traveled together for years, and it seemed to me as if I had lost a brother. All my main business was done with him, and when I looked around, in the middle of my work, and found a strange face in place of his, and remembered that I had just helped to put him in the ground, I nearly 'broke down.'"

As he said this, the eye of the humorist became moist, a slight tremor and huskiness was perceptible in his voice, and turning half round, so as to look another way, he suddenly asked a crowd of us to drink.

"Ah, gentlemen," said he, when we had all got our glasses, and he had cleared his throat, "You'll never see the like of poor Tom Briggs again! He was different from most other players. They seldom take any pride in their business, and are generally satisfied with any cheap instrument they can get; but Tom was very particular; he never stood upon the price of a banjo, and when he got a good one he was always studying some way to ornament and improve it. He had a light one and a heavy one for different kinds of work, and he played so strong that he had to get a piece of steel made for the end of his finger, as a sort of shield, like, to prevent his tearing off his nail. He was very fond of playing the heavy one, and, when we were coming up the coast, he would sometimes strike his strongest notes, and then turn round to me so proud, and say, 'Ah! Eph, what'll they think when they hear the old Cremona speak like that?'

It did not make any difference even when he took sick. He played away all the same. Only, after he got here, he could play only the light one. He used to have it hanging against the wall, so as he could reach it in bed. Most any time you went in you'd hear him talking to the old Cremona, as he called it, and making it talk back to him. But by'm-by he got so weak he could scarcely hold on to it, and I have sat by his bed and watched him till the sound became so faint, that it seemed as if he and the banjo were both falling into a dream. All the while, he kept a good heart—poor fellow; and we kept encouraging him along too; and every now and then he would raise himself up and say, 'Ah! how I'll make 'em look around when I get strength enough, once more, to make the old banjo speak!'

But at last he felt that he was gone; and after some straight, sensible talk, he told us that when he died, to take the two banjos and pack them up carefully and send them home to his father and mother. An hour before he went, he asked me to hand him his banjo. He took a hold of it, and looked at it for a minute as if he was looking at a person who he was going to part with forever; and then he tried to hit it. But he could merely drop the weight of his thin fingers on the cords. There was no stroke to his touch at all. He could just barely make a sound, and that was so fine that it appeared to vanish away like the buz of a fly. It was so dim that I don't believe he heard it himself, and he dropped his hand as if he gave it up. Then he looked at me as if he understood everything in the world, and, shaking his head, said, 'It's no use—hang it up, Eph,—I cannot hit it any more!' These were the last words that poor Tom Briggs ever spoke."

At this the speaker wiped a tear from his eyes; but it did him no discredit, for he had described the death of an artist, and given the best proof of a man.

- - - AMONG our contributors, this month, we number Mrs. L. H. Sigourney, for whose unexpected note, inclosing poems written for THE PIONEER, we tender sincere thanks. With a lively sense of the many shortcomings of our "Maga," we must be allowed to accept her compliments in the light of encouragement merely, and can only promise that our best endeavors shall be exerted to merit them in reality. We would remark, by the way, before closing, that Messrs. Phinney & Co., of Buffalo, have just issued a new work by Mrs. Sigourney, entitled "Sayings of the Little Ones and Poems for their Mothers." The general tenor of the book is faithfully indicated by the title. It abounds in diverse illustrations of youthful character, and, imparting on every page by precept and anecdote, in prose and verse, the highest lessons of morality and religion, it constitutes, emphatically, a Mother's Manual for the Nursery and the Fireside. The adult reader, also, will be sure to derive from it both entertainment and profit, for to an intelligent mind, nothing can be more deeply interesting than the gradual development of the mental and moral faculties of children. If any guaranty were needed of the literary excellence and moral influence of the work, it might be found in the name of its Author—a name synonomous with rare intellectual endowments, as well as the most genial and unaffected piety. - - - THERE is a good story told of General Twiggs while he was in Mexico, during the late war. It will be remembered that a certain battalion, seated before Vera Cruz, from a certain large city on the Atlantic sea-board, which, not to be invidious, we shall call the "Blank Battalion," was noted for the rascally character of its members, who were continually fighting among themselves, and thieving and robbing. One day Scott convened a council of war, to take into consideration the best ways and means for capturing the Castle of San Juan d'Ulloa. Twiggs was present. After many plans had been proposed, and much argument exhausted on their want of feasibility, Gen. Twiggs slowly arose and said—"Well, gentlemen, I have thought of a way of taking it, which I think none of you can object to;—Give me the "Blank Battalion" *and I'll steal it.* - - - AND this reminds us of another incident related of the same commander. As is well known, he was one of the strictest disciplinarians iu the army. It so happened that there was a miserable drunken fellow from Georgia among the troops, who, one day, swore that he was going to see Twiggs;—he had seen him in Georgia before, and he was determined to go to his tent and make him a call. His comrades, knowing him to be a good-for-nothing scapegrace, watched around to see him summarily repulsed. Parker sauntered up to the tent, and peered in, when, to the astonishment of his fellow-soldiers, Gen. Twiggs looked up from his work, and said—"Come in, Parker, come in;—I'm glad to see *a dog* from Georgia." - - - "THE LITTLE PILGRIM", is the title of an excellent monthly published in Philadelphia, and intended for circulation among the children of America. A sufficient passport, for it is to be found in the fact, that that charming writer, "Grace Greenwood," presides at its Editorial Table. In the list of its contributors we notice the names of some of the brightest literary ornaments of America. Its tone is genial and healthy; its terms are only four bits a year, and we trust that many a "Little Pilgrim" will wander to our far shores. We can heartily recommend it to parents for their children. - - - IN one of our Law Courts a short time since, an important case was on trial. The judge sat clothed in the awful majesty of his office, and twelve men sat at his right hand, with grave visages, carefully weighing the testimony. Two distinguished lawyers were conducting the trial, with much of that sharpness and address to which they owed their eminent position at the bar. A poor devil of a witness had been so badgered and battledoored about between them, that it became doubtful whether his testimony could be admitted. The two gentlemen of the law disputed about it. One proposed that the Court should decide, and the Court was inclined so to do. The other, on the contrary, preferred that the Jury should decide. The Court believed that it had heard the testimony, and could decide as well as the jury. "I beg the Court's pardon," replied the jury advocate, " I thought that as there were twenty-four ears in the jury, they might have heard better; but possibly your Honor's ears are longer."—A fact. - - - WE have seldom seen a more neatly constructed newspaper paragraph than the following, which we cut from a recent issue of that excellent daily, *The San Francisco Herald.* It is entitled "Old England *vs.* Young America."

"An amusing scene occurred in Murray's shipping office yesterday. While an officer from the steam frigate Susquehanna was engaged in superintending the shipping of seamen, a candidate presented himself in the person of an English sailor, who politely informed the officer that he would be happy to ship as captain of the maintop, in the laudable desire to instruct American sailors in the science of navigation. He said, boastingly, he was 'one of King George's men,' and flattered himself he 'knew a hawk from a handsaw.' He discoursed in an eloquent manner on the lamentable ignorance of American sailors in general; and intimated, that although a disgusting mission, he would generously sacrifice his own personal feelings, merely, as he very forcibly remarked, to teach the Americans a thing or two. The officer declined his offer, when he suddenly became rampant and exceedingly abusive—intimating at the same time, that he was fearfully perfect in pugilism, and that there was not a 'bloody American' in the house who could put him out. By this time his insolence had become unbearable, and the officer nodded to a light-weight little boatswain, who stood by in agony for a fight. 'Young America' first politely touched his hat to his superior officer, boarded the English craft, and in a very few moments 'one of King George's men' struck his colors in a sinking condition—going out of the action with an impression amounting almost to a conviction that American sailors were not such fools after all, and were certainly not the men he took them for."

- - - SOME of our readers may remember the old ship Globe. She was one of those clumsy, blunt-headed old crafts, that, when they came to a big wave, bump against it two or three times and finally sail round it. Nevertheless, her skipper, who was also weather-beaten and old-fashioned, and who had sailed in her many a voyage, was very proud of her, and, notwithstanding she had been for years beaten by every single craft that came anywhere near her on the ocean, Captain Pease still maintained his confidence in her unshaken. One day an old "hide drogher" hove in sight. She was a loggy old ark,—one of those tubs that were built in the year one. As usual, here was a chance for a race; and Captain Pease spread all his rags. The other craft was keen for sport also, and piled on every inch of patched canvass there was on board. There was a cracking breeze, and the two tubs thumped and stumped against the waves, and moved along all the forenoon, neck and neck, at the rate of four or five miles an hour. Every exertion was made by each party, and at last, late in the afternoon, the old Globe slowly began to pass her competitor. As she was almost imperceptibly drawing ahead, Captain Pease sauntered up to the weather tafferel, and leaning on his elbows, and shaking his head at his competitor, said, with a kind of drawling exultation—"Ah!—she's a hard 'un to look at,—but *she's a rum 'un to go!*" - - - WHILE we are on this subject, we may as well present the following description of the clipper ship "Highfalutin," which has been handed to us by a new and welcome contributor. "The discription," writes he, "was found inside of a sealed bottle, discovered floating near Point Lobos. It was adressed to the Editors of the San Francisco Journals. The note from the Captain which is appended, explains the object. (Thanks due to Adams & Co. for their down harbor favors):

EDITORS SAN FRANCISCO PAPERS: *Gentlemen:*—I have noticed from time to time, the glowing descriptions of the clipper ships arriving at your port, and, believing that my ship is equal to any "out," I would be much obliged if you would notice her arrival, and insert my description of her, which is inclosed; and you may rest assured that it is correct. I presume the agents of the ship will make it all right with you, and make the compensation satisfactory,—that is, if you do not consider their patronage entitles them to a puff as often as a ship comes to them. Please be particular about the proof, for those fellows who do that business in your office, make terrible mistakes sometimes, and get a ship all-aback. I send this by special current express, calculating that it will drift along a few days ahead of us; and you can have it all ready to put in, while we are within the usual "two hour's sail of the port for 24 days." Don't forget also to mention the fog, loss of sails, heavy weather, etc., and particularly "the light and baffling head-winds for a couple of months." But you can regulate that by the length of our voyage. No matter if you do make a little error of ten or fifteen days in our favor, in reporting us. If not noticed, we won't correct it; but if it is, then pitch into the d——d compositors, and call it a typographical error. All right, you understand. B. LAY BOOBYHATCH, Commander.

P. S.—Don't forget the usual mention about the gentlemanly officers, etc. Not that *I* care about it, but it will please my first mate, who belongs to one of the first families. B. L. B.

—

THE NEW AND SPLENDID CLIPPER SHIP HIGHFALUTIN——It affords us great pleasure to announce the arrival of the "Highfalutin," another splendid clipper ship, at our wharves, in sixty-two and a half days from Boston. She brings a large cargo, and is consigned to the sweet-scented, highly accomplished, elegantly behaved, energetic, enterprising and highly respectable House of

Doughboy, Fiddleinktum, Coozens & Co., who are well known in our community as upright merchants and downright clever fellows.

She will commence discharging to-morrow morning, under the supervision of Mr. Coozens; and we are assured by that voracious gentleman, that she will be entirely discharged and ballasted by four P. M., and will sail at six o'clock P. M., for China, *via* Petropoloski, where she will take on board the laurels won by the *all-lied* fleet. She will then keep a sharp look-out for the "Sitka," and serve that *Habeas Carcass*, as she has been offered the fees that the Sheriff *didn't* get. She has also been offered 12 shillings to capture Meiggs, and will endeavor to bait him up by carrying a bogus Controller's Warrant at the mast-head, and a couple of California Lumber Company's shares on the end of the bow-sprit.

The "Highfalutin" has had a succession of head winds ever since her keel was laid. The Captain, finding it impossible to make headway, "'bout ship," headed towards Boston, and finally made this port, on the principle that the boy adopted who went to school one slippery morning. She was six days to the equator on the other side; and dove under it on this side, and came up dry as a bone, two miles to the windward of the Farrallones.

She is 150 tons register, and carries 2,000 as measured in Boston, with the measurer's thumb inside the callipers, which (the thumb) being much swollen, and tied up in a rag, may have made a few feet difference in the measurements; but that don't amount to much. Her extreme length on deck, is 597¼ feet;—eight feet breadth of beam,—200 feet deep,—24 feet between decks. Her bow is a great rake, and the head is composed of a female carved figure, with one thumb resting on the extreme tip of her nose, fingers extended in the act of gyrating; the first finger of the left hand in the act of drawing down the lower lid of the eye; which the Capt. explains to us as a simile from the Heathen Mythology, denoting curiosity on the part of the figure to ascertain if anybody discovers anything verdant.

The "Highfalutin" is finished with the patent "Snogrosticars," indicating the millenium when it comes, and who struck Billy Patterson. She is rigged after the recent invention of Captain Blowhard, which consists of three topsail-yards on the bowsprit, the halyards leading down through a groove in the keel, up through the stern windows and belay to the Captain's tobacco box. She has also the "skyfungarorum," a sail something like a kite, which is set in light weather about 75 feet above the main truck, and made fast by a running double hitch under the binnacle and aft through the galley, and belayed to the cook's tea pot. It is sometimes (when the Captain carries his family) made fast to the baby-jumper. Her windlass is rose-wood, inlaid with clam-shells. She has also a French-roll capstan, with musical bars. The caboose is elaborately carved, with gilt edges, a Pike county gal-ley-sliding telescopic stove-pipe, of gutta percha, and a machine for making molasses candy for the sailors. Abaft the caboose, and just forward of the galley, is a parlor and berth-room fitted up elegantly, for the sole use of the cook, who retires to it for a siesta at 3 P. M., daily. The *chef d'œuvre* of the apartment consists of his coat of arms and crest over the dressing glass, being a gridiron and skimmer *couchant*, and a full grown "mutton" *ram*pant; the whole surmounted by a wreath of loaves of bread, hams and links of sausages.

The cabin, in its appointments, takes down anything ever before known. In richness of delicacy, and color of display of the blending, it beats all;—and the dreamy luxury, suggested by the cast-iron sofas and lounges, reminds one of opium smoke and chloroform. Each state-room is furnished with an orma-loo-loo card-table, a jack-knife bedstead, of a new pattern, the headboard containing a musical box, which so charms the fleas that they become absent-minded and starve to death; an elegant dressing bureau, furnished with all the appurtenances of the toilet—the far-famed Boston pomatum (its component parts being goose grease and peppermint) and lip salve, family jars of—cologne, bottles of—hair brushes, cards of—combs, several of—besides a dozen linen shirts—and under doings, and Hdkfs, suspended by golden cords within reach of the sleeper's nose while in bed; also a sheet-iron night-cap, billiard table and Bohemian glass boot-jack.

In the forecastle, the same good taste has been observed. The floor is richly carpeted with the —axe-the-minister carpet, from the "looms of the land;" berths furnished with the self-turning-over apparatus, which, being wound up on retiring, turns the sleeper over every two hours without disturbing him, and picks up the small change and keys that drop out of his pockets. Every sailor is provided with a rocking chair, with his name in gilt on the back, a copy of "Uncle Tom's Cabin," a moral pocket handkerchief, white kid gloves, five pounds of rose-scented cavendish, a gold pen and German pipe.

We assure our readers that the "Highfalutin" is well worth a visit; and visitors will be welcomed by "the gentlemanly and highly accomplished officers, whose urbane deportment," etc., etc. It will be easy to recognize the first officer by his distinguished air, aristocratic bearing and a patch of tar on the weather side of his pants, just astern of his starboard pocket. The Captain can be found doing the deportment on the quarter deck in a blue coat and brass buttons, with his right hand under the lee coat-tail, and has the appearance of undergoing the process of suffocation between a pair of chrome yellow side whiskers, and a sheet-iron shirt collar.

- - - By a recent number of the *Golden Era*, we notice that our old friend and cotemporary, Mr. J. E. LAWRENCE has become connected with that widely circulated weekly.   Mr. L. has long been connected with the California press ; in fact, if we mistake not, there are but three of our editors who rank him in point of seniority.   Early in 1850 he cast his destinies with the *Placer Times*, then published in Sacramento City, and he remained with that paper as proprietor and as one of its editors, through all its vicissitudes until a few weeks since, when he assumed an editorial chair in the sanctum of the *Golden Era*.   For energy, for activity and unremitting toil, for urbanity and warmness of heart he has long been distinguished.   His labors have tended to a great degree in establishing the *Times and Transcript* in the proud estimation in which it is held by the community, and the loss of his graceful pen must be seriously felt by that journal.   We congratulate our friends of the *Golden Era* upon their valuable acquisition, and wish Mr. LAWRENCE all success in his new undertaking.   - - - "THERE is probably no class of people," writes a friend, "more courteous to each other than Ship Captains; more especially do they illustrate the good feeling of their sait-water natures, when meeting a brother chip and ship in distress.   Not long since a Captain of a Whaler had the misfortune to lose his ship and all his personal effects ; but escaping with life, took up his residence on an Island of the Pacific, occasionally visited by Whalers, and at last had the inexpressible joy of discovering a sail in sight, which gave him some hope of renewing his inexpressibles, (which had become fit habiliments for a cook, being 'cool and airy,') and of leaving his lonely abode.   In due time the ship was ready to sail, and of course the shipwrecked Captain had become the guest of its commander.   But being impressed with the humble position he then filled, he kept himself very retired, and invariably took the lee side of the quarter-deck, where he stumped up and down with an uncertain and spasmodic gait—occasioned by one leg being an inch or two shorter than the other—maintaining a dignified silence.   For two days the rough old Whaler stood this reserve of his passenger ; but, his patience becoming exhausted, he at last addressed him as follows:—'Cap'en Brown, you have been shipwrecked hav'nt ye ?'—'Yes !'   'You've lost yer ship haint ye ?'   A mournful wave of the hand signified the fact—'You haint got no money neither, Cap'en Brown, in course not ; how could you have ?   Well, Cap'en Brown, I'm a plain-spoken man, and I hails from Cape Cod ; and I has feller feelings, Cap'en Brown.   What I says, I means ; and I say to you, Cap'en Brown, here's my ship at your sarvice ; you're "tu hum" here ; there's your stateroom, Cap'en Brown ; and there's my "chist ;" and there's my "licker," Cap'en Brown ; they are all at your sarvice.   I knows my duty to a feller sailor as is unfortunate and in distress.'   Cap'en Brown halted in promenade, turned towards his host, and after sundry mysterious gesticulations, indicating the utmost appreciation of his humble position, replied, 'Cap'en Skinner, I understands you.   But I knows my position.   'Tis true I haint got no ship,—she's "wracked," and I've lost my "vyge ;" I does'nt desarve but little or nuthin at your hands, and all I asks and expects, Captin Skinner, is civilities ; *civilities*, Captin Skinner, and those of the *most commonest kind*.'   'But Cap'en Brown, my chist and my 'pus' is at your .sarvice.' '*No*, Cap'en Skinner, I dont desarve 'em, and all I asks, Cap'en Skinner, is civilities, Cap'en Skinner, *civilities of the most commonest kind*,' and for the whole of that long voyage homeward, did Cap'en Brown adhere to the resolution to receive nothing but civilities, and those of the most commonest kind.

- - - THERE may be seen, almost any pleasant day, in Broadway, New York, a mild-looking, dreamy old gentleman, walking through the crowd, apparently lost in thought, unnoticed and unnoticing—who is well known about the War Department in Washington as "Old Captain T." He is also well known in the army, as an inventor of strange and intricate saddles, guns, mule-halters, and various other paraphernalia and trappings of war. The Capt. is decidedly a genius; but, like a large proportion of that class, is unappreciated. During the Florida war he invented a pack-saddle, which he took on to Washington, and bored the Quarter-Master-General, until he gave him an order for a few hundred to get clear of him. The saddles, in due time, arrived in Florida, and were one day brought forth for use. But, on investigation, they were found too scientific, the pamphlet, containing 150 pages of directions, nailed to each saddle, having been lost off. There were bands, straps, girths and croupers, things to tie, lashings to make fast, until officers and soldiers almost gave up in despair. But by hours of perseverance, one was finally secured to a mule; the heart-strap was drawn tight, and the crouper fairly lifted the animal up behind, like a severe curl in a little dog's tail. All was at length declared O K, according to their ideas of making a mule fast to it. The old mule, who knew more than all of them about pack-saddles, when free to see for himself what he had on his back, looked around at it a moment, gave a bray, kicked up behind, and away he darted, with straps and thongs streaming after him. But in kicking up, he made a great mistake, for the apparatus wouldn't let him down again; and the last ever seen of that mule and saddle, was a glimpse of them as he disappeared in the bushes, heels in the air, and going it on his fore-legs at a 2.40 pace, uttering the most hideous brays." - - - IT is very rarely that we see the following beautiful stanzas in print. Many of you may never have met with them. They are very touching, and were written by Philip Pendleton Cooke, who, had he been spared to us, would have been one of the most esteemed of America's poets. It is entitled

"FLORENCE VANE.

I LOVED thee long and dearly,
　　Florence Vane;
My life's bright dream, and early
　　Hath come again;
I renew in my fond vision
　　My heart's dear pain,—
My hopes and thy derision,
　　Florence Vane!

The ruin lone and hoary,
　　The ruin old,
Where thou didst hark my story,
　　At even told,—
That spot—the hues Elysian
　　Of sky and plain—
I treasure in my vision,
　　Florence Vane.

Thou wast lovelier than the roses
In their prime;
Thy voice excelled the closes
Of sweetest rhyme;
Thy heart was as a river
Without a main;
Would I had loved thee never,
Florence Vane.

But, fairest, coldest wonder!
Thy glorious clay
Lieth, the green sod under—
Alas the day!
And it boots not to remember
Thy disdain—
To quicken love's pale ember,
Florence Vane.

The lilies of the valley,
By young graves weep;
The pansies love to dally
Where maidens sleep;
May their bloom, in beauty vying,
Never wane
Where thine earthly part is lying,
Florence Vane!"

- - - The proprietors of the *Wide West,* with their accustomed enterprise and liberality, issued, last month, one of the best pictorial sheets ever published in California. The *Wide West* is an ably edited paper—every column in it bearing evidences of care—and for the credit of San Francisco it should be well supported. Now and then, we are compelled to differ from it in respect of its "critical judgments:"—for instance, we set much more value on "Theall the Philosopher," and much less on "The Mission by Moonlight," published in our December number than was attached to those productions by our cotemporary on Clay street. Again it must be remembered that an article, which is "prosy" to one class of minds, is exceedingly interesting to another; and an article which to many may seem feeble and too sentimental, may appeal to the heart of many others. Were there any one class of literary tastes in California sufficiently large to support a Magazine, we should appeal to that class alone—but in the present condition of affairs, we find it necessary to bring to bear upon such papers as are presented to us a species of catholic judgment which will enable us to please each of our patrons with something in accordance with his tastes. To make our selections so that every reader will be pleased with every article, is a moral impossibility. It must be remembered, also, that the California Poets are not, *all* of them, Miltons and Shakespeares. We think it can hardly be denied that in the main, The Pioneer presents a fair exposition of the literary talent of California. We propose to publish none but original articles. We shall endeavor to select the best from among the papers which are offered to us. If they are upon subjects intimately connected with California, of course they are the more acceptable; if not, we cannot help it. If our readers desire to peruse the current English and Transmontane literature, the counters of Le-Count & Strong—and Ullman, are well supplied.

THE PIONEER.

Vol. III.] FEBRUARY, 1855. [No. 2.

THE NATURE AND INFLUENCE OF POETRY.

BY C. E. HAVENS.

THE simplest analysis of poetry would reduce it to language and the ideas which language conveys. But such a definition would in no way distinguish poetry from prose, and we are forced to inquire further for its appropriate characteristics.

The ideas expressed being variously colored by the prismatic glow of the imagination and fancy, and the language being rounded into the one general law of harmony, curiously inflected and diversified through all its particular parts, those peculiarities which mark its difference from prose have been stated. There is no *philosophical antagonism* between poetry and prose. We believe both Coleridge and De Quincey concur in placing poetry and *science* in strict antithesis to each other; the former as the offspring of intuitive powers, the latter as requiring a severe logical basis. Science is lifeless fact. Poetry is spiritual truth. Science proves. Poetry affirms. Science is cold intellectualism. Poetry is warm with the impulses of the heart and glowing with the splendor of the imagination.

Science, whether in the domain of moral, intellectual or physical being, is always possessed with the same calculating prudence, the same slow and snail-like progress toward the goal of definite results. Poetry descends into the depths of experience, probes the springs and touches the chords of feeling and action. It is the glance of Apollo, illumining the world. When the golden veil of poetry is thrown over the naked reality of facts, we behold them transformed by passion, exalted by imagination, associated in every variety of manner by fancy. Poetry is the lyre of Orpheus, melting, by its tones, the rocks and the trees. Poetic inspirations are untrammeled licenses, coming and going like the winds, which start a thousand forms of waving beauty as they

flow on their invisible courses.   *Whence* these inspirations come, it is
not in the power of a final analysis to answer ; for the poetic rapture
and ecstasy, like the thrilling words of ancestral prophets, is inspired
by an oracle which is behind the veil.

The powers and faculties necessary to the production of poetry are
included under the names of observation, description, sensibility, invention, reflection, fancy, imagination and taste, or more properly, judgment.

That poetry may exist without involving all these qualities is very
true ; for we have descriptive poetry without imagination, and reflective
poetry without description.*   The predominating influence of one or
the other of these faculties in a poetical production justifies us in dis-
tinguishing the poetry as fanciful, descriptive, reflective or imaginative,
as the case may be.   Of *observation* and *description* we shall say little.
Their use and necessity as poetical agents are seen at a glance.   Of all
English Poets, Crabbe is the best illustration of these two faculties.
His close and accurate observation enabled him to describe objects,
even to their minutest details, in a style graphic enough, but calculated
to become in the end both wearisome and tedious.   A close affinity
exists between those old Dutch paintings, (which might almost be
styled humorous from their painful attention to details, were it not
for the evident sincerity and seriousness of the artists,) and the poetry of Crabbe.   The *intensity* of Crabbe's descriptions has more than
once disposed us to laugh.   Portions of Oliver Goldsmith's poetry are
characterized by these same faculties ; faculties, which, in connection,
with humor, may be traced in the paintings of Hogarth, the novels of
Smollett, Fielding and Richardson, and in connection with wit, in the
poetry of Pope.   We quote the following from Goldsmith's " Deserted
Village," as an illustration of the faculties of observation and description :

> " Imagination fondly stoops to trace
>   The parlor splendors of that festive place:
>   The white-wash'd wall, the nicely sanded floor,
>   The varnish'd clock that click'd behind the door;
>   The chest, contrived a double debt to pay,
>   A bed by night, a chest of drawers by day;
>   The pictures plac'd for ornament and use,
>   The Twelve Good Rules, the Royal Game of Goose;
>   The hearth, except when winter chill'd the day,
>   With aspen boughs, and flowers, and fennel, gay;
>   While broken teacups, wisely kept for show,
>   Rang'd o'er the chimney, glisten'd in a row."

The poetry of Goldsmith is destitute of the higher qualities of imagination.   He never paints with a single stroke of the brush, but
everthing is elaborated.

In poetry, even more than in prose, true sentiment inspires the most
heroic and truthful expressions.†   The language of the soul is always

---

* Reflective poetry is of two kinds.   That which *describes* our internal life ;
that which is purely didactic.   We here use the word *description* in a limited
sense.

† A taste and a genius for words!   An ear for the beautiful music of words!

the language of inspiration.   The poetic ecstasy is made known, like the Commandments on Sinai, amid thunders and lightnings.   It is only when imitation usurps the legitimate throne of inspiration, and learning is made to supply the place of intuition, that intensity of expression degenerates into a classic formality, and verbal melody is secured by an elaborate correction, revision and polishing.

Sensibility is perception by means of the senses ; and according to the refinement of sensibility, is the range and extent of perception.   In poetry, emotion and sensibility are so intimately blended, the former being the instantaneous result of the latter, that nothing is lost in omitting the philosophical distinction and treating them as one and the same thing.   Sensibility is the leading feature in English poetry, as imagination predominates in the poetry of Germany.   The Anglo-Saxon temperament is peculiarly open to the influence of external impressions, and undergoes every variety of modification in the changing condition of its outward circumstances.   English poetry is more truly emotional, than imaginative, or intellectual.   A great *heart* beats forever at its center and constitute the hidden spring which moves its delicate machinery.   Highly imaginative as are the works of Spencer, Shakespeare, Beaumont and Fletcher, and Coleridge, imagination is always used by them as an agent to heighten the effect of joy or sorrow, despondency or love.   On the contrary, in the poetry of Germany, all other qualities are subordinated to the grand and final triumph of imagination.   The German Poets enter the lists as knights for tilt and tournament, clad in all the gorgeous panoply of chivalry, and prepared with lance in hand for any display of imaginative prowess.

All the beauties of Nature,—the solitude of its immemorial forests—its stars and its sunsets—its sweet dews and flowers—its majestic rivers and everlasting hills,—are but the ornaments of the Muse, the decorations of the mind, the material garments that cover, but do not hide the profound emotions of the soul.   English poetry, alone, has scattered upon the dusty highways of life all the freshness of the cooling shower, shadowed them with the dark foliage of the pine and adorned them with wayside roses, sweet-scented with the dews of the morning.   Without overloading the sense and destroying the appetite, by an oriental superfluity, it has interwoven the beauties of Nature with the practical concerns of life, and, without seeking for ornament, has given it always in its proper place and in harmony with its ideas.   Vulcan at his forge is idealized by the red-hot glow of the anvil.   English poetry is a lake, whose surface is ruffled by the winds of sensibility, but it holds in the hollow of its hand, the perfect image of the surrounding scenery, and the moon and the stars are reflected in its depths.

Yet, perhaps, this exquisite sensibility has contributed more than

A happy justness in the perception of their strict proprieties!   A fine skill in apprehending the secret relations of Thought with Thought—relations along which the mind moves with creative power, to find out for its own use, and for the use of all minds to come, some hitherto uncreated expression of an idea—an image—a sentiment—a passion!   These dispositions and these faculties of the scholar in another mind falling in with other faculties of genius, produce a student of a different name—The Poet.—*Dies Boreales.*   No. II.

aught else to the sufferings of such men as Otway, Chatterton, and Keats, in grappling with the sterner and coarser realities of life.

"We learn in suffering, what we speak in song," says Wordsworth. But he was mistaken in framing this sentence into a general application. Neither the poetry of France,* nor that of Germany, shadows forth the personal experience of the poet's soul. The intellectual, with them, is of more value than the emotional ; and so it has happened that when the horizon was dark, and all the stars of sensibility had been extinguished, with a far-seeing worldly wisdom, they have turned their eyes from the heavens, and steered their vessels through the stormy waste by the unerring compass of reason.

Invention is that faculty which supplies and combines the material of poetry. It is not inseparable from genius, although in the highest poetic genius it always exists. Both Spencer and Shakespeare possessed boundless faculties of invention ; and, in our own day, Southey has exceeded all his contemporaries in the display of his inventive resources. Where the facts and outline of a poem are furnished by history, the sphere of invention is greatly limited; yet from the very fact that a poet voluntarily cramps and confines himself by the imposition of historic limits, his triumph is so much the more an evidence of power, and an imperishable record of genius.

In the dramatic art, especially, the freedom allowed by invention, is an invaluable assistance to the poet. It enables him to overleap the barriers of art, and, by a strong appeal to passion, so completely enlist the *feelings* of an audience, that the illusion is maintained without subjecting the drama to strict historical accuracy. Shakespeare never suffers an obstacle to stand between his genius and the ends of art, when it impedes the free development of action. He employs all the varieties of character, all the resources of passion, and all the illusions of scenery, in the exercise of his invention.

Shakespeare and his contemporaries never hesitated to seize and combine, not only the facts of history, but the plots of novels, and popular superstitions, for the purpose of supplying the pressing demands of the stage. The theater was, with them, comparatively a modern introduction. A *hiatus* existed, and was to be filled ; and as Dan Chaucer had made a wholesale appropriation of the works of Boccaccio and the poets of Italy, so Italian novels, Gothic histories, and Scotch and Danish traditions, were all fused together in the vast alembic of Shakespeare's soul, by the force of his inventive genius and the potency of his unequaled imagination. His intellect set at defiance all dramatic rules, and went forth into the spiritual world, conquering and to conquer.

Modern English poetry, with one or two exceptions, is deficient in

---

* The Poetry of France is *imitated* from the ancients. If popularity is *the* test of merit, it is not of an equal order of excellence with the poetry of England, Germany or Italy. Shakespeare is read, quoted and sung by the people. The vineyards on the Rhine re-echo the songs of Goethe ; and the Venetian gondoliers row by moonlight to the sweet measures of Tasso. Even Spain, in her degredation, has never forgotten her Calderon. But what do the French *people* know or care of Racine or Voltaire? Have the banks of the Seine ever given back the lyrics of Pascal and Rosseau?

any grand display of invention. It has been reserved for Goethe to unite, with a wild and boundless invention, the genius that controls and guides it, while overstepping the limits of art, and constituting his own judgment as the only acknowledged law.

A swan, imaged in a glassy stream, may stand for the symbol of *reflection* in poetry. Reflection is thought reproducing itself. Every thought that arises in the poet's mind is a representative of the *past*, and it is only by comparing his thoughts, that he is enabled to sum up the general truths of his experience.

Nature, herself, is the image of reflection. To the poet's soul, all her infinite variety is but a crystal transparency, through which he beholds in many-colored light the glowing ideal. The South American Amazon or our Missouri, are equally images of Time, as it travels to Eternity. Spring is the symbol of youth, and Summer of manhood. And, as the Autumn of life is rounded by the sleep of death, so the icy finger of Winter touches the heart of Nature into silence and sleep. Yet, as if even this did not suffice, she calmly reminds us, by the power of eternal reproduction, of our own mortality.

The reflective poetry of England is generally produced at the expense of imagination. Cowper, Young, Pope and Wordsworth, are reflective poets, but in the faculty of imagination they are deficient.

Reflection and imagination are only united but rarely, and then in the highest genius.

We find them both in the works of Spencer, Shakespeare and Coleridge; but their happiest development is to be found beneath the skies of Germany. The Germans are highly imaginative, and, at the same time, highly philosophical. Nature is ever reminding them of the great enigma of life. To intellectual pride and audacity, they unite a genuine love of flowers and streams, blue skies and singing birds; and, by the fortunate combination of the two, they are enabled to clothe the realm of barren abstractions with the purple haze of imagination.

An undue exercise of any one faculty must necessarily result in disadvantage to others. In poetry, especially, this end should be avoided. Universality in the arts, can only be attained by the equal and legitimate use of *all* the faculties; and where any one of these is developed to an unhealthy degree, the arts are diverted from their proper channels, and a radical defect will be found to exist in the judgment of the artist.

In the "Paradise Lost" we observe the operations of a well-balanced mind, in which the powers of description, reflection, imagination and fancy, are severally employed, and the dignity of the subject maintained equally, in the deepest reflections, and in the gentlest dalliance of fancy. On the contrary, in the "Night Thoughts," the impress of a gloomy meditation characterizes the work. The grave appears to be ever uppermost in the poet's mind. Nature has for him no "voice of gladness," no "smile and eloquence of beauty." She does not "glide into his *darker musings* with a mild and gentle sympathy." The path of our earthly pilgrimage is refreshed by no cool and lucid springs or "hedge-grown primroses," or enticing odors. No immortal youth, and beauty, and freshness, attracts the eye, and descends like sweet dew upon the heart. The enjoyments of life are treated as if they were its vanities.   The imagination is restrained, as if there were something unholy in its natural use.   And life clothed in sackcloth and sprinkled with dust and ashes, gravitates toward the tomb.

The faculties of *imagination* and *fancy* are perhaps best characterized by a display of their antithetical points.   The philosophical distinction between the two is of modern date, and is mainly due to the investigations of Wordsworth and Coleridge.*   The imagination, dealing with *plastic* images, gives the impress of unity to variety, resolves unity back again into its various parts, and confers upon one image properties inherent in another.   The fancy, dealing with images of a *limited* nature, produces its effects by the surprising facility of its associations.   We have sometimes thought that the imagination existed more in combination with genius and humor ; and the fancy, with talent and wit.   Milton concentrates his discription of the heavenly army in one magnificent line, in which all the splendid variety and gorgeous panoply of the advancing host is exhibited at a single glance, as the eye takes in all the details of a landscape.

> "Attended with ten thousand, thousand saints,
> He onward came, *far off his coming shone.*"

And this is imagination.

Again, he says of the fallen angels :

> "Through many a dark and dreary vale
> They passed, and many a region dolorous,
> O'er many a frozen, many a fiery Alp,
> Rocks, caves, lakes, fens, bogs, dens, and shades of death,
> *A Universe of Death.*"

And this, again, is imagination.

In the lines,

> "As when the sun, new-risen,
> Looks through the *horizontal* misty air,"

he confers upon the air, a property inherent in the sun.   The prose reading of it would be, "the new-risen sun looks horizontally through the misty air."

Thus Tennyson says "to roll the torrent out of dusky doors," instead of, "to roll the dusky torrent out of doors;" or, we might say, "twanged the barbed reed to its *swift goal*," the property of swiftness being not at all in the goal, but entirely in the reed.   We will take the description of the flowers from Milton's "Lycidas," and mark each line as imaginative or fanciful, as the case may be.†

> (imagination)
> "Bring the rath primrose that *forsaken dies.*
> (fancy)   (imagination)
> The *tufted crow-toe*, and *pale* jessamine,
> (fancy)   (fancy)
> The *white pink*, and the pansy *freak'd with jet*,
> (imagination)
> The *glowing* violet,

---

* Leigh Hunt, following in their footsteps, has, in his "Imagination and Fancy," analyzed these faculties, not so much by definition, as by illustrations from the poets.

† We believe Mr. Leigh Hunt has done this before us, but we can assure our readers that in this case memory is of no service to us.

(fancy)
The musk-rose, and the *well attir'd* woodbine,
(imagination)
With cowslips wan that hang the pensive head,
(imagination)   (fancy)
And ev'ry flower, that *sad embroidery* wears."

The imagination is the language of the soul. The fancy is the expression of the understanding. The imagination ministers to the eternal necessities of our being. The fancy weaves its flowery garlands, to crown the fleeting shows of our militant natures.

The workings of the imagination are calculated to fill the soul with awe, melt it into tears, or penetrate it with the sharp thrill of terror. The fancy moves our admiration, touches our gentler feelings, and seldom ministers to our deeper emotions. The imagination takes possession of the faculties, populates the soul with imagery of an undefinable splendor, and leads it upward to contemplate from its heavenly hight the center and the source of infinite glory. The fancy moves at the command of the will and draws its images from concrete nature, to effect only a temporary and passing emotion.

The fancy, *combines* by the power of association, and brings together all varieties of dissimilar images. The imagination, evolves by the power of its *creative* genius, new beauties, that exist not in Nature, but in the poet's mind.

"The Rape of the Lock" is perhaps as admirable a specimen of the powers of fancy as the English language furnishes. Its exquisite finish is the product of equal genius and taste, although in the highest development of genius Pope was deficient.

But in imagination, the poetry that illustrates the age between the reign of Elizabeth and the rise of Lord Byron, is lamentably defective. In the age of Elizabeth, poetry was less understood as an art, and poets were not troubled with self-consciousness. But modern poetry is founded and written on a knowledge of the laws which regulate its production, and the poet, not content with reproducing Nature, is constantly interposing his own personality. Shakespeare studied human nature in mankind. Byron studied it in himself. And the universality of the one is as refreshing and delightful, as the misanthropy and egotism of the other is forbidding and repulsive. We believe that civilization is eminently unfavorable to the arts, and especially to the art of poetry. What is gained in refinement, is lost in strength. The perfection of language appears to have been attained at the expense of imagination. The beauties of modern, English and Italian literature, are a poor compensation for the primeval strength of Spencer and Ariosto, Milton and Dante.

Taste is the presiding deity of poetry. It perceives whatever is excellent and beautiful, and maintains order and symmetry in the parts. It discriminates between the false and the true, and is an equal protection from vulgarity and exaggeration. It checks the riotous and disproportionate exercise of any one faculty, and preserves a due preponderance between all. And yet if we take the highest productions of poetic genius and subject them to a strict analysis according to the laws of art, we will often find that good taste is violated, while, at the same time, they inspire within us the most lively emotions. Good taste will not tolerate the conduct of Mariana in "Measure for Measure," and yet, when criticism has exhausted itself, we feel as completely, as ever, the self-sacrificing heroism of the deed.

The introduction of the witches into "Macbeth" and "Faust, is in violation of all the laws of taste ; but the effects of terror and of pleasure upon the imagination, cannot be dispensed with, because their proceedings are obnoxious to criticism.

The highest genius must ever be a law to itself. It will conform to the necessities of taste, so long as it can do so without clipping its own wings. But when the one or the other must be dispensed with, genius will cast off the shackles that impede its course, and give to its impulses a free development. "Genius," observes Madame de Stael, "provided it respect religion and morality, should be free to take any flight it chooses : it aggrandizes the empire of thought." The standard of taste is continually being corrected by every new flight of genius.

As we estimate the civilization of Greece by the degree of perfection she attained in the arts of poetry and sculpture, so in our own times, the state of the fine arts, next to the condition of Christianity, is the highest measure of national progress. This fact alone, should be a shield to ward off the critical arrows which are discharged at poetry. The moral argument against poetry is founded on a mistaken conception of the nature of imagination. Because it has been the means of effecting incalculable evil, it is argued that it is incapable of effecting infinite good. No sophistry could be more shallow. If Byron has written "Don Juan," does it necessarily follow that our children cannot read Shakespeare and Ben Johnson? Because he was a misanthrope, we are surely not to suspect all poets of misanthropy. Because Shelley wrote "Queen Mab," we must not denounce Chaucer as an atheist.

If the fact that poetry is sometimes made the instrument of evil, furnishes sufficient ground for its wholesale condemnation, then the same argument may be applied with equal force to the arts of painting and sculpture. Then the genius of Raphael and Phidias becomes of no avail ; and that which most illustrates and adorns the civilization of antiquity, loses at once its individual value and its historic glory.

Such an argument could, indeed, be only the product of a narrow intellect, and of a bigoted mind : nor could it be strengthened by affirming that the use of the imagination is inimical to the health of the understanding, as well as corrupting to the heart. On the contrary, we affirm that the exercise of the imagination enlarges the understanding, by incarnating sublime conceptions of important truths, and purifies the heart, by leading it out into the world of beauty, there to seek and identify itself with all that is beautiful and true. We believe that such as have *studied* Shakespeare with a scholar's love, must have arrived at altogether loftier conceptions of the nature of the soul, the strength, weakness and variety of character, the beauty, the grandeur and the sublimity of nature. The elevating character of poetry must be acknowledged by all who have understandings to appreciate it, and souls to feel. It lifts us, on the wings of imagination, above the sordid and unsatisfying vanities of life, into atmospheres of perpetual and unclouded beauty. It appeals to all the nobler impulses of our being, ministers to our infinite longings, and, on the pedestal of material life, erects the colossal statue of the ideal, the lineaments of whose divine countenance are radiant with the inspirations of hope and glowing with the rosy tints of youth and beauty.

In the Arcadia of Poetry flow lucid streams, whose clear and crystal depths reflect the beauty and sublimity of nature and of the soul. In its groves of stately palms resounds the sweet voice of the nightingale, and its vales luxuriate in all flowers of every hue. But if the serpent of evil enter that enchanted Arcadia, in evil's guile and crooked ways, how complete and instantaneous the transformation! The flowers are indeed as beautiful as ever, but their breath is poison. The song of the nightingale is as sweet ; but it is the song of the syren that allures to destruction. The shadow of its groves is delightful, but it is damp with the spirit of decay. We believe it to be impossible for the divine poetic genius to separate itself entirely from the good and the true. Some redeeming touches of the better nature will here and there appear. The faith which hopes everything for humanity, will not altogether cease to shine—will not degenerate into a despairing and bitter misanthropy.

Poetry is the natural language of praise and worship. "Man's body is the temple of the Living God," said Novalis : and in all climes and ages, from the heart's altar, in that temple, poetry has arisen, as at once, the sweetest incense and the purest praise. Every true feeling is poetic ; and love, the deepest of sentiments, always finds its fitting expression in a prolonged jubilee of mystic adoration.

Genius, in its highest developments, can never transcend the nature of humanity. When it strives to shadow forth the elysium of the Gods, its conceptions must be clothed in a human coloring. When it discloses the tragic extravagances of the passions—whether it be anger, whose eyes of fire "in lightnings own its secret stings," or "wan despair," or "impatient revenge" deaf to the entreaties of "dejected pity," or jealousy, flying from the extreme of love to the extreme of hate,—it always appeals to human sympathy, or invokes our sense of justice. When it describes the external beauties of Nature, it renews the immortality of youth and overwhelms the soul with a sense of indefinable joy. The poet is blessed with all the attributes of humanity ; but in him they are refined and intensified to an exquisite degree.

> "The Poet in a golden clime was born,
>   With golden stars above ;
> *Dowered with the hate of hate, the scorn of scorn,*
>   *The love of love.*
>
> He saw through life and death, through good and ill,
>   *He saw through his own soul.*
> The marvel of the everlasting will,
>   An open scroll,
>
> Before him lay : with echoing feet he threaded
>   The secret'st walks of fame :
> The viewless arrows of his thoughts were headed
>   And winged with flame,

Like Indian reeds blown from his silver tongue,
    And of so fierce a flight,
From Calpe unto Caucasus they sung,
    Filling with light

And vagrant melodies the winds, which bore
    Them earthward till they lit;
Then, like the arrow-seeds of the field-flower,
    The fruitful wit,

Cleaving, took root, and springing forth anew
    Where'er they fell, behold,
Like to the mother plant in semblance, grew
    A flower all gold,

And bravely furnished, all abroad to fling
    The winged shafts of *truth*,
To throng with stately blooms the breathing spring
    Of Hope and Youth."

A woman of genius has said, "It would be easier to describe the symptoms of genius, than to give precepts for the attainment of it. Genius, like love, is felt by the strong emotions with which it penetrates him who is endowed with it; but if we dared to advise, where Nature should be the only guide, it is not merely literary counsel that we should give. We should speak to poets as to citizens and heroes; we should say to them, be virtuous, be faithful, be free; respect what is dear to you, seek immortality in love and the Deity in Nature; in short, sanctify your soul as a temple; and the angel of noble thoughts will not disdain to appear in it."

We gladly adopt these words as *our* closing counsel.

ELLA ROBB.

—

BY A MINER.

—

AYE, welcome little traveler
    Across the drifted snow;
The fir-trees' shadows lengthen fast,
    And the evening sun is low;
The wolf is howling down the glen
    And scenting for his prey,
And the grizzly comes from out his den
    As soon as close of day.

Come, welcome to my fireside;
    I'll kiss thy infant brow,
For I left at home an angel child
    As innocent as thou.
And often in this lonesome cot,
    When wintry tempests wail,
I've started from my dreams, and thought
    Her voice was in the gale.

Our hut is made of shapeless logs,
    Our hands are rough and strong;
But long ago we listened to
    Thy mother's matchless song.
Then welcome, little pioneer—
    The kettle's on the hob,
And every one thou seest here
    Will welcome Ella Robb.

AT OUR CABIN, Yuba River, Cal., 1854.

OUR STREETS.

THE CHINESE—THE CANDY MAN.

BY J. P. ANTHONY.

PERHAPS no other place in the world presents so varied a panorama —so much that is at once striking and uncommon,—as the busy thoroughfares of our young city. The uncouth Chinaman, the showy and tawdry Mexican, the jabbering Frenchman, the hirsute miner, the rough backwoodsman and the elaborately got-up gent, jostle each other on the footway, whilst the languages of nearly all known nations, may be heard on every side. Faces, in which eventful histories are written; heroes, who seem just to have stepped out of volumes of adventures, meet you at every step. Here is, indeed, illustrated the romance of reality, and few there are amongst us, having sojourned a decade of months in San Francisco, but to whose ears are eventful narratives as familiar as household words. Few, but have listened to the adventures, hair-breadth escapes by flood and field, of some acquaintance, compared to which imagination's fictitious relations are vapid ; the manufactured, startling effects of the most popular romancist, spiritless and inane.

The battle of life is, or has, indeed, been here. How many in this stirring arena have succumbed to that black despair, which waged dread warfare beneath banners of fire ! How many have owned themselves vanquished, when, seeking in the bottle the appalling consolation of temporary oblivion ! How many, again—giants in spirit—the true heroes of the world, who, worsted in the conflict, fight on still, undismayed, unconquerable ! What histories are unwritten ! What biographies, teeming with rich teaching, could our young city furnish !

For men of broken fortunes, California would seem to have been peculiarly a place of refuge. We have seen a waiter at a leading restaurant, who had been at one time, a Colonel in the Austrian service ; —another, earning his livelihood as a paper-hanger, who had been an aid-de-camp to General Larmorcier,—a Doctor of great ability, in England, once eminent in his profession, driving a dray,—and another, an Emeralder, a good classic, educated at Trinity, Dublin, in the situation of a *rial* drinking house ; and doubtless there are numbers amongst us, who have passed through even greater changes. Shakespeare, who has something applicable to all classes and conditions, may fairly be supposed to have had such battlers with adversity in his mind's eye,—especially, those whose reverses have been self-entailed,— when he wrote,

> "There's a divinity doth shape our ends
> Rough hew them as we will ! "

To such, however, it becomes a question, whether the quotation may be well commended, or yet the practice of that comprehensive philosophy, which is embodied in the belief, that " all's for the best."

The frequent alterations which take place in the stores of our busiest thoroughfares, present a striking characteristic of San Francisco, effected, as they are, only less rapid than the changes in a pantomime.

Indeed, to observe the celerity with which some of these transmutations are accomplished, one might naturally look out in the expectation of beholding Harlèquin and Columbine flitting around the shifting scene. At the theater, beneath a single stroke of the magic wand, we see a butcher's changed into a barber's store,—and here, where in the morning you may have purchased pastry, in the evening, shall be in the hands of one who offers physic. In the same space of time, submitted to a discerning public, shall liquor take the place of literature.

And then the Chinese, with their frontispieces baffling all metoposcopy; whose nomenclature, in its strangeness, harmonizes so admirably with their very uncouth and grotesque looking selves! In one place we find a descendant, subject of the great Fohi, rejoicing under the appellation of "Sing Up;" (we believe that we were the first in one of our daily journals to surmise that these "Sings" were the Smiths of Chinadom.) Another, "Tong (tongue) Sing"; another, "Ah Sing," and one, still more altisonant, "King Lee"—at the first glance you might take for King Lear,—announcing washing at so much per dozen. One Celestial we have, the sign over whose door declares him to belong to no less a body than the well-known legion of the Smiths! Yes, a veritable pigtail John Smith! *Auri sacra fames!* Shades of the great Swee Gin Shee!—thou, who first discovered the production of fire by friction, and taught thy long-tailed, angular-phizzed countrymen to look up to Tien, the creating and destroying power, wilt thou tolerate such desecration—such absonant change of patronymic?

The Chinese may be a very clever people in their way ; but, in our opinion, their dramatic representations are conclusive as to the little progress they have made in the development of intellect. We advance this, presuming that the histrionic display by the Chinese company, who, sometime since, appeared in our city, was a fair specimen of their Drama. It is not the less true, that, notwithstanding their stage be destitute of anything indicative of a high order of mind, they may, nevertheless, have some shining lights, some mental Titans amongst them. The Bœotians, we know, were noted for their heaviness and stupidity ; yet had they Plutarch, Epaminondas and Pindar, glorious exceptions to the rule. We must tarry, until we know him better, ere pronouncing judgment on the intellectual capacity of long-tailed John. Meantime, on condition of their conforming to white men's customs relative to cleanliness and common precautions against fire, we would bespeak for them a continuation of that courtesy—so far in the absence of salutary correction much abused—the privileges of good citizens, and the protection of our laws, which have rendered these human macaws so much at home amongst us.

If the Chinamen's names are peculiar, there are numbers of others in our streets worthy of note for their singularity, and some of them for being particularly suggestive. We would instance two, that, at the moment, occur to us ;—a "Salvator Rosa," and a "Humboldt." These you may find within a few paces of each other, in one of our leading thoroughfares. As your gaze rests upon the first, it is scarcely possible that you do not recall some great work,—some landscape by the painter of the "Conspiracy of Catiline,"—some production displaying

"The vast, alone, the wonderful, the wild,"

that at some period of your life you may have had the good fortune to look upon ; whilst the name of Humboldt reminds you, in all probability, that after the cares of the day are gone by, the last edition of Cosmos awaits you with your slippers at home.

Considering its age, ours is indeed a wonderful city ! Our very candy men are orators ; our venders of tooth-paste, lecturers on anatomy in the thoroughfares ; and there are others, who, in offering compounds to remove stains from your habiliments, discourse on chemical properties and affinities with most marvelous skill.

Amongst these geniuses in the streets, there is one, in particular, to whose peculiarities, though often engaging the attention of the itemizers of our journals, justice has barely been done. It is almost superfluous to state, that we allude to " Everybody Buys 'Em," by everybody known.   Montgomery street knows the deep tones of his voice ; to the regions of Commercial street his addresses are as familiar as household words.   Like that Abbey, sung of by the poet, Night seems to be the time, when he is in his highest glory.   As Melrose is by moonlight, our Candy-Man is greatest in the hours of Gas.   His spirit burns up with the lamps, and the deep diapason of his voice rolls forth, as Byron has it, " like young earthquakes at their birth."   Has anyone, beside ourselves, ever speculated on the mental capacity of the " Ould Original," as he delights to call himself ?   That he indulges in profound reveries, we are quite assured ; for although his eyes may be riveted on his saccharine collection, often are his thoughts, like the dying gladiator's, far, far away.   Observe him attentively, and you shall find that, in the intervals of his stentorian addresses to the public, he starts at times as though from a reverie ; a reverie far too profound, to have been occasioned by mental problems on the future price of sugar, or whether a dime or quarter speaks in the eye of *hombre* or urchin approaching the stall with riveted gaze on its tempting store.   For our own part, we have no hesitation in regarding him as a profound thinker.   We believe him to be learned in many things, and great on sugar.   In his silent moments, we can easily fancy him pondering, for instance, on that passage from Jeremiah, which speaks of the sweet cane from a far country, clearly indicating that the sugar plant was then, like " Everybody Buys 'Em's " big lumps of the present day, an article of commerce.   Or, that his researches into his favorite subject have taught him how the word sugar was derived from the Hebrew, " Sachar," which signifies drunkenness ; proving a rich vein of thought in its suggestiveness to the " Ould Original."   Or, again, he may have discovered that, according to Pliny, " sakkarom," or sugar, was, in that great philosopher's day, found useful as physic ; that it was, moreover, first used in England as a medicine, and that old Chaucer, who, like our Candy Man, offered sweets to the public, alludes to sugre in his minstrelsy.   Popular fallacies it is well should be exploded ; and if he is cognizant of the fact, we can only wonder that our " Everybody Buys

'Em" does not strenuously, and in his biggest voice, declare that saccharine is not injurious to the carnivorous department of human development. It is possible, however, that, in the pursuit of his favorite study, this important fact may have escaped him, and we therefore venture, in the hight of our good will, to offer a suggestion which, if acted upon, may perhaps increase to the extent of a dozen dimes per day his commercial transactions. Let him convey to the public that sugar-eating rather preserves than injures the masticators of man, and, like a thousand of bricks, come down upon the skeptics with the fact, that the slaves of Jamaica have the finest grinders in the world. And then, as to its being wholesome, let him fire another broadside, by instancing the case of that certain Duke of Beaufort, who died at an advanced age in the year 1702 in England, and who was accustomed for forty years, to eat one pound of sugar every day.

We have said that we believe "Everybody Buys 'Em" to be a studious member of the human family. Certain it is, he discourses most learnedly on subjects which impress you with the conviction that his researches have extended to something beyond sugar. He is indeed great on the lungs! Listen to him, and you can scarcely fail to be convinced, that one of the most important facts in the economy of human life, is to swallow candy—"Take care of your lungs, gentlemen!" he vociferates, with a voice that indeed speaks volumes. "If candy be good for the lungs, then has he swallowed a heap of it!" you mentally exclaim, as his stentorian appeals make the pavement vibrate beneath you.

Our Candy Man is no copyist. He is, as his greatest pride appears to be to declare himself, "The Ould Original." He is no gatherer and disposer of other men's stuff, but one from whom others steal thunder. "Big lumps and strongly flavored!" How admirable, how succinct and expressive! No waste of words there, reader! "Everybody buys 'em!" Better and better; a sentence so comprehensive and concise is worthy of being blazoned in letters of his own candy. So Miltonish, it is almost sublime. It is as great, if not greater, than anything in Raglan's dispatches.

But our Candy Man is not always "i' the vein." There are times when he seems to be paying homage to Harpocrates. He stands before his stall, silent as that certain Mr. Patience, who upon a monument was found smiling at Grief. Lacking patrons, like that merit, which, according to the historian, languished to death under the cold shade of aristocracy, our Candy Man shuts up. He surveys the passers with a look, as though he pitied their ignorance; scorning to repeat his powerful addresses, he dives his digits deeper into his pockets, doubtless lamenting the degeneracy of the age. Tarry long enough, and you shall, however, behold this mood pass away. The first urchin who opens a trade with him, and tests the rate of exchange to the extent of a dime, rouses him as is roused a war charger by the trumpet blast. It is the sun of his Austerlitz! He gives himself a shake or two, his frontispiece is gaily illumined again by the light within, and his "Everybody Buys 'Em" rolls forth again with accustomed vigor. We believe that he has indeed a sincere and exalted opinion of the beneficial qualities of his saccharine stock. The earnestness which he displays in its recommendation to the public, stamps him a true philanthropist. Love of gain alone could not sustain him in the prodigious exertions which he makes to disseminate its virtues. Were the Olympic games re-established under his auspices, certain are we that the victor's wreath of wild olive would give place to one of candy.

In his physique and bearing we consider there is something of the heroic ; and it would require from us but little stretch of the imaginaation to behold him histrionically great. That he has been introduced to the stage is well known to all of us who are familiar with the transcendently talented local dramatic productions of our city. We had ourselves, by the way, a passing allusion to him in a Drama which we wrote for the Bateman prize, which said Drama, notwithstanding the Chairman of the Committee pronounced to be the best, neither got the cash nor the credit; both of which Mr. Bateman, we should say Mrs. B., did get. Had we been well posted in Barnumism, we should of course not have put lance in rest for the prize at all ; yet in committing to the flames our "Flying Gib," we had the satisfaction of reflecting, at all events, that our knowledge of "Ways and Means" had been considerably increased. Yes, we repeat, that we recognize something of the histrionic about "Everybody Buys 'Em." We have him at this moment in our mind's eye as the ninth priest in "Norma," and the first banner-bearer in "Brian Borohime." Of his antecedents we know nothing, yet should be prepared to hear they had been remarkable. It would not surprise us one whit to learn that he had been a grocer in Greenland, a tailor in Timbuctoo, or a candy man in Candehar.

We think it would be scarcely fair to institute a comparison between the "Ould Original" and the smaller fry of his calling. Adopting his striking, soul-stirring and palate-tickling addresses to the crowd, they have introduced others of their own,—setting off, however, to greater advantage the original master-pieces of our Candy Man. What vigor, what grandeur, what greater breadth of style is evinced in the cry of "Everybody Buys 'Em," when compared to the effete and feeble announcement that "It's *so* nice." Verily, a Titan to a pigmy— a Sebastopol to a Petropoloski !

Long may he flourish ! Long may he be heard in Montgomery street ! May Commercial street lose not the roll of his voice ! May his "Big Lumps" continue to be "Highly Flavored," and far, far distant the day when shall everybody cease to "buy 'em !"

L O V E .

BY **.

Every heart must have a shrine
Worshipping with love divine.
Souls must ever blend in one,
As the brooks together run.

Stars that shine upon the river
Waken answering star-gleams ever ;

Wild flowers where the fountains flow
Kiss the flowers that sleep below.

Thus do mortals ever find
Answering soul and kindred mind—
Feelings blending into one,
As the brooks together run.

CALIFORNIA, IN 1852.

BY SHIRLEY.

LETTER TWELFTH.

RESIDENCE IN THE MINES.

FROM OUR LOG CABIN, Indian Bar, January 27, 1852.

I WISH that it were possible, dear M., to give you an idea of the perfect Saturnalia, which has been held upon the river for the last three weeks, without at the same time causing you to think *too* severely of our good Mountains. In truth, it requires not only a large intellect, but a large heart, to judge with becoming charity of the peculiar temptations of riches. A more generous, hospitable, intelligent and industrious people, than the inhabitants of the half-dozen Bars—of which Rich Bar is the nucleus—never existed; for you know how proverbially wearing it is to the nerves of manhood, to be entirely without either occupation or amusement; and that has been pre-eminently the case during the present month.

Imagine a company of enterprising and excitable young men, settled upon a sandy level, about as large as a poor widow's potatoe patch, walled in by sky-kissing hills—absolutely *compelled* to remain, on account of the weather, which has vetoed indefinitely their Exodus—with no place to ride or drive, even if they had the necessary vehicles and quadrupeds,—with no newspapers nor politics to interest them,—deprived of all books but a few dog-eared novels of the poorest class,—churches, lectures, lyceums, theaters and (most unkindest cut of all !) pretty girls, having become to these unhappy men mere myths,—without *one* of the thousand ways of passing time peculiar to civilization,—most of them living in damp, gloomy cabins, where Heaven's dear light can enter only by the door,—and, when you add to all these disagreeables the fact that, during the never-to-be-forgotten month, the most remorseless, persevering rain which ever set itself to work to drive humanity mad, has been pouring doggedly down, sweeping away bridges, lying in uncomfortable puddles about nearly all the habitations, wickedly insinuating itself beneath un-umbrella-protected shirt-collars, generously treating to a shower-bath *and* the rhumatism sleeping bipeds, who did not happen to have an India-rubber blanket,—and, to crown all, rendering mining utterly impossible,—you cannot wonder that even the most moral should have become somewhat reckless.

The Saturnalia commenced on Christmas evening, at the Humboldt, which on that very day, had passed into the hands of new proprietors. The most gorgeous preparations were made for celebrating the *two* events. The bar was re-trimmed with red calico, the bowling alley had a new lining of the coarsest and whitest cotton cloth, and the broken lamp-shades were replaced by whole ones. All day long, patient mules could be seen descending the hill, bending beneath casks of brandy and baskets of champagne, and, for the first time in the history of that celebrated building, the floor (wonderful to relate, it *has* a floor,) was *washed*, at a lavish expenditure of some fifty pails of water, the using up of one entire broom, and the melting away of sundry bars of the best yellow soap ; after which, I am told that the enterprising and benevolent individuals, who had undertaken the Herculean task, succeeded in washing the boards through the hopeless load of dirt, which had accumulated upon them during the summer and autumn.   All these interesting particulars were communicated to me by "Ned," when he brought up dinner.   That distinguished individual himself was in his element, and in a most intense state of perspiration and excitement at the same time.

About dark, we were startled by the loudest hurras, which arose at the sight of an army of India-rubber coats, (the rain was falling in riversfull,) each one enshrouding a Rich Barian, which was rapidly descending the hill.   This troop was headed by the "General," who— lucky man that he is—waved on high, instead of a banner, a *live* lantern, actually composed of tin and window-glass, and evidently intended by its maker to act in no capacity but that *of* a lantern !   The "General" is the largest and tallest and—with one exception, I think—the oldest man upon the river.   He is about fifty, I should fancy, and wears a snow-white beard of such immense dimensions, in both length and thickness, that any elderly Turk would expire with envy, at the mere sight of it.   Don't imagine that *he* is a reveler ; by no means ; the gay crowd followed *him*, for the same reason that the king followed Madame Blaize, "because he went before."

At nine o'clock in the evening, they had an oyster and champagne supper in the Humboldt, which was very gay with toasts, songs, speeches, etc.   I believe that the company danced all night ; at any rate, they were dancing when I went to sleep, and they were dancing when I woke the next morning.   The revel was kept up in this mad way for three days, growing wilder every hour.   Some never slept at all during that time.   On the fourth day, they got past dancing, and, lying in drunken heaps about the bar-room, commenced a most unearthly howling ;—some barked like dogs, some roared like bulls, and others hissed like serpents and geese.   Many were too far gone to imitate anything but their own animalized selves.   The scene, from the description I have had of it, must have been a complete illustration of the fable of Circe and her fearful transformations.   Some of these bacchanals were among the most respectable and respected men upon the river.   Many of them had resided here for more than a year, and had never been seen intoxicated before.   It seemed as if they were seized with a reckless mania for pouring down liquor, which, as I said above, everything conspired to foster and increase.

Of course, there were some who kept themselves aloof from these excesses ; but they were few, and were not allowed to enjoy their sobriety in peace.   The revelers formed themselves into a mock vigilance committee, and when one of these unfortunates appeared outside, a constable, followed by those who were able to keep their legs, brought him before the Court, where he was tried on some amusing charge, and *invariably* sentenced to "treat the crowd." The prisoners had generally the good sense to submit cheerfully to their fate.

Towards the latter part of the week, people were compelled to be a little more quiet from sheer exhaustion ; but on New Year's day, when there was a grand dinner at Rich Bar, the excitement broke out, if possible, worse than ever. The same scenes in a more or less aggravated form, in proportion as the strength of the actors held out, were repeated at Smith's Bar and "The Junction."

Nearly every day, I was dreadfully frightened, by seeing a boat-load of intoxicated men fall into the river, where nothing but the fact of their *being* intoxicated, saved many of them from drowning. One morning, about thirty dollars worth of bread, (it must have been "tipsy cake,") which the baker was conveying to Smith's Bar, fell overboard, and sailed merrily away towards Marysville. People passed the river in a boat, which was managed by a pulley and a rope, that was strained across it from Indian Bar to the opposite shore.

Of the many acquaintances, who had been in the habit of calling nearly every evening three, only, appeared in the cabin during as many weeks. Now, however, the Saturnalia is about over. "Ned" and "Choch," have nearly fiddled themselves into their respective graves,— the claret (a favorite wine with miners,) and oysters are exhausted,— brandied fruits are rarely seen, and even port wine is beginning to look scarce. Old callers occasionally drop in, looking dreadfully sheepish and subdued, and *so* sorry,—and people are evidently arousing themselves from the bacchanal madness, into which they were so suddenly and so strangely drawn.

With the exception of my last, this is the most unpleasant letter which I have ever felt it my duty to write to you. Perhaps you will wonder that I should touch upon such a disagreeable subject at all. But I am bound, Molly, by my promise, to give you a *true* picture (as much as in me lies,) of mining life and its peculiar temptations, "nothing extenuating nor setting down aught in malice." But with all their failings, believe me, the miners, as a class, possess many truly admirable characteristics.

I have had rather a stupid time during the storm. We had been in the habit of taking frequent rows upon the river in a funny little toppling canoe, carved out of a log. The bridge at one end of our boating ground and the rapids at the other, made quite a pretty lake. To be sure it was so small that we generally passed and repassed its beautiful surface at least thirty times in an hour. But we did not mind *that*, I can assure you. We were only *too* glad to be able to go onto the water at all. I used to return, loaded down with the magnificent large leaves of some aquatic plant, which the gentle frosts had painted with the most gorgeous colors, lots of fragrant mint, and a few wan, white flowers, which had lingered past their autumnal glory. The richest hot-house bouquet could never give me half the pleasure, which I took in arranging in a pretty vase of purple and white, those gorgeous leaves. They made me think of Moorish Arabesques ; so quaint and *bizarre*, and at the same time dazzlingly brilliant were the varied tints. They were in their glory at evening ; for like an oriental beauty, they *lighted up* splendidly. Alas! where one little month ago, my pretty lake lay laughing up at the stars, a turbid torrent rushes noisily by;—the poor little canoe was swept away with the bridge, and splendid leaves hide their bright heads forever beneath the dark waters.

But I am not entirely bereft of the beautiful. From my last walk, I brought home a tiny bit of *out-doors*, which through all the long, rainy months that are to come, will sing to me silently, yet eloquently, of the blue and gold of the vanished summer, and the crimson and purple of its autumn. It is a branch, gathered from that prettiest feature of mountain scenery, a moss-grown fir-tree. You will see them at every step, standing all lovely in this graceful robe. It is in color, a vived pea-green, with little hard flowers, which look more like dots than anything else, and contrast beautifully with the deeper verdure of the fir. The branch, which I brought home, I have placed above my window. It is three feet in length and as large round as a person's arm; and there it remains, a cornice wreathed with purple-starred tapestry, whose wondrous beauty no upholsterer can ever match.

I have got the prettiest New Year's present. You will never guess what it is, so I shall have to tell you. On the eve of the year, as the "General" was lifting a glass of water, which had just been brought from the river, to his lips, he was startled at the sight of a tiny fish. He immediately put it into a glass jar and gave it to me. It is that most lovely of all the creatures of Thetis, a spotted trout, a little more than two inches in length. Its back of mingled green and gold, is splashed with dots of the richest sable. A mark of a dark ruby color, in shape like an anchor, crowns its elegant little head. Nothing can be prettier than the delicate wings of pale purple, with which its snowy belly is faintly penciled. Its jet black eyes, rimmed with silver, within a circlet of rare sea-blue, gleam like diamonds, and its whole graceful shape is gilded with a shimmering sheen, infinitely lovely. When I watch it from across the room, as it glides slowly round its crystal palace, it reminds me of a beam of many-colored light; but when it glides up and down in its gay playfulness, it gleams through the liquid atmosphere like a box of shining silver. "A thing of beauty is a joy forever;" and, truly, I never weary watching the perfected loveliness of my graceful little captive.

In the list of my deprivations, above written, I forgot to mention a fact, which I know will gain me the sympathy of all carniverously disposed people. It is, that we have had no *fresh meat* for nearly a month! Dark and ominous rumors are also floating through the moist air, to the effect that the potatoes and onions are about to give out! But don't be alarmed, dear Molly. There is no danger of a famine. For have we not got wagon loads of hard, dark hams, whose indurated hearts nothing but the sharpest knife and the stoutest arm can penetrate? Have we not got quintals of dreadful mackerel, fearfully crystalized in black salt? Have we not barrels upon barrels of rusty pork; and flour enough to victual a large army for the next two years? Yea, verily, have we; and more also. For we have oysters in cans, preserved meats and sardines, (*appropo*, I *detest* them) by the hundred box full.

So hush the trembling of that tender little heart and shut those tearful and alarmed eyes, while I press a good-night kiss on their drooping lids.

"THESE BE THY GODS, O ISRAEL!"

BY LUOF.

Immortal Gold! I worship at thy shrine!
I sing thy praise, Thou source of Life and Light!
Thy faithful worshippers have rights divine;
They quaff the pure elixir of delight,
In draughts more rich and deep than starry night.
For them stern Winter softens into Spring,
And Summer's sunbeams mellow on their sight;
All climes, all seasons their first offerings bring
To thine elect, oh Gold!   Our Saviour and our King!

Hail, Mighty Dollar! Belgie claims thy name:
Thou hast no ties of country,—none of creed;
Thou art the favorite harbinger of fame;
The good Samaritan in time of need;
The counselor of loving hearts that bleed:
Thou art the most substantial earthly friend;
The counselor, our every cause to plead;
With zeal sustain the right,—the wrong defend,
For in thy name the power of Gold and Silver blend.

Thou art the magic ring where extremes meet:
The princely hall, the cottage of the poor;
The trembling culprit and the judgment seat;
The devotee,—the God he doth adore.
Thou dost unlock the cherub-guarded door
Of that mysterious Eden, woman's heart,
And read with ease its hieroglyphic lore;
To it, Love's warm and gushing tides impart
Alike for youth and age, vice, virtue, nature, art.

Thy touch regenerates decrepid age;
Transforms to angels, maidens five times ten;
Changeth the clownish dolt into a sage;
With vestal bloom adorns the courtezan;
Transfigureth to saints unholy men.
Full many a sermon hath thy sheen inspired;
Full many a tome hath drawn from Genius' pen;
Full many a hero with dread thunder fired;
Full many a conquest won when courage had expired.

Great civilizer of Mankind! All hail!
Ark, Crescent, Cross, alike proclaim *Thee Great!*
Thy golden counsels evermore prevail
" In all the chief affairs of Church and State; "
Of conscience, Thou, " the measure and the weight: "
Alpha and Omega of created things!
Thou art the mighty Arbiter of Fate!
Thine orb sustains the thrones of mightiest kings,
And proud Republics bask beneath thy silver wings.

Rock of Eternal Ages! May we rest
Beneath thy shadow, through Life's pilgrimage!
Nor heed the storms which rend Earth's rugged breast;
Dream more serenely as Time's tempests rage;
To pleasure's tournaments our powers engage:
From thine auriferous clefts, divinely flow
The grace and beauty of the golden age,
Our souls melt in the rosy flood below
And on Love's blooming Ocean rise with immortal glow!

Oh, may our children's children, blessed Gold!
Luxuriate in thine inspiring beams:
Thy *sovereign* smiles their budding hopes unfold:
Thine *eagles* waft where joy and glory gleam;
Thine *unions* realize their fondest dreams;
May savage tribes thy grace appreciate;
Thy praise ascend from mountains, plains and streams;
Thine altars blaze in every Age and State,
And millions throng each shrine with the high impulse of Fate.

Oh, let us ever worship at thy shrine!
Let us discard the false philosophy
Of Moses and the Prophets! With Aaron join,
Free from all sanctimonious bigotry,
To worship Gold,—the only Deity
Worthy the aspirations of a soul
Panting for blissful immortality!
Gold is the God of man! From pole to pole,
Let the bold anthem on through endless ages roll!

THE SOUL UNTO HERSELF.

BY F. C. EWER.

Bereft?—Ah, when the forms of thy beloved
Ones vanish in the thick of life,
Stretch not thine arms forth after them,—
For here, is strife.

Press ever onward;—leave the past to die;—
Work out thy work with steadfast brow,
And let the mighty, headlong world
Its strange course flow.

For friends are sunshine,—they but help thee grow;
And when their work is done, they leave:
To other duties they must go,—
Why for them grieve!

Aye,—should pale Memory at thy side gaze back
To vanished scenes—neglectful friends,—
Look where she looks,—then upward soar
To thy high ends.

The past is gone;—the Future opens wide,
Plastic and grand! Then onward move
And mould it to thy will; and thou
Shalt have hand to thy hand, and love for love.

FAITH.

BY R. W. F.

FAITH is the hand that brings the spirit nigh
The shadowed things of far futurity;—
The vision of the soul invisible,
Piercing the mists, the mental gaze that veil;—
The bark that beareth sure to safety's haven.
The spirit to thought's restless ocean given;
The spider, cast by fate on tiny isle,
Gives to the breeze his silken thread the while,
And reaches banks where flowers in beauty smile;
So gulfs impassable are often seen
'Twixt soul and action;—Faith the bridge between,
That gives the mind the freedom to explore
The things of joy, that lie in shade before.

REST.

BY OLIVER OUTCAST.

"To distant countries I have been,
And yet I have not often seen
A healthy man, a man full grown,
Weep in the public road alone."

I KNOW it is thought unmanly to talk about a broken heart; I am aware that the man, who knows nothing of want of success, or who has never been crossed in his dearest object, or who, having been for awhile thwarted, has finally triumphed, will call that which I am about to write lack-a-daisical and sickly sentimental. But I write not for such. To the man full of hope, full of enthusiasm, and with a future to which he looks with pleasure, I have only to say, pass me by—leave others to read this essay if they list, for it is not written for you; you cannot sympathize with its spirit; you know not the feelings which I shall attempt to portray, nor will you admit the reasoning, by which I arrive at my conclusions. You are a healthy man, whose mind is free, clear and happy, and you cannot look with complacency or patience on the struggles of one different from you, weakening and still weakening to the final surrender and abandonment of the battle of life. You can have no charity for him, who has given up the strife while life lasted, for you see not how the heart-strings had been cracked, the springs of hope dried up. Your way of life has been calm and high, for hope and enthusiasm are yet left to you; and you have as little idea of the moving influences of one, who has parted with those incentives, as you have of the ruling motives of beings of another order. So pass on, and leave him, whose way of life has been rougher than yours, to read, perhaps, his own heart experience in my random thoughts.

It is not of unrequited love, that I have to speak. Whether there be some of so delicate and sensitive an organization as to be disturbed in their reason, or prematurely sent to the grave by this cause, I leave for the poets to decide. I speak of a nobler race; of men, earnest, gifted, enthusiastic men;—of men, bankrupt, ruined and broken down in youth; who feel nothing of pleasure in the present, see nothing but darkness in the future; of men, to whom the path, and the only path, in which they hoped to be useful or eminent, has apparently been closed, and closed forever.

In youth, men look forward to a certain position or avocation, which they believe necessary for them to reach, in order to fulfill their destiny. Each man has his mission. Each man has some course marked out for himself at an early period of life. No man resigns himself in youth to chance. He has some choice as to the road he will pursue, and all have aspirations of some kind. A fellow of low intellect and low tastes may aspire to no position higher than that of a day-laborer, yet, in youth, or early manhood he shall yet look forward to some change, social or domestic, that is to increase his happiness. Such a person, it is true, can never be seriously disappointed. His hopes are low, and the time may never come, when their fulfillment is not possible.

With the sensitive and the highly educated, however, it is vastly different. To them there is such a thing as disappointment; to them there may arise obstacles, such as no power within them can remove; they may see the way of life so choked up before them, that they can imagine no possible change of circumstances to open a field, wherein they may act and live the life they had fancied to themselves.

In no place in the world, probably, have so many of these waifs been cast as in California. Our land of golden promise has lured, alas! how many to disappointment and destruction! It is absolutely painful to contemplate, how many men of fine abilities and high promises have been crushed and ruined by the adversities of a life in California. I speak not only of those gross temperaments, which have given away under trouble to vicious indulgences. But I speak, also, of a different class; of men whose very sensibility has eaten into their heart's core, and consumed the ambition and enthusiasm that once impelled to action. They came here with their minds half-formed; their ideas of what they were best fitted for, vague and indistinct; impressed only with the idea, that a field was here opened for them, to work out their career and destiny. The country is full of such men. They may be found in every gulch and ravine throughout California—men who are buried to the world, and who wish not to hear of friends or home again, nor that any word of their life's failure should ever reach those whom they still love, but fear to meet. They thought to be men of distinction in the world. They had the talents for it, but in the whirl of the gold excitement they were thrown from the course, and after a few years of toil they find that their time is gone by, that they are poor as ever, and nothing opens before them but a life of toil. What else can they do? The country is full of people striving to live without work; and these men have no profession, no trade, no tact for speculation, and though educated within the walls of a college, perhaps, and all unused to toil, the life of a gold-digger is all that offers. It is a wonder that such men, after buffeting the world unsuccessfully for years, at length should long for rest? Is it a wonder that they become Pariah's and misanthropes?

I make no apology for such. They offer none for themselves, and they ask for no one's sympathy. You shall reason with them on the folly of their course, they will make no defense. They will admit that the road they are upon leads to a speedy death; yet they care not to prolong life by turning from it. "The day of their destiny's over," and their enthusiasm is gone.

I have been in the mines of California; I have worked in the gulches and the river beds; I have stood for hours in the cold mountain streams, till my limbs almost lost their feeling. I have slept on the ground when the cramp has caused me to cry out in an agony, and I know the thoughts that will run through the weary miner's head, as he lies looking at the stars, and contrasts his real condition with that his young imagination had pictured for his youthful manhood. Away, thousands of miles from all he loves, he finds himself doomed to work out a trying life by unintermitting toil. Of what does he dream at night? He sees old and familiar scenes, and when day comes to rouse him from his bed upon the ground, the long day brings the toil, and he thinks then of what is, and what might have been. He broods over his lost.estate, fallen from his youthful ambition and promise, to be a drudge without hope, and without any prospect, but one, of ceaseless, unrewarded toil; life, and such a life, hath for him no charm. When the morning comes he longs for the night, and when the night falls it brings him a couch of thorns, for it brings visions of blighted hopes, and joys never to be renewed. His only desire now is for rest; the world has used him so roughly, that he cares not to push against it again. You shall tell him of the heroic struggles of others under greater difficulties, and he will tell you how for years he toiled, how he worked hard and long, thinking that his labor would be rewarded, and how, that when he thought to grasp the bright gold, it vanished ; how that not discouraged, he applied himself with renewed energy to a new enterprise, and that too left him poorer than ever, until continued and unvarying disappointment had finally crushed out, and killed out all hope, and the single desire of rest was all that remained. To keep the body from want was the only remaining ambition, for it seemed that Nature had set to defeat him in all that he aspired to beyond that. Enthusiasm had died out, and when that is gone, man becomes a mere cumberer of the ground.

Enthusiasm! There is magic in the word. It is the great moving cause of all that is great and noble in human actions. It is enthusiasm that leads men to great and heroic deeds ;—it is that which impels to great efforts and great sacrifices. It is that which has made a Bacon, as it has made a Linnæus. Enthusiasm! O, it is the gift of God, and let him who hath it, beware that it be not dissipated ; for once gone, life is not worth its keeping. Let him beware lest he enter upon a road, where, if he fails, there will be no return. Let him cherish it as the apple of his eye, and never make a life-throw. Let him not take a step that may result in defeat, when defeat shall have no chance for redemption. Lose not enthusiasm ; for then the power to make the first effort towards redeeming a false step will be gone. When the spirit to make an effort is lost, man becomes a mere piece of drift-wood, to float down life's stream to oblivion's ocean. You shall see the man whose enthusiasm has left him, and wonder that he makes no bolder efforts. But he has no courage for an effort. You shall see him rarely gifted with talent, and shall listen to his discourse with delight, and you shall wonder that all his attainments and abilities avail him so little. But adversity has killed out his enthusiasm, and though he be honest and sincere as ever, and earnest, within a certain range wherein his own interest is not concerned, yet it is plain he acts from instinct rather than zeal, from duty rather than enthusiasm. If he shuns any action that might bring reproach, he yet will not care for fame. He would not even put forth his hand to grasp it, even though it were within his reach. Continued adversity had choked out the enthusiasm of his nature, and if he looks backwards on the past, he sees a dark road, varied only by the different disappointments that have checkered life's thorny path. And why should he look to the future for a change ? If it is darkness behind, it is gross darkness before, and why should he look forward with enthusiasm? Human nature does not admit of such indifference to the teachings of experience ; and when it has been so unvaried in its bitterness, is it strange, that the worn and heart-broken pilgrim sighs but for rest, till he is swept into eternity?

Cherish, then, enthusiasm; it is Heaven's impulse. And beware lest you see it dissipated from your nature ; for when that is gone you may well relinquish all else.

It is not the want of pecuniary success alone that kills our enthusiasm. Indeed success, in its true sense, depends in a small degree on pecuniary gain. A man may be ever so poor, and yet his life may be a splendid triumph. If he has had the opportunity of acting out himself, and of bringing forth his latent talent, it matters little what stock of worldly goods he may have acquired. The history of the classic writers of all ages, is but a record of struggles with the world for a subsistence. The exceptions to it are so few as to prove the rule. The unsuccessful man is he who cannot bring forth his mental lucubrations ; who is surrounded by circumstances that preclude him from ever proving to the world his genius and powers. If we will but read the lives of literary men, we shall see that, as a general, or at least, a frequent thing, it is chance that brought them before the world. Dickens was a mere reporter, and chance made him a reporter ; chance led him to take sketches that were so well received as to cause further attempts, which resulted in his becoming a famous novelist. Miss Bronte tells with what difficulty Jane Eyre was brought before the public, and had a slight mischance hindered or prevented its publication, we had never heard of Currer Bell. For aught we know, hundreds of volumes of equal power have been mouse-nibbled and destroyed in manuscript. Bulwer Lytton failed in all his earliest efforts, and had he not been a nobleman who could afford to publish his own works, and lose the outlay, and try again and again, he had probably never been heard of, but as a bad husband and licentious citizen. Shakespeare ran away, and chanced to be a hanger-on about the London theaters ; and to that circumstance may be attributed his dramatic productions. The fortunate circumstance, by which Goldsmith was thrown in the way of Dr. Johnson, is familiar to all, and it would be easy to find in the history of most literary men some trifling circumstance that changed the whole course of their lives. The same is true of everybody. May we not any of us call up some circumstance, by which our steps chanced to be directed, and which led us into a new way of thinking, living or acting? Perchance we debated long whether or no we should come to California, until some trivial occurrence, some unforeseen event, finally decided us. And on arriving here all were alike ; all, chance adventurers ; and our residence in San Francisco, or in the mines, was dependent on meeting an acquaintance, on arriving upon a certain day, on our ability to leave, or some circumstance esteemed of slight importance at the time, which changed the whole course of our lives. We are apt to attribute the success of men to their judgment, energy and perseverance, and to ascribe failure to the lack of these qualities. And yet every man, in looking over his past life, will admit that he himself has failed as often when he exercised the utmost caution and best judgment, as when he rushed into an operation with little reflection. I say it is chance that makes men rich or poor, though there be men whom no chance can keep rich, and no chance can keep poor. It is chance that has brought out great novelists and poets; yet there have been novelists and poets that no chance could repress. But if Burns could follow at the plow's tail through the day, and write his beautiful poetry by night, by the light of a fire of fagots, it is none the less true, that genius of another order can only flourish under a more genial sky. If the violet blooms in the cold winds of March, amid the sterile rocks, yet the warmth of summer must bring forth the moss-rose and the meadow-lily.

In estimating success, we are too prone to attach undue importance to wealth. A man shall be entirely successful, and yet never be worth a dollar in the world. It is not those who have accumulated the most money that are most envied, or to be envied. Girard, McDonough and Astor were examples of men successful in the race for wealth. But who envies them their fame? The best thing they ever did for the world was to die, and leave their property to be quarreled over, and divided up among ravenous lawyers and hungry heirs. And Daniel Webster was always poor, and probably never saw the day that he could pay his debts. And who does not envy him? Who would not be remembered as the most eloquent and sublime of American orators? We judge wrongly when we estimate success by the accumulation of worldly goods.

And what is this thing, success? and who is successful? We shall be told by the majority of people that Astor was eminently successful. So he was; he was successful in the only way that he cared for success. He shrewdly and cunningly managed his business affairs, lived niggardly, and died niggardly. Though he was beloved of none, except for his money, he was envied for his success. He left no monuments of good deeds, and the only monuments he left were those of miserly accumulation. Brinsley Sheridan is often mentioned as an example of brilliant genius, that gave no success to its possessor. It is true, that Sheridan lived in dodging creditors, and died in abject poverty. But could he be accounted unsuccessful, of whom Byron said he wrote the best opera, the best comedy, the best farce, the best monody, and made the best speech of any man who ever lived. If to die in a garret of starvation is ill-success, after such praise, from such authority, then our aspiration is that ill-success may follow us to the grave.

What is the verdict of the world on the career of the eccentric, melancholic and versatile Tom Hood? He died, poor as he had lived. When he was in his grave men said of him he was a true man—he loved his race; a rare wit and a genius, he deserved a better fate. "Poor Tom's a-cold," succeeded closely to his last joke, and he was accounted unsuccessful though his sad lyrics had touched the heart of the nation, and the great object of his life, the exposition of the wrongs of the working classes, was accomplished. "Poor Tom's a-cold;" yet the "Bridge of Sighs" and the "Song of the Shirt" shall cause the hot tear to flow, long after the lips of those who had been wont to utter thanks to him for his timely vindication, are cold and silent as his own.

It really matters very little, whether or no, a man accumulates wealth, if so be that he can act himself. The class of men of which I write are not mere hucksters, nor are they ambitious to get rich for any happiness that riches can bestow; but they regard it as a means to an end, and think, if relieved from the necessity of perpetual toil, they might develop whatever of genius or of talent they possessed. And when they see their youth wasting away, and feel themselves becoming callous, and know, that under no circumstances can it be different, and that they must repress all their higher aspirations, for that they can but lead to renewed disappointment, is it strange they think their lot a hard one? Is it strange they sigh for rest? It is not in their nature to be content, unless they have a prominence before the world. They were brought up under free institutions, and made to believe that it was a part of their mission to make themselves a name and a fame. It is impossible for them to settle down in any out-of-the-way path, even though surrounded by every comfort. They must mix in the busy throng, and be felt as men of power. Failing in this, they feel that they have made a failure; and when to this is added the trial of long physical endurance, they, at last, wilt under it, and their very ambition inverted inwardly, becomes a consuming fire; they cared not for wealth for its own sake, but they did care for it as a means to escape neglect. They could have toiled in the road to eminence, nor cared how difficult the way, how remote the goal. But this road has been closed to them, and now they care not whither fate may lead them.

It really matters very little how a man is housed or fed, the most greedy for wealth are willing to undergo almost any privation of the kind for the sake of increasing their stores. In these days a very light income will secure all the actual comforts of life, and many a man in our day, on a small salary, eats better and lodges better than did King Edward the First, if not better than Queen Elizabeth. Men desire wealth more for display than comfort; and, for that reason they are never satisfied. If they would separate comfort from ostentation, and the ephemeral applause of to-day from the lasting approbation of posterity, it is very likely they would put a different meaning on the word success from that which they now do. I say that a man is successful, if he is educated, in a position to enjoy the world around him, and to leave "foot-prins on the sands of time:"—

> "Foot-prints, that, perhaps, another
>   Sailing o'er life's solemn main,
> A forlorn and shipwrecked brother,
>   Seeing, shall take heart again."

Men do not consider that it is as important to learn how to enjoy wealth, as it is to get it. A rustic may know of no higher enjoyment than to eat, drink and carouse; of what use are all of the refinements and delicacies of life to him? He can see nothing beautiful in Nature or art; he can appreciate neither the elegant nor the sublime.

You shall see a man worth tens and hundreds of thousands, who never knew the difference between a crayon sketch and a lithograph; who can not tell the difference between a saltatory jingle and a psalm tune, and who thinks a grotesque combination of flashy hues the most beautiful of all possible arrangements of colors.

And this man shall be called successful, though he be too ignorant to enjoy wealth; yet if he possess it, there be many, who will say he has lived to a good purpose. His whole enjoyment consists in the miserly love of accumulation, and he has no taste superior to it; and still he is worshipped, honored and envied as a successful man by the masses, and too often by those who ought to despise such vulgar approbation.

This man, so envied, can never get beyond the most mercenary and common-place thoughts. If he has the bow of Ulysses, he lacks the strength to use it. He has no delight in beautifying his grounds, in stocking his library with books and his head with knowledge, nor yet can he enjoy active benevolence. He is like the man who hath lumbered up his house with useless wares; they are an incumbrance and annoyance; they bring him no pleasure, and entail ceaseless care and vexation. And yet men will envy him their possession.

But another man shall have the highest cultivation, the keenest sense of what is beautiful and grand in Nature, in literature and in the arts, and yet men shall pity him, and call him poor and unfortunate, because, forsooth, his income is small, and his wants pressing. Yet this man shall walk out into the fields, and shall see more to enjoy in one hour, than the rich man ever saw in his life; he shall sit down to the study of the "grand old masters," and derive more pleasure therefrom, than the other can get from counting over all his wealth. His mind is cultivated for enjoyment, and he has it, whether he be rich or poor.

True wealth is of un esoteric nature; it is in the man, and not the outward objects. The riches of Crœsus cannot enrich a mind not garnished with thought and culture. The world is full of wealth for him who can enjoy it; Nature hath spread her bounties for all; the morning sun breaks as beautiful and bright to the plowboy, as to the lord of thousands. If it be in the man to see and enjoy what is beautiful, nor monarchs, nor potentates can deprive him of this pleasure; God has given him this and man cannot take it from him.

An uncultivated churl will gaze on Niagara, and feel no inspiration of awe or grandeur; the beauties of nature are to him as a blank leaf, and he may pursue the avocations of life so successfully as to be known through all the country round as the wealthy man of the borough; his pleasures will be entirely gross and carnal, and he will know nothing of the higher kinds of enjoyment; his eye sees not the beautiful, his ear drinks in no melody, his mind appreciates not the sublime, yet, because of his wealth, men honor him. On the other hand, you may pick up a man in the street compelled to work for his daily bread with the most unremitting toil, and he shall descant with raptures on the poetry of Scott, Byron or Milton, and show you that, though his lot be hard, he hath a fountain of enjoyment within himself. You shall find one taken from the very *lazzaroni* of Italy, who never knew in the morning where he was to sleep at night, and if you show him a picture of suffering drawn by Raphael or Michael Angelo, he will gaze and gaze upon it, and each moment see new life and expression, till he comprehends the whole tale of sorrow that was in the artist's mind when he painted it. The tears shall trickle down his face profusely, for the conscious picture speaks to him of sorrow and pain. Let him turn to another picture of virgin beauty, and at once his eyes will dilate, and he will gaze with intensest rapture on the creation of genius; and, turning again to the delineations of the grotesque, he will laugh aloud at its whimsicalities. This man can enjoy what the other cannot, and who shall say that Providence hath not recompensed him.

The same is not true, however, of the class whose fortune we were considering. The earnestness of the American character is such that it cannot be satisfied with a sensuous philanthropy or with sensual gratification. The men of whom I speak have all felt that they had a mission, and they cannot, like the Italian or the Spaniard, be satisfied with the gratification of the senses. Though the taste be cultivated, and though they are educated in all the higher walks of literature and art, yet they have always regarded their education as a means to some great and high and honorable object and end; and when they see they are to fail, their sharpened wit and cultivated minds render it but more apparent that life to them is to prove a grand and utter failure. Though happiness be in the man, and not in his outward circumstances, yet when it has become a part of his nature to entertain ambitious thoughts, if he find they are all illusive, they turn inward and work to the utter wreck of his character and hopes. That which was good has been changed into a curse;—the best gift of Nature has been perverted from its good office to prove itself the cause of final self-abandonment, and, too often, of degradation.

With this rambling discussion of what constitutes success, we return to the unsuccessful Californian ; and we dare assert, that no country and no place before has ever been the tomb of so many youthful and brilliant hopes. It is painful to reflect upon the number of young and ardent men, who, led away by the glare of sudden wealth, rushed to California with their minds but partially disciplined, their education but half-finished, and with no fixed object in view, and have found themselves but waifs, purposeless and abandoned on the shores of the Pacific seas. It is a small matter to him, who had been brought up to the rough cares of life in youth, to be cast adrift on his own resources. But suppose no such wholesome discipline was vouchsafed at a time when it would have had the effect of discipline rather than disaster ? Then the unhappy outcast finds himself in a world of which he never dreamed, and straight enters on the downhill road to destruction and death.

It is a terrible thing for the young man, when he realizes that all his hope of future distinction and excellence were but castles in the air. To think that the whole course of life, which had been marked out in the exuberance of boyhood, is to be changed ; that, instead of honors, service and dependence are to be the price of existence— instead of wealth, poverty so severe that daily drudgery alone can save from absolute want—that, instead of being waited upon by men for opinions and ideas, deference is required to those who are known to be inferior, and it is no wonder that the light of hope dies out and misanthropy and indifference close out a life that has yielded only the bitter fruits of a disappointed ambition.

It is a fate that cannot be escaped. To what shall the young man turn, I care not how brilliant his intellect, if he has learned no trade and no profession? He has, perhaps, tried his hand in the mines, and finds that only by incessant labor can he maintain a precarious existence. He may be a poet; it will not give him bread. His logic may be faultless and his powers of analysis of the highest order; yet what can he do here? He never learned even to be a clerk or book-keeper. His talents or his acquirements can be put to no account that shall give him bread; and here a man cannot long be idle. He must labor, if poor, or else become a dependent on the charity of others—a street idler, despised by himself and respected by no man else.

It is a hard thing for a young man to relinquish the hopes of child-hood and youth, when the mind is vigorous and the body strong. To feel that the world is but a cruel prison-house, from which the spirit is ever crying to be delivered; to see that a great mistake has been made, and that life must be a humiliating failure. It is a dreadful thing, and alas! how many there be in this condition throughout this California, so often designated as the land of bright hopes and golden promises!

Advice is a cheap commodity, and there be few who are not more willing to give than to take it. How many, on reading of such forlorn interests, will spring up with indignation and say that what I write is all unmanly and weak! and how they will launch out with instructions on what such people are to do! "Go to work," say they; "be not discouraged; persevere, and in time you will come out right." Alas! it is easy to say "Go to work," and it is easy to work, provided there be anything to hope for in the future. But suppose that, after years of toil and rigid economy, the prospect of a respite is as remote as ever? Will not the heart get sick, when hope is so long deferred? It is easy to say "Persevere." But for what? For a mere existence, when it is obtained only by unyielding toil? He cares not for existence at such a price. He thought that fortune would use him more kindly, and so he indulged in dreams of fancy that have unfitted him for the life with which he has to cope. What right has he to volunteer advice who never yet was in need of it? Can he appreciate the feelings and the throes of one who looks forth upon the world only as a vast prison-house, from which there is no escape but through the portals of the tomb? The lives of men who have successfully struggled with fortune are often instances for the encouragement of others. But we find in most cases that a mere accident, the slightest chance, has brought them out successful before the public. How many of equal talent and equal perseverance have been crushed, because no such happy chance offered, is unknown. The world is said, by some, to know nothing of its greatest men. How many of the most brilliant intellects have been forever obscured by the clouds of adverse fortune, no man can tell, but they are many. It is within the experience of every one to have met with a variety of persons possessed of talent, wit and education that seem to be out of place in the world. They seem to have rare powers of mind, but they never could usefully apply them. The reason was they had made a mistake, like so many now in California, and had never learned to bring their powers into use and subjection. They jumped the future without preparing for it, and so they found, too late, that their life was to prove a failure, and that after worrying through a dissatisfied existence, they would at last sink unhonored—and they care not how soon—to the tomb. Poverty is not the misfortune that has broken them down. It has been because they could not act out their own character. It has been because they have been placed in a position that forbade their mental development, and they have seen whatever of talent and genius was in them choked up and killed. They feel themselves becoming callous, soured and misanthropic ; and so they see with never a regret the world and the life allotted them receding and vanishing away, and, like the prisoner of the Bastile, they would not stay the course of time for a day, but rather long for the only deliverance that awaits them. They now only wish for rest, and they see no haven of rest this side the grave; and all conscious and deliberate they pursue the path to speedy and unhonored death—they go deliberately and desperately to destruction. Who shall blame, or who shall censure one thus imprisoned in a living tomb ? Is not his lot hard enough without the cruel condemnation of one whose path has been all sunshine? Condemn not thy brother. " I will repay, saith the Lord."

It is a hard world we live in. If not to us it is to those whose case we have been considering ; and in the preceding remarks, desultory and unconnected as they may seem, it is believed and hoped that one lesson is inculcated, and that is a lesson of charity. We know not the trials through which many have passed who have succumbed before the battle of life was finished. If we have never yielded like them, it may not be because of any merit of our own, but rather because fortune hath dealt with us more kindly ; and it is for us to be thankful that our lot was cast in more pleasant places, and not to pass judgment on those whom the frown of Providence hath cursed, and to whom the whole world has already become but a picture of unvarying desolation.

MUSICIANS GOING TO CALIFORNIA.

BY L. H. SIGOURNEY.

BIRDS,—of a far-off region,
  A tuneful troop are we,
Mov'd to this bold migration
  From nest, and cliff, and tree,
Across two mighty oceans
  On wing of hope we fly,
And o'er the weary Isthmus bear
  The soul of melody.

We bring you many a message
  From tender hearts and true,
From cottage by the greenwood
  Where your happy childhood grew,

From sharers of your pleasures,
  From partners of your cares,
And from the kind old parents
  Who name you in their prayers.

We'll sing you stirring measures
  Of the glorious sires of old,
Who prompt with seeds of heaven
  To sow the land of gold;
And when we've sung our sweetest songs,
  Quick o'er the rolling main,
We'll fly with pleasant memories back
  To our blessed homes again.

THE SEASONS IN CALIFORNIA.

BY A. H. B.

It is now Winter, or, more properly speaking, the "wet season;" yet what a number of delightful days enliven the dark ones. It is strange that there should exist a prejudice against California climate, when it is really so genial; or that such erroneous opinions should be entertained of it by people in the older States, in spite of all that has been said and written.

It is generally believed, that our year consists of but two seasons, long and monotonous, "the one a perfect drought,—the other, a constant drench," with nothing either to vary or relieve their sameness. But what a mistaken idea! In what other country do we find a more delicious atmosphere and a milder temperature, at this season? Not even in sunny France or far-famed Italy.

The winter rains here do not bring the same chill, uncomfortable feeling that is experienced in the East, and to any person, not biased by old custom, the longest rainy season would be preferable to one of the cold and stormy winters of New England. Yet it seems in vain to plead the beauty of our clear Winter's day—the bland, yes balmy air, the soft haze overspreading the distance, and the complete calm that rests on everything,—there being no winds at this season,—for so completely are we the creatures of habit, that many, while they own these Winters are mild and genial, still cannot help having a lingering preference for the stern and icy ones of their old homes. "Oh!" say they, "the contrast of the Spring more than makes up for the severity of the Winter; at least, to our minds, trained from infancy to the wildest and most fitful moods of Nature." There seems a magic in them that moves the heart and inspires the soul. Indeed, I shall never forget the feelings, the rapturous excitement, with which I was accustomed to behold Spring, bursting from the chains of Winter,—with which I felt the sunbeams growing stronger day by day,—saw the icicles disappearing from the brook sides,—watched the willows putting forth their velvet catkins, and the fruit trees their coronals of blossoms, the lilies pointing their green spiral tops through the moistened earth, while the snow yet lingered by the garden wall,—marked the springing grass and the opening flowers, one variety appearing after another in quick succession,—and last of all, the crowning glory, the forest leaves, at first most fragile and transparent, but soon attaining strength, size and durability. Oh! I have stood amid a wilderness of such delights, and seen these jewels of beauty showered upon the earth. It is not strange that, having once rejoiced in these exciting scenes, we should in memory turn again to them with a kind of longing; and yet, what is there in all these which we lack, except the strong contrast of the Winter, which long habit and an acquired taste has taught us first to endure, and then to love? But what would a native-born Californian, a descendant of present Atlantic immigrants, say of the climate of his

Fathers', should he visit it in after years, when he had been brought up in, and become attached to, his own gentle clime? Would he perceive the beauty of a stormy Winter, or derive the pleasure from it that his Fathers did? Or how could he compare the Summer, with its continued days and nights of heat, rendering rest or sleep nearly impossible, to the cool and invigorating nights of his own fair land? Why, he would turn away with disgust, and wonder how people could live in such a country, and would return to his beautiful home better than ever satisfied, declaring it the finest land the sun rose upon. So much do our tastes depend upon surrounding circumstances, or, as some say, accident. The climate of California has had as yet but few advocates—for the simple reason that there were few to love it. This is not dear to many as the land of their birth or their home; but when the children of the country grow up, when they take their places on the public stage of life, and wield an influence—O, then shall we have effusions in praise of the golden hills, and exquisite climate of California,—*heartfelt, poetic* effusions,—not cold and formal; because, springing from glowing hearts, they will carry power and inspiration with them.

It is sometimes said that, since the great immigration of Americans, the climate has somewhat changed; the dry seasons becoming shorter, and the rains less constant. This has no doubt arisen from the ardent wish of some, that it might be so; as "We only paint as we would have things be." Yet, even could it be, I doubt whether old residents would be at all pleased with the change, as the experienced farmer has proved the summer not too long for the safety of his crops, which he now reaps and stacks in the field without fear of injury till they are thrashed, which is generally done in the open air. However, any material change is next to impossible; so fixed are the laws and influences which form the peculiarities of our seasons, that we may calculate, almost with certainty, not only the commencement and ending of the rains, but also have an instant check to any extreme of heat, since across the snowy Sierras, as along with the ocean currents, there sweeps a body of cold air, ever ready to rush to any point of greatest heat, to restore a healthful balance. There is scarce another country so blessed as ours with natural advantages and resources, and it but remains for our people to draw them out and profit thereby.

In an age like this, there is scarce a doubt that this will be speedily done, and, therefore, it need's no prophet's eye to foresee a glorious future for California. Her railroads, canals and interior improvements, are yet all to be; but she has commenced aright, and is laying a good foundation for future greatness. Her Schools and Churches rise on every hand. Intelligence and general knowledge are widely spread. Her Press is healthful and high-toned, her laws improving, and her legislators, chief officers and people disposed, we hope, to enforce and abide by them.

SCIENTIFIC.

THE COAST SURVEY OF THE UNITED STATES.

BY LIEUT. W. P. TROWBRIDGE, CORPS OF ENGINEERS, U. S. A.

In the year 1807, President Jefferson, in his message to Congress, recommended the establishment of a National Coast Survey, for the purpose of making accurate charts of our extended and dangerous coast. At that time, the only maps of our sea-coast, in existence, were isolated and unconnected charts, made by British navigators while we were Colonies, or by commercial houses of New York and Boston.

These charts were imperfect and often dangerous; and the object of the President was to cause a complete and accurate survey of our whole coast to be made on the most approved scientific principles. Congress, accordingly, passed an Act authorizing the President to organize such a survey, and the Secretary of the Treasury, Mr. Gallatin, immediately issued circulars to the principal scientific men of our country, requesting their opinions, individually, with regard to the best plan for carrying out the provisions of the law. Thirteen answers were received to these circulars, which were submitted to a committee of the American Philosophical Society for examination: the plan submitted by Mr. Hassler, a native of Switzerland, was adopted.

This plan was, essentially, to make a complete Land Survey along the coast and to base the Nautical Survey upon it; the Land Survey was to be made according to the principles of the science of *Geodesy*, the only method by which any extended portion of the earth's surface can be represented with accuracy.

This method involves the *figure of the earth*, and originated with the philosophers of the sixteenth century, in their researches for determining the relative lengths of the earth's axes.

Before giving the principles of Geodetic surveys in detail, a brief account of the progress of scientific investigation on the form of our planet is necessary, in order to show the importance which has always been attached to a correct knowledge of its figure, in the study of Geography and Astronomy.

It is well known that the earth has nearly a spherical shape, being flattened slightly at the poles of the axis, about which it revolves: the polar axis being about twenty-six miles shorter than the equatorial axis. The knowledge of this fact has resulted from a train of investigations, extending from the middle of the sixteenth century to the present time. To determine the lengths of the axes, it is necessary to measure the lengths of extensive acres on its surface, from which, by means of spherical Trigonometry, the lengths of the axes can be found.

The first attempt to measure an arc of meridian was made two hundred and fifty years before Christ, by the philosopher of Alexandria; the principle of the measure has remained unaltered till the present day, but the observations were extremely rude and gave no very definite result. On the overthrow of the Alexandrian school, the progress of science was interrupted and was not again revived until after the lapse of fourteen hundred years. During this long interval, however, the powerful Caliphs of Bagdad caused the works of the Greek astronomers to be translated and studied, but no important additions to scientific knowledge were made. An attempt to measure an arc of meridian, was made on the plains of Mesopotamia in 814, but the result has not been preserved.

The discovery of the true system of the Planetary Motions by Copernicus, in 1543, again aroused an intense interest in regard to Astronomy, and it soon became necessary, for astronomical investigation, to study more thoroughly the shape and dimensions of our own planet. During the half-century following, the telescope was invented and the science of Logarithms was first applied in making the tedious calculations. About this time, also, the science of Mathematics was extended and improved greatly, giving new facilities for theoretical investigations.

Philosophers still supposed the earth to be exactly spherical; and the discovery of its true shape was reserved for the wonderful genius of Newton. The first ideas of gravitation were entertained by Newton in 1666, and the discovery of the difference in the lengths of the earth's axes, was one of the first of the many brilliant results of the theory of Gravitation.

In order to test the correctness of his theory, Newton determined, by mathematical investigation, what the form of the earth should be, supposing it to have been at one time in a semi-fluid state; the particles being acted upon by the force of *gravity* and the centrifugal force due to the revolution. His investigations gave him precisely the figure which the earth is now known to have; he determined, theoretically, the relative lengths of the axes, and his results have since been found to agree remarkably with the results of measurement.

It is remarkable, that Newton was induced to give up his theory of Gravitation for a time, on account of the following circumstances, viz: Observations on the moon, gave also the means of testing his theory, by furnishing data for determining the *mean* diameter of the earth; the only actual measure to which he could refer, was that of a Parisian, named Fernel, who had made a rude measurement of an arc of meridian, near Paris, about one hundred and forty years before. This measure did not confirm his theory and he was led to doubt its correctness. A more accurate measure, by the French Academicians, three years afterwards, reassured him.

The measure of Fernel was nearly as rude as those of the Greek Philosophers, and the Caliphs: he measured a line on the earth's surface, sixty miles in length, by merely noting the number of turns of his carriage wheel, in passing over the line; his astronomical observations were also unworthy of credit.

The measurement near Paris, by the Academy of Sciences, three years after

Newton's discovery, was more accurate than any of the preceding measurements; the great principle of *Triangulation* was here first used to determine the distances between points on the earth's surface, and the work formed the basis of the first Geodetic survey ever made. It was the foundation, at this early date, of the very accurate map of France which has since been completed.

The test of Newton's determination of the earth's figure had not yet been applied. Shortly after he published his "Principia," the French Academy ordered another arc of meridian to be measured in France, founded upon the former basis; the object was twofold: to establish a basis for a complete map of France, and to determine the figure of the earth. To the great astonishment of the philosophers of the day, it appeared from the results, that the degrees of meridian shortened in going northward, which would make the polar axis the longest.

A conclusion so directly in opposition to Newton's Theory, now extensively received, excited a great sensation among the mathematicians of Europe: to settle the doubt, a degree of parallel was measured near Strasbourg, but the result seemed to lead to the same conclusion. To escape from this state of uncertainty, it was determined, that an arc should be measured near the Equator, and another in a high latitude, so as to separate them by as many degrees of latitude as possible: this was the origin of the famous French expeditions under Louis XV.

One was sent to Peru, where an arc was measured in the great valley between the two principal chains of the Andes; another was sent to the Gulf of Bothnia, and a third remeasured the French arc. These expeditions were equipped in a magnificent style, and were provided for several years' service: the expedition to Peru returned after an absence of three years, having endured many privations and hardships. The French arc had been remeasured, and the cause of the original difficulty was found to be an error in the measurement of the former *base-line*, upon which the triangulation was founded.

It is an interesting fact, that the Peruvian arc, measured in 1776, afterwards furnished, by comparison with an arc measured by order of the National Convention in 1791, the data for establishing the standard of weights and measures of France.

The French *mêtre*, equal in length to one-ten-millionth of a quadrant of the earth, has been adopted as a standard of measure in our Coast Survey.

It is unnecessary to give an account of the numerous other measurements, which have been made in Europe; although a great many have been completed, they are still insufficient to determine definitely the relative lengths of the earth's axes. One of the incidental results of the beautiful triangulation of our eastern coast, will be the measurement of several arcs, more accurately, perhaps, than any that have yet been made. The triangulations for measuring the European arcs are generally the foundations, also, of extensive maps.

The form of the earth has thus been dwelt upon, not only because its investigation has brought to great perfection the natural sciences necessary in a great work like our Coast Survey, but also because its different dimensions enter into the most important forms of mathematical computation; and a knowledge of these dimensions is therefore essential to a proper application of Astronomy and Geodesy to the work of making maps of our coast.

PRINCIPLES OF GEODETIC SURVEYS.

In making a survey of an extended coast, by the Geodetic method, the whole extent of the coast to be surveyed is covered with a network of triangles, formed by imaginary lines connecting certain selected points. The vertices of the triangles may be prominent points of the coast, the summits of the inland mountains, or temporary signals on the plains; and the lengths of the main lines may be ten, twenty, or even eighty miles, depending upon the nature of the country: generally a medium length of thirty or forty miles is preferred, and the triangles are made as nearly equilateral as possible.

As it is impossible to measure all the lines mechanically, their lengths are determined by trigonometrical calculation: for this purpose, it is necessary to measure one line only of the system, and the angles of the triangles; then starting from the measured line as a base, the lengths of all the others can be determined.

For convenience the line which is to be measured mechanically, is chosen on a level site, and is seldom over eight miles in length.

The determination of the lengths of the lines merely gives the *relative* positions of the prominent points; but does not give these points a definite place on the earth's surface. To accomplish this latter object, recourse is had to astronomical observations, by means of which the true *latitude* and *longitude* of the different points are found.

It is sufficient, in theory, to determine the latitude and longitude of the extremities of the *base line*, and the direction which this line has with reference to the meridian passing through one of its extremities; and to calculate, trigonometrically, the latitudes and longitudes of all the other points: but in practice, it is found necessary, in order to guard against errors, to verify the calculated determinations, at frequent intervals, by actual observations; and also to measure, at longer intervals, some of the lines of triangulation, as a verification of their computed lengths.

Such a system of triangles is called the *Primary Triangulation.* It forms a sort of skeleton of the coast, which may be filled up without the possibility of making serious errors in the positions of the intermediate points.

A *Secondary Triangulation* is then formed, by dividing each of the large triangles into several smaller ones, and, if necessary, a *Tertiary* system may be included within the secondary.

In the surveys of coasts, the primary triangulation generally extends many miles inland, advantage being taken of the highest accessible mountains, from which extended views can be taken. The secondary triangulation occupies a narrower belt along the coast; while the tertiary is confined closely to the shores, so as to furnish the basis of the Topography and Hydrography. The triangulation of our eastern coast now extends nearly unbroken from Maine to North Carolina, and it will soon meet the triangulation of the Gulf of Mexico, so as to form a continuous system along our whole eastern coast. The main triangulation of the Pacific coast now extends from a point above Benicia to a point below Monterey, while detached portions have also been executed in the vicinity of San Diego, San Pedro, and the mouth of the Columbia River.

The execution of the triangulation is, perhaps, the most difficult part of Geodetic surveying, and requires much scientific and practical skill on the part of an observer.   The first operation in order is the

RECONNOISSANCE.

The officer in charge of the triangulation first travels over the country in different directions, for the purpose of selecting such points for the scheme of triangles, as will fulfill, in the best manner, the required conditions.

A base line is selected on some level site six or eight miles in extent, the position of the line being so chosen, that it will be easy to form one or more triangles upon this line as a basis, the other sides intersecting on prominent points far enough distant to expand the triangulation, as successive triangles are formed. Rough observations are made, with the compass, to determine the approximate positions of the points, and a plot of the country, showing their relative positions, is drawn, for future reference.   The reconnoissance requires much judgment, as a great deal of the expense and accuracy of the work depend upon a judicious selection of the triangles.

After finishing the reconnoissance, the officer proceeds to the measurement of the

BASE LINE.

The extremities of the base are first marked by means of stone blocks, buried in the earth deep enough to prevent their being disturbed by anything that passes upon the surface: in the top of each block a metallic bolt is placed, upon which an extremely fine point is made; which is regarded as the true extremity of the base.   It is usual to erect a monument over each extremity, after the measurement is completed, to mark the locality.   The base is then graded where it may be necessary, and its length roughly ascertained by a common surveyor's chain.

For the more accurate measurement, various methods have been employed: the great difficulty is to avoid the errors arising from the change of temperature of the measuring-rods during the operation.   A line, six or eight miles in length, would appear shorter, by several yards, if measured in winter, than the same line, if measured in midsummer, if the measurement was made by simple iron rods: for slight changes in temperature, the change in the length of the iron rods would be proportionally less; but the difficulty of observing the changes of temperature, and of correcting the observations, has led to the invention of a compensating apparatus, which retains the same length for all degrees of temperature; the Coast Survey apparatus, for the measurement of Primary Bases, was devised by the present Superintendent, Professor Bache: it is probably the most accurate in the world.   Two measurements of a line, made by Prof. Bache, on the Atlantic coast, showed that the error in the whole line, seven miles in length, could not exceed *half an inch.*

The measurement of a primary base is justly regarded as the most important and difficult operation of the Survey: the triangulation for hundreds of miles may rest upon one measured base, and a slight error would become, if propagated through the whole system, wholly inadmissible in works of this character.

A single measurement often requires several weeks for its completion.

MENSURATION OF ANGLES.

After the measurement of the base, the next operation is the measurement of the angles of the triangles.   When the angular points, or *stations,* are selected, they are marked in a manner similar to that described for the base; and over each point a straight pole is erected, to serve as a mark, to which the telescope of the distant observer is directed. The angles at the extremities of the base are first measured, and then those of the adjacent triangles in regular order. The measurement is made with a Theodolite placed accurately over the station point: in the primary work, large Theodolites, one or two feet in diameter, are used; these often require to be kept three or four weeks in the same position, and are placed upon stone or iron supports. The angles of the secondary and tertiary triangulations are measured with smaller Theodolites of a more portable character.

For long lines the Theodolites are furnished with powerful telescopes, by means of which distant signal poles can be seen, when they would not be visible to the naked eye; even with the help of the telescope, it often happens that the weather is too smoky to permit the poles to be distinctly seen, and for long lines, such as are found on the coast of New England, a very beautiful instrument is used to mark the distant points. An observer is stationed upon the point to which the telescope is to be directed, with a little instrument called a *Heliotrope;* it is simply a small round mirror, mounted upon the barrel of a common spyglass, in such a manner that it may be turned in any direction by the hand. The spy-glass is furnished with a stand, and is placed accurately over the station-point; the Heliotroper then directs his glass to the station at which the Theodolite is placed, and, by turning the mirror, causes the rays of the sun to be reflected directly into the distant telescope; thus showing a small beam of light which may be seen at great distances. On the coast of New England this plan is always followed, and it is not unusual to see the rays from the Heliotrope, appearing like a distant star, at the distance of eighty miles, when the outlines of the hills are invisible.

To secure accuracy in the results, each angle is measured thirty or forty times and a mean of the measures taken.

A few hours just after sunrise, or before sunset, are the only portions of the day that can be employed in measuring angles; the heat, in the middle of the day, causing so much apparent irregular motion in the signals, as to prevent accurate observations.

From four to six weeks are often required to measure the angles of one primary station.

ASTRONOMICAL OBSERVATIONS.

The true position of a point on the earth's surface is determined, when its latitude and longitude are known; and the determination of these elements forms the principal object of the Astronomical Observations of the Coast Survey. The rough observations of mariners for the same purpose, depend upon the same principle as those of the Coast Survey; but while the mariner is often contented in getting his position within a few miles, in the latter case it is necessary to determine a point within a few feet.

The determination of latitudes is generally more simple and accurate than the determination of longitudes: the former may be obtained by measuring the zenith distances of some of the fixed stars, and are effected only by the errors of observation and the errors of the astronomical tables, from which the positions of the stars are taken. The determination of longitudes, however, involves the motions of the heavenly bodies and can only be accomplished by means of time keepers.

The difference of longitude between two places is, simply, the difference between the times indicated by ordinary time-keepers at those places, at the same absolute instant: thus, the difference of longitude between New York and San Francisco, is *three hours and thirteen minutes*, and a time-piece, brought from New York to San Francisco, should be three hours and thirteen minutes in advance of San Francisco time. To obtain the difference of longitude is therefore, simply, to determine this difference of time.

The first ideas of the difference of longitude and of the rotundity of the earth, arose from the observation of eclipses: As these phenomena are visible over large portions of the earth at the same time, different observers may see the eclipse at nearly the same absolute instant, but at different times by their clocks. The observation of these phenomena is the best means of obtaining the longitude, but as they are not of frequent occurrence, other methods are commonly used. The principal ones are the observation of the moon's passage over the meridian, and occultations of stars by the moon: the latter is the best, though it involves laborious computations; it requires an observer to note the instant, by his time-piece, at which a star disappears behind the moon or reappears on the opposite side, as the moon moves along in her orbit.

A spy-glass of high power is the only instrument neccessary for this observation, excepting the instruments for determining the time. The time, at the place of observation must, of course, be precisely known: to determine it, observations are made on some of the fixed stars as they pass the meridian, with an instrument, called the *Transit Instrument*. As the best time-keepers continually change their rate of motion, the transit observations are made during several successive nights, in order to determine this rate from day to day. The Transit, whether in fixed observatories or in the field, is the most delicate of all astronomical instruments and requires long practice and great skill, in its use, in order to obtain correct results.

One second of time at the parallel of 45° corresponds to about one thousand feet, and the various observations for longitude must therefore be reduced to a very small fraction of a second of time, in order to give the position of a point within a few feet: One second of latitude or of arc, corresponds to about one hundred feet at the same parallel; and the range of several hundred observations for latitude, at a single point, is frequently no more than four or five seconds; the latitude, may therefore, be found with much more certainty than the longitude. The magnetic telegraph furnishes a method, formerly unknown, of obtaining the difference of longitude with great accuracy. At some of our principal observatories, long series of observations are made for longitude, and by connecting the observatories with the Coast Survey Stations, by telegraphic wires, the longitudes of the stations may be very accurately determined. The observatory at Cambridge has furnished several years' observations for this purpose.

Another class of astronomical observations consists of those made for finding the directions of lines with reference to the meridian. These observations consist in measuring the angle between the given line and the vertical plane passing through the North star (or one of the close circumpolar stars) and the place of observation, when the star is on the meridian,

The observations are made with large Theodolites.

It has been remarked that it is necessary to determine all these elements at the base line only, as the same elements may then be computed for other lines. This is only true in theory; the errors of observation and incorrect estimates of the earth's figure, about which there is still much uncertainty, make it necessary to multiply the astronomical observations as much as possible; it is now known that the difference in the density and thickness of the earth's crust, at places not very remote from each other, will cause such a deflection in the level of an instrument, as to give sensible discrepancies between the astronomical and trigonometrical determinations of the same point.

Practical Astronomy requires the best instruments that mechanical genius can invent; and an observer should not only understand fully their construction, but should also be familiar with the principles of optics, upon which the telescopes are made. The instruments are usually placed, for observation, upon solid masonry supports, and are protected from the weather, by a temporary covering. The observations at each point occupy several weeks.

TOPOGRAPHY.

The work of triangulation being completed, the next in order is the Topography. This is the representation, on paper, by a peculiar system of drawing, of the features of the country; the drawing bears no resemblance to the face of the country as it usually appears to us; but by means of simple conventional signs, well understood by those who make use of maps, a topographical drawing represents a portion of the earth's surface as it would appear to an observer far above it; the forms of hills are represented by curved lines, such as would be cut from the surface by planes at equal vertical distances from each other. Rivers, forests, marshes and rocks, are represented by lines, drawn so as to suggest these objects.

The topographical drawing is a mere filling up of the triangulation, upon which it is based; the shore lines being the most prominent and important features.

The blank sheets of paper, upon which the drawing is to be made, are placed upon a portable table, called a *Plane Table;* the table is furnished with leveling screws, by means of which it may be placed in a horizontal position.

By directing a ruler towards the same object from two stations, in succession, and drawing lines along the edge of the ruler, the intersections of the lines will mark on the paper the relative positions of the object and the stations at which the table was placed. In this way all prominent objects are placed upon the sheet: the delineation of the surface, representing cultivated ground, marsh, or woodland, is left to the taste and skill of the draftsman.

The Topography is thus a continuation of the system of triangulation, or a minute subdivision of the larger triangles.

The topographical sheets are copied on a reduced scale by skillful draftsmen, in the Coast Survey Office, before they pass into the hand of the engraver.

HYDROGRAPHY.

The Topography of the coast forms the basis of the work of Hydrography. Under this head are embraced all those important researches, which have for their object the determination of facts which directly influence Navigation; such as the form and character of the bottom of the sea, the depth of the water, the ebb and flow of the tides, the positions of rocks, shoals and reefs; and the direction and velocity of currents.

The Hydrographical Department is the source from which the most important results to Navigation directly flow: the determination of sites for light houses, beacons, buoys and so forth, are intrusted to this Department; and, in general, the Hydrographer is required to investigate all circumstances, which may obstruct or facilitate Navigation. The principal part of the work is the operation of sounding, to determine the depth of the water in different places. Along the shore, and in bays, and tidal rivers, numerous lines of soundings are run in every direction, so as to leave no part of the bottom unexamined; at a great distance from land, general lines of soundings are made to determine the general features of the bed of the sea. The positions of the boats, while sounding, are determined by observations from the shore, made by observers stationed at suitable places for that purpose.

PROGRESS AND ORGANIZATION OF THE U. S. COAST SURVEY.

The law of 1807 appropriated $50,000 for the Survey of the Coast, but, on account of the disturbed state of our relations with Great Britain, nothing was done to carry out the provisions of the law, until 1811. Mr. Hassler, whose plan had been adopted, was then sent to Europe for the purpose of obtaining the necessary instruments and standards of measure, for carrying on the work. On the declaration of war, he was detained abroad as an alien enemy, and did not return until 1815. He was formally appointed Superintendent of the Coast Survey in 1816, and immediately commenced his labors in the vicinity of New York Harbor.

Before he could publish the results of his first year's labors, the Coast Survey was effectively discontinued by an Act of Congress, passed in 1818. From this period until 1832, it was exclusively under the administration of the Navy Department; but it was no longer conducted upon the complete system established by Mr. Hassler: local surveys, at different points of the coast, were made, but the cost of the work was found to be enormous, and the charts were pronounced, by the Hon. Samuel L. Southard, Secretary of the Navy, in 1828, to be "unsafe and pernicious;" "though executed as well as the circumstances, under which the officers were placed, would allow."

Mr. Southard was a firm friend of the Navy, and yet he earnestly urged upon Congress the necessity of reestablishing the Survey upon the original plan.

Mr. Hassler was accordingly reappointed to the charge of the work in 1832, and continued in this position to carry it on, until his death, which took place in 1843.

On the recommendation of most of the scientific men of our country, the President appointed Alexander D. Bache, L. L. D., to the office of Superintendent soon after the death of Mr. Hassler.

Professor Bache graduated with the highest honors at the U. S. Military Academy in 1825, and received a commission in the Corps of Engineers of the Army.

After four years' service in the Corps of Engineers he resigned his commission, and was appointed Professor of Natural Philosophy and Chemistry, in the University of Pennsylvania.

This position he occupied about eight years: in 1836 he was appointed President of Girard College, in which capacity he visited Europe. He there had an opportunity of making the acquaintance of the most illustrious men in the European Academies, and received from them the most flattering consideration.

Under his energetic and skillful administration the Coast Survey received new life, and now stands first among our scientific Institutions. The investigations, incident to the work, require frequent application of almost all the practical sciences, and Professor Bache directs the detailed operations of all the departments of the Survey, with equal skill and ability.

In 1848, when a bill was introduced into the U. S. Senate, providing for the transfer of the Coast Survey to the Navy Department, thus depriving it of the services and talents of Professor Bache, the chief commercial and scientific bodies, throughout the country, presented remonstrances against the transfer: the " Insurance Companies" of Boston, the "American Philosophical Society," the "Franklin Institute," the "American Academy of Arts and Sciences," the " Chamber of Commerce" of New York, the "Board of Trade" of Philadelphia, the " Chamber of Commerce" of Charleston, the Citizens of Mobile, and several other societies, united in addressing Congress in favor of the present organization. No better evidence is needed, of the favor in which the work is held by those who can best appreciate its useful results.

The distinguished philosopher Humboldt, on hearing of the proposed change, expressed himself in a letter to Professor Schumacher, of Altona, thus: "You know, better than I do, in how high an estimation the direction of the work for the Survey of the Coast stands, not only among us, but among all the most illustrious men, who, in France and England, are interested in the study of Geography and Nautical Astronomy." "To the most solid knowledge of Astronomy and Mathematics, Mr. Bache unites, in an eminent degree, that activity of mind and extent of views, which render a work of practical utility profitable to the science of the Physics of the Globe;" "I should be glad to think, that in a country where I am honored with so much good feeling, my feeble testimony might contribute to enliven the interest which is due to the excellent labors of Mr. Bache."

Arago, in addressing Professor Schumacher on the same subject, speaks of the possible loss of the services of Professor Bache, as a "misfortune, which he desires to unite with all that Europe has most distinguished in science, to prevent;" and Prof. Schumacher in transmitting these expressions to Prof. Bache says: "You will see by the inclosed letters from our common friends, Mr. Arago, and the Baron de Humboldt, how anxious they are to know if the great work you have undertaken, will remain in the hands to which the whole scientific world have intrusted it."

This testimony to the scientific attainments of Prof. Bache, and the character of the Coast Survey, needs no comment.

In the administration of the work, Professor Bache shows the same prëeminence which distinguishes his scientific researches. In the expenditures, there is greater economy attained, than in any other public work of the country. According to the Reports of the Secretary of the Treasury, the average cost of the Coast Survey, notwithstanding its greater accuracy and detail, is less than the cost of the public land surveys with the magnetic compass. Compared with the Ordnance Survey of Great Britain, which was commenced in 1791, our Survey costs only about one-third as much as the English Survey; while for rapidity of execution, and accuracy of detail, we have no reason to shrink from a comparison.

The organization of the Survey requires the Superintendent to employ civilians, and such officers of the Army and Navy, as may be detailed for this duty; and his kindness and courtesy, in directing their combined operations, produces the utmost harmony; while there are but few who are not inspired with the same zeal which marks his labors.

The present organization of the Coast Survey was established in 1843, on the recommendation of a Board of Army and Navy Officers and Civilians, who were appointed by the President to make a report on the subject.

The Secretary of the Treasury directs the executive details of the work, and its administration is intrusted to a Superintendent, who has chief control over all its operations, subject to the approval or disapproval of the Secretary.

The Superintendent is authorized to employ such Civilians as he may choose, to execute the details of the work; and also the services of eminent scientific men throughout the country, in the discussion of difficult questions of science, or in making special observations of importance. The plan of organization authorizes the President to detail officers of the Army and Navy for service in the Coast Survey; and places the Hydrography exclusively under the charge of Naval officers.

At the beginning of the year 1853, there were fifty-two Naval officers and fourteen Army officers, attached to the Survey.

The force of Civilians engaged in field and office duty, at the same period, consisted of about twenty *Assistants* and twelve *Sub-Assistants;* besides Aids, Clerks, Draftsmen and Engravers.

The land work is executed by Civilians and officers of the Army, each one having special and definite duties. The work of the office, consisting of computations of the work of the field parties, drawing, engraving, printing, and so forth, is superintended by an officer of the Corps of Engineers of the Army, under the direction of the Superintendent.

All work done in the field is recomputed in the office, and subjected to the most scrutinizing examination, before it is given to the public.

The rigid mathematical forms of computation, the regulations with regard to making and transmitting observations, the reductions of maps, drawing, engraving, electrotyping, printing, and so forth, all present interesting features; detailed accounts of which might show the order and regularity with which the whole system of field and office work is conducted.

On the acquisition of California, a special appropriation for the Survey of the Pacific Coast, was made by Congress; and the most accomplished officers of the Survey were sent out to take charge of it: the duty was considered by the Superintendent as one of great responsibility, and he selected officers in whom he could place the greatest confidence. Conducting operations at a distance of six thousand miles from the Department, these officers were often obliged to assume responsibilities which belong to the Superintendent alone; with very limited means, they found the whole country looking for the immediate production of charts of the coast; money flowed in profusion from every source except the National Treasury; and in the excited state of the country, but little assistance or encouragement could be expected from the people.

The able manner in which the Survey was conducted, under these circumstances, has frequently called forth the warmest commendations from the Secretary of the Treasury and the Superintendent.

The Hydrography of the coast was first placed under the charge of the lamented Lieut. W. P. McArthur, U. S. N., who was succeeded by Lieut. Alden. The triangulation and topography were intrusted to R. D. Cutts, Esq., Assistant in the Coast Survey, and the astronomical work to Assistant Geo. Davidson. At present there are seven parties engaged, acting independently of each other, and under the *special directions* of the Superintendent.

A hydrographical reconnoissance of the coast was made by Lieut. McArthur, from the Columbia River to Monterey. Lieut. Alden subsequently extended this reconnoissance to San Diego; and has since reëxamined the whole coast from San Diego to Puget Sound, making a complete reconnoissance chart of the coast, besides numerous local charts of the principal bays and anchorages.

The mouth of the Columbia River and the Bay of San Francisco, have received special attention. A triangulation was made by Mr. Cutts, for the survey of the Columbia, extending thirty-five miles up the river, and resting upon a base near Cape Disappointment. A thorough hydrographical survey of the dangerous *bar* of the Columbia, by Lieut. Alden, was one of his first operations on this coast.

The latitudes and longitudes of about thirty prominent points of the coast have been determined by Mr. Davidson, in connection with the hydrographical reconnoissances.

The primary triangulation of the coast rests upon a base line measured on the Pulgas Rancho: as before stated, it extends Northward to Suisun Bay, and Southward to a point below Monterey.

The Topography is progressing rapidly under the charge of Mr. A. F. Rodgers and Mr. W. M. Johnson.

The peculiarity of the Tides of the Pacific, has, no doubt, been remarked by every one who has had occasion to observe them. This peculiarity is the great inequality in the *hights* of successive tides and in the *intervals* of their occurrence. It may be gratifying to know that this subject has not escaped the attention of Prof. Bache. In April, 1853, an officer was sent to this coast charged with the special duty of making systematic observations on the Tides. The observations are made by *self-registering* machines, which trace a continuous curve upon paper, corresponding to the rise and fall of the water.

Observations have been made at intervals of about eighty miles, between San Diego and the Columbia River, with these self-registering instruments, and the results are now undergoing investigation, by Prof. Bache. The irregularity of the Pacific Tides (called by sailors "Tide, and Half-Tide,") is caused by the varying positions of the sun and moon: it is observable in almost all ocean-tides, but nowhere to such an extent as in the Pacific.

The investigations of Prof. Bache will not only furnish data for constructing tide-tables for this coast, but will also throw new light on the mathematical theories of the Tides.

The subject of Magnetism also receives its share of attention in the Coast Survey. A magnetic needle, if suspended so as to move freely in all directions, will rest in a horizontal position at the Equator, and in a vertical position, nearly, at the Poles. At the latitude of San Francisco its inclination is over sixty degrees. In common magnetic compasses, this tendency to incline is overcome by a mechanical contrivance for its suspension.

The direction of the needle, it is well known, varies continually as we pass from East to West. There is no variation from the true meridian at certain places on the Eastern Coast, while on the Pacific, the needle falls about fifteen degrees to the East of North. For the study of this mysterious force of Nature, observations are made at numerous points along the coast, with instruments constructed for that purpose; the observations required at each place are, to determine the *inclination*, the *intensity* or *strength* and the *variation*, of the magnetic force.

Systematic observations upon the weather are also made at all the Coast Survey Stations.

In making appropriations for this important work, Congress has heretofore dealt with a sparing hand.

In order to carry on the Survey at all points of our coast at the same time, it is divided into eleven Sections, the first commencing in Maine, and the last ending at the Northern Boundary of our Pacific Possessions: each of these sections requires its Triangulation, Hydrographical and Topographical parties; and yet the annual appropriation for the Coast Survey, is less than the cost of a first-class steamship.

The question may be asked, when will the Survey be completed? The time of its completion will depend, in a great measure, upon the favor which it meets at the hands of our enlightened Representatives in Congress.

SAN FRANCISCO, CALIFORNIA, Jan. 5, 1855.

MONTHLY SUMMARY OF EVENTS.

—

"With news the time's in labor and brings forth
Each minute some."

—

December 3. The Baptist Church, situated on Bush street, above Dupont was dedicated. Rev. Mr. Rollinson preached the dedication sermon. Rev. Messrs. Brierly, Briggs, Willis, Pieson and Bannister officiated in the proceedings.

December 4. Burgoyne & Co. moved to their new Banking House on the corner of Battery and Washington streets. . . . Charles P. Duane was re-elected Chief Engineer by the Firemen by 189 majority. . . . The third meeting of the indignant citizens of the First Ward was held, and a committee was appointed to obtain signatures to a protest against Alderman Hyde retaining his office. . . . The new American Theater was opened; an Address written by Mr. Frank Soulé, to commemorate the event, was read by Mr. Neafie, the manager. The plays were the Rivals and the Two Bonnycastles. A large audience were in attendance. . . . The Grand Jury for the November term made their report. It called attention to the Chinese Brothels and Gambling Houses as a nuisance not to be tolerated; praised the condition of the County Jail, and recommended that Prisoners for long terms be made to work upon the streets. Applauded the practice, results and condition of the Common Schools; deemed the County Building Fund Scrip illegally issued and thought it should not be paid. Decided that the basement, and several other rooms of the City Hall were entirely unfit for the purposes for which they are used. Directed attention to the effect the filling in of water lots was leaving upon the business between the wharves and the harbor. Praised the cleanliness and good order of the State Marine Hospital, but suggested that a better location should be found for it. Considered the condition of the County Roads, and the manner in which the contracts for constructing them had been fulfilled. Paid a high compliment to the Orphan Asylum, and returns thanks for kind and gentlemanly treatment received from the Court, District Attorney Byrne and Officer Ryan.

December 5.   A large sale of Real Estate was made by the Sheriff, under a judgment obtained in the suit of C. K. Garrison *vs.* Elias L. Baird, Charles Hopkins and others.   The property consisted of two blocks, one bounded south by Washington, west by Davis, north by Oregon, and east by Drumm; the other south by Washington, west by Drumm, north by Oregon, and east by East street. The total amount of sales was $209,000, that of the judgment being $199,000. The report of the City Treasurer for the year ending November 30, 1854, showed the total amount of receipts to have been $199,241 27, and the disbursements $179,678 94.

December 7.   The Nic. S. S. Cortez arrived in eleven days from San Juan, bringing 245 passengers, and among other important news an account of the expulsion from France, and insulting treatment of Mr. Soulé our Minister to Spain.

December 8.   Judge Ogier, of the U. S. District Court, confirmed the claim to the "Pulgas Rancho," with the exception of that portion known as the "Cañada de Raymundo;" that is, from the Bay up San Mateo Creek, one league westward, to the summit of the hills on the east side of Cañada Raymundo; and from the San Mateo Creek parallel with the Bay to San Francisquito Creek and the Peralta grant, upon the grant from Sola to the *Cerito*. . . . Robert Bruce was hung at Sonora for murder.

December 9.   In the U. S. District Court, Judge Ogier granted an injunction restraining Palmer, Cook & Co., from collecting the rents and profits in the Central Government Reserve, bounded by Pacific, Jackson and Sansome streets and deep water.   During the pendency of the suit brought to foreclose the leases granted by Capt. Keyes to Steinberger and Shillaber, and assigned to Palmer Cook & Co., on the ground of non-payment of rent, Mr. C. J. Brenham was appointed receiver. . . . About sixty Mexicans and Negroes were arrested while holding a masquerade ball in a dance house on Kearny street. . . . The steamship Sierra Nevada left for San Juan, with treasure to the value of $677,220 00. . . . James Cavanaugh died in consequence of a stab received from the hand of Wm. Ray during an affray at the Nonantum house.

December 10.   Early in the morning quite a thick frost was observed on the planks of the streets. . . . The steamer New World struck a snag about nine miles below Sacramento, on the Yolo side of the river, which stove a hole in her bow, causing her to fill rapidly.   She was run upon shore, when her passengers and most of her freight were taken off by the Bragdon and carried to Sacramento. The damage did not prove to be serious. . . . The Queen City also ran aground about forty five miles below.

December 11.   Mr. and Mrs. Stark commenced an engagement at the American with the tragedy of Othello, they were supported by Mr. Neafie as Iago, and Mrs. Burrill as Desdemona. . . . A shock of an earthquake was felt at the Mission Dolores about four o'clock in the morning. . . . Of the Mexicans and Negroes arrested in the dance house, the men were fined $5 each, and the women set free. . . . The pews of the Bush street Baptist Church were sold at auction for prices ranging from $110 to $220. . . . Mr. T. D. Green was elected City Sexton by the Common Council. . . . The San Francisco Blues had a grand ball at the Metropolitan Theater.

December 12.   One of the largest mass meetings that ever gathered together in San Francisco, was held at Musical Hall to discuss the subject of the Pacific Railroad.   His Honor, S. P. Webb presided, supported by Thos. O. Larkin, Esq. and Dr. O. M. Wozencraft, as Vice-Presidents.   The meeting was addressed by Col. Baker, Fred. Billings, Esq., Dr. Wozencraft and others, and after passing a series of resolutions adjourned to meet on the 20th of December. . . . Mr. Napier Lothian died very suddenly while conducting the orchestra at the ball of the San Francisco Blues.   He was for a long time the leader of the Union Band, and the founder of the first military band organized in the City. . . . Signor Bassani the leader of the Italian Opera Troupe had a benefit at the Metropolitan Theater.

December 18.   The body of Mr. Napier Lothian was attended to the grave by the San Francisco Blues and a number of his professional friends. . . . The new steamboat Surprise, intended for the Sacramento river trade, arrived from New York via Panama, under the command of Capt. Edgar Wakeman.

December 14.   The P. M. S. S. Golden Age arrived, bringing news of the terrible shipwreck of the ship New Era, near Shark river, on the Jersey shore, with the loss of 250 lives; and that Louis Napoleon had withdrawn his prohibition of Mr. Soulé's passing through France. . . . A fire broke out on Market street, between First and Tremont, by which property to the value of $1,500 was consumed. . . . A statement published in the *State Journal* showed the number of licenses for foreign miners, issued in the State during the year 1854, to be 109,140, yielding a revenue of $412,500, of which the State receives one-half, the remainder being divided among the respective counties in which they were collected.

December 15. A statement in the *Herald* exhibited the Civil Debt of the State of California to have been on the 1st July, 1854, $2,588,666 07, and the War Debt at the same date, $990,483 12.

December 16. A man while passing at night along Powell street, near Union, was attacked by two midnight marauders, and robbed of his watch and purse.

December 17. A Policeman named Harry Kerrison was stabbed by a woman named Elizabeth Sullivan, *alias* Howard. . . . An ordinance was passed admitting Peterson Engine Company No. 15 into the Fire Department.

December 19. An agreement to have the question as to the precise location of the Capital decided by the Supreme Court in Chambers, was sent up to Benicia. . . . James McCabe, formerly Probate Judge in Michigan, was stabbed by a man named Ackey. The cause of the act was jealousy produced in the mind of the latter by a misconstruction of certain polite attentions which the former had paid his wife. . . . The woman Sullivan, *alias* Howard, was removed to the county jail. . . . A man named W. D. Carr was brought before the Recorder, charged with burglariously entering a house on Greenwich street and robbing it of various articles of value. He was sent up to the Court of Sessions. . . . Jim Peeler, the great Southern walker, accomplished at Mokelumne Hill the unparalleled feat of walking 102 consecutive hours. . . . Mr. John Hogan, Marshal of Oakland, decamped privately with from ten to fifteen thousand dollars of that city's funds. . . . A meeting of the Emigrant Road Committee was held, and, after passing several resolutions, adjourned to the 2d inst. . . . Mr. John Smith was married.

December 20. The Nicaragua Company's S. S. Uncle Sam arrived, bringing news of the definitive settlement of the Soulé affair, and of the terrible battle of Inkerman on the 5th of November, in which 13,000 of the Russians and 5,000 of the allied troops were killed and wounded. Among her passengers were Rev. Dr. Scott, with his wife, four children and four servants. . . . A number of Chinese women were convicted in the Court of Sessions of keeping brothel houses, under an indictment from the Grand Jury, whose object was to have them removed from the city as a nuisance. , . . The schooner Falmouth, Capt. Bowden, arrived from Margaretta Bay with a full cargo of salt of fine quality.

December 22. The Rincon Point Public School, under the superintendence of Mr. J. Swett, had its semi-annual examination. Many of the pupils, in the elocutionary and other exercises which had been prepared for the occasion, acquitted themselves to the gratification of their parents and satisfaction of their teacher, and at the close the latter received from them the handsome testimonial of a gold watch, which he acknowledged in a neat and appropriate speech. . . . The New England Society, by a banquet at Wilson's Exchange, celebrated the 234th anniversary of the landing of the Pilgrims at Plymouth Rock. Some of the most eminent citizens, with many members of the press, were present, and the festivity was distinguished by the greatest hilarity. . . . A destructive fire occurred at Vallecito, Calaveras county, which destroyed property to the value of $12,000. . . . The young ladies of the Powell street Academy, held a fair in Burgoyne's Building of articles, chiefly of their own manufacture, the proceeds of the sale of which were to be devoted to the Protestant Orphan Asylum.

December 23. The choice of pews in St. Mary's cathedral, corner of Dupont and California streets, was sold at auction in the church. The premiums ranged from $150 to $175. . . . A large audience assisted at the complimentary benefit to the popular manageress of the Metropolitan theater. The performances passed off pleasantly, and the occasion was further distinguished by a poetical address, which was gracefully delivered by Mr. Mark Leman. . . . The new Hall of the Turn-Verein Society, situated on the corner of Powell and Bush streets, was dedicated with appropriate ceremonies. . . . The suit of B. F. Latimer and Wife *vs.* The City, brought to recover the sum of $8,482 25, for a lot of ground situated on Merchant street, corner of Montgomery, was decided against the plaintiffs. . . . E. F. Norton was elected by the Board of Aldermen Collector of Street Assessments. An ordinance providing for the registry of deaths was passed; also one to increase the pay of the police, making the salary of the captain $250 a month, the assistants $225, and that of the officers $175. . . . Intelligence was received of an extraordinary and terrible affray, which occurred on the 20th ult. at Rock Cañon, between three miners and a band of robbers. The miners were Mr. Jas. C. McDonald, Dr. Bolivar A. Sparks, and Capt. Jonathan R. Davis. When passing through the almost inaccessible cañon above-named, they were suddenly attacked by a party of robbers. McDonald fell dead at the first fire. Sparks fired twice at his assailants, and then fell, severely wounded; but Capt. Davis killed or wounded eleven of his adversaries, and escaped almost uninjured, although his friends counted twenty-eight bullet-holes in his clothes—seventeen in his hat and eleven in his coat and shirt. Probably a hoax.

December 24. The handsome four-story building and banking house of Dr, A. S. Wright was opened to the inspection of visitors; and those who availed themselves of the opportunity to examine the edifice in the city were not only delighted by the attractive appearance of its lofty rooms, and the extensive view afforded from its cupola, but were courteously received and hospitably entertained by its gentlemanly and enterprising proprietor. . . . A young man named Lee, who escaped sometime since from the station house, was arrested by Capt. McDonald with a carpet-bag which was completely filled with various articles of jewelry. . . . The mechanics had an adjourned meeting to consider upon the means of establishing a library. A proposition to join the Mercantile Library Association was discussed and was concurred in by many, but the meeting adjourned before coming to any action. . . . St. Mary's cathedral was opened for divine service for the first time.

December 25. *Christmas day* was celebrated by the usual festivities and religious ceremonies. . . . The jewelry store of Victor Lang, situated on Dupont street, near Jackson, was robbed of various articles of the value of $2,300. . . . The Turn-Vereins gave a grand ball in their new hall. . . . Two pedestrians, named Kennovan and Phillips, commenced walking a match against each other: he who held out the longest was to be declared the victor. . . . Major Roman arrived in the steamship Southerner, having resigned his office as consul at Guaymas. . . . A man named William Johnson was hung at Iowa Hill for stabbing a man by the name of Montgomery on the 22d ult.

December 26. The State Educational Convention commenced its session in the Union street schoolhouse.

December 27. The Supreme Court decided that Sacramento should be the capital of the State. . . . A number of convicts overpowered their guard and succeeded in making their escape from the State Prison at Point St. Quentin.

December 28. By a statement in the *Herald,* the total yield of the mines for the year 1854 was shown to be $49,619,821 85, and for the four years from the 1st January, 1851, $186,684,088. The product of the Almaden mines (quick-silver) was 1,449,000 lbs. during the year 1854, amounting in value, at the rate of 50 cents per lb., to $724 500; during the year 1853, 18,800 flasks, or 1,410,000 lbs.; value, $683,189. . . . The number of vessels entered at the Custom House during the period comprised between the 1st January to the 26th December, 1854, was from domestic ports 261, or 215,822 tons; 12 have been sold by the marshal, the proceeds amounting to $166,000 00. From foreign ports, 356 vessels, or 191,663 tons—making the total number of those arriving from all quarters, 617, with an aggregate tonnage of 407,485. In the year 1853 the total number of arrivals was 862, with a tonnage of 413,979; showing a decrease during the present year of 245 vessels, but only 6,494 tons: from which the inference is that those which arrived in 1854 were generally of larger burden than of previous years.

EDITOR'S TABLE.

THE KNICKERBOCKER GALLERY.

It is almost needless for us to direct the attention of our patrons to this forth-coming volume; for it is not hazarding too much to say, that all who read THE PIONEER are aware of its objects. But although of course it is not for us, to hold a leading part in the splendid tribute, which many of his compeers in literature are about to pay to Mr. Louis Gaylord Clark, editor of the *Knickerbocker Maga-zine*, yet we desire to add our mite to the graceful compliment, by presenting to our patrons the claims of THE KNICKERBOCKER GALLERY, and urging our friends, for the sake of ill-requited merit, to lend a helping hand in the good work of surrounding a gentleman, who has devoted the best years of his life to the en-couragement and purifying of American Literature, with the comforts and ele-gancies of a home. You, who have for years watched for the monthly coming of *The Knickerbocker*, and laughed and wept over its world-renowned gossip,— you, who have felt the mild influence of its humor and its pathos stealing into your character, and, therebecause, have looked more kindly upon the world around you,—you, who feel a pride in the growth of American Literature,—you, who would scatter a flower along the pathway of a man who has spent twenty years of his life in encouraging young talent and teaching young genius to fly—it is to you, that such men as Washington Irving, Henry W. Longfellow, William Cul-len Bryant, Nathaniel P. Willis, Geo. P. Morris and a host of others, bright orna-ments of America, appeal. In the words of another, "a volume so unique in its conception, and so expensive in its illustrations, and yet so moderate in price, de-serves complete success. While the work is intended as a compliment to Mr. CLARK, its express design is for the *benefit* of the popular editor. The committee intend, if a sufficient sum can be realized by the sale, to purchase a cottage in the vicinity of New York as *a home* for Mr. CLARK and his family. To secure a result so desirable, the friends of Mr. CLARK, and all lovers of good literature, will, we trust, use more than ordinary effort. Every reader of *The Knicker-bocker* should feel a pleasure in taking some copies, and in asking his friends to do so also. They will thus have the satisfaction of laying a brick or fastening a nail in their friend's new home."

We give below the

PROSPECTUS

OF THE

KNICKERBOCKER GALLERY,

A MISCELLANY OF LITERATURE AND ART.

In one splendid 8vo. vol., comprising original Literary Papers by the most eminent living American Authors, with forty-seven Portraits on steel, from original pictures. A complimentary tribute to Louis Gaylord Clark, Esq., for twenty years editor of the Knickerbocker Magazine.

Considering that Louis Gaylord Clark has been, for the unexampled period of **twenty years,** Editor of a leading Literary Magazine in this country; that his labors meanwhile have been constant, arduous, and ill-requited; that they have been eminently creditable to his abilities and character, and of great service to the country in developing its intellectual resources, several of his friends met together last December to devise some suitable plan for tendering to him a substantial Complimentary Benefit, in all respects appropriate for the literary class to offer, and for him to receive. The result was a project for publishing such a work as is above described; **and** upon submitting the plan to Washington Irving, Fitz-Greene Halleck, Henry W. Longfellow, and other literary men of the United States, it received their cordial approval; so that the committee having the matter in hand are able to announce for the ensuing season a Literary Souvenir, beyond all parallel in the eminence of its writers, and in mechanical execution equal at least to any similar production ever issued from the American press. The collection of Portraits of American writers will be far more complete than any hitherto attempted.

THE KNICKERBOCKER GALLERY

will be published, under the direction of the committee, by Mr. Samuel Hueston, 348 Broadway, New York, and will be ready for delivery to subscribers in November next. Subscribers will receive the first impressions of the plates, and the series will possess a value much beyond the cost of the volume. The entire profits of the work will be invested for Mr. Clark.

JOHN W. FRANCIS,	RUFUS W. GRISWOLD,
FREDERICK W. SHELTON,	RICHARD B. KIMBALL,
	GEORGE P. MORRIS.

The Publisher has the pleasure of announcing as contributors to this Literary Testimonial, Washington Irving, William Cullen Bryant, Fitz-Greene Halleck, Nathaniel P. Willis, Rev. George W. Bethune, D. D., Hon. William H. Seward, George William Curtis, Donald G. Mitchell, Henry W. Longfellow, John G. Saxe, George Lunt, Rev. Frederick W. Shelton, Richard B. Kimball, George P. Morris, Henry J. Brent, Dr. Oliver Wendell Holmes, Samuel Osgood, Epes Sargent, Alfred B. Street, George H. Boker. George H. Clark, R. H. Stoddard, J. L. McConnell, Theodore S. Fay, J. Russell Lowell, Charles G. Leland, Dr. Thomas Ward, John T. Irving, P. Hamilton Myers, T. B. Thorpe, Henry T. Tuckerman, Ralph Roanoke, George D. Prentice, Samuel S. Cox, Frederick S. Cozzens, W. H. C. Hosmer. James T. Fields, R. S. Chilton, Park Benjamin, George Wood, Hon. R. T. Conrad, Bayard Taylor, Donald McLeod, and others.

All the subscribers and readers of *The Knickerbocker* are hereby authorized and requested to act as agents for this book. It will be seen that the expense of such a work must be very great, and the only way to make it profitable is by a large sale. The publisher hopes for the active co-operation of editors and publishers with whom we exchange. The price of the volume will be Five Dollars per copy, in elegant cloth binding, gilt edges; and in Turkey extra, Seven Dollars. All subscriptions payable on delivery of the work. Those who wish the work, and who may feel interest enough in its success to get some of their friends to take it, will confer a special favor by sending the names as early as possible, that the publisher may be able to judge how many to print for the first edition.

☞ *The Knickerbocker Gallery* will be sold *only* by Subscription and by Agents.

Agents wanted in every city, town and village in the United States, to whom a liberal discount will be made. Please apply for terms, &c., *post paid,* to

SAMUEL HUESTON, 348 Broadway, New York.

We doubt not the volume will reach California soon, and we bespeak for it a liberal sale.

—

GOSSIP WITH READERS AND CORRESPONDENTS.

IN some unaccountable manner a large roll of poetry selected for insertion has been mislaid, and can nowhere be found. It is exceedingly provoking, as well as mortifying to us to be compelled to make this statement to our kind contributors, since not only were many of the poems excellent, but we are put to the necessity of asking the indulgence of our friends and requesting the favor of second copies. Some of the poems had been waiting for insertion as long as six months,—space of the exact extent not having presented itself for their admission. We shall endeavor not to have the like happen again. - - - IT WILL be seen by the date of the note apologetic below, that "Our John" is luxuriating himself at the Mission Dolores. He has left his "observatory" at San Diego, and having given the world, in his widely copied lectures, the results of his glances at the ridiculous and the stars, is, as we strongly suspect, extending his researches into the peculiarities of the Vegetable Kingdom. At any rate we are promised a contribution for our next. But meanwhile, for the letter:—

LETTER FROM JOHN PHŒNIX.

MISSION OF DOLORES, 15th January, 1855.

Dear Ewer :—It was my intention to furnish you, this month, with an elaborate article on a deeply interesting subject, but a serious domestic calamity has prevented. I allude to the loss of my stove-pipe, in the terrific gale of the 31st December.

There are few residents of the city, whose business or inclination has called them to the Mission of Dolores, that have not seen and admired that stove-pipe. Rising above the kitchen chimney to the noble altitude of nearly twelve feet, it pointed to a better world, and was pleasantly suggestive of hot cakes for breakfast. From the window of my back porch, I have gazed for hours upon that noble structure; and watching its rotary cap shifting with every breeze, and pouring forth clouds of gas and vapor, I have mused on politics, and fancied myself a Politician. It was an accomplished stove-pipe. The melody accompanying its movements, inaptly termed creaking by the soulless, gave evidence of its taste for Music, and its proficiency in Drawing was the wonder and delight of our family circle. It had no bad habits,—it did not even smoke.

I fondly hoped to enjoy its society for years, but one by one our dearest treasures are snatched from us: the soot fell, and the stove-pipe has followed soot. On the night of the 31st of Dec., a gale arose, perfectly unexampled in its terrific violence. Houses shook as with tertian ague, trees were uprooted, roofs blown off, and ships foundered at the docks. A stove-pipe is not a pyramid, —what resistance could mine oppose to such a storm? One by one its protecting wires were severed; and as it bowed its devoted head to the fury of the blast, shrieks of more than mortal agony attested the desperate nature of its situation. At length the Storm Spirit fell upon the feeble and reeling structure in its wrath, and whirling it madly in the air with resistless force, breaking several tenpenny nails, and loosening many of the upper bricks of the chimney, dashed it down to earth. But why harrow up the feelings of your readers by a continuation of the distressing narrative. The suffering that we have endured, the tears that have been shed since this loss will be understood, and commiserated, when I add—the next morning the kitchen chimney smoked,—and has been doing it intermittently ever since!

Since my last, scarcely a gleam of fun has come to illumine the usual dull monotony of the Mission of Dolores,—

> "The days have been dark and dreary;
> It rains, and the wind is never weary."

A little occurrence at the toll-gate, the other day, is worthy of notice, perhaps, as betokening "the good time a-coming." A well-known gentleman of your city, who frequently drives forth on the Plank Road, perched on one of those little gigs that somebody compares to a tea-tray on wheels, with the reins hanging down behind, like unfastened suspenders, in an absent frame of mind, drove slowly past the Rubicon without bifurcating the customary half-dollar. Out rushed the enthusiastic toll-gatherers, shouting, "Toll, sir, toll! you've forgot the toll!" "Oh! don't bother me, gentlemen," replied the absent one, in a lachrymose tone and with a most woful expression, "*I'm an orphan boy !*" This appeal to the sympathies of the toll-men was effective; their hearts were touched, and the orphan went on his way rejoicing.

It is amusing to observe the shifts a maker of Poetry will resort to, when compelled to make use of an irrelevant subject to eke out his rhyme, to convince himself and his readers, that the *faux pas* was quite intentional, the result of study, and should be admired rather than criticised. In a poem called "Al Aaraaf," by Edgar A. Poe, who, when living, thought himself, in all seriousness, the *only* living original Poet, and that all other manufacturers of Poetry were mere copyists, continually infringing on his patent,—occurs the following passage, in which may be found a singular instance of the kind alluded to:

> "Ligeia! Ligeia!
> My beautiful one!
> Whose harshest idea
> Will to melody run:
> Oh, is it thy will,
> On the breezes to toss;

> Or capriciously still,
> * Like the lone Albatross,
> Incumbent on Night,
> (As she on the air,)
> To keep watch with delight
> On the harmony there?"

Observe that note: " *The Albatross is said to sleep on the wing.*" Who said so? I should like to know. Buffon didn't mention it; neither does Audubon. Coleridge, who made the habits of that rare bird a study, never found it out; and the undersigned, who has gazed on many Albatrosses, and had much discourse with ancient mariners concerning them, never suspected the circumstance, or heard it elsewhere remarked upon.

I am inclined to believe that it never occurred to Mr. Poe, until having become embarrassed by that unfortunate word "toss," he was obliged to bring in either a *hoss*, or an albatross; and preferring the bird as the more poetical, invented the extraordinary fact to explain his appearance.

The above lines, I am told, have been much admired; but if they are true Poetry, so are the following :

> Highflier! Highflier!
> My long-legged one!
> Whose mildest idea
> Is to kick up and run:
> Oh, is it thy will
> Thy switch-tail to toss;
> Or caper viciously still,
> † Like an old sorrel horse, [*pron. "hoss,"*]
> Incumbent on thee,
> As on him, to rear, [*pron. "rare,"*]
> And though sprung in the knee,
> With thy heels in the air?

A note for me, and the man waiting for an answer, said ye? Now by the shade of Shadrach, and the chimney of Nebuchadnezzar's fiery furnace! 'tis the bill for the new chimney! Bills, bills, bills! How *can* a man name his child William! The horrid idea of the partner of his joys, and sorrows, presenting him with a *Bill !*—and to have that Bill continually in the house—constantly running up and down stairs—always unsettled,—Distraction's in the thought! Tell that man, Bridget, I'm sick; and, lucky thought, say it's the small-pox; and ask him to call again when I've got better and gone to San Diego for my health.———He's gone. I see him from a hole in the window curtain, flying off in a zig-zag direction, and looking back timorously, like a jacksnipe, with his long bill. I shall write no more; like that bill, I feel unsettled. Adieu!

I am, Ewer, Ewer obedient servant,

JOHN PHŒNIX.

- - - GREAT is California of the Americans! True is she to her reputation! How proudly have we read that "the peoples" have contributed from among their best to build up her population. And who shall deny that among us—hid away among us,—*very much* hid away among us—are such inventors, such historians, *such* poets, such geniuses of all descriptions as the world never before saw! Show us the man who would venture such an assertion, and we will hold up before him one GLASS (John W. of Columbia, Tuolumne county,) as a living, withering refutation to his slander. MR. GLASS has given to the world "an 'umble effort." It is before us in yellow covers. It is called "The California Sacrafice or the Last of the Montezuma's—a poem," and we cannot refrain from giving our readers a specimen or two of its beauties. It opens as follows, viz:

"CALIFORNIA SACRAFICE OR THE LAST OF THE MONTEZUMA'S.

The folowing Poem is founded upon an Indian Tradition, particularly detailed in the notes; but bearing in general that Lonoma, the '*The last of the Montezuma's,*' was discovered by a gold hunter in California, upon the summit of the dividing ridge between Bear River and Steep Hollow, and with him Loneta,

---

* " The Albatross is said to sleep on the wing."
† The sorrel horse is said to be the most vicious of quadrupeds, *and to sleep standing !*

his maden child; They informed him they were the Last of the Montezuma's;— That California was their fathers *native* land, the land of Ophir;—That they were driven thence by Volcanic Eruptions to Mexico;—distroyed there by Cortes; and that they, the last of all their race had sought their father land to offer up, upon the altar themselves—a human sacrifice; also of some pale Indians; (supposed to be the same now found to the East of the Sierra Nevada.)

"Driven thence *by Volcanic Eruptions into Mexico!*" Think of it!—"also of some pale Indians!"—alas, what an uncertainty hangs over their fate!

"THE POEM.

I have stood on Nevadas snow capped mountains
And by their sparkling fount:
On Arabia's drear and sandy plains,
And Italy's burning mount:
Thirty years I 've been a wanderer o'er
This vast earth:
And ever more my onward course I go
To the North, South, East, and West,
Of what I reep, or what I sow,
My roving ways I love the best.
Of late I stood upon a craggy mount,
A listening to the gushing fount,
When lo! a voice broke on my ear
Saying; 'Father! Oh! father dear
Let me die with thee:—my sire
Yes, by thy side expire
In fiery flames with thee.'
'It shalt be so;' the red man said
For red they were.
And there they knelt before a shrine,
T 'was built long years before their time,
When formed no one on earth can tell;
Since then nations have formed and fell;
Like dew they have dissolved and fled,
Or like the brave have fell, and bled,
To save their land from tyrants power;
But fate in that dark and trying hour
Gave the palm of victory, to men of blood,
Who o'ped the gates; then freely flowed
The purple drops of the red chief's vains,
And sank within the Earth.
Me thought 't would never rise no more,
But lay where it had sank of yore,
Though in him who kneels before that shrine,
I see the last of Montezuma's line."

The poet, GLASS, as he becomes heated by his subject, bursts out at last into the following sublime rhapsody:

"The chieftain paused;—and gazed around,
Then bent his looks upon the ground.
His grey hair's shook: he seemed
As one destracted, one who had dreamed
Fearful, and bloody dreams.
His clenched hands, and hard drawn breath,
Gave token of approaching death:
Moments passed thus; a calm at last
Settled o'er his brow, and the blast
Swept past him with a mournful sound;
When with a yell, and bound,
He once more spake.

'Pale man I 'm soon to leave this earth,
I cannot live in the land of me birth;
I have been driven from me native shore,
And sought me fathers land of yore,
To offer up upon this shrine,
The last of Montezuma's line.
Me hand if it could speak, would tell
Of many deeds, and how well
My oath of revenge has been kept.
How I have crawled by night, and crept
Stealthily upon my foe,
And gave the fatal blow,
And cried, strike; Lonoma for your sires
Strike for your altars, and your fires,

That long since perished by sword, and flame,
They blessed in Montezuma's name;
Blessed by the God who rules above,
Blessed by friendship, truth, and love;
Held dear by every parting breath,
And cherished even until death,
Now? where the temples of our land;
Fallen by the destructive fire brand.
Yet still a remnant may be found
On hill, in vale, on mount, and mound,
To show where once the good, and brave,
Flourished ere they became the slave
Of jealous war.

The time of waging war's now o'er;
I have fought my last battle; oh! more;
For to-day with me ends mortal strife,
This day I offer up my life.
Thou shalt see my spirit ascend in fire,
On wings of light to join my sire;
I, with me daughter here so fair,
Will sing our songs where angels are.
Our sands of life 's soon run; an hour more
And then, ah! then, me sire of yore,
We join thee in thy sports again,
Where, no sorrow pain or strife
Will reach us more
On that flowery shore,
But happy w 'll forever be
From this to all eternity.
Ages will circle here away,
And leave no sign's of our decay,
Now hear me fathers, hear me pray.

Ye spirits of the mighty dead
Who bravely fought and fearless bled,
To shield the red man in his right,
I come to join you in me sprite,
To join with you the heavenly strain;
And as the blood that flows me vein.
Has come from pedegree so rare,
I pray my spirits blessings, are
Through this my daughter of thy blood,
Borne safely o'er the darksome flood,—
Far from the reach of mortal hands,—
To join thee in they heavenly lands.
And as our spirits wing their flight,
To our eternal heavenly site.
Procured by thee;
We pray thy spirits have but blessed
The final Montezumas rest.'"

There's rare poetry for you! The work concludes with "The death-bed conviction of a California miner and his Requiem":

"These lines were prompted by peculiar circumstances. Being called to witness the death of one of my fellow miners, the scene I there witnessed made such an impression upon my mind, that I voluntarily penned the following, which I respectfully submit:

Mark that, he *voluntarily* penned them.

The day's aurora with its beam
Gilds hill and mountain, vale and stream;
It is a lovely morn ; as when
Fitz James first sought clan alpine's glen,
Or Adam,—e'er he took the leave
To eat, and give to knowledge—Eve;
As beautiful the morn the broke
On Linden's fleecy unstained cloak;
Or that which made Palermo own,
The arm that restored Palermo's throne;
But hark ! what sad *convictions* come
To call the softening breeze's home,
And there indorse e er they depart,
The sorrows of a miner's heart.
Ah! Sol; e'rr thou again decline,
And bid the queen of night to shine;
Take note and tell, if eer thou know
Such anguish, such relenting woe,
As from this miner's bosom flow.

'For twenty years have I enjoyed the blessings of the blessed,
With a loved wife, family and friends; I then could rest,
Assured in sickness, pain, or strife,
I had enough of worldly gain for sustenance for life;
Among the scenes of childhood, I loved so much to dwell,

For every hill and rivulet some pleasing tale would tell,
The orchard, and the meadow, the schoolhouse and the oak,
The mill where with my bride I sung to the tune of the sawgate's stroke;
But rumors told me there was gold for all 'twould venture o'er
To where Nevada's snow capped peaks bind the Pacific shore,
I not content with wealth enough left all that I adore,
To try the hidden treasury of California's shore,' &c."

But we must bid farewell to MR. GLASS, merely copying the following from the last page of the cover:

"ADVERTISEMENT.

Will be published, shortly, by the author of the 'CALIFORNIA SACRAFICE;' two new works, entitled '*California and its Mysteries*,' and '*California from* 1848 *to* 1854.'"

- - - A NEW and welcome contributer sends us the following:—"There is a French lady of my acquaintance in San Francisco, who is making strenuous and laudable exertions to learn to speak our language. When she hears an English word pronounced that is new to her, she writes it down in order to impress it upon her memory. A day or two since, she asked a friend what was the word for '*semaine;*'—he told her 'week.' She repeated it over two or three times—'week—week,'—and then, 'for sure,' wrote it down in her tablets '*ouic.*' Is there any French scholar who will not be pleased with this characteristic and (to her) most natural spelling? It beats 'k a u g h p h y' out of sight and is a historical verity." - - - THIS reminds us of a "French gentleman," to whom we dropped a hint, one day, touching a change in his affairs, which we deemed might be for the better. "Ah!" said he, "I believe in 'Letting better alone.'" "No," responded we, "you mean 'Letting *well enough* alone.'" "No, no, no," said he thoughtfully, "Hold on to *well enough*, and let *better* alone." We said no more. - - - ON the twenty-third of last month a change occurred in the management of the ALTA CALIFORNIA, the chair vacated by Mr. Edward C. Kemble, the late editor of that journal, having been assumed by Mr. Charles C. Washburn. Mr. Washburn is an able, argumentative writer, and whatever may be the difference of opinion with regard to the positions he may assume, we are well assured that the popular daily, over whose columns he presides, will be characterized by dignity and manliness of tone. In entering upon his new duties, Mr. W. was of course compelled to resign his position as editor-in-chief of the *Evening Journal*. His chair in the last named daily is now occupied by Mr. Edward Pollock, the late junior editor, a gentleman well known to all our readers. It is needless for us to allude again to the high estimation in which we hold his talent. Worth finds its level; and we congratulate him on the rapidity with which he has arisen from obscurity to a leading position before our community. On the retirement of MR. KEMBLE from the post he has so long held in the *Alta California*, the relationship which has heretofore existed between us, prompts us to at least a passing notice of the services he has rendered in behalf of the public, and to the expression of sincere regret at the severance of the editorial bond, that has so long united us. We are the more prompted to this, inasmuch as MR. KEMBLE and ourself were the only editors remaining in San Francisco, of the few that worked shoulder to shoulder in the far-off days of "Forty-Nine." As one by one, who ranked us in seniority, vacated his place,—some, alas, for the solemn ways beyond the grave,—it was natural for us to find growing within us an unusual regard for the lessening band around us, and it is not without feelings of the sincerest regret—nay melancholy—that we are at last called upon to extend the farewell hand to our only remaining senior. We cannot but trust, that we shall soon have an opportunity to welcome him back to our ranks again.———Mr. Kemble was one of the early pioneers to California. In fact he had scarcely passed beyond the verge of boyhood, when he landed upon these shores. Soon after the *California Star* (the first newspaper published in San Francisco) was established, he assumed its editorial management. Many months did not elapse before *The Californian* (the first number of which was issued at Monterey somewhat in advance of the appearance of *The Star*) was removed to this place. Both papers were compelled to stop their issues during the summer subsequent to the discovery of gold at Sutter's mill, Mr. Kemble himself being at last seized with the prevailing epidemic, and leaving for the *placeres*. At the opening of the subsequent autumn, (1848) however, he returned to San Francisco, and, having gained the control of both papers, united them into the weekly *Star and Californian*, which he published until the first of January, 1849; when, having associated with himself the late Mr. Gilbert, the first number of the *Alta California* was issued under their combined charge. The career of Mr. Kemble since that time is doubtless well known to most of our readers. His labors have been constant and arduous; he has ever shown himself a staunch friend of the land of his adoption, and leaves the post with which he has so long been identified, bearing with him the regrets of numerous friends. - - - Our new contributor "Podgers," well known for his rich satires, given to the world through the New Orleans press, and who, by the way, penned the burlesque, entitled "The Clipper Ship Highfalutin," which appeared in our last, favors us again. If we knew the number and trench outside the walls of Sebastopol, where that valorous Englishman is to be found, who wrote home so Falstaffean an account of the number of "Russian Serfs," he caused to bite the dust, during a charge at Inkermann, we should certainly mail him a copy of this month's Pioneer.

PODGERS HAS A DREAM.

On the arrival of the John L. Stevens, last Saturday evening week, being anxious to learn the news from the East and eastern world generally, I procured a New York paper, retired to my room, stirred up the cheerful fire, and after proceeding to ensconce myself comfortably in bed, with the candle conveniently placed, I lighted my cigar, unfolded the paper, commenced its perusal, from the "Terms" at the head of the first column, and went straight through, up hill and down, over accidents and incidents, plunging head-foremost into political articles, and emerging in a "prices current." But the last hour I gave to the War in the Crimea. I went into the battle of Inkermann, and drank in the wondrous exploits of the Munchau——heroes, I mean, and "War Dogs," who committed such havoc in the enemy's ranks; particularly the "fire eater," who "sabered" twelve Russians into the next world, and, as he says, "put twelve more on the passage there." My cigar was finished, and so was the paper; and I dropped into a gentle slumber, and began to dre. 'n. Gradually I "wandered in dreams," and fancied myself on the way to the Seat of War, fully commissioned as European reporter and correspondent of THE PIONEER MAGAZINE. I arrived at the Crimea, and, by special permission, was permitted to pitch my tent on an emi-nce, where I could obtain a bird's-eye view of the camp of the Allies and the Russian defenses. was aroused early the next morning by the roaring of cannon and sharp rattle of musketry. Hastily donning my accouterments, mounting a piebald charger I had purchased the day before, and putting my note-book into my pocket, I joined a squadron of Cavalry, passing on a gallop, bound for the fray. My old charger gave a snort, and assumed a position on the right of a company as naturally as if accustomed to it all his days. An officer hailed me with "Who the devil are you?"—to which I answered. "Nobody in particular, and Special Correspondent of the California Magazine generally;"—"All right," said he, "report *that!*"—as a shell exploded over our heads. Our speed was quickened, and we rapidly approached a dense column of Russians, who were blazing away at our front ranks, mowing them down by dozens. I thought it about time to halt and take a safer position, and pulled away at the bit to stop my "*cavallo;*" but he never deigned to notice my efforts. I pulled harder, stronger; it wouldn't do. I holler'd "Whoa!"—struggled away; but the old beast only snorted and plunged ahead. Just then I heard the order "'Charge!"—and so did my old war-horse; and away we dashed. I saw it was no use, and made up my mind, my time had come. There was a confused mass of human beings and horses struggling before my eyes;—a clashing of steel, a whistling of bullets;—all was noise and confusion. I just had time to see myself and horse rushing down a slight declivity, right straight for a six-foot Russian, on a large black charger, with saber upraised. "Oh, Lord!" thinks I, "here goes the Pioneer's Special Reporter! Wouldn't give three cents for his chance." There was a shock. I felt myself performing a somerset and the duties of a projectile; "plunk!" went something, and an exclamation, sounding like "Schweitzbtxlpbxopki," roared out just over me, conveying the idea of a tremendous oath in the most impressive Russian. I felt myself going somewhere, and somebody going with me. The next instant, I was rolling under the feet of plunging horses, and, as I rolled over and over, caught sight of my Russian friend just beyond, going through the air still, with his hand on his stomach. The thought struck *me*, that I must have struck *him*, head-foremost, thereabouts, like a battering-ram; and the concussion had sent him flying from his horse into a locality somewhat safer, and I envied him. At that moment, down came a horse on me, falling across another dead animal, that had obstructed my further progress, which in a measure protected me. I couldn't move, but I could see out between his fore legs; and, finding myself very snug from danger, I got out my note-book with much difficulty, and prepared to jot down items. What a scene! Russians and English in one general *mêlée*, cutting and slashing! I saw the man who so decimated the Czar's army. I know it must have been he, for he was whacking away with all his might, just as he said he did; the only difference being, he didn't hit 'em *every* time. I noticed every time he brought his saber down, he yelled out two, four, five, seven, nine, twelve, etc. I presumed he was taking the census of the damage *he* was doing;—but he was evidently no mathematician. Being a non-combatant, and being very much "opinionated," as was the woman who looked on and saw the bear and her husband settling their differences, I couldn't lay there and see any unfair play on either side, and such an outrageous construction of Daboll. Such counting would have soon annihilated the entire Russian army. "Hold on, old fellow!" said I, "you aint counting straight." He answered, "'Old your tongue, or I'll 'ave your 'ead off, too;" and just then, happening to have a Russian on the point of his saber, (one of the twelve he had "stuck,") he pitched him at me; who, falling across my look-out, shut out a further view of matters. The din of battle having ceased, I fell into a doze, while waiting for whatever might come next. The next thing that *did* come, was a big Russian, who, in poking about, collecting the wounded, stumbled over my heels, which projected somewhat; and, fancying a pair of boots thereon, he commenced pulling at them; and I very naturally commenced kicking. Whereupon he went around, changed ends, and began to pull at my head. Grabbing me by the collar, and giving two or three heavy surges, he finally brought me to light. Holding me up at arm's length, he looked at me and exclaimed, "Hello, *you!* say!" "Good God!" said I, "do you speak English? Hello, yourself!" "Englisher?" said he. "No Siree!" said I. "Vat man?" "One of the free and enlightened Yankee nation," said I. "Goot!" he replied; and lugged me off with him to Sebastopol. I was led into a sort of court-yard, where quite a number of soldiers were lolling about, and an old woman sat knitting in the corner. Every thing seemed very comfortable. While looking about I heard a whizzing sound, followed by a tremendous explosion, that nearly stunned me. "What's that?" I exclaimed, thinking everybody was killed, and things knocked crazy. The old lady, who was knitting, stopped a moment to brush a little dirt from off her apron, and went on with her work, without even changing countenance. I looked around, and discovered that a shell from the camp of the Allies had exploded just over us, and the pieces had fallen among us, without disturbing the equanimity of anybody but me. It was but a commencement, and all day the balls rolled around the place, and shells threw the dirt all over me, scaring me half to death; however, they seemed to be accustomed to it, and evidently considered it a great waste of powder and ball. Parties of soldiers now and then gathered up the latt and, taking them to the batteries, returned them where they came from. Resolving to escap watched for an opportunity. During the night, when all was quiet, I managed to scale the wall, and, dropping down, ran for the river. I knew the banks were high. I had gone but a few yards, before I heard them after me. Away I dashed. with balls whistling past my ears. I came to the bank, and, making a leap, I felt myself treading on nothing, and going through the air *somewhere* very rapidly. At that moment my pursuers fired a volley at me "on the wing." I felt three bullets go through and through me, then came a plunge into the river.   Oh! how cold that water was!   It took my breath away; but I rose and struck out for the opposite shore, where I saw the watch-fires of the piquet guard of the Allies.   I reached it amid a shower of bullets from *them*, who, supposing me a Russian spy, gave me a volley.   One musket hung fire, and, as I rose from the water, the bullet went through my heart, and I fell back into the river again.   The guard ran down to the water's edge, and, as I was sinking, a soldier made a drive at me with his bayonet; pinking me beautifully and bringing me to the surface, shouldered musket and all, and running to the fire, held me towards the light on the bayonet, exclaiming "My heyes! 'ere's a go!—he's a Hinglishman."   "No," exclaimed another, "I twigs the cove; it's that 'ere bloody Yankee, that came 'ere takin' his haccount of hus;" and without further ceremony, he pitched me back into the river.   Down, down I sank, until I bumped on the bottom—a *slew'd* individual—the defunct Reporter for the Pioneer Magazine, who had died in the service of that valuable publication, and expected a splendid obituary and "epithet."   I was killed "deader nor thunder."

I don't know whether it is worth while or not, to mention how an individual, about my size, woke up and found himself out of bed, sprawling on the floor, with his head under the bureau, the table capsized, and himself laying about loose generally, among the fragments of candle-ends and broken pitcher, the contents of which had completely deluged him.   The water of the Alma *may* be cold; but the water from that pitcher I *know* was.   PODGERS."

- - - On a dark and rainy evening some time since, a friend of ours left San Francisco in his private carriage, for his residence on the San José road. After passing the last toll-gate, he drew about his legs a blanket, laid himself comfortably back, and placing perfect reliance in the driver and Divine Providence, incontinently went asleep. In his dreams, he was present at a meeting of the " E. Clampsus Vitis ; " and, fancying that he was about to jump the sickle, gave a tremendous bound in the air and came down "plunk" in a mud-hole. He was awakened by a tremendous lunge of the carriage, and the voice of the trusty driver ; "Mr. ——," exclaimed that individual, "where on airth have we got to? Its dark as a wolf's mouth; I've been driving about here for more than three hours; we're stuck in the mud and I *think* we've got off the road." Ever calm and self-possessed in the moment of danger, our friend alighted, and, wading slowly and painfully through the mud, his boots sucking at every step, he at length came to a fence. It was a picket fence, composed of short piles, driven firmly into the ground in close juxtaposition. "Eureka," exclaimed he, "you are all right! This is Sanchez's fence, on the right of the road; keep on, and occasionally get out and feel for the fence; keep it constantly on your right, and we'll soon be at home." With this remark he returned to the carriage and again sank to sleep. On rolled the carriage,—hour after hour tugged on the weary horses,—whipped and groaned the driver,—and placidly snored our friend in the darkness. At length the driver, who, following his directions, had many times alighted and felt of the fence, which remained the same fence, had his patience exhausted. "Mr. ——," shouted he, " *somebody has been and stretched this fence;* we ought to have got to *San José* by this time, it's most daylight! " "Drive on! " was the response. On they went ; the horses, wearied out, struck into a slow walk ; the driver, a man of religious inclination and a taste for music, sang "It's a hard road to travel over Jordan I believe," and from the back seat, loud resounded the snore of our somnolent friend. Slowly the darkness of night gave place to the first grayish indication of dawn ; the endless fence became indistinctly visible ; the light increased, the fence appeared distinct ; the driver stretched up his neck and stopped his horses. "Whoa! " he shouted; but while giving utterance to that melancholy ejaculation, he laughed. His companion on the back seat awoke, and gazing o'er the landscape, now plainly visible in the dim light of morning ; "Good Gad! " he exclaimed, "*we've been driving round Sanchez's corral all night.*" They had,—exactly ; and the outside of the *corral,* an enclosure about a quarter of a mile in diameter, presented the appearance of a well-trodden turnpike. There *are* occasions, when a little profanity may be excusable ; but we forbear giving the comments of the excellent driver and his companion. - - - To our friend, Mr. Stephen C. Massett, a man of "infinite jest" and exquisite taste, are we indebted for a copy of the following poem, which he had stored in his fertile memory. It is from the German of Herder, and to our mind is most beautiful and touching :

"THE BROTHER AND SISTER.

FROM THE GERMAN OF HERDER.

In a lone grove, with richest verdure clad,
An image of the Virgin Mother stood ;
Round which two children oft were seen at play,—
Brother and sister ;—with them played the while
Sweet Grace, pure Love and childish Innocence.

And often, too, beside that holy shrine,
Their mother sat ; and there with gentle voice
Spoke to her children of the child Jesus ;—
How good he was while in his mother's arms,—
And how he lov'd all children that were good.
'And does he love us yet?'　'Yes, when you 're good:
Whate'er I say to you, he hears it all.'

One evening, while the sunset's richest glow
Streamed o er the faces of the pair at play,
Sudden the sportive boy exclaim'd : 'I wish
The child who loves us yet, our mother says,
Would come down but for once and visit us.'
'Oh! I would give him all the fairest flow'rs,'
The sister said.　'And I,' the boy replied,
'Would gather for him all the sweetest fruits—
Oh! holy mother, let us see thy child.'

With mild rebuke the mother chid the twain ;
But in her heart their words remained impress'd ;
And in a dream, ere long, one night she saw
The Virgin Mother from her home descend,—
And with her children the child Jesus play'd ;
Pleasant was the dream ;—the child of heaven
Spake thus : 'For your fair fruits and flow'rets fair,
What present shall I make ?　Thou, oh brother,
In greener meadows shalt play with me,
And I will bring thee sweeter fruits by far,
Than e'er thy lips have tasted yet.　To thee,
Oh sister, I will yet come down again,
And round thy brow the bridal chaplet twine.
A mother shalt thou be of children good,—
Good, e'en as thou art, and thy mother too.'

Such was her dream.　In fright she started up,
And went and knelt in pray'r before the shrine :
'If it be possible, oh! holy child,
Leave me my boy ;—if not, thy will be done.'

Brief space elapsed.　The dream was soon fulfill'd.
The boy lay dying ;—but e'en then he saw
(Such were his words) a gentle child of heav'n
Approach, who offered him the sweetest fruits—
These sweetest fruits are still his portion fair.

But the girl lived and grew ; and she became
Her mother's image.　Beside the altar
As she knelt in all her bridal beauty,
And pray'd, the child appear'd and crown'd her brow
With flow'rs ;—the garland (to her it seem'd)
Was mostly woven of the lily and the rose.
Dark blossoms there were few.　Her life of love
And innocence was aptly emblem'd there."

- - - WE call the attention of our readers to the article, given in this number, entitled "Rest." It takes a most kindly view of the sad condition of, alas, hundreds—if not thousands—of our young men, who, as manhood opened upon them, hastened away to California, flushed with ambition and hope,—but who, having struggled for the realization of their anticipations, and fallen again and again, have at last given up the great battle of Life, ere their earthly career is over. It is not saying too much, we think, to state that, so far as its genial, sympathizing tone is concerned, it reminds one of the "gentle Elia;" and if it does not appeal to the hearts of many of our readers, then are we a-wrong in our judgment of human nature. Mr. J. P. Anthony's sketch—"Our Streets,"—will amply repay perusal. Our New York contributor, Mr. C. E. Havens, to whom we tender many thanks for finding time in the midst of his literary labors at home for remembering the far-off PIONEER, presents us this month, with another paper, entitled "The Nature and Influence of Poetry." - - - THE too prevalent practice which many, who are in no way connected with the Press, have adopted for obtaining nightly admission to the various theaters of our city, by means of uttering to the door-keepers a similar phrase to those magic words, "The Press," is no less annoying to those who conduct our weekly and daily journals, etc., than it must be to the various liberal managements, who suffer from the imposition. But the following exercise of small tactics was too good, it seems, to pass unrewarded. A bit of a wag, who either had spent his last cent, or was desirous of listening to the popular strains of "Bobbin' areound and 'reound," and at the same time of saving his sixteen "bits," walked with an air of easy unconcern, up to the door of one of our theaters, and mumbling over abstractedly the words "The Press," was about to pass in, when the faithful Cerberus brought him to a stand-still, by politely suggesting—"Name, if you please, sir?" "The Press!" responded our *nonchalant* friend. "But, sir, the *name;* will you give me the name of the paper?" "Well, it's not much known at present;—I told you 'The *press*,' sir!" responded the unknown, with an air of semi-insulted dignity. "But, sir," was the answer, "the *name!* I must insist upon having the *name.*" "Well, we only started it a week or so ago, but have met with such unexpected success, that we are about to make improvements and enlarge. Mrs. Sinclair always admits the Press." "The *name!* the *name!* what press is it, sir?" urged Cerberus, as he grew confident of an imposition. "The CIDER *Press!*" quickly responded the applicant, as he looked Cerberus full in the eye. "You may pass in, sir," was the equally prompt answer by the appreciative outside guardian. And our waggish Jeremy Diddler sauntered leisurely towards the Dress Circle. As he took his seat in the front row, a close observer might have noticed a somewhat peculiar expression lurking around his "off eye." - - - "JOHN PHŒNIX's last has the "bead" still on, and we serve it up as though the cork had just been "popped." A day or two since, he left the bosky precincts of the Mission Dolores,—whereat he holds a country-seat, doubtless for the prosecution of vegetable inquiries and the investigation of the mysteries of equine physiology,—for an hour's visit to that nervous little locality so reminding one of a certain "*ridiculus mus,*" spoken of by the Latin classic, viz: Oakland. On the return trip in the ferry-boat, a "lady friend," (if we may be permitted to use that convenient, but vile phrase,) called his attention to a breastpin, which one of their fellow-passengers was sporting, about two inches above his top vest-button. It was no less than a curiously-twisted lady's broach, about two inches long by an inch wide. The friend suggested that it might have been presented to him by his wife. "Well," replied Phœnix, "in presenting it to him, it's very evident she *broached a very disagreeable subject.*" - - - WE have received the following epitaphs and epigrams, many of which may be new to our readers. At any rate, they will bear repeating:

EPIGRAMS.

To wonder now at Balaam's ass, is weak:
Is there a day that asses do not speak?

No wonder that science and learning profound
At Haven and Cambridge so greatly abound;
When such numbers take thither a little each day,
And we meet with so few who bring any way!

Some men there are two wives would crave,
    Their appetite is such:
Not so with me—but one I have,
    Yet find that one too much.

While Adam slept, from him his Eve arose:
Strange! his first sleep should be his last repose.

How fitly joined—the lawyer and his wife!—
He moves at bar, and she at home, the strife.

"I am unable," yonder beggar cries,
"To sit or stand." If he says *true*, he *lies!*

Says Harry, "My wife and I are two,
    Yet faith I know not why, sir!"
Quoth Dick, "You're ten, if I speak true:
    She's one, and you're a cypher!"

ON A LADY AFFLICTED WITH STRABISMUS.

If ancient poets Argus prize,
Who boasted of a hundred eyes,
Sure greater praise to her is due,
Who looks a hundred ways with two!

"With folded hands and lifted eyes,
Have mercy, heaven!" the parson cries,
"And on our sun-burnt, thirsty plains,
Thy blessing send in genial rains!"
The sermon ended and the prayers,
The parson to be gone prepares;
When with a look of brighten'd smiles,
"Thank heaven, it rains!" cries farmer Giles.
"Rains!" quoth the parson—"sure you joke!
Rain! heaven forbid! I've got no cloak!"

And now for the

EPITAPHS.

ON MR. RICHARD QUICK.

Quick living, and Quick dead; lo! here he's Dick,
Who was, and is, and ever shall be, Quick.
Nor Quick, nor Dead, from Death we now can save,
Since Quick and Dead lie buried in one grave.

Underneath this stone doth lie,
As much virtue as could die;
Which, when alive, did vigor give
To as much beauty as could live!

Reader, a soldier here lies dead,
Who oft from fields of battle fled;
And should he hear the trumpet's sound,
Tho' dead, he'll rise and quit the ground.

Here lies my wife! Reader, enough is said—
Good only must be spoken of the dead!

While on Epitaphs, did you ever see the following curious specimen of this species of literature?

Here Churchill lies, ah sacred name!
Revere him, nor be silent fame!
Impart applause nor praises spare,—
Desert, not fortune lieth here.

If each line is read from the end to the beginning, instead of from the beginning to the end, it will run as follows, viz:

Name sacred,—ah, lies Churchill here.
Fame, silent be, nor him revere;
Spare praises, nor applause impart;—
Here lieth fortune, not desert.

- - - SAYS Elia, in his never-to-be-too-highly appreciated essay on the "Two great Races of Men," viz: the borrowers and the lenders, in speaking of his library and of old Ralph Bigod or somebody else, to whom he "lost" many a precious volume: "One justice I must do my friend, that if he sometimes, like the sea, sweeps away a treasure, at another time, sea-like, he throws up as rich an equivalent to match it. I have a small under-collection of this nature (my friend's gatherings in his various calls) picked up, he has forgotten at what odd places, and deposited with as little memory at mine. I take in these orphans, the twice deserted. The proselytes of the gate are welcome as the true Hebrews. They stand in conjunction; natives and naturalized. The latter seem as little disposed to inquire out their true lineage as I am. I charge no warehouse-room for these deodands, nor shall I ever put myself to the ungentlemanly trouble of advertising a sale of them to pay expenses." Thus is it with the library of the sanctum. Many an "ugly gap" has stood on the shelves waiting long for its inmate. And many a strange little orphan volume lingers upon our table tarrying for its adoption. Among these "deodands," is a copy of *The London Times* purporting to be published in the year of our Lord 1953. It was left we don't know when, nor by whom. But it is a kindly companion, and has served to while away many a weary moment. From the advertisements and extracts which we give below, it will be seen that very important changes took place in the world between the years 1850 and 1950. Those who inhabited the earth as far back as the years 1850 '51, '52, etc., considered that they were very far advanced in the sciences and general enlightenment; but as we peruse this Times newspaper before us published in our own day, and read of the applications of science which were made to the arts between 1850 and 1950, and compare the advancement which even the advertisements argue our race to have made, with the condition of affairs during 1850, as chronicled by our historians, how like folly, sound the recorded boastings of our ancestors of Queen Victoria's time, and how ridiculously appears the epithet, " a fast people," which the Americans during the days of the Republic arrogated to themselves. Franklin, it will be remembered, was a cotemporary of the celebrated orator Noah Webster, both having been born about the same time, during the Archonship—the Presidency, we should have said, of Frederick Pierce; and should they, with the great General and Statesman, George Washington, visit the earth and peruse this journal before us—should they behold America under the happy reign of its present Emperor, how would they wonder that they should ever have advocated a democracy. We give, as illustrations to a portion of our remarks above, the following advertisements, selected from *The Times Newspaper*, dated Jan. 1st, 1950, before us.

FOR BOMBAY DIRECT.

The Original Nassau Balloon leaves Vauxhall, New Town, (the once royal property,) Mondays, Wednesdays and Fridays, returning every Thursday, Saturday and Tuesday.

FARE.

Car..An Albert.
Bird-Cage..A Victoria and a half.
On the Wings...Half an Albert.

The Director of this highly popular and much-patronized conveyance, begs to assure the public that he still continues to soar higher than any aerial machinist whatever, performing the whole distance in the quickest possible time, and with the least motion. For the safety of his passengers, he hereby warns all persons against flying kites, letting off rockets, or holding umbrellas at more than one mile from the earth, as it is his intention to drop down upon all offenders. No smoking allowed in the Bird-Cage.

RAPID COMMUNICATION WITH INDIA.

The aerial ship the "Highflyer," Capt. Bott, takes wing positively on Monday next from the Terminus, at old Nelson Column, Trafalgar Square. The "Highflyer" is a safety ship, but guaranteed by its owners to perform the journey almost as quick as the Mails. For freight or passage, apply to the Captain on board.

THE NEW HOUSES OF PARLIAMENT.

The Commissioners of Public Works are willing to receive tenders from Builders agreeable, to finish this Great National Undertaking. It will be recollected that the edifices in question were commenced in the reign of King William the Fourth. Some little progress was made towards completion during the reign of Queen Victoria, but as they are now at a stand-still, the Commissioners beg applicants to state the exact number of years required to complete the job.
Board of Works, January 1, 1950.

ROYAL SOCIETY OF GREAT BRITAIN.

At a Meeting of the above Society, held at their Rooms on Monday last, it was unanimously resolved to dissolve the Society, nothing now remaining to be learnt or discovered. Subscriptions are earnestly solicited from the Benevolent, to enable the Council to discharge a long arrear of rent.
Albermarle Street, January 1, 1950.

EMIGRATION TO THE ANTIPODES!

For Cardahar Gulf and Port Proserpine.—Regular Tubes descend through the earth to these celebrated places, Every Tuesday. These very superior Tubes are fitted up expressly for the comfort and accommodation of Levelers, with separate Mouths for families and married people. There is a Library in the Leather, and the passage is thoroughly lighted and ventilated. For descent or plunge, apply to   R. R. BOREHAM, Grand Tower street.

INLAND MAIL POST LETTER BALLS.

The Postmaster-General notifies to the public that letters are now put into balls, and discharged by cannon. Steam every ten minutes, from Central Station, at Albert Bridge, to the various suburban villages. The Postmaster-General begs to state, that, in order to prevent accidents, the Mail Post Letter Balls are preceded by Couriers of thin wood, which, having holes in their sides, collect the wind as they go along, making a whizzing noise, to admonish people to keep out of the way of danger.   A. POP, Secretary of this Department.

THE PIONEER.

Vol. III.]   MARCH, 1855.   [No. 3.

ANNIE SEABROOK:
A Story of a Returned Californian.

BY EDWARD POLLOCK.

PERHAPS no country in the world could show a history, at once so
brief, and so full of romantic adventure and change, as California, since
the discovery of gold. The story I have to tell, however, is not indirectly connected with this history, for it antedates it ; but it is one of
a kind, that has had too many recent parallels.

On a spring evening, in the year 1847, the ship, in which I had made
a long and tedious voyage on the Pacific, came to anchor in a well-
known Atlantic port, the name of which I need not mention. "Home
again," is usually a thought of inexpressible joy, to one who has been
long a wanderer on the sea ; but the place in question was not my
home, and I regarded it with little interest. I do not know that I
would even have gone ashore, (as the vessel to which I was attached
was to make but a short stay) but for a dear friend ; one, who had
been my dear companion through the many months of our voyage.

Seabrook was his name, and this was his native city. To his return
to it, and to the meeting with his father and mother, who lived there,
and to the meeting with his young wife, who lived with them, many
and many an hour of anticipation had been given, during the silent
night watches, amid the ice islands, and under the bitter storms of the
cape, or on the flashing sea, and beneath the deep blue starry sky of
the tropics. Many and many a time had I listened to him, chanting
in a subdued tone—he had a voice as sweet as the west wind—some of
his wife's favorite songs, until I fancied that the breeze, singing
through the cordage, was her voice answering him from afar over the

unlimited ocean.   Many and many a time had he painted to me the
sparkle of her eye, the flush of her cheek, the wave and hue of her
hair, until I fancied I saw some trace of her beauty in every curl of
the breaking wave, some shade and touch of her loveliness in every
change of the varying clouds.

We were alike in many things. We were alike in an education far
above the situation in which we were placed—we were alike in the
eager, romantic spirit of adventure with which we hurried on in quest
of something new; we were alike, if I may say so, in the daring
of our natures, and in a kind of poetical enthusiasm, which gilded
the hardships of a life upon the sea.

But he had a heart far deeper in its sympathies for others than
mine.   Not that I was deficient in feeling, but that he was of a tender
and loving nature, beyond any man I ever knew ; and while I was of
a variable temperament, and liable to moments of melancholy, and
even gloom, nothing, it appeared to me, could damp the strong fire of
enthusiasm, that continually burned within his bosom.

Quite a little romance had been connected with his wedding and
wooing ; all of which he had told me twenty times, and all of which I
heard with fresh delight every time he told it.

It seemed he had had a rival, (one quite formidable too) wealthy,
aristocratic, handsome and young ; a kind of competitor, apt to be
very successful, when the prize is but a poor man's daughter, with no
dowry but her surpassing beauty.

The girl's parents, though not a whit richer, had still some pretensions to social superiority over Seabrook's family, and consequently
favored the wealthy gentleman, as is too often the case, while discoun-
tenancing the poorer suitor in a proportionate degree.

But the penniless enthusiast triumphed.   A clandestine marriage
terminated the struggle, and sweet Annie Wilson became the delighted
and delightful Mrs. Henry Seabrook.

Of course her parents were unmanageable ; no attempt at reconciliation would they listen to ; and the aristocratic, but unsuccessful suitor
heard of his rival's triumph with a contemptuous curl of his white,
exquisitely chiseled lip, and a few words pregnant with menace, bitterness and scorn.

However, Seabrook paid but little attention to these things.   "You
know," he would say, "I could not quarrel with the father and mother
of Annie, and as for Vincent,"—his rival's name—"I held a secret
that kept him pretty well in check.   Despite his grandiloquent pretensions, he was but an illegitimate son, and I knew it, and he knew that
I knew it, and was modest accordingly.   Not that I would have used
my power, but he was morbidly sensitive on the point.   It was known
to but very few, and I did'nt trouble him with any parade of forbearance."   So Seabrook took his beautiful bride home to his father's, with
a heart elate with joy, and swelling with the proud consciousness of
ability to obtain fortune, through any channel, no matter how dangerous or stormy it might be.

But he had neither trade nor profession ; nothing but a good, yet
imperfect education ; and he soon discovered, that it would be neces-

sary for him to hold some direct and distinctly marked course, if he ever hoped to reach the honors and comforts of life.

To one of his temperament, and in his situation, the sea—with all its unexplored regions of adventure and indistinct visions of wealth and power—would naturally first suggest itself. Decision soon follows consideration; he determined to become a sailor. He proposed to give one voyage to the acquirement of a practical knowledge of navigation, and trusted to his education, and the energies which he felt restless in his heart, to soon place him at the top of his profession.

He opened his plan to a kind friend who had some interest among sea-faring men. It was approved, and he went out on his first voyage, under a captain, who, of all men, was best calculated to be of use to him. A man of sound, good sense, who had spent his life from a boy, upon the ocean, and had maintained, through all vicissitudes, a heart as fresh as when he first slept to the rocking of the sea.

On this first voyage, Seabrook had been fortunate and successful. He had bent his mind with untiring industry to the study of his pursuit, and on his next voyage was to go out first mate, passing over the subordinate rank. He had made some money too. His friend, and some of his friend's friends intrusted to his care a few little ventures, in the management of which he displayed great tact and ingenuity; and the profits arising therefrom were quite important. Altogether, he had been highly successful and fortunate, as I have said; and it was no wonder he looked forward to a reunion with parents and wife with an eager enthusiasm, that, even while it rejoiced me, made me sad, by forcing me to contrast with his, my own dreary and forlorn situation.

So much for his previous history. I had joined the ship abroad, and our close and sincere intimacy had been, as it were, the natural result.

It was just nightfall, as we stepped down the plank leading from our vessel to the wharf, on our way upon the long promised visit. The afternoon had been squally, with occasional showers, and the daylight, brief enough at the best, was fading before a gray, premature twilight. We turned, when we reached the shore, to glance a moment at the vessel, the tempestuous sky, and the turbid, rushing river, swollen by recent rains, and a spring tide above its ordinary level.

"It will be a wild night, Frank," said Seabrook, "and there's many a craft along the coast, at this moment, would give a good deal for morning. Well, there's a heaven above all! and we've had our own share of the tempest, Frank; and we've purchased the right to be merry for once, let the wind blow as it will. So *vaya!* there is a pleasant home, and there are happy faces waiting to welcome and receive us."

"Don't know of any one as wants to ship, messmates?" inquired, in a voice hoarse as a nor'-wester, a rough looking seaman, who had approached us while we were looking at the darkening prospect.

"I do not!" returned Seabrook, eyeing the speaker curiously, "its hardly the weather, comrade, I'm afraid, to expect any one to turn up."

"Neither it is," replied the other with a hitch of his pantaloons, and an increase of the backward inclination of his tarpaulin. "But d'ye see, we're bound out t' night—time's short, and complement a'nt full—we're bound out to-night."

"Its a venture," returned Seabrook, "these gales are long winded."

The seaman shrugged his shoulders and glanced suspiciously at the sky. He, however, ventured a suggestion that it might break when the moon rose, which would be about eleven—at any rate, that they must drop down with the tide, which would flood between twelve and one.

Seabrook inquired where his vessel lay. He pointed out between two of the ships, that lay along the wharf, to a low, rakish-looking barque near the middle of the stream, tossing and struggling, with her bows to the current and the ebbing tide, straining on her cable as if impatient to begone. The gathering darkness rendered her somewhat indistinct, but she had a taut, trim appearance, and her whole contour, with the spray dashing up round her black cutwater, was, to a sailor especially, highly suggestive of motion, loveliness, liberty and the open sea.

Seabrook looked at her for perhaps a minute with a steady, melancholy eagerness, and then passing his hand through my arm he drew me away. "Come Frank," said he, "let us be going—I don't know, sir, any one who would be likely to ship with you ; but I wish you well out of the channel, plenty of sea-room, and a lighter wind. Good night."

Two or three times, as we ascended the straight, steep street, that leads up from the river, my friend stopped to look back upon the vessel fast disappearing in the haze and gloom, and I could not help noticing with what an ineffable sadness his beautiful countenance was clouded.

"I've been thinking, Frank," said he, at length fairly stopping and facing the stream, "what a suitable craft that would be for any desperado to embark in, who held existence his worst enemy. If I were at odds with life and fortune now, as I sometimes imagine I may and shall be—for I have my fits of melancholy like other men—I would ask nothing better than to ship on board some such desperate thing as that, and dash out into the ocean under the very shadow of tempest and destruction."

"Why, Seabrook," I said, "you are unsaying your own philosophy of enjoyment in the present."

"So I am," he replied, rallying himself, "I am growing mopish when I should be merriest. Away with such fancies ! Come, Frank, they are waiting for us. Kindle your imagination with that—we are bound for happiness and home."

We moved on rapidly. The night had by this time completely fallen, and the darkness was but partially dispersed by the dingy, flaring oil lamps along the street. The wind blew in gusts, and now and then, as a stronger blast and heavier cloud than ordinary swept over the city, a few scattering drops of rain would dash into our faces, or go pattering away over the housetops. Distant thunder too, and an occasional flash of lightning with an uncomfortable chilliness in the air, conduced to heighten the effect of as dreary a night, as ever darkened on land or water.

Notwithstanding my companion's enforced gayety, it was evident he labored under mental depression. I did not wonder at this. I had often noticed with what increasing distrust, a person, instinctively as it were, approaches the scene of an expected pleasure ; as if experience, unasked, were whispering remembrances of past joys, dashed from the hand while on the way to the lips ; or as if some unsuspected monitor lurked in the human heart, whose office it is to warn men how fleeting and uncertain is all earthly happiness. I remembered this, and endeavored to engage him in conversation ; but in spite of all my efforts his replies sunk into monosyllables ; he increased his speed, and it was in complete silence that, on turning a corner, we were startled by a sudden blaze of light streaming across our way.

On examination—for we stopped simultaneously—we found that it proceeded from the front windows of a stately mansion, within which some festival seemed to be proceeding ; for occasional strains of music rippled out into the night, only indeed to be instantly scattered by the rougher waves of the storm. As Seabrook stood in the light, and looked up at the tall dwelling, the cheerful glow seemed to shine away the gloom from his face, and he turned to me with a smile.

"It is a good omen," said he pleasantly—"my father lives but a short distance further on, and in the same street. I will go into his house with a thousand times lighter heart, than if I had not passed through this cheering light." While he was speaking, the curtain on one of the windows was drawn aside, and a woman looked out into the air. I touched his arm, and he looked. The glimpse I had of her was but momentary, for she immediately withdrew ; but I could see that she was young, and beautiful, and probably happy, and her appearance gave me pleasure. Seabrook, too, seemed delighted. He caught me by the arm and drew me away. "She's as like Annie, as one star is like another ! I am impatient—let us begone."

The remaining moments of our journey were passed in silence and anxious expectation. The distance seemed but a span, the time but a minute, until we burst into a quiet room. An old man dropped his book and started up with a wild, bewildered look. A woman, also aged, with the quicker apprehension of her sex, had, with a cry, folded the wanderer to her breast, before the husband and father had time to collect his senses ; and then came a storm of tears, and sobs, and convulsive laughter, during which I stood aside unheeded, with heavy drops of joy, and sorrow, and sympathy, rolling down my face.

"And Annie, mother, where is Annie ?" exclaimed Seabrook, the moment the confusion had subsided. "I cannot be half-welcomed, I cannot believe I am here even, until I have seen *her*."

Ah God !—the descent from life into death is not briefer, than is sometimes the plunge from rapture into woe, eternal and unspeakable ! How happy, how blest a fate would it be, at some point in life, the one ecstatic moment in a long career, when the great wish of our humanity, love or ambition, is fulfilled to the utmost, to pass away from existence and be seen no more !

The mother's countenance fell.

"What!" he cried, "is it possible she can be absent on the night her wild lover returns! Is it possible!" The faces of both parents change more and more. "Mother! father!" he exclaimed in quick alarm—"O my God! can anything have happened? Is she sick? Is she—is she—"

Poor fellow! he paused, unable to pronounce the fatal word which his agitated fancy dictated.

His father dropped his eyes, full of distress and gloom, upon the floor, his fingers playing in forlorn abstraction with the massive old seals of his watch. His mother, ere he had time to calm his agitation, or make the dreaded inquiry, again threw her arms around his neck and burst into tears—alas! not this time tears of startled joy, but of bitter, bitter sorrow.

He said nothing, but after a moment unwound his mother's arms, and drew her gently to a chair; then, sinking himself into another, he silently buried his face in his hands.

How the wind moaned, as if it knew of his great grief! How, in the sudden absence of all sound within, the violence of the storm was redoubled without, and the showers might be heard coming down at a great distance, passing with a tempestuous sweep, and dying gradually away!

For some minutes he struggled—with an energy that made me tremble—with the wild agony that I well knew was tearing his very heart. His large masculine frame quivered from head to foot, in the silent but deadly conflict. But resolution, pride—everything at last gave way, and he burst into sobs so passionate and violent, that it seemed as if, with every one, his heart would burst. My heart bled for him, yet I could say nothing. The frightful and unexpected *denouement* of a scene that opened so brightly, had struck me dumb, and I stood, silent and motionless, apart from the suffering three. Indeed, I doubt if the parents noticed me, or were aware of my presence, so sudden had been the surprise, so rapid the transition from delight to grief.

At length Seabrook mastered, in some sort, his emotion—or, rather, its own violence, for the moment exhausted it—and wiping the tears from his face, with a simple dignity, more touching than any violence, said, fixing his eyes on his mother, and pausing, to steady his voice, between every word: "Poor, dear Annie! How—long—mother—is she—dead?"

An unaccountable embarrassment now mingled itself with the old man's deep dejection, and he glanced in a curious, inquiring manner towards his wife. She noticed it; the mystery was soon explained. She rose suddenly, came forward rapidly, and knelt by her son's knee.

"O my son! my son!" she cried in a voice broken and tremulous, yet with a deep, earnest solemnity of look and tone, "you have to listen to a bitter truth. Annie is not dead—would, O would to God she were! She was not worthy of you, my noble boy; she was false to you, and to her vows, my darling; from this poor home, and our quiet fireside she has fled to wealth, and fashion, and pleasure, and *shame!* Don't think of her, my child ; or think of her only as one not worth your trouble and care. Think of us ; of your old father— of your poor mother, who would die this moment, if that would save her son from the disgrace and pain an unworthy woman has brought upon him ! "

It appeared to stun him. For a moment his eye glazed over, and his cheek blanched like one that faints with pain. But he rallied a little, and raising his mother, said in a voice, low, but alarming in its singular calmness, " I can't understand you, mother—I don't rightly ; will you speak it again—plainer ? Annie false ? Annie not dead ?— did you say not dead ? "

It really seemed for a moment as if his reason were becoming unsettled ; his mother saw it, and her grief changed at once to fear and alarm. " My child ! " she cried, catching his arm, " O for God's sake don't look so, don't let it master you so much ; you will break my heart if you look so wild ! "

" No, no, mother," said Seabrook, putting her gently aside, " I am well enough ; only I don't quite understand—father will you—will you explain this a little ? "

" It's only too true," said the old man, weeping, and speaking in a voice of subdued suffering, infinitely more pathetic than the woman's stormier grief, " She was but a light o' love, after all, Harry, and not worth a man's thought. I tried—God knows how hard I tried—to make the old place comfortable, and let a little light in on our dull, gloomy ways. But she soon got tired of the old home and the old folks, and no doubt longed for lighter company ; young hearts don't easily fall into beating along with ones that are dull with age. There was no want of people to help her discontent, you may be sure. Vincent never lost sight of her, and his agents were everywhere in her way. This much I'll say for her, that her temptations were of a kind, difficult for a young unsettled heart to withstand. They met in secret, it seems, and—and, the sum of it is, she's away, to present pleasure and gratification, no doubt, but I fear to a sad end of disgrace and sorrow. We must learn to think of her as of the dead."

There was a pause The old man spoke with a dead, hopeless tone, such as rises from a crushed heart ; and when he relapsed into silence, he stood just as he had stood while speaking, never lifting his eyes from the floor, his fingers playing listlessly with the seals of his watch, and the unheeded tears flowing down his worn and chastened face.

Seabrook had heard this simple revelation of his wife's faithlessness with a face that changed, as he listened, from stupor into a strange and abstracted attention. His eyes were fixed, not as if bent on any definite object, but rather as if he were examining something invisible to all but himself. He continued so for some minutes, all the time beating with his fingers a slow, measured stroke on the table beside which he sat ; his mother, who had wept bitterly through the recital of her son's wrongs, now watching him narrowly. As he sat thus, I could see, I thought, a singular change come over his face—a dark purpose clouding it, as it were, not suddenly, but with the slow, almost imperceptible gradations by which a blue sky fades into the leaden hue of the coming storm. His features, always eminently handsome, grew stern and rigid as a stone Nemesis, and a clear, steady light sprung up in his gray eyes so intense as to dissipate, I fancied, every trace of the moisture in which they had lately been suffused.

I thought, too—so easily do we color outward circumstances with the momentary hue of the mind—that the very appearance of the room, and the indications of the weather without, sympathized with the spirit I traced on his features. The chamber seemed to grow cold and lose its cheery air of comfort—the wind had a sharper, keener, angrier cry, as it went past, and the thunder—for it still thundered—reached us with a deeper and more alarming sound.

At length Seabrook glanced at me for the first time since our entrance, and instantly started to his feet.

"Dear father and mother," said he, extending a hand to each, "I intended to introduce a friend to you to-night, but that's all over now. My wandering is not done—I must bid you farewell."

His father took the proffered hand in silence, but his mother, with a look of apprehension, sprung between him and the door, as if to prevent his egress.

"Harry! Harry!—what are you thinking of!" she exclaimed. "You must not—you *shall* not go out again to-night. O think, my dear boy, you would kill me if you did anything rash, or wrong. What is done is done—leave the rest to God."

"Mother," he replied, with a trembling kindliness in his voice, "God knows how much I would do to please you, or relieve you of any trouble or distress. But this thing is now past all reason—I must go, mother," he cried, clasping her to his breast. "Farewell! God comfort and protect you—for me, you may never see more!" She hung insensible on his breast—she had fainted. He kissed her white cheek again and again, and, turning, placed her in his father's arms. "Take her," he cried, "and O, father, forget me and be happy! But that is mockery. Well, bear your load of misery as lightly as you can. Come!" he cried to me, and opening the door he rushed blindly and precipitately from the house. The old man made no attempt to stop him, but gazed after him into the dark with those lusterless, streaming, utterly hopeless eyes, and with a last glance at the room and its afflicted inmates, I followed my friend into the street.

The storm had greatly increased in violence. Still it rained but little, and that little, coming as it did in inconstant showers, appeared to bear no proportion to the other elementary turmoil. The wind blew high, the thunder rolled louder and nearer, and the surging clouds were so heavy that the lamplight—insufficient as it was for the illumination of the street—occasionally cast a gleam on the gray, watery breast of one flying lower than the rest.

I believe, as I pressed to his side, I hazarded some words of expostulation. I do not positively recollect such to be the case, but I think so, from the fact that he suddenly stopped and turned to me.

"Comrade," said he, "you remind me of what I might otherwise have forgotten. I am going on a dangerous adventure, which, let it end how it will, cannot end well. Now I am desperate, and it does not much matter what becomes of me; but there is no reason in the world why I should drag you after me into ruin. So let us part at once, and say farewell."

"You know," said I, "that that is impossible. What is it you propose to do?"

"Call Vincent to account," he replied with a sudden burst of energetic fury. "In his own house, by his own fireside, within this present hour—by the God of Justice and of Vengeance"—and he swept his hat off, and stood bareheaded, his face turned to the sky, awful in its turbulent gloom—"I swear to visit my poor wife's wrongs and dishonor on the head of that villain, or add my death to the sum of his crimes!"

I grasped and pressed his hand, instantly overcome and swept away by the headlong torrent of his passions.

"Say no more," I cried, "come life—come death—old, true friend, I will never leave you!" "It is well—it is like you—I expected nothing else," he replied. "Listen then to what we shall do. The house where we stopped to night is his. That I should have stopped in that light—that I should have found pleasure in anything coming from under his roof! The cursed—but no matter. I did not recollect it at first, but I do now. She, that we saw at the window, is my wife; O! I might have known that the world could not hold another like her! But I was blinded by hope and delight. By the illumination and the music I judge that he holds some infernal revel with his debauched associates—for a greater libertine, than he always was, never tempted God. We will go directly there—find him wherever he is, and let fate and vengeance direct the rest."

He ceased, and we proceeded rapidly—retracing with hurried strides, both of us in gloom and sorrow, and one, at least, in desperation—the road which we had traversed not half an hour before in light-hearted expectation and joy.

As my excitement was not so intense as Seabrook's, so my resolution was scarcely so equal to the approaching crisis. Of the distance now to be traveled I had taken no note, and as we made it rapidly shorter, and minutes after minutes went by, it was, I confess, with some apprehension, that I watched for the strip of light across the pavement marking out Vincent's abode.

When at length it did appear, however, it was so gradually rising from a narrow glimmer to a broad bright glow, that I had time to partially recover my self-possession; nevertheless, when Seabrook raised the heavy knocker, I could not help drawing a deeper breath, and its loud repeated fall went stunning through my heart.

I stole a glance at him, as he stood waiting a response to his summons, but I could therefrom guess but imperfectly what his feelings were, even with my knowledge of his usually impressive features.

He had wrapped himself up, on leaving the ship, in a large dark cloak, both as a protection from the storm, and as more seemly on land than the heavy dread-naught coat, as it was called, with which he defied the weather at sea, one of which, on the present occasion, was my own less picturesque costume.

He had cast this off on entering his father's, but had recollected to snatch it up again when leaving, and now wore it muffled round his throat, and across the lower part of his face. His hat, a broad-leafed Chilian felt, was drawn down low on his brow, and shaded his eyes ; but even in the gloom I could see their brightness, and his face, when visible, appeared as rigid and almost as white as marble.

The door opened and we went in ; a gust of the cold night wind preceding us, like a dismal herald, swept along the hall and nearly extinguished the lamps in its imperious progress.

The servant held the door partly open, after we had passed him, and glanced inquiringly at our, no doubt, unexpected persons and strange attire.

"To your master, sir !" said Seabrook in answer to his look of dubious inquiry, "we wish to be shown to your master, Mr. Vincent !"

The man shut the door, but yet hesitated. "Mr. Vincent," he said, "has something of a party to-night. "Would it do to see him here ?— or in another room."

"No !" said Seabrook sharply. "Go on straight to wherever he is now."

"I really," returned the servant with increased confusion, "I really —but wait a moment and I will let Mr. Vincent know."

"Stop !" exclaimed Seabrook, detaining him forcibly by the arm. "Stand aside—we will introduce ourselves," and he pushed the man out of his way and passed on.

There was naught in my companion's manner now to indicate that he was on anything but a grave, though not uncommon duty. He paused, however, a second or two, with his hand on the handle of the door. Through the panels the sound of revelry, laughter and music, came deadened to my ear, and I thought my friend heard the sounds with a firmer compression of his lips, and a fiercer sparkle of his eye. But there was no time for observation, he flung the door wide open and we were within the room.

The blaze of an hundred wax lights of various colors and brilliancy for a moment dazzled me, and rendered my impression of the room confused ; but I was soon able to perceive that the apartment was furnished in a style of great splendor, that the statues and pictures, of which there were not a few, had been selected under a somewhat Cyprian taste, that the company was large, and the women, who were in the majority, pushed the then prevailing fashions, in themselves no way delicate, to what I thought a somewhat indecent extreme.

These things I saw at a glance ; indeed there was no time for more, for Seabrook advanced across the floor, neither looking to the right nor the left, and I kept close beside him, ready for whatever part in the scene, chance, or my friend might assign me.

He bent his steps directly toward a group which occupied the further end of the room, and as he moved on with an even, steady stride, the guests fell back in dismay from his gloomy and forbidding presence.

We were not long in discovering the object of our search. He was standing before a large mirror, a costly, and, at that time, a rare importation from France, supporting on his arm the girl whom I had seen through the window—Seabrook's beautiful but faithless wife.

Although it was only his shadow in the glass which we saw as we came up—for they were regarding themselves playfully therein—I knew him at once from my friend's description, and, truth to say, my heart beat loudly as we drew near.

He caught our images, and something of the agitation of his guests, in the mirror at the same time, and turning with quick surprise and displeasure on his haughty face, at once fastened his eyes ou Seabrook. He evidently did not know him, for there was real curiosity mingled with the displeasure of his voice, as he asked, "Who are you, sir, and what brings you here?"

Seabrook paused a moment after the question, and then lifting his hat and throwing back his mantle at the same moment, dropped both on the floor. Vincent knew him at once. With the rapidity of lightning every trace of color fled from his face—from his very lips even, and he staggered like one who had received a blow. On the part of Annie, the recognition was as instant and still more startling. With a short, shivering scream, she sprung forward, and would have fallen at Seabrook's feet, had not Vincent, despite his own dismay, interposed his arm and caught her as she sunk fainting on the floor.

Seabrook never moved, nor in any way recognized his wife, either by look or gesture, until some of the women offered to take her away; then he ordered them sternly back and she was laid insensible on a sofa.

Vincent stood for a moment in utter confusion, with writhing lips, and cheeks flushing with rage or paling with fear, evidently feeling keenly how much his manhood and dignity suffered by his silence, but as evidently undetermined whether to treat our intrusion with wrath or scorn. The appearance of the latter, however, he at last adopted, probably from its furnishing the readier screen for his real fears, and as being easier to support. "You are profoundly welcome, sir," at length he said, with an enforced smile of irony, which his white cheek and apprehensive eye sadly belied. "You have found us in some confusion—will you be pleased to let us know how we can serve you?"

"I have come," said Seabrook slowly, and regarding him with a glance of concentrated hatred and contempt—"I have come to look after an unfortunate and erring wife, and to open some account with her shameless and unprincipled seducer."

"Bless my heart!" exclaimed Vincent, as if he had just recognized him, "you astonish me! Gentlemen," he pursued, glancing round at his company, "behold the most constant of men! Ladies—look, and admire the truest-hearted of swains! Let me present you, sir—the husband, friends, of our Queen of Beauty—of my own adored, but unfortunately, at present, unconscious mistress!"

"Your friends," returned Seabrook, with a hurried glance round the room, "will no doubt consent to see your crimes in whatever light you may choose to place them; but how, sir, will you answer to me—here to demand of you why you have brought disgrace on two unoffending families, drawn from virtue into ruin a young and thoughtless wife, and injured a husband in the highest degree."

"Good Lord!" ejaculated Vincent, still maintaining, but evidently with increasing difficulty, his ironical tone and manner. "How well the gentleman talks! Ladies, it will do you good to listen to him. The runaway, the sailor, the vagabond who could not stay at home to care for his own goods, he speaks like a king! Bless me! Will it please you, sir, to delight the humblest of your servants by proceeding?"

It was soon evident, that whatever effect Seabrook proposed creating by exposing the seducer of his wife before that person's own friends, would, by the very evident character of those friends, be neutralized. My companion saw this, and merely saying—"You are a villain, Vincent—and I will teach you presently how a villain should be punished," went and stood a few moments beside his wife, who had not yet recovered from her swoon.

After looking at her a little while, he knelt by her side, and taking her hand in his, gazed long and mournfully into her face. The persons round, despite their constitutional and habitual levity, were for the moment over-awed, and Vincent vainly strove to cover his rage and shame, with his ill-fitting mask of scorn and indifference. As he continued to look, the deep-settled determination on his face seemed for a moment to waver. His lip quivered—I even thought a tear dropped from his eye—and he appeared to be fast forgetting his situation. I was fearful of this, and was about rousing his attention, when the mercurial crowd around saved me the trouble, by various whispers and titters at, what was to them, no doubt, an unusual display of feeling.

Seabrook caught the smothered intimations of mirth, and dropping his wife's hand, rose slowly to his feet.

"You must excuse me," he said, "it is hard to look on so fair a thing, wrecked and destroyed without being grieved. But I am wasting your time—Vincent, without more delay, than what going from one room to another of this brothel of yours, will make, I demand what, if you are not a coward, you will not deny—the satisfaction due to an injured husband and an insulted gentleman."

A burst of affectedly scornful laughter was the first answer to this proposition. "You are extremely modest, sir," said Vincent, when his assumed mirth had subsided. "Is there nothing else I could do to show my regard to your sailorship! But this," he pursued, changing his tone and manner to what severity he could muster, as if aware that jeering would serve him no longer—"this is lasting too long; I have listened to you from deference to the proverb that allows a losing man to scold. I have heard enough—begone, before I am compelled to have you turned forcibly into the street."

Seabrook made no answer, but walking up to him, before any one could interfere, struck him so forcibly on the face with the back of his open hand as to draw blood.

They were instantly separated. Vincent fell back, and several persons interposed. Loud words rose everywhere, and angry glances were directed to us. Over the tumult I could see the insulted and infuriated man gesticulating violently, and hear him vociferating— "Thomas—William—Stephen"—the servants crowded into the room— "Throw him out—into the street. Damnation, villains! don't you hear me?" and he extended his arm and stamped his foot upon the floor, actually foaming with rage.

Seabrook stood perfectly still, until he saw the domestics and some of the male guests gathering round him in a threatening manner. "Have patience a moment," he said ; then with a wave of his hand, "and if he does not give me the satisfaction I require I will go without a word. Vincent," he pursued, striding up to within a yard of him—and so threatening had his appearance by this time become, that not the slightest attempt was made to impede his progress—"I thought I could have insulted you into some courage, without having recourse to a somewhat unmanly threat ;—it seems, I cannot ;—if you do not at once agree to meet me, I will through all the city proclaim you a coward and a ————." He bent down and whispered the concluding word ; what it was I could not hear, I could only judge of its import from my knowledge of his preceding history taken in connection with its singular effect.

Never was change so sudden—never was word so effectual—the man stared at his assailant as if he had been changed into stone. Slowly he turned, and laying his arm upon the mantel-piece behind him, leaned his head upon it, and remained for perhaps a minute, as if busied in thought.

During the pause, the unfortunate and guilty cause of this discord had recovered from her swoon and lay sobbing in unavailing grief on the sofa ; every moan so low and pitiful, it seemed rising from a breaking heart. But no one noticed her ; the whole assembly seemed as stricken with inaction as its leader.

"Well," said Vincent at length, raising his head and speaking with a dogged sullenness, "if it must be, let it be at once. Come, Chester, I will require your services—all the rest of you may stay and be as merry as you can."

He nodded to a man dressed in the hight of fashion, who, without much concern had watched the whole proceeding, and who, now, with a ready bow and smile, came to his side. We followed them out of the room—Seabrook only pausing a second on the threshold to cast a last glance on his guilty wife ;—"God pity and forgive you, Annie," he said, "as I do from my heart," and the door closed behind us.

In the hall, Vincent beckoned to one of his servants. He gave the man a key and desired him to bring the case to the library, after which he passed his arm through his companion's, and with a slight intimation to us to follow him, moved on. We ascended a flight of stairs, traversed an entry, crossed what appeared to be a bed-chamber, and entered a large room dimly lighted, which the tall, oaken Gothic cases, with their innumerable rows of books declared to be our destination. The servant arrived with the case—which I at once conjectured contained pistols—at the same moment with us, and was again dispatched with a whispered order, of which I could catch only, "more lights."

I took occasion of the pause caused by his absence, to draw Seabrook aside—"For God's sake !" I said in a whisper, "what are you going to do? This man is probably a professed duelist, and you, I suppose, know nothing about it."

"If I really knew nothing about it," he replied in the same tone, "it would make no difference ;—I must still act exactly as I am doing. But I do—I am not so ignorant as you think. Take your cue from Vincent's companion and do as he does ; agree to all he proposes—make no demur—and leave the rest to me. We must not talk. My old friend—if anything should happen—farewell !" I wrung his hand and left him, as I saw Chester advancing as if to speak to me.

He greeted me with the most complaisant of bows, and an easy carelessness that rather irritated than conciliated me. Perhaps, indeed, he intended such to be the case. "Quite annoying, this little affair, now," said he with an air of affected sympathy. "These hot-headed fellows are, upon my life, such fools ! And about a woman, too—ridiculous ! "

"I quite sympathize and agree with my friend," said I, in the gravest tone I could command. "I suggest that we confine ourselves to our duty."

"Ah—very well !" he replied. "And I suppose reconciliation now—"

"Is out of the question," I answered.

"And your friend now is a dead shot, I dare say—eh ? "

"Mr. Chester," I began, but at that moment the servant, with candles, re-entered, and I cut short what I was about to say with, "Let us, if you please, proceed," in which he acquiesced, and we entered at once upon our arrangements. We agreed on pistols for weapons—the distance ten paces—and Chester to give the word. As I led Seabrook to his place, he asked me in a whisper if the door was open behind him—he seemed not to like turning his eyes from his adversary. I answered that it was. "Keep your eye on it, then, and see that no one closes it. Now give me my pistol, and stand aside."

The weapons had been loaded and primed under my eye, but as I returned to the table on which I had left them, Chester had both in his hands. I thought, too, as I approached, that I heard the click of the shutting of a pan. A suspicion of I know not what treachery, flashed across my mind for a moment ; but recollecting Seabrook's caution, I took, without comment, the pistol which Chester gave me, with his lowest and most insultingly obsequious bow.

There was a dizzy whirl in my brain, as I stood gazing on the two antagonists, standing in deadly opposition. It seemed all for a moment like a frightful dream. The black, gaunt book-cases, with their numberless gilded volumes, so suggestive of associations strangely different from our present business,—the candles, clustered together in two principal places, insufficient for general illumination, but shedding a strong light on the persons of the combatants,—the white busts and statues, standing round on pedestals, in niches and in obscure corners, looking pale and impalpable against the blackness of the wall—as if the dead were stealing out from the gloom to witness the unusual and terrible scene,—all this for a moment reeled and wavered before me like a vision. I was roused by the fatal words, and the report of a pistol—only one—Seabrook's had missed fire. I sprang to his side—he handed me the weapon, simply saying, "Not primed." "Scoundrel!" I cried, as I recollected Chester's behavior. But Seabrook instantly interfered. He laid his hand on my arm. "Not a word," said he—"let them re-load quick."

As he spoke I perceived that Vincent's bullet had grazed his cheek, and the blood was flowing pretty rapidly down his face. I restrained my temper with difficulty, while Chester jestingly re-loaded; but I took care this time to look to Seabrook's pistol myself. I put it into his hand—I drew aside—the interval was short this time, and there was no haze on my apprehension. The words were given slowly—one—two. I was looking at Vincent;—suddenly his face was dashed all over with blood, and with an awful yell of anguish and horror, his hand sprung up to his face, he leaped half his length into the air, and fell headlong, with a crash, on the floor. "Follow me, Frank," cried Seabrook in a loud voice, and I instantly turned to obey.

It was time. A crowd of angry faces was blocking up the door. I recognized the servants, and some of the guests, whose sinister and threatening glances suggested the worst kind of apprehensions. On this barrier Seabrook threw himself, with all his great strength, and all the energy of his nature. Felling a man here, and another there, dealing desperate, yet discriminating blows, with the heavy butt of his pistol, he clove his way through all opposition, across the room, along the entry, down the stairway, and out the front door. I kept beside him, step by step, doing my best; and the crash of breaking lamps, the extinguishment of candles, the blows, curses, and falls of men, together with the shrieks of women, made a scene more hideous than any that fancy could conceive. The last object that my eyes rested on, as I turned for a second on the threshold of the house, which we had found in gayety and left in confusion and blood, was the guilty wife, beautiful even now in her utter ruin and shame, her black hair streaming loose upon her shoulders—her eyes, face, attitude, her wildly extended arms, all making an ineffaceable picture of wild abandonment and despair. The spectacle was before me but a moment. We were swept into the street, and plunging through the darkness, the house was soon far behind.

Through all the singular adventures of this singular evening, I imagined that the progress of the storm kept even with the incidents which succeeded each other so rapidly. It now streamed and lightened, and thundered, with a violence beneath which the earth appeared to rock. It seemed raining jewels; the precipitate torrent shone with a glittering splendor that fairly dazzled the eye, in the continual and appalling glare of lightning; and at length, when we had gone perhaps two hundred yards on our way, one blaze like twenty suns, one tremendous report that stayed the very wind, at once formed the climax and termination of the tempest. The rain ceased almost immediately, though it still lightened; the thunder was no longer near—the wind resumed its course, but with a less hurried sweep, and, stunned and dizzy, we reeled upon our way. In a minute, it seemed, the distance between us and the shore was passed;—in a minute we stood by the swollen, rushing river; Seabrook, his hat and cloak gone—his hair streaming in the wind—the blood flowing down his face—gazed eagerly into the driving mist that went scudding down the stream.

"Made a short trip of it, messmates," said a hoarse voice behind. It was the seaman who had hailed us on our first coming ashore. Seabrook started. "I wanted you," he said; "Frank, come here," and he drew me and the sailor into a low drinking-house on the wharf, from which the latter had probably just emerged. "Frank," he said, when we were under cover, "here we part. Don't speak—its useless. I have one thing more to ask, which you will, I know you will, attend to. Find out my poor wife—take her to my father; tell him it is my last request that the wife of my bosom, my first and only love, should never come to want. I know you will do this—and if a man so guilty and desperate as I am, may ask a blessing for any one—may God forever bless you. Farewell!"

He wrung my hand, and I was alone in the house. I could not speak—scarcely see—but on hurrying out to the brink of the river, I heard above the dying storm the plashing of oars, and caught a glimpse of the boat that bore him away. Some three hours later, by the gray light of a waning, clouded moon, I saw the ship he had joined dropping down the stream, and I half-fancied I could trace through the gloom his mournful but noble features, yet wet with blood, looking to the city, where he had hoped to find welcome and delight, but where he had found disgrace and left disaster and violence.

My mind ran back through the spent storm, through the terrible fight, through the bitter interview with his parents, and rested with awe on his gloomy but too prophetic words—"If I were at odds with life and fortune now, I would ask nothing better than to ship on board some such desperate thing as that, and dash out into the ocean under the very shadow of tempest and destruction."

LIFE.

BY G.

ALL Nature beats with an eternal pulse
 In ev'ry altitude, in ev'ry clime,
Ages on ages roll, and still it throbs
 Strong and unwearied by the lapse of time.

Mysterious Life! antagonist of death,
 Conquered and conquering; in thy onward course
Thou dost not pause, but with man's latest breath,
 Leap'st with his spirit in resistless force.

The withered grass, the fetid sepulcher,
 The moldering carcass, and decaying tree,
Increase thy volume and extend thy power,
 In slow and solemn strides, eternally.

Almighty God, who art of Life the source,
 And from whom Life perpetually springs,
Teach us to know more fully of this force
 Which penetrates and vivifies all things,

That we may learn from e'en the lowliest plant
 Which on thy footstool rears its tiny head,
That all the glory's thine, and Life, and Death,
 But humble agents, acting in thy stead.

CALIFORNIA, IN 1852.

BY SHIRLEY.

LETTER THIRTEENTH.

RESIDENCE IN THE MINES.

FROM OUR LOG CABIN, Indian Bar, February 27, 1852.

You will find this missive, dear M., a journal, rather than a letter; for the few insignificant events, which have taken place since I last wrote to you, will require but three lines apiece for their recital. But stop; when I say insignificant, I forget one all-important misfortune, which, for our sins I suppose, has befallen us, in the sudden departure of our sable Paganini.

> Yes; Vattal Ned to the valley hath gone,
>   In a Marysville kitchen you'll find him;
> Two rusty pistols he girded on,
>   And his violin hung behind him.

His fiddle is heard no more on all the Bar, and silence reigns through the calico halls of the Humboldt. His bland smile and his dainty plats, his inimitably choice language and his pet tambourine, his woolly corkscrew and his really beautiful music, have I fear vanished forever from the mountains.

Just before he left, he found a birth-day, which belonged to himself; and was observed all the morning thereof, standing about in spots, a perfect picture of perplexity painted in burnt umber. Inquiry being made by sympathizing friends as to the cause of his distress, he answered, "that having no fresh meat, he could not prepare a dinner for the log-cabin, worthy of the occasion!"

But no circumstance can put a man of genius entirely *hors du combat*. Confine him in a dungeon, banish him to an uninhabited island, place him solitary and alone in a boundless desert, deprive him of all but life, and he will still achieve wonders. With the iron hams, the piscatory phenomena referred to in my last, and a can of really excellent oysters, Ned's birth-day dinner was a *chef d'œuvre*. He accompanied it with a present of a bottle of very good Champagne, requesting us to drink it (which we *did*, not having the fear of temperance societies, or Maine law liquor bills before our eyes,) in honor of his having dropped another year into the returnless past.

There has been a great excitement here, on account of the fancied discovery of valuable quartz mines, in the vicinity of the American Rancho, which is situated about twenty miles from this place. Half the people upon the river went out there, for the purpose of "prospecting" and "staking claims." The quartz apparently paid admirably; several companies were speedily formed, and men sent to Hamilton, the county seat, to record the various claims. F. himself went out there, and remained several days. Now, however, the whole excitement has turned out to be a complete humbug. The quicksilver which was procured at the Rancho, for the testing of the quartz, the victims declare was "salted," and they accuse the *Rancheros* of conniving at the fraud, for the purpose of making money out of those who were compelled to lodge and board with them while "prospecting." The accused affirm, that if there was any deception (which, however, is beyond the shadow of a doubt) they, also, were deceived ; and as they appear like honest men enough, I am inclined to believe them.

Just now, there is a new quartz mine excitement. A man has engaged to lead a company to the golden and crystalized spot. Probably this, also, will prove like the other, a mere yellow bubble. But even if as rich as he says, it will be of little value at present, on account of the want of suitable machinery ; that, now in use, being so expensive, and wasting so much of the precious metal, that it leaves the miner but little profit. It is thought, however, by men of judgment, that in a few years, when the proper way of working them to advantage has been discovered, the quartz mines will be more profitable than any others in California.

A few days ago, we had another specimen of illegal, but in this case, at least, extremely equitable justice. Five men left the river without paying their debts. A meeting of the miners was convened, and "Yank," who possesses an iron frame, the perseverance of a bulldog, and a constitution which never knew fatigue, was appointed, with another person, to go in search of the culprits, and bring them back to Indian Bar. He found them a few miles from this place, and returned with them in triumph and alone—his friend having been compelled to remain behind, on account of excessive fatigue. The self-constituted court, after a fair trial, obliged the five men to settle all liabilities before they again left the river.

Last week, the Frenchmen on the river celebrated the revolution of Feb. 1848. What kind of a time they had during the day I know not ; but in the evening (*apropos,* part of them reside at Missouri Bar) they formed a torchlight procession, and marched to Rich Bar, which, by the way, takes airs upon itself, and considers itself as a *Town*. They made quite a picturesque appearance as they wound up the hill, each one carrying a tiny pine tree, the top of which was encircled with a diadem of flame, beautifully lighting up the darker verdure beneath, and gleaming like a spectral crown through the moonless, misty evening. We could not help laughing at their watchwords. They ran in this wise ; "Shorge Washingtone, James K. Polk, Napoleon Bonaparte ! Liberté, Egalité, Fraternité ! Andrew Jacksone, President Filmore and Lafayette !" I give them to you, word for word, as I took them down at the time.

Since the bridges have been swept away, I have been to Rich Bar but once. It is necessary to go over the hill now, and the walk is a very wearisome one. It is much more pleasant to live on the hills, than on the Bar, and during our walk we passed two or three cosy little cabins, nestling in broad patches of sunlight, and surrounded with ample space for a promenade, which made me quite envious. Unfortunately, F.'s profession renders it desirable that he should reside where the largest number of people congregate, and then the ascent to the habitable portion of the hill is as steep as any part of that leading into Rich Bar, and it would be impossible for him to walk up and down it several times a day, a task which he would be compelled to perform if we resided there.   For that reason I make myself as happy as possible where I am.

I have been invited to dine at the best built log cabin on the river. It is situated on the hill of which I have just been writing, and is owned by five or six intelligent, hard-working, sturdy young men.   Of course, it has no floor, but it boasts a perfect marvel of a fireplace. They never pretend to split the wood for it, but merely fall a giant fir tree, strip it of its branches, and cut it into pieces the length of the aforesaid wonder.   This cabin is lighted in a manner truly ingenious. Three feet in length of a log on one side of the room is removed and glass jars inserted in its place; the space around the necks of said jars being filled in with clay.   This novel idea is really an excellent substitute for window glass.   You will, perhaps, wonder where they procure enough of the material for such a purpose.   They are brought here in enormous quantities containing brandied fruits ; for there is no possible luxury connected with drinking, which is procurable in California, that cannot be found in the mines ; and the very men, who fancy it a piece of wicked extravagance to *buy* bread, because they can save a few dimes by *making* it themselves, are often those who think nothing of spending from fifteen to twenty dollars a night in the bar-rooms. There is at this moment, a perfect Pelion upon Ossa-like pile of beautiful glass jars, porter, ale, Champagne and claret bottles lying in front of my window.   The latter are a very convenient article for the manufacture of the most enchantingly primitive lanterns.   Any one in want of a utensil of this kind has but to step to his cabin door, take up a claret or Champagne bottle, knock off the bottom, and dropping into the neck thereof, through the opening thus made, a candle, to have a most excellent lantern.   And the beauty of it is, that every time you wish to use such a thing, you can have a *new* one.

But to return to my description of the cabin.   It consists of one very large room, in the back part of which are neatly stored several hundred sacks of flour, a large quantity of potatoes, sundry kegs of butter, and plenty of hams and mackerel.   The furniture consists of substantial wooden stools, and in these I observed that our friends followed the fashion—no two of them being made alike.   Some stood proudly forth in all the grandeur of four legs, others affected the classic grace of the ancient tripod, while a few, shrank bashfully into corners on one stubbed stump.   Some round, some square, and some triangular in form ; several were so high that when enthroned upon them, the ends of my toes just touched the ground, and others were so low, that on rising I carried away a large portion of the soil upon my unfortunate skirts.   Their bunks, as they call them, were arranged in two rows along one side of the cabin, each neatly covered with a dark blue or red blanket.   A handsome oil cloth was spread upon the table, and the service consisted of tin plates, a pretty set of stone China cups and saucers, and some good knives and forks, which looked almost as bright as if they had just come from the cutlers.   For dinner, we had boiled beef and ham, broiled mackerel, potatoes, splendid new bread, made by one of the gentlemen of the house, coffee, milk, (Mr. B. has bought a cow, and now and then we get a wee-drop of milk,) and the most delicious Indian meal parched that I ever tasted. I have been very particular in describing this cabin, for it is the best built, and by far the best appointed one upon the river.

I have said nothing about candlesticks as yet, I must confess that in *them*, the spice of life is carried almost too far. One gets satiated with their wonderful variety. I will mention but too or three of these make-shifts. Bottles, *without* the bottoms knocked off, are general favorites. Many, however, exhibit an insane admiration for match boxes, which, considering that they *will* keep falling *all* the time, and leaving the entire house in darkness, and scattering spermaceti in every direction, is rather an inconvenient taste. Some fancy blocks of wood, with an ornamental balustrade of three nails, and I *have* seen praise-worthy candles making desperate efforts to stand straight in tumblers ! Many of our friends, with a beautiful and sublime faith in spermaceti and good luck, eschew everything of the kind, and you will often find their tables picturesquely covered with splashes of the former article, elegantly ornamented with little strips of black wick.

The sad forbodings mentioned in a former letter have come to pass. For some weeks, with the exceptions of two or three families, every one upon the river has been out of butter, onions and potatoes. Our kind friends upon the hill, who have a little remaining, sent me a few pounds of the former the other day. Ham, mackerel and bread, with occasionally a treat of the precious butter, has been literally our only food for a long time. The Rancheros have not driven in any beef for several weeks ; and although it is so pleasant on the Bars, the cold on the mountains still continues so intense that the trail remained impass-able to mules.

The weather here, for the past five weeks, has been like the Indian summer at home. Nearly every day I take a walk up on to the hill back of our cabin ; nobody lives there, it is so very steep. I have a cosy little seat in the fragrant bosom of some evergreen shrubs where often I remain for hours. It is almost like death to mount to my favorite spot, the path is so steep and stony, but it is new life when I arrive there, to sit in the shadow of the pines, and listen to the plain-tive wail of the wind as it surges through their musical leaves, and to gaze down upon the tented Bar lying in somber gloom,—for as yet the sun does not shine upon it,—and the foam-flaked river, and around at the awful mountain, splashed here and there with broad patches of snow, or reverently upward into the stainless blue of our unmatchable sky.

This letter is much longer than I thought it would be when I com-menced it, and I believe that I have been as minutely particular as ever you can desire. I have mentioned everything that has happened since I last wrote. O ! I was very near forgetting a present of two ring doves, (alas ! they had been shot) and a blue jay which I received yes-terday. We had them roasted for dinner last evening. The former were very beautiful, approaching in hue more nearly to a French gray, than what is generally called a dun color, with a perfect ring of ivory encircling each pretty neck. The blue jay was exactly like its namesake in the States.

Good-bye, my dear **M.**, and remember, that the *same* sky, though not quite so beautiful a portion of it, which smiles upon *me* in sunny California, bends lovingly over *you* in cold, dreary, but in spite of its harsh airs, beloved New England.

INVOCATION AT MIDNIGHT.

A LOVER TO HIS MISTRESS DURING ABSENCE.

BY EDWARD POLLOCK.

Come dearest sunlike mingle with my dreams,
Come from the East, thou fairer than the morn ;
On me thy shadowy smiles shall shine like beams
Poured down at dawn on blossoms newly born.
The sun will soon be jeweling the corn
Around thy dwelling—ere he wake the night,
Haste—haste in spirit to these arms forlorn,
Ere day divide us, meet my sleeping sight,
And thrill my heart anew with dreams of old delight.

The sea is near thee in thine East countrie,
The sea is near me on this Western shore,
O, could we both now rove by either sea,
As once we wandered—when the wild waves' roar
Was music to us ! O to be once more
Where thou hast being, and to taste the bliss,
That earliest warmed my bosom to its core;
Once more thy hand to press, thy cheek to kiss—
All powerful Love ! canst thou no marvel work like this ?

O Love ! thou wert a God in the past days,
When Earth was young and Passion in her prime ;
Immortal Love ! the poet's antique lays
Have charmed thy followers from the touch of Time;
Wake once again, and if the minstrel-chime
Of tuneful numbers please thee, hear me now,—
Responsive to the worship of my rhyme,
Give me to gaze upon that dear-loved brow—
Great are the Gods alone who list a votary's vow.

What comes ? bright Heaven, 'tis she ! Lo, on the air,
I see her misty image dawn like day ;
The wind flows under and uplifts her hair,
And as I gaze upon her, fast away
Roll these dim scenes ; I feel the cool, white spray
Sprinkle my fevered forehead,—and I stand
Beside her—doth she see me not ?—I lay
My trembling fingers on her lifted hand—
She starts not—feels not—sees nought save the sea-washed sand.

O, if I dream, then sleeping let me die !
If this be phrensy, let me mad remain !
Alas ! she fades—her form eludes my eye—
Farewell the vision—all is dark again !
Now to my lonely couch, this ceaseless pain
To drug with slumber : yet, immortal Love,
Accept the homage of my humble strain,
That, bending from the placid realms above,
Thy magic hand for me this dear delusion wove.

Once more I call thee, darling, to my dreams,—
Come from the East thou fairer than the morn;
Shed on my sleep thy shadowy smiles, as beams
Are showered at dawn on blossoms newly born;
And, ere the dews are jewels on the corn
Around thy dwelling—ere the drowsy night
Wakes, starts and flies—oh seek these arms forlorn,
Chase the sad shadows from my clouded sight,
And thrill my hushed, cold heart with dreams of old delight.

SOME HINTS ON THE MORAL INFLUENCE OF THE COMMERCIAL SPIRIT OF THE AGE.

[Delivered in Calvary Church, at the Second Anniversary of the Mercantile Library Association of San Francisco, January 25, 1855.]

BY REV. W. A. SCOTT, D. D.

MR. PRESIDENT AND DIRECTORS,
        LADIES AND GENTLEMEN:—

You are aware that the sages of the great cities and empires of the old world, in the fullness of their wisdom and the brilliancy of their imagination, could not see beyond the pillars of Hercules. They sailed across the Styx long before the compass enabled Columbus to unfurl—

> "An eastern banner o'er the western world,
>   And teach mankind where future empires lay,
>   In these fair confines of descending day." *

Columbia's early bard was more prophet than poet, in writing of empires in the future of these climes of "descending day." And "westering still," says another poet of a later day ; but I beg pardon for quoting so much poetry, I will leave that to the poet of the evening, my Hon. friend here on my left.† Well, prose or poetry, "westering still" is the star that leads

> "The new world in its train,"

and *westward* will the stream of humanity, in its best forms, continue to flow, and it may be, sometimes, with the gush of a cataract, until it shall run *eastward* and the circle be complete.

As citizens of public spirit, you desire to see the physical resources and wealth of the country developed, and for this purpose you are constantly urging the erection of railroads and telegraph lines. You are striving to facilitate emigration by having a road across the mountains, and the great plain opened and safe for the wagon and children of the hardy pioneer. These, and a thousand other appliances for bringing out the resources of the country are all right ; they are to be commended. But it is my purpose, now, to look in a brief and simple manner at the MORAL INFLUENCE OF THE COMMERCIAL SPIRIT OF OUR AGE.

The subject at once commends itself to you, both as a subject of history and of experience. It is too great, however, for me to attempt anything more than to suggest hints, and them, only, such as relate to national experience. Every one of you must feel that our commercial relations are interwoven with the very frame work of our national existence.

The history of free cities, and of the commerce of nations, is now receiving more attention than at any former period, but our language is still shamefully poor in its contributions to this subject. The history of commerce is a most interesting one, because of its great antiquity, for as soon as men learned the difference between *meum* and

* Barlow.   † Hon. F. S. Soulé.

tuum, which was doubtless very near the beginning of their existence, they began to bully, barter, swap and exchange *meum* for *tuum*, with the hope of obtaining both. The history of human migrations, which is essentially connected with the commerce of nations, is also interesting to every one that studies the progress and destiny of mankind. The migrations and traffic of nations are developments of national mind. It is as the national mind is awakened and enlightened and directed towards utility, that the schemes of commerce are apprehended ; in the mind of a nation are all the springs of its activity ; as we trace, therefore, the outgoings of commerce, we see the progress of mind. The progressive power of a nation is always in proportion to its progressiveness of mind ; the extension of a nation's commerce is, therefore, evidence of its growth, both in intelligence and in the development of its resources. We must guard against the idea, however, that our commercial greatness can be segregated from our mechanical skill or agricultural power. This cannot be done. Commerce is nothing without the products of the farm and the manufactory. Commerce and agriculture are joined together by the Creator through the mechanic ; not a single vessel can go to sea without the help of the stalwart "tiller of the ground," and the handicraft of the knight of tools. The oaks, and pines, and hemp, without which the carpenter cannot build the ship, and the products which make the ship's cargo, are all to come from the farmer's soil.

"Our commerce and agriculture, like the twins of Hippocrates, must flourish or must die together ; one cannot exist and prosper without the other. The lords of the sea will be strongest, when the lords of the soil are most honored."

In modern times no nation can be truly great without a powerfully awakened mind and opportunities for the development of its national resources ; millions of sinews, muscles, bones and heads ; thousands of bays, harbors, rivers and lakes ; millions of millions of treasure in coal and lead, and in the precious metals ; the savannas and the sierras ; the forests and all the wealth that lies undeveloped in the soil and streams of a continent, are nothing without mind to bring it out and to place it before mankind, so as to increase the influence of the nation. The produce of the soil, the products of the mills, and the wares of the shop, and the riches of the mines are *exponents* of the activity and skill of the national mind. As it was the Creator's design for man to labor, to till the earth and subdue it, and have dominion over it, so it was, doubtless, the Divine intention that men should trade one with another, and this divine beneficent intention is the MAGNA CHARTA of human progress ; and every contribution obtained from air and water, from the ocean and the clouds, from chemistry and geology, to the advancement of human science and art, is a fulfillment of the Divine mind in giving man dominion over the earth. The commerce of nations is evidently, then, agreeable to the Great Father of all ; it is one of Heaven's approved agencies for overcoming the barbarism of the savage, and for elevating the moral feelings of the civilized. It is by diffusion and reciprocation that the necessities of our race are to be supplied. The Creator has wrought into the soil of the globe a capacity to feed all its tenantry ; the overplus of one portion in any article of consumption is evidently intended for the deficiency of another portion, and the transfer of such commodities is left to the industry and intelligence of the human family.   It is thus that the Creator has given to every unit of the human family a specific part to do for the well-being of himself, and through his individual well-being to promote the well-being of the whole race.   The object of commerce is not to enable one man to live from the misfortunes of another ; not to enable one man by his wits to overreach another, and live on his brother's losses.   The legitimate object of commerce is to meet the necessities of one part of mankind, by supplying them with the over supplies of another part.   If there are wrongs perpetrated, and evils connected with the extension of commerce, they are chargeable to its abuse, and not to its legitimate fruits ; its blessings far transcend its evils ; they are as the stars of the firmament, while its evils are but fire-flies in the swamps, or fire-damps in the mines.   It is not the fault of commerce that some are left in want, and some are defrauded in trade ; this is owing to the clogs that human depravity has fastened to its wheels—" it is man's inhumanity to man," and not any of the Creator's laws, " that has made countless thousands mourn."

The laws of commerce are good.   It is only when the moral sense is blunted, that the friction of its vast machinery is dangerous.   The real basis then of the commerce of nations may be, as it has well been styled, the *mutuality of self-interest.** By this is not meant selfishness.   For the moral evil of self-interest is neutralized in a pure commerce by its mutuality, and " every man engaged in commerce, whether he knows it or not, consents to this mutuality of self-interest ;" that is, while he honestly watches over his own interests, he allows and expects his neighbor to do the same thing, and so long as honorable principles govern men's actions, the *self-interest* of trade is kept from degenerating *into selfishness.* The importance of rightly understanding this point may be illustrated by a comparison suggested by another, and which he uses on a kindred subject ; suppose, which is necessary to the very existence of commerce, that there is a common stock for human subsistence and well-being, and that this common stock is represented by a reservoir, which contains the water that is to refresh and nourish the vast population of the city, and that each individual in the city needing supplies from the reservoir is equally interested in maintaining its embankments in strength, and its waters healthful.   Now it is evident, that the well-being of the aggregate of the city's population is dependent on the faithfulness of each individual to the performance of his individual duty, in keeping up the embankments, and in watching over the purity of its waters.   Now suppose that this reservoir represents the common stock of America and of all the nations with which she trades : and again, that the United States and each nation she trades with has its own reservoir, and that each individual of each nation is intrusted with a specific duty, in reference to the keeping up of the embankments, and the preservation of the purity of the water, and you cannot fail to see how each individual in the United

* By Rev. Dr. Fisk of England. See his Lecture.

States, and in every nation we trade with, is interested in the individual honesty and skill of every farmer, artisan, banker, tradesman and sailor engaged in all these nations. And what but intelligence can keep up the embankments and keep the water pure? I am sure the history of mankind will show that those nations that are the most pure in their principles, are the greatest in their power and glory. Commercial extension is in proportion to the prevalence of Christian intelligence and integrity. And additional importance is affixed to this part of our subject when we consider that the age of barter in shells, hides, animals, stone and the such-like things, has given place to an age remarkable for a circulating medium, called money, consisting of precious metals, and that on this basis, credit has become as available as money. On this point, I will not say much, for it is in the line of my friend of the " Flush Times of Alabama." * The abuses of credit have been and may be great, but the exigencies of commerce require it. Public credit is and must be coined and stamped with the die of public approbation, in such a form as to make capital as available as the actual presence in force of the precious metals. The commerce of nations cannot now be carried on without express offices and bills of exchange; but what is commercial credit without moral worth? It is by confidence in the honesty of those engaged in banks and trade, that capital becomes as available as the precious metals themselves. But what stability can there be in such momentous transactions—transactions that stretch round the circumference of our globe, and require even with the facilities of travel that we now have, almost a year to bring a bill of exchange home, without abiding moral principles? And I am happy to say, and from some little personal experience in different quarters of the globe, that the mercantile honesty of Great Britain, the reliability of her merchants, is one of the mightiest bands of her strength. The continentals may affect to despise her as "a nation of shopkeepers," and attempt to rival her in arms and in arts, but they are compelled both to love and fear her for her commercial integrity. I am not speaking of the haughty aristocracy, nor of the government of Great Britain, nor of her huge, imperial monopolies, but of her private bankers, manufacturers and merchants. It is to their credit more than to her prowess in arms, great as it is, or to the gold in the vaults of her bank, that she owes her greatness; and the way for us to extend our commercial power, is to make our flag the herald ensign of national integrity. When heathen nations learn that the word of an American skipper is equal to an oath, and the promise of our merchantmen sacred as a covenant, then will they open their hearts and their treasures to us; we must gain their confidence by mildness, forbearance, firmness and truth, The interflexions of commercial life are so numerous and so vast, that, like the nervous system of the human body, you cannot touch one nerve without having a response from all. The individual and aggregate well-doing of all commercial nations is, therefore, the necessary basis of their individual and aggregate wellbeing. The dishonesty of the artisan in making a clock, or of the weaver in making a print, of the weigher or measurer, or of the clerk,

* J. G. Baldwin, Esq.

shipper, consignee, vendor or banker, affects the whole transaction
from the inception of the design of the fabric to its consumption, and
is reflected back in the product of the consumer by which the article in
question was purchased ; and there is as much dishonesty in the consumer, who wishes to purchase an article below its value, as there is in
a vendor who sells it for more than its worth ; and the dishonesty of
the purchaser who wishes to get an article for less than it can be
honestly afforded at, leads the artisan to make a cheap article that will
resemble the high-priced one, and to sell the inferior article as the
high-priced one, to such customers as are not familiar with the qualities and value of such things.   It is evident that the *moral spirit* of
commerce is a subject that interests, not only the CONSCIENCE and the
soul both here and hereafter, but is, also, deeply connected with the
progress and success of commerce itself ; it is not merely a moral habi-
tude that gives intensity and coloring to an existence in a state of
endless retribution, but it is necessarily interwoven with success in business, and still more with the enjoyment of the fruits of success in
business even in this life.

But how shall I draw a picture of the commercial spirit of our age ?
Whither can we fly to escape from its presence ?

The "snowy cones" and green woods of Oregon, the jungles of India,
the canals of China, the sands of Coromandel, the gulches of the Sierra,
and the mountains of Africa are witnesses of its adventures, failures
and successes.   I know not that there is a sea on which our ships do
not float, nor a wind that does not unfurl our flag, nor a haven, upon
earth, into which our merchants do not send their vessels, nor a nation
on the globe with which we do not transact business.   The goings
forth of our commerce have covered the Atlantic with our sails, and
while the Great Powers of Europe are measuring their strength for
mutual destruction, to gain an ascendancy over the little bright blue
Mediterranean sea, it is ours to make the vast Pacific an American
"lake."

The Westminster Review rather piquantly admits, that "cousin Jonathan does a vast stroke of actual work in the practical way ; preparing
the wilderness for the use of man ; transforming things unowned into
property, and European pauperism into American prosperity."   " A
very respectable, useful and valuable relative, indeed," of his English
uncle.   " Altogether modern, and with a history of only two short
chapters—Puritanism and Revolution"—we are nevertheless "a remarkable family of cousins—of singular, and perhaps, the most expand-
ing, mobile, multiplying, 'go-a-head' human creatures that ever
'exploited' this terrestrial globe.   *   *   *   Hardly more settled
than the halt of the exploring traveler, whose night's rest is hurried
and feverish with onward thoughts for to-morrow ; *our* keen faculties
and energies are all set on 'progress'—working for times that are not,
but will be—for a Future that is to 'beat all creation.'"

And even *The London Daily News* finds time amidst its pictures to
say, "To watch the spirit of American commerce is to witness some of
the finest romance of our times."   The equator and the poles, the
mountain passes and desert oases, the forest, lake and water-fall, the

sunny South and Arctic snows are as familiar to our traders and explorers as of any other nation.   In traffic ours are the pearls of the South, "with bird's of bright plumage," the gums and the sweets, and the spices and teas, even of "prussic blue" of the East, and the gold and silver and gems of the New World.   Our Salem rivals the fame of the Hanse-Towns, and of Old Venice, the bridegroom of the sea, that has been dead and hearsed many a year.   But the spirits of the Adriatic Queen have already witnessed the nuptials of the beautiful Pacific with her bridegroom of the Golden Gate.   And brilliant is the wedding, and numerous as the stars will be the offspring when Santa Claus shall come sailing in steam vessels, and riding on iron horses to pour the *bonbons* of both the East and the West into her lap on Christmas Eve.

In sober reality our merchant princes are the aristocracy of Neptune ; the lords of the sea.   Their scepter is the trident of the floods, and ocean's waves are their baronial acres.

In our harbors we see ships of the most distant nations riding safely. Pactolian streams literally flow into our lap ; and we are in a fair way to gain the lion's share of the wealth of the world.   Many of our ships carry the treasures of kings, or sufficient wealth to have founded an empire, or have created a new dynasty.   Every day witnesses something contributive to our resources and mercantile power ; when we consider the shipping connected in the outlet of the St. Lawrence, the Hudson, the Chesapeake, the Mississippi and San Francisco, and anticipate the day when our valleys and mountains, from the Northern Lakes and the Eastern Atlantic to the Pacific, shall be reticulated by railroads, and filled with prosperous villages and cities, farms and manufactories, and bound into one web of affection and reciprocal advantage, and of Christian principle, we cannot refrain from uttering the great Statesman's prayer : THAT WE MAY EVER BE ONE PEOPLE, WITH ONE CONSTITUTION AND ONE DESTINY.

What, but the urgencies of the commercial spirit could have enacted the neutrality laws now existing between us and the belligerent powers of Europe ?   The treaties now between the United States and Russia, and the other great nations, are an acknowledgment of the power of our commerce.   The magnitude of our commercial interests, I am not able to set before you in detail.   The report of the Secretary of the Treasury and of the Census Bureau are in your hands ; our tonnage and marine transactions are equal to the greatest, and superior to that of any other nation, with, perhaps, one exception.   The mightiness of our commercial interests, the magnitude and extent of our mercantile operations far surpass the expectations of our forefathers, and just in the proportion of their greatness, is there danger in them involving our interests.   But vast as are our commercial transactions, the spirit that is in them, is still *progressive and aggressive.*   You know that the great weight of a body once in motion on an inclined plane increases its velocity, and that its progress is accelerated with every revolution of the wheel.   In proportion then to the magnitude of the commerce of our nation, and the number and power of the various facilities by which it can be increased, will be the rapidity and force of the progress which it makes.   The spirit that broods over the workshop, the plough, the loom, the ledger and the bank, cry out for progress ; there is a cry for the extension of the area of trade, whether there is for the widening of "the area of freedom" or not. In every mail that brings the news that some improvement has been made in ship-building, in agriculture, in railroads, telegraphs and steamships, or that some new port is open to trade, some new mine discovered, or some invention made, by which elements and things already known can be turned to account ; in every breeze that fills the sails of the clipper, and in the lashing of the restless waves of the great ocean at our gate, there is a loud voice calling for progress, saying to us, from the nations beyond, "come over and help us"—and we are going ; we have already gone. Loo Choo and Niphon bay have saluted American keels, and the waters of Jeddo itself have fondly embraced "the Lady Pierce." And one of the necessary results of this vast increase of mercantile pursuits IS A POWERFUL AWAKENING OF THE HUMAN MIND.

Every improvement in manufacturing, or discovery in agricultural chemistry, and every new channel that is opened up for trade, is a stimulus to human activity. The whistle of the steam-car and the click of the telegraphic key have not only awakened old Rip Van Winkle from his sleep of ages, but have created in his history an era of new and terrible thinking, where there was scarcely a thought before The old order of society is disintegrating everywhere ; everywhere cracking and crumbling to pieces. The vast armies of Europe are but police forces to preserve order among those very refined and well-behaved people called kings and emperors, and their families. The current of men's thoughts is quickened ; the old tread-mill round of business is forsaken ; the circle of knowledge is enlarged. The field of vision extended, and the mind awakened to the idea, to the possibility, to the actual effort of achievement ; and the world has yet to see what the product will be on these glorious shores of the Pacific, of Anglo-Saxon blood warming and multiplying in an Asiatic climate. The poetry, the dreaming enthusiasm of the East, is here in living contact with the eternal activity and courage of the descendants of the followers of the Odin religion, converted to Christianity. Our blood through Cromwell and Luther runs up to the aspirants for Valhal. The Anglo-Saxon is here for the first time since the primeval emigrations from Asia westward, on a soil and under such stars and sunshine, and in the face of such hills and mountains and oceans, as have heretofore been identified with the developments of Oriental mind. Who can tell what will be the progeny of the blood of the heroes of Western Europe, flowing in the veins of freemen, under the mighty stimulus of Republican Institutions, and warmed by a Syrian sun, and fanned with breezes like those of the sacred mountains ? The generations to grow up here under the ministry of life and joy from the ocean air and mountain skies, and watched over by such a galaxy of stars, and playing by springs like those of Siloa and Jordan, and wandering in valleys like those of Sharon and Esdraelon, and gazing on mountains like Lebanon and Carmel, must be generations of deep and pious thinking, and high and noble daring ; and if I could say it without interrupting my thread of discourse, I would say positively, that there is no climate in Italy, or on the Mediterranean, equal to that of this State.

ANOTHER RESULT OF THE EXPANSION OF COMMERCE IS A LIBERALIZING OF OUR VIEWS.—Just in the proportion that we are well acquainted with other nations, will our prejudices and dogged notions be removed. "Every body and his wife" now travels and trades, and in the hard jostlings of the dusty thoroughfare many of the sharp corners of humanity are rubbed off. The inhabitants of those countries, as of China and Japan, that are the most closely shut up against intercourse with other countries, are the most bigoted and narrow minded, and filled with the idea of their superiority to other nations. But as "the John's," and "John Bull's" and "Jonathan's," and the F. F.'s of the "Old Dominion" travel abroad, and see the world, they become more and more tolerant and kindly disposed, and at last begin to feel that there may be, after all, some other country beside their own on the globe. As there are many beautiful objects in nature that we do not admire, because we do not see them, we are ignorant of them. So there are good and great people in all nations that we do not love, because we are not acquainted with them. Intercourse with mankind must, therefore, *liberalize* our views and remove many of our prejudices. In this point of view, the Congress of Nations at the World's Fair, where the various improvements in the modes of agriculture, methods of education, and uses of the mechanical arts were exhibited, did much good. And as the knowledge of different nations is mutually extended, so may they be bound together in bonds of mutual respect, affection and interest. Every ship that plows her way from this port to the seas of the Flowery Kingdom, is a chain that draws the two continents nearer and nearer to one another. Every new trail of the hunter over the mountains ; every new path *blazed* through the forest by the buckskinned pioneer to his log cabin on the hill side, and every sod that is turned up by the spade or the plow, and every stream that is harnessed and put to work at the mill, and every railroad and telegraph wire that is stretched across this great continent, is a band of iron binding the different races and portions thereof more firmly together.

Among the dangers growing out of, and in some measure inseperable from the amplitude of our commercial transactions, are RECKLESS SPECULATIONS. Men are now found who play with ships, land lots, and "water lots," that cannot be confined by stakes, and ingots of gold as with dice ; invoices, rents and commissions are staked at the gambling table, and even legitimate business is pursued as a game of chance. And of near a-kin to this demoralizing speculation, is the tendency of the day to bring down every thing to the level of the market. The Rule of Faith on 'change is the *Rule of Three*, and the Rule of Practice is—*will it pay ?*

ANOTHER DANGER IS THE TOTAL ABSORPTION OF THE FINEST AND BEST FEELINGS IN A COLD AND NARROW SELFISHNESS.—It is a natural law of the mind, that in proportion to the strength with which it is fixed upon any one object, it will be drawn from all other objects. There is danger then that the mind, absorbed in the magnitude and progressiveness of commerce, will be withdrawn too much from higher and noble things. The claims of God and man, of body and soul, of family and society are too often neglected through an intense application to business.

Perhaps such men think or say—this is true ; but we cannot help it ; it must be so. The vessel is to be steered over dangerous seas and threatening rocks, and under the lowering clouds that may break over it at any moment. The pilot must, therefore, ever be at the helm. This may be so sometimes. But is it not often allowed to interfere with the improvement of the mind and heart when there is no absolute necessity for it ? Is it not the making haste to be rich, that dares not look up to heaven, and dares not take time to bend the knee in fervent supplications for divine blessings, rather than the pursuits of a legiti- mate and well regulated commerce that absorbs the mind and draws it from mental and social recreations ? Would it not be a gain to your families and to society, and to business in general, if there was more reading, and more domestic enjoyment among merchants and business men ? Would it not be a great guide to healthfulness both of body and heart, if the mind were more perfectly drawn from the trammels of office, and allowed to escape to the library and the picture gallery, or to enjoy the sweetness of domestic repose ? There is great danger of mental contraction in our day. The horizon of some men's minds is so fearfully knit together at the corners by rent-rolls, per cents. and de- posits, that they live and move and have their entire being in a hogs- head, a ship, a house, or a bag of gold. Several thousand of such souls may be baled up in a single package, and leave sufficient room to breathe. So intently and strongly do they gaze upon their gains, that while they have no range without, and never lift a telescope to the glo- ries of the vast Universe, they resort to the microscope to see how fast the grains increase their "pile." Multitudes of men, who might with proper mental, moral and social discipline have grasped the world of science and the wealth of history, and "walked in the starry way of intelligence, and have gone up to the highest places of spiritual enjoyment," are groveling like worms in the dust, and in a circle of exceedingly small dimensions. They turn their meals into seasons of calculation, and their homes into counting houses. So ter- rible is the despotism of the heart once yielded to the love of money, that there are not wanting some who would blast down Mount Sinai for lime or for a railroad track, if its stock could be made to pay ten per cent. O ! there is terrible injustice and cruelty upon the father of a family, who allows his business to rob them of what is beyond the price of all merchandise—high moral culture and religious elevation. What if a man does gain wealth for his children, and go down to the grave with the approbation of his fellow citizens as a successful, honest merchant, and still leaves them without a *mental* or *moral* capacity to profit by it, and to enjoy or do good with his wealth ? The case is a painful one, but it is often seen. The absorbed father with his heart and mind filled with the objects and affairs of every day, returns late, wearied and worn, yet anxious for the morrow, and utterly unfit for the holy duties of his office as the head and priest of his household. The rest of the sabbath comes in vain. The exhaustion of the week hangs over it, so that it is not a day of recreation or improve- ment, much less a foretaste of that rest which remaineth for the people of God. The commercial spirit of our day is so incessant, so unrelaxing in its demands upon mind, time and strength, that it cuts off opportunities and even strength for the proper consideration of higher objects.   Now, fellow-citizens, it is with such views of commerce, its mighty influence and the progress of mind of which it is both a fruit and an exponent, and at the same time aware of the dangerous tendency of the absorbing, ubiquitous spirit of trade in our day, that wise and good men in this and other cities have established Mercantile Library Associations, and have sought to awaken attention to the high morals of commerce, and to diffuse intelligence and sound principles among the masses of men engaged in trade.   It is chiefly owing to the efforts of the agents, committees, lectures and publications of such institutions in Great Britain, that the hours of business have been so shortened, as to give young men employed in manufactures and counting houses opportunities for repose, for instruction and for moral and religious cultivation.   It is in the example of heads of business houses, in the anunciations of Chambers of Commerce, and in the lectures and libraries of Mercantile Associations that we see the power to awaken and spread abroad such a moral spirit as may elevate society, and make the gains of commerce contribute to national prosperity.   The purity of the conscience of our commerce is the tower of our strength.

The right reading of the brave old nations of yore, shows that as the idea of supernatural beings was lifted off from their minds, they became gross and stupid.   "As Jupiter vanished out of their sky, conscience faded in the heart."   As a sense of the presence of Divine beings and of a personal accountability hereafter for the deeds of this life became feeble, and a dull and dreary Atheistic night shut down on their vision, so their energies died out and the darkness of falsehood and of ignorance settled over them in terrible gloominess.   Kings may confederate and sow the earth with dragon blood ; but "God makes facts."   And all God's facts are revelations speaking of a glorious future for man.   Happy the day, when commerce that swings the great hammer—"the Miollnir of Thor"—shall have broken the mountains of tyranny to pieces ; and when the spirit of commerce, itself, and the toiling of the field, shop and mill, shall be baptized into the spirit of Peace, then will the iron of the mountains be beaten into railroads and ploughs, and not into muskets, shells and sabers ; and our great ships shall be the messengers of plenty and joy, and not be the floating batteries of death and wo.   Happy the day when on earth's every high place, the Janus temple of the Cross shall point its soiled, dustworn and weary millions to glory and immortality, and the din of our great cities shall be mingled with the holy music of the Gospel.

The nature of our population and our local influences, render such an Institution as this, more important to us, perhaps, than to any other city in the world.   A large proportion of our population, are young men, who have some knowledge of the world and of books,—young men of enterprise and noble daring,—who are just entering upon the active pursuits of life, far away from home influences, and often placed under strong temptations to vice.   This Association throws open to them its doors and its thousands of selected volumes.   It is intended to continue their education which was begun at home—to cultivate the mind and so elevate the heart that it will scorn vice and bear misfortunes.

In the libraries of this society, they will find friends that no adversity can alienate, and gain ornaments for society more precious than rubies. Here the *young man from home* may find solace in a weary hour, and acquire knowledge, that will dissipate prejudice, overthrow superstitious fears, chasten vice, guide, virtue, and give grace and government to genius. In building up, therefore, this useful and noble Institution, you throw around young men, at a most critical period of their lives, the example of intelligent and high, moral, business men; and you promote harmony and good feeling among citizens, and contribute to elevate the standard of public morals.

THE CHILD AND FLOWER.

BY J. P. ANTHONY.

HE was a beauteous Child! Upon his cheek
　Reigned ruddily the hue of health; his eyes
The very language of his soul did speak,
　Telling of joy which, ere contentment flies
With riper years is childhood's day's alone;
　When all is bright and fair as summer skies,
Ere murky clouds their giant forms have thrown
　Upon its azure arch, and seem to rise
Against each other in tempestuous strife,
'Midst which bright sunbeams fitfully are rife,
Like joy amidst the clouds and cares of life!

In childish sport I saw that lovely Boy,
　Amongst a throng where every heart was light,
O'er whom might Time, the mighty spoiler, fly,
　And be unnoticed in his gloomy flight:
I saw him in his gambols pluck a flower,
　And toss it in the air, and as it fell
In fragrant particles, a mimic shower,
　His voice with theirs did joyous laughter swell;
Nor did they cease their rude and boisterous mirth
Until the lovely flower, which gave it birth,
In fragments lay all trampled on the earth.

Again I saw that Boy,—he was alone,
　And in his hand a flowret's stem he held,
Gazing upon it as though spell had thrown
　Thereon its magic;—his bosom swelled,
And he was weeping tears of bitter grief;
　For one who loved him well had said, to chide,
'Twas crime to injure ay a single leaf;
　That He who made that flower, and dyed
Its leaves with beauteous hues, did from on high,
Watch all his works with an all-seeing Eye,
To punish him who dared those works destroy.

I saw him once again, when months had passed—
　A little sufferer on his bed he lay;
For fell disease upon his frame was cast,
　Slowly to bear the vital spark away:
Ah! he was dying, and in dying pressed
　To his pale lips a flow'ret's shriveled stem,
Which he had prized for long, and in his breast
　Had constant treasured it as a sacred gem!
Yes, from the moment he in illness lay,
That stem had with him been, by night and day,
And kissing it his spirit passed away!

CHINESE LETTERS.

TRANSLATED BY QUELP.

An eminent writer has observed, that foreigners may be regarded as a sort of cotemporaneous posterity, whose calm and impartial views on the moral and physical condition of a people, if given and received in the proper spirit, may sensibly augment their happiness and prosperity. The justness of this observation is obvious enough to a thoughtful mind, and must seem plausible to those bigots even, who claim that those only who live under peculiar institutions, can appreciate their working. If this be granted, it follows as a fair sequence, that the more intelligent the stranger, and the more diverse his habits and modes of life, the more interesting and instructive will be his observations.

With so much of preface, I will introduce to your notice a Chinese gentleman of my acquaintance, of the name of Luchong. He has resided in San Francisco many years, in the pursuit of commercial operations, but concealing behind his knavish occupation an intellect and soul of the finest texture. Although born in the heart of China, and warmly cherishing the religious and political institutions of his native land, he knows no pride of birth, and claims no respect for the high social position which his forefathers have earned for him. He has taught himself to look with the calm and philosophic eye of a cosmopolitan upon all classes and conditions of men, and has steeled his heart against the vagaries of fortune and the corroding accidents of an adventurous life. It is to his zealous friendship I owe the little knowledge I possess of the Chinese letter, whilst his superior strength of mind and enlarged experience have many a time given an impulse to my energies, when exhausted by ill fortune, and my heart, when pierced by domestic affliction. Though I be despised for it by my countrymen, I respect and love Luchong quite as much as any of my own people.

But to proceed. A short time ago, Luchong received a letter from an old and highly esteemed friend of his, the distinguished Whang-hi, a mandarin of Pekin and a lineal shoot of the chief disciple of the great Confucius. Whang-hi is regarded in the Oriental schools as the most eminent living sage within the walls of China. He was told by some emigrants, who had returned to Pekin with their pouches filled with gold dust, that Luchong, though he sought after wisdom more than after wealth, had obtained great success in the distant land of Ophir, and had taken up a permanent abode there. Whereupon Whang-hi, ever thirsting to extend his knowledge of human affairs, even by so trifling an addition to his stock as the barbarians of California could furnish, wrote to Luchong, and begged him to send every species of information that would serve to paint the manners and customs of the curious people among whom he was living. The kindly nature of Luchong, that knows not how to deny a request of friendship, easily consented. He also added to the many favors already shown me, by consenting to my urgent request for copies of his replies to turn into my own language for the benefit of my countrymen. A sense of justice to my friend, however, urges me to admit, that my powers are utterly insufficient to portray the glowing and picturesque style in which his thoughts are set. The Chinese tongue abounds with quaint allegory and sumptuous metaphor ; and is at times above the reach of our vernacular. I have, therefore, made no effort to reflect the gorgeousness of his style, but, esteeming the jewel above the casket, have studiously searched for the idea, and when a conversion of language did not render it to suit me, I have taken the liberty to paraphrase. Luchong arrived in the country in the latter part of 1850. The first letter of the series was written in the fall of 1853, and was followed by others, at intervals of about three months, from that period up to the present.

LUCHONG'S LETTER.

My Beloved Cousin, Whang-hi, guiding Star and delight of my Soul :

Your book, bathed in the perfume of the precious waters of Do-di, was placed in my hands by your worthy slave, Moon-Cheek, who warmed my heart by the eager account he gave me of your health and happiness. I wish I could believe your words were not the expression of your feelings, when you say I have it in my power to make so valuable a contribution to the literary wealth of my country. O! Whang-hi, my friend, most gladly do I respond to your flattering appeal, while yet my breast misgives me that your expectations will be sadly disappointed.

I propose then to give you merely the incidents of my checkered career while in this land of strangers, passing over the many curious places and people I have met with, from the time I tore me from the loving hearts at Pekin, until I trod upon the fabled sands of California. As my eye caught the first glimmer of the surging gate, every sense was strained to catch the golden hues, with which imagination had invested this famous entrance. Nought gratified my gaze, however, but the stone-clad giants, crowned with fogs, which guard the mouth of the harbor; and these were piled up mountain high, until their tops were lost amid the fleecy clouds. I looked then for the turrets and fortifications, which should guard the industry and wealth of so ambitious a people. But no frowning battlements and masonry and metal were there to check the daring, and punish the presumption of hostile nations; and I reflected, that I was now crossing the threshold of a country possessed of buoyant hopes and peaceful views; whose people claim that their hearts are a sufficient shield, as well from domestic treason, as from the jealous invasions of foreign foes. I thus felt the necessity of casting aside the educational prejudices of my youth, and of observing every novelty with a mind freed from the fetters of custom and past association. You can judge, my friend, how well I have succeeded in doing so.

As we rounded the point of Telegraph Hill to gain our anchorage, a most beautiful and imposing landscape opened upon our view ;—the limpid waters of the bay, extending as far as the eye could reach, were studded here and there with rock-bound islands, while to the left lay a long stretch of verdant plain, and to the right what seemed a vast bee-hive of a city, and all around, in the distance, huge rolling hills, softening away against the blue horizon. In the quiet of the morning, with the rising sun shedding light and life upon the scene, it is an enchanting picture, and, once seen, too impressive ever to be forgotten. We dropped anchor about a stone's throw from one of the wharves that line the water front of the city, and the great emporium of Western America lay spread out before me. The anchor chain had hardly ceased to vibrate, when our vessel was surrounded by a fleet of pirate boatmen, who sprang upon the deck, and seized at random the property of the passengers on board. A number of packages belonging to me were clutched up, as I turned about to appeal to the officers of the ship for protection; but they told me, with great alarm, it was as as much as their lives were worth to interfere with these men. I then strove by signs to make them understand I would not permit them to rob me of my goods;

when, on a sudden, I was gathered up from behind by one of these marine monsters, and hurled into a little dingey, that had scarce strength to survive the shock of my fall. A severe contusion on the head caused a dizzy faintness to seize upon my senses, and I lay insensible until my captor scooped up a dipper full of water and dashed it in my face. This application restored me to myself, and, as I opened my eyes, there sat before me a huge, brawny fellow with a face almost completely disguised with hair. The ferocious manner in which he gazed upon me, increased the agitation of my nerves, already quite feeble from the injuries I had received, and in a fit of trembling I cast myself upon my knees and supplicated for my life. I implored him by signs, aided by the little broken English I had picked up on the voyage, to strip me of my little all, and make a servant or a slave of me, but adjured him to have mercy on me and to spare my life. He made no reply to my petition, but tugged on his oars, making up in action what he lacked in words; and in the twinkling of a star the little shell quivered against the wharf pile. Fearful of my fate, I remained in the attitude in which I had thrown myself, until he spurned me with his foot and motioned me ashore, when I rose up, and stood upon the wharf. As I did so, my persecutor seized me by the hair of my head, and by a significant gesture made me understand that he wanted my purse. Eager to escape from him on any terms, I tore my doublet open, and strove to remove from about my waist the girdle, which contained all the money I had brought with me from China. He saw my struggles, but supposed (as I afterwards ascertained) that I was searching for a concealed weapon, according to the custom of the country, so he stripped me of my silk jacket, and ejaculating the single word—*get*—showered his foot on my person with such warmth as to make me writhe with pain. After tying me by the hair to one of the wharf posts, he spit upon me, and with a dreadful imprecation on his lips, descended into his skiff and pulled away.

Thus, O! illustrious Whang-hi, did I stand, a lonely and friendless wanderer, outraged in body and in mind in the bleak atmosphere of San Francisco. Thus, was I heralded into a country, that, with such liberal inducements invites the stranger, and so earnestly pledges him her protection and her hospitality. * * * * It was upon the deserted end of Long Wharf where first I landed, and never shall I forget the time, place and other circumstances of that fearful adventure; or the sensations which flitted through my half-crazed mind at that time. The loving and tender memories that were twined about my heart, reproached me that, for this, I had madly torn asunder the chords of affection and the ties of home. I took a small blade from my pouch and cut the braids of my hair, until I had freed myself, when exhaustion made me sit down on the parapet of the wharf, and hiding my face beneath my arms, I gave the reins to my fevered fancy. Though philosophy had taught me to submit without a murmur to the strokes of fortune, this rugged welcome to America's boasted shores overcame my fortitude, and I dwelt long and bitterly on the hollow and false pretences blazoned forth by her people.

After a while, cooler thoughts came to my relief; and I reflected on the unfairness of passing judgment on a great nation, at the instance of highly wrought feelings, and the evidence of a few amphibious plunderers, who were not worthy of the name of Tartars. These reflections calmed my feelings, and gave me back my self-possession; and getting up I wandered slowly along, gazing with a delighted surprise at the grotesque collection of sights that greeted me on all sides.

The costumes of the people, in particular, afforded me much mirthful entertainment. The hats of the men are shaped exactly as the flower pots in the botanical hongs of Chee-long; only they are worn inverted: while those of the women cannot be approached by any description. They are the most unique adornments for the head, so far as my observations have extended, that female taste has yet adopted in any part of the world that affects to be civilized. My memory is at a stand for a complete comparison; though they resemble in shape and general appearance the scalloped shells that abound along the shore of Whampoa. In no single particular do they answer the objects for which hats were originally worn; as they neither furnish protection from the rays of a noonday sun, nor from the rigors of a northern winter, while at the same time they give a disagreeable effect to the appearance of the face. The other parts of the costume of either sex, also, afford an illustration of the lengths to which a foppish fashion will go, when directed by the caprices of the wealthy, and not, as in China, by the sober decrees of a wise government.

My attention was so absorbed by the new and striking objects that surrounded me, that I wandered along, regardless of my course, until I found myself clambering up a rocky eminence at the foot of Telegraph Hill. Before I had attained the summit I was overcome by fatigue, and casting myself upon the ground, I took a survey of the straggling city, which lay spread out, like a map, at my feet. The natural surface of San Francisco is undulating, and if possessed by the Chinese could have been made as beautiful as Ning-po or any city in the Imperial domain. From what I have seen and learned from other sources, however, I gather that profit is the great ruling spirit of the American mind. The grandeur and sublimity of Nature, with all the graces of art and design, have to bow down to, and obey the stern decrees of this iron-handed monarch. The people seem to have little or no taste for the natural beauties of the country, but, on the other hand, have been, for the past year or two, expending vast sums in removing picturesque hights, which might be fashioned into terraces and elegant plateaus. The whole site will soon be reduced to the flatness of a Tartarian plain, and before the lapse of many years, when this emporium of the West shall have been despoiled of all her charms, a people yet to come, will rise up and curse the Vandalism of the present occupants.

A sense of grateful pride throbbed within me, as I reflected on the great superiority of my countrymen in all that pertains to elegance and refinement of taste. The Chinese beautify and embellish nature by art, which latter they deem but the handmaiden to arrange the drapery in such a way, that the symmetry and elegance of the former may be the better perceived. They think whatever the hand of God has made, or his finger has painted, to be far more grand and beautiful than the highest achievements of the children of this world; and in their view the artistic is worthy of praise, only according to the measure of its faithful resemblance to the natural. On the other hand, these people think there is nothing that cannot be improved upon. They would gild the rays of the sun. Their vanity or ignorance, or both, is apparent in all their outward appearings. In their dress, nature is distorted, until by lacing up and padding out, a once comely form is shorn of its loveliness, and made to appear ungraceful and disproportioned in its parts. In their social customs, stiffness and constraint are the chief elements of their etiquette, as well as in their religion. Whether in physics or in morals, with them everything is veneered. The beautiful simplicity of nature is either entirely banished, or it is so disguised by art and affectation that it might as well be. They seem to be utterly lacking in natural appreciative taste; while at the same time they presume to think themselves in advance of every other people in all matters of this kind. It is true, their schools teach a species of intellectual discernment, which is honored by the same name, but they are, of course, as different in their character, as the sources from which they respectively draw their illustrations, art and nature. I will dwell upon this subject more fully as I treat in order upon their social and political peculiarities.

Awaking from the revery into which these thoughts had led me, again I looked about until my head grew weak and giddy at the new and gaudy scenes around me. The eye sought in vain for a solitary object of grandeur or antiquity on which to rest. Not a glimpse of any thing that varied, in any important particular, from the dull monotony that lined the view in every direction. More than to compensate, however, for the absence of all striking or prominent features in the landscape, the heart was gladdened to view the amazing evidences of the energy and wealth of this infant Hercules among cities; clusters of masts, surmounted by the colors of every nation that trades upon the waters, snake-like wharves that extended their broad folds into the very bosom of the bay, huge cormorant warehouses stuffed with the products of every section of the globe, long streets of ornamented brick buildings, and a forest of wood in the shape of houses, ranging from one to three stories in hight, thickly studding the picture, as far as the eye could reach. The judgment staggered at the contemplation of such a fairy-like reality as San Francisco presented. The fabled lore, that inflamed and glowed upon our youthful imagination became disenchanted, and shrunk into insipidity before the stupendous creation of the wand of the Golden Wizard of California.

But shall the physical axiom apply here, as to all else in the material world, that rapid growth is followed by speedy decay? Will the gradual disappearance of gold sap this prosperity, unexampled in the annals of events, and the turn of a century, perhaps, find the memory of these things embalmed among the traditions of the past? California alone can solve the interesting problem. I am told by travelers through other sections of the country, that San Francisco is a fair specimen of most American cities. They all have a new, showy, unsubstantial appearance, and are full of animation and bustle all the time. The reason is obvious enough. These people have no national genealogy; their history is spanned within four-score years, and their ancestry is tinged with the blood of every nationality of Europe. There is little in the past for them to recur to, and their hearts and hopes are thus dependent on the present and the future. Having thus no origin to be proud of, few national achievements to commemorate, and few obelisks to raise to the memory of any great warriors or statesmen, they have little veneration of character, and would raze from the ground the last monument of their country's greatness, would defile the ashes of their heroic dead, did they wish to erect a granary, or build a public road.

In the midst of these reflections I was-startled by the approach of a very distinguished looking personage, who stepped up and regarded me with deep but respectful interest. Upon his left breast shone a silver decoration in the form of a star, his apparel being of the most elegant and costly texture, and he wore the air of a high imperial mandarin. I instinctively plucked the covering from my head and greeted him with a profound obeisance, when he politely touched me on the arm, and beckoned me to follow. I jogged along by his side, flushed with pride and pleasure at what I esteemed the civilities of one of the high dignitaries of the country, until we approached a rather fine looking and substantial edifice of brick. A crowd of noisy idlers were standing about the doorway, who dropped their voices as we came up, and gazed curiously upon me as I passed through the entrance. After threading a short hall-way my conductor opened a door, and led me into the presence of about a dozen similarly dressed personages, all of whom where equally distinguished by the stellar badge. With the politeness of a Chinese gentleman, I sought to perform the Kotoo of respect, and was in the act of going through the first prostration, when I was visited by a salute upon my person that deranged my equilibrium, and cast me sprawling and breathless upon the floor. Indignant at my discomfiture, and the yell of coarse laughter that accompanied it, I arose and found myself, not the guest of an assemblage of the great of the land, but, O! can you believe me, Whang-hi, my friend, a prisoner of the police. The horror of my feelings, as the shocking fact was revealed to me by the police interpreter, passes the power of language to describe. I was arrested on suspicion of being an accomplice in a robbery that had taken place the night previous, on the hill near where I was found. O! dreadful thought, to be stained by so foul a charge at the very outset of my career in a strange land. I protested in the most earnest and solemn manner against the outrage that had been done me, assured them I had just arrived in the country that morning, and again and again offered to prove my story true, if they would permit me to accompany an officer to the ship that had brought me here. My appeal, however, fell upon stony hearts and disbelieving ears, and before I had time to speculate on my fate, I was seized by the nape of the neck, hurried down a dark staircase and thrown like a sack into a dirty, dingy little cell. I now gave myself up as a lost man, and muttered a prayer to Buddha to grant me strength and courage to comfort myself as became a Chinaman and a true believer. A few pious thoughts soon calmed the beating of my heart, and gave me fortitude to face manfully, whatever doom my destiny had in store for me. I then turned to my household gods, and besought them to guard with a tender solicitude the devoted beings who were wafting blessings to me, myriads of miles away.

O! illustrious friend, it is only when the body is racked by pain, or the head bowed down by grief in the wilderness of life, that man can realize the full value of the priceless gifts of friendship and of love. May it never be your fate to experience this truth. I lay down upon the floor of my cell, and enjoyed a peaceful sleep, which closed my first day's adventures in California.

THE TWO SERENADES.

ANONYMOUS.

FIRST.

Diana on her queenly throne sits in the azure sky,
The lulling evening wind has breathed its latest gentle sigh,
And all along the turret hights, and o'er the city spires,
The diamond dew is glittering, like sparks from altar fires.

O, night! so beautiful, so still, who givest sweet release
From toil and anguish of the earth, thou messenger of peace!
We praise thy solemn majesty, and step with gentle tread
To couches where soft pillows wait to woo our weary head.

Now, sleep hath come and waived his wand on every mortal eye;
The gay forget their sunny joys, the sad have ceased to sigh;
The rich man dreams of woeful want—the poor, of hoarded wealth,
The prisoner, of his liberty,—the sick, of rosy health.

But listen! music's softest notes! are they from earth or heaven?
Ah, yes! I wake and comprehend; the serenade is given.
O, gentle strains! the thoughts ye strike from out this drowsy brain,
Are mixed with memories of friends I ne'er shall see again.

Aha! yon lattice moves! and by the dim moon's misty ray
I half discern the graceful form of one who hears the lay;
I solve the mystery at once; the wand, which sleep hath waved,
Finds Cupid's shaft hath parried it, and all its power braved.

SECOND.

Again the moon is on her throne, the dew upon the flower;—
Each leaf is now a diamond in greenwood and in bower;
I pause upon the lonely shore, where shells and sea-sands lie,
And music creeps among the rocks, where sleeping mermaids sigh.

The wind is out upon the night, and deeper, louder notes
Are swelling in their harmony from many brazen throats;
I see grand forms, with snowy plumes, all marching to and fro;
I'm deafened with their thunder songs, as o'er the sea they go.

Great ships are laid in ocean's bed, their crews shall sail no more;
And fragments of a thousand wrecks are strewn along the shore;
The mountain waves but laugh at this, and merry, merry still,
They shout and dance, and all the more their brazen trumpets fill.

A mermaid takes me by the hand, and, pointing up to Mars,
She says, " King Neptune and his Court do serenade the stars;
And truly now methinks I see each lattice of the skies
Half-open, and, O Angel forms, with beautiful bright eyes!

In solemn awe I bow me down, and hide my face in fear.
O, Nature, Nature worships God, and Angels come to hear!
Poor, puny man,—thy arm so weak, thy trembling heart so frail,
Think not without that worship too, thy fragile bark to sail.

If ocean from his couch arise to sing his midnight praise,
And tune his vesper organ notes to worship's holy lays,—
If moon and stars look out and smile from windows in the sky,
Shall man not love and worship God, who sees with sleepless eye?

SCIENTIFIC.

METEORS AND METEORIC SHOWERS.

The following extracts were taken from *The S. F. Herald*, of Nov. 7th, 15th and 23d to which they were communicated by Mr. Alex. S. Taylor, of Monterey:

METEORIC SHOWERS.—On the night between the 12th and 13th of November, 1833, occurred the most wonderful of meteors or aerolites recorded in history. It was seen over the whole Atlantic and Gulf coast of the United States, and its phenomena minutely described by Professor Olmstead, of New Haven, in a memoir which has made his name celebrated among philosophers. These meteoric showers have been historically noticed as falling more or less in the months of October (latter part,) and during all November, ever since A. D. 902—nearly one thousand years ago. The great celestial fireworks of 1833 are said to return, and enter within the influence of the earth's attraction, every twenty-one years—which will be on Sunday night next, 12th instant. All persons who are on marine or terrestrial look-outs on that night, or possibly the 13th and 14th, are likely to have a rare opportunity of sight seeing.

METEORS AT MONTEREY.—Meteors or aerolites were seen at this place, (Monterey,) on the evening of Thursday, the 9th instant, between the hours of 6 and 8.30 P. M.—the night very clear. It is likely that on the nights between the 12th and 23d of this month, large numbers of them will be seen. The old Californians say that the Meteoric Showers of November, 1833, '34, '35, were seen in this country, and were extremely brilliant, particularly that of the 12th of November, 1833, which Olmstead describes so fully. From the clearness of the atmosphere in California, when unaccompanied by fogs, it is likely these phenomena will be found more brilliant here than on the Atlantic shores. The Placer people, from the elevation of the country and the rarity of the air, ought to have a better view of them than on the coast. Your readers will get an excellent idea of these celestial bodies by referring to Alexander Humboldt's "Cosmos," vol. 1, pp. 98, 125, which can be seen at the Mercantile Association Library.

A large meteor of great brilliancy was seen at Monterey on the night of the 15th inst., at 10 o'clock. The light was so strong that it cast a shadow like a young moon. It fell from a point nearly due south, and slightly declined to the west.

In addition to the references made by Mr. Taylor, the attention of those readers, who are curious in this matter, is called to p. 57, and pp. 204 to 226, "Cosmos," vol. 4, and "Dick's Celestial Scenery," pp. 141 to 149. With the exception of the above notices of meteoric phenomena in California, none, to the writer's knowledge, have been published; from which it is fair to conclude, either that the meteoric shower did not occur as was predicted, or that the soporific influence of our climate fell so heavily upon our savans, as to prevent their making those necessary observations which would have enabled them to report. This is much to be regretted, for, as Mr. Taylor says, there is no doubt that the climate of California offers peculiar and superior advantages for their proper observation.

The periodicity of the occurrence of these showers is not generally conceded by philosophers. Dick says that they have occurred, and may occur at all times, and in all places on the earth, but he makes no distinction between sporadic and periodic showers.

Humboldt does, and shows that while the former may occur continually, the results of his observations and those of his friend, Herr Julius Schmidt, of the observatory of Bonn, would lead to the conclusion that the latter were more frequent and brilliant in the months of July, August, November and December, or during the latter months of the year; but by a comparison of the accounts of those which had been observed at different times, it is difficult to fix upon definite periods for their appearance. The mean number of *sporadic* shooting stars had been found to be from four to five in the hour, and of periodic of 13 to 15. It has been remarked, that the frequency of meteors increased with the length of time from midnight, and that the greatest number fell between the hours of two and five in the morning. Humboldt also says, "Cosmos," page 219, vol. 4, "Meteoric stones fall the most rarely in a quite clear sky, without the previous formation of a black meteor cloud, without any visible phenomena of light, but with a terrible crackling, as upon the 6th of September, 1843, near Klein Wenden, not far from Mülhausen: or they fall, and this more frequently, shot out of a suddenly formed dark cloud, accompanied by phenomena of sound, though without light: finally, and, indeed, the most frequently, the falls of meteoric stones present themselves in close connection with brilliant fire-balls."

With regard to the character and composition of solid masses that fall from the air, he says, "All aerolites, wherever found, have a certain physiognomic resemblance; still upon closer investigation they present great differences. Many contain 96-100ths of iron, others scarcely 2-100ths, (Siena); nearly all have a thin, black brilliant, and at the same time, veined coating; in one (Chantonnay) this crust was entirely wanting. The specific gravity of some meteoric stones amounts to as much as 4.28, while the carbonaceous stone of Olais, consisting of crumbling lamellæ, showed a specific gravity of only 1·94. Some (Juvenus) have a doleritic structure, in which crystallized olivin, angite and anorthile are to be recognized separately; others the masses of Pallas, afford merely iron, containing nickel and olivin, and others, again, are aggregates of hornblende and albite, (Chateau Renard), or of hornblende and labrador, (Blansko and Chantonnag). Of the simple substances hitherto detected in meteoric stones, there are eighteen —orygen, sulphur, phosphorous, carbon, silicium, aluminum, magnesium, calcium, potassium, sodium, iron, nickel, cobalt, chromium, manganesium, copper, tin and titanium. The proximate constituents are (*a*) *Metallic:* nickel iron, a combination of phsphorus with iron and nickel, sulphuret of iron and magnetic pyrites; (*b*) *Oxydized:* magnetic iron ore and chrome iron ore; (*c*) *Silicates:* olivin, anorthile, labrador and augite."

These meteoric masses have long excited the wonder of philosophers, and many and ingenious are the theories which have been promulgated to account for their origin and formation. Some held that they were generated in the upper regions of the air, where for a time they performed certain orbits round our globe, till from some unknown causes, their courses being disturbed, or their centers of gravity lost, they fell, and finally struck our earth; others thought that they were projected from volcanos; but the fact that they were found at too great a distance from their birth-place, rendered this opinion untenable. La Place, with many distinguished astronomers of his day, believed that they were cast from the moon; but as it was necessary to prove first that volcanos existed there, and if they did, that they had sufficient force to project those large masses beyond the power of her own attraction, this theory had few supporters, and La Place, himself, finally abandoned it. On the supposition that the bursting of a large planet was the origin of the small planets, Vesta, Juno, Ceres and Pallas, Sir David Brewster broached the following opinion: "When the cohesion of the planet was overcome by the action of the explosive force, a number of little fragments, detached along with the greater masses, would on account of their smallness be projected with very great velocity; and being thrown beyond the attraction of the greater fragments, might fall towards the earth, when Mars happened to be in the remote part of his orbit. When the portions which are thus detached arrive within the sphere of the earth's attraction, they may revolve round that body at different distances, and may fall upon its surface, in consequence of a diminution of their centrifugal force; or being struck by the electric fluid, they may be precipitated upon the earth and exhibit all those phenomena which usually accompany the descent of meteoric stones." An hypothesis, which, if not entirely satisfactory, is, perhaps, the most plausible that has yet been advanced.

In the pages to which the reader has been referred, he will find many accounts of meteoric phenomena occurring at different periods and places, whose interest is unsurpassed by those of the most thrilling incident ever woven into a table of romance. The compiler regrets that the narrow limits to which he is confined prevented him from transcribing a few of the most striking. The following, however, is one which will not be found there. It was published in the Connecticut Journal of December 24th, 1807. The meteoric mass which it describes, was seen by the writer of this article many years ago in the Trumbull Gallery, at Yale College, where it was deposited soon after it fell.

REMARKABLE PHENOMENON.—On Monday, the 14th instant, at about the break of day or a little after, the weather being moderate, calm, and the atmosphere somewhat cloudy and foggy, a *meteor* or *fire-ball* passing from a northern point disploded over the western part of this State with a tremenduous report. At the same time several pieces of stony substance fell to the earth in Fairfield County. One mass was driven against a rock and dashed in small pieces, a peck of which remained on the spot. About three miles distant, in the town of Weston, another large piece fell upon the earth, of which a mass of about thirty pounds weight remains entire, and was exhibited the same day at town meeting. A small mass has been sent to Yale College and examined by a number of gentlemen. It was immediately perceived by Professor Silliman to contain a metal, and on presenting it to a magnet, a powerful attraction proved it to be iron. This is, we believe, the first instance in the United States in which the substance of this species of meteor has been found on the earth, though it has often been found in Europe. Fortunately, the facts respecting this wonderful phenomenon are capable of being ascertained and verified by precision, and an investigation will, we understand, be commenced for the purpose. We request gentlemen, who may have observed it in distant parts of the State, to favor the public with their observations. It is desirable to ascertain the course or direction of the meteor, the point of compass in which it appeared at different places, the general appearance and velocity, the manner of its explosion, and the time between the explosion and the report.

MONTHLY SUMMARY OF EVENTS.

—

"With news the time's in labor and brings forth
Each minute some."

—

December 29. Statements in the *Herald* showed the total number of passengers arrived during the past year to have been 47,730, and of those departed, 24,477—a net gain of only 23,253, of which a large proportion consists of Chinese. . . . The Revenue Cutter Polk was sold at public auction by Messrs. Smiley, Yerkes & Co. for $3,500, cash. Daniel Gibb, Esq., was the purchaser. . . . John Welch, "Scottie," and others of the escaped convicts, were recaptured by the police. . . . The opinion of Judge Heydenfeldt, dissenting from that of his associates, regarding the location of the capital of the State, was published in the papers.

December 30. Judge Satterlee denied the application of a Chinaman to be admitted to citizenship, on the ground that he did not belong to the Caucasian race. . . . Officers Hampton, North and J. Nugent returned from a pursuit of the escaped convicts. They proceeded as far as San Pueblo Bay, but though they overtook a party with Bill Powers at their head, the latter succeeded in effecting their escape at that point in a sloop.

December 31. By a statement in the *Herald*, the number of brick buildings in the city at this date is 638, whose value is $18,618,750. . . . The steamship Sonora, on her downward trip, was robbed of $27,000. The carpenter and boatswain were arrested on suspicion.

January 1. A statement in the *Herald* showed the total amount of duties collected at the Custom House from the 1st of January to 29th December, 1854, was $1,461,160 31; for 1853, $2,652,208 59, a falling off of $1,191,648 28. . . . "Jimmy from Town," one of the escaped convicts arrived in the Goliah and was recommitted to prison. . . . The Legislature commenced its session. . . . A terrible storm visited the city which did a great deal of damage in many quarters.

January 2. A statement in the *Herald* showed the total number of cases disposed of by the U. S. Land Commission, during the year 1854, was 330, of which 224 were confirmed and 106 rejected; the total number of acres confirmed was 3,064,195, and rejected 3,692,368. . . . The schooner Pilgrim arrived bringing two chests containing $34,000 recovered from the Yankee Blade.

January 3. A man named Philips accomplished the feat of walking 104 consecutive hours. . . . Mr. Stowe, of Santa Cruz was elected Speaker of the Assembly.

Jan 4. H. B. M. Frigate Pique arrived 14 days from the Sandwich Islands, bringing news of the death of King Kamehameha III. on the 15th December, and of the accession of Prince Liholiho as Kamehameha IV. . . . A fire broke out in the segar store kept by Mr. Andrews, and caused damage to the extent of $1,000. . . . I. C. Woods, Esq., was chosen President of the Atlantic and Pacific Railroad Company; Samuel J. Hensley, Vice-President; Capt. C. P. Patterson, Treasurer; and Sherman Day, Secretary. . . . The Board of County Supervisors passed a resolution authorizing the committee to advertise for proposals for the construction of the House of Refuge at a cost not exceeding $30,000.

January 5. Henry Vaughn and John Nichols were examined before Commissioner Schell, of the U. S. District Court, on an alleged robbery of $27,000 on board the Steamer Sonora, and were discharged. . . . Six of the escaped convicts were captured near San José.

January 6. The Governor's Message was published in the daily papers.

January 7. The French Corvette La Moselle arrived from Tahiti, having on board the Governor of the Society Islands, Commodore Page. She also brought news that the barque American, having on board Henry Meiggs and family, had arrived at Tahiti and sailed Nov. 21, for parts unknown.

January 8. Five of the recaptured convicts made their escape from the Jail at San José. . . . News was received that Santa Anna had been almost unanimously reëlected President of Mexico.

January 9. The Nicaragua Steamship Uncle Sam left for San Juan, conveying treasure to the value of $642,000.

January 10. Mr. and Mrs. Philips were examined before the Recorder on a charge of inhumanly treating their daughter Julia Riley, but as no specific assault or outrage could be proven against them they were dismissed; the girl was, however, taken from them and placed in the care of a gentleman of this city.

January 11. The Board of County Supervisors passed a resolution vacating the room occupied by the Law Library, and awarded the same to the use of the Board of Delegates of the Fire Department; Mr. Olds the proprietor of the Library refused to vacate the room and procured an injunction against the action of the Supervisors. . . . A letter was published from one of the members of the Cocos Island Expedition which expressed great hopes of being able to obtain the treasure. . . . The opening of the New Merchants' Exchange was celebrated by a large assemblage of merchants and an appropriate festivity. . . . An important case which had been on trial for nine days before the Fourth District Court, involving the question whether a neglect to improve a lot caused a forfeiture of the grant, as against a subsequent grantee who had improved and remained in possession, was decided in the affirmative.

January 12. Mr. Farwell of the Assembly Introduced a bill for "An Act to provide for the survey and construction of a Wagon Road from the Sacramento Valley to the Eastern Boundary of the State."

January 14. A fire broke out in Chase's Planing and Turning Mill on Stevenson or Second street, which destroyed a considerable quantity of valuable lumber. . . . The new Congregational Church, on Bush street, under the pastoral charge of Dr. Scott was consecrated. . . . A contractor, Lyman Mowry, was shot by one of his employees named Blake.

January 15. A new local burlesque called the "Lady Killer of San Francisco," written by Mr. Simmonds was brought out with great success at the American. . . . The Steamer Goliah arrived from San Diego, bringing news of the hanging, by the people at Los Angeles, of Brown and Alvitre, for the murder of a man named Clifford; also, of a man named Johnson by the "King" boys. . . . Mr. Johnston, of San Francisco, introduced a bill for "An Act to Fund the Debt of San Francisco County." . . . The matter of the Law Library being brought before the Fourth District Court, Judge Lake decided against Mr. Olds, and the latter made preparations to remove.

January 16. News was received of the loss of the Steamship Southerner, about sixty miles to the southward of Cape Flattery while on her passage down from Columbia. The Steamship Sonora left for Panama, carrying treasure to the value of $1,430,389. . . . A destructive fire occurred at Yreka and destroyed property to the value of $11,800.

January 17. The Legislature commenced balloting for United States Senator, the principal candidates were Gwin, Edwards, McCorkle and Broderick.

January 18. Mr. Buffum introduced a bill to increase the jurisdiction of Justices of the Peace in the City and County of San Francisco, in Civil Cases, to all claims amounting to $500. . . . By order of the California Land Commissioners, a sale was made of the State's interest in a large amount of water property, the proceeds of which were $23,479. . . . The Mercantile Library Association elected officers for the ensuing year: for President, Henry M. Hall; Vice-President, W. H. Stevens; Corresponding Secretary, F. A. Woodworth; Recording Secretary, J. H. Gardner; Treasurer, Spear Riddle; and nine Directors.

January 19. Joseph Heslep, the acting Treasurer of San Joaquin County, was brutally murdered by a man named Griffith and his office was robbed of all the money it contained, with the exception of about $2,506. The murderer was soon captured and hung by the people.

January 20. The seat of Mr. Galvin, Senator from Tuolumne County, contested by Mr. McCurdy, was declared vacant, and the contestants referred to their constituents. . . . The corner stone of the New Custom House was laid with appropriate ceremonies.

January 22. John Tabor, who shot Joseph Mansfield of the San Joaquin Republican in June last, was sentenced to be hung on the 16th day of March. . . . Wilson and Mathews charged with feloniously taking $34,000 of the lost treasure of the Yankee Blade, and who had been a long time under examination before Commissioner Schell, were discharged.

January 23. The Governor appointed John G. McNair, Judge of Sonoma County, in place of F. Shattuck, resigned.

January 24. The Steamship Sierra Nevada left for San Juan, carrying treasure to the value of $533,889. . . . A German, named Oldman, was shot by Mr. Rodman Backus of Wells, Fargo & Co.'s Express. . . . That portion of Merchant street, known as the Latimer claim, was fenced in, Judge Norton having decided that there was no evidence that the city had accepted the property.

January 26. The Grand Jury indicted John Blake for the murder of Lyman Mowry. . . . Capt. Randall, of the Yankee Blade, charged with taking a quantity of gold dust from the wreck, was examined before Commissioner Schell and discharged.

Jan 27. A fire broke out in a stable on First street, opposite Jessie, communicating to the Clipper Flouring Mills, and other buildings adjoining it, destroyed property to the value of $10,000. . . . Mr. Thomas Murray, a brave and efficient Fireman of Company No. 11, received a severe injury which resulted in his death. . . . The Steamboat Pearl from Marysville, just as she passed the conflux of Sacramento and American Rivers burst her boiler and destroyed the lives of from fifty to sixty human beings. The boat itself was a complete wreck. . . . Mr. Bay, tried for the number of James Cavanagh at the election affray of the 7th November, was acquitted.

January 28. The remains of the Fireman, Thomas Murray, who lost his life at the late fire were attended to the tomb by a long procession of his brother Firemen. . . . Mr. Bay who was acquitted of the murder of Kavanagh was murdered on the old mission road near the toll-gate.

January 29. A man named George Lendrum was arrested in a house on Bullard's Rancho on suspicion of having murdered Mr. Bay. . . . Mr. Leach had a benefit at the Metropolitan Theater, on which occasion he was presented with a handsome service of silver as a token of the esteem and regard in which he was held by his many friends.

January 30. Two men, named Robert Parker and George Sheldon, were arrested at Oakland for horse stealing.

January 31. Of the two men named, George Sheldon was hung by the people of Oakland, and Parker set at liberty. . . . A notorious desperado named Wm. Smith was arrested by the police on his return to this county after an absence of three years.

February 2. A bill was passed giving each member of the Legislature $1,000 cash. . . . In the case of Miss Sullivan alias Howard, tried before the Court of Sessions for an assault upon Kerrison with intent to kill, the Jury were unable to agree, standing nine for acquittal and three for conviction. She was accordingly discharged upon her own recognizance. . . . In the same court, Sanchez, who had been tried in the Fourth District for the murder of Miguel Savadra, was admitted to bail in the sum of $5,000 by Judge Freelon, notwithstanding it had been refused in the latter court by Judge Lake. . . . The Grand Jury presented an indictment against C. D. Carter and C. K. Garrison for embezzlement of $75,000 in goods and chattels belonging to the city, which they held as trustees; also, against Smyth Clark on the same count; also, against Henry Meiggs for forging to a note of $15,000 the name of Wm. Neely Thompson & Co. . . . A young man, named McClure, while stopping at Wilson's Exchange, was assaulted and cowhided for his supposed share, as the people's sheriff, in the hanging of Johnson at Iowa Hill; the persons who attacked him were a brother of the unfortunate man and a number of his friends; the affair made a great excitement.

February 6. News arrived by the brig Susan Abigail from the Sandwich Islands of the funeral of the late King, and of the crowning and installation of Kamehameha IV. . . . In the case of C. K. Garrison and Charles D. Carter, indicted for converting to their own use $75,000 of the city's money a *nolle prosequi* was entered. . . . Sanchez after having been admitted to bail by Judge Freelon was rearrested by Judge Lake, he was this day brought, upon a writ of *habeas corpus* before the former and again discharged.

February 9. The U. S. Revenue Cutter Jefferson Davis, arrived from Puget Sound. . . . The Nicaragua Co.'s Steamship Cortez sailed for San Juan with treasure to the value of $621,059. . . . Sanchez was discharged by Judge Freelon for the third time on bail.

February 10. A number of merchants met at the new Exchange and fixed the hours at meeting on 'change at from half-past 12 to half-past 1 o'clock.

February 11. The new Germania Society gave their first Concert at the Farmer's Hall. It was well attended.

February 12. A new play called the "Daughter's Vow," written by M M. Noah, Esq., was brought out at the American. . . . The steamer Goliah sailed with a large number of passengers *en route* for the Kern River Diggings.

February 13. The Fourth Anniversary of the San Francisco Oryhan Asylum was celebrated with appropriate ceremonies.

EDITOR'S TABLE.

[Scientific.]

OFFICIAL REPORT OF PROFESSOR JOHN PHŒNIX, A. M.

—

Of a Military Survey and Reconnoissance of the route from San Francisco to the Mission of Dolores, made with a view to ascertain the practicability of connecting those points by a Railroad.

—

MISSION OF DOLORES, Feb. 15, 1855.

IT having been definitely determined, that the great Railroad, connecting the City of San Francisco with the head of navigation on Mission Creek, should be constructed without unnecessary delay, a large appropriation ($120,000) was granted, for the purpose of causing thorough military examinations to be made of the proposed routes. The routes, which had principally attracted the attention of the public, were "the Northern," following the line of Brannan Street, "the Central," through Folsom Street, and "the extreme Southern," passing over the "Old Plank Road" to the Mission. Each of these proposed routes has many enthusiastic advocates; but "the Central" was, undoubtedly, the favorite of the public; it being more extensively used by emigrants from San Francisco to the Mission, and, therefore, more widely and favorably known than the others. It was to the examination of this route, that the committee, feeling a confidence (eminently justified by the result of my labors) in my experience, judgment and skill as a Military Engineer, appointed me on the first instant. Having notified the Honorable Body of my acceptance of the important trust confided to me, in a letter, wherein I also took occasion to congratulate them on the good judgment they had evinced, I drew from the Treasurer the amount ($40,000) appropriated for my peculiar route, and having invested it securely in loans at three per cent. a month, (made, to avoid accident, in my own name) I proceeded to organize my party for the expedition.

In a few days my arrangements were completed, and my scientific corps organized, as follows:—

JOHN PHŒNIX, A. M...........Principal Engineer and Chief Astronomer.
LIEUT. MINUS ROOT...........Apocryphal Engineers. First Assistant Astronomer.
LIEUT. NONPLUS A. ZERO......Hypercritical Engineers. Second Assistant Astronomer.

Dr. Abraham Dunshunner .... Geologist.
Dr. Targee Heavysterne... Naturalist.
Herr Von Der Weegates... ↑otanist.
Dr. Fogy L. Bigguns .... Ethnologist.
Dr. Tushmaker.. Dentist.
Enry Halfred Jinkins, R. A..................................... ⎱ Draftsmen.
Adolphe Kraut.. ⎰
Hi Fu... Interpreter.
James Phœnix, (my elder brother)............................... Treasurer.
Joseph Phœnix,   ditto, ... Quarter-Master.
William Phœnix, (younger brother)............................. Commissary.
Peter Phœnix,   ditto, ... Clerk.
Paul Phœnix, (my cousin)...................... .... Sutler.
Reuben Phœnix, ditto, ... Wagon-Master.
Richard Phœnix, (second cousin)................................ Assistant ditto.

These gentlemen, with one hundred and eighty-four laborers employed as teamsters, chainmen, rodmen, etc., made up the party. For instruments, we had 1 large Transit Instrument, (8 inch achromatic lens), 1 Mural Circle, 1 Altitude and Azimuth Instrument, (these instruments were permanently set up in a mule cart, which was backed into the plane of the true meridian, when required for use,) 13 large Theodolites, 13 small ditto, 8 Transit Compasses, 17 Sextants, 34 Artificial Horizons, 1 Sidereal Clock, and 184 Solar Compasses. Each employee was furnished with a gold chronometer watch, and, by a singular mistake, a diamond pin and gold chain; for directions having been given, that they should be furnished with "*chains and pins*,' —meaning of course such articles as are used in surveying,—Lieut. Root, whose "zeal somewhat overran his discretion," incontinently procured for each man the above-named articles of jewelry, by mistake. They were purchased at Tucker's (where, it is needless to remark, "you can buy a diamond pin or ring,") and afterwards proved extremely useful in our intercourse with the natives of the Mission of Dolores, and, indeed, along the route.

Every man was suitably armed, with four of Colt's revolvers, a Minie rifle, a copy of Col. Benton's speech on the Pacific Railroad, and a mountain howitzer. These last named heavy articles required each man to be furnished with a wheelbarrow for their transportation, which was accordingly done; and these vehicles proved of great service on the survey, in transporting not only the arms but the baggage of the party, as well as the plunder derived from the natives. A squadron of dragoons, numbering 150 men, under Capt. McSpadden, had been detailed as an escort. They accordingly left about a week before us, and we heard of them occasionally on the march.

On consulting with my assistants, I had determined to select, as a base for our operations, a line joining the summit of Telegraph Hill with the extremity of the wharf at Oakland, and two large iron thirty-two pounders were accordingly procured, and at great expense embedded in the earth, one at each extremity of the line, to mark the initial points. On placing compasses over these points to determine the bearing of the base, we were extremely perplexed by the unaccountable local attraction that prevailed; and were compelled, in consequence, to select a new position. This we finally concluded to adopt between Fort Point and Saucelito; but, on attempting to measure the base, we were deterred by the unexpected depth of the water intervening, which, to our surprise, was considerably over the chain bearers' heads. Disliking to abandon our new line, which had been selected with much care and at great expense, I determined to employ in its measurement a reflecting instrument, used very successfully by the United States Coast Survey. I, therefore, directed my assistants to procure me a "Heliotrope," but after being annoyed by having brought to me successively a sweet smelling shrub of that name, and a box of "Lubin's Extract" to select from, it was finally ascertained, that no such instrument could be procured in California. In this extremity, I bethought myself of using as a substitute the flash of gunpowder. Wishing to satisfy myself of its practicability by an experiment, I placed Dr. Dunshunner at a distance of forty paces from my Theodolite, with a flint-lock musket, carefully primed, and directed him to flash in the pan, when I should wave my hand. Having covered the Doctor with the Theodolite, and by a movement of the tangent screw placed the intersection of the cross lines directly over the muzzle of the musket, I accordingly waved; when I was astounded by a tremendous report, a violent blow in the eye, and the instantaneous disappearance of the instrument.

Observing Dr. Dunshunner lying on his back in one direction, and my hat, which had been violently torn from my head, at about the same distance in another, I concluded that the musket had been accidentally loaded. Such proved to be the case; the marks of three buckshot were found in my hat, and a shower of screws, broken lenses and pieces of brass, which shortly fell around us, told where the ball had struck, and bore fearful testimony to the accuracy of Dr. Dunshunner's practice. Believing these experiments more curious than useful, I abandoned the use of the "Heliotrope" or its substitutes, and determined to reverse the usual process, and arrive at the length of the base line by subsequent triangulation. I may as well state here, that this course was adopted and resulted to our entire satisfaction; the distance from Fort Point to Saucelito by the solution of a mean of 1,867,434,926,465 triangles, being determined to be exactly *three hundred and twenty-four feet*. This result differed very much from our preconceived ideas and from the popular opinion; the distance being generally supposed to be some ten miles; but I will stake my professional reputation on the accuracy of our work, and there can, of course, be no disputing the elucidations of science, or facts demonstrated by mathematical process, however incredible they may appear *per se*.

We had adopted an entire new system of triangulation, which I am proud to claim (though I hope with becoming modesty) as my own invention. It simply consists in placing one leg of a tripod on the initial point, and opening out the other legs as far as possible; the distance between the legs is then measured by a two foot rule and noted down; and the tripod moved, so as to form a second triangle, connected with the first, and so on, until the county to be triangulated has been entirely gone over. By using a large number of tripods, it is easily seen with what rapidity the work may be carried on, and this was, in fact, the object of my requisition for so large a number of solar compasses, the tripod being in my opinion the only useful portion of that absurd instrument. Having given Lieut. Root charge of the triangulation, and detached Mr. Jinkins with a small party on hydrographical duty, (to sound a man's well, on the upper part of Dupont Street, and report thereon) on the 5th of February I left the Plaza, with the *savans* and the remainder of my party, to commence the examination and survey of Kearny Street.

Beside the mules drawing the cart which carried the transit instrument, I had procured two fine pack mules, each of which carried two barrels of ale for the draftsmen. Following the tasteful example of that gallant gentleman, who conducted the Dead Sea Expedition, and wishing, likewise, to pay a compliment to the administration under which I was employed, I named the mules "Fanny

Pierce," and "Fanny Bigler." Our *cortège* passing along Kearny Street attracted much attention from the natives, and, indeed, our appearance was sufficiently imposing to excite interest even in less untutored minds than those of these barbarians.

First came the cart, bearing our instruments; then a cart containing LIEUT. ZERO with a level, with which he constantly noted the changes of grade that might occur; then, one hundred and fifty men, four abreast, armed to the teeth, each wheeling before him his personal property and a mountain howitzer; then the *savans*, each with note book and pencil, constantly jotting down some object of interest, (Doctor Tushmaker was so zealous to do something, that he pulled a tooth from an iron rake standing near a stable-door, and was cursed therefor by the illiberal proprietor,) and finally, the Chief Professor, walking arm in arm with Dr. Dunshunner and gazing from side to side, with an air of ineffable blandness and dignity, brought up the rear.

I had made arrangements to measure the length of Kearny Street by two methods; first, by chaining its sidewalks; and, secondly, by a little instrument of my invention called the "Goitometer." This last, consists of a straight rod of brass, firmly strapped to a man's leg and connected with a system of clock-work placed on his back, with which it performs, when he walks, the office of a *ballistic pendulum*. About one foot below the ornamental buttons on the man's back appears a dial-plate connected with the clock-work, on which is promptly registered by an index each step taken. Of course, the length of the step being known, the distance passed over in a day may be obtained by a very simple process.

We arrived at the end of Kearny Street and encamped for the night about sundown near a large brick building, inhabited by a class of people called "The Orphans," who, I am credibly informed, have no fathers or mothers! After seeing the camp properly arranged, the wheelbarrows parked and a guard detailed, I sent for the chainmen and "Go-it-ometer" bearer, to ascertain the distance traveled during the day.

Judge of my surprise to find that the chainmen, having received no instructions, had simply drawn the chain after them through the streets, and had no idea of the distance whatever. Turning from them in displeasure, I took from the "Go-it-ometer" the number of paces marked, and on working the distance, found it to be four miles and a-half. Upon close questioning the bearer, William Boulder, (called by his associates, "Slippery Bill,") I ascertained that he had been in a saloon in the vicinity, and after drinking five glasses of a beverage, known among the natives as "*Lager Bier*," he had danced a little for their amusement. Feeling very much dissatisfied with the day's survey, I stepped out of camp and stopping an omnibus, asked the driver how far he thought it to the Plaza? He replied, "Half-a-mile," which I accordingly noted down, and returned very much pleased at so easily obtaining so much valuable information. It would appear, therefore, that "Slippery Bill," under the influence of five glasses, (probably $2\frac{1}{2}$ quarts) of "*Lager Bier*," had actually danced four miles in a few moments.

Kearny Street, of which I present above a spirited engraving from a beautiful drawing by Mr. Kraut, is a pass about fifty feet in width. The soil is loose and sandy, about one inch in depth, below which, Dr. Dunshunner discovered a stratum of white pine, three inches in thickness, and beneath this again, sand.

It is densely populated and smells of horses. Its surface is intersected with many pools of *sulphuretted protoxide of hydrogen,* and we found several specimens of a vegetable substance, loosely distributed, which is classed by Mr. Weegates as the *stalkus cabbagiensis.*

It being late in the evening when our arrangements for encamping were completed, we saw but little of the natives until the next morning, when they gathered about our camp to the number of eighteen.

We were surprised to find them of diminutive stature, the tallest not exceeding three feet in height. They were excessively mischievous and disposed to steal such trifling things as they could carry away. Their countenances are of the color of dirt, and their hair white and glossy as the silk of maize. The one that we took to be their chief, was an exceedingly diminutive personage, but with a bald head which gave him a very venerable appearance. He was dressed in a dingy robe of jaconet and was borne in the arms of one of his followers. On making them a speech, proposing a treaty and assuring them of the protection of their great Father, Pierce, the chief was affected to tears, and on being comforted by his followers, repeatedly exclaimed, " da, da,—da, da ; " which, we were informed by the interpreter, meant "father," and was intended as a respectful allusion to the President. We presented him afterwards with some beads, hawk-bells and other presents, which he immediately thrust into his mouth, saying " Goo," and crowing like a cock; which was rendered by the interpreter into an expression of high satisfaction. Having made presents to all his followers, they at length left us very well pleased, and we shortly after took up our line of march. From the notes of Dr. Bigguns, I transcribe the following description of one of this deeply interesting people :

" Kearny Street native; name—Bill;—height, two feet nine inches;—hair, white ;—complexion, dirt color ;—eyes, blue ;—no front teeth ;—opal at extremity of nose;—dress, a basquine of bluish bombazine, with two gussets, ornamented down the front with *crotchet* work of molasses candy, three buttons on one side and eight button holes on the other—leggings of tow-cloth, fringed at the bottoms and permitting free ventilation behind—one shoe and one boot ;—occupation, erecting small pyramids of dirt and water; when asked what they were, replied 'pies,' (word in Spanish meaning *feet ;* supposed they might be the feet or foundation of some barbarian structure)—religious belief, obscure ;—when asked who made him, replied 'PAR,' (supposed to be the name of one of their principal Deities.)"

We broke up our encampment and moved North by compass across Market Street, on the morning of the 6th, and about noon had completed the survey as far as the corner of Second Street.

While crossing Market Street, being anxious to know the exact time, I concluded to determine it by observation. Having removed the Sidereal Clock from the cart, and put it in the street, we placed the cart in the plane of the Meridian, and I removed the eye and object-glass of the transit, for the purpose of wiping them. While busily engaged in this manner, an individual, whom I have reason to believe is connected with a fire company, approached, and seeing the large brazen tube of the transit pointed to the sky, mistook it for a huge speaking trumpet. Misled by this delusion, he mounted the cart, and in an awful tone of voice shouted through the transit " *Wash her, Thirteen !*" but having miscalculated the strength of his lungs, he was seized with a violent fit of coughing, and before he could be removed had completely coughed the vertical hairs out of the instrument. I was in despair at this sudden destruction of the utility of our most valuable instrument, but fortunately recollecting a gridiron, that we had among our kitchen apparatus, I directed Dr. Heavysterne to hold it up in the plane of the true Meridian, and with an opera glass watched and noted by the clock the passage of the sun's center across the five bars. Having made these observations, I requested the principal computer to work them out, as I wished to ascertain the time immediately; but he replying that it would take some three months to do it, I concluded not to wait, but sent a man into the grocery, corner of Market and Second, to inquire the time, who soon returned with the desired information. It may be thought singular, that with so many gold watches in our party, we should ever be found at a loss to ascertain the time; but the fact was that I had directed every one of our employees to set his watch by Greenwich mean time, which, though excellent to give one the longitude, is for ordinary purposes the meanest time that can be found. A distressing casualty that befel Dr. Bigguns on this occasion may be found worthy of record. An omnibus, passing during the time of observation, was driven carelessly near our Sidereal Clock, with which it almost came into contact. Dr. Bigguns, with a slight smile, remarked that "the clock *was nearly run down,*" and immediately fainted away. The pursuits of science cannot be delayed by accidents of this nature, two of the workmen removed our unfortunate friend, at once, to the Orphan Asylum, where, having rung the bell, they left him on the steps and departed, and we never saw him afterwards.

From the corner of Market to the corner of Second and Folsom Streets, the route presents no object of interest worthy of mention. We were forced to the conclusion, however, that little throwing of stones prevails near the latter point, as the inhabitants mostly live in glass houses. On the 8th we had brought the survey nearly up to Southwick's Pass on Folsom Street, and we commenced going through the Pass on the morning of the ninth. This pass consists of a rectangular ravine, about 10 feet in length, the sides lined with pine boards, with a white oak (*quercus albus*) bar, that at certain occasions forms across, entirely obstructing the whole route. We found no difficulty in getting through the Pass on foot, nor with the wheelbarrows; but the mule carts and the "two Fannies" were more troublesome, and we were finally unable to get them through without a considerable pecuniary disbursement, amounting in all to one dollar and fifty cents ($1 50). We understand that the City of San Francisco is desirous of effecting a safe and free passage through this celebrated cañon, but a large appropriation (220,000) is required for the purpose.

The following passages relating to this portion of the route, transcribed from the Geological Notes of Dr. Dunshunner, though not directly connected with the objects of the survey, are extremely curious in a scientific point of view, and may be of interest to the general reader.

"The country in the vicinity of the route after leaving Southwick's Pass is very productive, and I observed with astonishment, that red-headed children appear to grow spontaneously. A building was pointed out to me, near our line of march, as the *locale* of a most astounding agricultural and architectural phenomenon, which illustrates the extreme fertility of the soil in a remarkable degree. A small pine wardrobe, which had been left standing by the side of the house, (a frame cottage with a piazza) at the commencement of the rainy season, took root and in a few weeks grew to the prodigious height of thirty feet, and still preserving its proportions and characteristic appearance, extended in each direction, until it covered a space of ground some forty by twenty feet in measurement.

This singular phenomenon was taken advantage of by the proprietors; doors and windows were cut in the wardrobe, a chimney erected, and it now answers every purpose of an addition to the original cottage, being two stories in height! This phenomenon appears almost incredible, but fortunately the house and attached wardrobe may be seen any day, from the road, at a trifling expense of omnibus hire, by the sceptical. Some distance beyond, rises a noble structure, built entirely of cut-wood, called 'The Valley House, by Mrs. Hubbard.' Not imagining that a venial species of profanity was conveyed by this legend, I concluded that Mrs. Hubbard was simply the proprietor. This brought to my mind the beautiful lines of a primitive poet, Spenser,* if I mistake not:

> 'Old Mother Hubbard went to the cupboard
>   To get her poor dog a bone;
> But when she got there, the cupboard was bare,
>   And so the poor dog got none.'

Feeling curious to ascertain if this were, by any possibility the ancient residence of the heroine of these lines, perchance an ancestress of the present proprietor, I ventured to call and inquire; and my antiquarian zeal was rewarded by the information, that such was the case; and that, if I returned at a later hour during the evening, I could be allowed a sight of the closet, and a view of the skeleton of the original dog. Delighted with my success, I returned accordingly, and finding the door closed, ventured to knock; when a sudden shower of rain fell, lasting but about five seconds, but drenching me to the skin. Undeterred by this *contretemps*, I elevated my umbrella and knocked again, loudly, when a violent concussion upon the umbrella, accompanied by a thrill down the handle, which caused me to seat myself precipitately in a bucket by the side of the door, convinced me that electrical phenomena of an unusual character were prevalent, and decided me to return with all speed to our encampment. Here I was astounded by discovering inverted on the summit of my umbrella, a curious and deeply interesting vase, of singularly antique shape, and composed, apparently, of white porcelain. Whether this vase fell from the moon, a comet or a passing meteor, I have not yet decided; drawings of it are being prepared, and the whole subject will receive my thorough investigation at an early day.†

I subsequently attempted to pursue my investigations at the 'Valley House,' but the curt manner of the proprietor led me to suspect that the subject was distasteful, and I was reluctantly compelled to abandon it.

Near the 'Valley House' I observed an advertisement of 'The Mountain View,' by P. Buckley, but the building in which it is exhibited being closed, I had no opportunity to judge of the merits of the painting, or the skill of Mr. Buckley as an artist. A short distance further I discovered a small house occupied by a gentleman, who appeared engaged in some description of traffic with the emigrants; and on watching his motions intently, my surprise was great to find his employment consisted in selling them small pieces of pasteboard *at fifty cents a-piece!* Curious to know the nature of these valuable bits of paper, I watched carefully the proprietor's motions through a window for some hours; but being at length observed by him, I was requested to leave—and I left. This curious subject is, therefore, I regret to say, enwrapped in mystery, and I reluctantly leave it for the elucidation of some future *savant*. The beautiful idea, originated by Col. Benton, that buffaloes and other wild animals are the pioneer engineers, and that subsequent explorations can discover no better roads than those selected by them, would appear to apply admirably to the Central Route. Many pigs, singly and in droves, met and passed me continually; and as the pig is unquestionably a more sagacious animal than the buffalo, their preference for this route is a most significant fact. I was, moreover, informed by the emigrants, that this route was 'the one followed by Col. Fremont, when he lost his men.' This statement should be received *cum grano salis*, as on my inquiry—

---

* The Doctor is in error; the lines quoted are from Chaucer.   J. P.

† This curious antique, to which I have given the name of the "Dunshunner Vase," has singularly the appearance of a *wash basin!* When the drawings are completed, it is to be presented to the California Academy of Natural Sciences.   J. P.

'What men?' my informant replied 'A box of chessmen,' which answer from its levity threw an air of doubt over the whole piece of information, in my mind. There can be no question, however, that Lieut. Beale has frequently traveled this route, and that it was a favorite with him; indeed, I am informed that he took the first omnibus over it that ever left San Francisco for the Mission of Dolores.

The climate, in these latitudes is mild, snow appears to be unknown, and we saw but little ice; what there was being sold at twenty-five cents per lb.

The geological formation of the county is not volcanic, I saw but one small specimen of trap during the march, which I observed at the 'Valley House,' with a mouse in it. From the vast accumulations of sand in these regions, I am led to adopt the opinion of the ethnologists of the 'California Academy of Natural Sciences,' and conclude that the original name of this territory was Sand Francisco, from which the final 'd' in the prefix has been lost by time, like the art of painting on glass.

Considering the innumerable villages of pigs to be found located on the line of march, and the consequent effect produced on the atmosphere, I would respectfully suggest to the Chief Engineer the propriety of changing the name of the route by a slight alteration in the orthography, giving it the appropriate and euphonious title of the '*Scent*ral R. R. Route.'

Respectfully submitted,

ABRAHAM DUNSHUNNER, L. L. D.

P. G. C. R. R. R. S."

From Southwick's Pass, the survey was continued with unabated ardor until the evening of the 10th instant, when we had arrived opposite Mrs. Freeman's "American Eagle," where we encamped. From this point a botanical party under Prof. Weegates was sent over the hills to the S. and W. for exploration. They returned on the 11th, bringing a box of sardines, a tin can of preserved whortleberries, and a bottle of whisky, as specimens of the products of the country over which they had passed. They reported discovering on the old plank road, an inn or hostel kept by a native American Irishman, whose sign exhibited the Harp of Ireland encircling the shield of the United States with the mottoes

"Erin go unum,"
"E Pluribus bragh."

On the 14th the party arrived in good health and excellent spirits at the "Nightingale," Mission of Dolores.

History informs us, that

"The Nightingale club at the village was held,
At the sign of the cabbage and Shears."

It is interesting to the Antiquarian to look over the excellent cabbage garden, still extant immediately opposite the Nightingale, and much more so to converse with Mr. Shears the respected and urbane proprietor.

The survey and *reconnoissance* being finished on our arrival at the Mission, it may be expected that I should here give a full and impartial statement as to the merits or demerits of the route, in connection with the proposed Railroad.

Some three months must elapse, however, before this can be done, as the triangulation has yet to be perfectly computed, the sub-reports examined and compiled, the observations worked out, and the maps and drawings executed. Besides, I have received a letter from certain parties interested in the Southern and Northern routes, informing me that if I suspend my opinion on the "Great Central" for the present, it will be greatly to my interest,—and as my interest is certainly my principal consideration, I shall undoubtedly comply with their request, unless, indeed, greater inducement is offered to the contrary.

Meanwhile I can assure the public, *that a great deal may certainly be said in favor of the Central Route.* A full report accompanied by maps, charts, sub-reports, diagrams, calculations, tables and statistics, may shortly be expected.

Profiles of Prof. Heavysterne, Dr. Dunshunner and myself, executed in black court plaster by Mr. Jinkins, R. A., one of the Artists of the Expedition, in his unrivaled style of elegance, may be seen for a short time at Messrs. LeCount & Strong's—scale ½ inch to 1 foot.

In conclusion I beg leave to return my thanks to the Professors, Assistants, and Artists of the Expedition, for the energy, fidelity and zeal, with which they have ever co-operated with me, and seconded my efforts; and to assure them that I shall be happy at any time to sit for my portrait for them, or to accept the handsome service of plate, which I am told they have prepared for me, but feel too much delicacy to speak to me about.

I remain, with the highest respect and esteem for myself and every body else,

JOHN PHŒNIX, A. M.,
Chief Engineer and Astronomer, S. F. A. M. D. C. R.

—

The annexed sketch of our route, prepared by Messrs. Jinkins and Kraut, is respectfully submitted to the Public. It is not, of course, compiled with that accuracy, which will characterize our final maps, but, for the ordinary purposes of travel, will be found sufficiently correct.   J. P., A. M. C. E. & C. A.

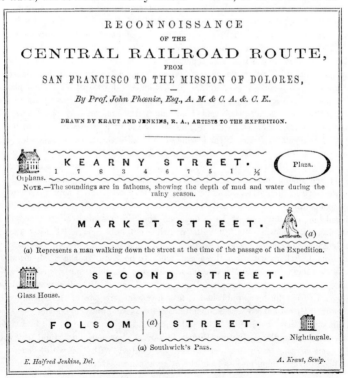

RECONNOISSANCE
OF THE
CENTRAL RAILROAD ROUTE,
FROM
SAN FRANCISCO TO THE MISSION OF DOLORES,
—
By Prof. John Phœnix, Esq., A. M. & C. A. & C. E.

DRAWN BY KRAUT AND JINKINS, R. A., ARTISTS TO THE EXPEDITION.

KEARNY STREET.
1   7   8   3   4   6   7   5   1   ½   Plaza.
Orphans.
NOTE.—The soundings are in fathoms, showing the depth of mud and water during the rainy season.

MARKET STREET.
(a)
(a) Represents a man walking down the street at the time of the passage of the Expedition.

SECOND STREET.
Glass House.

FOLSOM (a) STREET.
Nightingale.
(a) Southwick's Pass.

E. Halfred Jenkins, Del.   *A. Kraut, Sculp.*

GOSSIP WITH READERS AND CORRESPONDENTS.

IF there is anything that is amusing to the quiet looker-on, it is to see a Yankee—we use the term in its broad sense—become exasperated, when he is brought into contact with a Mexican or Indian (in crossing the Isthmus, for example) and curse the poor *hombre* because he does n't understand English. Of course it is the poor fellow's fault that he was n't born among "the Universal Yankee Nation," and, in the self-sufficient air of mingled disgust and indignation with which his superior "gives it up" and turns away, do we notice a trait in the character of our people, which we possess in common with no other nation on earth. A good story is told of a Yankee, who had taken up his residence for several months in Rome, the delicate humor of which cannot fail to be appreciated. He persisted in speaking English wherever he went. If there was anything which he did despise, it was Italian. The subjects of the Pope were not born either North or South of Mason and Dixon's Line, and, of course, were an inferior race. As Jonathan was walking one day down the "Corso," he came to a pastry shop, and after looking into the windows sometime, he sauntered into the establishment, and up to the counter, behind which stood a soiled Figaro with a red fez cap upon his uncombed locks. After gazing all over the counter and among the shelves, he looked at Figaro, and said—"Have you got any regular, old-fashioned, down-east, Yankee, pumpkin pies?" Figaro was non-plussed. Jonathan repeated—"Have you got any regular, old-fashioned, down-east, Yankee, pumpkin *pies?*" Figaro looked off, then back again, shook his head and shrugged his shoulders in intimation of his utter ignorance of what his customer wanted. Jonathan then leaned over the counter, looked the *pasticciere* directly in the eye, and, repeating very slowly and distinctly each word by itself, in order to insure no misapprehension this time, said once more— "Have—you—got—any—regular—old-fashioned—down-east—Yankee—*pumpkin pies?*" Figaro shrugged his shoulders again, and was evidently no nearer the point than before. "O," said Jonathan, with mingled pity and contempt upon his countenance, and with the peculiar tone of a man who gives it up— "O, you do n't *understand*," and walked out with the most self-satisfied air imaginable. - - - UP among the Green Mountains there dwells a family by the name of Slocum. They were very numerous and very clanish—always marrying among themselves. They were never known to pay a bill or to do a day's work in their lives. Among them was a dry old fellow yclept "Job," who spent his days and nights mostly in the tavern bar-room. One of his neighbors asked him, one day, how it happened that the Slocums always intermarried— cousins with cousins, etc. "Well," drawled out Job, dryly—"I do n't know, unless it is *to keep the property together.*" "At that blessed moment," states our informant, "there was n't a three-cent piece to be found in the whole crowd." - - - MANY thanks to Mr. GEO. PEN. JOHNSTON, Assemblyman from San Francisco, for Legislative documents. We were much amused, by the way, with a curt card from his pen, published a few days since in one of the Sacramento papers. Mr. JOHNSTON has shown himself to be no puny opponent. - - - PROBABLY a more miserable, filthy and degraded race do not tread the surface of the earth than the California Digger Indians. They certainly stand at "the far end of the last point" of humanity. Contact with the whites has not sufficed to raise them an iota from their degradation. During a visit to Marysville, a few weeks since, we stopped at one of their villages, while on a ride to Hock Farm, in order to show the natives to "THE DAME." Of course, having visited the place before, we were confident of a thorough acquaintance in the premises. So the ladies descended from the carriage, and we accompanied them in the important and responsible capacity of *cicerone.* To our surprise, many of the holes in the ground (their former habitations) were deserted—the bush and mud coverings having fallen in. Supposing, of course, that the race were rapidly thinning out, we philosophized on the interesting subject, and pointed out several piles of rubbish and torn sail-cloth as evidences of increasing civilization among them. THE DAME, however—having a practical turn of mind, withal—quickly discovered, while we were remarking upon the dissolving touch of the Anglo Saxon race, etc., that "the filthy creatures" had left their holes, and were actually living *upon* the earth, and that these rude piles were hollow, being in fact their present habitations. Slightly foiled, we turned confidently to point out the high, cylindrical, wicker-work receptacles, which every old Californian will remember as their garners for gathered acorns. But we looked in vain. The "creatures" had actually come to use barrels instead, and we gave it up, and concluded that we did n't know anything more about them than our neighbors. We however took occasion, as a desperate resort, to remark upon their high advance in civilization; but, on a close inspection into their huts, THE DAME thanked her stars "she was not as other men," but expressed her gratification at an opportunity of witnessing this "interesting people," while yet they had a *few* remnants of their primitive condition about them, and before they had become *entirely* enlightened. THE DAME has a vein of sly humor and a streak of concealed satire, at times, exceedingly annoying. - - - SPEAKING of "The Diggers," one of the most singular facts connected with them is their irreligious belief. Every "good Indian," say they, passes after death to the sun; every "bad Indian" to the moon; while all the women "go nine days into the earth, and there stay." This is being "quietly inearthed" with a vengeance. - - - IT's a large, indefinite region of country, between the Alleghanies and the Pacific, and our Eastern cotemporaries appear to be so short-sighted that different individuals of merit who happen to dwell West of Ohio, lose their distinctness and seem to blend together into one generality. "*Some fellow* 'out West' says"—and then will follow a gem of thought or a witticism that would do credit to Longfellow or Holmes. Now it's a small piece of business, this complaining at such matters, but we have held our peace until patience is no longer a virtue. John Phœnix's, and Pollock's, and Shirley's, and Anthony's best, are scissored again and again by our cotemporaries "out East," and nine times in ten are introduced by the eternal generality—"Some fellow out West says." The phrase is becoming almost as stale as the well-known simile—"The oasis in the desert." Our protest may be feeble, but we most decidedly enter it. - - - A FRIEND of ours, who has a house on Dupont street, hired a son of Erin a few days since to put it into order for a new tenant. Pat met his employer shortly afterwards, and accosted him thus: "Well, Mr. S——, I've fixed up iverything in the house, and claned up iverything, and put it in complate orther." "Well, that's all right, Michael," responded our friend. "But what," said Pat, "what will yez be doin' with that back window there?" "Which window do you mean, Michael?" "The window in the back o' the house, sir."

"Well, but which window do you *mean?*" "Arrah, sir," responded Pat, true to his nativity, "that one that has the three *wooden panes o' glass* in the bottom of it, sir." At this stage of the proceedings our friend burst into a roar. "What the divil are ye larfin' at?" said Pat. "I'm laughing at you, Michael," responded our friend. "Well," said Pat, conscious enough that he had made a bull, but too much of an Irishman to know how to correct it, "how the divil would *you* say it, thin?" We strongly suspect that many of the published bulls are charged unjustly upon the poor sons of Erin, but the above we can vouch for as "A GENUINE." - - - SOME fellow out East has written the following beautiful poem:

"THE EMPEROR'S BIRD'S-NEST."

Once the Emperor Charles of Spain,
   With his swarthy, grave commanders,
I forget in what campaign,
Long besieged in mud and rain
   Some old frontier town of Flanders.

Up and down the dreary camp,
   In great boots of Spanish leather,
Striding with a measured tramp,
These Hidalgos, dull and damp,
   Cursed the Frenchmen, cursed the weather.

Thus, as to and fro they went,
   Over upland and through hollow,
Giving their impatience vent,
Perched upon the Emperor's tent,
   In her nest they spied a swallow.

Yes, it was a swallow's nest,
   Built of clay and hair of horses'
Mane or tail, or dragon's crest,
Found on hedgerows, east or west,
   After skirmish of the forces.

Then an old Hidalgo said,
   As he twirled his gray mustachio,
'Sure this swallow over-head
Thinks our Emperor's tent a shed,
   And our Emperor but a macho.' *

Hearing his imperial name
   Coupled with these words of malice,
Half in anger, half in shame,
Forth the great campaigner came
   Slowly from his canvas palace.

'Let no hand the bird molest,'
   Said he, solemnly, ' nor hurt her!'
Adding then, by way of jest—
'Golondrino is my guest—
   'Tis the wife of some deserter.' †

Swift as bow-string speeds a shaft,
   Through the camp was spread the rumor;
And the soldiers, as they quaffed
Flemish beer, at dinner, laughed
   At the Emperor's pleasant humor.

So, unharmed and unafraid,
   There the swallow sat and brooded,
Till the constant cannonade
Through the walls a breach had made,
   And the siege was thus concluded.

Then the army, elsewhere bent,
   Struck its tents, as if disbanding;
Only not the Emperor's tent—
For he ordered, ere he went,
   Very curtly, ' Leave it standing!'

And it stood there all alone,
   Loosely flapping, torn and tattered,
Till the brood was fledged and flown,
Singing o'er those walls of stone,
   That the cannon-shot had shattered."

- - - OUR readers will recollect that in our last we extracted a number of advertisements from the issue of *The London Times*, purporting to be published on the first of January, 1955, in which the advancement made in the arts and sciences, and the changes in government, during the last half of the nineteenth and the first half of the twentieth centuries, were shadowed. We resume our extracts from the same sheet:

SCHOOLS FOR ALL.—Useful instruction having hitherto been chiefly confined to the productive classes, and many in the upper ranks still remaining in a desperate state of ignorance, it is proposed to establish SCHOOLS FOR THE HIGHER ORDERS, in order that, being equally well informed with the rest of the community, the plea of ignorance may no longer be allowed as an excuse for the want of knowledge in the duties of life. Applications for particulars to be made to DR. CHILDRENS, Light House, Brompton.

IMPORTANT TO INVALIDS.—The NEW MAGIC ELIXIR, which cures all diseases by the smell. The public will not be surprised at this announcement, as it has been discovered that the whole Materia Medica can be carried in a ring, and that the instruments of Surgery may be compressed into a snuff-box. To be had of JOHN FRANKENSTEIN & CO., German House, Spa Fields.

   * Spanish for "mule."   † Golondrino, in Spanish, means a swallow and a deserter.

FAMILY MOURNING.—Ladies and Gentlemen obliged to go into Mourning suddenly, will find the quickest and most economical method is to dip in the PATENT CALIGRAPHIC BATH, Dyer's Buildings.   One trial will prove the efficacy of this truly valuable invention.

GENERAL QUARTER SESSIONS FOR LONDON AND MIDDLESEX.—Notice is hereby given that Her Majesty's Justices of the Peace for the City and County, knowing the general corruption and inaccuracy of the witnesses, do intend, at the next Sittings of their honorable Court—viz: the first of the month next ensuing—to reject verbal testimony altogether, and form their correct and infallible judgments upon the sure and undeviating basis of that most profound and useful of all sciences—Craniology.   JAMES BUMPUS,
    SESSIONS HOUSE, January 4, 1955.   Clerk of the Peace.

TO ACCOUNTANTS AND OTHERS.—Any person who will undertake to unravel the Bank Accounts, find real Claimants for the unclaimed Dividends, and point out an easy and effectual way to pay off the National Debt, may have constant employment, on application to JOHN BULL, No. 1 Bullion Street.

NOW OPEN.—The AERIAL SUSPENSION TERRACE, from the Iron Gallery of the Monument to the Ball and Cross of St. Paul's Cathedral.   This delightful promenade is open daily for the use of children and invalids, and is entirely free from the smoke of the Railway trains passing through the City of London.   For the accommodation of Visitors, the Proprietor has made arrangements with the Aerial Omnibus Company for one of their Balloons to stop at either Entrance of the Suspension Terrace every five minutes. Toll: Adults, 1d.; Children and Servants, Half-price.

SINGULAR CURIOSITY.—To be seen alive, at 229 Regent Street, a remarkably fine specimen of that noble animal, the HORSE. It is perfectly tame and docile, and is supposed to be the last of the species which formerly drew the cabs, broughams, etc., of the Metropolis. As this extraordinary animal will not long remain in London, an early visit is suggested, it being the Proprietor's intention to exhibit the Horse in the Provinces. Admission: Front Seats, 2s.; Back do., 1s. Visitors are allowed to mount, as a real Saddle has been borrowed for the occasion from the British Museum.

RAIN FOR PEAS.—ELECTRICAL POCKET MACHINES, for Dissolving Clouds instantaneously. Of immense utility and assistance to Gardeners. To be seen in full operation in the Parterre of Messrs. FIELD & WATERS, Meadow Lane, Moorfields.

COMFORT IN TRAVELING.—Messrs. Walker and Flight beg to invite the attention of pedestrians to their portable walking sticks, which contain, (conveniently stowed away,) in their interior tubes, a bed, bolster and pillow, ready for inflation; also, a bedstead, linen sheets, Whitney blankets, soap, pens, ink, sealing-wax, paper, boot-jack, fire, knives, forks, spoons, Milton, Shakespeare. Byron, easy-chair and comfortable velocipede. At prices varying from 2s. 6d. to an Albert. Budge Row. Copy the address.

LOST.—In England, between the years 1840 and 1850, all interest in the productions of one William Shakespeare. The missing article was sadly mutilated in the 19th century, by persons of the names of William Macready, Charles Kean and James Anderson. Being of little use to any but the owner, and not much to him, no very great reward will be given. Address Legitimate Drama, Humbug Street, Drury Lane.

We extract the first leading article entire. It is as follows, viz:

"In these days of progress let us sneer at nothing because it is new. We may smile and doubt, but still let us—think! Nearly two centuries have passed since our journal first started into existence; and, during that brief period, we have chronicled changes and improvements which have shaken the earth to its very center. We now print off more than one million copies of *The Times* newspaper per day, and are enabled to effect this great desideratum by means of air-pressure, which has completely superseded the use and power of steam. We now *blow* off fifty times the number of impressions we were formerly enabled to do by the then all-powerful use of steam. But even this is nothing compared to what we are preparing to effect for our readers in future. Within one little week from the present date, we shall dispatch our broad sheet to the remotest corner of the habitable world within fifteen minutes from the time of its leaving Printing-House Square. The number of impressions required to be worked for the supply of all the earth will be, as our readers are aware, incalculable; but we have entered into an arrangement for the construction of a cylinder which is to throw off 5,000,000 copies per hour. The sceptical may, perhaps, deem this an exaggerated statement. Let them do so. We say that we are about to achieve this miracle; and what *The Times* promises it always performs. But it may be said that the thing is impossible. The same observation has been made from time to time upon any advance in art or science. Little progress is made without perseverance. The man who invented printing was burned for a wizard;

the first applier of gas was neglected, and starved on a dunghill; and the first English maker of a steam-packet was treated as a mere visionary, although he happily lived to see his model cross the Atlantic. Again we say—readers, smile if you will, and *doubt*, but think—as sure as the sun rises in the East and sinks in the West, we will perform what we promise. Every day is suggestive of some important improvement in our present wonderful machinery; and we will not rest upon our oars until we have annihilated both time and space."

The following is an article in which a *résumé* of the doings in Parliament on the previous evening is given, viz:

"LONDON, Thursday, January 6, 1955.

In the House of Peeresses last night, their Ladyships agreed to a motion brought forward by the Duchess of Brompton, by which, in future, the journals of Parliament are to record what is left undone, instead of narrating every trivial circumstance of fact, as heretofore. On a motion of Lady Peel, their Ladyships agreed to a return of the expenses incurred bringing the waters of the Nile to the Metropolis.

MRS. BROTHEROE gave notice that she should move the House to repeal the standing order which prohibited the admission of the other sex during the debates.

MRS. BATHURST, in a most forcible, eloquent, and feeling speech, called the attention of the House to the distressing particulars of a death from actual starvation, which had occurred in the metropolis, and held it monstrous that such a casualty should take place while the Sisters of Charity took so large a stipend from the public purse for the sole purpose of preventing the possibility of such destitution.

MRS. HOME SECRETARY HAWES proved the death of the individual alluded to arose from a mistaken spirit of pride on his part. The man had barricaded himself in a lonely house near the ruins of St. James's Palace, and had positively refused to be seen by, or receive aid from, the Sisters of Charity. She was, however, perfectly willing to consent to any inquiry upon the subject which the House might suggest.

MRS. COCHERANE laid upon the table her bill for the observance of a proper dietary by all ranks of society.

MRS. BATHURST opposed the motion, and moved that the bill be read that day six months. The Hon. and learned Lady called the attention of the House to the primitive history of America, and drew a forcible picture of the horrors of Democracy. She placed these horrors in juxtaposition with the blessings which had occurred to the same country by its after adoption of monarchical government; and she did not think that England could, consistently with the true dignity due to its own character, interfere to make this monarchy elective. The bill before the House invested England with a most arbitrary power, and she should be sorry to see any of her countrywomen or countrymen called upon to interfere with America in her choice of a Queen. The Hon. Lady was exceedingly happy in her allusions to the policy, or, rather, impolicy of England in bygone times, and completely roused the risible faculties, if she did not actually rivet the more serious attentions, of her auditory, by detailing the petty schemes and maneuvering of our own country in endeavoring to entrap poor Samuel Binks Columbus into accepting the crown of America. The Hon. Lady concluded a speech remarkable for its bitter irony by calling upon her countrywomen to reject the bill as an interference at once uncalled for, unconstitutional and unwise.

MRS. SKEFFINGTON declared it to be her intention to support the amendment of Mrs. Bathurst, if Mrs. Home Secretary Hawes persisted in pushing the motion to a division. England, she contended, had suffered for ages from interference with the political government of countries for which, in fact, it did not care one farthing.

MRS. COCHRANE said at present England had the whip hand of America, and she thought her countrywomen could not do better than keep that turbulent nation in its present subjection.

A discussion then ensued upon a petition presented by Mrs. Lushington from

Hounslow, praying for a return of the practice of burying the dead instead of burning them, as at present ordered by law.

Mrs. Peel objected to the reception of the petition, and called attention to the fact that it was only in the unenlightened ages of the last century that the indecent practice of burying the dead in the midst of the living was tolerated.

The petition was rejected, and the other orders of the day having been gone through, the House adjourned."

And, to conclude, we give the following additional advertisements:

HOT AIR PIPES.—The Commissioners appointed by Government to protect the lives of the middle classes of society, hereby give notice that they are ready to receive tenders for an immediate supply of Gutta Percha Tubes, to be laid down for the dissemination of hot air in the streets of the Metropolis, as the Act will come into operation on the first of March. Entitled "An Act to prevent Persons Perishing of Cold in the Streets of London and Villages adjacent." Blanket House, Dec. 26, 1954.

POCKET SHIRT-WASHER.—This invaluable article for the toilet may be had of Messrs. Combes & Sweet, Lavender Hill. By this simple, but useful, contrivance, gentlemen's shirts wash, iron and starch themselves whilst on the backs of their wearers. Price one Edward. In waistcoat boxes, two Edwards.

BRITISH ASSOCIATION.—An extraordinary meeting of the Members will be held on the 1st of February next, Professor Wageman in the chair. A full attendance is particularly requested, as Professor Jackson is prepared to prove as an indisputable fact, that the Antediluvians kept cows and vended their produce like Christians; the learned Professor having discovered during his travels in Belgraria, a petrified milk-walk with a fragment of a fossil pump-handle at the end of it.

WHO'S FOR GOLD.—The Lucifer Line of Omnibuses across the Rocky Mountains, starts from "The Swan with Two Necks," to the Kingdom of California, every other hour. Fare half-an-Albert. No gold will be received.

ECONOMISE YOUR TIME.—John Sears would inform to the public, now that coal has become scarce, that having perfected his wonderful invention, the Composition-Warming-Blocks, a large supply of the article is to be found at the Suspended Warehouse, ninety-eight feet S. E. from the ball of St. Pauls. Carrier balloons every five minutes from Hyde Park grand gate. Professor Sears would state for the information of the public that he has an article of Composition-Warming-Blocks, in a corner of each of which, a match is inserted, which being touched with sand paper, speedily ignites the Block, thus avoiding the vexatious delays heretofore suffered in the kindling of a fire. Prof. S., having patented his invention, is now a marriageable man within the letter of the law, and is ready to receive proposals.

HIFALUTIN LETTER EXPRESS.—Letter Wings, with Clock-Work attached, will be supplied cheap at 92,451 Strand, to such as cannot afford to pay the exorbitant price of one penny to Wells, Fargo & Co's Ancient Grand Air, Earth and Water Express, for the transportation of Packages across the Island. Tables giving the number of turns to the key for each distance, and showing to an inch the different distances between door-step and door-step, throughout the south and center of England, furnished gratis.

- - - The following, writes "our John," is what K. N. Pepper Esq. would call a Nepigram,—it dropped from the pen of a literary friend on a warm day of ye present month:

> 'The Seasons drive Time's circling Car—
> And this the unwelcome fact explains,
> Why 'times' so dull and sluggish are
> For Winter *holdeth back the rains.*"

- - - While promenading Montgomery Street the other day, we fell in with an old friend who has not done so well in this country as he probably would have done, had the art of distillation never been discovered. "What are you doing now, Blossom?" said we. "Sir," replied Blossom, with great solemnity, but a rather vacant expression of countenance, "I'm taster of liquors to Patty & Barren, *office hours from 9 P. M. till daylight*"—and then he hiccoughed. His salary should be large, poor fellow, for he is undoubtedly very attentive to business. - - - The following, from the archives of the "Mission of Dolores—Asylum for vagabond puns," was committed by Judge T——, after incredible labor and exertion, during some four months occupied principally in watching it. "Who was the mother of St. Luke?" "Probably a Mameluke." This pun is evidently antique and of Hebrew origin, being a "*Jew d' esprit.*" - - - IN a country town in Vermont, whilom, there dwelt a waggish character who was nicknamed by the townsfolk, "Drug." He was a man who could carry out a practical joke, as well as appreciate one. It so happened, that on a certain Sabbath, there was no minister to officiate in the small Presbyterian church of the village. In the dilemma, one Deacon Hicks, voluntered to mount the pulpit and read a sermon. The choir appeared to be empty and the good deacon commenced the services. To eke out the time, he selected the longest Psalm in the book, to read after the prayer. There were fifty mortal stanzas; the deacon waded through every one of them, and took his seat, merely because it was customary, and was about to arise a second afterwards to read a selection from the Scriptures, when he was surprised to observe lank "Drug" rearing himself, solitary and alone, in the choir, showing full half of his person over the curtains, and commencing in a most nasal tone to sing the first stanza. The Deacon took his seat again, quite gratified that his friend "Drug" was sedate for once in his life, and that he had come so kindly to his (the Deacon's) assistance. After some nine stanzas had been sung, he began to grow nervous, wishing to proceed to the sermon. But "Drug" continued on, with imperturable face, and notwithstanding the Deacon hemmed, and skook his handkerchief and tried all ways imaginable to arrest the attention of the wag in the choir, the latter quietly persevered, neither looking to the right nor the left, until he had sung out the entire fifty stanzas. This done, he took his seat as though nothing had happened. The Deacon eat a cold dinner that day and concluded that he had adopted a profession which was "not at all in his line." - - - ONE of the best conducted and pleasantest hotels that one can meet in his journeyings through California, is "The Merchant's" at Marysville. Convenient, quiet, elegant and home-like, are the terms best expressing its condition. Mine hosts, Messrs. Stephenson & Churchill, leave nothing undone to secure the comfort and pleasure of their guests. It is rarely that one sits at a better table, rarely that one meets a more polished and agreeable company than are to be found at the establishment just west of the Plaza. Most agreeable is it to meet in your host, a man who can sympathise in your "creature wants,"—but if, peradventure, he be an educated gentleman and one *au fait* in the elegancies of life, as are our friends of "The Merchant's," then is it doubly to one's advantage to place himself under their social roof. - - - During the sojourn of Christy's Minstrels among us, "Our John" was called upon to prepare a local song for them, to be consigned to the pleasant flats and spaces of "The other side of Jordan." The song of course "took," excellent well. We have a few stanzas by us at this present writing, the best of which we cannot refrain from transferring to our pages. They run as follows :—

> "The British and the French feel just as good as new,
>   Sebastopol is now all their burden,—
> But if all accounts from Petropol'ski are true,
>   They were walloped on the other side of Jordan."

>   *   *   *   *

> "Henry Meiggs built this hall, a year or two ago,
>   It's a long un, a high un, a broad un,
> But he made a bigger *haul* just before he went away,
>   And—he *tuk* it to the other side o' Jordan."

Alas, too true! - - - AN esteemed contributor has prepared for us the following account of a scene which occurred not long since, not a thousand miles away from Powell street, or Bush street, there or thereabouts: "What do you think!" exclaimed a friend of ours, as he rushed into his house the other evening in a high state of nervous excitement. In his hand he held a basket, covered with a white cloth, which he deposited very carefully on the floor. "What do you think! I've found a baby!" "A baby! when? where? how? Why *Charles!* What in the world did you bring it here for?" remarked his wife with great astonishment. "Do you think we need an addition to the family? Have we not babies enough already, I would like to know? How came you with other folks' babies? Where did you get it?" During this outburst, our friend was pacing the floor with hurried strides, the top of his hat crushed in, and his agitated face expressing the fearful responsibility he had assumed. Coming to a halt, and folding his arms in an exceedingly impressive and solemn manner, he said—"My dear, this innocent child has been abandoned, and left in the streets to perish; and had not Providence directed my steps toward it, the rising sun would have found it cold in death. Just opposite the Lager Bier Saloon, I nearly stumbled over this basket, when a low, piteous moan made me aware of its contents. Take it, my dear; cherish and protect it, and when in some future time we see it occupying a high and distinguished position in society, our hearts with pleasure will recur to this most happy hour." As he gently raised the basket from the floor to place it in her hands, something very like a cry seemed to issue from it, striking with painful distinctness upon their ears. All the latent chords of the mother's sympathies were aroused. She forgot her previous annoyance, her already sufficiently numerous family—everything, in fact, except the helpless creature before her thus imploring for relief. "Poor little thing!" she exclaimed. "It's nearly starved, I expect; there, there, there—don't cry; bless his little heart"—and, carefully removing one corner of the napkin, she discovered what appeared to be the outline of a very diminutive, dark complexioned child. Starting suddenly back, she indignantly exclaimed—"O, horror! It's *black!*" and, covering her face with her hands, sank into a chair. A boisterous shout of laughter was the only reply. Not appreciating the joke, and being rather angry at having her feelings thus trifled with, she said, somewhat tartly—"I'm sure *I* don't see anything amusing in all this. You bring home a nigger baby in a basket, endeavor to enlist my sympathies in its favor, and then make fun of me. Charles, I am ashamed of you!" A renewed burst of laughter cut short the lecture, nor could any answer be obtained to the oft-repeated question—"What in the wide world *are* you laughing at?" while our friend was rolling on the floor, holding his hands on his sides, kicking out his legs, and displaying many other very decided symptoms of insanity. Finally he managed to gasp forth—"It——may——not be——very ugly;——why——don't——you——examine——its *features?*" Hastily approaching the basket, she tore off the cover, and disclosed——*a large, cold, roast goose,* beautifully cooked, and quite brown. The mystery was solved—a kind friend had presented the said goose, and the creaking of the handle had been mistaken for a cry. It was a severe struggle between anger at being made the victim of such an *unfeeling,* practical joke, and the extreme ludicrousness of the whole affair. Natural good humor, however, prevailed, and many were the jests on the subject of an increase in the family, and the extraordinary philanthropy displayed by "Charles" in his effort to save a young soul *slightly off color.* - - - READ, mark, learn, and inwardly digest the following excellent paragraph, which we cut from that well-edited and sensible sheet, *The Chronicle :*

"WE have never seen in this city so many beautiful women collected together on a similar occasion. There was not as much extravagant dressing as we had anticipated,—a very good sign. This has been a vice as well as a folly here. But a better taste seems to have found a commencement. Elegance, the true type of correct taste, is not to be bought with dollars. She who wears the most costly dress, is not necessarily the best-dressed lady. We have seen fair ladies in muslin appear to better advantage than their neighbor with a month of her husband's salary upon her back. There were rich, as well as beautiful dresses displayed upon the occasion, but, comparatively, little of foolish extravagance."

- - - To L. H. F. we would say, that

> " *Would that never*
> *Thou shouldst ever*
> Cease thy soulfull sounding song,"

will scarcely pass muster. The rest of the poem is very good, but not quite excellent enough to induce us to overlook the slight mistake above alluded to. - - - A FRIEND relates the following as an instance of the readiness with which the sons of Erin adapt themselves to any land service in which they may happen to be engaged. When Napoleon meditated the invasion of England, it was proposed to enlist some of the Irishmen who at that time in large numbers made France their home. It was believed that hatred to the "Ould Country" would make them good fighters. Gen. Humbert was detailed upon the recruiting service, and soon collected quite a large battalion. While in Bordeaux, one of his new recruits met an Englishman, a domiciled resident of the city. With true Irish heartiness Pat clapped him on the shoulder, saying "Yer my Prisoner!" "Prisoner! to whom?" inquired the Englishman. "Prisoner to the Frinch!" - - - THIS reminds us of an incident which occurred in this city, a day or two since. A lady who resides on "Sophia Terrace," had requested a storekeeper, from whom she had purchased a work-box, to send it up to her residence. The same afternoon the Irish porter was dispatched with the package. He was told to go to No. 20 "Sophia Terrace," and the *locale* of this little street was accurately described to him. He wandered round until he thought himself about in the right place, and then going up to a door, which happened in fact to be the very place to which he was sent, he rapped. The door was opened, and Pat, holding the box carefully in his hand, asked with the utmost innocence—"Sure, and does Sophia Terrence live here?" Pat delivered the box, but couldn't for the life of him understand why the laugh should happen to come in just at that point. - - - AMIDST the recent changes in San Francisco, one of the most noteworthy is the gradual but certain transfer of business from Montgomery down to Battery street. Upon the latter thoroughfare, Page, Bacon & Co. have recently erected one of the most classic structures in the city. Here also stands the new Merchants' Exchange, and opposite the latter, the corner-stone of the new Custom House was recently laid. A large crowd were assembled on the occasion, and the ceremonies were exceedingly interesting, Mr. SAMUEL J. BRIDGE, the Appraiser-General, officiating. His eloquent address, replete with information touching the past and present commercial condition of our city, was listened to with marked attention by the merchants and citizens generally who were present. We understand that arrangements have been made to complete the structure this year. - - - WE are in **regular receipt** of the *Sierra Citizen*, published in Downieville, and one of the most neatly edited papers in the State. Its editor, Mr. C. B. McDONALD, is a polished writer, and we are happy to learn that the *Citizen* is rapidly growing into favor wherever it appears. Its first volume was completed on the third of last month, and we cannot refrain from copying a short extract from the leading article, which is entitled "Finished." Here it is:

> "However little we have accomplished, we have tried to do right, never wantonly assailed our neighbors, or aught set down in malice—never lent our assistance in a bad cause. Now we have turned a leaf to a page that is yet unwritten, and perhaps ere it is finished, some one else may be called to write in black letters, at the bottom of the page, the last word that is spoken of so many thousands of Earth's inhabitants—DIED! Then
>
> Tap! tap! says the hammer
To the nail in the coffin-lid.
>
> The rattling of the clods in the narrow prison house, the snow drifts over the fresh-dug earth, and all is finished—here!
>
> Our lives are made up of anniversaries. One day the roaring of cannon, and the merry peals of the village bells proclaim the nation's jubilee; another day breaks silently and unheralded, revealing an empty seat in the chimney corner, or some memento of a friend whose work is finished. One man sits in his counting-house, reckoning up the gains of the past year, while his schoolfellow sits beneath a hedge, thinking that just one year ago, a cloud appeared in the horizon, at first no bigger than a man's hand, and how that it grew blacker and heavier, until it sank round him, and all his hopes and fortunes melted in its damp folds. In one place youth and beauty are celebrating their birthday with dance and song, and in another, the chill of death is creeping over the wounded soldier on the battle field. One day the Moslem turns his face toward his shrine, and utters "God is great!" Another, the Christian looks to the East for the Star of Bethlehem. Time goes on in an endless cycle, and in threescore and ten years, all have finished."

- - - WHAT can be more agreeable as a center-table companion than Morris & Willis's *Home Journal.* To say the least, it is a rare privilege to commune weekly with two of the leading poets and prose writers of America. The *Home Journal* has long ranked with the leading magazines, and if the fireside of a gentleman of intelligence is not complete without the *Knickerbocker, Putnam's, Blackwood's, Punch,* and the *London Illustrated News,* it most assuredly is not furnished without the *Home Journal.* We have long considered this American classic as the embodiment of taste in Literature. Its price is a mere nothing in California, and if those of our citizens who are not in the habit of purchasing it, will call at LeCount & Strong's or Ullman's, and possess themselves of one number, we are confident that they will not thereafter allow their homes to be uncheered by its genial rays. - - - AND, by the way, we would say before closing our Gossip, that we are happy to be informed that a limited number of "*The Knickerbocker Gallery,*" a full description of which we gave in our last, has arrived, and is for sale at LECOUNT & STRONGS'. - - - MR. EDWARD POLLOCK, who has too long "held silence," presents himself once more to our readers this month. In "Annie Seabrook" he has chosen the commonest materials for a story, and has worked them up to the very best advantage. The tale which he offers to the public in this number, although similar in character to many of the tales that appear in our magazines, stands among the leading ones of its class. - - - In one of the western towns in Massachusetts, not long since, there was a general gathering of the faithful for the good of the Baptist cause. "Old Drug,"—an individual who figured above as having assisted a deacon to eke out the services by singing fifty mortal stanzas of a psalm,—desirous of seeing what might be interesting on the occasion, left the farm, up in Vermont, and went down to spend a week at the gathering. It was a very warm day, and after several clergymen and deacons had relieved themselves, one Elder Beaman arose to address the assembled crowd. He said that the heat was very oppressive; that he was very unwell, and in fact was scarcely able to speak at all;—he hoped his brethren and sisters would excuse him from making a long address, as it would be utterly impossible for him to speak at length, owing to the weak state of his lungs and his general debility;—that after saying a few words he would "yield the stand to Brother Whippey, yonder." The good Elder then went on with his remarks. He shouted and bellowed and roared, and flung his arms about in the most violent gestures, and in short preached on in this strain for fully two hours and a-half, when he wound up with an exhortation, bellowed forth so loudly that it could be heard a half a mile, and took his seat. "Old Drug" rose to his feet, put his hands in his pocket, stretched himself up to his full hight, and said to himself distinctly enough to be heard by most of the congregation— "I'd like to hear that man once when he was well!" - - - The following will bear embalming. It is entitled "The Hen," and was translated from the German Lyrics of Count Von Auersberg, by "some fellow out East:"

"A famous Hen's my story's theme,
Who ne'er was known to tire
Of laying eggs, but then sh'd scream
So loud o'er every egg, 'twould seem
The house must be on fire.

A turkey cock who ruled the walk,
A wiser bird and older,
Could bear't no more, so off did stalk,
Right to the hen and told her;
'Madam, that scream, I apprehend,
Does nothing to the matter;
It surely helps the eggs no whit,

Then lay your egg, and done with it!
I pray you, madam, as a friend,
Cease that superfluous clatter!
You know not how't goes thro' my head!'
'Humph! very likely!' madam said,
Then proudly putting forth a leg:—
'Uneducated barnyard fowl!
You know no more than any owl,
The noble privilege and praise
Of authorship in modern days,—
I'll tell you why I do it;
First, you perceive, I lay my egg,
And then—*review it.*'"

- - - Almost every one, writes a new contributor, has in his mind's eye a case which he may have been cognizant of, indicative of a meanness of disposition. One or two have just been brought to the writer's memory, of which the following is a sample: A certain young man in Northern Ohio invited a couple of ladies to ride with him one evening. They called at a store while out, and he had the liberality to buy three sticks of candy, one of which he divided between his companions, and kept the two for his private eating. That was very small, but the next is smaller, if possible. . . Old H. had been to town one day, and, on his return, had clubbed a quart of chestnuts from a tree by the roadside. Soon after, meeting a neighbor, he inquired of the latter if he wanted some chestnuts. Of course, he did, and holding his hand, old H. deposited therein *three*, remarking at the same time, "Perhaps you would like to buy a quart?" . . The following was related to me by a friend who witnessed the performances: A party of some six or eight couple, from a neighboring town, had been sleigh-riding one afternoon, and had brought up about three at the hotel in which my friend was boarding. They ordered their horses baited on *hay*, and instead of calling for supper, the young gents walked down town and invested some change in gingerbread and candy, which they brought back and distributed among the ladies, and had a good time generally. About dark they called out the teams, and that each one of the company might bear his proportion of the expense, the whole amount of moneys expended in horse-feed, candies and gingerbread, was averaged and apportioned; but, owing to a scarcity of small change, one of the party found himself out of pocket just three cents. This was more than he was willing to bear, and several ineffectual attempts were made to set matters right. At last an old stage-driver, who had overheard the whole, helped them out of their difficulties by giving the sufferer three coppers, which he pocketed with much satisfaction, and the party then drove off.

THE PIONEER.

Vol. III.]   APRIL, 1855.   [No. 4.

THE GREAT ORDER OF THE CAVE.

BY F. C. EWER.

THE very existence of an association, whose plans are conceived behind the impenetrable veil of secrecy,—whose growth is in the dark, —and whose might, exercised in quick succession upon towns, upon counties and upon states, threatens at last to grasp the whole Union and mould it to its will, is justly cause for alarm, unless the great end at which it aims, is known to be pure and worthy the plaudits of the patriot.

Through the life-giving influence of a momentous discovery, whispered frightfully into the ear of this, that and the other man,—imparted with alarm to a few friends in secret conclave at the midnight hour, has such an association sprung suddenly into life upon the American Continent, like a monster at the tap of the magician's wand.— Whence are the Know Nothings,—what is the great end of their mysterious movement,—in the far depths of whose mind did the dim idea take shape, which has resulted in this perfect machinery,—what is the great secret which has summoned these Americans forth from their peaceful homes, as the innumerable blades of grass answer all over the land to the beckoning of the summer sun,—what is this whispered discovery, that has been potent to gather them into the newly thrown-up wigwams, and, strangers to each other though many of them were before, to so bind them together in a day—in an hour, that we see them in the moment of trial standing shoulder to shoulder, even unto death,—such are questions which we hear upon every street corner.

The obligation of secrecy touching what I shall write is not upon me. It is no longer with trembling hand that I lift the pen to the subject. Americans have banded together for America's sake, and the order is too strong now to fear the machinations of demagogues. There was a time, when defeat at the hustings was inevitable to such as dared breathe a regret at the rascality with which the ballot-box had been corrupted. And the only safe way to rear a dam to check this corruption, was to do it in secret. Thank God, the dam has been reared, and the first step towards the great end has been taken. The true patriots have learned in secret how great is their strength ; they tread boldly forth in the broad light of day, in closely-knit phalanxes, which sweep everything before them, and those, who would strike axe at the very root of our institutions, stand aghast.

Secrecy is no longer an absolute necessity for success. Nay, America has stood the test applied to her, and open publicity is perhaps required now, for the completion of the work, which is as yet but *begun,*—the finishing of those ramparts, behind which we can successfully ward off the impending and awful blow, whose coming was so opportunely discovered.

From the relation which I hold to the Know Nothings—more fully to be explained below—I believe no one can gainsay my right to assume my present position. I am bounden to no man—save perhaps to one. I am free to speak as I list, notwithstanding his objections. I have faithfully kept the secret during the trying times, and as I believe the above questions can now be answered with safety, nay with profit to my countrymen, as I am fully convinced of my clear right to answer them, I have decided to lay this paper before the public, let the consequences be what they may.

It is supposed by many not connected with the order, and indeed by most of those in the order, who have not passed behind the veil of that "secret degree"—that *sanctum sanctorum,* the very existence of which is unknown except to a few only of the leaders, that the main and ultimate objects of the Know Nothing Association are to sweep away the political hacks, who for years have ridden down the country,—to clean out the filth from the hustings,—to put a stop to double, triple and quadruple voting,—to the stuffing and breaking up of the ballot-boxes,—and to hurl away the muscle-suasion which has so long deterred many well-disposed citizens from exercising their right of suffrage. That these are important preliminary objects of the society is true. But it must be remembered that illegal voting is mainly confined to the cities. The great rural districts are intact, and so far exceed the urban in population as to preclude all apprehension for the safety of our country from the evils mentioned. It must be remembered, too, that the presence of this monster association is not felt in the cities alone, where only it would be needed, were the above-mentioned the sole objects of the society. Wondrous in its ubiquity, it finds its home also among the villages of our land, and at the magic disclosure the indweller of the quiet hamlet passes from his fireside and joins his comrads. A great American heart is beating, and throughout the remotest veinlets, as along its central arteries, are the pulsations distinctly felt. It is not merely to save some half-dozen cities, that the natives of our land, rural as well as urban, are gathering their strength.

—It is ripe time that the true relation, which these immediate objects of the Know Nothings bear to the great ultimate object, should be known, not only by those without the pale of the order, but by those within, who have advanced only through the *well-known* "degrees." It is time that the threatening cloud, which has so suddenly called forth these preliminary preparations for defense should be pointed out as it approaches, and that the nature of the *grand end* for which the movement was put under way, should transpire and be thoroughly understood.

It was an innocent curiosity that led me to a discovery of a most important character, a full account of which I propose to lay before the public. In the spring of 1852—I think it was about the latter part of April—while I was out of employment, and waiting for a position on one of our daily papers which had been promised me, I was in the habit of wandering out of the city with a few biscuits and a flask of sherry in my pocket, and spending hours among the hills around the Mission Dolores and the Presidio. At that time San Francisco had not run up to the summit of Russian and Clay Street hills, much less scattered its suburbs down the slopes on the other side, and he was considered as an adventurer indeed, who built his cabin beyond Larkin Street. My walks on these occasions were frequently extended to the shore of the Pacific, and I loitered away many an hour, watching its rollers, as they came sweeping inevitably towards me, and finally breaking into sunny crests, and tumbling in long surfs far up the beach. On one of these occasions as I was sauntering back—the twilight approaching—I struck into a short path on the western side of a hill which lies about midway between the ocean and Lone Mountain. I was surprised to find that the path, after growing rapidly more and more distinct, suddenly stopped. As I walked on ruminating upon the circumstance, the singularity of the fact grew upon me so much, that I resolved to turn back and investigate the mystery. I was not long in discovering near the end of the path a hole, concealed by growing bushes and leading into the earth. I stood for a moment wondering what it could be, and irresolute whether to explore further, or to pass on and return to it at some subsequent time. I had little occasion to think it was aught else than the work of human hands, for a board was lying near among the bushes, and there were unmistakable footprints in the vicinity. It would be with no little difficulty that I could enter, for the hole was comparatively small, and it was at least natural for me to feel, that the attempt would not be without risk. But curiosity conquered, and I placed myself upon my hands and knees and crawled in. I found the passage descending gradually in an irregular curve, and enlarging as I proceeded, until at last it was of sufficient hight to admit one to stand erect, and about eight feet broad.

The first object that I met was what seemed to be a loose pile of cloth. It was dark in the passage, and I could not distinguish very clearly what it was. I continued, however, crawling stealthily on, and at last came upon a niche in the side of the passage, which contained, as nearly as I could tell by the sense of touch, a large, rough wardrobe. The doors were open, and it was empty.

I had proceeded but a short distance further, when I distinctly heard a footstep approaching me. I rose to my feet, and moved back to conceal myself in the wardrobe. But I could not have been so far from it when I started to return as I supposed, for in commencing (as I thought immediately) to run my hand along the wall to feel for it, I found I must have already passed it, as I soon felt the pile of cloth beneath my feet. Under this I quietly concealed myself instead. The footstep approached nearer and nearer, and at last passed me.

I waited until I supposed the individual had made his egress into the open air, and then attempted to explore the passage again. But, to my surprise, found my movements impeded by a second personage ; and suffice it to say, between curiosity on the one hand and the two unknowns on the other, I found myself a prisoner, so to speak, for five long hours.

As the evening waned into night, there seemed to be preparations going on within ; of what nature I could not, of course, discover. It must have been about half-past eleven, when a torch was brought into the passage, which served dimly to light it up. One of the unknowns then posted himself within a few feet of my place of concealment, and, although he varied his position somewhat, standing at times so near me that I could have touched him, yet from his motions, taken in connection with other maneuvers, I could come to no other conclusion than that a meeting of some kind was about to assemble, and that he was acting as a guardian over the entrance.

By the dim light I discovered, to my surprise, that his features were masked, and that he was clothed in a domino, on the breast of which, in large, distinct figures, was the number "29." As can well be conceived, there was no other course for me to pursue, than to lie without a single motion, and await breathlessly the result.

It was not long before I heard some one entering. The guardian moved a few feet down the passage, while the new comer selected from the pile above me a domino, and from another pile in the vicinity which, strange to say, I had not noticed before, a mask. After concealing his person and face, he said a few words to the guardian and disappeared within. Shortly afterwards another entered, and went through with the same maneuvers. Then another, and another, and another, at different intervals, until the number reached about twenty-five.

Meanwhile, I had come to the frightful conclusion, that my place of concealment was a pile of dominos, which threatened in a short time so far to decrease, as to discover me. And I thought, tremblingly, of the necessity to which I might be forced, of endeavoring to make my exit unheeded by the sentinel, and of the possibility that I might be stopped by some one outside. I waited anxiously, but fortunately for me, the assemblage was not numerous that evening.

As the stragglers came in, I endeavored to catch the magic words which permitted advance beyond the sentinel. At times, when he happened to be standing near the pile of dominos, I could almost distinguish them, and had I commenced earlier to make the discovery, I should doubtless have been successful the first night.

In about two hours the meeting seemed to have adjourned, for the parties passed out, one by one, as they had entered ; in no instance did two go out together. Seizing an opportunity when, as I supposed, the last one had departed,—at least, when the guardian had gone down the passage, I stealthily left my place of concealment, and crawled out. I shall never forget the sense of relief which I felt as I gained the open air, and the trepidation with which I ran up the hill, stumbling among the bushes.

It was quarter of four when I reached my room, and throwing myself upon my bed, I revolved in my mind the singular events of the night. An ungovernable impulse had seized me to ferret out the mystery. I felt charmed on, even though it was to my destruction. And, during the subsequent two months, my mind was occupied with little else. I visited the spot, night after night, under the cover of darkness, and at last, when Saturday evening rolled round again, I found that the board was removed which, during the other nights, seemed to have been carelessly thrown over the hole. But should I be as successful now in gaining admission? Where would the unknown be, as I approached my place of concealment? Would he endeavor to come out, as I was entering? What would be my fate, were I discovered?

I was early upon the spot. To enter, I was determined; and I knew that my only hope was extreme caution, watchfulness and slowness of movement. I placed myself flat upon the earth and moved in, an inch at a time. In this way I at last gained the pile of dominos, and waited for the assemblage to gather. I determined to lose no time, but to devote all my attention towards catching, if possible, the phrase which served as a password for admission. I listened long and closely. I caught one word, then another, then another, and listened to the repetition until, at last, I satisfied myself that I was master of the phrase.

After the meeting broke up, a domino, bearing the number "5" upon his breast, approached the guardian to say a word, when I overheard the latter remark, that it was dull business for him there, and that he would like to change places on the next evening, and stand at the entrance; to which the latter assented.

I believe my curiosity is no greater than that of most men, but I had gone too far to recede. The more I saw, the more I was determined to see; and when the next Saturday night came, I was promptly at the mysterious passage.

I remembered the remarks of the two guardians, and as I knew the wardrobe was this side the " entrance," alluded to by the unknown number 27, my course was clear. I waited until several had passed in, and then, not without trembling heart, essayed myself. The guardian was at his post. I carelessly selected a domino and a mask, and having put them on, passed to him, whispered into his ear the strange phrase, " LANDMARK, OUR GUIDE," was permitted to proceed, and, as though nothing were unusual, sauntered carelessly down the crooked passage, until I was out of his sight. My course, as I have said, was clear. It was necessary for me to gain the wardrobe. I stepped stealthily along and discovered that it was only about fifteen feet from the entrance of what I found to be a lighted, subterraneous chamber. Strange to say, there was no door at the entrance, as I believe is usual in such cases.

But, unfortunately, the second guardian was posted near the wardrobe. Here was a dilemma. I could neither return, nor go on. While I was waiting in utter doubt as to what I should do, I heard footsteps behind me. I pretended that I was stopping to arrange my garments, and the unsuspecting individual passed me and entered. As he walked on, the inside guardian, in saying something to him, accompanied him to the entrance ; and seizing the opportunity, (for I knew not when another would occur,) I moved rapidly and stealtily along, hugging the wall as I proceeded, and slipped into my new place of concealment, where I found several swords and two or three dominos.

But it is needless for me to recount the minutiæ of my movements. Suffice it to say, what I at first considered as a misfortune, to wit, the position of the inside sentinel so near the wardrobe, proved of the utmost advantage to me. It was, however, only after three nights of anxiety and care that I was enabled to obtain the second pass-phrase. "GOD AND HIS EMPIRE. WE DESTROY TO SAVE," were its ominous words ; and each member who repeated it, received from the sentinel a sword. My curiosity was only excited the more.

But, although I had persevered until I could easily pass the two sentinels and reach the entrance, how was I to become acquainted with the formalities, should there be any, necessary for me to go through, in the cave, before I could pass to a seat.

I arranged a plan for the next Saturday night, and determined to take at least one step in advance. When the time came I entered, clothed myself, gave the pass-phrase "Landmark, Our Guide," to the outside sentinel, passed on, repeated the sentence, " God and His Empire. We Destroy to Save," to the inside sentinel, received from him a sword which I buckled around me, and went without hesitation to the entrance, where I stopped. I looked down and found that I was bearing the number " 28 " on my breast. I leaned unconcernedly against the edge of the entrance, looking into the cave, and was not at all astonished to find that the guardian, after regarding me a moment, approached me. His question did not at all surprise me. He asked me if I didn't intend to go in. I answered that I should enter shortly,— that I desired to wait a moment for a friend who had not arrived. I little knew how nearly I approached making a most fatal error in answering as I did. The guardian hesitated a moment, but as, partly from sheer ignorance, I manifested no trepidation, he seemed satisfied and resumed his post.

As I anticipated, I had not to tarry long before an individual duly received his sword, and passed me. The cave was oval—the longest diameter being about thirty feet in length, and the shortest about seventeen. At the end opposite the entrance, and on a platform, which was ascended by two steps, stood an altar. It was so painted or covered, to say the least, that it had the appearance of having been constructed of crystalized substances. Upon it lay an open book, behind which stood a crucifix, with three lighted candles on each side. While on its front were the letters "I. H. S.," in appearance as though made of crystals, but in color of gold. Near the altar, and on the right side of the cave as I was facing, stood a black canopied cathedra; above the chair was a shelf on which rested a miter, and over the shelf was the canopy, projecting as a roof to the chair. Upon the short, black curtain, hanging from its front, was a representation in white, of a sword and crosier crossed ; and the cathedra held a masked figure, clothed in a white domino. At the end of the cave opposite to the altar was a rostrum, canopied with blue and containing a crowned and masked figure in a crimson domino. On the front of the rostrum was a representation, in crimson, of a sword crossed with a scepter. The crimson domino seemed to be acting as a presiding officer over the assemblage. Around the sides of the cave were ranged benches, upon which sat brown, green and purple dominos ; and distinct upon the breast of each was a number in large figures. The numbers did not range very high, 31 being the highest that I saw in the room. The sides of the cave were boarded up, and across the ceiling stretched rafters with boards on top of them. I discovered afterwards in the center of the ceiling a large hole, which I subsequently learned reached perpendicularly through the hill, and came out a short distance below its summit. Over it was a shanty, into which, as I ascertained afterwards, the iniatiate was led, and after being blindfolded, was made to walk across a trap-door, which fell with his weight, and precipitated him through the tunnel into the cave, where he struck upon a machine so arranged with weights as to break his fall. I afterwards thanked my stars that I had gained admission without suffering the frightful initiatory ceremony and swearing the fearful oaths.

With this description, the movements of the individual who passed me, as I have said above, and by whom I learned how to work my way in, will be understood. He stepped to the center of the room, knelt facing the altar, bowed his head and crossed himself, then rising to his feet, he turned, faced the rostrum, drew his sword and gracefully saluted the scarlet domino with a " Present Arms," being saluted by the president in return, who rose to his feet during the formality. He then sheathed his sword, passed to the figure in the cathedra, knelt upon one knee and lifted his scabbard with his left hand, while the domino in the cathedra drew the sword from its sheath, touched him upon the shoulder with its blade, addressed him with " Arise, my Son, Sir Knight of my Faithful Order of the Cave," and, still retaining the sword, laid it upon a pile at his side. The individual whose movements I was casually observing, as were also the rest, then arose to his feet, and took his seat upon one of the side benches. It is needless for me to say that, having waited sufficiently long for my friend to come in, I at last gave it up, and formally entering the cave, passed to the center of the room, knelt, crossed myself, presented arms to the president, and having yielded my sword to the service of the white domino in the cathedra, was dubbed Sir Knight of the Faithful Order of the Cave, and took my seat also.

Thus much I have deemed it necessary to detail for the satisfaction of my reader. I cannot be expected to linger longer among particulars. I would simply state, that the proceedings were to me of a most interesting, not to say startling, character. Of course I could not learn the objects of the gathering at once. I obtained on the first night, however, glimmerings of such a nature, as to excite in me the most serious apprehensions, and to urge me to persevere in my investigations at all hazards, even to that of death itself.

I attended the meetings regularly during the next two months ; and, to come to the point, the result of my investigations was as follows, to wit :

I found that the assemblage, of which I formed a temporary member, was a lodge of an association entitled " Le Grand Ordre de la Caverne." To ensure the utmost secrecy, the lodges are always held in subterraneous chambers. Hence the name of the institution—"The Great Order of the Cave."

As I have said, the members are always masked and dominoed while in the cave, and they call themselves stalagmites. The presiding officer is entitled the royal stalactite. No names are ever mentioned, but when a proposition is made, the motion is put as having come from Stalagmite Number 22, or whatever number the member may happen to bear on his breast that evening. Of course each knows that the person who introduced him, and the individual whom he has introduced, (the oath allowing to no one the privilege of proposing more than one candidate) are members of the order. But, in theory, this is all. The greatest care is taken that none shall know the rest of their comrades, nor be able to recognize them on the street, had they the desire to do so. Of course it is impossible to carry this out to the fullest extent, but so perfect is the machinery of the order, that it is enabled to effect its objects notwithstanding this peculiarity, which is considered as one of the safeguards to secure, so far as possible, the desire of the Institution, that its very existence shall remain a secret to the world, until such time as it has gathered means to itself to accomplish its aims.

I propose to hold nothing back which I have learned. I have not discovered all—but fully enough. I am aware that my life will be in danger from this time forth. But, if so be a timely exposure shall serve to break up the march and influence of the Order, at least, upon this continent,—if so be it will serve to awaken Americans and Englishmen, and Prussians, to the true state of affairs that is surrounding them, I am ready to assume the responsibility and danger of tearing open to the light the designs of this greatest monster that ever cursed the earth,—this enemy to our country,—this throttler of freedom,— this secret murderer of science, general advancement and the happiness of the people. The die is cast, even though the kidnapper stalks behind me upon the morning of publication. It is an insufferable weight upon my mind. I have borne it until it is a torment, and, like the secret of the murderer, it must *out*.

This order—and they *know* it—extends throughout France, Italy, Austria and Upper Germany, Spain, England and Ireland. By whom it was started I know not. As nearly as I could ascertain, it is about sixty years old. Its head-quarters and stronghold are in France. It knows that the past, and with it its appliances for the securing of universal empire, are gone, and gone forever. But it sees in the nineteenth century—elements, which however dissimilar they may be, can possibly be so combined, or used one after the other, as eventually to secure its object. It finds the world cut up into independent nations, in each of which a spirit of aggrandizement is rife ;—it finds that jealousies, bloodshed and wars are the inevitable result of this state of affairs, and, urged by another motive, more powerful to itself, perhaps, than all the rest, it is gathering and strengthening with the utmost aution,—it is enlisting none but leaders, to carry out the stupendous project of bringing the principal nations of the earth within range of the temporal power of one potentate. The murder is out—*is out*, and let me be calm as I finish my recital.

France is gained, and with it, Italy. The mine is now laid in Austria. Foreseeing that a great rising of the people must come, it brought on the revolutions of Europe prematurely, in order that the despots might seize by a firmer grip. It is folly to suppose, for an instant, that the *coup d' état* was the sole work of Louis Napoleon. He is a member, and a very willing instrument of the immense order. With the keenest Machiavelism the tremendous vote by which he was elevated to the presidency was rolled up. When the ripe time came, he vaulted in a night to the imperial throne, and, through the immense influence of the Cave was it, that 36,000,000 of Frenchmen looked on in quiet.

France is a great point gained. And through that country, its wealth, its internal resources, its people,—its power, do they hope to commence the great movement upon other leading nations of the earth, before which, if successful, the lesser powers must inevitably yield.

But meanwhile, the Greek Church was advancing from the East. She must, of course, be checked. The fleets of the Czar must by no means pierce the Bosphorus. Russia must be driven back. The game became extensive. Their hands were full. Nevertheless, inaction would be fatal, and France rushed to the rescue and has been followed by the kingdom of Sardinia. Unwitting England, while she fondly hopes to preserve her commercial power unimpeded, is the veriest tool of "Le Grand Ordre de la Caverne." France is *using* the British armies and moneys merely to assist in driving back the Greek Church,—a work she could not have accomplished alone. Meanwhile, all is bright for the order. For England, although at her zenith, and, perhaps, tottering to her decline, would, nevertheless, had it not been for the war, have remained, too long, immensely powerful, to answer their purposes well. England was too enlightened, too free, and would never succumb, unless brought down to the grade of a second class power. To this position they hope now to reduce her. For the members of the Cave know full well that in default of men, England must *pay* heavily towards the expense of the long campaign. They know that her immense debt, although at present an element of her stability as a nation, can be made so large, that payment of the interest alone, will be intolerable, and that her liabilities will inevitably become to her in time an element of weakness, instead of strength. And there is Ireland too !

But England will be sustained through the influence of the Order of the Cave and by France, until the war is over. For by sustaining her, they but weaken her. And when Russia is driven back, perhaps cur-

tailed of some of her proportions, then can exhausted England be
easily managed. The order knows meanwhile, that it can command
money in abundance, and that it has nothing to fear on that score. To
secure the permanency of the Imperial throne of France, has its plan
to interest the people (through their pockets) in sustaining the present
dynasty, been carried into execution. And the world knows how
greedily Frenchmen swallowed the bait,—cashed the "People's Loan"
bonds, and of course became unwittingly the supporters of the stability
of that government which has so gladly become their debtor.

The order is so strong in Austria already, that it is beginning to feel
confident of ranging her power, sooner or later, side by side with France.
Russia driven back, therefore, Austria gained, and England humbled,
they will be possessed of such a combination of strength, that they
hope easily to subdue Prussia. This done, the smaller kingdoms and
principalities will be but battledores in this immense game of nations.

Their great engine of power is "The Spoils." And there are enough
in Europe, who are ready to occupy the kingly, the grand ducal, the
ducal palaces, etc., under this new system, if the reigning dynasties of
the duchies, the grand duchies, the principalities, and the smaller kingdoms are disagreeably obstinate. The plan works well thus far. God
send against them the strugglings of the people !

But while the order was slowly gaining ground in Europe during
fifty years, it was all at once astounded to find, that a weak nation
in the new world had suddenly arisen to an equal rank with the five
great powers. Its game was becoming as extensive as it could well be.
Nevertheless, while its attention was directed to the management of
affairs in Europe, it was certain that the United States must be cared
for, and emissaries of the order were sent among us. This was about
ten years ago. And since that time, "Caves" have been established in
every leading city of our Union.

The order acts either directly and with considerable boldness, as in
France and Italy, or, as in Austria and England, indirectly, by using
and moulding to its purposes the circumstances of the times as they
arise. None but the shrewdest men are admitted within its precincts ;
and the extremest care and the utmost surveillance—extended for a
long time in secret over the actions and opinions and prejudices of a
candidate—are used, before he is admitted, and allowed to swear the
oaths by which he assumes the terrible responsibility of a leader in the
movement.

The hateful monster is well aware, that if the United States are allowed to continue on their course for fifteen years longer as an entire
nation, our country will become too powerful for them to cope withal.
It knows that if we are broken up, the pieces can be managed, one
by one, with comparative ease. And its great object among us is to
effect if possible, and as soon as possible, a dissolution of the Union.
It is *using* the rabid abolitionists and the rabid secessionists towards
its ends. It is exciting bitterness of feeling among us, wherever it
can. And a certain great high priest in New York, who wields a wide
influence, and the high priests of Boston, who nurse mobs in Fanueil
Hall, and the authoress of "Uncle Tom's Cabin," are just as much the

veriest tools of the order against the glory of our country, and its moral influence in Europe as a great enlightened nation under a republican form of government, as is England in the present war.

The plan to import by an arranged system, thousands of starving ones, and to scatter them among us—thousands, who they know will be useful, when their great hour for "interference" arrives, is perfected, and he who reads the papers, can see how admirably it is working. The late insult to Soulé was but a second blunder of the "Nephew of his Uncle," which, from its prematureness, it was necessary for the power behind the throne to patch up and smooth over.

I could go on, but I have told enough. The dissolution of our Union! The moral effect of our country blown to the winds! What was I to do with this fearful secret! This damnable mine laid throughout our fair land to burst upon us unawares!—I thought over my acquaintances and friends. To whom was I to tell it? It tormented me night and day.

At last I bethought me of Mr. Thomas Southwick of Salem, Massachusetts;—a man in whose patriotism and mental ability I had the utmost confidence. To him I addressed a long letter, announcing the existence of "The Great Order of the Cave," exposing its designs, and asking him what we should do. He responded, that after mature deliberation, he had opened the matter to a few friends, and that they had agreed with him, that a secret American Order should be established, to operate against "The Order of the Cave,"—to approach its borders in every direction, and hem it in. He thought this the best way to test the strength of the American sentiment throughout the Union, and to find out what inroads "The Order of the Cave" had made among us thus far. The existence of the Lodge, and such others as they could succeed in starting to join them, was to be kept a profound secret. And the appropriate name of "Know Nothing" was adopted for it. What the internal organization of the new order is— what its immediate plans are, I know not.

But it is an Institution not to be confined alone to this continent. It is essentially cosmopolitan. It is destined yet to spread over England and Prussia, and to meet this monster, whose designs I have exposed, hand to hand in the most unique and momentous struggle for liberty, science and general advancement, that the world ever knew.

TO SALLIE.

BY G.

My Love is all mine own. To me
  The treasure of her spotless heart
Is freely given. In extacy
  She hails my coming; when we part,
Her last, long, lingering look of love
  Leaves its sweet impress on my soul,
And then, I feel a joy above
  The world's contumely or control.

Beats my pulse high with health, her smile
  Adds vigor to the fount of life:
Doth care corrode, her lips beguile
  The subtle demon from his strife.
Nor fell disease, nor worldly loss,
  Man's hatred, nor the ills of life
Can cast one gloomy cloud across
  The love of my angelic wife!

EPITOME OF THE TRAGEDY OF FAUST.

BY JOHN S. HITTELL.

A WORK of art of the first rank, has an inexhaustible attraction and an ever new meaning to a man capable of appreciating it ; and of such a work, it can never be said, that it has been worn out as a subject for consideration. No matter how competent a man may be when he has the work immediately before him, to think of all its beauties and to combine them as a unit, yet let it be forgotten for a short time, and it slips from his grasp. No one can keep Hamlet full in view before his mind's eye, except by committing the play to memory.

Goethe's Faust has been acknowledged for the last half-century to be a work of art of the first rank. It has been the subject of more comment in Germany, than Shakespeare's works, in England. Professorships have been endowed for special and lengthy courses of lectures upon it. It is said, that one hundred different translations of it have been written in English, and many have been made into other modern languages. But no translation can give a fair idea of the original. Haywood's and Birch's, the best English translations, are barely readable, and would not be readable at all, except for the great curiosity excited by the fame of the original. Faust, in German, is the most attractive of all poetry.

I know that what I here offer is not so well done as the translations of Haywood and Birch, but it is short, and in a shape different from theirs. In beginning, I thought of Carlyle's " Epitome of the Action of the Niebelungun Lied," but the work resembles the ideal about as much as the deeds of the man fulfill the visions of the youth.

Faust is concise, complete and clear as the best models in any language. It is simple and joyous as Burns,—grave and sad as " Hamlet,"—bitter in expression of discontent and hate as " Manfred " and the " Vision of Judgment,"—sublime in description of Nature as the choicest passages of " Childe Harold " and " Paradise Lost,"—humorous as Sterne,—almost as regardless of chasteness of idea as the human soul can be to itself, and sweet and perfect in melodious rhythm as " Midsummer's Night Dream." The plot, though full of action and variety, presenting a multitude of pictures and episodes, yet preserves its unity ; and the supernatural machinery of Satan, wizards and spirits, never shock our notions of possibility or even of probability. Carlyle justly observes, that Shakespeare's ghosts are introduced as if their existence was of the same class with that of the mind itself. Goethe's spirits, on the contrary, are mere phantoms, which have been proved to have no positive existence, and, themselves ignorant that they are only phantasms, are permitted to come upon the stage by the managers, who understand their unsubstantial nature.

The passion of the piece is frightful ; the climax of agony heaped upon the heroine is unequaled by that of Ædipus or of the most unfortunate of the doomed house of Athens, as portrayed by the Greek tragedians. Faust says, truly, mind cannot conceive that more than one human being ever suffered such pain as Margaret's.   The misery of Hamlet, Othello and Lear, is simple, in comparison.   Manfred was plagiarized from Faust, but is only a caricature.   The misanthropic discontent is master of Byron, and his poetry holds the mirror up to himself, far more than to nature.   Faust is more fierce than Manfred in his curses of all existence, but the misanthropic mood rules him only occasionally ; the poet is far above the passion, and instead of being governed by it, he uses it only as he uses the other passions.   Goethe is that which Shakespeare might have been had he lived in this century, and spent a long life under the most favorable circumstances, in assiduous study as poet, philosopher, naturalist, artist and statesman.

The following meager abstract of Faust, is offered in the hope that it may interest the general reader, and, perhaps, give in a short space as good an idea of the plot of the tragedy, as could be obtained from a complete traslation.   Many of the scenes and episodes are entirely omitted ; the original work being at least fifteen times larger than this abstract.   Faust is understood here, to mean the First Part ; the Second Part was not published until about thirty-five years after the First, and is not understood by one out of a hundred of those who read and understand the earlier production.

The tragedy of Faust is founded on a popular tradition prevalent throughout Europe, of a very learned professor or president of a university, who some four hundred years ago, when fifty years of age, became dissatisfied with life and sold himself to the Devil.   The poet refers to some customs of Catholic Germany not known here,—the hymns in churches on Easter morning,—the habit of spending religious holidays in festivities in the open air, etc.   The popular belief that the witches congregate on the Harz mountain on the night of the first of May, furnishes the foundation for a wild scene.

PART I.

The poet begins with a short "invocation."   He addresses the figures which arise in his imagination.   They throng upon him, and he surrenders himself to their dominion, in the hope that he may catch and hold them.   With them arise, dim, like the dying echoes of a song, the recollections of early days of love and friendship, joy and sorrow. Time and the labyrinth of life have robbed him of the friends to whom he sang his first songs ; the sounds of their applause have died away, and he shrinks from the praises of a new and strange generation. While sorrowing over the wreck of early pleasures and hopes, he is seized and hurried off to the spirit world.

PART II.

The preface or prologue on the stage is a conversation between a stage manager about to open a theater, the poet, and a friend of theatricals.   The manager appeals to the poet for aid.   He desires to gratify the public because they live and let live.   He hopes to see them crowding fiercely in the afternoon about the ticket box, like the poor about bakeshops in time of famine. This is the miracle to be wrought by the poet. The latter replies that he wishes not to hear of the rabble ; his spirit forsakes him at the thought of bowing down to them. The muse loves seclusion and seeks not the glitter of the moment. Her joy is in that which will exist for the future as for the present. The friend of theatricals damns posterity ; if the future only is to be thought of, who will provide amusement for to-day ? The manager expresses a desire to have a piece full of action and variety, with love, fire, flood, storm and battle scenes, from which every one can select something to his taste. He advises the dramatist to remember his audience. They go to the theater for pastime ; the woman to exhibit her dress ; the man in the expectation of a night at cards, or in other worse dissipation. Why storm Olympus to gratify such people ? The poet refuses to become a buffoon or a bombastic rhymer ; —rather a cave for his dwelling and acorns for his food, than accept such dictation. The manager yields, and begs a play, reminding the poet that he may, at least, be prodigal of sun, moon and stars, water, fire, mountain peaks and all animals and vegetables, and that the muse need not be prevented by any poverty of the scenes, from coursing through the whole range of Heaven, Earth and Hell.

PART III.

The introduction, or fore-piece in Heaven, represents the Court of the Almighty on reception day, after the manner of the first chapter of Job. The Archangels, Michael, Raphael and Gabriel, sing in rotation, of the majesty and beauty of the universe. After they have closed, Mephistopheles (Satan) presents himself. He confesses his inability to hymn the praises of Nature like the Archangels. His spirit is open only to observe man, the little God of earth, who uses his spark of reason to no purpose except to excel the brutes in beastliness, and who recalls to mind the long-legged grasshopper, which flutters in the air to sing for a few seconds, and then falls to bury its nose in the earth.

The Almighty. Do you know Faust?

Mephistopheles. I do. He is superior to his race; his mind sweeps beyond the bounds of earth; yet if I had permission, I would soon make him my slave.

The Almighty. Permission you have. While man lives, he errs. I have given you to him as a companion, that he may not rot in idleness. Fear no restriction from me, for I never hated the devil.

PART IV. Scene 1.

The main piece, the tragedy of Faust begins in the study of the hero, where he soliloquises. He complains that he is weary of life ; he has mastered law, medicine, theology and science, and all that he knows, is, that he can know nothing. His thirst to learn the great secret of existence, mocks and tortures him. Of what use to look down on the doctors, lawyers, priests and fools ? Of what pleasure to laugh at scruples and doubts, hell and the devil ? He has neither honor nor wealth—he can possess nothing—he is sick of the empty dream. As a last hope he has sought in magic the key to unlock the stores of positive knowledge.

By incantations, he calls up a horrible phantom, which he does not understand and from which he shrinks. While engaged in the incantation and in conversation with the spirit, he speaks aloud, and a pupil (Wagner) overhearing and thinking that his master was reading a Greek drama, comes to listen and learn. The spirit had previously been dismissed by Faust, but the pedantic conversation of the word-monger disgusts the philosopher in his present mood, and he soon gets rid of his visitor.

Left to himself he falls into despair. He curses the vanities of earth, resolves on suicide and grasps a vial of poison. The resolution to rush into the wide sea of existence, fills him with joy. Taking a glad leave of earth, he places the vial to his mouth and is about to empty it, when he is arrested by hearing the hymns of women in the neighboring church rejoicing in the resurrection of Christ. (It is Easter morning.) The deep, religious, worshipful tone of the hymns delights him, he hesitates ; old associations of the pious teachings at his mother's knee arise ; he casts the vial from him, bursts into tears and is again of earth.

SCENE 2.

During the day, Faust walks out with Wagner to see the people celebrating the occasion. Different personages are introduced upon the stage, expressing their simple tastes in pithy expressions. The peasants collect about Faust in reverence, an old farmer offers him a mug of wine, praises the affability of so great a man in being present at the rustic dance, and recalls to his mind the services which the Fausts, father and son, had rendered during a pestilence, by saving multitudes of people. As they walk away, Wagner expresses his envy of the feelings of the man, at whose presence the music and the dance are stopped, before whom all bow, who is pointed out by father to son, and who is looked to as a saviour from past and future danger. Faust replies that the praise of the multitude sounds to him like scorn. His father and himself had blindly used their pills and powders, which killed more than they cured; and yet to them were credited the cures, and the deaths to the disease.

While returning home, Faust notices, at a distance, a black dog coursing about them in a singular manner. He calls the dog to him, and it follows him into the house.

SCENE 3.

Scene in his room with the dog ; Faust begins to study. He turns to the New Testament—the best revelation—reads the first sentence of St. John's Evangel and comments on it. The dog becomes restless and howls. Faust orders him to be still and comments further. The brute continues to howl, and his form changes to that of a hippopotamus. Faust, satisfied that the dog has some super-canine spirit, turns to his magic to exorcise it. He uses incantation after incantation in vain, and finally tries the most terrible form known to him, when the animal is hidden by a vapor, and Mephistopheles, in human form, steps out.

Faust. So ho! You were the kernel hidden in the dog-shell.

Mep. It is true; you gave me a good sweating.

F. Your name?

Mep. That matters little to you, who despise words and look only at the essence of things.

F. But let me have it; I can perhaps judge your nature from your name.

Mep. I am part of the power which always seeks evil but does good. I am the spirit which denies and destroys. But my labors are almost in vain: though I cause earthquakes, floods, storms and fires, yet earth and sea remain the same; and with the cursed men and brutes, I can do nothing; they breed two, while I kill one. May I retire?

F. I know not why you ask. I know you now; return when you please, here are the door, window and chimney.

Mep. I must confess the chalked figure on your threshold stops me. The corner this way is closed; the outer corner is slightly open, through that I came.

F. Lucky accident! But why not out at the window?

Mep. It is one of our laws that we must go out where we came in.

F. Hell itself has its laws? You stick to your bargains then, I suppose?

Mep. Certainly; all my promises are kept faithfully. But let me go.

F. No.

Mep. Then I will exercise my art for your amusement? The fairies shall dance and scatter incense through the room?

F. Yes.

Faust goes to sleep under the effect of the music—Mephistopheles calls a mouse—drops some oil on the chalked figure—the mouse gnaws it away, and Mephistopheles goes.

Scene 4.

Mephistopheles. Take my advice, and dress like me in gold-braided scarlet coat and breeches, and cloak of rustling, heavy silk, and we will go out together to enjoy life.

Faust. In every dress I must feel the pains of slavish life. I am too old to play—too young to be without wishes. What can the world afford me. It forever cries, "Be a stoic, deny yourself;" but in vain. No man can forget or renounce his right and desire for content. Two irreconcilable spirits dwell within me, and the better scorns the worse. Life is hateful.

Mep. But death is never welcome.

F. "O, happy he, about whose brows He binds the bloody laurels in the hight of battles' splendor;" and whom after an exciting dance, He takes from a maiden's arms.

Mep. Yet you did not empty that vial.

F. You were eavesdropping! Accursed be the bright colors which the soul throws upon life. Accursed be reputation and riches, and all possessions—wife and child—servant and friend! Cursed be the juice of the grape! Cursed be hope and faith; and cursed, above all, be patience!

Mep. Cease to tear your vitals with such thoughts. Even the basest company teaches you that you are a man like other men. I can give you a more cheerful mood, if you desire me for a companion through life.

F. On what condition?

Mep. I will serve you here, and you shall serve me yonder.

F. Agreed. This earth furnishes my joys—this sun shines upon my sorrows. After I leave them, let come what will. And more, if ever I should desire to prolong a moment, for the pleasure it may bring, then strike me down; let time be past for me. The Great Spirit has left me an orphan; the thread of thought is broken; I am sick of knowledge. I ask no joy—I give myself up to passion, unrest and discontent. Let my spirit feel in their highest and deepest phases all the passions, and wants, and feelings of mankind. Heap upon me all good and evil—make me to be in myself the whole human race, and let me at last like it be crushed.

Mephistopheles spreads out his cloak upon the floor; the two sit upon it, and it flees off with them.

Scene 5.—*A witch's den, hung about with a multitude of disgusting objects—skeletons, skulls, dried snakes, etc.*

Mephistopheles. You will receive from the witch a drink to make you young again.

Faust. Is there no other means of rejuvenation?

Mep. Yes—go into the country—dig the ground from morn till night—live upon unmixed food—keep the soil moist with your sweat—raise everything you consume.

F. Give me rather the witch's bowl.

The witch appears and gives Faust a mug of her magic brewing. The liquid bursts into a flame as soon as poured out, but Faust drinks it down. Turning around he discovers in a mirror the figure of a woman and wishes to stop to admire it, but Mephistopheles forces him away, and says, that with that drink in his body, every woman shall be a Helen in his eyes.

Scene 6.—*Cathedral Door.   Margaret coming out.*

Faust. Beautiful lady, allow me to escort you home.

Margaret. I am neither a lady, nor beautiful, and I can go alone.

Scene 7.

Faust orders Mephistopheles to give him immediate possession of Margaret. Mephistopheles replies that she is perfectly innocent and cannot be had at once; besides, the pleasures of possession would be much enhanced by the prologue of an interesting courtship—as described in French novels. He promises to furnish a present to begin with.

Scene 8.

During Margaret's absence, Faust enters her room, and leaves there a box of very rich jewelry. She returns and finds it, supposes it to have been taken by her mother as security for money loaned, and takes it to her mother. The old lady suspects something wrong, and gives the box and jewelry to the priest. Margaret grieves, and begins to suspect that Faust was the donor.

Scene 9.

Martha Schwerdtlein, abandoned by her husband, who has gone to the wars, laments her fate. Margaret visits her and tells her that another box of jewelry, much richer than the first, has been placed in her room. Martha advises her to not inform her mother, for fear that it too would go to the priest. While in conversation, Mephistopheles enters and, finding Margaret dressed in the jewels, bears himself toward her as toward a noble lady. She says that she is a poor girl and the jewels are not her own. He insists that her bearing, far more than her rich dress, mark her as a lady of rank. Turning to Martha he informs her that her husband is dead and that he brings a message from him, requesting her to have prayers said for his soul's repose. She grieves and asks whether he sent nothing save the message. Mephistopheles replies, that is all.

Martha. He might, at least, have sent me some memento. Every journeyman mechanic, on his travels, saves some trinket for his mistress, and rather will beg and starve than part with it.

Mephistopheles. Your husband repented his faults and grieves over his misfortunes. He expressed his detestation of himself for having deserted his wife and trade.

Mar. [*Weeping.*] I have long since forgiven him.

Mep. But he said you were more in fault than he.

Mar. He lied.

Mep. He said you left him no peace.

Mar. O, the villain!

Mep. Not so! He said he prayed often for the welfare of his wife and children; Heaven heard his prayers, for off Malta his vessel took a rich prize, of which he received his share.

Mar. O, how? O, where? Did he perhaps bury the money?

Mep. The Lord knows. A young lady took him in tow as he wandered friendless about Naples, and gave him many tokens of her affection.

Mar. The vile rogue! No misery could stop his shameless life.

Mep. Well, he is dead. Go into mourning for a year, and then look out for another.

Mar. Alas, he was a good, harmless soul. I'll never see such another; only he was too fond of strange women, and strange wine, and the cursed cards.

Mep. Don't take it so much to heart. I feel tempted to ask you to count me as a suitor, when you begin to receive suitors.

Mar. O, you're joking.

Mep. [*Aside.*] Its time for me to go; she'd take the devil at his word.

Mar. Tell me. I am a great friend of order. I wish to see my husband's death announced in the newspapers. You will appear before a notary and testify to the fact.

Mep. Two witnesses are necessary, and I have a young man with me. I will return hither this afternoon with him. He's a traveled young man, and will be glad to meet this young lady here, to whom he will show all honor.

SCENE 10.—Martha's *Garden.* Margaret *upon* Faust's *arm.* Martha *upon* Mephistopheles' *arm.*

Margaret. I feel it well; you stoop to talk to me, only out of kindness. My poor conversation cannot entertain a man who has seen so much society as you have.

Faust. A word—a glance from you, has more interest than all the wisdom of this world.

[*He kisses her hand.*]

Marg. How can you? It is all rough with the hard work from which I have no rest.

They cross to the rear of the stage, the other pair occupy the front of the stage a few minutes, cross over, and Margaret and Faust are again in front.

Marg. Alas! your politeness comes easily. You have numberless friends more wise than I. You will forget me when I am out of sight.

F. O, best one, believe me, what is called wisdom is often only arrogance and vanity.

Marg. How?

F. O, that innocence—that simplicity—never understand themselves and their own worth—that humility, unpretending sincerity, the highest gifts of loving, lavish Nature—

Marg. Think of me but a moment—I shall have time enough to think of you.

F. You are much alone?

Marg. Yes, our household is small. We have no maid. I must cook, sew, sweep, knit, and run from morn till night; and my mother is so exacting. And yet she is not so poor but that we might live in more style. My life is quiet. Mother is a widow. My brother is a soldier. My little sister is dead; poor thing, how I nursed it!

F. An angel, if like you!

Marg. I reared it, and it loved me dearly. It was born after my father's death. We thought mother would not live. She could not suckle it, and I fed it as I could, with milk and water. It became mine; in my lap it grew, was happy, and became large.

F. You have tasted the purest pleasure.

Marg. And many bitter hours too. The cradle stood by my bed. At night, if the child moved, I had to feed it, and carry it up and down; and then in the morning, go to the washtub, and look out for the marketing and see to the cattle. After that, food and sleep were sweet.

Faust and Margaret cross to the rear of the stage : Martha and Mephistopheles occupy the front awhile in conversation, retire, and the former pair again come forward.

F. You little angel, knew me when you saw me come in.

Marg. Did you not see! I could not look up.

F. And you pardon my boldness at the church?

Marg. I was confused. No one could say that I was to be approached by strangers without ceremony. Indeed I was angry with myself that I could not be more angry with you.

F. Sweet darling.

Marg. Leave me a moment.

[*She plucks a rose and pulls off leaf by leaf.*]

F. What's that? a boquet?

Marg. No, only a play.

F. How?

Marg. Go away; you'll laugh at me.

[*She pulls and murmurs to herself.*]

F. What are you saying?

Marg. [*Half aloud.*] He loves me—loves me not.

F. Angelic face.

Marg. Loves me—loves me not; loves me—loves me not. [*Pulling out the last leaf.*] He loves me!

F. Yes my child, let this flower-word be Heaven's decree. He loves you. Do you comprehend it?

Marg. It overthrills me.

F. O, tremble not. Let this glance, let this hand's grasp speak what words cannot tell—all trusting love—endless delight—endless! Its end would be despair! No end—no end!

[*She presses his hands—and then turns away. He follows her.*]

SCENE 11.

Marg. Promise me, Henry.

F. What I can.

Marg. Are you religious? You are a good man, but I think you do not go to church.

F. Leave that, my child. You know I love you and would give my life for my love. I wish to rob no one of his belief: I would hurt no one's feelings.

Marg. That is not enough; you must have religion.

F. Must I?

Marg. Alas! if I could only influence you. And you do not respect the Sacraments.

F. Indeed I do.

Marg. But not with love. And you have not been to mass or confessional for ever so long. Do you believe in God?

F. My dear, who can say "I believe in God?" Ask priest or philosopher, and the answer is like mockery.

Marg. Then you do not believe in Him?

F. Mistake me not, you angel. Who dare name Him? And who can say "I believe in him?" Who that feels, dares say "I have no God?" The all-embracer, the all-sustainer, does he not surround you, me, Himself? Is not the Heaven arched over us? Is not the earth firm beneath us? Do we not see each other eye to eye, and does not all existence rise to your hand and heart, and float in infinite majesty before you? Let your heart, big as it is, be full of the great idea, and when you are perfectly happy in the thought, name it what you will, Good—Heart—Love—God. I have no name for it. The feeling is all in all; the name is but noise and smoke clouding celestial glory.

Marg. That is all right and good; the priest says it too, only, in other words.

F. All men say it; each in his way. Why not I in mine?

Marg. But you are not a Christian.

F. Dearest child!

Marg. Then I grieve to see you in such company.

F. How?

Marg. I hate your companion from the bottom of my heart. The sight of his face makes me unhappy.

F. Fear him not.

Marg. His presence stops my blood. I like everybody else, but as much as I love to see you, so much I shudder to think of him. He is a villain. God forgive me if I do him wrong.

F. There must be such chaps too.

Marg. I see it on his forehead that he never loved a living soul. I must go.

F. And can we never have an hour to ourselves, to spend arm in arm and bosom to bosom.

Marg. If I only slept alone I would gladly let you in to-night, but my mother does not sleep soundly; and if she were to see us, I would die on the spot.

F. You angel; there is no difficulty about that. Here is a vial. Three drops from it will cause her to sleep soundly.

Marg. What would I not do for your sake? It will do her no harm?

F. Would I otherwise give it to you, dearest?

Scene 12.—*At the Well.*

Eliza. Have you heard of Barbara?

Margaret. No. I never get out.

E. She's made a fool of herself.

Marg. How?

E. When she eats, she feeds two.

Marg. What a pity!

E. Serves her right. How she courted the fellow; always out promenading, going to balls and shows, eating and drinking; and she even took presents from him.

Marg. Poor thing!

E. Do you pity her? When we were spinning in the evening she was off in the dark with her lover. Let her repent now.

Marg. He will surely marry her.

E. He's not such a fool. He'll find plenty of fun elsewhere. Besides, he's gone.

Marg. That's mean.

[*Eliza goes.*]

Marg. How I used to blame the poor girl who made a slip. I could not find words enough. I could not make the offense black enough. And now I am the sinner. And yet all that led me to it, was—O, God! how good! how dear!

SCENE 13.—*Night.   Street before* Margaret's *door.*

Valentine—Margaret's Brother.   There was a time when it was a pleasure to me to sit at our mess table in the evenings, and hear the fellows bragging of their favorites among the village maidens; and I would sit and listen to it all, and stroke my beard with satisfaction, and after they had done, I would take my full glass and say, "Everybody to his taste, but is there another in the whole land like my Gretchen? one that can hold a candle to sister Margaret?" Then all cried, "He's right; she's the ornament of the whole sex." And the braggarts were dumb. And now! O, I could tear my heart out. Every rascal turns up his nose at me, cuts me with insulting hints. I must fret at every accidental word: and yet I cannot give them the lie. Who's coming there? If it be he, I'll kill him on the spot.

Mephistopheles and Faust enter.   Mephistopheles sings an indelicate, serenading song.   Valentine attacks Mephistopheles.   Faust draws his sword and runs Valentine through.   The two make off.   A crowd collect about Valentine—Margaret and Martha at his side.

Val.   Margaret, come near—I'm dying.   It's soon said, and sooner done.   I want to tell you in confidence—you're a strumpet.
Marg.   Good Lord!
Val.   Let the Lord alone.   What's done is done, and what's coming can't be helped.   You begin with one in secret, soon others come to you, and then the whole town has you.   Sin is born in the dark, and is at first covered over with the veil of night.   Men would destroy it, but it grows, and soon uncovered dares the light of day.   The more hateful it is, the more public it becomes.   I already see the time when all decent people will shun you like a plague-infected corpse.   Your heart shall freeze when they look at you.   You shall never more be admitted to communion, never more attend the dance.   You shall spend your days in rags and filth in a dark corner among beggars and cripples; and if God forgive you in Heaven, you shall yet be cursed upon earth.
Martha.   Commend yourself to God: heap not sin upon your soul as you die.
Val.   You shameless bawd!   If I could but run through your dry body, I should thereby obtain a rich measure of forgiveness for all my sins.
Marg.   O, Brother! what agony!
Val.   Stop your tears.   When you lost your honor, you gave me the severest wound.   Jesus receive the soul of a true soldier.   [*Dies.*]

SCENE 14.—*Cathedral—Catholic service in progress.*   Margaret *in the crowd.*
Evil Spirit *behind her.*

Evil Spirit.   How different was it, Gretchen, when you, all innocence, came hither to the altar and repeated the prayers from the misheld book, half-child's play, half God at your heart?   Margaret, where is your head?   In your heart what misdeed?   Are you praying for your mother's soul, sent, by your act, over to the long, long, painful sleep?   Whose blood is that at your threshold?   What swelling in your bosom is it that fills you with anxiety?
[Margaret *swoons.*]

SCENE 15.

Harz Mountain.   Walpurgis Night.   Grand assemblage and festivities of witches.   Earth and air are full of witches, young and old, clothed and naked, riding on brooms—goats and sows, dancing, flying and carousing.   The whole scene is full of the witch element—wild, crazy, obscene.   Faust and Mephistopheles are present, and each with a partner join in the dance.

SCENE 16.

Faust. In misery! In despair! Long a pitiful outcast on earth, and now in prison! As a criminal incarcerated to suffer fearful agony! The good and unfortunate being! So miserable! Treacherous, villainous spirit, and you concealed this from me! Stop there, stop! Turn your fiendish eyes about in rage! Stand there and disgust me with your intolerable presence! Imprisoned! In indescribable misery, given over to evil spirits and pitiless, persecuting mankind! And you rocked me in insipid pleasures, while you left her to suffer without help.

Mep. She is not the first.

F. Dog! Hateful Monster! Turn to the hound that you were, and crawl in the dust again on your belly before me that I may crush you. Not the first! O, agony! The human mind cannot conceive that more than one ever suffered such pain. Not the first! The sufferings of this one burn through my vitals! And you grin in mockery at the sufferings of thousands!

Mep. Now we are at the end of our wit, and when sense fails to you men, you make insane raving take its place. Why seek our companionship, if you cannot go through with it. The dizzy-headed must not try to fly. Did I press myself upon you, or you yourself upon me.

F. Snap not your teeth like a wolf at me. You sicken me! Great Spirit, you, who have thought me worthy to recognize you, who know my heart and soul, why rivet me to this shameful companion, who delights in suffering?

Mep. Are you done?

F. Save her, or woe be yours! I will heap the most fearful curses upon you for thousands of years.

Mep. I cannot break the bonds of justice. Save her! Who caused her ruin, you or I? [*Faust looks wildly about.*] Would you grasp the thunderbolts? It is well that they were not given to miserable mortals.

F. Take me to her; she shall be free.

Mep. And the danger to which you expose yourself! They are still on the watch for the murderer.

F. Silence of that. Take me thither I say and set her free.

Mep. I will take you and do what I can, but I have not all power in Heaven and Earth. I will cloud the senses of the jailer and you can lead her off. Here are the magic horses! Away!

SCENE 17.—*Prison.   Before daybreak.*

Faust at the door of the prison hears Margaret within singing a crazy but affecting song of her dishonor and desertion, and of the murder of her child. When he enters, she supposes him to be the executioner.

Margaret. O, take pity on me. I am so young, and must I die? Have pity, I never did you harm! Let me at least suckle my child. I nursed it all night; and then they took it away; and, to make me miserable, said I had drowned it. I will never more be happy.

After trying in a low voice to make her understand that he has come to take her away, Faust throws himself at her feet.

Marg. O, let us kneel and pray! See how hell boils under us. Hear how the Evil One roars.

Faust. [*Aloud.*] Margaret! Margaret!

[*Margaret springs up. Her chains fall off.*]

Marg. Where is he? I heard his voice. I am free. Nobody shall stop me. I will fly to his heart. I will lie on his bosom. He called Margaret. He stood in the door.

F. Here I am.

Marg. You here: O, say it once more! [*Embracing him.*] I have you. I have you. Where is my pain? Where is the agony of the prison, of the chains? You are here. Do you come to save me? I am saved!

F. [*Urging her forward.*]   Come with me.

Marg.   O, stay! I stay so gladly where you are.

F.   Make haste or we must suffer.

Marg.   How, can you not kiss? My friend, so short a time away from me, and you have already forgotten how to kiss? Why am I so sad on your bosom? Once a whole Heaven used to pour upon me with your words, and you kissed as if you would smother me. Kiss me now or I'll kiss you. Alas! your lips are cold.

F.   Come, follow me, dearest! Take courage!

Marg.   Are you Henry? Are you certain?

F.   Indeed I am, come.

Marg.   Will you take me to your bosom? Do you know who I am? Do you not shun me?

F.   Come, it is getting light.

Marg.   I killed my mother. I drowned my child. Was it not given to you and me? Is it you? Do I not dream? Give me your hand! It is moist. Wipe it off, there is blood on it. Good God! what have you done? Put up your sword, I beg you.

F.   Think not of the past; you torment me when you mention it.

Marg.   No, you must survive me. I will describe the graves to you. You must provide for them to-morrow. Give the best place to mother, and a place for Valentine by her side. And put me not too far off, with the child at my right breast. I dare not hope that you will lie by my side: it would be too much happiness for me. I fancy that you push me away from you, and yet your looks are kind.

F.   Then let us go.

Marg.   Out there.

F.   Yes, out of the prison.

Marg.   Death and the grave are out there, watching. From here to the eternal rest is only one step for me. Are you going, Henry? O, that I could go with you.

F.   You can if you will, the door is open.

Marg.   I dare not—there is no hope for me. Of what use to fly? They will catch me. It is so miserable to wander about and beg, and with a bad conscience at that.

F.   I will stay with you.

Marg.   Quick, quick, save your child! Quick, there in the forest pond on the left where the planks are; catch quickly—it cries—save it! save it!

F.   Collect yourself—only one step and you are free.

Marg.   There sits my mother shaking her head. She slept that we might enjoy ourselves. She slept so long that she will never wake again.

F.   Here's no use of entreaty or advice. I'll carry you with me.

Marg.   Let go—I'll suffer no force. Let go; your hold is murderish. Is this the reward of all that I've done for you?

F.   The day is breaking. Dearest! Dearest!

Marg.   Day? yes, the last day is breaking; it shall be my wedding day. Tell nobody that you have been with Margaret. They are taking me to the block—how the sharp axe glitters!

F.   O, that I had never been born!

Mephistopheles. [*At the door.*]   Haste, or you are lost.

Marg.   What rises out of the ground there? He! He! Send him off. What does he want in a sacred place? He wants me.

F.   You shall live.

Marg.   Good God preserve me!

Mep.   Come or I leave you with her.

Marg.   Father, save me! I am thine. Ye angels! ye heavenly hosts, surround, protect me. Henry, I tremble for you.

Mep.   She is lost.

Voices from above.   She is saved.

[Mephistopheles *and* Faust *fly off.*]

Voice from within.   Henry! Henry!

CALIFORNIA, IN 1852.

BY SHIRLEY.

LETTER FOURTEENTH.

RESIDENCE IN THE MINES.

FROM OUR LOG CABIN, Indian Bar, March 15, 1852.

This fifteenth day of March, has risen upon us with all the primeval splendor of the birth-morn of creation. The lovely river—having resumed its crimson border, (the so-long idle miners being again busily at work,) glides by, laughing gaily, leaping and clapping its glad waves joyfully in the golden sunlight. The feathery fringe of the fir-trees glitters, like emerald, in the luster bathing air. A hundred tiny rivulets flash down from the brow of the mountains, as if some mighty Titan, standing on the other side, had flung athwart their greenness, a chaplet of radiant pearls. Of the large quantities of snow which have fallen within the past fortnight, a few patches of shining whiteness, high up among the hills, alone remain ; while, to finish the picture, the lustrous heaven of California, looking "further off" than ever, through the wonderfully transparent atmosphere, and for that very reason, infinitely more beautiful, bends over all the matchless blue of its resplendent arch. Ah ! the heaven of the Golden Land. To you, living beneath the murky skies of New England, how unimaginably lovely it is ! A small poetess has said that "*She* could not love a scene, where the blue sky was *always* blue." I think that it is not so with me ; I am sure that I never weary of the succession of rainless months, and the azure dome, day after day so mistless, which bends above this favored country.

Between each stroke of the pen, I stop to glance at that splendor, whose sameness never falls ; but now, a flock of ringdoves break for a moment, with dots of purple, its monotonous beauty ; and the carol of a tiny bird, (the first of the season,) though I cannot see the darling, fills the joyful air with its matin song.

All along the side of the hill, rising behind the Bar, and on the latter also, glance spots of azure and crimson, in the forms of blue and red-shirted miners, bending steadily over pick-axe and shovel; reminding one involuntarily of the muck-gatherer in "Pilgrim's Progress." But, no, that is an unjust association of ideas ; for many of these men are toiling thus wearily for laughing-lipped children, calm-browed wives, or saintly mothers, gathering around the household hearth, in some far-away country. Even among the few now remaining on the river, there are wanderers from the whole broad earth ; and, O ! what a world of poetic recollection is suggested by their living presence ! From happiest homes, and such luxuriant lands, has the golden magnet drawn its victims. From those palm-girdled isles of the Pacific, which Melville's gifted pen has consecrated to such beautiful romance ; from Indies, blazing through the dim past with funeral pyres, upon whose perfumed flame, ascended to God, the chaste souls of her devoted wives ; from the grand old woods of classic Greece, haunted by nymph and satyr, naiad and grace, grape-crowned Bacchus and beauty-zoned Venus; from the polished heart of artificial Europe, from the breezy backwoods of young America, from the tropical languor of Asian Savannah ; from *every* spot shining through the rosy light of beloved old fables, or consecrated by lofty deeds of heroism or devotion, or shrined in our heart of hearts, as the sacred home of some great or gifted one, they gather to the golden harvest.

You will hear in the same day, almost at the same time, the lofty melody of the Spanish language, the piquant polish of the French, (which, though not a *musical* tongue, is the most *useful* of them all,) the silver, changing clearness of the Italian, the harsh gangle of the German, the hissing precision of the English, the liquid sweetness of the Kanaka, and the sleep-inspiring languor of the East Indian. To complete the catalogue, there is the *native* Indian, with his guttural vocabulary of twenty words ! When I hear these sounds so strangely different, and look at the speakers, I fancy them a living polyglot of the languages, a perambulating picture gallery, illustrative of national variety in form and feature.

By the way, speaking of languages, nothing is more amusing, than to observe the different styles, in which the generality of the Americans talk *at* the unfortunate Spaniard. In the first place, many of them really believe, that when they have learned *sabe* and *vamos*, (two words which they seldom use in the right place,) *poco tiempo, si,* and *bueno,* (the last they *will* persist in pronouncing *whayno,*) they have the whole of the glorious Castilian at their tongue's end. Some, however, eschew the above words entirely, and innocently fancy, that by splitting the tympanum of an unhappy foreigner, in screaming forth their sentences in good solid English, they can be surely understood ; others, at the imminent risk of dislocating their own limbs and the jaws of their listeners, by the laughs which their efforts elicit, make the most excruciatingly grotesque gestures, and think that *that* is speaking Spanish. The majority, however, place a most beautiful and touching faith in *broken English*, and when they murder it, with the few words of Castilian quoted above, are firmly convinced, that it is nothing but their "ugly dispositions" which makes the Spaniards pretend not to understand them.

One of those dear, stupid Yankees, who *will*, now and then, venture out of sight of the smoke of their own chimneys, as far as California, was relating *his* experience in this particular the other day. It seems that he had lost a horse somewhere among the hills, and during his search for it, met a gentlemanly Chileno, who, with national suavity, made the most desperate efforts to understand the questions put to him. Of course, *Chileno* was so stupid that he did not succeed, for it is not possible that one of the " Great American People" could fail to express himself clearly, even in Hebrew, if he takes it into his cute head, to speak that ancient, but highly respectable, language. Our Yankee friend, however, would not allow the poor fellow even the excuse of stupidity, but declared that he only " played possum from sheer *ugli-*

ness." "Why," he added, in relating the circumstance, "the cross, old
rascal pretended not to understand his own language, though I said as
plainly as possible, ' *Señor, sabe mi horso vamos poco tempo?* ' which, perhaps, you don't know," he proceeded to say, (in a benevolent desire to
enlighten our ignorance and teach us a little Castilian,) "means, 'Sir,
I have lost my horse, have you seen it?' " I am ashamed to acknowledge, that we did *not* know the above written Anglo-Spanish sentence
to mean *that!* The honest fellow concluded his story by declaring,
(and it is a common remark with uneducated Americans) with a most
self-glorifying air of *pity* for the poor Spaniards, "They ain't kinder
like *eour* folks,"—or, as that universal Aunt Somebody used so express-
ively to observe, "Somehow, they ain't *folksy!*"

The mistakes made on the other side, are often quite as amusing.
Dr. Cañas related to us a laughable anecdote of a countryman of his,
with whom he happened to camp, on his first arrival in San Francisco.
None of the party could speak a word of English, and the person referred to, as ignorant as the rest, went out to purchase bread, which
he procured, by laying down some money, and pointing to a loaf of that
necessary edible. He probably heard a person use the words "some
bread," for he rushed home, Cañas said, in a perfect burst of newly
acquired wisdom, and informed his friends that he had found out the
English for *pan*, and that when they wished any of that article, they
need but enter a bake-shop, and utter the word *sombrero*, in order to obtain it! His hearers were delighted to know *that* much of the *infernal
lengua*, greatly marveling, however, that the same word which meant
hat, in Castilian, should mean *bread* in English. The Spaniards have
a saying, to the following effect, "Children speak in Italian, ladies
speak in French, God speaks in Spanish, and the Devil speaks in English."

I commenced this letter with the intention of telling you about the
weary, weary storm, which has not only thrown a damp over our spirits,
but has saturated them, as it has everything else, with a deluge of
moisture. The Storm King commenced his reign (or rain) on the
twenty-eighth of February, and proved himself a perfect Proteus during his residence with us. For one entire week, he descended daily
and nightly without an hour's cessation, in a forty Niagara power of
water ; and just as we were getting reconciled to this wet state of
affairs, and were thinking seriously of learning to swim, one gloomy
evening when we least expected such a change, he stole softly down,
and garlanded us in a wreath of shining snow-flakes, and lo! the next
morning you would have thought that some great white bird had shed
its glittering feathers all over rock, tree, hill and bar ; he finished his
vagaries by loosening, rattling and crashing upon this devoted spot, a
small skyful of hailstones, which, aided by a terrific wind, waged terrible warfare against the frail tents, and the calico-shirt huts, and made
even the shingles on the roofs of the log-cabins tremble amid their
nails.

The river, usually so bland and smiling, looked really terrific. It
rose to an unexampled hight, and tore along its way, a perfect mass
of dark-foamed, turbid waves. At one time we had serious fears that

the water would cover the whole bar, for it approached within two or three feet of the Humboldt. A sawmill, which had been built at a great expense by two gentlemen of Rich Bar, in order to be ready for the sawing of lumber, for the extensive fluming operations which are in contemplation this season, was entirely swept away,—nearly ruining, (it is said,) the owner. I heard a great shout early one morning, and running to the window, had the sorrow to see wheels, planks, etc., sailing merrily down the river. All along the banks of the stream, men were trying to save the more valuable portions of the mill, but the torrent was so furious that it was utterly impossible to rescue a plank. How the haughty river seemed to laugh to scorn the feeble efforts of man? How its mad waves tossed in wild derision, the costly workmanship of his skilful hands! But know, proud Rio de las Plumas, that these very men, whose futile efforts you fancy that you have for once so gloriously defeated, will gather from beneath your lowest depths the beautiful ore, which you thought you had hidden forever and forever, beneath your azure beauty!

It is certainly most amusing, to hear of the different plans which the poor miners invented to pass the time during the trying season of rains. Of course, poker and euchre, whist and nine-pins, to say nothing of monte and faro, are now in constant requisition. But as a person would starve to death on *toujours des perdrix*, so a man cannot *always* be playing cards. Some *literary* bipeds, I have been told, reduced to the last degree of intellectual destitution, in a beautiful spirit of self-martyrdom, betook themselves to blue blankets, bunks and Ned Buntline's novels. And one day an unhappy youth went pen-mad, and in a melancholy fit of authorship wrote a thrilling account of our dreadful situation, which, directed to the editor of a Marysville paper, was sealed up in a keg and set adrift, and is at this moment, no doubt, stranded, high and dry, in the streets of Sacramento, for it is generally believed, that the cities of the plain have been under water during the storm. The chief amusement, however, has been the raffling of gold rings. There is a silversmith here, who, like the rest of the miserable inhabitants, having nothing to do, discovered that he could make gold rings. Of course every person must have a specimen of his workmanship, and the next thing was to raffle it off. The winner generally repeating the operation. Nothing was done or talked of for some days, but this important business.

I have one of these rings, which is really very beautifully finished, and, although, perhaps at home, it would look vulgar, there is a sort of massive and barbaric grandeur about it, which seems well-suited to our wild life of the hills. I shall send you one of these, which will be to you a curiosity, and will doubtless look strangely enough amid the graceful and airy politeness of French jewelry. But I think that it will be interesting to you, as having been manufactured in the mines, by an inexperienced workman, and without the necessary tools. If it is too hideous to be worn upon your slender little finger, you can have it engraved for a seal, and attach it as a charm to your watch chain.

Last evening, Mr. C. showed us a specimen ring which he had just finished. It is the handsomest *natural* specimen that I ever saw. Pure gold is generally dull in hue, but this is of a most beautiful shade of yellow, and extremely brilliant. It is, in shape and size, exactly like the flower of the jonquil. In the center, is inserted, with all the nice finish of art, (or rather of Nature, for it is her work) a polished piece of quartz, of the purest shade of pink ; and between each radiant petal is set a tiny crystal of colorless quartz, every one of which flashes like a real diamond. It is known beyond doubt, to be a real live specimen, as many saw it when it was first taken from the earth, and the owner has carried it carelessly in his pocket for months. We would gladly have given fifty dollars for it, though its nominal value is only about an ounce, but it is already promised, as a present, to a gentleman in Marysville. Although rather a clumsy ring, it would make a most unique broach, and, indeed, is almost the *only* piece of unmanufactured ore, which I have ever seen, that I would be willing to wear. I have a piece of gold, which, without any alteration, except, of course engraving, will make a beautiful seal. It is in the shape of an eagle's head, and is wonderfully perfect. It was picked up from the surface of the ground, by a gentleman, on his first arrival here, and he said that he would give it to the next lady to whom he should be introduced. He carried it in his purse for more than a year, when, in obedience to the promise made when he found it, it became the property of your humble servant, Shirley.

The other day a hole caved in, burying up to the neck, two unfortunates, who were in it at the time. Luckily, they were but slightly injured.

T. is at present attending a man at the junction, who was stabbed very severely in the back during a drunken frolic. The people have not taken the slightest notice of this affair, although for some days the life of the wounded man was despaired of. The perpetrator of the deed had not the slightest provocation from his unfortunate victim.

BOAT SONG.

—

BY G.

—

Merrily sing, though day is closing
　And the shadows lengthen'd fall,
We on cheerful hopes reposing
　Heed not evening's gloomy pall ;
Though the god of day forsake us,
　We've a god within our breast,
And the power of Love shall make us
　In the darkest hour blest.

Merrily sing, Heaven's arch is gleaming
　With the stars' eternal light,
And the gentle moon is beaming
　Silvery glory on the night ;
O may we, when Life's day closes,
　Safely reach the promised shore,
Where undying day discloses
　Light and life for evermore.

RECOLLECTIONS OF INCIDENTS IN ENGLAND.

BY J. P. ANTHONY.

NO. I.—THE STRANGE HOUSE AT DOLGELLY.

> WHEN draw the prosperous near me, I forget
> The Gods of Heaven ; but where
> Sorrow and suffering in my sight are set,
> The Gods, I feel, are there.
> SCHILLER.

IN introducing the recollections to the readers of *The Pioneer*, the writer would observe, that he seeks no higher object than that of amusing by the narration of incidents, which somewhat deviate from the common occurrences of every-day life.   On the attention of lovers of the marvelous, he has no claims—possessing not the gift of imagination to embellish, nor indeed, the desire to coin strange things, to add to the interest of his story.   To those, however, who in the calm, unruffled repose of a stationary life, care but to know the romance of reality through other media than self-experience, these incidents may fairly be presumed to possess some interest, penned, as they will be, by one who has seen much variety in life, and in the quiet village as well as the crowded city, mingled with almost every grade of the great family of man.

In the words of the " Rambler," however, the reader is requested to accommodate his mind to the author's design ; and as he will have no interest in refusing the amusement that is offered to him, not to interrupt his tranquility by studied cavils or destroy his satisfaction in that which may be already well, by inquiring how it might be better—to be content without pleasure, or pleased without perfection.

With this brief preface, will I now proceed to my story of " The Strange House at Dolgelly ; " and in the event of any of my readers being familiar with the part of the habitable globe, where the narrative opens, they will readily admit, that a more remarkable spot to harmonize with the singularity of such a meeting, as my story will reveal, could not be chosen, were I framing a fiction, and selecting from the most remarkable places in Britain.

By lovers of the grand and beautiful in combination, the scenery of North Wales has ever been enthusiastically admired.   It is worth a pilgrimage, alone, to look upon Cader Idris, that, like our own Diabolo, soars to Heaven a landmark of grandeur!   It is a sight never to be forgotten, to behold the giant Cader from the deep and dark ravine, through which winds the road from Machynlleth to Dolgelly, over whose path beetle huge rocks, as pile on pile in majestic ruggedness they mount in aspiring grandeur to the clouds.   Here, turning his gaze towards the opening in the hills, which admit him to the rocky pass, the traveler may behold low in the distance, a far-spreading lake, whose waters are not unfrequently lashed into waves by the wild winds that here prevail, and which howling, rush onward with a sound like the cries of troops of demons, or the voices of spirits of the frowning rocks and sterile regions around.   Never have I visited the place without pausing at this romantic pass to gaze with increased interest on the scene.   On the left of the road, partly hid by a low, unmortared stone wall, in many parts shattered by the winds, the rocky hight shelves sloping down, some two hundred feet to its lowest depth, where, parted by a narrow gullet, whose stream takes its way amidst fragments of rocks, it rises again more abrupt and precipitate on the other side, forming a part of the base of the all-majestic Cader.   It has been observed, that mountain scenery the most impresses the mind with a sense of the greatness of the works of the Creator ; certain it is, mountains, barren though they be, ever possess grandeur and sublimity.   Here, where crested with granite, they raise their unadorned heads to the clouds, they possess a language, which must address itself to every beholder, in their boldness of outline and their giant magnitude.   Reader, picture the scene I have attempted to describe, for here it was I met with the subject of my narrative.

It was on a boisterous October evening, that I had left Machynlleth (so well known for its mementos of Glendower) and night was drawing rapidly on, when I arrived at the wild ravine, and at that part of the road which, cut out of, and winding round the cloud-capped battlements of rock, leads again to the open country and the snuggy little town of Dolgelly.   Walking beside my horse as he ascended the road, and occasionally checking his willingness to proceed, whilst I paused to drink deeply from the rich fount of Nature's grandeur, presented to me in nearing the summit of the ascent, I beheld, a few paces in advance of me, the stationary figure of a man.   His back was towards me, and he appeared to be absorbed in reflection, intently gazing on the majestic Cader, the sides of which a grayish mist was wreathing, whilst the summit was hid in a dense cloud of vapor.

The sound of the approaching wheels of my gig, seemed for a moment to rouse him from his revery.   Turning suddenly round, he cast a hasty glance upon me, and immediately resumed his original position.   Seemingly, he was advanced in years, and to judge by his dress and general appearance, a gentleman.   Night was drawing rapidly on,—old age ever commanded my reverence and respect, and knowing, also, that we were miles distant from any habitation, I did not hesitate, on coming up to the spot where he stood, to offer him a seat in my vehicle, should his way chance to be the same as mine.   The reader may judge my surprise, when the mountain gazer declined my offer almost rudely ; he could and would walk, and not even thanking me, turned on his heel, and again appeared to become absorbed in the contemplation of the wild scenery before him.   I made no reply, but with an inward ejaculation against human nature in general, and this discourteous old gentleman in particular, I resumed my walk by the side of my steed, and in a few moments had gained the summit of the ascent.   Whilst engaged gathering up the reins and preparing to take my seat, a voice from behind hailed me, and almost at the same moment, the old gentlemen, whom I had so recently passed, with more agility than I should have given him credit for possessing, placed his hand on the side of the gig and sprang in.

He had been running, and for a moment or two, was almost breath-less ; as soon, however, as he was able, he commenced apologizing for his former rudeness, and to express how sensible he was of the kind-ness of my offer. He would now gladly avail himself of it. His conduct was somewhat extraordinary, but there was a frankness in his manner which pleased me, and taking my seat beside him, I drove on, not a little amused at the singularity of the proceeding.

I did not, however, hesitate to declare, how much the conduct for which he expressed his regret, had annoyed me at the time, and that I hardly knew how to reconcile the sincerity of an apology, following so closely on the heels of an offense. So earnest was the manner of the old gentleman, on again expressing his regret that he had acted so boorishly, that I at once banished my half-feigned displeasure, and soon entered with him into an animated and amusing conversation.

There was an unmistakable polish about the stranger, a felicity in the choice of words, a happiness of expression, and a cheerfulness of manner most engaging. For an old man, however, he appeared to be somewhat excitable. As we proceeded, he seemed to make himself quite at home with me, and, somewhat to my surprise, evinced not the slightest hesitation in putting the most direct questions, as to the plea-sure or business, which had called me into that part of the country. Such seeming impertinences, ill-accorded with his otherwise gentlemanly bearing, and yet, in return for the little information which I gave him on the subject of his inquiries, I must do my companion the justice to say, that he was very communicative to me. Indeed, when he had learned that I was only on a brief visit to Dolgelly, purposing return-ing on the following day, he immediately proceeded to inform me, that he was almost a stranger to the place, that his residence was within a mile of the town, and that he had chosen the locality for a few month's sojourn, on account of its quietness and salubrity.

When he spoke of the scenery in the neighborhood, he became posi-tively eloquent, and appeared to be doubly delighted to have found in me a congenial worshiper at the all-glorious shrine of Nature.

There was something so truly original, so much pleasing enthusiasm and buoyancy of spirit in my companion, that I could not resist the opportunity afforded me, of seeing more of him ; the reader will there-fore scarcely wonder, that we parted with an acceptance on my part, of the invitation which he gave me to sup with him, and as I put him down at the gate, which through an avenue of trees led to his residence, I assured him he might rely upon my attendance.

It may be easily imagined, that I had not long been an inmate of that spacious and comfortable hostelrie, yclept, " The Golden Lion " at Dolgelly, ere I instituted inquiries relative to the occupants of the mansion, which my late companion had pointed out to me as his home. The information which I received on the subject, was calculated not a little to increase my curiosity and desire to learn more of that eccentric individual. It appeared, that the family consisted, besides the old gentleman, of an elderly and a young lady, who, by their hermit-like habits, had much puzzled the denizens of Dolgelly. They never entered the town, had been seen by very few, and the servants, since the arrival of the family in the neighborhood, had proved invulnerable to all attempts made by the curious, to learn whence they came, with other particulars which they were desirous of ascertaining.

One person, alone, Doctor Price, was on visiting terms with the family, and that chiefly in his professional capacity. And he, even to his most intimate friends, was as close on the subject as the grave. And so the mansion was known to the natives as the strange house, and its occupants, as the strange people.

The worthy hostess of the Lion was not a little surprised, when, in return for her liberal communication of all she knew—and what she thought, I informed her, that I was about to visit the old gentleman ; and having seen my steed comfortably housed for the night, and devoted a few moments to the toilet, I lost no time in proceeding to the place of invitation.

It was a lovely night. The cloudless, star-gemmed heavens seemed to touch the majestic mountain-hights around, whilst on the very crest of the towering Cader, one bright planet was glittering in glorious effulgence, seeming like some Queen of Light, enthroned and giving audience in that vasty court, whose boundaries were Heaven and Earth, to the innumerable myriads of attendant luminaries beaming around. How beautiful, indeed, is unclouded starlight amidst the mountains !

My coming was evidently expected by the liveried functionary, who answered my summons at the door of the mansion ; he silently proceeded to usher me into a room, which I had scarcely entered, ere I was joined by my host. The apartment was spacious, richly furnished and ornamented with numerous choice paintings, which the old gentleman seemed not a little proud of, whilst introducing each separately to my notice.

As in his description of the grand and beautiful in Nature, he was scarcely less an enthusiast in his admiration of the works of art, the productions of the master spirits of the age, which he had here gathered together, and which were chiefly modern. As I then beheld him, I think I see him now, standing before a large painting, which he highly prized, and changing the position of the candle which he carried, until he had obtained the proper light in which I was to inspect it. The subject of the picture was a mountain lake—time sunset;—the waters of the lake and the angular masses of rocks which bounded it, were cast in deep shadow,—whilst the summit of the mountain, with its heathery clothing, catching the last rays of the sinking sun, presented itself in contrast as beautiful as it was striking. Such dark green water, such blackish gray rock and such sunshine, were never surpassed, perhaps, but rarely equaled on canvas. An eagle, on the wing, was seen crossing the lake, as though it were about to ascend to some eyrie in the rocks ; the whole scene presenting a picture of wild beauty and grandeur, such as would alone impress the beholder, that Nature itself, and Nature only, had been followed by the painter-poet's hand; ay, in verity, none but a poet, if not in language, in the depths of his soul was he, whose master-hand had produced that exquisite work of art. The subject chosen revealed how much had he of the poetry of the beautiful within him, and its surpassing excellence, that it had been with him a labor of love alone. That he had, with all a poet's fondness, sought and communed with Nature amidst the hills many a time, and oft watched the sinking sun, and gathered from fleeting ray and spreading shadow, subjects for that pencil, which should gain him immortality. It was indeed a surpassing production of true genius. The artist appeared to have had complete dominion over the powerful materials of light and darkness, and had so varied and disposed them under the influence of a poetical mind, as to produce effects, whose beauty was only equaled by their close fidelity to Nature. I dwell upon this subject as affording a revelation of the enthusiasm of my entertainer ; and in the description, which I have given of the painting, to the best of my memory, have repeated his language. Yes, I think I now behold him whilst expatiating on this prized gem of his collection ; his eyes seemed to beam with additional luster ; and, as the glowing terms with which he expressed his admiration, and the beauty of the object before us, drew from me scarcely less warm expressions of delight, he appeared to work himself into a state of excitement almost rapturous.

Our inspection of the painting over, we drew up to the fire, and I now observed an embroidery frame, a piano forte, and several ornaments on the massive marble chimney-piece, indicative of there being members of the gentler sex occupants of the house. Strange, although my entertainer must have noticed my gaze resting upon these evidences of such proximity, he never alluded to them ; but led the conversation, in which I soon found myself discussing the popular subjects of the day, politics and phrenology, music and mesmerism, and I know not what besides. My host's conversational powers were considerable, yet I could not but observe, that he endeavored to prevent the conversation resting on one subject long ; and by the time that we sat down together to supper, a listener would have had reason to suppose, that we had pretty nearly exhausted the whole range of ordinary conversable matter. The supper provided for us was first-rate,—the cookery worthy of a first-class professor, the appointments of the table superb, and the liveried functionaries who attended, glided around us noiselessly as spirits.

My entertainer certainly spared no efforts to make me enjoy his society, and yet withal, I did not feel exactly at my ease. There was an indescribable something about him, that kept my curiosity continually on the alert, and yet baffled it. I could not divest myself of the impression that he was acting a part, and that there was, moreover, a something of the forced in his seeming gaiety and joyousness. Besides, the absence of the rest of the family was calculated to induce me to believe, that my visit had been to them not altogether acceptable ; the reflection of which, to some extent, prevented me from entering fully and freely into the humor of my host, which, by the way, rapidly increased, as he paid close *devoir* to a delicious punch of his own concoction, the which won from me, with its peculiar excellence, most honest and unqualified praise.

The time wore on, and with the flying hours at length vanished the unpleasant cogitations, which, on account of the reasons I have mentioned, since my entering the mansion had been mine. Seeing that there was no likelihood of an addition being made to our party, and that the ladies, if in the house, had, in all probability, retired for the night, I no longer hesitated to enter fully and freely into the jocular spirit, which seemed to inspire my entertainer. The old gentleman was possessed of a tolerable stock of anecdote, most of which to me was new ; his acquaintance, also, with the German and French, as well as our own Drama, was surprising, displaying a memory wonderfully retentive in the various readings which he gave. But his perception of the ludicrous was, perhaps, the most striking feature in his character ; he was highly imaginative, and the odd and whimsical imaginings and conceits which he gave utterance to, were not unworthy of being chronicled in Punch or Diogenes. In return, I gave him the best things I was acquainted with, and our united cachinations at times were certainly somewhat trenching on the boisterous. My companion would occasionally rise from his chair, and pacing the apartment, repeat the point of anecdote which had tickled his fancy, and whilst repeating the words, burst out afresh into louder laughter. At times, too, it appeared as though he were endeavoring to repress the mirth kindled within him, by changing the theme to more sober matters, and so I imagined, with this view proceeded to recite some lines, which he told me were a translation of his own from his favorite Schiller. Most admirable was his elocution, and I was not a little vexed when in the midst of the piece, he suddenly came to a pause, a peculiar expression, which I had not observed before, spread over his features, and to my great astonishment, when he again broke silence, it was with an exclamation of mingled surprise and terror, whilst with starting eyes he looked at me, as though I had suddenly become an object of aversion. By a strong effort, however, he seemed to master this sudden emotion, and resuming his seat, the position of which I observed he so altered as no longer to confront me, declared that he had forgotten the remainder of the passage, and challenged me to another bumper from the capacious bowl. Deeply now did he quaff the nectar; again came a change over his humor, and again did his boisterous laughter break on the stillness of the night.

It was during one of these loud bursts of merriment, that I was turning on my chair to the table to replenish my glass, when my attention was suddenly arrested by perceiving in a distant part of the spacious room, where the candles threw but a glimmering haze, the figure of a woman. Scarce had my glance rested on her, ere she disappeared in the gloom ; a slight noise as of a door gently closing, leading me to believe that she had been on the watch, or probably intending to speak to us, and changing her intention, had suddenly retired.

From the stationary position in which I had seen her, the first supposition appeared to be nearest the fact, and as the other extremity of the large room in which we sat, was almost in total darkness, I conceived it to be not unlikely that others might be there concealed observing us. The old gentleman had not noticed my look of surprise, nor heard the half-smothered exclamation, which, on discovering the figure, I had involuntarily made. From the moment, however, that I beheld the form that had so suddenly vanished, a change came over the spirit of my merriment, and with tenfold force my former uneasiness returned.

My host's late extraordinary display had somewhat tended to lessen the enjoyment which I had previously derived from his society, but this last most singular proceeding on the part of some other, to me, mysterious member of the establishment, completed the effect. I resolved to quit the place, and rising from my seat, intimated my intention of returning to my inn.

My entertainer seemed somewhat astonished at the suddenness of my resolve, and appeared determined, if possible, to induce me to prolong my stay. I had, during the earlier part of my visit, in the course of our conversation on the subject, expressed myself as a lover of music ; and my host now backed his pressing entreaty for me to remain, by volunteering something on the piano forte, if I would but consent to stay another hour. Fond as I am of the concord of sweet sounds, I must confess to feeling somewhat annoyed at finding my intention of retiring thwarted, unless I became positively rude, by the remembrance on the part of the old gentleman, of an expression made at an early part of the night, and at finding it made subservient to detain me longer. To do my host justice, he played as few amateurs can play ; he sang, also, and though age had much impaired the quality of his voice, sweet was it in its feebleness, whilst his execution revealed how thoroughly grounded he had been in the science of song.

Behind the instrument, forming as it were, a panel in the wall, was fixed an immense mirror, and as the old gentleman played without notes, and as there was nothing before him to intercept the reflection, I had presented to me, as I stood at his side, his countenance therein fully shown. I know not why, but my gaze was irresistibly attracted to a contemplation of his features thus presented in the bright mirror before me.

A few gray hairs were scattered over his brow, lofty and broad ; his features marked with the lines of age, but yet handsome ; whilst their general expression of high intelligence with a cast of sadness, confirmed my previously formed opinion, that the hilarity, which I had witnessed, had in some measure been forced, and his joyousness anything but from the heart.

After singing two or three sweet compositions of a plaintive character, he suddenly ceased, nor did he make an observation for full five minutes afterwards, but continued playing a beautifully wild and touching melody, which, from his silence, I judged to affect him deeply. Indeed, he appeared so much absorbed in his performance, as to have forgotten me altogether. I remember well, that it was just as I was about to address him, when he suddenly came to a pause, resting his fingers on the keys of the instrument, and raising his eyes;—in the huge, bright mirror before us, his gaze met mine. Great Heaven ! how strange ! what fearful fascination ! I could not take my eyes away ; whilst my heart felt as though it had been suddenly frozen to ice. The glare of a madman was upon me. It was deep night, and we were alone ! The muscles of his mouth, as his eye met mine, contracted in a fearful manner ; his face became blanched,—his lips livid. Uttering a cry, which was something between a howl and a scream, on the instant he sprang to his feet, throwing himself upon me, whilst I felt his hand grasping at my throat. So sudden, so impetuous and unexpected was the attack, that I stumbled backwards and fell. Rescuing me from his attempted grasp, my fall enabled him to snatch one of the irons from the fire-place, which, quick as light, he raised to strike me. Springing to my feet, I succeeded in partly escaping the intended blow, by catching his descending arm, and seizing him round the body, and after a brief struggle, I hurled him to the ground, and throwing myself upon him, held him firmly down. For a few moments, nay not so much, and yet it seemed an hour, I held that poor maniac there; and the expression of his eyes, as they then glared upon me, will never pass from my memory.

Whilst we were struggling on the floor, a loud scream rang through the room. I heard approaching footsteps, and in the same moment a young girl throwing herself on her knees beside us and placing her arm round the neck of my antagonist, sobbed out the name of Father.

Two of the servants, strong, powerful fellows they were, who, unseen by me, had rushed into the room, soon released me from the old man, bearing him to a sofa, despite his violent exertions to break away. Standing by the sofa, and bending over the lunatic, I now beheld an elderly lady, who, like her companion, was attired in deep mourning. She appeared to give instructions to the servants, addressing them in a suppressed tone of voice ; and they, apparently acting under her directions, cooly bore the old man, who was still making violent efforts to break away, past me, whilst a female domestic, who stood with a light, evidently prepared for the case, led the way out of the room. The elderly lady and her young companion were about to follow them, when the former, turning to me, hurriedly expressed her regret for what had occurred, begging me to be seated, and to excuse their absence, which for a short time was indispensable. I silently bowed ; they left the room, and a few moments after, I heard the sound of voices, as though in high altercation ; then the noise of a closing door, and all became as still as death.

I was too much excited to sit calmly down, and paced the apartment with all kinds of strange conjectures crowding in upon me. It was evident I had been completely deceived in the character of my host—that I had been indeed for hours unconsciously sitting in the company of a madman. There was a mystery, also, in the whole affair, which bewildered me ; and it may easily be conceived, that I was impatient for the return of the old lady, when I might expect to have some little light thrown on the matter.

I had not to wait long. With her younger companion, she again entered the room, and after, with much apparent concern and kindness of manner, inquiring if I had received any hurt, proceeded to offer me a room for the remainder of the night, if I would accept it in preference to returning to town. I declined the offer, and observed that I was sorry to find myself the unworthy cause of circumstances, which, as well as for the old gentleman, on their account I so much regretted.

"You are very considerate, very kind, sir," said the youngest of the ladies, addressing me ; "but we feel that we have much to apologize to you, for my father had apprized us of your meeting, of your coming, and we have much to regret that we did not prevent or prepare you for that dreadful visitation of mind which, in consequence of severe domestic affliction, has ———"

Emotion prevented her finishing the sentence. The melancholy melody of her voice, the expression of her dark, hazel eyes, which, despite her efforts to suppress, tears were rapidly suffusing, caused me to experience a peculiar sensation about the organs of vision, and I am not sure that I did not a little play the woman myself.

"I assure you, sir," said the old lady, interposing to the last speaker's relief, "that Mr. —— has never before been so violent as you have seen him to-night. Indeed, it having been so long since he had a paroxysm at all, we more readily consented to allow him to make his own arrangements to sup with you alone; it was an error in judgment which we must be careful not to repeat. In extenuation, however, I must observe, that we had no conception that the evil, with which Mr. —— is so unhappily afflicted, was so deeply rooted and so serious as this night has revealed it to be." She paused, but before I could offer a remark, again resumed.

"If we have understood aright, you are making but a short stay in the neighborhood?"

"To-morrow evening I purpose quitting Dolgelly," I replied; "allow me to leave my card. I had not one to present to Mr. —— on our first meeting, since which I had forgotten it;" and, drawing one forth, I handed it to the elderly lady, adding "that my quarters were at the Lion Hotel."

"You will very much oblige us," she rejoined, whilst hastily glancing at my name, "by not caring to communicate the particulars of your visit here to any of the curious in the town who, having heard of your visit, may interrogate you about us. By thus obliging us, you will truly show that sympathy, which I am sure you feel for Mr. —— and for us."

The reader will readily conceive that I assured the old lady she might rely upon her wishes being attended to; and, feeling that my presence longer could not be otherwise than painful to them, I rose from my seat to depart.

Ere bidding me good-night, they gave me a pressing invitation to dine with them on the morrow, by which time they believed Mr. —— would be so far recovered as to be able to join the party; he would then have an opportunity of apologizing to me for that which had passed, without which the recollection of the event would be to him a continual source of pain. Pleading a prior engagement to visit the mountain, Cadir Idris, I begged to decline, expressing at the same time a hope that the old gentleman would soon recover, and that on some future visit to Dolgelly, I should hear of his health being thoroughly established. With an understanding that I was to pay them a visit when I next came to that part of Wales, and a good-by and cordial shake of the hand with both ladies, I took my leave. Ushered by a servant, I soon found myself at the entrance-gate and on the road to Dolgelly, with the events of the last five hours flitting across my brain like the unconnected fragments of a strange and half-forgotten dream.

It was somewhere about two o'clock in the morning, when I aroused that useful functionary—the Boots—from a sound sleep enjoyed in an elevated domicil of the Golden Lion. I retired to rest in anything but a composed state of mind; the events of the night had been of so exciting a nature, that in my fitful slumbers I again joined in boisterous mirth with the old gentleman, again beheld in the huge mirror his eyes glaring upon me, and with his hand at my throat, felt myself struggling with him again.

In the summer following, I once more visited Dolgelly, and on inquiring, learned that the strange house was untenanted, the mysterious family had left, none knew whither. I never saw or heard of them more.

On reviewing the circumstances which I have related, the reader will probably conclude with me, that they present one of the many instances which, in this world's ever-changing scene, try and develop the most sterling and beautiful qualities which characterize woman. He will with me perceive, that the two individuals of the gentler sex, of whom these pages tell, had—the one sacrificed friends, and comforts, and that peace and tranquility, which should ever smooth the declining years of life,—and the other, the world, kindred, young fresh hearts like her own, society which she was so highly calculated to adorn, to cheer the hours of a decaying and darkened mind, to watch and tend that which in its state of wreck had become than ever more endeared, and by self-sacrifice and watchfulness to avoid the dread alternative of immolating in the gloomy walls of an asylum, one so well beloved. Honor to Woman! such instances so exalting to humanity, are not rare. Honor to Woman for her self-denial, her patient suffering, and her undying affection! Woman, who in harmony with that glorious creation which gave the sun to gladden the earth, despite of the clouds which lower over the paths of life, with her smile irradiates the scene, and until time shall be no more, will be, as she hath ever been, the brightest gem of this beautiful world.

LINES SUGGESTED BY THE VIEW FROM TELEGRAPH HILL.

BY J. P. ANTHONY.

SOUL inspiring sight!
　　Waters magnificent!　Bay of vasty spread!
When Nature fashioned thee in wondrous might
　　Bidding a world of waves from ocean's bed
With whelming power yon rocky portals smite
　　Until they ope'd their ponderous jaws for thee,
Did grace with wondrous grandeur then unite,
　　Designing all—as less than seer may see—
　　For some great acts in "Human Destiny."

Diabolo! high soaring from the plain,
　　A mountain monarch, mountains for thy throne,
Though now o'erlooking but a vast domain
　　That scarce the tread of human foot hath known,
Ere long awaking from inaction's reign—
　　Plains, hills and dells, adorned by culture's hand
A very Eden shall thy regions gain,
　　Whilst 'mid the hamlets o'er the smiling land
　　Shall tapering spires bespeak a Christian band.

And thou, young city, of all wondrous birth!
　　O'er whose rude cradle glared the fiends of fire,
Of greatness or of grandeur, nought has earth
　　But to surpass, methinks, thou mayst aspire;—
Thou, that came forth a giant at thy birth,

(Bespeaking such a dawn what manhood's glory)
With big events I read thy future rise—
  Ay, here, shalt thou and Time, that wizzard hoary
  Eclipse the wonders e'en of Eastern story.

Slaves of the lamp!—the genii of the ring!—
  How pale their fires, with all their fabled magic,
Compared with thee, and all that thou canst bring
  To thy strange history—so trying, tragic.
Thee more than conqueror of dread fire, I sing,
  Ocean, defeat before thy march hath known,
O'er its once realm thy vanguard banners spring
  Thou Ocean Queen—proud title, all thine own,
  Right well becomes thee, the Pacific Throne.

THE PAGAN CHALICE.*

ANONYMOUS.

QUAINT scriptures of old pagans, dug from the mouldy past,
Record a rich designing, some painter's skill had cast—
A rare and deep contrivance, by which a cup of wine
Was made to deck with emblems the pagan's idol shrine:
Yet when the wine was absent, the cup no emblem bore.
That antique art lies buried along pagan shore.

The painters and their emblems, the temples with their priests,
Their Gods, like coiling serpents, or all unsightly beasts,
Their mysteries of worship and all their rude conceits
Still haunt benighted Asia with faith in jugglers' feats;
But yet that Chinese Chalice—the emblem cup of wine—
That antique art lies buried far under some old shrine.

The priests of shrines more modern have sought, yet sought in vain,
To make an emblem chalice to stand on christian fane,
On which the Jewish rabble, the cross and dying Lord
Shall rise, when Priest or Pontiff the sacred wine hath pour'd.
New generations moulder with those the dust of yore,
And still that art lies buried on some wild, pagan shore.

Rich scriptures of old patriarchs, saved from the wreck of Time,
Teach histories of virtue in hearts of men sublime.
The royal bard of Israel, when bowed with grief and care,
Drew from his sore affliction the soul of holy prayer.
Until that soul was sorrow'd, no contrite prayer it bore—
Like empty antique wine-cup in pagan days of yore.

The man of Uz was prostrate before his chast'ning God,
Yet faith his eyes unsealing, wrote patience on the rod.
Pure faith and deep affliction paint in the human heart
Fields of far richer blazon than any pagan art—
High thoughts of the Eternal—the God of sea and shore,
When pagan arts lie buried in dust for evermore.

When Christ, the Lord's anointed, of martyr-hosts the chief,
Became our great example, he taught that shame and grief
Are like the milk of kindness to all of woman born—
As gentle rains of Heaven nurse infant fields of corn—
They warp the soul to goodness, they fill the heart with lore,
No art can ever bury on Time's eventful shore.

O, Christ! thou King of martyrs—A King of Kings the Chief!
Thou wert a man of sorrows, acquainted well with grief!
The teachings of thy mission were bathed in many tears—
Baptismal emblems shining around our hopes and fears.
Thou gavest grief for priestly wine, man's heart the chalice-bowl,
When Thou of Nazareth put on the sackcloth of the soul.

The christian prayer is spoken, the pagan is forgiv'n—
The Chalice is forgotton, the worship is of Heav'n—
The Chinese gods are melting before that great design
Which Calvary attested in ancient Palestine.
The archives rest in Heaven, while things of earthly lore,
Like Chinese arts, lie buried on many a pagan shore.

---

* "The Chinese formerly knew how to paint porcelain with fishes and other animals, in such a way that the figures never appeared to the eye till the vases were filled with liquor. This art, like that of the Aztec feather-work, is entirely lost."—*A Lady's Scrap Book.*

LAW REVIEW.

ABSTRACT OF THE DECISIONS OF THE SUPREME COURT.

THE decisions of the Supreme Court, since our last issue, are so voluminous, that we are compelled, for want of space, to present our readers with an abstract merely.

BURGOYNE *vs.* SUPERVISORS OF SAN FRANCISCO, 424.—The first session of the Legislature conferred upon the Court of Sessions the entire management of the financial business of the counties. Among other duties enjoined was that of purchasing suitable buildings for Court Houses and public offices. In compliance with this power, the Court of Sessions of San Francisco County purchased certain real estate in the City of San Francisco, for the use of the county, upon credit.

Held, that the Legislature could not confer this power upon the Courts of Sessions, but that their jurisdiction is limited to criminal cases alone; that the law was unconstitutional, and consequently the contract was void. Judgment affirmed.

JOHN C. HAYES AND AL. *vs.* JOHN HOGAN, 484.—*Held*, that an appeal will not lie from an order sustaining or overruling a demurrer. An error committed on such ruling can only be taken advantage of on an appeal from final judgment. Appeal dismissed.

THE PEOPLE *vs.* AH CHUNG, 252.—*Held*, that the Court of Sessions could not be holden by the County Judge and one Associate Justice. Judgment reversed.

GEORGE W. GARKINS *vs.* JAMES B. LAKUE, 449.—Dispute as to the right of possession to a lot. Garkins claimed as pre-emptioner, but failed to prove the inclosure of, or any visible boundaries embracing the lot. *Held*,

1. That Lakue, having erected a house upon the lot, could not be dispossessed in the manner sought by the defendant.

2. The exclusion of the record of defendant's claim, as evidence, was not injurious to him upon the trial, since, if admitted, it would not have been of itself evidence of a right of possession.

3. The motion for a nonsuit was properly overruled, as it was the province of the jury to pass upon the question of possession, as well as to estimate the damages suffered by commission of a wrong. Judgment affirmed.

J. G. FRAZIER *vs.* THE CITY OF MARYSVILLE, 419.—Demurrer to a complaint for negligence.

Held, that in an action against a city for injuries received by the plaintiff from the neglect of the city in cutting a sewer, and allowing the same to remain open to the danger of passers by, must allege, that the plaintiff was injured by such negligence; that the obstruction could not have been avoided by ordinary care and diligence; and that such care and diligence was used by the plaintiff. Judgment reversed and demurrer sustained.

PINKHAM ET AL. *vs.* MCFARLAND ET AL, 474.—The indorsements of the notes are not denied with sufficient certainty by the answer. If they were, the defendants should have objected to their introduction in evidence. Not having done so, the plaintiffs were warranted in supposing the objection waived, and the subsequent motion for a non-suit was a surprise upon them.

The power of a court to open a case after it has once been submitted, rests on the sound discretion of the Court hearing the case. In this case, however, the plaintiffs have been misled by the acts of the defendants, and justice demands that a new trial should be granted. New trial ordered.

BERRYMAN ET AL. *vs.* WILSON ET AL., 418.—The evidence of a juryman will not be received to implicate a verdict on the ground of the misconduct of the jury.

The mode of making up the verdict was the same as that adopted in Dana *vs.* Tucker, 4 Johns R., which we think correct.

We will not interfere with the decision of the Court below, in granting a new trial, where no gross abuse of discretion is exhibited. Judgment affirmed.

STUART *vs.* TREAT, 382.—1. The plaintiff in an action of forcible entry and detainer, must show an actual forcible possession in himself at the time of the entry.

2. A landlord cannot in this form sue in his own name for an unlawful entry upon the possession of his tenant.

3. The remedy is a summary one, given by statute to protect the possession, and cannot be extended by implication to any others than real occupants.

JOHN THORNTON *vs.* DANIEL DOUGHERTY, 386.—1. The Judge who tries the cause must find the facts, and state his conclusions of law separately. The case of Russel *vs.* Amador, 2 Cal. Rep. Approved. Judgment reversed.

CAIPMAN & AUGENBAUGH *vs.* JOSEPH EMERIE, 440.—Decision the same as in the preceding case.

J. R. WEST *vs.* SMITH & DOWNER, 323.—Both parties agree that the rule of damages, adopted by the Court below, was erroneous, and a new trial will be necessary, but seek the opinion of the Court upon other points of law arising on the record.

"This Court has invariably refused to decide questions not directly involved in the case and necessary to a judgment of reversal or affirmance. This Court cannot be expected to anticipate the rulings of the Court below on points that may not arise on the new trial, or to furnish inferior tribunals with directions as to the manner of disposing of questions which may possibly come before them." Judgment reversed.

BROOKS *vs.* TOWNSEND, 389.—Bill to quiet title.

1. The plaintiff's bill contained matter sufficient to give a Court of Chancery jurisdiction, and the demurrer was properly overruled.

2. If the defendant had no title or outstanding deed to the premises, it was his duty to enter a disclaimer. As he has chosen to pursue a different course, he cannot complain if he is compelled to pay the costs of his proceeding.

3. In regard to the final judgment entered against the defendant after the Court had granted him a stay of proceedings, in order to allow him to perfect his appeal, we are of opinion, that it was a surprise upon him; and whatever may have been the power or duty of the Court below, no substantial right should be lost to him on account of a mistake induced by the Court.

Judgment upon the demurrer affirmed, and final judgment reversed with leave to the defendant to answer over. Costs to be paid by the appellant.

CHIPMAN *vs.* BRIGGS, 441.—When land is sold for a gross sum described by specific boundaries, —and as containing so many acres, more or less, the vender cannot recover for the overplus, if on survey it be ascertained that more land is contained in the tract than the precise amount mentioned in the deed.

The findings of fact by the Court below, are conclusive upon the right of the appellant. Judgment affirmed.

WM. H. LADNER *vs.* JACOB FOURE ET AL., 485.—Appeal dismissed because there was no statement of facts signed by the Judge or agreed upon by the Attorneys.

HENRY PIERCE *vs.* FORD, LATHROP & CO. ET AL., 347.—1. Guarantees of a note are strictly indorsers and entitled to notice of non-payment.

2. Riggs *vs.* Waldo, 2 Cal. Rep., approved.

3. The maker's absence will excuse presentment and demand on him.

4. If an indorser receive security from the maker, it will sometimes fix his liability without notice. Judgment affirmed.

ENGELLS, HOOPER & CO. *vs.* MCKINLEY & GARRIOCH, 432.—Mowbray assigned to the defendants to secure the payment of a loan of five thousand dollars, and was to remain in possession until the discharge of the debt and interest, paying the defendants one-half the net profits until the liquidation of the debt, when the relation of the parties was to cease. The defendants never entered upon the premises.

1. This assignment can only be treated as a mortgage.

2. The defendants were not entitled to possession until breach of the agreement. Mowbray might at any time have compelled a cancellation of the assignment upon payment.

3. It is not sufficient to show that the defendants have a proper title and a legal right which might be enforced against their assignees. They are not entitled to the reversion on the ground of privity of contract, but by privity of estate or the actual occupation and beneficial enjoyment. Judgment reversed.

CUNNINGHAM & BRUMAGEN *vs.* STEPHEN D. HARRIS, 491.—The third instruction asked for by the defendant and refused by the Court, was,—

"That if the jury find that the plaintiff sued Bryan & Saunders for the same cattle here in controversy, in the action of which the record of this Court is in proof, and that the said defendant holds under said Bryan & Saunders, then the judgment and record in said cause is a bar to this action against this defendant, and plaintiffs cannot recover."

Held, that this instruction ought to have been given. Judgment reversed.

STEARN *vs.* AQUINE & ARGUELLO, 434.—Demurrer to answer. The allegation in the answer that the plaintiff extended the time for payment, in consideration of a change of the place of payment, is a good defense and discharges the surety, Aquine, from liability. Judgment reversed.

GETT ET AL. *vs.* CASTRO, 481.—1. Affidavits of jurors will not be taken to contradict the verdict.

2. A description of the land by name, is sufficient, without setting it out by metes and bounds.

3. It is immaterial that the name (a Spanish one) may be translated into English so as to mean nothing.

4. If notice to quit was necessary, the objection should have been made at the trial.

5. A party's possession is not always confined to his actual inclosure. Sherne *vs.* Leonard & Thompson, approved.

6. It is not for the jury to determine whether joint possession is evidence of title. It is so declared by law.

7. Nor is it for the jury to determine that "the possession was of such a character that a grant could be fairly presumed." Judgment affirmed.

PARSONS *vs.* TUOLUMNE WATER CO., 443.—1. In conferring upon the County Courts the power to prevent or abate nuisances, the Legislature exceeded their constitutional authority, and that portion of the Act is invalid.

2. The term "Special Cases," in the Constitution, was not intended to include any class of cases for which the Courts of general jurisdiction had always supplied a remedy, but is confined to those cases which are the creation of statutes and are unknown to the general framework of Courts of Common Law and Equity.

3. The cases of Hudson *vs.* Caulfield and Reed's Heirs *vs.* McCormick, cited and approved. Judgment reversed and cause dismissed.

RAMERO *vs.* RAMERO ET AL., 490.—Demurrer to complaint. The complaint must show that the work was done at the instance of the defendants, and that they promised to pay the amount demanded, or what it was reasonably worth.

Order overruling demurrer reversed, with leave to plaintiff to amend.

HOWARD ET AL. *vs.* HARMON, 492.—Appeal from County Court. The objection that there was no proper appeal bond filed with the Justice, should have been made in the Court below. It is too late to make it in this Court.

The Court below, upon proper excuse shown, would have had power to allow the party to file a bond. Judgment affirmed.

STEMTHALL *vs.* LONSDALE.—The Judge gave an improper reason for refusing a new trial, but for want of a statement settled or agreed upon, the judgment must be affirmed.

HAVENS *vs.* CADWELL.—The case of Baldwin et al. *vs.* Kramer, 2 Cal. Rep. 582, cited and approved.

RYAN *vs.* JOHNSON.—The "Act to prevent extortion in Office," C. L. 214, is constitutional. The defendant may have a jury trial.

The "Act regulating Fees in Office," is not an Act of a general nature.

DUELL *vs.* THE BEAR RIVER CO.—1. To make the doctrine of estoppel (in pais) apply, the defendants must show that the declarations of plaintiff's grants were inducements to the purchase by the defendant.

2. The Court will not reverse the order of a Judge refusing a new trial, unless there is a gross abuse of discretion.

3. The Court will not review the verdict of a jury where the evidence is contradictory or where the jury refuse to give full credit to the testimony of witnesses. Nor if there is sufficient evidence whereon to base the verdict of the jury.

SAMUEL F. SERREY *vs.* WELLS, FARGO & CO.—There must be a statement settled or agreed upon. The certificate of the Clerk is not sufficient.

PEOPLE *vs.* THURSTON.—An indictment found by a Grand Jury of twenty-four persons is wholly void, and all proceedings based upon it are void.

This objection may be taken in the Supreme Court.

BERNARD EXLINE *vs.* S. P. SMITH ET AL.—So much of the Practice Act as provides that "the Court may prescribe by rule what shall be a waiver (of jury trial) in other cases," is unconstitutional. C. R. L. 55.

2. The constitution has imposed the power, as well as the necessity, upon the Legislature of determining in what cases a jury trial may be waived, which cannot be transferred or delegated to any other department of government.

3. Legislative duties cannot be conferred upon judicial officers.

THE PEOPLE *vs.* HORACE BREWSTER.—The defendant was convicted of manslaughter and moved an arrest of judgment, because the indictment charged more than one offense.

The first count charged the defendant and one Horton, with the crime of murder. The second charged the defendant as accessory.

There is no irregularity in this. The offense of the principal and accessory are the same, (C. R. L. 639.) Both parties were indicted for murder.

MCDERMOTT *vs.* DOUGLASS.—Judgment affirmed.

BENNETT *vs.* WOODS.—Judgment reversed.

BUCKELEW *vs.* ESTELL ET AL.—The Court properly refused to dissolve the injunction. There are several defendants and only two have answered. The answer admits the grant through which the plaintiff claims. A stranger cannot question the performance of the conditions of the grant. The question as to boundary is the only one which is to be determined—and until then, the injunction, to stay waste, should be continued in force.

WALKER *vs.* SEDGWICK.—1. In Chancery Cases the Judge need not find the facts and conclusions of law.

2. In Chancery Cases, this Court has to examine the facts, and is not concluded by the findings of the Chancellor.

3. The statute does not apply in such cases, but is intended for those cases where the trial by the Judge supplied the place of a trial by jury.

4. In Chancery Cases the parties are not entitled to a trial by jury. Judgment affirmed.

JOHN SAUNICKSON *vs.* EZEKIEL BROWN.—Accounts for labor and services, and goods and materials furnished, and defendant's request made out in writing, under which was written "audited and approved," or "certified to be correct," and signed by defendant, are instruments in writing, and are not barred by that portion of the statute of limitations applying to accounts. Judgment reversed.

PEOPLE *vs.* DAVID DAVIDSON ET AL.—S. P. AS PEOPLE *vs.* HORACE BREWSTER ANTE.—Under an indictment for "An assault with intent to commit murder," a verdict of "Guilty of an assault with a deadly weapon, with intent to commit great bodily injury," is regular.

MANTINEZ *vs.* GALLARDO.—After the dismissal of an appeal for the want of a proper bond, a new appeal may be taken at any time within the period allowed by law.

JOSEPH T. MCCLINTOCK *vs.* DAVID BRYDEN ET AL.—1. A settler upon public lands of the General Government may maintain ejectments against a mere intruder.

2. A settler upon mineral lands acquires no title or right under the laws of the United States.

3. Any person entering upon such settlement, to dig for gold, is not a trespasser, but is in the pursuit of a lawful occupation, and in exercise of a lawful right.

4. The precious metals in the earth belong to the General Government.

5. By the uniform practice of the General Government, she has permitted her citizens and those of other States, to enter upon the mineral lands and take therefrom the precious metals.

6. The State of California has undoubted right to pass laws regulating the manner of defending and possessing the public lands of the United States, by her police powers.

7. The General Government will issue no patent to a pre-emption claimant upon mineral lands, who claims the same for agricultural purposes.

8. The wants and interests of a country must govern the application of principles of law, and rules must be relaxed which are unsuited to its condition.

IRWIN *vs.* PHILLIPS ET AL.—1. Where a river flows through lands subject to private ownership, it cannot be lawfully diverted from its natural channel.

2. But this rule does not apply to water flowing through the public lands.

3. The owner of a canal in the mining regions of this State, constructed for the purpose of supplying water to miners, has the right to divert the water of a stream from its natural channel, as against the claims of those who subsequently take up lands along the banks of the stream for the purpose of mining.

4. Courts are bound to take notice of the political and social condition of the country which they judicially rule.

5. Query? Whether the mineral lands are the property of the State or the United States?

6. Mining canals and water races, are property.

7. The case of Hicks *vs.* Bell et al., cited and approved. (The right of miners to dig for gold.)

DARTIN *vs.* ENDICOTT.—The instruction asked for and referred, was included in another instruction which was given. The refusal has no error.

STOKES *vs.* BARRETT & CO. ET AL.—1. A settler cannot maintain trespass against a person entering to dig for minerals.

2. The mines of gold and silver in the State are the property of the State, whether in public or private lands. The doctrine laid down in Hicks *vs.* Bell, re-asserted.

3. Every citizen has the right to enter public lands to dig for gold; but not upon private lands without further legislation.

JOHNSON *vs.* SEPULBEDA.—1. Where bills of exceptions are taken and signed by the Judge at the trial, they become a part of the record, and it is not necessary to prepare a statement.

2. It is not necessary to embody matter of record in the statement.

3. Every intendment must be in favor of the decision of the Court below.

4. Judgment will not be reversed for error of law, where no injury has ensued to appellant.

5. A tenant in common, may maintain an action of ejectment, alone.

6. Semble—that *all* the tenants in common may join in the action—but a part may not.

EDWARD W. TAYLOR *vs.* ANDREW RANDALL.—Suit upon a promissory note. Motion to set aside the judgment, for surprise, on the ground of the necessary absence of his counsel from the trial.

The affidavit alleged material alteration of the note, but did not show in what the alteration consisted. *Held* insufficient.

The attorney of record admitted in writing, on the back of the note, the amount due.

Held, that such admission, when not done in fraud of the rights of his client, must destroy the effect of the denial in the answer. Judgment affirmed.

SCIENTIFIC.

WE devote our entire Scientific Department this month to a graphic account of the celebrated Calaveras Cave. It was written by Mr. W. P. Blake, recently attached to Lieut. Williamson's surveying party, first published in the *Times and Transcript*, and afterwards in the *Calaveras Chronicle* of the 23d September, 1854, from whose columns we extract it:

"GEOLOGICAL FORMATION OF THE GREAT CAVE IN CALAVERAS.

The Cave in Calaveras County, which has attracted considerable attention by reason of its extent and the beauty of portions of its interior, is about twelve miles from Murphy's, and fifteen from the grove of Mammoth Trees. Rich *placeres* are found in the immediate vicinity of the Cave, and mining is conducted with energy and success. The visitor will find accommodation in the adjoining town, called Cave City, or at the house erected for the purpose, near the entrance of the Cave.

This Cave is in a hard crystalline limestone, which is not of secondary age, as has been represented, but belongs to the granitic group of rocks, and is popularly termed *primitive limestone*. It is intercalated with the talcose and clay states, and forms a wide belt which extends in a nearly north-west and south-east direction through Calaveras County.

This rock is sub-crystalline, and may be called a granular marble. Many places were seen where abundance of fine building-stone or slabs for ornamental purposes could be procured. It is thickly veined with light blue lines, which are all parallel, and give a structural character to the mass, that resembles stratification. These lines of structure give a distinct trend to the formation, which is generally north-west and south-east, but at the Cave I found it to be north 50 degrees to 75 degrees west, dip east.

Limestone of this character, found imbedded in the old slates and granites, are considered by some geologists to have once been horizontal strata laid down under water and filled with the relics of organic life. They account for their present peculiar crystalline character and the absence of organic remains, by supposing them to have been metamorphosed by great heat and pressure, so that all their original characteristics have been destroyed. Others conclude that they were formed from igneous action nearly in the condition which we now find them. In either case, they belong to the foundations of the earth, and underlie the superstructure of geological history, which records the birth of animate existence.

The road from Cave City to the Cave house skirts along the base of a ridge of this limestone. The entrance to the Cave is near the road, and was cut at a lower level than the natural opening, and resembles a mining tunnel. Within the opening the passage descends gently for twenty or thirty feet, and then expands into an irregular chamber, which communicates by various passages and openings with different parts of the Cave.

There are several rooms or chambers varying in size from twenty feet square to over fifty feet in length. Some of these chambers connect by large open passages so that they may be considered as forming one continuous cavern. Their form is exceedingly irregular, and the hight of the roof does not exceed forty feet.

These caverns in the rocks have evidently been formed by the eroding action of water, either standing in great pools, or slowly flowing in and out. The evidences of this action are visible on the sides and tops of the chambers, which in some places are distinctly marked with water-lines, and in others are eaten away below a certain level, leaving projecting angles and overhanging masses.

Several pools of water of unknown depth are found in different parts of the Cave, and there are doubtless many chambers which are thus completely filled. The water used at the hotel is obtained from one of these pools, near the entrance. It is delightfully cool and clear, and is highly charged with lime. It is evident that there is a constant infiltration of water through the seams of the rock forming the roof, and that it becomes highly charged with lime in its downward passage. This is shown by the great number of stalactites hanging pendent from above, some of them being several feet in length and very perfect in form. In one of the chambers where the stalactites are very numerous they are nearly snow-white, and hang like icicles from all parts of the roof. At many places in the Cave the direction and dip of the planes of structure in the limestone were clearly visible; some parts of the limestone having been eroded more rapidly than others, so that long grooves and lines were formed in the roof. It was interesting to observe that long lines of stalactites had been formed on these prominent portions. One of the chambers contains a beautiful grotto, formed by a fringe of broad but thin stalactites hanging like drapery from the edge of a table-like projection of the rock. These pendents are so thin as to be translucent, and a beautiful effect is produced by lighting up the interior with candles. The light becomes mellowed and softened as if inclosed in vases of alabaster.

Wherever the infiltrating water has coursed down the sides of the chamber, large and massive accumulations of snow-white lime have been formed, covering up all the irregularities of the walls and heaping up on the floor so as to resemble a frozen waterfall. The similarity of form and appearance is nearly perfect, and they might be called *petrified cascades*. The floors of the chambers are dotted in many places with stalagmites, that rise like stumps or posts above the general surface. It is hardly necessary to remind the reader that these are formed by the calcareous waters that drop down from the roof. These stalactites and stalagmites are all carbonate of lime, and it is an interesting fact that complete crystallization appears,to have extended throughout the lime that has been deposited, in whatever shape it is found. One of the accumulations that resembles a waterfall is brilliant with myriads of crystalline facets, and reflects the light of a candle in all directions. This mass appears to increase by successive additions upon the outside in their crusts or layers; but the molecular forces appear to bring the particles into mathematical order, and a crystal results. It is, however, frequently the case, that lines of discoloration corresponding with each successive layer of material, will remain in the crystalline mass and indicate the former shape of the surface.

The crystallization of the stalactites renders them compact and elastic, so that when struck they produce a clear sound like a bell. It is soft and musical, and in one chamber there is a group of stalactites, varying in length and thickness, that give a variety of tones.

In most parts of the Cave there appears to be a thick deposit of fine earth or loam upon the bottom. Portions of this earth are crusted over with stalagmite, which makes an apparently solid, rocky floor. There are, however, several places where the soft earth has been washed away from under the crust, and it is left projecting out from the walls, and marked the hight of the former surface.

It is desirable that this accumulation of earth should be examined for the remains of animals, which are often found in such places.

A skull of a small carniverous animal had been taken out not long before my visit. All bones found in such places should be preserved, as they are often remains of extinct species of animals.

This Cave does not compare in size or interest with those in Virginia and in the limestones of the western States; but it presents interesting and instructive lessons in geology, and is a good example of the solvent power of water when charged with carbonic acid. Portions of the Cave are beautiful, and those who have not seen the extensive caves of the eastern United States will not regret making it a visit."

MONTHLY SUMMARY OF EVENTS.

"With news the time's in labor and brings forth
Each minute some."

February 14. The bill for an Act to Fund the Debt of the State, as exhibited in Controller's Warrants, now outstanding, passed the Senate.

February 15. The Board of Aldermen passed an ordinance to Fund the Floating Debt of San Francisco, amounting on the first of January last, to $1,562,391. The loan to be taken at twenty years, at an annual interest of 8 per cent., payable in New York, and the principal in San Francisco. . . . Six State prisoners, convicted of robbing in El Dorado County, arrived in charge of Sheriff Buell.

February 16. The P. M. S. S. Golden Age left for Panama, carrying treasure to the value of $1,287,364 57. . . . The first floor of a building south of the Herald office, fell through, with a crash, injuring a quantity of goods which were stored upon it. The accident was caused by a species of wood-ants, who had perforated the beams to the depth of two or three inches. . . . The Electoral Convention having balloted for U. S. Senator many days in vain, was adjourned *sine die.* . . . The new Telegraph line connecting Stockton, Jamestown and Columbia, was completed. . . . Day celebrated by the Chinese as the first day of their new year.

February 17. The P. M. S. S. Oregon arrived, bringing news of the failure of Messrs. Page & Bacon, of St. Louis. This intelligence caused a "run" upon their house in this city, and during the day the excitement was intense. It was said that the suspension of the house was but temporary. . . . The St. Charles Hotel, situated on the corner of Davis and Washington streets, and a portion of Hillman's Hotel adjoining, were consumed by fire. Loss $10,000.

February 18. A bill was introduced into the Legislature, claiming that the Public Lands in the State, belong to California, and not to the United States. . . . The brig "Sophie," lying at Stuart street wharf, was burglariously entered and robbed of $1,500 and various articles of value.

February 20. The first number of a new German paper called the *San Francisco Journal*, and edited by Mr. Julius Froebel, was issued. . . . A fire broke out at Nevada, destroying property to the value of $50,000.

February 21. A destructive fire raged at Stockton, and consumed property to the value of $50,000.

February 22. The Birthday of Washington was celebrated by the entire Fire Department, who marched in procession through the streets. All the Fire Companies were dressed in full uniform, and their engines tastefully decorated. They were accompanied by fine bands of music. The procession was preceded by carriages bearing Gen. J. E. Wool and Staff, Lieut. Gov. Purdy and other distinguished persons. After marching through the principal streets, it proceeded to the Metropolitan Theater, where Col. E. D. Baker read a poem, written by Frank Soulé, Esq., for the occasion, and the Department was addressed by Major Gen. Wool, Mayor Webb, and others. . . . The Banking House of Page, Bacon & Co. suspended payment. . . . The Court House of San Leandro, valued at $4,500, was burned to the ground. The fire was supposed to have been the work of an incendiary.

February 23. The suspension of Page, Bacon & Co. on the day previous, caused an intense excitement, and a run on the other banks in the city. Adams & Co., Wells, Fargo & Co., Robinson & Co. and A. S. Wright's Miners' Exchange Bank closed. Lucas, Turner & Co. had a severe run, but remained unshaken. Drexel, Sather & Church and B. Davidson met the attack with proper resistance and survived. Palmer, Cook & Co., Tallant & Wilde, and Sanders & Brenham had a slight run, which interfered but little with their ordinary business.

February 24. Henry Haight, Esq., tendered his resignation as President of the Board of Assistant Aldermen. Assistant Alderman Maynard was elected to fill his place. Assistant Alderman Perry resigned as a member of the Board. . . . The sale of City property, for the payment of State and County taxes, advertised to take place to-day, was restrained by an injunction issued from the Superior Court, upon the ground that the assessment-roll upon which the taxes were based, was not properly made out. . . . The America arrived from Los Angeles, confirming the favorable news which had been received of the Kern River Gold Mines.

February 25. The creditors of Messrs. Page, Bacon & Co. had a meeting in the new Banking House of that firm, when a statement of its affairs was presented to them, and a proposition that if $500,000 of its liabilities was extended for two, four, six and eight months, at 1 per cent., the house could resume payment. The proposition was received with enthusiasm by those present, and a bond entered into by a number of citizens to the amount of $1,500,000, guaranteeing the ultimate payment of every sum that should be extended in accordance with such proposition. . . . Henry M. Nagle was appointed Receiver in the House of Wells, Fargo & Co., and A. A. Cohen in that of Adams & Co.

February 26. The steamship "Uncle Sam" left, carrying treasure to the value of $92,322. . . . Adams & Co. published a circular, proposing to their creditors that they should be allowed to go on, provided they paid 25 per cent. on all claims in 30 days from date, and the balance as fast as the Receiver could declare the dividends. . . . Mr. Farwell introduced a Bill in the Legislature, providing for the construction of a Plank Road from the intersection of Bush and Larkin streets to the Pacific Ocean, either to the Seal Rock House or the Beach House.

February 28. A meeting of the depositors and creditors of Robinson & Co. was held at the San Francisco Hall. That gentleman made a statement that if he was allowed time, he might be able to pay 37½ cents on the dollar, which was not at all satisfactory. The meeting was very disorderly. A committee was appointed to examine the books of the concern and report thereon. . . . By a statement in the *Chronicle*, it appeared that the Mint had coined during the month of February, $1,375,000 in double eagles and $200,000 in bars.

March 1.   The P. M. S. S. Golden Gate left for Panama, carrying only $391,-270 17. . . . The members of the Mechanics' Institute met in the rooms of the Board of Aldermen and adopted a constitution. . . . The Express of Adams & Co. stopped.   The employees of the House formed an association to do business on their own account, under the name of the Pacific Express; and James King of Wm. and H. Reed, Esq., formerly connected with Adams & Co., started a new Bank, under the name of James King of Wm. & Co. . . . The Sacramento *Statesman* was sold to P. Dunlap, Esq. . . . The sailors in port struck for wages and caused a great excitement about the wharves.

March 2.   The celebrated actress, Miss Davenport, arrived by the Sonora. . . . The steamship America arrived from Los Angeles, bringing still more favorable news of the Kern River Mines.

March 3.   The steamboat Antelope made the quickest trip from Sacramento on record, being 5 hours and 56 minutes. . . . The statement of Dr. S. A. Wright published in the *Herald*, showed an excess of his assets over his liabilities to be $41,020 78.

March 4.   The vault of the Banking and Express office of Adams & Co. at Sonora was broken open by a mob, and about $45,000 taken out, which was distributed by a committee. . . . Five Mormon converts were baptised on North Beach in presence of 500 persons. . . . The creditors of Messrs. Page, Bacon & Co., in Sacramento, had a meeting at Jones' Hotel.   It was addressed by Messrs. Page and Crockett, and a proposition for extension was presented, which was signed by a number of those present. . . . By a decision of Judge Norton, Messrs. Gordon & Stein were exempted from liability for damages by the explosion of the Steamboat Secretary.

March 5.   General Allen, editor of the *Margsville Herald*, was elected Mayor of Marysville.

March 7.   The depositors of the Miners' Saving Bank had a meeting in which they agreed to submit a proposition to Dr. Wright, permitting him to resume business, on condition of his agreeing to pay 25 per cent. on his deposits at the expiration of every succeeding two months, until the whole were paid. . . . In the Fourth District Court, John Blake was convicted of the murder of Lyman Mowry. . . . A mandamus, issued from the Supreme Court, commanding Judge Shattuck to revoke an order made by him, transferring a case from his Court to the U. S. District Court, was presented, which he refused to obey. . . . Judge Norton decided that Controller's Warrants were not evidences of indebtedness, and third parties could not recover upon them against the city, unless the original audited account, upon which the Warrants were drawn, were also assigned.

March 8.   Gov. Bigler granted an unconditional pardon of John Tabor, of Stockton, who had been convicted and sentenced to execution, for the killing of Mansfield. . . . Mozart's grand opera Don Giovanni was brought out at the Metropolitan, with the full cast of the Italian troupe, Madame Anna Bishop and Madame Barili Thorn appearing at the same time.

EDITOR'S TABLE.

THE CRIME OF DELAY.

—

You ask, dear Jim, why I took so much interest in that boy? I will tell you, but mark me, you must never allude to the subject again. I had thought, that for my own credit, no one should ever know the reason of my solicitude concerning him, or why his death has affected me so deeply. But he is dead now, and lest you should misconstrue my interest in him to my prejudice, I will tell you frankly all that I know of him, so far as it affects myself.

I was not always, you are aware, dear Jim, the man you have recently known me. I once had position and influence, and when you first knew me, had never done any act to bring a blush of shame to the cheek of friend or relative.

But of this, enough. It sufficeth, that one year ago, or thereabouts, as I went to my office on a beautiful morning in March, I noticed a boy walking down the street, just ahead of me, looking pale, emaciated and yet beautiful. There was a peculiar—an exceedingly anxious look, that I had never seen before. There was the face of a boy with the anxiety of a man. It struck me as peculiar at the first glance, and I stopped to look at him. I perceived that it was with difficulty he could restrain himself from sobbing aloud. When he saw me, he repressed his emotion, and spoke up with an obvious effort of unconcern.

"Please, Sir, are you not the editor of the ———?"

"I am," said I, "my fine fellow, and what can I do for you?"

"Mother's sick, sir, and we are very poor, and I want to get a place to work."

"What can you do," said I.

"O, I will try to do anything;" he replied, "but I don't know what I can do, for I always went to school before I came to California; I will try to do anything."

The boy had interested me, and though I am a callous man, whom buffeting with the world has hardened prematurely, I could not allow him to leave me, till I had given him a word of comfort.

"My fine fellow," said I, "can you come to my office at seven o'clock this evening?"

"I will," he answered—"I will do anything to earn some money for my poor, sick mother."

I took a five dollar piece from my pocket, and put it into his hand. Had I a right to do it? I had often said I ought to pay my honest debts, before I thought of charity. Had I a right to do it? Yes.

The boy looked at the money; then he looked at me, and then—burst into tears.

Dear Jim, believe me, I had a great mind to cry, too. Said he, "Did I act like a little beggar?" As he spoke the word "beggar," he burst out again, and the tears gushed forth afresh.

"No my lad," said I, "but take that to your mother, and this evening I will have a place for you, so that you can earn the money, and when you have enough of it, perhaps you can pay me back."

He held the coin towards me and said, "Take the money,—I am not a beggar, and as my father, who is dead, and my mother, who is dying, told me to starve sooner than beg—I shall not take it."

He was so earnest, that to have refused, would have offended him the more, and so requesting him to call on me at seven o'clock in the evening, I told him to go home to his mother, and tell her that he had found a friend who would get him a situation.

He tripped away with a lighter heart. I went my way, thinking how I could and would befriend him. It was only the day before, that a friend had told me he wanted a boy of about his years, and if he was faithful and trustworthy, would pay him a liberal salary. I resolved in my own mind, I would go and see him immediately after breakfast. But,

> The flighty purpose never is o'ertook,
> Unless the deed go with it.

At the breakfast table I got engaged in an angry, political discussion. The Senatorial election was on the *tapis*, and we had got news that morning, that a reverend Senator, belonging to our side, had sold out and gone over to the enemy. I went down town after breakfast to learn the facts of the matter. I talked with one and another, till the case of the poor boy was quite driven out of my head. Before I returned, the dispatches began to arrive from the Capital, and what with talking to interested friends, and writing for the next morning's paper, I quite forgot the pale-faced boy and his dying mother.

At seven o'clock he came. My heart smote me when I saw him, for I had neglected and forgotten my promises. But I told him,—God forgive me,—not so much for the deception as the neglect,—that I could not see the man whom I thought would employ him, but if he would come the next day at two o'clock, I would get him the situation, and pay him the first month's salary in advance. Dejected, he turned upon his heel and left the office. The next morning I went to my friend's store; he was out for a few minutes. While I was standing in his door, an acquaintance with a fine horse and buggy, came along, and asked me to ride with him to the Mission. I at once consented, thinking to call as I came in. We went to the Mission, from there to the race-course. Time flew swiftly, and before I was aware of it, two o'clock had passed, and I came home to find that the boy had been to see me and had gone away. I did not suppose I would see him again that night, and would put off the matter—so important to him—till the next morning. But he came again in the evening, and I had to tell him, that I had been away. The next day, at twelve, however, should see him in his new place.

It was nearly twelve of the next day, when I bethought myself of my promise. I hastened down to see my friend, and found that I was too late; the vacancy had been filled about an hour before. Conscience smitten, I returned to my office, and I met the boy's anxious look as I entered the door. I told him I had just been to see about the promised situation, and it was taken. Yet, I thought I could get him a place soon. He thanked me, but his heart was bursting. I saw that an anxiety, terrible for one so young, was wearing his life away.

The next day I found him a place, and engaged it for him. I sat in my office writing, when the door softly opened, and he entered. He was pale, but calmer than I had before seen him.

"Well, my fine fellow," said I, "I have got you a place at last. You are to have twenty-five dollars a week, and you shall have a whole month's salary in advance, if you like."

He came towards me and handed me a slip of paper. It was a notice for the newspaper, and announced the *death of his mother!*

I have had many severe crosses, my dear Jim,—I have felt that all was lost, and that my life was not worth a rush. I have seen my fondest hopes crushed by one fell blow, and I have felt to cry out in an agony at the cruel fate that pursued me. But all, that I had ever suffered, was nothing to what I felt when I looked on that pale, calm, intellectual boy, with his bright, big, blue eye, gazing supernaturally into mine, and thought how that, perhaps, but for my neglect, his mother might then have been alive. I know not how I looked, or how I acted, but I know that man never suffered more in a short space of time, than I did. I have never got over it yet, and I never shall. You may not be able to realize the full force of it, but "I would not have the same touch of heart-break again,—no, not for all the lands ever owned by McGregor."

After that, I tried to do what I could to drive away the deep melancholy, that seemed to have settled upon him. But he would not be comforted. He seemed to be impressed with the idea, that here, in San Francisco, where so many live in extravagance and splendor, his only friend, his beloved and affectionate mother, had been allowed to perish in abject poverty and neglect. I attended the funeral, and interested some of my friends in the case, so that she had a decent burial. But the boy thanked me not. How could he? Could he feel gratitude, that I had shown an interest in the dead, which I had denied to the living? He seemed disinclined to receive any favor from me, and his clear, calm, mild eye, was too much for me to look at. I quailed before it, as I never quailed before. That he might not suppose that it was I who was acting in his behalf, I got a friend to offer him a situation, where he could earn more than his support. But he did not keep it long. He grew paler and paler each day, and soon was too weak to attend to his duties at all. I watched him with more than fraternal interest, and I often went to see him at his room. It was evident that he would soon die. I procured a watcher for him, for my own presence seemed to trouble him, and when I went the next day to see him, I found that he was dead. He died, as he had lived cursing me, I believe, in his heart. I felt, while he lived, that his curse was justly upon me, and have often recalled the terrible lines of Coleridge:

> "An orphan's curse would drag to hell
>   A spirit from on high;
> But oh, more terrible than that
>   Is a curse in a dead man's eye!"

He is dead now, dear Jim, but this lesson I have learned ;—never again to put off the business of another for the sake of my own. Life or death may depend upon his, while mine, you know, is of little importance; for though life be at stake, I ask why I should perpetuate so fitful an existence.—[OLIVER OUTCAST.

MUSICAL AND THEATRICAL.

FROM DEC. 20 TO MARCH 20.—We confess to great remissness during the past three months, touching our friends of the sock and buskin. We would feign lay the blame to the fact that there had been little of interest at the Metropolitan and American, were we not aware that we had played truant from the Theaters so much during the interval, that we were positively unable to post our friends in California and at the east, as has heretofore been our wont. That peculiar species of "moon" having waned, which every Benedick experiences once in his life, we are ready to take up the *stylus*, and recommence our monthly notices of the stage.

Indeed there has been very much of interest at both temples of the Muses, since our third volume opened; and even if there had not, the recent appearance of a new star at the Metropolitan, together with the brilliant opening of the American by the combined Monplaisir and Italian Opera Troupes, were enough to awaken a very Romeo to his duty. Such a mass of matter is before us, that we hardly know how to handle it. We must, however, "cut the Gordian Knot," by passing over the last week in December and the months of January and February with a hop, skip and jump, and coming down full upon the Ides of March.

THE AMERICAN—CLOSE OF THE SEASON.—In our last notice we alluded somewhat at length to Mr. Stark. As artists who have received the *American* stamp visit us, one after the other, and fail to elicit the enthusiasm of San Francisco audiences, we are no longer surprised, that a reputation in the transmontane States weighs not a feather in England, and are more than ever sure of Mr. Stark's triumph, sooner or later. His engagement closed on the 25th of December, when Mr. Henry Sedley made his first appearance, with Mrs. Woodward, (a sterling stock actress,) in the leading female characters. This lady had just returned from a visit to her friends in Boston. Mr. Sedley is young upon the stage. He, however, gives promise of excellence. The remainder of the season, after Stark's engagement, was not marked by full houses, and the theater closed on the 28th of February. Mr. Neafie has not succeeded in California as a star, having in this respect followed in the footsteps of Miss Laura Keene. They are both sterling artists, but cannot be ranked among the great.

Mr. Stark performed at Marysville after his engagement at the American, and then appeared at Sacramento, where he was warmly received, filling the house for three weeks.

THE METROPOLITAN.—Mr. and Mrs. Barney Williams appeared at this establishment during the last week in December and the first half of January, giving way to the opera until the last of February, when they performed their farewell engagement in this city, and left to appear for the last time at Stockton and Sacramento.

The nights of the opera were, in the main, very brilliant. A combination was formed by Mrs. Sinclair, between the Italian and the Madame Anna Bishop Troupes, and "La Favorita," the "Elixir of Love," "Robert the Devil," "Lucia," the "Bohemian Girl" and the grand opera of "Don Giovanni," were produced.

We have had no manager in California, that could be compared with Mrs. Sinclair in liberality and enterprise.

The Italian Troupe undertook to please the Sacramentans during the last of December, but the Levee City preferred Mr. and Mrs. Barney Williams to music.

MISS DAVENPORT.—On the evening of March 12th, at the close of Mr. Williams's farewell engagement at the Metropolitan, Miss Davenport made her first appearance. Up to the time of our writing, she has performed Julia in the "Hunchback," The Countess in "Love," Pauline, Parthenia, Juliet, and Adrienne the Actress.

In their opinion of her, the community seem to be divided into three classes; first, those who regard her as a great *artiste*—far superior to any we have had here; second, those who are vastly disappointed in her, and who can in no way be induced to rank her among the really great; and third, those who are endeavoring very strenuously to be pleased with her who, although they like her, perhaps, are at a loss to account for the fact that they do not find in their hearts any very great enthusiasm for her,—who, nevertheless, are doing all they can in her behalf, and dislike to hear her spoken disparagingly of. This is a singular condition of affairs, but it is made plainly visible by the size of her audiences and their invariable conduct. For, since her first night, the houses have not been overflowing—not even full—yet they have been respectable in size. And, again, while they have been invariably attentive, they have been by no means enthusiastic, except in occasional instances, where Miss Davenport has burst out of her usual manner and given evidences of high tragic power.

On the first evening the attendance was large, the seats being filled with one of the most intelligent and critical audiences we have ever seen gathered. It was an audience of whose plaudits any artist upon the boards might justly be proud. It was a study to watch the faces; and a careful observer could not fail to see that those present were weighing every word, every gesture, every look; that they were awake for "points," and that when they applauded, they knew well whether it should be with five claps or *ad libitum*. As a final result, we can say truly that, on the whole, Miss Davenport made a favorable, but not *highly flattering* impression.

More than a year ago we tossed aside the old system of puffing with which the press of California had been stained from the first, and commenced to speak candidly of the merits and demerits of artists who presented themselves to our public. It is almost needless, perhaps, for us to say, that the course of our periodical in matters theatrical has been too long established, to permit us, even under circumstances of the warmest friendship and the heartiest desire for success, to deviate from our rule in any one instance. This Magazine has been called by a well-known commedian and tragedian, whose coldness upon the stage we took occasion to notice frankly, "An infernal *Stark* affair." We confess to the warmest friendship for Mr. Stark,—a friendship engendered by a very high esteem of his *genius* as an actor; but we appeal with confidence to our December number as giving evidence of a want of any partiality in criticism. Friend or the contrary, we took occasion candidly to point out what we considered as his defects. We shall endeavor in the present instance to be equally candid. We write in the spirit of kindness—nay, friendship. It has been said by one of the shrewdest critics of the present century, who has, alas, solved the Great Mystery, that it is not the business of the critic to point out excellencies—they speak for themselves;—but to notice those points in which improvement may be made. If we follow this rule too closely, it will not be because we admit its correctness, nor by any means because we rank ourselves among the second class spoken of above,—those who consider Miss Davenport as so destitute of the elements of greatness, that she can not be ranked above our approved stock actresses.

When we find an *artiste*, who, in the position which she seeks to hold, commands the respect, and retains the attention of audiences of unusual critical ability, and, to say the least, moderate in size, and yet who clearly does not awaken very general *enthusiasm*, we are naturally led to cast about for the reason. Such an *artiste* cannot certainly be considered as mediocre, and should not be degraded in our estimation to the rank of a merely excellent stock actress; for she aspires to be a star, and at least commands respect in that aspiration. But on the other hand, she cannot be ranked among the very brightest ornaments of the stage, for overflowing audiences do not follow her, nor has she the ability—shall we call it *genius*—to fan mere admiration into enthusiasm. We should be equally at error, therefore, in judging her by the standard of the Keans, the Cushmans and the Fanny Kemble Butlers of the boards, as are they who seek to compare her with our mere approved stock actresses. We need not say that we have Miss Davenport in mind while making these remarks. If, then, she is not to be classed with the more brilliant stars on the one hand, nor with the leading stock actresses on the other, where between these two grades does she stand?

It has been justly remarked by the present professor of modern languages and literature at Cambridge, that talent, although it may be larger in frame and stronger of muscle than genius—lacks the wings. Is Miss Davenport possessed of remarkable talent merely, which through long training and care has been polished to great excellence, or is that spark of genius within her, which, whatever may be its faults, kindles a conflagration wherever it falls? There is scarcely any judge who is not pleased with her in some particulars. What is it that pleases us—in how far do we admire her—why is our admiration cold—why are we not enthusiastic?

Before we proceed, let us ask ourselves first, what are the elements that go to form a great *artiste?* And by applying our ideal as a touchstone, we shall be able to see in what respects she abides the test, and how far she falls short.

In such an analysis, we shall not fail to find some qualifications implied by others, and several so running into each other as to render separation difficult. But let us, for the nonce, proceed as though this were not so, to separate the elements that make up a perfect *artiste*.

First in order, although by no means in importance, we mention form—general appearance. The *figure* should be such as not to offend in any, the slightest particular. It should possess sufficient *physique* to render the stormier passages, without suggesting a fruitless straining for the point aimed at. It should possess grace and be accompanied by a carriage which is always appropriate to the occasion.

Second, *gesticulation* capable of earnestness, vigor or mere grace, at will; in short, gesticulation which always adds force to the sentiment uttered or the feeling represented.

Third, a *face capable of infinite expression*—of reflecting the passion or feeling within; a face which shall not scowl for indignation, upon which there shall not be the appearance of a smile for grief, but upon which there may be thrown at the instant when needed, and sustained so long as needed, the unmistakable expression for every passion, for the shades of each, and for combinations of two or more.

We have placed these in the order of their importance. By all means, the artist should have an expressive face. Leaving now the externals, we come to those more essential elements still, which, for the sake of classification, we may designate the internal.

Fourth, *voice,* which should be capable of every variety of modulation, of accompanying truthfully with its tones—its deepness—its whisperings—its strength—its softness—its pathos—every thought expressed.

Fifth, the *reading;* that ability (acquired of course by study) so to render every sentence and phrase that its best meaning shall be clear; that ability to modulate phrases, even when they are similar in structure, when they are similar in sound, when they vary but little in meaning, (the last three sentences for instance,) so to tone such, that there shall be variety in the rendering—that the ear shall not be pained by identity of modulation in each.

Sixth, and more important than all we have yet mentioned—*intellect* polished by education. In fact, this is an element only equaled in importance by one other, which we shall mention below; for it stands as the director—the stern tyrant over at least four out of the five elements we have given above, and, in addition to that, is the sole element to which we can look for that all-important requisite in good acting—*conception of the character to be taken.* With intellect but moderately developed, how many nice shades in Lady Macbeth's—in Parthenia's—in Julia's character will escape the *artiste,* even during careful study; how many concealed motives will be overlooked; in short, without intellect of breadth and power, the *artiste* will fail to depict correctly those changes which are developed in the character she assumes by the circumstances of the different scenes of the play—she will fail to compass and present true and great conceptions. As a faculty included in the intellect, we would allude in a line to taste, that element which, among other things, enables the actress to adorn her person elegantly or appropriately; nor should we forget a general air, indicative of good breeding.

Intellect will atone for many faults. In it we forget peculiarities of the person; it gives to the face that appearance which invariably commands respect; where the *artiste* is capable of gesticulating well, it guides the movements of the arms; it suggests readings; and if the voice be not wanting in proper qualities, it is its ruler. It lies at the bottom of all excellent acting. Even with the other elements in perfection if the intellect be moderate only, the *artiste* cannot rise above the grade of the stock actress.

It commands our admiration; but unless it is combined with one other element, which lies side by side with it in the composition of the truly great *artiste*—of her who possesses *genius,*—it commands but our cold admiration.

That other element, which we place last in our catalogue, we may call, for the want of a better phrase, *sympathetic feeling;* that indescribable objective faculty, which leads the actress to forget herself—to abandon herself to the character; which so exalts and sublimates her, that, ere she knows it, she is *living* the scenes upon the stage, instead of coldly *acting* them, until at last the audience themselves forget the *actress*—grieve, suffer, rejoice and exult with the *character*, and are carried away in a storm of enthusiasm.

It will be found, on consideration, that some artists—Mrs. Woodward and Mrs. Baker, for instance—possess feeling without remarkable intellect. Such can never be ranked higher than good stock actresses. Others, again, possess intellect with feeling either totally wanting, or but partially developed —Mr. Murdoch, for instance. Such may aspire to be stars, but can never be brilliant. Others, again, possess the two elements to a certain extent, but are wanting in voice, in gesticulation, or in expressiveness of feature. In fact, we shall find either a part or all of the above elements combined in every variety, if we glance among the various actors and actresses of the present day—stock as well as stars of the different magnitudes. For *true greatness* a high degree of intellect and feeling, combined to some considerable extent, at least, with the other elements, is required. Of course, we do not allude, in this connection, to the comic faculty.

We wish not to be understood as carrying our ideal, by which we are to judge of artists, to a Procrustean extreme. It would be folly to say, that to be great—really great, the actor or actress must come up to our ideal in every respect. But it is useless to attempt to criticise without a standard. With an ideal, we are ready, by applying it, to tell why we like, where we like, and how much we dislike.

It only remains for us to apply our standard to the *artiste*, whose performances are under review. It is a simple and brief task. In what respects is she perfect—in what deficient? One cannot say she is wanting entirely in any of the particulars we have specified. She is, however, deficient to a certain extent in each.

Her gesticulation is at times angular, feeble and inappropriate; and, on the contrary, at other times singularly expressive, graceful and appropriate. We are convinced that there are those, who, in noticing her deficiencies in this respect, fail to give her proper credit in instances where it is justly deserved; and, on the other hand, we cannot but think there are those, who, in admiring her excellent gestures, are willingly unprepared to notice and remember those instances, equal in number, in which she fails to add force or expressiveness, through angularity, rapidity, or feebleness of movement.

In depicting the passions upon her face we cannot regard her as successful. Of course we do not look for perfection. We ask not, that she should align herself exactly upon our ideal in order that we may render a verdict in her favor. But we should at least have a considerable degree of excellence in this respect. We do not find this excellence in Miss Davenport. We find but a limited variety of expression upon her features. We find the scowl for indignation; we find the same scowl for dislike; we find, at times, an expression, which we have frequently deplored in Mrs. Woodward and Mrs. Baker—an expression bearing resemblance to a smile, when the look of sorrow or grief should have been present. We find no delicate shades—no combinations of expressions, such as at times we noticed in Miss Heron; (of course we do not allude to the grimaces of Miss H., which she affected many times during her late engagements in this city.) We never find an expression (appropriate to the occasion) underlying all others, and kept up during the entire scene, when it should be. In short, however exactly Miss Davenport may give a proper expression at rare intervals, she cannot but be regarded as, in general, at fault in this respect.

On the contrary, her voice is remarkably expressive—at times wonderfully so; now touching, now strong and forcible, now sweet, now playful, now indignant, now whispering with terrible intensity—in fact, capable of such variety and modulation as leaves little to desire.

In general, her readings display considerable care and intelligent thought; and not seldom has she astonished and pleased her auditories with new and excellent "points." At times, however, they rather suggest an early familiarity with the stage than a close intimacy with the closet.

That she has intellect, none can deny. This explains the fact that she commands the attention of her audiences through a long play. It is this, that calls forth and holds their respect. It is this, that carries her above the grade of the stock actress, and enables her to compass and render conceptions, not perhaps of the highest order, but certainly, at times, most excellent. Nevertheless, why is it, that she does not excite a sustained enthusiasm? Why is it that we are not so much pleased with her in our heart of hearts, as we really desire to be? It is because she is lacking in feeling. To repeat a phrase which we have used above, she *lives* her character only in isolated passages, where deep passion is aroused. Then it is, that she gives evidences of high dramatic power. But it is only for the moment, and during the long intervals between these bursts, we feel that she is but *acting*. It is only during these displays of power, that we forget the *artiste* in the character, and that the audience breaks forth in enthusiasm;—an enthusiasm which is speedily chilled by her coldness, and which ere long gives place, again, to mere admiration. It is this state of things—this singular combination of merit and fault in her, which explains the anomaly of an attentive, but cold audience, enthusiastic only by fits and starts; and here can be found the reason, why our community are divided into those who like, those who dislike, and those who are striving to like.

It is but rarely, we say, that we can forget Miss Davenport. If at times she excels in depicting feeling, at other times her dashes at nature are too broad and glaring. If at times she is powerful, we cannot but feel that she is wanting in that nice appreciation of character which disarms criticism. In short, the main faults in her performances, are their general coldness, and their unevenness. There is a want of harmony in the pictures she presents. The prevailing hue is tame, with here and there a dash of brilliant color across it. The lights and shadows are too abrupt; they are not properly toned into each other. Although possessed of much talent, the spark of genius does not glow within her.

We have spoken only in general terms of Miss Davenport as an actress. Space will not permit us, on the present occasion, to allude in detail to her representations of the different characters in which we have seen her. Nor is it, perhaps, required at our hands. It may be, that from what we had heard, we expected too much of her. Certain it is, that however great may be our admiration for some of her powers, we are, in the main, disappointed in her.

We regret that we could not have seen Miss D. in Camille before preparing these remarks. This is a piece that comparatively few have witnessed, and we understand that the leading character is Miss Davenport's great part. We doubt not that in it she will please much better than she has heretofore, as there will be on the evening of her benefit not only a display of her abilities in their best light, but the added interest of the play itself; the pleasure to be derived from which it will be difficult to separate from the pleasure to be derived from the *artiste's* abilities in the part.

Mr. Ryer. is a valuable acquisition to the stock company of the Metropolitan. Mr. Chas. Wheatleigh is unassuming, but is too neat an actor to be passed over without notice. He understands his business well. For two years a member of the stock company at the Princess Theater, London, while under the management of Mr. Chas. Kean, he was selected by that gentleman to perform in the plays which were produced with so much splendor before the Queen at Windsor Castle.

We have learned casually, that the play of "Adrienne, The Actress," as presented by Miss Davenport, was translated for her some five years since by William Barber Esq., a distinguished member of the legal profession in this city. Those who listened to it, can testify to the excellence with which the polished scholar accomplished his work.

THE AMERICAN THEATER.—On the evening of March 18th, this establishment was opened by one of the most brilliant theatrical combinations ever formed in California. The Italian Opera Troupe and the Monplaisir Ballet Corps constitute, we believe, the management. No one who has ever heard the former, or witnessed the finished performances of the latter, can have any doubt as to the high character—the excellence of the entertainments, which they will present to the public. It will be long ere such attractions will be offered to us again. The company are richly deserving of success, and we were happy to see a full house on the evening mentioned. We have only witnessed one performance, and shall speak more at length in our next. We trust our citizens will not forget old and deserving favorites.

Miss Laura Keene arrived from Australia on the 20th instant. We understand that she is intending to return to New York, prior to a second visit to Australia, and that she will appear at the Metropolitan before her departure.

MADAME BISHOP.—We cannot close without calling the attention of our citizens to the fact that we shall soon lose the presence among us of the favorite Madame Anna Bishop. By the advertisement which we give below, as our last tribute to her worth, it will be seen that she proposes an early departure for Australia. Her services in behalf of music among us have been invaluable. She has been untiring in her efforts to please the public, and the late tremendous demonstration at her benefit showed clearly how amply her endeavors and her distinguished merit have been appreciated. The prestige of her name alone will fill her houses in Australia, and her talent as a singer will, we are sure, serve to keep them filled, so long as she remains among our friends across the Pacific.

We are confident, as it will be the last opportunity our community will have to listen to her, that the houses during her final series of entertainments in San Francisco, will be overflowing, and trust that measures will be taken to tender her a monster farewell benefit.

The advertisement, as it appears in the morning papers, is as follows:

"LAST PERFORMANCES

OF

MADAME ANNA BISHOP

IN CALIFORNIA.

MADAME ANNA BISHOP respectfully announces, that previous to her departure from the country, she has secured Musical Hall, for one week only, commencing on Monday Evening, the 2d of

April next, when she will take final leave of her patrons and the kind public of San Francisco, in a series of novel entertainments, aided by eminent Vocalists, a full Chorus, a grand Orchestra and the prestige of new Scenic Effects.

On the first night will be presented a Grand Biblical Spectacle, consisting of Haydn's stupendous sacred work of the "Creation of the World!" The various phases of the Wonderful Six Days, so beautifully described in Haydn's sublime composition, to be all through clearly illustrated by an extensive and superb Moving Panorama, painted expressly for this occasion by the eminent artist, Monsieur CLAVEAU.

During the Series, Madame ANNA BISHOP will (for the last time) go through the range of some of her most popular Lyric Rôles, besides offering admired Italian, German, French and English Operas, each performed in their respective languages, with appropriate Costumes, Decorations,—and carefully compressed, to insure on each evening a quick succession of the various attractions.

The whole under the direction of M. BOCHSA, who will on the last night perform, on the Harp, one of his bardic effusions.

For these entertainments, the whole interior of Musical Hall will undergo an entire change. A *Fantasie Theatre* will be erected; raised Dress Circle and Amphitheatre Boxes will give a commanding view of the Spectacles, and new arrangements will allow upwards of one thousand persons to be comfortably seated.

All the seats are numbered; due notice will be given when and where the sale will commence.

> Raised Dress Circle..$2 50
> Amphitheatre Fauteuil... 3 00
> Floor Sofa... 2 00

Full particulars of each night's performance will be speedily announced."

—

GOSSIP WITH READERS AND CORRESPONDENTS.

OUR kind contributor, "Mr. Mullet," once more presents his welcome face among the guests around the board. "Mullet" is an "odd FISH." Who would suppose, that beneath that quiet, unpretending exterior, there lurk so many living fountains of genuine humor? Who expects his puns, his dry jokes, his oddities, his side-splitting conceits, when they come out; and though they drop —it almost seems by accident—in quick succession, he is so imperturbable, so sober, so bashful through all, that we cannot but think each joke the last that we shall have, and somehow can't help being surprised at every new one that falls. Incomparable Mullet! It was a new moon to-night, but she has long since gone down. One by one our worthy burghers have left their offices, or reading-rooms, or clubs, and have entered their mansions and closed the front doors behind them for the night. Not a footstep has been heard upon the sidewalk for an hour. The gas lamps are shining upon deserted streets, and the watchful stars are gazing upon a quiet city. "The family" has retired, that we may chat through ten pages or so without "let or hindrance," and all is silent around us, save the nervous little clock upon the mantle-tree, which swings its diminutive pendulum with energy, and jerks out the quarter-seconds gleefully, almost laughing as it scatters the time. We are without a companion, besides; and yet, as we lean back in the big arm chair, and puff complacently, with up-lifted face, lest the smoke should curl into our lee eye and leave its sting therein, we glance to the other side of the fireplace, and seem to see our genial friend seated, as not long erewhiles, in yonder easy chair;—our quiet friend, from whom so little is expected, yet who so often sets the whole room upon a roar. God bless thee, Mullet! thy memory is green. And God preserve thee, as thou wanderest, homeward-bound, across the waters! But whither are we straying? What is this letter, signed with a representation of a fish? Ah, it is private, and we cannot read it here. We must, however, steal one sentence: "I think" writes he, "the 'pome' is 'excessive stupid,'" but we are fallible mortals, and I may be mistaken." Verily, Mullet, thou art a fallible mortal. But *this* we can venture to lay before you. Read it:

MY DEAR EWER: I send you a nautical "judy spree," which I hope may be of service, with a valentine which I picked up somewhere, I think in an old newspaper of 1830, or thereabouts. I do not know who is the author, but it seems to me a most exquisite and dainty conceit, well worthy of republishing; but of course you will judge for yourself. I also send you a hideous pun, which may perhaps do for your "Gossip." I regret to say, it was made by a friend of mine under the following circumstances: He was taken ill with some cutaneous eruption, which was at first thought to be small-pox, but afterwards decided to be varioloid. Whereupon he remarked, "If that was the *very* alloyed, he should prefer the *un* alloyed." He recovered from his illness in three days, and from the joke in six months—a striking instance of tenacity of life.

Yours, &c.,   MULLET.

THE SAILOR BOY'S DREAM.

BY MR. MULLET.

JACK BROWN was a sailor boy, well versed in all
    That is useful in sailing or steaming,
He was ripe for a frolic, and prompt in a squall,
    He also was good at blaspheming.

He had sailed in all sorts of craft,—brigs, schooners, sloops,
    From catamarans up to clippers—
In vessels with flush decks, and vessels with poops,
    With every description of skippers.

One fair, fine, summer night, in the ship Fly Away,
    His trick at the wheel he was steering:—
Although he was spokesman, he had nothing to say,
    The second mate probably fearing.

He looked all around, took a nautical view
    Of the weather, the sails too, inspecting—
He hitched up his trowsers, and took a fresh chew,
    And then, tried his hand at reflecting.

But he very soon found that it wasn't his forte,
    And so, after some vigorous winking,
He fell fast asleep, and in dreaming, he thought
    That the good ship was suddenly sinking.

He rose again quickly and looked for the wreck,
    His eyes for the loose fragments straining;—
But alas! there was nothing more from "a full deck,"
    But the Jack and the Deuce left remaining.

He attempted a prayer, but even his thought
    Was embellished with maritime graces,
And all he could utter, amounted to naught
    But naughty and nautical phrases.

He thought of the probable fate of his bones;
    Like most men who have been in the navy,
He believed in the locker of old Mister Jones,—
    Better known by the prefix of Davy.

At length some small fragments rose near our poor tar,
    Though fortune still seemed to deride him;
For he just escaped breaking his head by a spar,
    Which fell, heavy as felspar, beside him.

He grasped at an oar; 'twas like most ores, in vein.
    He attempted a thwart, but was thwarted.
But he finally mounted a settee of cane,
    Which just from its lashings had parted.

As soon as Jack fairly was into his place,
    He began thus his loud lamentation;
With a visage most rueful, each line of his face
    Denoting deep disapprobation.

      I'm surfeited with surf; and salt
        Is making fast around my head.
      The sea runs high as C in alt,
        It's wrath and kelp on me to shed,—
      And Neptune's self could not go far,
      If perched on such a low-backed car.

      To bitter fate I needs must bow;
        Poetic justice here I see;—
      I've followed long the seas, and now
        The angry seas are following me.

And I could weep, but that my hair
Drops tears enough, and some to spare.

O Grog! my much loved glorious Grog!
    Annihilator of dismay!
Thou—only thou couldst lift the fog,
    That hovers o'er my latest day.
I feel I could my eyes resign
    For gin or whiskey, rum or wine.

I cannot even spin a yarn,
    Still less a line to give me hope;
My craft is loose from stem to starn,
    And since stern fate denies me rope,
But one thing want these hands of mine,—
To grasp a ball of cotton twine.

If I had but some ratline stuff,
    I'd give the ransom of a Guelph;
The waves have lashed me long enough,
    I would much rather lash myself;
But I must sink beneath the wave
Without a rope-yarn stretched to save.

But Jack all this time was fast nearing the shore,
    Though his frail bark was breaking asunder;
He had been half-seas over quite often before,
    But now he was down half-seas under.

He at length reached the land, as the warmest embrace
    Of his kind mother earth convinced him,
And he soon made his toilet by scraping his face
    With a clam-shell, which lay there forninst him.

He rose on his feet, and he looked on the earth;
    He knew he could not be mistaken;
He was sure that he gazed on the land of his birth,
    And he felt some old feelings awaken.

He looked once again with a lingering glance,
    Then resolved he would visit his mother;
For he sagely considered he now had a chance,
    And would never, perhaps, have another.

This strange resolution might well cause surprise,
    Since the sailor in general is rather
More often accustomed to d—ning his eyes,
    Than to eyeing his dam—or his father.

He started at once, lest his zeal should abate;—
    For one's good resolutions are fleeting;—
And in due time arrived at the old lady's gate,
    And received an affectionate greeting.

He dwelt there contented and much at his ease;
    Although verdant in matters bucolical,
Yet in all that related to ships and to seas,
    He was held as a salt-water oracle.

He once went to church with a serious air,
    And well might the good parson falter;—
He had ne'er seen a tar with a prayer book, and ne'er
    Had beheld an old salt with a psalter.

But the sermon was all thrown away upon Jack,
    Who into the next pew was peering,
Where he just caught a glimpse of two fine eyes of black,
    And a view of a neat weather ear-ring.

Jack declared that the sermon was all "bloody fine,"
    But the damsel "a bloody sight finer,"—
And he vowed with the usual true lovyer's whine,
    He would perish before he'd resign her.

And soon our poor sailor was fairly entrapped
    By her feminine wiles and cajoling;
For his dear Mary Ann proved exceedingly apt
    In the use of the manrope and beauline.

He built him a cottage in strict rural style,
    With everything 'round it in keeping;
And he spent his time basking in Mary Ann's smile,
    And in feeding the poultry and sleeping.

But—alas! even sailors are nothing but men,
 And few can live always in clover;
His felicity all was demolished, and then
 "The house that Jack built" was knocked over.

For here his fond dream was dispersed into air,
 By a form at his elbow appearing,
And the second-mate blandly demanded—"Where
 In the"—(no matter what)—"are you steering?"

Now we often hear the remark made, ridiculously enough, "That is worthy of Shakespeare," or "That is worthy of Byron." But, *do* we deviate very far from the truth in saying that the above *is* worthy of Hood? The "Valentine" shall have due attention. - - - An esteemed friend sends us the following batch of anecdotes: A gentleman of my acquaintance, just returned from Sacramento, was giving me an account of an individual whom he saw there, very well and favorably known in the financial community, who was cooling himself in the lobby of the Legislature, while endeavoring to get a certain Bill through, which he believed would have a most important effect upon his fortunes. He was exceedingly nervous and anxious, but possessed such extraordinary self-control, and concealed his agitation under so calm an exterior, that a careless observer, noticing his among the numerous careworn and anxious faces that fill the State-House, would have considered him the most unconcerned person there. But he had his revenge for this constraint. When he thought himself alone and unobserved, he vented his long pent-up feelings by muttering curses, not loud but deep, clenching his fists, and gesticulating in a most remarkable manner; and, said my informant, the exhibition he then made of himself was laughable in the extreme. Yet the instant he perceived that any one observed him, every token of impatience, every sign of agitation vanished, and he presented the same unruffled and placid exterior which was his wont. At this point of the description, one of his hearers broke in with, "That reminds me of old Captain Snow, who used to command a packet-ship. His ordinary demeanor was as cool and polished as the substance whose name he bore. Always cheerful and attentive, kind and complacent, it was believed that he never allowed anything to disturb his equanimity, and, what was unusual with a sailor, he was never known to use a profane expression; while his invariably polite manners made him immensely popular with his passengers, who unanimously distinguished him as 'the most gentlemanly captain in the line.' One day, however, a passenger saw him go to a retired part of his vessel, and deliberately taking off his hat, stamp upon it repeatedly with the greatest earnestness and energy, throwing his arms about the while, and uttering volley after volley of well chosen oaths in a most extravagant manner. Surprised at such behavior in a man usually so equable in his moods, he approached him with, 'Why, what's the matter, captain? Has anything happened?' 'Ah,' said the captain, discovering his interlocutor and resuming his accustomed urbanity, while every trace of his vexation vanished, 'I beg you to excuse me; do not interrupt; this is my *swearing time.* I will be through in a few moments. Leave me alone now, if you please.' And as the passenger, with eyes opened wide in wonder, sauntered off, the polite captain continued his safety-valve occupation, and thus exploded the resentment and irritation which had probably been accumulating for a month.".. Another story occurs,—it is very old, yet some whose eye passes over these pages may not have heard it. Capt. Jones was the roughest old salt that ever trod the deck of a ship; rough in voice, in manner, and in look; rough as—we can think of nothing at the moment rougher than a terrier dog—to which animal he bore no slight resemblance. Yet, within this forbidding exterior, he concealed a good heart and kindly nature. But he never could speak without an oath, and in moments of excitement or danger he used a great many. His passengers and crew thought nothing of this, or no more perhaps than that it was a bad habit that the "old man" had got into, and the latter obeyed him as readily as if he spoke "honied words of kind persuasion." There was a Quaker on board, however, who did not view it so lightly; but though he sometimes winced and lifted up his eyes in horror, when a torrent of oaths poured from the quarter-deck and stirred the men to their duty, he kept his annoyance to himself. At length the spirit moved him to speak. He found the captain in a very placable mood, and took occasion to accost him thus: "Friend, thee uses a great many vain words." "Oh yes, I have to swear sometimes." "Swear not at all." "But I must; [with an oath]—I could not command my men unless I did. They would not understand a word I said." "Verily, thee could have as much discipline and as much command without thy oaths. Try and refrain from them." In fact, he wrestled strongly with the captain, and after a long exhortation upon the evil practice, gained from him a promise that he would not use another "vain word" during the voyage. The old sea-dog kept his promise for one whole day strictly. The weather happened to be calm, and he had few occasions to give orders. But at night a wind sprang up; it increased, and finally blew great guns. He vociferated the necessary orders through his speaking-trumpet, but always in accordance with the terms of his promise to the Quaker. The men, missing the usual accompaniment of these orders, as the captain had predicted, could not understand them, and ran wildly about the ship, doing nothing. The captain was enraged—furious; but, true to his promise, he *would not swear.* Confusion outside, confusion inside the ship, the Quaker looked at the tattered sails flapping in the wind, heard the howling of the blast and the dashing of the waves, and saw that, in the midst of the universal turmoil, the ship was upon the waters, as it were, without a director. His fears got the better of his sense of right and his steadfastness. Going quietly to the captain, who, chafing like a caged lion, was pacing the quarter-deck furiously, he touched him upon the shoulder and said, "Friend, I think thee might *swear a little* now." There was no misunderstanding the orders that came after that, and the ship rode out the gale gallantly. [It's old, nevertheless it's very good.] .. I have not read Barnum's autobiography, but have been informed by a gentleman who has read it that the following story about Barnum is not to be found in it: About the time when the great Baron Hum, as the English have lately entitled him, assumed the management of the famous American Museum, he entered into an agreement with a certain editor of a widely-circulated and highly popular journal, according to which the latter should be continually on the lookout for natural marvels and phenomena, while the former should have the use of its columns to puff and advertise them. The arrangement for sometime acted charmingly. People came in crowds to see the strange things their favorite journal told about, and the treasury gradually lost its vacuity. But the editor was a waggish fellow, and suddenly took it into his head to play tricks upon his coadjutor, by sending him off on a wild-goose chase after several things that never existed. The showman bore several of these experiments with exemplary patience, and finally determined upon a plan to cry quits with his funny friend. One day he sent for him in great haste. The editor, obeying the summons, found Barnum walking his office in a state of great excitement. He had scarcely time to open his mouth ere he was greeted with, "George, I am so glad you are come! I want your advice now more than I ever did. I never was in such a fix!" and Barnum rubbed his forehead and temples violently with his perfumed handkerchief. "Why, what's the matter?" said G; "they haven't found a *real* mermaid, have they?" "No, hang the mermaid!" "Nor Joice Heath?" "Curse Joice Heath! Don't provoke me, George. I have something on my mind too important. Listen—an Egyptian has just arrived in the city, direct from Egypt, with a most unparalleled, most incredible phenomenon; a wonder of wonders. He found it in a little pool of water in the darkest corner of the catacombs, where it has probably been for three thousand years, if not longer; and having heard of me—(my fame has reached even that point; gratifying, isn't it?)—he came straight to give me the first chance at it. He says that, although a fish now, as it has doubtless been for numberless years, strange as it may seem, in a few days it will become an animal." "How does he know?" "Because he has watched other creatures of the same species go through the same transformation. In fact, there is no doubt it is all as he says it is. But he asks such an unconscionable price, I'm beggared at the thought of it. Will you believe that the rogue has the conscience to ask *one hundred thousand dollars*—think of that!" "It's a big price to be sure, but then you might say as Alexander did, "Too much for him to receive, perhaps, but not too much for you to give." "Good! egad, I'll have that put in the bills." "Besides, you'd soon realize that sum, and more too, with your talents for advertising and giving a thing notoriety." "Well, I might get over the price, but the name is a sticker. I couldn't draw a dozen people together with such a name. There is everything in a name. The *Ornithoryneus Paradoxus* is an object of intense interest, but call it a New-Holland Otter, and no one would look at it. Can't you think of some good name, high-sounding you know, and descriptive of its habits?" "Where is the creature?" "Oh, the Egyptian keeps him safe enough; he let me take one peep at him, that's all. But get up a good characteristic name. It lives in the water now, like a fish, but in a week, or ten days, will have legs before and behind, in fact become an animal, and go upon land." "Very wonderful, truly; but *what is the name* which the Egyptian gives him?" "That which every one else does—the *Tadpole!*" shouted Barnum. The editor reflected a moment, then took his hat and left; but he never tried a second time to humbug the "Prince of Humbugs.".. "Maggie L.," writes a friend, "was the prettiest, merriest little fairy that ever gladdened a mother's heart, or filled a father's soul with pride. With her winning, affectionate ways she stole every one's heart, while her smart sayings went from mouth to mouth. When about seven years of age, she came to make us a visit, where she had our son Bob, a rough, clumsy lad of twelve, for a playmate. They quarreled at play, and she vowed she would never speak to him again. Her mother reproved her, and said she must pray for Bob, that he might be a better boy. It had been this good woman's custom to make her child repeat a prayer every night before she went to sleep; but Maggie soon became such a proficient that she could lead off as well as the best camp-meeting revivalist. She had, too, a peculiar stammer, which made her speeches seem funnier sometimes than they really were. On the night after the quarrel, when she was nicely tucked in bed, the family gathered around to hear how she would acquit herself. Clasping her little hands, she lifted up her voice and eyes, and said, 'Oh Lord, bless father and mother; bless uncle and aunt, and bless Bob—if he *is* a naughty boy. Bless *all* the b-boys; they are all n-naughty—all just alike; for they all s-steal, and l-lie, and s-wear, and do all s-sorts of wicked things, but we girls don't. Amen.'" - - - Don't fail to cast your eye over "The Crime of Delay." With it we commence our Editor's Table. It is from the pen of "Oliver Outcast," and is very characteristic. - - - The black plumes are waving—and the beat of the muffled drum sounds in slow cadence—and upon the breast of every "brother" there is a sprig of green—as the long, mournful procession winds itself among the hills of our city, and at last files slowly through Pacific street, where from the window at our side we drop our pen and push back the curtain to gaze upon it and listen thoughtfully to the solemn funereal dirge. Yes, and as we look again, there moves the hearse!—there follow the carriages, while from far up above us, as it passes into the gorge at the foot of Russian Hill, and issues from the city, the music sounds fainter and fainter, and at last dies away. One more gone to his long home. An hour, and the sod will be above him—he will lie alone and deserted to-night upon the side of the silent hill! And yet how shall the world be merry and laugh as though Death had not taken his reluctant hand. And must it be *thus* with us all? Is the time so certain when one by one we shall lie cold and lifeless in the coffin, for others to lift us and bear us silently away? It is even so; and as we gaze upon the slow hearse and the pall-bearers with their downcast heads, moving among the stir and heedless haste of our city, how involuntarily do we repeat, in the beautiful language of the Prayer-Book, "In the midst of life we are in death!" Strange are the contrasts around us! and this, stranger than all. O, how much better is it to give, than to receive! A kindly word—a cheering look to the downcast—a touch of sympathy for the sorrowing—ah, we are none so poor but that we can be wealthy in these. And when it is *ours*, in turn, to lay aside the pen forever, and fold our hands in an eternal sleep, may there be many hearts behind us that will beat kindly for a time in that they are richer from such "goods" at our hands. - - - "Pipesville" is not a myth. It standeth no longer in the day-dreams of its owner, but just back from Mission street in painted and garnished reality. Its door is as open and its welcome as warm as the heart of its proprietor. There it rests, perched upon an eminence, like some castle of yore, while the hut of the solitary "retainer" standeth in the vale below, and a thick cloud of genial associations, visible to the mind alone, surrounds it. There it stands, with its tiny green blinds, and its neat little parlor—(*and* its closet)—and its center-table, covered with the latest periodical literature, and its *bijouterie*—(the gifts of many friends)—and, shall we forget the hung-up slippers?—all making up the very picture of a bachelor's habitation. We visited it, a day or two ago, in company with several friends; and although before we departed, we found ourselves all ale-ing, a right merry time of it did we have.

THE PIONEER.

Vol. III.]   MAY, 1855.   [No. 5.

REPUBLICATION

OF

𝕿𝖍𝖊 𝕰𝖛𝖊𝖓𝖙𝖋𝖚𝖑 𝕹𝖎𝖌𝖍𝖙𝖘 𝖔𝖋 𝕬𝖚𝖌𝖚𝖘𝖙 𝕿𝖜𝖊𝖓𝖙𝖎𝖊𝖙𝖍 𝖆𝖓𝖉 𝕿𝖜𝖊𝖓𝖙𝖞-𝕱𝖎𝖗𝖘𝖙,

THE

EDMONDS CORRESPONDENCE RELATING THERETO, ETC.

—

On the 16th of April, the following letter was placed in my hands by Judge S. Heydenfeldt, viz:

SAN FRANCISCO, April 16th, 1855.

F. C. EWER, Esq.:

Dear Sir:—Since the publication of your letter in *The New York Herald,* and the reply of Judge Edmonds, much inquiry has been made for, and much interest felt in obtaining the article which has produced the controversy. Will you therefore favor the public, if not inconsistent with your other arrangements, by republishing in the next *Pioneer* "The Eventful Nights of August 20th and 21st," together with the subsequent correspondence on the subject, and thus place it within the reach of a large number who are anxious to read it?

Respectfully,

J. G. KELLOGG,	S. HEYDENFELDT,
C. C. BOWMAN,	J. G. BALDWIN,
JOHN H. SAUNDERS,	JOHN H. WISE,
O. C. HALL,	E. J. C. KEWEN,
N. HUBERT,	J. R. McCONNELL,
LOUIS BLANDING,	J. B. PEACHY.

My reply was as follows, viz:

SAN FRANCISCO, April 17th, 1855.

GENTLEMEN:

I acknowledge the receipt of your kind note of yesterday, and in response would say, that in accordance with its request the article and correspondence alluded to will appear in the May Number of the *Pioneer Magazine*.

With Respect,

Your Obd't Servant,

F. C. EWER.

To MESSRS. S. HEYDENFELDT, J. G. BALDWIN, and others.

THE EVENTFUL NIGHTS OF AUGUST 20TH AND 21ST.

BY F. C. EWER.

I AM about to undertake a task,—here in the silence of this room,—to which I feel impelled by a combination of circumstances, such as I believe never surrounded mortal man before. I am hurried to its accomplishment—to the unburdening of my mind, from certain strange intelligence, not only on account of an express order, which I have received,—the nature and particulars of which will more fully appear below,—but because I feel that I can only relieve my mind from its insufferable weight by laying before the public the occurrences of the last two nights.

I am in a house on McAllister Street, between Hyde and Larkin. The room in which I am seated contains little furniture, save a poor bed, a large pine table, one of smaller dimensions, and a chair. The paper I write on,—this is the second night I have been here,—I was compelled to bring with me, together with the pen, ink and candle. At every whisper of the breeze, as it sighs among the bushes outside, I shudder and look around me, where lies the body of a man whom I knew not until yesterday—yet to whom I feel bound by a spell such as I never experienced before. And yet I know that all is over and quiet now. The hush of silent death is in this room; and I can distinctly hear my own breathing and that of a little child—she tells me her name is Jane— who is sitting on a box at the foot of the bed, and who, although young, is just old enough to realize that she is stricken by an awful calamity, and yet knows not whether the more to be amazed or grieved. At times she will come to my side, and the tears will rise into her eyes; but at a word from me, she will check them, return to the dead body of her parent, and there gaze into the cold, still face, silently and with a mingled expression of awe and uncertainty. She, too, has been a witness of the events of the past forty-eight hours, and now that she is at last left alone, she clings to me instinctively for protection—she knows not from what nor why. May God give me health and strength to support her, and guide her in the uncertain ways of the dark future!

She has just stolen quietly to me, put her little arms about my neck and said—

"What are you writing, sir? Come with me. I am *very* lonesome. Come with me to father and make him talk."

I kissed her upon her fair white forehead, and said—

"Hush, child! Father will not speak to us any more to-night. You shall go with me to-morrow,—and we'll take father with us."

I led her back to her seat, and turned quickly,—for the tears were gushing to my eyes. But I must hasten to my recital.

I shall endeavor to state the plain facts, as they occurred, as briefly and in as simple a style as possible. For I find that it is already half-past two in the morning, and I feel quite exhausted from the excitement I have passed through. In bringing these facts before the public, I am aware that I shall subject myself to the taunts of the street, and be pointed at by the world as one of the "insane dupes of the Spiritual Rappers,"—and nothing but an imperative sense of duty, (mistaken, it may be thought by some) urges me to submit myself to such an ordeal.

I will not (at least upon this occasion) go into the *rationale* of "Spiritualism." The public are already sufficiently acquainted with the modes in which the "manifestations" are given, to understand thoroughly all I shall have to say. I will not speak of the singular facts of "Odism," which have been established by Reichenbach and Liebig, with a clearness only less satisfactory than that with which the truths of electricity are proven. I will not state that no evidence of the Odic fluid can be discovered in paralyzed limbs; I will not speak of the supposition, therefore, of the above named physicists, that as mind cannot act directly on matter, and as it is impossible by an effort of mind to move a paralyzed limb, the Odic fluid may be the condition necessary to lie between the mind and the arm or foot (which are matter) to account for the mysterious effect of the will in moving our bodies. The relation of these facts and suppositions is not at all necessary to a clear understanding of my story.

Night before last, (the nineteenth of August) after I had retired and extinguished my candle, I was surprized on laying my head upon my pillow, at discovering a pale, bluish brush of light at the other side of the room, apparently hovering over a portion of a tea-poy, on which is a Parian statuette of Venus, one or two daguerreotypes, a small pearl cross, and several other little matters of ornament. I was struck by the suddenness with which the light ceased to waver as I directed my attention to it. I started up, but immediately came to the conclusion that the strange appearance resulted from a diseased retina. (My eyes have been affected for the past six months.) I looked away, supposing, of course, that if the apparition could be traced to the cause mentioned, it would display itself wherever I gazed. This, however, I found not to be the case. And as I looked again towards the tea-poy, I thought I heard a series of faint tickings. Determined to have my curiosity satisfied, I arose and advanced towards the apparition. The tickings here grew more active. I re-lighted the candle; there was, however, no unusual appearance about the stand. But I soon found that the sounds proceeded from a small pocket-compass that was lying thereon. I opened it, and the needle was trembling and vibrating quite violently over N. Soon the north pole moved round to the south-west, and back again; and so on, three distinct times—each time pausing a moment at N., trembling violently, then sweeping round and reaching the S. W. point with a jerk. Thinking this a very singular circumstance, I hurriedly threw on some clothes, and sat down to watch it. After a pause, and while my eyes were directed intently upon the needle, it moved slowly round again, reaching the south-west point with a jerk,—repeating this three times, and then stopping. It seemed to me to act almost with *intelligence;* and I involuntarily uttered,— "What *does* this mean?" To my surprise—for I was a firm disbeliever in anything like "Spiritualism"—the needle, as though in answer to my ejaculation, made a rapid curcuit entirely round the card, passed the north point, and resting for an instant at south-west, or rather over the fifty-first degree point, returned slowly and steadily to its place at north.

I now, (half ashamed of myself) commenced a series of questions in whisper. Yet, although the needle seemed to act intelligently, I could not discover what was the nature of the information (if any) intended to be conveyed, and why, after each series of unsuccessful questions and answers, it swept with more and more vigor to south, fifty-one degrees west; and at length I reluctantly retired.

Last evening, about ten o'clock, I received a note, written in pencil, which, I was told, had been left for me by a little girl. It was brief, but exceedingly urgent in a request—nay, it was almost a command—that I should go out to the house of the writer,—Mr. John F. Lane. It stated that I need fear nothing, but should start immediately upon its reception, bringing with me paper, a pen and candles.

I learned that the little girl could not read, but by showing the superscription of the note containing only my name, had at last succeeded in finding the *locale* of my apartment on Kearny Street. But she had gone, and I could therefore learn nothing of the nature of the riddle from her.

I cannot tell how, but by some strange intuition, I associated unconscionably the note, with its singular request, its lack of any cue by which I could discover why my presence was required in a desolate and lonely part of the city at the dead hour of night, with the singular occurrence of the compass the night before. The only bond of connection between them, it is true, was the unexplained mystery that hung around both. But the human mind often finds itself at conclusions without any known steps by which it could have arrived at them, whose subsequently ascertained correctness staggers reason, and leads to the belief that there are mental processes and strange sympathies and connections in nature whose character and depths are to be sought for in the Infinite God alone. At length, however, I became convinced that some villian was working upon my curiosity, to entrap me among the sand-hills and rob me; and I determined not to go, and to pay no heed to the affair at all. But I could not drive the subject from my mind, and at last I deliberately resolved, come what would, to go out to the spot designated and solve the mystery. For precaution's sake, I relieved myself of my watch and purse, put my pistol in my pocket and procured a lantern before sallying forth.

At the corner of Kearny and Sacramento Streets I met two of my friends— Mr. H. and Doctor L. Mr. H. asked me where I was going in that Diogenes style. In response, I related the circumstance of the note, and my determination to see the end of the affair. The two expressed their willingness to accompany me, and we proceeded together. It was then half-past eleven o'clock. We passed without molestation to the corner of Sutter and Mason Streets, and thence struck off in a diagonal direction over the sand-hills toward Yerba Buena Cemetery. Contrary to our expectations, our devious walk to McAllister Street was undisturbed, save by the occasional barking of a dog. When we reached the corner of what we found on inquiry at a neighboring house to be Hyde and McAllister Streets, one of my friends called my attention to a noise that sounded like a faint groan. We approached in the direction whence it came, and found ourselves nearing a small house that stands on the north side of the road, just before you come to Larkin Street. This was the house designated in the note. I rapped at the door, and the little girl, who answered the call immediately, said—

"Father wants you to come in."

Mr. Lane, who was lying upon the bed, reached forth his hand in welcome; but was evidently surprised on seeing Mr. H. and the Doctor following me into the room. After apologizing for not having chairs enough for us, he called me to the bedside and stated that he knew I must have been surprised at receiving his note; that he was too weak to write more; that he had told Jane to see me in person, but that she, becoming alarmed at her long absence from him and at the lateness of the hour, had hastened back without obeying his instruction. He said that it was very kind of me to take so much trouble, but that he was a dying man, and had information of importance to impart to me.

"But, my dear sir," said I, "something must be done for you. Fortunately one of my friends is a physician,"—and I called Doctor L. to the bed-side.

Mr. Lane was evidently in the last stages of consumption. In fact, the Doctor told me in a whisper, that it was too late; that nothing could be done, and that his end was very near.

He overheard us and said that he knew all; that nothing remained for him but to fulfill a duty to me and to the world. Before proceeding to the business before us, he told me briefly, his previous circumstances,—his early education, which was liberal,—his poverty, and the fact that his little child—this patient, sweet little Jane, who, exhausted with watching, has laid her head in my lap and sunk, at last, into a slumber,—would by his death be left alone in the world. He besought me, with tears in his eyes, to watch over her when he was gone, and see that she did not suffer. He did not care about her being poor. He expected she would have to work. He did not wish her to be a burden to me. But oh ! he prayed that I would guide her footsteps away from sin and its influences; that I would instill into her a love of purity, and so guard her, that she would grow to womanhood, an honor to herself and a blessing to those around her. I drew little Jane to me, kissed her, and satisfied the dying man by promising solemnly that I would do my utmost to comply with his last wish.

His mind was then apparently relieved from its only care, and he turned his attention to the business before us.

"My friend," said he, "I must premise my remarks by stating that I am a firm believer in the Great Doctrine of the present century; that we have at last reached that momentous period, when the spirits of the departed can, through the medium of a principle newly discovered, communicate their thoughts and wishes to mortals upon earth. I have been led to this belief by the surest of all processes—personal experience. When I am alone and find a table moving under my passive hands—moving intelligently—moving in such a manner as to give me information of events which are happening in the distant East— and which I subsequently find to have occurred exactly as stated through this mysterious agency,—nay more, when I feel a nameless sensation—half chill, half tremor—running through my whole body, apparently penetrating to the innermost recesses of my brain, and find my arm and hand moved over the paper beneath it by some influence which I cannot convince myself is not foreign,— when I find my hand writing strange, grand thoughts, such as I never conceived of before—such as at times it takes me days thoroughly to understand,—when I close my eyes and so divest myself of attention, that I know nothing, except that my hand is moving, and when I find afterwards thoughts worthy of the angels, penned, I cannot but believe we are upon the threshold of one of the most eventful changes that ever occurred upon the surface of the earth. Geology has told us of mighty epochs in the far past history of the world. Look back my friends. Remember that whole races of the animal and vegetable kingdoms have been swept away,—that whole periods of the world have moved into the still past, leaving their history legible to the mind of a subsequent period on the everlasting rocks and strata. Remember that whole continents have gone grandly down and been swallowed up in the depths of ocean; that whole oceans have swayed in volumes around the earth—from pole to pole, from the Orient to the Occident. If we stand amazed, as we contemplate the mighty changes that rest entombed in the past, ever receding from us, is it unreasonable to suppose that other changes equally momentous are approaching the world from the future? O, deceive yourselves not; for mankind tread toppling upon the verge of a tremendous epoch; that in which Finity can speak to Infinity,—that in which the Greatest Seal shall be broken, and the secrets of hereafter whispered from strange intelligences to man! I know it—I know—know—."

Mr. Lane here sank back upon his pillow, exhausted.

I had stood wrapt in wonder and admiration, as I listened to such sentences coming from a man apparently so humble in life. The shadow of death stretching up to meet him seemed almost to inspire him. The deliberate enunciation with which the remarks were uttered, coupled with the soul-felt earnestness with which he spoke, impressed us all; and for a moment we stood at the bedside, gazing with rapt attention at that pale face with its spiritual expression and its closed eyes. The eyelids seemed to me so thin, as to be powerless to conceal the large jet black eyes within, which almost appeared to be displayed *through* them.

I know not how long our silence would have lasted, had not the Doctor called my attention to the fact, that the last struggle of mind had hastened the dying man towards his dissolution; and that if he had any important information to communicate, we must be brief.

I looked again, and the large, black eyes were upon us,—they seemed larger and blacker than any I had ever beheld before—and Mr. Lane continued—

"I wish this conversation recorded. At first, I regretted that you had brought your friends with you; but I am glad that you have done so, as one of them can be of service to us."

I then took the writing materials which I had brought, and after recording, as nearly as I could recollect, the remarks set down above, I delivered them to Mr. H., who moved the large table into the center of the room, and proceeded to take the notes which now lie before me, without whose assistance I should have great difficulty in preparing these remarks for the press.

Mr. Lane resumed—

"As I have told you, I am not only a believer in Spiritualism, but am a medium myself. Four days ago, I was informed, by one of the spirits, that he desired me to procure some gentleman either connected with the press, or to whom the columns of some paper were open, to be with me during my last moments; that what should occur at our interview, would be of importance. I knew none of the editors. I had heard, however, that you had devoted several months to the investigation of Spiritualism, previously to which time you were atheistically inclined. The fact that an atheist should have looked into this matter, with any degree of assiduity, convinced me that you were a candid man, open to conviction. Was I rightly informed with regard to your previous tenets, and your investigations?"

I answered in the affirmative.

"I am surprised, then, that you have not exercised your advantages, by publishing some of the extraordinary proofs of the science. I suppose you have recovered from your atheism, and that you are somewhat of a believer in Spiritualism!"

I responded that, with regard to the former, I was still quite skeptical, and inclined to a belief in materialism; and as for the latter, that my earnest investigations had only led me to the conclusion that it was an unmitigated humbug so far as any *spiritual* agency was concerned.

Mr. Lane appeared astonished, and after a pause, asked me if I had any objection to remaining with him, and awaiting the result. I told him that I certainly had none.

At his request the small table was then drawn quite near the head of the bed. Mr. Lane, who was lying upon his back, stretched forth his thin, white hand, placed it, with the palm downwards, upon the side nearest to him, and then closed his eyes as though he were settling himself for death. I sat at the end towards the foot of the bed, and was in such a position that I could see his face distinctly. The Doctor and Jane were at the opposite side of the bed, while Mr. H. was seated at the table in the center of the room. After a pause the table tipped toward me, lifting Mr. Lane's hand. We all remained in silence, during which the dying man appeared to be putting mental questions; to which the table answered. At length he stated that the spirit desired to transmit a written communication. Paper and a pencil were procured. The sick man's hand was moved very gently, but the paper moved with it. I then secured the sheet with my hand, and the first communication was as follows, viz:

"The time is ripe. The great truth has entered into the circle of the world silently, and powerfully,—as the 'still small voice.' There is sublimity in its silence. And thus it appeals to man. We cannot trumpet forth the truth. For voice is not to us, as hearing is to you. We appeal to you through sublimity, and silence, and an unheard, though felt power. Behold, how the great change has manifested itself in every city, and town, and hamlet in America! This is one of the great voices of your great country. She announces the glad tidings—crying '*The gates of Death are open, the ladder of Jacob is reared, and angel voices are ascending—descending—from us to them—from them to us!*' We are hovering above and around and among your republic of *thought*. It was the fitting field. Had the seed dropped too early, or upon the unenlightened, it would not have fructified. Years were to roll. Years have rolled. The intellectual soil was at last prepared, and the sowers joyfully went forth. At first, the great change broke slowly upon man. It was right. There must have been doubters. But the truth is mighty and prevails. The Spiritualists are numbered by hundreds of thousands. And thus as it is, that the seed has taken root sufficiently for permanence and ever-growth, spite of all calamity of skepticism and ridicule, it is right that you should advance one step further. Attend. The meaning of Death is the mission of this interview. Then mayst thou indeed exclaim, 'Where is thy sting, and oh Grave, where is thy victory!' Attend, while the passing spirit performs his privilege and his high duty."

Mr. Lane's hand then ceased moving. The whole was calculated to render us breathless. After a pause I remarked, that the solemnity of this time would not, I freely confessed, permit me to doubt the honesty of the dying man. But I ventured to ask the spirit—if spirit it was—whether he would not give us some certain proof of the genuineness of the communication as a *Spiritual message.*

Mr. Lane's hand immediately traced the following—

"Willingly. The whole shall be in itself a test. For true it is, that one of the first elements of success in this new movement is, that you believe. *Mr. Lane shall hold a conversation with you prior to, during and after death.* In which he will give you his experience of Death, and the facts and scenes, so to speak, to which he first awakes, after the heart has ceased to beat. Farewell."

I willingly dispelled doubt from my mind, and was for a time lost in thought at the solemn import of the spirit's message. The silence was only broken by the low sobbing of this dear little creature, exhausted, and pale and scantily clad, who, thank Heaven, has forgotten her affliction for a time in sweet slumber. Her dreamy eyes have seized upon my heart. Ah! what a shadow within them lies! Will she live to womanhood? O! will she always love and trust me, with all my faults? Well-a-day! At length, as I gazed into the emaciated face upon the pillow before me, the lids opened—the large black eyes turned upon me, and with a faint voice he said—

"I am sinking—sinking—"

His eyes then turned upon Jane with a gaze of sadness, then rolled slowly round to me again. The look was enough. I leaned toward him, and assured him with a low voice that henceforth she should be my daughter. The little thing ran round to me and fell upon my breast, sobbing violently.

"And now," said he faintly and with pauses between his sentences, "I am ready to die.—I feel that it is good.—It grows dim—dim—dim.—I am losing earth—losing you all.—I know that I live.—It—it is a solemn passage—but what, I know not.—Are you here?—Touch me—touch me—that I may know that I live."

I pressed my hand gently upon his as it lay upon the table before me. It was cold.

"Are you—are you here?—*Can* you not touch me?"

I stooped over him and whispered into his ear that his hand was in mine.

"In mine?—in mine?—There is no angel here.—What was it whispered?—I am in no one's keeping. I am passing—O," said he, making a faint effort to rise, "O! that I could stay!—Janie—Janie—that—that this solemn journey were but over."

Exhaustion succeeded, and for a moment he ceased breathing. I quietly respread his hand upon the table and resumed my seat.

"I seem hovering—I know not where.—No one is around me—no one comes to me to lift me on through this solemn gloom.—I hear nothing—solitary—solitary in this fearful way.—This is—indeed—the valley—of the shadow of Death. —Where are they, my friends of the Future?—Is this *Death?*—Is this the Future?—*Is the spirit theory then untrue?*" at last he cried in despair. "And am I —am I to live thus—*thus?*—Oh! the fearful *Hell* of an Eternal Existence *alone!* —no sight—no hearing—no God—no Heaven—(as I had been told)—no light— Great God! *no darkness!*—all thought!—My soul is consuming—*consuming itself!*—— *Can* I live thus forever?—O! for annihilation, for anything but this solitude!—Why can I not peer through this gloom!—Horror, horror—where are these limbs of mine—*I feel not my body around me!*—Oh! lost at length—lost to the green earth—and to my Janie—lost to the sweet harmony of companionship! —— The past, *gone,*—the Future, a *blank!*——Great Eternity, am I a God? —am I creative?—will a world spring at my thought?————Yes, I create— but it is *thought* alone—for that is of my own essence.————I *must* be dead. —If you are here and I am not yet dead—tell Janie I will *try* and seek her,—I know not how.—Tell the world that in death the spirit is fearfully and forever *alone!*—Tell the world that Death is terrib————"

The nervous twitching about the under jaw stopped; and from the very instant when he ceased to articulate, I was startled by finding the table slowly rising and leaning toward the bed. And as the jaw dropped and the strange shadow of death swept down like a curtain over his face, the table rose quickly and pressed firmly and steadily against the bed-side, as though it were attracted towards the dead body by an immense power.

We were all now around him. The Doctor, who was on the side opposite to us, slowly laid the right hand, which he had been holding during the dying scene upon the breast, and we remained gazing awe-struck at this strange death. I believe that, for a moment, my heart actually ceased beating. There was an oppressive pause, which must have lasted at least five minutes. During all this time the table maintained its inclined position, and we still stood speechless—almost breathless. At length we were awakened from our trance by finding the table quietly descending to the floor. It then commenced tipping on two of its legs with a gentle rocking motion. I know not why, but I shuddered at the thought of breaking the death-like silence, so I took up the pencil and wrote—

"Will you finish what you were saying?"

Imagine our terror at seeing the dead arm and hand which had been lying on the table, strike into rigidity, as though it were a piece of mechanism pulled by wires,—rise slowly from the table and move toward me. When it had reached within a few inches of me, like lightning it darted forth and down upon my hand in which I was still holding the pencil. Its fingers grasped suddenly and tightly around mine. The touch was as of an icicle. A nameless thrill and terror seized me. Mr. H. fell back;—and slowly the locked hands before me moved across the paper. The dead hand was so tracing the words that *I* could read them. *They were upside down to itself.* The following was the

RESPONSE.

"No,—not that death is *terrible.* The silence and the solitude were *the Dying* —not *Death!* Tell them that it was a fearful, silent passage to me and those before me. But that it shall be so no longer *in secula seculorum!* Silent and strange—yes.—But fearful—no. It was terrible and has been terrible from its *uncertainty.* Every spirit hath known not, when it feels that it has at length lost Earth, but it was doomed to silence and solitude *forever!* The struggle to know what it is, the futile efforts to see—to hear,—followed by the great, all-absorbing consciousness and conviction, that it is simply an *existence,* are fearful! But let the living listen! Hereafter, let those that die, be content to pause through the change;—for the solitude lasts but a moment, when the dormant spirit gradually develops. *Then,* there was nothing around it;—*now* it knows itself and that into which it enters."

"Are you in the midst of spirits?" I asked aloud; and my voice seemed to resound unnaturally through the felt silence of the room.

RESPONSE.

"I had lost you for a time. I could see and hear nothing. I almost forgot the circumstances of my death. But then, I was not dead. Slowly a sensation of lightness came over me, and I remembered all. I knew you all. I felt calm. I saw your motions as of something apart from me;—very much as you look down through clear water and watch the motions of the strange monsters of the deep;—whose element is different from yours,—whose actions are sometimes strange and unaccountable,—with whom you have nothing in common."

Here was a pause again for about five minutes, during which the cold, dead hand relaxed from around mine. At length, I asked again,

"Are you in the midst of spirits?"

The strange, invisible wires were pulled again,—for the blue death-fingers tightened around my own, and the locked hands traced the following

RESPONSE.

"I found myself gradually taking *form*—and *moving* through a long, grand, misty, undulating arch-way; towards a *harmony,* as it were, of far-off music. All was indefinite. I felt the intense consciousness of my own existence. Nothing more. At length, clearer and clearer I understood the new Universe into which I was entering, and a part of which I formed. I was alone. I heard no voice. But as I swept through the arch, I said as it were distinctly to myself this strange word, 'FORMS.' At length it changed to 'FORMS—MOTION.' After I had swept on still further, it changed to 'FORMS—MOTION—HARMONY.' And then after a pause, to 'FORMS—MOTION—HARMONY—THE ARCH.' Why I repeated them I know not. Soon I was, as it were, uttering 'FORMS—MOTION—HARMONY—THE ARCH—CONNECTION.' At length the word 'BEAUTY' was added; and finally I found myself repeating over and over again—

 'FORMS—MOTION—HARMONY—THE ARCH—CONNECTION—BEAUTY—ETERNITY—ETERNITY—ETERNITY !'

I knew not what it could mean. I know now. I will tell you more to-morrow night. I thought, and those in the flesh think, that all they conceive of, is everything that exists, save God and the disembodied spirits. Hence they call it the 'Universe.' I find myself now forming a part of a second Universe; as I have formed unknown through all ages. All have lived and shall live forever. I know it in the dim distance. You are immortal as truly in the past, as you shall be in the future. Finity at the beginning must lead to finity at the end, and as you shall live forever, so *have* you lived forever: for your life is *infinite*. I will explain to-morrow night. Your first stage was non-self-sentient. Peer not into the past. It will not advance HIS GREAT LIVING. Look to the future. You are wearied. Remember Janie—see, she sits weeping. Farewell."

 "But are you in the midst of spirits?" cried I.

RESPONSE.

 "O, wonderful—wonderful!—O, altogether inexplicable. As you may suppose the rose unto her leaves,—as you may suppose music unto the consciousness of man,—as you may suppose the harmonious, and ever crossing, and unheard, and dimly understood converse always going on between the elements of a landscape,—the cascade and the rocks—the liquid water ripples and the shore—the forest and the sunbeams—so do the hosts of the new universe around me hold communion with each other. Direct, not impeded—silent, and dreamily beautiful and sublime! As different from the converse of man with man, as is color from weight. Remember Janie—see she sits weeping. Adieu."

 "But I am *not* weary—*I am not weary*," cried I, quickly. "More—*more !*"

We asked and asked again for one more response—*but* one. The spirit had, however, left us. I wished to know if they experienced the passage of time in the other world. But not one word could we obtain. At the word "adieu," the dead hand fell off from mine. The clock struck three,—and, bewildered with the strange occurrences of the night, and intoxicated with excitement, I staggered out into the air. My friends soon joined me.

—

I will not say—I need not say—that for us there was no sleep that night. As I have remarked above, I staggered, bewildered, from the room into the open air, where I was followed by the Doctor and Mr. H. Not a word was uttered. In the awfulness of the occasion each seemed to respect the other's feelings. Great, silent waves of thought had rolled upon us out of profound Death. And the majesty of the new Universe,—from whose solemn depths a soul had just now whispered to us,—as it pressed down and around me with painful reality and grandeur, overwhelmed and stupefied me. Where was the invisible spirit, upon whom its sublimity had just burst?—the great liquid eyes, forth from which he had looked upon us, were glazed now, and set. Where was the *Soul?* —could it be here, standing, silent, at my side, and gazing serenely upon me? Whence had issued those strange whispers—those fragments of knowledge?— There, in the room, were the arm and the hand—that had traced the thoughts—relaxed, and left by us in our bewilderment outstretched upon the table. But where was the *spirit*, that had stirred it—from *without !* Where was the spirit? —Fled:—fled into those unknown, strange regions, whither we all shall go!— Fled! Yet co-existent, co-knowing co-working with us. I burned to learn of the NEW UNIVERSE.

—While we stood in the still, dark night, thus wrapt in thought,—with the stars looking down from afar,—with the invisible wind sighing around us—we knew not where,—with the great city of the dead before us, where glimmered faintly in the starlight the white tombstones of the unnumbered departed,—and with the lowly, silent hall of death behind us, whence another spirit had just now—lifted and sped,—as we stood thus wrapt in thought, a soft hand stole into mine, and I felt upon my fingers the pressure of a gentle kiss. I looked, and it was Jane. She was kneeling at my feet—kneeling upon the damp ground, and weeping. In her desolation—sweet child—she had left the dead to cling to the living. She had silently singled me out from the rest, with an instinct that knows no premeditation.

"Janie, my dear child," said I, "let us return to father."

I lifted her into my arms, and she clasped her little hands around my neck, and laid her head upon my breast, and wept—wept bitterly. I need not say that my own tears were flowing full and fast,—and dropping, and mingling with hers.

—We moved slowly along towards the silent room and, as we entered, Mr. H. passed noiselessly to the mysterious bed-side, and disposed the body decently.

—We stood gazing upon it for a time in silence,—and then—recollecting ourselves—consulted in a low voice upon our position.

For us to inform our acquaintances with what had passed, was not to be thought of. We should have had the town upon us in an hour. We had received no instructions,—but the sentence, "I will tell you more to-morrow night," clearly indicated what was expected from us. At last, it was decided that Mr. H. should remain with the body during the day, (it was now nearly four o'clock in the morning,) while the Doctor and myself should return to our respective duties in the city. To prevent inquiry, it was thought best that Jane should stay with Mr. H. And we agreed to meet here to-night—or rather, last night, (for it is now nearly daylight of the 22d,) at eight o'clock, punctually. The preliminaries being arranged, the Doctor and myself took our silent way across the hills toward the city, while Mr. H. bowed farewell to us from the door, with little Janie in his arms looking tearfully after us.

—Oh, the long, weary hours, that dragged, leaden-footed, until night! It seemed to me that sunset would never come. Need I say that the Doctor and myself, although we separated at six in the morning, could not remain apart? The imperative call of duty summoned me at ten to my desk in the Custom House; and when I went in, I found him there waiting for me. Our eyes met,—but not one allusion was made to the occurrences of the previous night. Each felt intensely the other's knowledge. A mysterious spell bound us together. I dared not have him stay, lest remark should be excited; and yet I could not *bear* to have him leave. And so—he lingered, all day. Now and then we would steal a word together. But, oh, need I say, what an effort it caused me to attend to the details of my desk, and to talk cheerfully and carelessly of the trivial events of the morning? —oh, so trivial, they seemed to me, beneath the shadow of the great event, that had towered about me in a night! —No,—I will pass all this. Suffice it to say, evening came. And at half-past seven we were at the threshold of the darkened chamber. I entered—with Janie in my arms;—for she had watched for us from the edge of the widow-curtain, and had run out to meet us, chiding me sweetly and artlessly for my long delay.

With the exception of a little more neatness in the arrangement of the simple furniture of the room, everything was as we had left it, even to the small pine table at the head of the bed.

—Well, the momentous hour had arrived. The solemn arcana of Hereafter were to transpire. I know not why, but we hesitated at meeting the great intelligence, and we lingered in conversation at least an hour, before we prepared to receive those communications, which we knew were in store for us. We re-read those we had already received:

"Mr. Lane shall hold a conversation with you prior to, during, and after death,—*in which he will give you his experience of death, and the facts and scenes, so to speak, to which he first awakes, after the heart shall cease to beat.*"

He had only given us a part of his experience of death, and to-night, then, he would finish the recounting of his solemn, solitary passage through the shadowy valley, and open to our view, in language, the structure and appearance of the NEW UNIVERSE. Where *was* this Universe? What manner of beings were the spirits? What was their form,—their destiny? Did they increase in knowledge? That *must* be so, for the soul had declared it. How then was the paradox to be explained, of a spirit living on forever.—forever increasing in knowledge,—forever—forever—and yet never equaling the changeless God!

—At length we took our seats around the table at the head of the bed, and placed our hands upon it. For fifteen minutes we remained in silent expectation, but received no manifestations of the spirit's presence. This was strange. It was, however, suggested, that Mr. Lane's hand was not upon the table; and that possibly this might be the reason of our want of success. But the body had become stiff, and the hand, when outstretched, slowly arose from the table, and returned to its place upon the breast. We then held it down; and soon found that the Odic fluid (if fluid it be) was penetrating it; or, at any rate, that the arm and hand were becoming limber. Another fifteen minutes elapsed without result. The table neither tipped, nor manifested any disposition to slide, or even stir. The only indication we had received thus far was a single rap, which startled us by its loudness and brevity. Finally, in the silence of almost hopeless expectation, and as a last resort, I resumed the pencil, and, without saying anything to my friends, lifted the dead hand, placed it around my own in the position it had assumed of itself last night, and held it there to keep it from dropping off. Another anxious pause ensued, when, what was my delight, at feeling the cold fore-finger pressing gently, but very perceptibly upon the back of my hand. I ejaculated with almost profane gleefulness—

"It is clutching me!"

"Hark!" said the Doctor, quickly, while both leaned forward with painful anxiety for the result.

Slowly the middle finger commenced to press down. Then the third finger. Then the little finger.—And at last, the spell of death seemed to break, for the arm violently stiffened, and the whole hand grasped mine with a suddenness that startled us, notwithstanding we were so anxiously hoping for some such result.

We breathed freely again. And I could not but contrast our feelings of placid joy, with those of terror which filled us last night, when first we beheld the hand and arm rising mysteriously from the table.

But, if the reader is as anxious to learn the tenor of the communications as were we to procure them, he will wish me to come to them without more delay. In short, I must hasten to the conclusion of my task, for I have been writing since two this morning, and the dawn has already broken.

To proceed then:—My first question was, "Are you happy?"

—No response.

QUESTION, again—"Are you happy?"

After a pause—

RESPONSE.

"That is a singular interrogatory for this occasion,—and one, for obvious reasons, I am not able to answer."

QUESTION.

"Why are you not able to satisfy your friends on so important a point?"

RESPONSE.

"If those who are happy could communicate the fact to their friends,—*those who are unhappy* could do the same.

—"But I do not see the point," said I.

RESPONSE.

"Silence is the best answer."

QUESTION.

"Perhaps if I put the question in an abstract form, the difficulty will be removed. Is there happiness and misery in your Universe?"

—No response.

—After a pause, Mr. H. remarked as follows, viz: "But I am anxious to have you finish your experience of death. You told us last night that you found yourself repeating the words—'Forms, Motion, Harmony, The Arch,' etc., and that you would tell us more to-night."

RESPONSE.

"While moving in the midst of your Universe, I had been blinded by the glare of particularities. Numberless individuals and species were around me. I saw not that which underlay and ran up through all things.

Motion—in all its infinite varieties—is sublime. Whether I watch it flitting in the butterfly, curling gracefully in the rising smoke, or darting in the lightning,—whether I contemplate it in the majestically wheeling worlds,—or grasp it with far-reaching conception in the slow decay of an abbey ruin,—it is the same mysterious condition of nature. The boy passes into the man. It is motion. Nations rise and sink. It is motion. 'Rest' is a relative word. As the word ghost sprang from man's fear, and expresses something which never had existence, so does the word 'rest' spring from man's egotism, and expresses what never had existence. That which moves faster than man's knowledge is as much rest to man as that which moves slower, and that which moves without his knowledge is as much rest as either. The landscape appears at rest, while silently grow the trees, fabricating their slender tissues from the earths, the air and the water, with magic fingers;—slowly, unseen by mortal eye, unheard by mortal ear, are the chemical and mechanical forces of nature tapping at the life-essence of the rocks and strata;—shine on the stars in the heavens unseen by you,—move on the worlds of the Universe unfelt,—flows on the eternal circle of vapor, clouds and the rain-storm. So, could you enter more minutely into nature, would you find that *all* is motion. Rest is not life. Rest is death—is non-existence. And your Universe lives. It is all working—working—*God cannot rest!*—Rest means that thou movest faster than some things, and slower than others. Motion is not merely a fact in your Universe, here and there. It is a condition pervading your entire Universe, running down to every—even the minutest part. MOTION underlies and runs up through all things.

Your Universe exists by entering into forms. In its present phase it has entered as a whole into the form of revolving suns and earths, with all the forms that on and in them are. All things around you are in forms.—FORMS—MOVING.

Come now to the 'Arch.' How do the forms of your Universe move? The seed drops into the ground. The plant springs up. Watch the arching of the flower. First the tender embryo upon the stem—the unshaped silky chaos. This is soon a bud. The bud swells. It bursts. The ripe flower opens to the full its fragrant form, and the sunbeams come there, and nestle in the warm beauty. The maturity is on. The key-stone is reached. But not one instant does the motion stop. Less and less grows the fragrance. Duller and duller is the blushing white—the yellow—the crimson;—petal and sepal and stamen and pistil drop away;—and what was a flower—is nothing. And what of the plant! Certain particles have married into that form. But in the course of the months, or the years, or the centuries, the form dissolves and disappears. The *particles* are eternal. But the *form* is no more. The arching of the flower is typical of that of every form, and all the arching forms make up your Universe. All forms come into being—pass, however slowly, however rapidly, up to maturity,—and so—however slowly, however rapidly, down to dissolution. Where is Hundred Gated Thebes? The small makes up the great. This is the answer to the autumn leaf, that flits across your pathway, and to the dying girl. The great Motion, which pervades your Universe, is its flowering to culmination. And hearken. When it shall have reached its acme, it will descend along a bright pathway, and, entering into, be lost in another grand form, into which it will expand. FORMS—MOVING—in ARCHES.

Why wonder at the fitness of things? The horse's head and neck are just long enough to enable him to reach the ground, and crop the grass which is his food. And you lift your eyes, and admire the harmony, and say it was so designed. Designing is a process of mind, requiring more or less time, and arguing imperfection. Forget the great man, who is thy God. God weigheth not, nor doth he consider. God resteth not, but liveth out his nature of necessity. For he cannot be any one else, as a square cannot be a circle. Men wonder at the fitness of the horse's head and neck for the purposes for which they are used. They do not consider that were his neck and head too short to reach his food, the whole race of horses would die. Discord would defeat itself. And they are astonished, because they discover only a part of the harmony of Nature. Harmony prevails everywhere from the necessity of the case. It pervades your Universe.—FORMS—MOVING—HARMONIOUSLY—in ARCHES.

There is action and reaction around you. Who was he that said 'Each grain of sand is the center of all things'? This is truth. Each form acts upon every other, and is reacted upon, in turn, by every other. Mind, even, works upon your Universe. Your Universe works upon mind. CONNECTED—FORMS—MOVING—HARMONIOUSLY—in ARCHES.

Beauty is universal. To the mind of man a part is free. The rest is latent. This, too, is well. For mind must build, first a hut—then a house—then a temple. Mind upon earth must search out beauty—must be educated for higher works in the future. God is not discordant;—so is He all beautiful.—CONNECTED —and BEAUTIFUL FORMS—MOVING—HARMONIOUSLY—in ARCHES.

Therefore is your Universe not a heterogeneous mass of disjointed parts. It is a homogeneity. It is distinct and different from our Universe.

Rise now for a moment to a contemplation of Deity. To gain a conception of Him, conceive of any form around you—a golden goblet. It has certain qualities —color—hardness—extension—weight—by which you know it.—So has God essential qualities, which constitute Him the being He is. He is an infinite being —therefore are each of his qualities infinite. Your Universe is the expression of one of those qualities. Mine, of another. Both are, therefore, infinite;—infinite in extent,—infinite in duration, from the past and into the future. But as God, too, is an infinite being, He has not a *finite* number of qualities, as has the golden goblet; but an infinite number of qualities, each of which expresses itself in an infinite Universe. The soul has within itself a germ of every universe, and it sinketh on ever from one to another. The Universes are infinite in number, therefore is the soul everlasting;—ever growing in knowledge, yet never exhausting that through which it passes. For it would require an infinity of years to exhaust the secrets of one single infinite Universe, how much more then to exhaust those of an infinite number of Universes, each of which is infinite in itself! Glorious art thou, oh man, the everlasting! Glorious art thou, oh man, that ever sinketh through the Universes.——Glorious art thou, oh infinitely greater—Exhaustless God!

Thus then do I describe to you your Universe.

CONNECTED AND BEAUTIFUL FORMS
MOVING HARMONIOUSLY IN ARCHES THROUGH ALL
ETERNITY."

This extraordinary communication was followed by a long, thoughtful pause on our part. What subjects for contemplation did it not open up!—the connection between Universe and Universe;—the connection between God and His Universes:—the meaning of death:—its necessity, as a link, between Universe and Universe, etc. At length I broke the silence by the following remark, viz: "But in all this—for which we are truly grateful to you—you have not given us what we so anxiously wait for—to wit: the remainder of your experience of Death. What of the Arch in which you found yourself? And what species of place is the New Universe, into which the soul passes at death?"

RESPONSE.

"The spirit frees itself from the cloudy arch by reasoning and testing. It finds itself *alone*. The solitude is oppressive. At first it knows not what manner of being it is. It struggles, in the solitude, to bring into existence something besides itself, that it may not be alone. But tell those that shall die, to pause patiently, until the dying has ceased. Each soul will then involuntarily test itself. At first, it supposes that all its faculties were suited to its condition and surroundings upon the earth alone. Its eyes and ears, with their corresponding mental faculties, seemed fitted alone to enable it to act in the world. Love bound it to its fellows. Sublimity and ideality enabled it to enjoy the beauty and grandeur of nature. But it knows that it has dropped Nature. What use then for these mental faculties? for benevolence, since the sick and suffering and needy are left behind; for its moral faculties, since mankind is gone; yes, even for its pious faculties, for it finds no God. Thus does it eliminate *itself* from every condition of earth. But forthwith I realized that I was *reasoning*.—I recognized the action of *selfish faculties;* for I was alone, and yearned for companionship.—I remembered that I had been *observing* the long archway, with its gentle wavering, its form, its vast length, its soft, variegated opal colors. I realized that I was appreciating the surpassing beauty and the grandeur of this my passage. I noticed that I was *remembering;*—and when I reached where I now am, I knew within myself an ardent desire for knowledge,—I was charmed with the new scenes around me,—I found new companions to love,—new grandeurs to enjoy,—new duties before me,—new works to accomplish. I see no God. But I know that He exists. Thus did I learn myself, discovering that I still possessed all the mental faculties I had on earth."

QUESTION.

"And when you looked around you, what species of place did you find yourself in?"

RESPONSE.

"There is no 'passage' with me, as you move on earth. There is no 'place,' as you speak of 'locality' on earth. There is no 'form,' as you speak of shape on earth. The archway of death was but a condition in which I remained while testing myself, and becoming prepared to enter into my present state. Our condition here is such, that that by which each soul seems surrounded, is an out-creation from itself. When you are in a grove, the grove actually exists; and would exist were you not there. Not so here. We cannot speak of 'locality,' for there is no such thing in this life; and therein consists the difficulty of making you comprehend our condition. But that, here, which is analogous to your 'locality,' I must express by using your word. The locality, in which is each soul from time to time, does not exist outside of itself, as, for instance, does your grove, or street, or habitation; but it is an out-creation of the soul itself; and I appear to live in the midst of my out-creations,—they are all in effect as actual to me, as are your surroundings to you."

"But this being the condition of affairs," remarked I, after a pause, "your Universe must be very heterogeneous in appearance."

RESPONSE.

"Beware of Materialism,—for its hand-maiden is Atheism. The landscapes of Earth 'appear' to the vision—and the dark blue vault of the heavens with its stars! I comprehend your difficulty, however, and will explain as best I may.

—True,—each soul lives in the midst of its out-creations; and you might suppose our Universe heterogeneous in its character. But consider the various localities of earth, how they differ from each other. Where is there similarity between a room and a river flowing between its leafy banks?—Bear in memory, that no two persons on earth can occupy, at the same time, the same space, and witness their surroundings from precisely the same angles, else would they be one person. So, no two souls live in the same out-creations, else would they be one soul. But, as all the different spirits—which, with their ever-varying, ingenious and beautiful out-creations, compose this Universe—have, nevertheless, that something in common, which throws them together into the one class 'SOULS,'—our Universe has a general effect of unity in itself, analogous to that unity which is possessed by the Universe you have not yet left.

Motion pervades this Universe also. All the souls are continually varying their out-creations. Therefore is it like a vast kaleidoscope—heaving itself into new, grand forms of beauty, forever and ever!

Thus can I dimly only tell you of that to which I awoke."

QUESTION.

"But how can your Universe be infinite,—when the number of spirits who have left earth is finite?"

RESPONSE.

"Look into thy heavens. Thou beholdest but a thousand of the infinite lights!"

"But *where* are you?" asked I.

RESPONSE.

"Is color above extension? Is weight above, or beneath, or even among color? And yet each is different from the other, while all are qualities of the same golden goblet. Neither can I say, that we are above, or beneath, or even among your Universe:—and yet each Universe—yours and mine—is a part of God."

—Well, we were at length satisfied with regard to the general character of the abode of the departed, and our conversation about it was long and rambling. I will not detail what we said, as no notes were taken of it, but will leave the reader to his own reflections.

At length I asked the spirit, if he could give us any information in relation to the appearance of the soul;—its form, its structure.

RESPONSE.

"Mankind are wrong. The earth and their senses clog them. Every man, when he thinks of a spirit, attains to a conception of it by passing through an unnoticed, subtle series of rapid steps. He thinks of some material object,—water;—he passes thence to steam;—thence to air, and, finally, by a further etherealization, he reaches a conception of spirit. This unremembered, but invariable process leads inevitably to a conception, tinged with materiality. To gain an idea of spirit, think of a single thought. It has no shape;—it occupies no space;—and yet it is distinct and different from every other thought. Pass thence to a spirit;—which has no shape—which occupies no space, and yet is distinct and different from every other spirit. A tree is a material unit—non-self-conscious. A thought is a spiritual unit—non-self-conscious. A soul is a spiritual unit—self-conscious."

This was a new process—to me a simple and reasonable one—and I wondered that it had not struck me before.

QUESTION.

"Do the relationships of earth—the friendships—the filial loves last beyond the grave?"

—No response.

—"Have you friendships in the other world?"

RESPONSE.

"By how much the better was the spirit at death, by so much the more lovely are his out-creations as he sweeps hither-among. Thus there are grades among us, as there are among you. Thus there are similarities and dissimilarities of disposition. Free intercourse exists among the souls;—free-will. Thus are there opportunities for advance and improvement, or for the reverse. Could you pass to a contemplation of the other Universes—which do exist, although I see them not—then would you feel how important is improvement at every step. Awaken to a conception of a life forever! For each Universe which the soul has passed through is lost to it forever with all the means of advance contained therein. And, as capacity for enjoyment widens and deepens the further we sink along the Universes, so does the disadvantage of a single unimproved Universe, in the past increase in awful, irremediable proportion, the further we advance through the future. An unimproved Universe is a clog forever! Beware, beware, O, beware! Act purely,—speak purely,—but, above all, *think* purely and with dignity. For in two Universes, at least, selfishness is the mainspring of the spirit's life."

QUESTION.

"But how do you converse, having left the organs of articulation upon earth?"

RESPONSE.

"As it is with you, neither can soul here pierce the depth of the soul. Each recognizes the other's out-creations, but can not pass within them into the motives and thoughts of the soul with which he is communicating. The conversation of the pure in heart on earth is truthful;—that of the vast intellect embodies great thoughts; the words of the vile are either vile or deceitful. Thus is it here. Our out-creations each arranges at will. The noble, the great, the improved, can and do naturally surround themselves with corresponding out-creations. They bear an influence among us. There are souls that originate, and souls that copy. And truth and deceit is mingled here as it is with you. You can judge of a man's motives notwithstanding his remarks;—we can judge of a soul's motives notwithstanding his out-creations. Thus, as it were, do we communicate with each other,—originating and improving—or retrograding, as you do on earth. Death will necessarily make no one happy;—free no one from cares;—release no one from labors. Our condition is no happier than yours. Not only does the individual have duties to perform here,—as you suppose,—for which he should prepare himself on earth by purity and a strengthening of the mind, but races have also grand works to perform."

QUESTION.

"Must the souls advance to a definite point of perfection before they can pass from your Universe to the next?"

RESPONSE.

"Why do you ask this, when it is not so with you?"

"It is generally supposed to be the fact," said I.

RESPONSE.

"No soul knoweth when it shall be summoned away—we know not whither. Our out-creations are to us here, as are your bodies on Earth. When the soul is no longer able to surround itself with out-creations, it becomes unfit for duties in this Universe; it cannot act among us, any more than can a corpse among you. And the soul—the 'me,' when its out-creations die from around it, remains for an instant a torpid entity, and vanishes, ere we can think,—we know not whither.—*This is Death with us.*"

QUESTION.

"Do the friendships of earth continue beyond death?"

RESPONSE.

"Lift yourself to a contemplation of an *Eternal Existence*, and think of the fleeting friendships of earth and their uses. Is not the useless cast away?"

"It is sad to think of parting forever from a loved mother or sister," said I,— "It is sad to think, that when we stand by the deathbed of a dear father, we shall see him no more."
—No Response.
—"I say, it is sad to feel that at death we leave our friends forever."

RESPONSE.

"The useful remaineth. God is Great."

—"Can you not answer us more definitely?"

RESPONSE.

"Would you have me say, that the soul of a vile son shall forever pollute the purity of a sainted mother? Or—that a loving sister shall forever be separated from a kind brother?"

"I would have you tell us the truth."
—No Response.

QUESTION.

From the Doctor. "Is the doctrine of transmigration of souls correct in whole, or even in part?" At this moment I noticed the other hand and arm of the corpse moving slightly. The odic fluid had evidently penetrated the entire body.

RESPONSE.

"Can the tree call back its leaves? We press ever onward. Death is a barrier, across which we may look back,—but over which we may not pass again."

QUESTION.

"Is there communication between your Universe and the one beyond you?"
—No Response.

QUESTION.

"Can you tell us of the Universe beyond you?"

RESPONSE.

"Did you know aught of this—until now—save that it existed?"

"It is true," said I "but what—what of the next?"

RESPONSE.

"Knowing 'color' and 'extension' only, how could you judge what manner of quality 'weight' might be? Neither can we conceive what manner of Universe the next is, for we have nothing to judge from. We only know it to be as different in its character from ours as ours is from yours—as color is from weight."

We had scarcely received the response, when I was amazed at finding the entire body strangely agitated. The odic fluid, passing through the arm, had indeed penetrated it throughout. But before I could speak, the hand dropped away from mine, and I was stupefied at seeing the corpse rise slowly to a sitting posture,—evidently without any internal muscular action, but as though it were willed up from without by its disembodied soul. It was stiff and stark. The lids opened,—the black eyes—they were the glazed, soulless eyes of Death,— stared forth into vacuity,—and, to our horror, the chin dropped, the organs of articulation were moved,—*the corpse spoke!*

"Great Heavens!—I am—I am—*leaving my Universe!*—my out-creations die from around me!—I am passing to the next——O where!—*where!*—I am DYING!—dy——Fare—— "

And the body fell relaxed upon the bed—the right arm bounding as it struck.

—When we had recovered partially from our stupefaction, we looked around us, and could scarcely believe what we had seen and heard. Could it indeed be possible, that the corpse had moved—*had uttered words?*—Yes,—we were all awake—all dismayed—terror-stricken;—and in the ears of each of us still rang those words of awful import—"I am leaving my Universe!—my out-creations die from around me!—I am passing to the next!"—— Could our senses have deceived us?—And yet if the disembodied spirit could, through the medium of the odic fluid, move the table, or, the arm and hand that once were his, why *indeed* could it not will the inhaling muscles and the organs of articulation into action?—Yes,—strange though it seemed, the one was no more unreasonable than the other.

—We laid the body into a proper position again, reclosed its eyes and resumed our seats.

—But the spirit——the spirit—whither had it flown?—It was now not even within *our* reach!—A whole Universe was between us!

What more is there for me to say? My task is done. I have related the strange occurrences to which I have been witness during the past forty-eight hours, as faithfully as lies in my power,—and my duty to the world is performed.

The Doctor and Mr. H. left me at two this morning, promising to return at noon. The reader knows the rest,—Stealthily, hour by hour, has the night stolen away,—the silence only broken by the rustling of my papers. Janie still sleeps sweetly and confidingly.— One lock of hair must I clip from the marble forehead—one single memento of the departed for her who is left alone.

—

Five days afterwards, two passed over the hills toward that silent city, beneath the shade of whose trees and among whose winding paths all eyes are closed— all hands are peacefully crossed forever. And as they left the city of the living behind them, and the din of its crowded streets died away in the distance, peace fell upon their hearts, and I knew they drew closer together, as they walked hand in hand. It was the blessed Sabbath morning. Nearer and nearer sounded the solemn, mournful roar of the great Pacific. To the elder, it seemed like the far-heard, commingled converse of the innumerable departed!

—Thus they moved in silence, and entered the broad avenue, with sunny hearts. Path after path they threaded,—and at last they stood before a new-made grave. Flowers were freshly planted around it, and on the head-stone were graven these simple words—

"Farewell—Father."

—And as the elder threw himself upon the grass, he knew not which was the fairer,—the younger, or the flowers she tripped among.

FLOWN: A REVERIE.
A SEQUEL TO "THE EVENTFUL NIGHTS," ETC.

—

"When she had passed, it seemed like the ceasing of exquisite music."

SHE lies in the little chamber. All is hushed around her. The crimson cords are loosed, and the curtains hang heavily to the floor.—They speak in whispers around me; the doors are closed noiselessly, and footsteps in the hall are softened;—for they could not but love my orphaned one,—my sweet, my playful, gentle sister. The light falls crimsoned around her. Her arms lie folded upon her breast—as soft and snowy as the pillow where rests her head. And outflowing is the wealth of her chestnut ringlets,—how rich,—oh, how soft and warm and rich, upon her marble shoulders,—how beautiful in their light and shade,— how graceful in their negligence! Her lids are closed,—they do not even tremble. Her lips are parted.—And she lies so still,—so fair, and pale, and still, —that I cannot think but she is dead.—And I have just passed noiselessly to the bed-side,—and I have just leaned forward and listened for her breath,—and I have just placed a single white rose upon her breast, that she may know I have watched her, and am near.—O, how beautiful is sleep!——

——Why do they whisper around me! Why do they look at me so mournfully—so mournfully and silently!—And why did they move her little stand away,—and why—*why* does he not come? Did he not say there were hopes? ————She is very—very still!——

——How gracefully the tassels fall!—How beautiful the colors of her room! —The crimson and the gold!—Ah, she rests richly!—She shall suffer no more. Never again shall she ask for bread—for a single crust from the neighbors, because her father is sick, and she is hungry. Never again shall she wander, obediently and patiently, in the dark night, for a stranger to come to her lonely home. Never again shall the tear-drops melt in her mournful eyes; for I shall kiss them all away. Never again in the chill winter shall her fragile limbs lack raiment. For God will give me strength for her sweet sake.—God *shall* give me life and health and strength;—and her little room shall always be next to mine, —shall always be beautiful;—as she is beautiful.————The crimson and the gold;—and the white lace canopy above her,—and her little book-case,—and her play-things,—and, by and by, her little work-table in the corner. Yes, she must not—*cannot* die! God shall spare her,—even for my guilty, guilty sake! Has He not already taken father and mother,—and shall He take the child? —She is *not* left alone,—oh, she is not alone! She need not go. Has he not reared for her a protector—a brother?—Yes, I shall never ask again, Why have I lived?—I see it—know it, now. And God has spared me, that she may be happy.——

——In the little chamber;—so statue-like and still!—The door is open between us. And they have all gone, and left us alone in the night. And everything is hushed.——She had begun to smile again. And she would clap her little hands as I came in, and run to me for the kiss,—and many a happy hour would I spend with her among her play-things.——And now, she lies so quiet;—and her face, and neck, and shoulders are so like marble;—and her ringlets lie so peacefully, —that I cannot think but she is dead.—It was a gentle hand that laid them ;—I know it was no mother's hand,—but it was a gentle, loving hand that laid them, —and she kissed it, and said—
"Dear brother, why are you weeping?—Have I not been a good little girl?— The Doctor told me I should be well soon. And, then, you shall play with me again;—shan't you;—and read to me again;—about Joseph and his brethren." ——O God! God! Whither shall I turn!——

——It seems but a sennight ago, that the mournful rites were over, and, after they had borne him to his grave, that we stood together in the silent room.—— She knew nothing but that he was gone now, and that she was left alone; and so, with the instinct of helplessness and innocence, she looked to *me*, she scarce knew why;—I felt that she was clinging to me. And as I moved around the room, she watched me, or hovered near me, knowing not what was to be done, nor whither she was to go. Oh, that sweet face, with its silent expression of uncertainty and mournfulness!

When all was ready, I could not leave, but sat down for a moment, and took her into my lap. And as the tears rose, and I leaned forward and wept, she looked into my face with sympathizing gaze, and almost wept, too, because *I* was sad.—At length, as I arose, and looked for the last time upon the bed, now empty, she stood silently by my side,—looked where I looked,—put her little hand in mine, and, with the same mournful, uncertain expression in her eyes, followed, yieldingly, whithersoever I led her.——

——And then she grew cheerful again. Her little room was *very* pleasant,—and it was next to mine,—and Mrs. B. was very—very kind to her.—And her little chair was next to mine at the table.—And, when the sun-light fell upon the corner of my book-case, she knew it was time for me to come,—and she would watch for me along the street,—and she would run down to meet me at the door and tell me, she had been a good girl.——And at last her little dresses came, and her hat; and she was very happy, and light, and fairy-like:—for I had left all these to Mrs. B.—And then, in the evening, I would stay with her. And when Margaret came for her, she would kneel by my side, and say her little prayers, and kiss me, and bid me good night. Ah! she was very sweet and sunny to me,—and I know she loved me,—and I believe I grew to be a better man.——

——And then they told me, one day, that Janie was sick, and had asked for me;—and they had sent for the Doctor.—And she was so glad to see me as I came in.—And then, the windows were darkened;—and they were all so kind to her:—and she was very—very grateful.—And then, she sank lower and lower. O, how I have watched her these last five nights!—And as her voice grew weaker and weaker, how have I fallen upon my knees in anguish, and prayed God, that he would but spare her!————But, alas! they have moved away her little stand;—and they have opened the window;—and they are all weeping around me;—and she will never—*never* take the rose from her breast, and know that I have watched her and am near!——

EXPLANATORY SEQUEL.

–

During several months subsequent to the publication of the above paper in *The Pioneer*, so much had been said and written, concerning the article,—so many letters had been addressed to me on the subject, from strangers in different parts of the Union,—so gross a blunder had been committed by one or two of the leading "Spiritualist" editors in republishing the fiction as a narrative of facts, that I decided to write an explanatory communication on the subject to Mr. James Gordon Bennett.

The communication was published in the *New York Morning Herald* of March 12th, accompanied by the following brief notice from the editor, viz:

"Astounding Revelation from the Spirit World.—We publish to-day a curious communication from San Francisco, which will fall like a bombshell into the camp of the Spiritualists. It appears that some months since, the writer, Mr. F. C. Ewer, of San Francisco, took it into his head to prepare for the *California Pioneer Magazine* a fiction of rather a bold and original conception, undertaking to describe the sensations of a dying man during the moment of dissolution, and sketching the scene which opens to the soul as it enters upon its second existence. Some two or three months after it was published, the writer was surprised by receiving a letter from Judge Edmonds, stating that he had copied the first part of it into the November Number of the *Sacred Circle*, and adding the astounding fact that he (the Judge) had had several spiritual interviews with the defunct fictitious hero of the narrative, "John F. Lane!" The best part of the joke is, that the article contains assertions in physics which are impossible, and which, to minds less credulous than those of Judge Edmonds and his fellow dupes, would have at once suggested doubts as to the sincerity of the writer. The value attached to the Judge's adhesion to the new sect will, after this exposure, be considerably lessened. If his present convictions have been arrived at on such loose evidence as the above, we can only say that, however much we may admire the extent of his faith, we can have very little respect for his professional acumen."

Doubtless the *New York Herald* of the 12th of March has already reached the eyes of nearly all that perused "The Eventful Nights" in *The Pioneer*, nevertheless I cannot but regard it as proper, that the explanatory communication should appear in the same medium, through which the article to which it relates was first presented to the public. I give it therefore below, merely remarking that the "heading" was prefixed to it by the editor of the *Herald*; viz:

"ANOTHER BOMBSHELL THROWN INTO THE CAMP OF THE SPIRITUALISTS.
A NUT FOR JUDGE EDMONDS TO CRACK.

To the Editor of the New York Herald:—

I trust it is not asking too much to beg the favor of a short space in your columns for an explanation to which I find myself forced by Judge Edmonds and the editor of the *Christian Spiritualist*, in relation to a fiction prepared by me for *The Pioneer Magazine*, which, I must say, singularly enough, they have seen fit to republish as fact, and as an evidence in proof of 'Spiritualism,'—the former in his magazine and the latter in his newspaper.

In order to render the matter clear to you, it is, perhaps, necessary for me to state that, in casting about for a subject, it struck me that no one had ever passed in imagination across the line of the solemn Shadow of Death, to record what may be the sensations of a dying man during the moment of dissolution, and to sketch a picture of the scenes, so to speak, which may open to the soul as it enters upon its second existence.

Knowing that the subject would necessarily involve me in ideas somewhat metaphysical in their character, I determined, in order to render what I had to write the more attractive, to surround it with a story in the narrative style.

My first difficulty, was to account, apparently, for the manner in which the strange information concerning death and the *physique* of the future world was to reach the earth; and it occurred to me that the best mode of overcoming this difficulty would be to assume a fictitious character, describe his death, represent him as conversing up to the last moment, and then allow him to give the remainder of his experience of death, and a description of that which was opening to his gaze, by means of 'spiritual manifestations,' so called. I gave the name of 'John F. Lane' to my leading fictitious character, located the occurrences in San Francisco, and entitled the article, 'The Eventful Nights of August 20th and 21st.'

Two or three months after it was published, I received a letter from Judge Edmonds, in which he stated that his attention had been called to the article by a friend in San Francisco, and that he had copied the first half of it into the November Number of *The Sacred Circle.* This was quite a surprise to me, but the surprise was as nothing, to my astonishment on being made acquainted by him with the fact, that he had had several 'spiritual' interviews with my defunct fictitious character, 'John F. Lane.'

I must confess I scarcely knew what step to take under the circumstances. At first I was about to write to Judge Edmonds; but on maturer thought, I decided, for several reasons, to adopt the course of addressing the public, with your liberty, through these columns. In the first place, if I am to judge anything from the numerous letters on the subject of 'The Eventful Nights' which I have received from strangers, the article has gone broadcast over the Union. In fact, I know this to be the case, from the republications which are before me; and I cannot but feel that the minds of many who have perused it, and believe it to be a narration of facts, should be disabused of their error. And in the second place, I am the more impelled to the step I am taking, inasmuch as the argument used by so many thousands—namely, that Judge Edmonds has for years been in the habit of weighing testimony, and that if there is enough in Spiritualism to convince him, 'there must be something in it'—can now be easily refuted. The fact is made too evident for contradiction, that he has shown himself to the thousands who look for and implicitly believe his views on the subject, and to the world at large, as a man incapable of weighing testimony touching Spiritualism, carefully; and not only one whose mind can be easily tossed about by the designing, but, as in this instance, to be one who is anxious to deceive himself.

Had he merely republished an imaginary case of 'Spiritualism,' which contained no assertions in physics impossible in themselves, or which, granting the correctness of the 'Spiritualist' theory, might have occurred, the blunder would not have been so unfortunate for him as a leader in the new theory. He could only have been charged with indecent haste in accepting testimony.

But how utterly incompetent he is to stand prominent among what has become a very numerous sect in America—how utterly unworthy he is of wielding the wide and increasing influence he unquestionably wields—will be plainly seen by any calm, thinking man, who may peruse 'The Eventful Nights of August 20th and 21st.'

How stands the case? In the first place, the article contains assertions in physics which cannot, in the nature of things, be true. For instance, a circumstance is recorded which, stripped of all surroundings, and reduced to plain English, amounts simply to this: that a magnetic needle turned away from its place at the north, and went around to the south-west point with a jerk, several times, and of its own accord. Why, it seems to me almost incredible that this fact alone should not have sufficed to stagger the Judge's credulity, great even as he has shown it to be.

In the second place, any one who is not over-anxious to believe in Spiritualism—who is not willingly blind—could hardly fail to see that the article, as a whole, is the argument *reductio ad absurdum*—to be applied to Spiritualism. I assume the ground of the Spiritualists, viz: that all matter conducts this mysterious 'odic fluid,' and that it is the necessary condition to interlie between mind and matter, to enable the disembodied soul to move matter, as the embodied mind moves the arm or foot; and, finally, at the close of the article, show to what an absurdity these positions will lead: viz: that the departed soul will have a power over its dead body, which common sense and the universal experience of mankind teach it does not and cannot have. For, while the 'circle' present at Lane's death are charging the table all night with the 'odic fluid,' they unconsciously charge Lane's entire corpse, which, after his soul has given all the information promised, suddenly interrupts the conversation by rising bolt upright in the bed, opening its eyes, and announcing that the soul feels itself at that instant dying very suddenly in the next world, and passing into a third state of existence. And yet, instead of seeing this absurdity, Judge Edmonds, forsooth, clutching tightly his premises, moves placidly, like a sheep to the slaughter, into any ridiculous conclusion to which his assumptions may lead him.

Nor is this all that should have arrested the attention of the Judge, of his collaborateur of the *Christian Spiritualist*, and of the Spiritualists generally. The very communications purporting to come from Lane, present a theory with regard to the Creator, the soul, this world, the next, etc., utterly contrary to the theory maintained by the Spiritualists. Lane, for instance, denies that the soul is etherealized matter, and that it has shape; he denies that the immaterial particle occupies time to pass through space—(that if it 'doesn't know,' forsooth, whether our absent friends are well or not, it can 'go and see,' and 'return and let us know.') He denies that one must become purer and better before he can advance from one state of existence to another hereafter, etc. etc. And yet Judge Edmonds, in his infatuation, and his brother editor of the *Spiritualist*, in his infatuation, have blindly republished as true, and corroborative of their theory, an article distinctly announcing a theory before which their own magnificent hierarchy of 'spheres' and 'circles,' and their own fine drawn materialism, must utterly fall. It really seems as if these astute investigators had adopted what the Frenchman called the Americans' motto, 'Go 'head—no mind.'

I might allude to the ill-disguised differences of style between Lane's remarks, the remarks of another spirit, and the narrator's remarks, as well as to other internal evidences, going plainly to show that the article could not have been a narration of facts, but will only make one more statement in this connection.

Not to go into minutiæ, according to the theory developed in 'The Eventful Nights,' the soul, at death, passes into a second state of existence, as different from this as extension is from weight, and, in the process of time, dies there, and passes on to a third state, as different from the first and second as the color blue is from a mass meeting; and so on, there being no possible intercommunication between the spirits in the third state and men upon earth. And yet Judge Edmonds, while he publishes as true a statement, according to which he could have had no 'spiritual' intercourse whatever with Lane—even granting that such a character had ever existed—gives to the world a communication from him.

That those who stand at the head of a class of religionists in America numbered by thousands—that those who are the Sir Oracles of 'Spiritualists'—should have republished in their own journals, as a remarkable proof in favor of their theory, an article which, as a whole, is an argument against themselves; which, besides, contains statements in physics that could not be true, and which, in addition to this, propounds a theory before which their own must utterly fall; and to crown all, should report a conversation which they have just announced could not have taken place—seems almost too ridiculous for belief. The whole affair is too glaring an evidence—I will not say against 'spiritualism'—but of the blindness of its devotees, to justify my taking any other step than that of exposing it to the world.

To complete this singular history, allow me to state that Judge Edmonds, in laying before his readers the first half of my article, publishes the letter from his friend, Mr. J. E. Austin, of this city, with a statement that he gives the article for what it is worth. In his December Number, however, he publishes the conclusion, with a prefix, in which he says, that although some who have read the article doubt its truth, there is nothing in it too marvelous for him to believe; and, finally, settles the matter, so far as he is concerned, by an additional prefix, dated November 4th, in which he publishes a report of a spiritual conversation about the affair between himself and Lane, containing, among other curious announcements from the latter, a promise to the effect that further communications were to come from him through me. I merely desire, by way of parenthesis, to inform Judge Edmonds and his friends that I said all I wished to say in 'The Eventful Nights'—that I consider Mr. John F. Lane exceedingly dead, and that I do not intend to write another fiction in which he shall figure.

I find also, that after the second half had been republished in the *Sacred Circle*, the editor of the *Christian Spiritualist*, for fear it should not be thoroughly placed before the believers in the new doctrines, and those who were wavering, republished it again, and, to settle all cavil, writes an article nearly a column long, to prove that it is utter folly to disbelieve in 'The Eventful Nights' as a narration of facts.

I fear that I am encroaching on your space, but the position in which I find myself demands a word or two more of explanation from me.

Mr. A. states in his letter that there is 'much doubt existing in the minds of some of our community as to whether said article is fiction or fact;' that he knows me, and believes me to be 'entirely incapable of giving publication to so important a falsehood as this would be were it not true, and one calculated to do so much injury.' I find myself, therefore, reduced by this either to the necessity of remaining silent, and thereby implying that 'The Eventful Nights' is a narration of facts, or to the disagreeable necessity of obtruding myself upon the public with the announcement that the article is a fiction, and with an explanation, to clear up my character for veracity. I conceive that I have a perfect right, as a truthful man, to propound a theory which I have never seen in print before, and which, I believe, may not be without interest to some —to hold up (even at a charge of arrogance) the result of an unaided mind on earth, in contrast with a theory purporting to come from a world beyond the grave—to contrast a theory which is, as I think, consistent in all its parts, and, to say the least, not impossible, with a theory which contradicts itself, and therefore cannot possibly be true. I believe that I have a perfect right to weave this theory into a fiction which, as a whole, is the argument—*reductio ad absurdum*—to be applied against spiritualism, without subjecting myself to the charge of being a man regardless of the high dictates of truth. I shall say no more on this point here; but propose, now that I have become interwoven with the Spiritualists, to treat the matter more at length, through the pages of my own periodical.

Mr. Austin also writes that the little girl—alluding to 'little Janie,' another character in the tale—was living at the house where I resided, and that I am a 'writing medium.' This reminds me very forcibly of the story of the 'Three Black Crows,' and only shows how eager Spiritualists are to believe what they wish to be true. It is but another evidence that their investigations are searches, not after truth, but after proofs for their theory. It may not be irrelevant for me to say that after the article was published, if I happened to be in a ball-room where there was a little girl, or was anywhere in the neighborhood of a little girl, the question was frequently asked, 'Is that little Jane Lane?' And it is probable that Mr. Austin's story originated from the fact that at the house where I occupied a room there was a little girl, an adopted daughter of the landlady. With regard to my being a 'writing medium,' I had never had any hesitancy in saying that my hand was at times moved in a very singular manner, without any direct volition on my part, to my knowledge. And I may also take this occasion to say that, after months of calm investigation, I could and can discover no evidence of the interposition of disembodied souls. My hand has never given me information of any importance whatever, although I have given it a fair chance, and has never answered any test question correctly. On the contrary, by careful introspection and delicate memory, I have been able to trace every answer which it has penned while in this abnormal condition to the indirect action of my own mind. I cannot, of course, state this with the same positiveness with which I can state that this paper is before me; but I state it with the same positiveness with which I can assert any fact of memory.

If Mr. Austin had made inquiries—as he should have done—he would have found, as others did, that there was no house in the locality designated as the spot where Lane died.

But all this is as naught. Whatever confidence Judge Edmonds may have had in the coolness and judgment of his friend, the gentleman's statement regarding the doubt existing here, should have sufficed to lead him to caution. But, this out of the question, I cannot conceive how anything could have weighed an iota against the glaring internal evidences in 'The Eventful Nights' noted above, as so plainly indicating that it could not be a narration of facts—that 'the wayfaring men, though fools, could not err therein.'

The grammatical errors that have crept into the article during the last six months, I propose to say nothing about; but I conceive it to be proper to remark, that the title which I gave to the article was not 'Wonderful Revelations—The Eventful Nights,' &c., nor 'Wonderful but True, or The Eventful Nights,' &c., into which it has been variously altered by other hands, but simply, 'The Eventful Nights of August 20th and 21st.'   F. C. EWER.

SAN FRANCISCO, Feb. 7, 1855."

That the above letter should enter quite fully into particulars, and appear to some unnecessarily long, seemed to be proper from the fact that it would probably be read by many, who had never seen nor heard of "The Eventful Nights," and who knew nothing of the circumstances connected with the fiction. With regard to a few repetitions, which will doubtless meet the eye of the reader below, it should be borne in mind, also, that the several papers which make up this article were penned at different times, and addressed to different sets of readers.

—

I understand, that the fiction, to which the above letter relates, has been considered, by some, as bearing a close similarity to "Facts in the case of M. Valdemar," by Edgar Allan Poe. Indeed, after I had published a fiction entitled "The Great Order of The Cave," as a handmaiden to "The Eventful Nights," (the latter taking in its range the whole Heavens—and the former, the whole Earth) an ably edited journal of this city, *The Wide West*, intimated that I was evidently aspiring to be the "Poe of the Pacific."

It is proper for me to state, that after I had prepared the first part of the fiction and a portion of the second, a friend, to whom I read what I had written, remarked to me, that it bore resemblance, in some respects, to one of Poe's papers. I was rather surprised, but requested her to say nothing more, since I preferred to finish the fiction, before I heard or read anything which might influence me even unconsciously to myself. It is a melancholy admission for me to make, perhaps, but the truth is, I had never read anything of Poe's, save "The Raven" and "The Bells." So soon as I had completed "The Eventful Nights," I purchased his entire works, and read the article to which allusion has been made above. There were some three or four points of similarity between Poe's "Valdemar" and "The Eventful Nights," it is true, but any reader who has perused both, cannot but have seen, that the few respects in which the two bore resemblance to each other, were, so far as my article is concerned, of very slight moment, as compared with the important respects in which they utterly differed. The gist of Poe's article consisted in the fact that, through the process of Mesmerizing, which was attempted *in articulo mortis* as an experiment, Valdemar's soul still remained attached to the body after the latter was dead. In the case of "The Eventful Nights" on the contrary, Lane died a natural death, described his sensations through spiritualism and announced to us the condition of the great Future.

Finding, however, that—although at a far distance in the rear of Poe's—my mind was apt to run in a similar train of thought, I considered it as absolutely essential for me to read all that he had ever written, in order not to meet him, even in unimportant particulars, in any fiction that I might write subsequently. The reader may therefore judge of my surprise, on finding myself charged with precisely that which I most desired to avoid.

—

So many interesting facts and letters had collected around "The Eventful Nights," that in order to preserve those which had not already been lost or destroyed and to put them into a compact form, I gathered them into a private volume for my library, believing, moreover, that such a volume would be entertaining to my relatives and more intimate friends.

Among other things in the book, is a paper, showing the analytical and synthetical process of my mind during the writing of the article ; which I prepared under the conviction that the volume would not be complete, unless it contained a recounting of the motives which led me to write the fiction, and a history, so to speak, of its conception and composition.

I have been advised by a number of friends—one or two of whom, on reading the paper, recognized the process of mind recounted, (having been kind enough to sit patiently through my "calls" and allow me to "talk at" them, before writing the fiction)—I have been advised, I say, by these and several others to extract the paper from the volume and lay it before the public. Members of that peculiar species of bores who can get along much better if they utter their thoughts aloud, half to themselves and half to some one else, while arranging an argument or conceiving a fiction, will understand well what I intend to imply by the somewhat colloquial phrase "*talk at.*"

The pronoun in the first person is necessarily repeated innumerable times in the paper. While there would be nothing objectionable in this, so long as the article remained private and open to the perusal of my relatives and friends only, I cannot of course but feel that in presenting it to the world, I lay myself open to a charge of egotism. But recent events have called "The Eventful Nights" so prominently before the public, that I am not sure but that it would be advisable for me to explain myself, even more fully than I have done in the letter given above, particularly since it seems to be believed by many in the States, who did not credit "The Eventful Nights" as a narrative of facts, that I wrote it while in a trance, or under the influence of opium, or something of that sort. It is to satisfy such, as well as to explain myself fully, once and for all, that I have decided to undergo the opprobrium of a charge of egotism, and follow the advice of my friends, by giving extracts from the paper above alluded to, as contained among the manuscripts in my private volume.   The article is entitled :—

THE COMPOSITION

OF

THE EVENTFUL NIGHTS OF AUGUST 20TH AND 21ST:

Being a Paper showing the ANALYTICAL *and* SYNTHETICAL *process during the writing of the article.*

—

I FREELY confess, that the idea of preparing the present paper was suggested by an article of Edgar A. Poe's, entitled "The Philosophy of Composition," in which he describes the *modus* of construction, which ended in the production of "The Raven."

I have for years—I may say from early boyhood—been in the habit of watching the operations and changes of my mind. I could sit down and trace most of the actions of my life—important as well as unimportant—to the motives and combinations of motives from which they sprang, and the operations of my mind prior to and during the composition of "The Eventful Nights," having a bearing upon that article, are so vivid in my memory, that I can lay them bare to whomsoever the exposure may promise entertainment.

In his "Philosophy of Composition," Poe says:—

"I have often thought how interesting a magazine paper might be written by any author who would—that is to say, who *could*—detail step by step, the processes by which any of his compositions attained its ultimate point of completion.   Why such a paper has never been given to the world, I am much at a loss to say—but, perhaps, the autorial vanity has had more to do with the omission than any other cause.   Most writers—poets in especial—prefer having it understood that they compose by a species of fine frenzy—an ecstatic intuition—and would positively shudder at letting the public take a peep behind the scenes, at the elaborate and vacillating crudities of thought—at the true purposes seized only at the last moment—at the innumerable glimpses of idea that arrived not at the maturity of full view—at the fully matured fancies discarded in despair as unmanageable—at the cautious selections and rejections—at the painful erasures and interpolations—in a word, at the wheels and pinions—the tackle for scene-shifting—the step-ladders and demon-traps—the cock's feathers, the red paint and the black patches which, in ninety-nine cases out of the hundred, constitute the properties of the literary *histrio*."

Although this *paper* was suggested by Poe's "Philosophy of Composition," the mental process which I used in the preparation of "The Eventful Nights" was by no means suggested by Poe, since (I am ashamed to confess) the article was entirely written before I read Poe's works. But the analogy which existed between Poe's process of mind in writing "The Raven," and my own in writing "The Eventful Nights," was so striking, and Poe's article interested me so much, that I determined for once wittingly to act upon his hint—follow in his footsteps and record my own mental operations, as he had recorded his, in the belief that, as the "Philosophy of Composition" had been entertaining to me, this might not be without interest to some others.

*   *   *   *   *   *   *   *   *   *   *

In casting about for a subject my great aim was originality. I determined to write *nothing*—rather than follow in the footsteps of another. I have no sympathy for those would-be authors who run about to ring the thousandth change where nine hundred and ninety-nine have been rung already. Give me vileness with originality, rather than respectable triteness. The former has at least something to recommend it—the latter nothing.

While searching for a subject, I remembered a lecture which I had delivered before the Sacramento Mercantile Library Association in June, 1851—the subject of which was "The Universalities of Nature."   In it I had stated that there were certain conditions in nature underlying it and running up through all things.   These were Motion – Forms—Harmony—Connection—Beauty—The Arch—and Eternity. So that the sentence by which we may describe the universe is "Connected and beautiful forms moving harmoniously in arches through all Eternity." I could not but feel that there was some originality in the lecture—at least I had never seen the same thoughts in print nor heard them from the lips of others. It suggested itself to me that what I had said in the lecture was but a part of a system which I had believed, and which I might develop clearly by a little thought. And at first I had an idea of presenting that system to the public. It would be new, and might at least satisfy some who were in doubt as to what they should believe. But although I much desired to publish it, I could not but feel that it was of too metaphysical and dry a character to attract the attention of the general reader.

For the most complete success, I should adopt some subject which was very prominently before the community as a matter of discussion, and combine originality with that.

At the same time it struck me that no writer had ever carried a soul through the gates of death and into the regions beyond—that no one had ever described what may be the sensations and thoughts of a dying man from the time when he ceases to speak—his experience immediately after death, and that strange condition of affairs to which the departed spirit may first awake. Here, at least, was an attractive and—what was of all importance—untrodden field before me, with all the breadth that I could desire. I determined in an instant to enter upon it, but at the same time I did not wish to give up the idea of presenting my system of former belief to the public, for the good of whom it might concern; and I immediately saw that I could combine the two, and at the same time gain another point by interweaving a subject which was agitating men's minds to a remarkable degree—the subject of spiritualism.

These thoughts passed through my mind in about one-fiftieth of the time it has taken the reader to peruse them.

I determined, therefore, to write an article, in which I would describe a dying man, who should converse with me up to the time when his tongue should cease to act and give me the remainder of his experience of death, together with a description of that to which he was awakening, by means of spiritual manifestations. My lecture and former system of belief could then come from him as communications, with a temporary effect upon the reader's mind, arising from the fact of its having apparently all the authority of an announcement from the mighty Spirit Land. I foresaw that my great difficulty would be to create in imagination a state of things—a *physique*, so to speak—for the world after death, which should be entirely original, *totally* different from the condition of affairs surrounding us here—as totally different as is the spirit from the body—but which at the same time would not be impossible. Feeling confident, however, that when it should become necessary for me to describe such a state of things, I could in some way, I knew not how, accomplish the *desideratum* to my satisfaction, I gave little thought to it at the time.

The article would depend for its success upon the excellence of two distinct effects—first, that to be produced from a description of death: second, that to be produced by the development of a new and complete theory of the Infinite God, His works, and the connection between His works and Himself. The latter was somewhat metaphysical, and I foresaw that it would be necessary for me to bring to bear what of ability was within me so to attract the interest of the general reader to the first half, as to induce him to read the last half, which would not otherwise be perused by him. At the same time I felt that however much the first half might attract for the moment, the real value of the article would depend almost entirely upon the originality and consistency of the last half.

Meanwhile I had enough to do to succeed in bringing about the first effect of the article by carrying the man through death; and I approached with determination the more minute portions of my work.

The first point that arose was, what should be the character of the recital—should it bear about it the fictitious air, or not? The answer was clear. For effect's sake, it should by all means be written as a narrative. The great point that I was to bear in mind was, therefore, a combination of probability with originality. The next question was, should the party whose dying is to be described, be an acquaintance of mine or a stranger to me? For obvious reasons, which will appear from a perusal of "The Eventful Nights," I decided that the effect would be hightened were the fictitious character represented as a stranger to me. How then was I to know that he was in a dying condition? The most probable way was through a note sent to me by him. At first, I thought the note should be brought by a little boy; but it struck me the reader would be apt to be rather more interested in a little girl, as the more delicate of the two, and I promptly adopted the latter. It was at this point that I determined to relieve the article from its somber cast, and to add interest to it, by weaving a thread of pathos through its entire length. The father must be in indigent circumstances. The little girl must be in want. A wife would be in the way and would complicate matters too much. The little daughter should be the sole companion of the dying man. Although poor, he must be educated, for he had important truths to acquaint me with. He must live in some cheap tenement on the outskirts of the city.

But as the article opened before me in this condition, I did not fail to see that it would be little else than an enormous lie. And for a day or two, I gave up all thoughts of writing it. It struck me, however, that it might be made the means of good, provided I could make spiritualism a very prominent element in it, and so write it as to deceive at first, but to appear very evidently, on a second and more careful perusal, to be the argument *reductio ad absurdum* to be applied to spiritualism. It might awaken the eyes of some to the fact that they had been in the habit of accepting testimony touching the new doctrines, with too little thought. It might show them to how great a degree they were anxious to believe, rather than properly to search for the truth.

I resumed the matter again, and decided not only to make the whole paper the *reductio ad absurdum*, but to leave concealed improbabilities in the article which would be so great as to amount very nearly, if not quite, to impossibilities.

This suggested to me the self-moving compass, an account of which appears in the early part of the story. The house, too, where the scene occurred, should be near others, and yet no neighbor should visit the dying man to furnish him with anything to eat, or in fact to offer the slightest humane attention. It would not be proper to locate the scene upon a lot where a tenement stood, lest the owner or occupant should object. I thought of selecting my own lot, south-west corner of Sacramento and Hyde streets. But it was too near town, and many might remember that there was no house there. For while keeping in mind the necessity of improbabilities, I did not wish to sacrifice the verisimilitude of the article, upon which in no small degree depended its success. I then decided upon a location in the vicinity of Yerba Buena Cemetery, believing that if I could conceal any appearance of effort in locating the scene there, the solemnity of the place would have a slight effect upon the mind of the reader, the cause of which would not be noted by him at the time. For success, I depended in no small degree upon the *number*, rather than the *intensity* of the effects, which I should thus seek to produce prior to the climax of the fiction. I consulted a map at Wainwright & Randall's office, and selected a lot on McAllister street, (facing the cemetery,) upon which there was no tenement.

The question then arose—Why should Lane send for *me*, rather than any one else? It now struck me, that, from the importance of the information to be gained from him, the reader would think it natural that the spirits should desire its publication, that they should acquaint Lane (who of course must be a believer in spiritualism) with the fact that he was to be the medium of presenting to the world important information, and instruct him to send for an editor, or some one who had access to the columns of a paper. As I have said, I had been the subject of some little remark in 1852 from my connection with the Spiritualists, having been considered as weak-headed enough to believe in the new doctrines. It would not be improbable that he, being a Spiritualist, had heard of me, and if he were represented as unacquainted personally with any editor, it would be the most natural thing in the world for him to send for me. Here the idea that the spirits would know of his decision, and that they might be represented to use the compass to endeavor to communicate to me the fact I was to go out in a south-west direction to Lane's house, occurred to me.

The sympathies of the reader must be gradually awakened for the little girl by slight circumstances, and must be made eventually to cluster strongly around her. To begin with, she must hunt me up in this great city. She must be old enough to be able to go upon such an errand, and yet too young to render her father any material assistance in his sickness. She must persevere in the search for me, but not find my whereabouts until about dusk, when the little one must hasten back, through the darkness, over the lonesome hills to her poor dying father—to her far-away home. There would be no apparent effort in this—it was natural, and at the same time it would tend gradually to awaken the sympathies of the reader.

The next thought that I had about the matter was, that it would by no means be proper for me to go out to the house, and allow the man to die like a dog, without assistance. Besides, I should have witnesses, and one of these should clearly be a physician. Some little skill was to be exercised in keeping from the reader the object of my visit to Lane's house, and at the same time letting drop casually a sufficient motive for my being accompanied while there with friends. The necessity of witnesses seemed, however, to be clear. Accordingly I opened the matter to ———, and ———, told them the plan of my article, and asked them if they had any objections to my using their names in it. They said that they had none, and I determined to make them my companions in the fictitious adventures. Subsequently, however, while writing the article, I changed my mind with regard to this, as I saw that it would give the paper too near an approach to a lie. I rejected real characters for companions, and selected the fictitious titles of "Mr. H." and "Dr. L.," believing that the reader would say, "Well, if this were true—if Mr. E. were sincere in this matter, of course he would have given the names in full of parties to whom we could refer."

My next point was—How should the whole article be planned to be the *argumentum reductio ad absurdum?* Brief thought enabled me to decide upon adopting the grounds of the Spiritualists—that the "odic fluid" is generated in the human system—that all things conduct it—that it is the necessary condition to interlie between mind and matter to enable the former to will the latter into motion—and then show to what an absurdity this theory would lead, by representing Lane's corpse, which of course is matter, as thoroughly charged by us with the fluid, during our final experiments, as bursting open the top of the coffin while we were bearing him in the midst of a crowd (attracted to the spot) towards his grave in Yerba Buena, as rising (of course by means of the willing of hosts of departed spirits)—as rising slowly in a horizontal position, while we stood with the coffin in our arms gazing upward at it—as changing gradually in its upward course from the horizontal to a perpendicular position—and as finally (its grave-clothes fluttering in the wind) entering a small white cloud, which in its course from the east across the heavens bears it out of our sight into the western horizon. This plan I adhered to without a thought of changing it, until the second part was nearly written, when I became convinced that it would not be an appropriate and dignified conclusion to that which preceded—that with it the paper, as a work of art, would not be considered as successful. Acting upon this belief I drew my pen through that portion of the conclusion which I had already written, and wrote that conclusion which appeared in print: giving (in accordance with the theory of the Spiritualists) Lane's soul that power of motion over his dead body, which, from what preceded, would not strike the reader as being equally ridiculous as impossible, while at the same time it was a power which common sense and the universal experience of mankind teach the soul does not and cannot have. This conclusion was also selected, from the fact that it would put a natural and complete close to the article. For if Lane were represented as still having the power to commune with us, the close of the article would have the appearance of depending entirely upon my will, and the reader might still desire and expect further communications at some subsequent time.

But to resume. I now reviewed the work I had gone over. The climax of the fiction was to be the announcement that Lane, during the process of dying and entering the other world, should, through spiritual "tippings," give us his sensations, and describe to us that to which he was awakening. The article must be toned gradually up until this point was gained. The nature of the climax was to be entirely concealed prior to its announcement, while at the same time such hints were to be dropped as would arouse the reader's wonder and curiosity. Although the climax would occur early in the fiction, comparatively, the reader would not be satisfied, as he would still wish to read on and learn what *was* the experience of Lane while dying, and what he saw after death. Had the article been different in this respect, I should not have attempted to write it, since I could have anticipated nothing else than failure. The article would be in two distinct parts, each complete in itself;—the first containing the story of Lane's death, the second, the theory of Deity, Here and Hereafter. The latter would depend for its success upon originality of idea, strangeness, clearness, and beauty of diction. The whole was a hazardous experiment, and the least I could do was to try.

I had now proceeded sufficiently far to take pen in hand. But a difficulty met me at the threshold. Of course, I desired that the article should be read. It should be so commenced, therefore, as strongly to attract the reader's attention at the very outset. The first line should be such, that if any one glanced at it, he would be likely to read the whole sentence. This should be so written as to entice him into reading the second, which should only awaken his attention the more; so that the first paragraph would perhaps cause him to settle himself in his chair for at least a page or so.

Accordingly, for my opening sentence I penned the following, viz:

"I am about to undertake a task—here in the silence of this room—to which I feel impelled by a combination of circumstances, such as, I believe, never surrounded mortal man before."

Having satisfied myself that this would have the desired effect, I endeavored to awaken the reader the more to a wish to peruse what was to succeed, by the following, viz:

"I am hurried to its accomplishment, to the unburdening of my mind, from certain strange intelligence—not only on account of an express order which I have received—the nature and particulars of which will more fully appear below,—but because I feel that I can only relieve my mind from its insufferable weight by laying before the public the occurrences of the last two nights."

Thinking that these two sentences would accomplish my purpose—that I was perhaps sure of the reader's attention for at least a page or so, I decided so to write that page—to give the reader such glimmerings merely of some strange important matter that was to follow, as to induce him fairly to compose himself to accompany where I should lead him, even though it were through the dryer parts of my recital.

I fancied myself, as the narrator, seated in Lane's room, the description of which sprang into my mind at once from I know not what source. I fancied myself as having just taken my pen after the occurrences to write the very article which I was about to write. I described my position and imagined sensations, keeping in view the fact that I was not to prëexpose any of the important points of the article. In this condition I wrote the page, (about three pages of manuscript.) I was, in fact, seated in my own room. But so vivid were my feelings, that I actually felt as though I had witnessed the occurrences I was about to describe. I heard my own loud breathings as I stated, and involuntarily turned round with a shudder towards my bed with a feeling, which some may understand when I say it was akin to a mad wish that I might see the body of a man lying there, lifeless and grim. I should say that during this time, I kept in mind that I should so write as to lead the reader to suppose perhaps that a murder had been committed. I imagined the child seated on a box at the foot of my bed behind me, and as finally stealing to me, putting her arms around my neck, and saying in simple tones and language—

"What are you writing, Sir? Come with me; I am *very* lonesome. Come to father and make him talk."

I wrote on that—"I kissed her upon her fair white forehead and said—'Hush, child! Father will not speak to us any more to-night. You shall go with me to-morrow,—and we'll take father with us'"—when I burst into tears myself. I wrote that "I led her back to her seat and turned quickly,—for the tears were gushing to my eyes," when I threw down the pen, unable from excitement to write any more that night. I could not but feel satisfied that I had attained the effect desired; for if I (foolishly enough, it must be confessed,) had been moved to tears, it was reasonable to suppose that the reader's mere *interest* would be excited sufficiently to induce him to accompany me over the commencement proper of the article, which was now about to follow, and so far beyond, that he would begin to rise towards the climax with me, and not leave me until he had finished at least the first half of the article.

The next evening I sat down to my work to pen the commencement proper of the fiction. The reader will see that there remains little else for me to say, save to record a few incidents that occurred during the writing of the paper, and to note one or two other changes in the minutiæ of the plan at first decided upon, which occurred to me while composing.

I need not say why the dash at the scientific was made at the commencement proper of the recital. I need not say that the parenthesis occurring in the first sentence of that commencement, viz: "I will not (at least upon this occasion) go into the *rationale* of Spiritualism," was inserted to gain a slight effect upon the reader's mind;—as though I had said, "Well, I cannot stop now to do this—but as I am thoroughly committed to the new doctrines, I may as well, after publishing one paper, undertake the matter seriously." Such facts will be sufficiently clear without a hint from me. In addition to the reasons given above for the insertion of the spirit-guided compass, I felt that it would act upon the sentiment of the superstitious in the reader, already prepared from what had gone before to be awakened, and would at the same time be to him, should he review the article carefully after reading it once, a most positive evidence of its fictitious character. The tea-poy, statuette, cross, etc., were actually in my room as I described them. The name of "Little Janie" was adopted principally from the fact that there was no straining for effect in it.

When the article was advanced to the point where the narrator and his friends had reached the house, a difficulty occurred to me which I had not thought of before. I saw that it was necessary for me to write in four different styles, viz: first, the style of the narrative, which from the fact that it was represented as written late at night and hastily, should have an air of simplicity and carelessness about it;—second, the style of Lane while living, serious and impressive;—third, the style of the Spirit who announces what is to be done; and, fourth, the style of Lane while in the Spirit Land. For the style of the unknown Spirit, I affected short disconnected sentences. For the style of Lane after death, I affected—if I may use that convenient and expressive term—the "hyfalutin'." But the first part of the paper succeeded so fully in permanently deceiving large numbers, that I became alarmed, and concluded to leave the internal evidence of the fictitious nature of the article more apparent in the last half, by attempting no disguises of style whatever. The difficulty of accounting for my exact repetition of Lane's words, was easily overcome by representing Lane—in view of the importance of our interview—as instructing us to note down upon the spot all that was said or done.

Lane's first conversation with me was inserted, that I might have an opportunity of showing the reader that the narrator, after investigation, had not been a victim of spiritualism—that therefore his narration was at least worthy of respectful consideration; and that I might also have an opportunity of preparing the disbelieving reader for what was to follow, by presenting what I thought a sensible argument, going to show that the Spiritualist theory was not impossible in the nature of things, nay, that it might be considered as actually probable, since it announced no greater change in the order of things, than science shows has already occurred many a time upon the earth. My object, as will be remembered, was to make the reader believe the article was true until he reached the *denouement*, or until he had carefully looked over the fiction a second time.

Without wishing to reflect upon myself as inclined to the "hyfalutin'" style, I would state that by all means the most difficult part of the article for me to write, was the narrative, that portion which, in fact would seem to be the simplest. This was written several times before I was satisfied with it. Next to the narrative in difficulty of composition, were the disconnected remarks of Lane just before the spirit parted from the body, which were re-written three or four times; and although I finally accepted the last version, I was by no means satisfied with it.

My aim in the death scene was originality. And yet I saw, of course, that it would be folly for me to run counter to the knowledge and universal experience of mankind. I was *forced* therefore to represent Lane's senses as growing dimmer and dimmer, until he could not see and could scarcely hear. I felt that if I could once get him thoroughly dead, I could then enter upon a field where I could range at will in search of originality.

I would state that in order to write as effective a description of the dying of Lane as was possible for me, I lay down upon my bed one evening at eight o'clock, put out the light, and fancied myself going through the process of dying. My imagination became so excited, that in less than five minutes I sprang up alarmed, and had to light the lamp, feel my pulse and look round a little to convince myself that I had not actually died. The next day I wrote the dying scene as it appeared in print.

Consumption was the decease which I selected for Lane as being that around which Melancholy and Beauty hover as attendant angels.

When I had carried Lane through death, it struck me that the process of eliciting information by putting questions and receiving answers from him through "tips" of the table, would be so tedious as to be impracticable; and I decided to represent him as willing the hand of his corpse to grasp a pencil and write what he wished to communicate. For effect's sake, however, I so altered this, that his hand should grasp mine, which should be represented as holding a pencil and writing a question; and I therefore was further urged to endeavor to make the scene at the death sufficiently impressive to warrant, in the eyes of the reader, my *writing* the question, instead of uttering it aloud.

I was engaged in writing the first half during the leisure hours of about a month. I did not, at any time, advance more than a page a day.

The main difficulty in the last half, was so to commence it as to awaken the reader's attention once more after a month's delay, by suggesting to his mind what had preceded, without repeating myself,—to awaken, again, his sympathy for "Little Janie"—and to remind him of precisely what information had been promised from Lane, that he might not expect too much.

My lecture was altogether too long to be inserted as a communication, so I condensed it into two pages and published it in that shape.

I was occupied but a brief space of time in conceiving what I was to write as a description of the condition of things in which Lane found himself after death. Several ideas suggested themselves to me, and the questions which I put to myself, were: Has this been thought of or published before? If so, it was rejected. Would any one be likely to think of this? If so, I rejected it. When I struck upon something which I thought could not but be original, the remaining questions which I asked myself, were: Is this state of things as *utterly* different from this world as is spirit from body? Is it impossible, to say the least for it, to be *true*? Having satisfied myself on these points, I proceeded to write again. The spirit-land should be represented as composed of souls and their ever-varying out-creations. I endeavored to attack materialism by showing that it was possible to conceive of spirit as being without shape, as not occupying *time* to pass through *space*. I endeavored to analyze Infinity and show the reader what a vast difference there was between the Infinite God and man, though his life were infinite in duration. I endeavored to show that it was folly for us to seek to learn (admitting the spiritualist theory to be true) whether, or not, the souls of our friends were happy. I endeavored to make my whole theory harmonious and consistent in all its parts—which cannot be said of Spiritualism. I endeavored to make the answers, purporting to come from the spirit-land, contain something of real moment, and not the insane generalities about progress, and the ridiculous materialisms of "spheres and circles," which we are in the habit of receiving through the instrumentality of the so-called mediums. In fact, I was determined to make Lane *say something*, which, if true, would be of importance to the world.

I was occupied in writing the second half, about five or six evenings. The selection of a title gave me no little annoyance.

When the article was finished, I found that it was complete in all respects, except the disposition of Little Janie.

To have represented her as growing up under my care, and as becoming a staid matron with six bouncing children, or anything after that style, was impossble from the nature of things, and would have been simply ridiculous. What was there for me to do but to kill her and so put an entire completion to the fiction? Accordingly, for the November Number I wrote "Flown." It was intended to be a reverie, in which my thoughts were traced as I sat in my room immediately after her death, while she was lying in her little bed in a room opening into mine. It may strike some readers as an ineffectual attempt at the pathetic. It may be so, but all that I can say is, it was written without effort, and was the dearest flower of my soul, torn up by the roots and offered to the world. If it is rejected of all, I shall still love it tenderly.

—

In the *New York Herald* of the 14th March appeared the following rejoinder from JUDGE J. W. EDMONDS to my letter given above, viz:

"*The Late Spiritual Revelation from San Francisco.*
LETTER FROM JUDGE EDMONDS.
No. 85 CHAMBERS STREET, March 14, 1854.
To the Editor of the Herald:

Your paper of the 12th contains a letter from San Francisco, with the signature of F. C. Ewer, from which it appears that I was fool enough to receive as true an article under his own name, published in the *Pioneer*, a monthly magazine, edited by him, and which purported on its face to be the relation of facts within his own knowledge.

It is true I did so receive it. But I also received a letter from a gentleman of San Francisco, assuring me of its truth. I learned on inquiry that Mr. E. had an office under the General Government. Mr. Lecount, one of the publishers of the *Pioneer*, at that time in this city, and one or two others who professed to know him, gave the assurance that Mr. Ewer was a gentleman utterly incapable of perpetrating such a fraud as that would be if not the truth. Mr. Ewer himself sent to me, by a gentleman direct from San Francisco, a copy of his magazine, without the slightest intimation on his part that the articles were otherwise than what they professed to be, namely, the relation of an actual fact, but that, on the contrary, he had said to his messenger, when interrogated by him, 'Do you think I would publish a lie under my own name?' And twice, through a medium in whose communications I had been in the habit of placing a good deal of confidence, I received messages which tended in the same direction.

It was under these circumstances that I trusted in the truthfulness of Mr. Ewer; and now it would seem—if this letter to you is genuine—that I was gulled and imposed upon by a fabrication.

If the object of the device, and all the pains taken to carry it out, was to impose on my confidence, it has been successful.

If the object was to show me the dangers of spiritual intercourse, and how liable we are to be deceived by false or fabricated communications, it was quite unnecessary; for I long ago learned that, and have earnestly, once and again, given utterance to a warning against that danger.

If the object was to give me the pain of learning that a gentleman occupying a public station, and appearing before the world as the editor of a magazine having some pretension to a standing in our literature, was unworthy the confidence I had reposed in his word—it was equally unnecessary; for I had already learned the public use he had made of a private letter which I had written him in the confidence which I hope will always obtain among gentlemen, and it was not demanded that he should superadd to it the humiliation of proclaiming his own fraud.

If the purpose was to convince me that men having a fair exterior could still be otherwise than what they seemed, it was also unnecessary; for I had not presided so long over a criminal court without learning something of the degradation to which the influence of evil passions, and a perverted education, may sink the fairest seeming among us.

But if the purpose was to induce me to withhold all confidence in my fellow man, or all reliance upon spirit communion, it has signally failed.

I have been imposed upon many times in my life, and, as I grow older and the instances multiply around me, I am admonished to greater caution than was habitual with me in my more confiding years. But I cannot yet withhold all confidence in my fellow man, or in the testimony on any subject, which may reach me through his instrumentality.

                                                  J. W. EDMONDS."

The following letter from one W. J. BAUER was also given immediately after JUDGE EDMONDS', viz:

"*To the Editor of the Herald:*

One or two facts in relation to F. C. Ewer's letter, published in Monday's *Herald*, should be stated, in justice to the Spiritualists of this city.

The first is, that with the exception of Judge Edmonds, and Mr. Toohey, the editor of the *Christian Spiritualist*, the fiction of Mr. Ewer was received with universal skepticism. This is shown by the fact that at a large conference of Spiritualists, held a few evenings after Mr. Ewer's fiction was published in this city, there was but one man possessed of sufficient credulity to manifest the slightest faith in this story, and this man was Mr. Toohey

The next fact that should be mentioned is, that Judge Edmonds, though he has achieved a deservedly high position in this community, both as a man and a jurist, is by no means a Sir Oracle among Spiritualists. Indeed, it is more true of Spiritualists than of any other class of people in the world, that each individual is obliged, from the nature of the facts brought before him, to stand distinctly upon his own judgment, and to refuse positively to have his reputation for sanity or common sense placed upon the shoulders of any man, however high his reputation for sagacity or worldly wisdom.

If you will allow the above statements to go to the world through the medium of the *Herald*, you will greatly oblige   Yours, truly,   W. J. BAUER.

NEW YORK, March 14, 1855."

My response sent to the *Herald* was as follows, viz :

"REPLY TO JUDGE EDMONDS.

To the Editor of the Herald :

With your liberty, I desire to say a few words in response to the letters of JUDGE J. W. EDMONDS and one W. J. BAUER (published in *The Herald* of the 20th March) having reference to me and to 'The Eventful Nights of August 20th and 21st.'

It is perhaps folly for me to state so evident a fact, as that the Judge's letter is utterly wide of the controversy. He does not make the slightest pretension to meet the real merits of the affair, at all. He incontinently packs up, without saying one word, and leaves the field.

Yes, it is even so ;—he has been weak enough to re-publish as true—as corroborative of his theory, a fiction from which the slighest analysis would have developed several impossibilities and numberless improbabilities—a fiction, which is evidently an argument showing his own proposition to be absurd—a fiction, which, even it were not an argument against himself, contains a theory before which his own must fall,—and to crown all, he has held solemn conversations with a fictitious character, with whom, even if the tale were true, he could not, according to its statements, have held any communication whatever. Not one item does he deny, and the controversy is in fact closed.

But he is not utterly undeserving of praise in the affair. For it cannot but be admitted that he has had the frankness to come out and acknowledge (humiliating, though it may be,) that he is in a corner. Frankness is a jewel. Whether he could have taken any other step, is not perhaps to be inquired into too closely. It is—one must confess—no very pleasant admission for a man to be compelled to make, that, after having been for years upon the bench, deciding upon the soundness or fallacy of arguments, he should have been so far led astray—he should have been 'fool enough,' to use his own phrase, to admit and re-publish an argument going decidedly to disprove the very proposition which he seeks to establish. Indeed, Mr. Editor, on the principle of not kicking a man when he is down, I have no desire to do aught else than to commend the Judge to the kind sympathies of the public.

But what does this lame rejoinder of his amount to? Why, finding himself in an inextricable predicament, he struggles to get out of his corner by explaining how it happened that he got in, and, under the circumstances, crying 'Mercy!' The ridiculousness of his pitiful situation, would induce me, now that the controversy is virtually closed, to say no more: but as his explanation contains several assertions, expressed and implied, which call for a flat denial from me, I am forced to the melancholy resort of driving him out of his corner and from the last beam where he has a foothold.

His explanation appears to be that, first, he learned on undoubted authority, I was a truthful man, and incapable of publishing a fraud. I commend him to the same kind authorities still, and to that portion of my letter in the *Herald* of the 12th March, to which he has forgotten to allude, in which I stated, that, I conceived I had a perfect right as a truthful man to propound a theory which I had never seen in print before, and which I believed might not be without interest to some—to hold up, even at a charge of arrogance, the result of an unaided mind on earth in contrast with a theory purporting to come from a world beyond the grave—to contrast a theory which is consistent in all its parts, and to say the least, not impossible, with a theory which contradicts itself, and therefore cannot possibly be true. I believed I had a perfect right to weave that theory into a fiction, which as a whole. would be the argument *reductio ad absurdum* to be applied against spiritualism, without subjecting myself to the charge of being a man regardless of 'the high dictates of truth.' It may be an evidence of unusual sagacity in the Judge, that he has not attempted to violate *all* common sense, by denying the truth of the above. But until he shall have done so, he must not expect me to exhibit an equal want of common sense with himself, by noticing further a mere assertion of his, which has already been fully answered.

His second explanation is, that I sent him a copy of the Magazine by a gentleman direct from San Francisco, saying to that gentleman, 'Do you think I would publish a lie under my own name?' My memory is tolerable, and it only serves me with the fact that I sent an exchange to Judge Edmonds of the *Sacred Circle*, while the other exchanges were preparing for the mail. But this is child's play. What could the Judge desire to establish, more than that I wished to have a Magazine go direct to him? If, in his agitation, he is anxious to excite sympathy for himself through this fact, I will give him the opportunity. I did direct a Magazine to him, put it into the mail, and, of course, positively intended that it should reach him. But before I proceed further, let me in this connection make an extract from his letter:

'If the object of the device, [says he,] and all the pains taken to carry it out, was to impose on my confidence, it has been successful.'

I positively deny that there was any *device* on my part. I positively deny that I took any pains to deceive the Judge. I sent him the Magazine, and I had a perfect right either through private hands or through the mail, to place it beneath his eyes. The theory developed in it was utterly opposed to his, and I supposed it would be entertaining to him. I thought, of course, that he would read it with interest. But I gave the man credit for ordinary sagacity ; he had been ' for years upon the bench of a criminal court,' and I was never more astonished in my life than when I received his letter announcing that he had been rash enough to publish the first half. Even then I supposed that when he should see the last half, he would certainly find out his error. But no, he completed his humiliation by republishing that also, and giving several communications, which he, forsooth, had received from the fictitious character, John F. Lane, who, as I have said above, even if the article were true, was represented as utterly beyond the reach of communicating with any one on earth.

But whether I or any one else did or did not send him the Magazine, the Judge seems to forget, in his agitation, that it really makes no difference. Supposing, for the sake of argument, that I sent a Magazine to him by a messenger direct,—it will not help the matter for him, since he none the less blindly overlooked all the internal evidences of the fictitious character of the article, and disregarded the advice of his friends who cautioned him against it.

There is little else for me to state. The Judge remarks, that 'if the object of the *device* [forsooth!] was to show me the dangers of spiritual intercourse, and how liable we are to be deceived by false or fabricated communications, it was unnecessary, as I had long ago learned the fact, and cautioned others in relation to it.' It is to be regretted that the Judge was not guided by the light of his experience.

' If,' says he, ' the object was to give me the pain of learning that a gentleman, etc. etc., was unworthy of confidence, it was unnecessary ; for I had already learned the public use he had made of my private letter to him, and it was not demanded that he should superadd to it the humiliation of publishing his own fraud.' As for making public use of a private letter, I would state that the Judge is misinformed. I have not allowed either his letter, or any copy of it, ever to leave my hands. I consider it equally sacred with a letter from my sister. If 'publishing my own fraud ' is not beneath the Judge to charge, after my first letter to the *Herald*, completely refuting it, (and still unanswered,) I assure him that I consider any response to it beneath me to make.

' If,' says he, ' the purpose was to convince me that men may not be what they seem, it was unnecessary : for I had not presided so long over a criminal court without learning something of the degradation to which the influence of evil passions and a perverted education may sink the fairest seeming amongst us.' His Honor grows facetious ;—but really he reminds one a little of ' Patience on a monument smiling at Grief.' He seems to intimate, that he has seen such fellows as I am before, at the bar of a criminal court. Oh, Judge—Judge ! I cannot assert that this is another evidence that his Honor's mind is a little shaken from its balance, for my associations during life have not been very intimate with criminals; but I will state, that curiosity led me once to visit the Insane Asylum at Stockton, in order to investigate somewhat the condition of the unfortunates placed there for a restoration of mental health, and really the Judge's condition calls up to my mind recollections of a most sad and unpleasant character. But admitting what he would intimate, he only makes the matter worse in his agitation, the further he goes. For even if I were a man regardless of the dictates of truth, his Honor but admits that his experience has availed him naught.

' But if,' says he, ' the purpose was to induce me to withhold all confidence in my fellow man, it has signally failed.' Ah, Judge, it should teach you to have less confidence in yourself.

But with regard to all these ' ifs,' I beg the Judge to bear in mind once again, that there were *no* intentions whatever on my part, for I sincerely assure him, that I had not the slightest idea he would be ' fool enough ' to re-publish ' The Eventful Nights of August 20th and 21st.'

If it would not be considered as arrogance in me to drop one little word of advice to him, I would say, that by far the sagest plan for him to have adopted, when he found himself in his corner, would have been to remain there, looking up with an air of unconcern, and when the laugh was over, and his agitation was calmed, he could have slipped quietly out, and gone on his way into obscurity, unnoticed by any one.

One word more, and then farewell. The world will hardly believe, Judge, that there are not truthful spirits enough among the ' spheres and circles ' to tell you (if you have not sagacity enough to see it yourself) whether the next document you would gladly devour, be genuine or not. Alas for that man, who putteth not his own theory into practice !

And now, one line for Mr. Bauer. I am very ready to believe that large numbers of the N. York Spiritualists saw the fictitious narrative of ' The Eventful Nights.' It would be a sad commentary on the acumen of many of my friends in that great city, if this were not so. Moreover, were it not so, I should really be alarmed for fear that I *had* composed a downright enormous lie, and was unworthy of being regarded as a truthful man. But if Mr. Bauer will come to San Francisco, I will show him by letters from New York, that he was misinformed with regard to the fact that ' The Eventful Nights ' was discredited by *all* there. But the most unfortunate affair of the whole is, that this man, Bauer, should, now that the Judge is in his sad—his pitiful predicament, turn against him and seek to cast him overboard. Well may his Honor exclaim, ' Save me from my friends.' Why—why—why—Mr. Bauer, *isn't* Judge Edmonds a Sir Oracle of the Spiritualists ?   F. C. EWER.

P. S. I notice that *The Christian Spiritualist* promises me a blast. It would be ungenerous in me not to allow the galled jades to wince. And so, without more remark, I touch my hat and retire from among their writhings, leaving them ' to settle it, somehow, among themselves.'
San Francisco, April 16, 1855.   F. C. E."

To conclude, I would remark, that on the 16th of April, the following brief communication appeared in the *Daily Chronicle* of this city, viz :

" THE COCK AND BULL STORY—'JOHN F. LANE.'

Editors Chronicle :

It is a curious fact, if Mr. Ewer's ' John F. Lane ' be fiction, that there did live and die in our own day and generation, a real ' John F. Lane.' He was a young gentleman of distinguished

ability and attainments, but impatient of distinction.   He died by his own hand, during the
Florida war.   The following is an extract from the list of graduates of the Military Academy,
published in 1850:

'JOHN F. LANE—Brevet Second Lieutenant of Artillery, July 1st, 1828.   Second Lieutenant
Fourth Artillery, same date.   Acting Assistant Professor of Mathematics, Military Academy,
from August 31st, 1828, to February 1st, 1829.   Assistant Quarter-Master from June, 1834, to
May 17, 1835.   Captain Second Dragoons, June 8, 1836.   Colonel, commanding regiment Mounted
Creek Volunteers, serving in Florida war, from September 1, 1836, to October 19, 1836.   Died,
October 19, 1836, at Fort Lorane, Florida.'

There, Messrs. Editors, is a veritable, genuine 'John F. Lane,' and no mistake.   When Judge
Edmonds summoned the spirit of 'J. F. L.,' who is authorized to say that the genuine John did
not respond?   A."

MR. NISBITT has himself so neatly plunged the point of his penknife
into this soap-bubble, that no further remark is required from me.
Says he :

"Oh, there are lots of *liars* in the other world, so the Spiritists tell us.   What matters it
whether the 'Cocklane Ghost' itself, or the 'spirit' of Baron Munchausen, or of the 'genuine
John,' trotted out and 'sold' this crazy Judge Edmonds?   To adopt the sentiment of Lord
Grizzle's excellent remark to Queen Dollalola, we may say:

'Spirits !—why, madam, 't is all flummery :
He made the spirits first, and then he saw them.' "

OFF CAPE HORN.

BY LAWRIE.

HERE Ed. my boy, here 's to you, though the howling of the deep,
Gives angry warning that the gale, has waken'd from its sleep;
What if it be? no better time to pledge a friend so true!
With storm and darkness round me then, I drink a health to you.

I 've pledged you oft, in many a scene, where all was bright and fair,
Around the festive board at eve, with many a friend to share;
Ah me! how chang'd is all since then, for time has taught us how
Some hearts, that pledg'd the truest then, breathe little friendship now.

I ve pledg'd you in the wilderness, where none could see or hear
Our fun, except the forest trees, or some wild forest deer;
As leaning on our rifles, by the watch-fire burning bright,
Our laughter has reecho'd, 'mid the stillness of the night.

'Tis but a little time ago, since all these joys were ours,
And all our dreams of future years, were bright as summer flow'rs;
I dream no more ; the brightest hope, that ere my vision drew,
Is fled—but here, I fill and drain, a brighter dream to you.

And here's to those who still are true, as they were wont to be;
Old friends, my heart is with you all, though I am on the sea:
And midst the storm that's raging, and the howling of the blast,
I drain a goblet to you all, though it should be my last.

DREAMY REVERIE.

BY J. SWETT.

I AM dreaming, I am dreaming
Of my pleasant mountain home,
Where the morning sun is beaming
On the hills I loved to roam.

I am dreaming, I am dreaming
Of meadows green and sweet,
Where the brooks so brightly gleaming,
In quiet beauty meet.

I am dreaming, I am dreaming
Of little mountain dells,

Where the evening sunlight streaming
In mellowed radiance dwells.

I am dreaming, I am dreaming
Of maidens I loved best,
Of dark eyes brightly beaming
And lips that mine have prest.

I am dreaming, I am dreaming,
My fleeting life away—
And my darkest hours are teeming
With visions bright and gay.

THE WAR IN EUROPE—THE ORIGIN—THE COST—THE END.

—

THE mass of the people in both Hemispheres can take but little real interest in the present war, or the objects designed to be accomplished by the parties engaged in it. It is a war of ambition and conquest, on both sides. Russia wants more Turkish territory and a free outlet for her naval and commercial marine through the Dardanelles into the Mediterranean. England and France resist these designs of Russia— not because the Czar is despotic, and his subjects barbarous,—not to promote freedom in Turkey, or to protect the integrity of that Empire, but simply to maintain their own supremacy in the affairs of Europe.

The origin of the war has grown out of a desire to prevent Russia acquiring more territory and political power in Europe, and to maintain intact and inviolate, the present balance of power among the large maritime States on that Continent. In other words, to confine Russia to her present territorial limits, rather than to protect the weak, and redress the wrongs of the human race, or give freedom to the oppressed. The English Government, when speaking its honest sentiments on this subject, has had the candor to acknowledge, that jealousy of the Czar, and the prospective ascendency of Russia in the affairs of Europe, constitute the sole reason for the war. Even Napoleon has had the fairness to justify the war on this ground. In his late speech upon the opening of the French Chambers, he declared that this war had separated France from a " Power, which for forty years had menaced the independence of Europe." For the proof of our declaration, that this war was not commenced and is not prosecuted, to protect the integrity of the Turkish Empire, and to defend the weak against the strong, let us appeal to history.

A few years since, when Russia united with Austria, and hurled her legions upon the brave and struggling Hungarians, neither Great Britain nor France had any sympathy for the weak and oppressed. When appealed to by the Hungarians for aid, they gave the patriots to understand, that they could not interfere in their behalf, nor offer them any assistance. They therefore permitted Austria and Russia, with their combined armies, to overwhelm those brave and struggling defenders of the liberties and independence of their country. Indeed, Louis Napoleon not only operated against the oppressed and struggling Hungarians, but he refused the exiled refugees an asylum in France, and sought even to have them expelled from the dominions of every country in Europe. Not only this, but more. After the war was over, he complimented the Emperor of Austria and the Czar of Russia, for " crushing out," the spirit of liberty in Hungary, and for reducing its people to slavery.

Now, if Great Britain and France desire to convince the world, that they are leagued together for the defense of the liberties of the oppressed and the rights of the weaker States, how are they going to justify their conduct to the world, in not having protected Hungary—in not having resisted then, the conquering armies of the Czar ? How was it they did not then (as they are now doing,) appeal to the civilized world to unite with them in protecting the brave defenders of independence ? They had no sympathy then with suffering humanity,—on the contrary, they took sides with its oppressors.

What makes the present position of the French Emperor more singular and inexplicable, is the fact, that the Czar of Russia and the Emperor of Austria, refused to acknowledge Louis Napoleon as the reigning monarch of France, until he had justified their conduct toward the Hungarians, and until he had, at their request, sent a French army to Italy, to put down the Republican Revolution in that country. It was not until after he had carried out all of these menial and humiliatory demands and instructions, that they consented to overlook the obscure origin of his family, and acknowledge him as the head of the French nation.

And how stands the case with England ? When Napoleon accomplished the overthrow of the French Republic, and caused himself to be proclaimed and inaugurated Emperor upon its ruins, Lord Palmerston, then the British Secretary of Foreign Affairs, complimented him for the act ; for doing which, he was indignantly expelled the British Cabinet. The Government of England considered that he had insulted the whole British nation by his conduct, and the Cabinet and people drove him into obscurity. But this once French-Emperor-hating British Cabinet, soon after, reversed its decision and openly justified Napoleon ; and, although they too have been expelled from power, it was by no means for this cause, since Lord Palmerston is now Prime Minister.

When Russia, Austria and Prussia invaded and conquered Poland—destroyed her Constitution—abolished her Government—dismembered and divided her territory—murdered and exiled her sons—neither France nor Great Britain interfered for their protection ; neither offered aid, nor came to the assistance of the brave and struggling defenders of Poland. No, to their eternal shame, neither of those Powers even remonstrated against this act of barbarism. The deed was done in mid-day, and in the face of all Europe ; and the record will stand as a monument to the eternal perfidy of the parties who inflicted this outrage, as well as to those who permitted it to be done.

When the oppressed people of Italy rose in their own right, and by their sovereign authority, to redress the wrongs which they and their country had suffered for so many centuries, and to overthrow one of the worst systems of Governmental tyranny and despotism in the world, the present Emperor of France dispatched an army to uphold the Government, and to conquer and subdue the people. The French Emperor was successful ; and the Republicans, who commenced the revolution, and who would have succeeded in establishing the freedom and independence of the Italian States, had not this mercenary foreign army been sent against them, were either all slaughtered in cold blood, or banished their country. Here France and Austria combined to oppress the weak, and to fasten tyranny around the necks of a people who were gallantly defending their rights. Although England did not send an army to conquer the patriots, she permitted those two Powers to inflict this outrage on a people over whom they had no legal control. To the best of our knowledge she did not even remonstrate against the deed.

The history of the acquisition of the Crimea, the present seat of war, by Russia, is another striking case in point. This country, from the year 1474 to 1783, belonged to Turkey. Catharine II. of Russia, however, in 1783, succeeded in corrupting the Khan, or native Prince, induced him to abdicate in favor of Russia, and the armies of that Empire marched into the Crimea. The Turks, as well as the native Tartars of the Crimea, waged a long and bloody war with Russia to recover this part of the Turkish Empire, but Catharine succeeded in wresting it from them. The Turks on that occasion received no support from either France or England in maintaining the integrity of their Empire, and in resisting the aggressive policy of Russia. Since then, other Turkish territory has been seized by Russia, and annexed to her dominions without any interference from either of the Allied Powers. At present, however, they are seriously concerned and incensed at the ambition of the Czar, and are now appealing to all nations to aid them in arresting further acquisition of territory by Russia. Time will show with what success.

The history has as yet been but imperfectly written, in which the world beheld England uniting with the Czar of Russia to overthrow in France the Great Napoleon, the uncle of the present Emperor, for establishing the very same character of institutions and government which now exist in that country. Then she defended the claims of the Bourbons against the Napoleons, and to uphold them she waged war for the space of a quarter of a century, sacrificed oceans of the best blood of her people, and squandered countless treasure. The result was, the Napoleons were all banished, and the Bourbons once more ascended the throne of France. Now she has deserted the Bourbons, and to uphold the Napoleons, her former enemy, she has leagued with them to wage a deadly war upon the Czar, her former friend and ally. The Bourbons are all exiled, and the nephew of the great Napoleon now wears their diadem. What solemn mockery, in the face of these facts, is the present interest professed to be felt by the Allies for the rights of humanity !

Why should England go abroad, or at least out of her own dominions, to give protection to the weak and redress the wrongs of the human race ? Is she just now suffering remorse for the wrongs causelessly committed upon the untutored and unarmed inhabitants of what is now called British India ? Can she, with her present professions, justify herself for invading the numerous principalities and kingdoms of India, and, without any provocation, violently seizing and annexing, as she then and there did, whole States to her Empire—for dethroning their princes—dispossessing the natives of their lands and their homes—for slaughtering in cold blood millions of men, women and children—condemning thousands to drag out life in dungeons and prisons, out of the reach of the sympathies and support of their "kith and kin," and for consigning all the living to bondage, and placing over them English task-masters, who were allowed to rule with a rod of iron ? Can she justify such acts as these, with her present professed devotion to the rights of the weaker States and the liberties of the human race?

What has she done for Ireland, her neighbor—her companion in arms—her chief ally in war and resource in peace ; Ireland, whose statesmen, warriors, poets, philosophers and historians have spread the fame and dominions of Great Britain to every quarter of the world? What has she done for her? Where are the monuments of England's love and philanthropy for the Emerald Isle? Has she not smitten her people with penury and want—yea, with disease and death? Is she not "thinning out" Ireland, as one of her statesmen expresses it, of her native inhabitants, to give place to their conquerors? England's love for the weak and defenseless is like that which the vulture shows to the lamb.

If England be sincere in her present professions, she should first begin at home to protect the weak and oppressed. In the very center and core of her own dominions she can commence the work, in the language of one of her greatest statesmen, "to redeem, regenerate and disenthrall" mankind. Let her cease to overtax the dissenters and other classes to support a sumptuous and princely order of Government clergy and nobility. Let her abolish the unnatural, corrupt and corrupting union of the Church and the State. Under her own eyes and in her own dominions she can find a field large enough for the exercise of her charities and good will to man, without going abroad to discover objects for her sympathy and benevolence. Charity begins at home.

What has France been for the last three-quarters of a century? What at this moment but one vast slaughter-house of liberty—where the sons of freedom have been butchered in cold blood, or shipped by thousands to the pestilential marshes of Cayenne—where freedom of speech is prohibited, and the liberty of the press is gagged—where the Legislature is but the tool of a usurping and perjured despot, from whose Government every vestige of Constitutional liberty has been "rooted out," and whose exiled sons, driven from their own country, are living in poverty upon the soil of that Empire now leagued with her in close alliance for the championship and defense of Constitutional liberty throughout the world. History, indeed, might be searched in vain, to discover more glaring imposture and ranker hypocrisy than the Allies have exhibited and offered to the world as an excuse for the war. The reasons they assign as a vindication of their united attack upon Russia, belie their nature—are contrary to their policy, and are a libel upon the whole history and practice of their Governments.

It has been semi-officially published in England and France, that should these Powers succeed in humbling the Czar and in wresting from him a part of his dominions, they will then turn their united attention and energies to "putting things in order" in the United States. What things do these two Powers propose to put in order in this country? The people are not suffering here from foreign invasion—from domestic tyranny, or from penury and want. We are all peacefully cultivating the soil—extending our commerce, foreign and

domestic—increasing our products, manufactories and mechanic arts—
multiplying our churches, public schools, colleges, and other seminaries
of learning, and are enjoying in a large degree peace, prosperity and
contentment.   What are they then coming here to do?   Our country
has generously opened its arms to receive the poor and oppressed of
every clime—given them homes for themselves and children, and
shielded and protected them in all things.   Our people are free—conscience is free, speech is free, the press is free.   What, then, is it they
propose to put in order?

We suppose they consider that our country, too, is very likely to
have some influence in the affairs of States—something to do with
the common destiny of the world, and they would restrain our influence and restrict our progress.   Well, let them come.   They will find
that the Young Giant of the West is prepared to meet them.   We
fear them not.   If they should be fool-hardy enough to attempt it, they
would soon find a mighty nation in arms at once, and united to a man
—ready to meet them on the beach, and dispute every inch of ground,
rather than permit the foot of a foreign enemy to invade and contam-
inate the soil of our country.   But England and France will attempt
to do no such thing—they would be guilty of no such folly.   They
want our cotton, rice, tobacco, sugar, breadstuffs, provisions and gold;
and besides all these, however much they may bluster, they want,
above all things, peace with the United States.

We have shown, we think, conclusively, from the whole history and
practice of the Governments of the Allied Powers, that it was no love
for Turkey—no desire to protect her people from the tyranny of the
Czar, that induced them to espouse her cause against Russia—but
jealousy of the ambition of the Czar, and the prospective ascendency
of Russia in the affairs of Europe.   And the historian, who will
truthfully narrate the origin of this war, will so record it.

We now propose to consider the cost of the war.   The English
Government at this time is struggling under a heavy National Debt,
growing out of the last European War.   That war, into which the
Younger Pitt plunged England, in order to overthrow Napoleon and
reinstate the Bourbons on the throne of France, added £600,000,000
sterling to the National Debt; or in Federal Money, $3,000,000,000.
The mere annual interest on this sum, is nearly £23,000,000, or
$115,000,000.   The cost of the last Continental War, to England,
alone, from 1803 to 1815, was £1,159,729,256, or $5,798,646,280.
During the five last years of this war, the annual expense to England
was as follows :

In 1812 the war expenditures were			£103,421,538
In 1813 " " "			120,952,657
In 1814 " " "			116,483,889
In 1815 " " "			116,491,051

Total in four years................ £457,709,135

All this vast sum, too, was incurred, in addition to the loss of human
life, to put down Napoleon and to place upon the throne one of the
Bourbons, over a people who would greatly have preferred his room to

his company. The end of this war—a war extending through nearly a quarter of a century—resulted in overthrowing Napoleon, and in sending him captive to St. Helena, where he died a prisoner in the hands of that Government now leagued with his nephew, against the Bourbons and the Czar. Truly the times have changed.

This immense National Debt, let it be remembered, was created then by paying, as she is now doing, the expense of the armies of her allies. The expense of arming, equipping and transporting to the Crimea is estimated by Government at £150 for each infantry soldier, and for each cavalry soldier, £300. From this official estimate of the cost of transporting troops, in addition to the outlay for provisions, ammunition, tents, monthly salaries for officers and privates, horses, contingent expenses, etc., necessary to carry on the war, it is reasonable to suppose, that the allies have already expended over £100,000,000 sterling, or $500,000,000. The heaviest part of the expenses of the war must necessarily fall upon England. This sum does not include the expenses of the navy. The theater of the war, on account of its great distance from the point of embarkation, will make the cost of conducting the struggle fully as expensive to Great Britain, as was the last European War. From this statement it will be seen, that the cost of the war to the allies, is destined to be immense, should the contest be extended for even one year longer. If they should not be successful in the meantime, we apprehend that the Cabinets of both Governments will be seriously embarrassed, and it would not be unreasonable to expect to find Louis Napoleon once more exiled from his country, and to see France again changed from an Empire to a Republic. That it will shake England from center to circumference, we think is clear, and it may end in the overthrow of the Throne, the Nobility and the Church, and in placing the Government in the hands of the people and the commoners of the "Fast Anchored Isle."

We now propose to consider the probable end of the war. We can see and know but little of the real political condition of Europe from the military and diplomatic movements of the several despots, who rule over it. They just now, manage the war, and shape the affairs of Europe to suit themselves. This exclusive privilege cannot, however, always belong to them; the continent of Europe is on the eve of great events,—events more important to the welfare of the human race, than have ever yet occurred. Kings and rulers cannot forever keep in force their present Balance-of-Power System—or confine the States of Europe to their present rulers and territories. The people of Europe, ignorant as they may be—priest-ridden and enslaved as they are by their masters, have yet independence and strength enough left, to overwhelm their oppressors, and disenthrall themselves. They need but the opportunity to strike the blow and free the world from bondage ; and this war may enable them to do it.

The great struggle of the Allies now is, first, to keep down the threatened republican revolution in Italy,—second, to force Austria and Prussia to join them against Russia. This will be found very difficult—but they may be successful. Should Austria join the Allies, the Czar will strike her such a blow, as will make the very throne of the imbecile Joseph totter to its base. Never did the head of a great nation possess ampler means for overwhelming an enemy, than the Czar at this time possesses, to humble and punish Austria, should she take sides with the Allies against him.

It is well known that the Czar exercises a powerful influence over all those who profess the faith of the Greek Church. The insurrection at Epirus and Albania was stirred up by the Greeks. They have adhered to the cause of Russia against the Allies throughout, notwithstanding the occupation of Athens and Piræus by a French army. The secret, and even open, opposition experienced by the Allies from the Greeks at Balaklava, Varna and Gallipoli, prove that their sympathies are with Russia, and not with the Allies.

The Serbs, a warlike nation contiguous to Austria, and numbering more than a million of people, form the principle focus of the Slavic and Greek Christians in the Turkish Empire. The Austrians south of the Danube, the Save and the Drave, to the shores of the Adriatic, are almost exclusively inhabited by Slavic tribes, such as Illyrians, Serbs, Croats, Marlachs, Dalmats, etc., all of whom profess the faith of the Greek Church, and of course sympathise with Russia. All of their traditionary and historical recollections—all of their sentiments of religion and nationality are concentrated into a deadly and unrelenting hostility to the Turks and the Mohammedan faith. These people never would take up arms to support Austria in defending Turkey against Russia.

So well convinced is the Austrian Government of this fact, that she only ventured to send to the Principalities of Moldavia and Wallachia (in dispute between Russia and Turkey,) those regiments in her service, in which the Germans, Magyars and Italians prevailed. Indeed, so great is her dread of these people, that in a dispatch of the Austrian Secretary of Foreign Affairs to Count Colloredo, the Austrian Minister at the Court of St. James, which was officially read to Lord Clarendon, the Vienna Cabinet thus confesseth its fears. The Secretary says, " If Russia should decide to carry on the war beyond the Danube, vigorously, a rising of the Christian populations might have incalculable results." In other words, the Vienna Cabinet acknowledges, that a rising of the Christians in Turkey in favor of Russia, might easily extend to their brethren in Austria, who, united with Russia, would soon menace the very existence of Austria herself.

From these facts, it is easy to see that, should Austria join the Allies, the Czar would only have to make an appeal to all the Slavonic tribes of Turkey, cross the Danube with a powerful army, set fire to Servia, Bulgaria and Greece, in order to extend the conflagration to Austria. Nicholas would dread such a tempest as those Christians would create, and which might, under any other circumstances, become in the long run too terrible to control. He would put himself at their head, only in the event of Austria joining the Western Powers. Not even an alliance with Prussia would equal in magnitude and efficiency an alliance with these Eastern Christians. They would furnish myriads of fanatical warriors, who would fight with furious desperation. They could hardly be more than prepared to take the field either, before they would also be joined by all Hungary, and with the Czar at their back, they would soon carry their victorious banners into the very streets of Vienna.

The united army of these tribes and Hungary would not long be pouring into Austria, before a formidable rising of the Republicans of Italy would take place, and thus complete the ruin and humiliation of Austria. Should Prussia likewise join the Western Powers, the Czar would have at his command, an army equally formidable to assail her, as that with which he would assail Austria. He would be forced for his own protection to proclaim the re-establishment of the independence of Poland, and to pledge himself to support it. Such an announcement as this, would call forth every Pole in Russia, Prussia and Austria. Armed for freedom, they would pour their united legions on Austria and Prussia, with deadly effect. The Poles would fight in such a war with desperate courage. Thrice, therefore, is the Czar armed for vengeance on his enemies. In such a condition of affairs, he would be willing to lose Poland and content himself in retaining the remaining part of his present dominions, for the pleasure of seeing the thrones and principalities of his enemies crumbling into ruins.

The Allies would find themselves in such an event, so impaired and harrassed at home, that they could render neither Austria nor Prussia any material assistance. The small German States would gladly embrace such an opportunity to free themselves from the tyranny of Austria and Prussia. Ireland would be found also ready then to break with England, and this would give the Allies ample reasons for work at home. They would find as much as they could do to keep down anarchy and revolution in their own States. Indeed, it is natural to suppose, at least, that France would be convulsed with civil war. This state of things, too, would have the effect of removing the seat of war from Russia to the heart of Europe. The Czar, thus far removed from these terrible scenes of battle and confusion, could afford to see anarchy and revolution waving their horrid scepter over the broken thrones of his enemies. Such a result as this, would also change the character of the present war. It would no longer be a contest between despots for supremacy and power, but a deadly conflict between an infuriated and enraged people against their rulers. In such an emergency, the Czar could say to his foes, " You have 'sowed the wind, and you may now reap the whirlwind,'—your people have hurled you from power, and broken your thrones in pieces,—Europe is now all Republican, and Turkey has been stricken from the list of nations.

This must be the winding up and end of the war, should Austria and Prussia join the Western Powers. Such a change in the objects and designs of this conflict, would be hailed with delight by the Republicans of Europe and America. The change would be auspicious to man's deliverance and liberty everywhere. Europe then indeed, would be "redeemed, regenerated and disenthralled, by the genius of universal emancipation." The bondsman would then no longer wear the livery of his lord and master—kings no longer sway an iron scepter over their subjects—no longer live sumptuously in their palaces, and sport with the sufferings and toil of the people. With Europe free, and

America free, the world would present the gratifying aspect of approaching the dawn of the earth's great jubilee.

In conclusion, we may remark, that, while we condemn the policy of the Governments concerned in the war,—while we cannot sympathize with that policy, we deeply sympathize with their people—and regard them as belonging to the great brotherhood of man. When they shall strike a blow for the independence and liberties of their countries, and assert their rights as freemen, they will find Americans ready to sympathize with them—to bid them God speed in their efforts. We who know the value of liberty, cannot—will not side with the present projectors and managers of the war. They are fighting to maintain their own supremacy in Europe, and not to secure freedom and happiness to their people, and while this is the case, we shall be unconcerned spectators of the struggle.

HOME LYRICS: THE GOLDEN GATE.

BY CAXTON.

Old Thebes could boast of her gates of brass,
  As they grated on hinges hoary,
And loosened their bolts for a monarch to pass,
  On his errands of guilt and glory.

But their portals were closed on a nation of slaves,
  Kneeling low at the foot of a Pharaoh,
And the Nile now waters an Egypt of graves,
  From sepulchral Philæ, to Cairo.

Remorseless Time, in his journeyings on,
  Like Samson, at Gaza, of old,
On his shoulders her hundred gates have bore,
  And covered their sheen with mold.

But further than Ind, in the western world,
  Unknown to the sages olden,
Young Freedom, at length, has her banner unfurled,
  In a city whose Gate is Golden.

Its glittering bars are the breakers high,
  Its hinges are hills of granite,
Its bolts are the winds, its arch is the sky,
  Its corner-stone a planet!

Inside of its portals no slave bows his head,
  To priestess of On or of Isis,
Or covers the ground a monarch may tread,
  With the slime of a minion's kisses.

But proud of his home in a city so fair,
  Enthroned on her hillocks seven,
He stands like a Roman, and breathes the free air,
  And kneels to no God, but in heaven.

No giant can tear from their pillars away,
  The Golden Gate of his glory,
For as long as the winds and the waters play,
  It shall swing on its hinges hoary.

OLD HARVARD.

BY OUTIS.

Do you remember with what an air the gray-headed Sam, venerable Ethiop, drove the old carryall, ('twas muddy that day,) round the carriage-sweep, and drew up, all standing, before the front door? Phœbus looks not more benignly on earthly worms than did Sam on us that morning. There we stood; you, with your mother and sisters clustered anxiously around you,—sisters, encouraging with sympathy, slightly touched in Nelly's case, I recollect, with covert satire, which was so kindly acid as to make the whole agreeable and piquant,—mother, half in admiration, half in fear, now smiling cheeringly, now dropping an anxious word that revealed the inward turmoil, now with trembling fingers smoothing some imaginary wrinkle in your coat, (that coat, donned for the first time that day,) as all the while she gazed with pride upon her boy. Meanwhile, you, half-turning from those kindnesses as all too puerile for one of your estate, still did not take your seat beside me until one long, heartfelt kiss, by its humility, had told that mother an assuring tale of filial love. I, among the party, yet not of it, crowding down the bitter sense of loneliness which years of orphanage had not quelled, smiled a laughing adieu to all, pulled you down on the seat beside me, and away we went for the freshman examination at Cambridge.

We had just reached the head of the little lane which led by the Moselys, when down the road came their old family ark, drawn by that wonderful beast, quadruped by nature and by birth, but tripod by use and age, who had always performed the first mile of any journey upon three legs, until exercise and use rendered the fourth sufficiently elastic for practical purposes.

We shouted our mutual greetings, and then, on we went, for Sam was all too dignified to allow such uproarious proceedings to continue any longer than was absolutely necessary. Indeed, I think, had he been in a condition to use the elective franchise, he would have voted the Mosely turn-out low. It was seedy, that's a fact.

You and I talked big for the first two or three miles; called the tutors we were to meet by slang names, learned from the rusticated who frequented our little village—the purgatory which intervened between the heaven of college and the hell of the wide world—from the suspended ones, who, unlike California banks, were compelled to be suspended from the too free use of coin, both the baser sort and that more precious money, time, in amusements odious to the faculty. Them had we seen in all the effulgence of faded dressing-gowns, flashy vests, and French boots, rather the worse for wear, smelling wondrously of the Virginia weed, sometimes with the odor of strong drink upon their breath, swaggering through the village lanes, bristling to the hawbucks and kindly leering to the rosy-cheeked lasses, and as to us, they had appeared the very epitome of deep, dark and reckless dissipation, we had hung on the horrid eloquence of their lips, and learned to speak bluffly of "Bobby Boots," "Old Conny," *et id omne genus*, our rulers that were to be. But I have traveled off the road nearly as far as my thoughts roamed that morning, when you, responding with a sickly smile to my first remark, that "It would be rather rich, if we 'deaded' after all," threw yourself back despondingly upon the seat and left me to the luxury of my own imaginings—an extravagance I would have gladly dispensed with, just then.

"Time and tide wait for no man ;" neither did Sam and our good old horse. Sure, and disagreeably fast, as the thirty days when we have "promised to pay," the old fellow jogged on, and one by one the well-known buildings came in sight. On we went, by Washington's head-quarters—by Benny Pierce's—(we called him Benny then ; smart, wasn't it ?)—by the famous old elm, under whose shade a patriot army mustered—by the church—through the college gates—into the yard—up to the steps of University Hall—out of the carryall—up the aforesaid steps into the entry, among a crowd of impatient, uneasy victims, very like ourselves.

Off drove Sam, turning as he went, to give us an encouraging grin, for Sam was proud of us. It lacked just fifteen minutes of nine ; so said the clock on the church, though that was two minutes wrong. At least, that large young man in satin vest, with a silver watch and gold chain, (I presume it was gold, for he told me so in confidence at the close of the first day, as we were coming down the steps together,) said so.

The clock clanged forth the hour, a door opened, and in we went, rather quietly for such a crowd of boys, though some audacious creatures actually pushed and snickered ; how could they ? We were alphabetically numbered and classified in divisions. You and I, thanks to the kind divinity who presided over the Cadmean arrangement of our names, were in the same set. The other divisions filed off, some to one recitation-room, some to another. Our set remained in the room we had first entered ; we were to be examined in Greek. Ugh ! The door closed after the last retiring form. By the way, do you know I always believed that fellow winked as he was shutting the door ? Poor wretch, if he really thus derided us, we were amply revenged, for he was turned by.

How shall I describe Sophocles ? Short, stout, thick, stubbed ; head like the ball, into which at desire the hedgehog manufactures himself ; disposition like that generally attributed to the hedgehog aforesaid ; dress Tutonish ; ornaments antediluvian—including that venerable bull's-eye, from whose broad face he computed the exact amount of torture he could inflict on each of us. Ecce Sophocles ! a modern Greek !

Shades of the graceful Alcibiades, could a gazelle-eyed sylph of fruitful Greece have produced such an one as I have described ? He must have suffered some "sea change" before he reached our shores. He was no myth, though ; but a scornful, snarling reality, as we discovered to our cost, as we blundered and stumbled along through our recitation, reckless of the future in the desperation of the present. Lord ! how he "screwed" us ! All bad things, as well as good, come to an end ; rotten banks, muddy walking, restaurant dinners, dull razors, tight boots, tight times, all must have an end. So had that examination. With relieved respiration we passed to the Latin room, lingering yet a moment by the way to say one to the other, "Well, what do you think?" Before we had time to think, we stood before "Bobby Boots." We had often laughed about "Bobby Boots" with the rusticated and suspended aforesaid ; but we felt no inclination to laugh then, and, if memory serves me, we had no very strong desire to call him "Bobby Boots." His boots were of the thickest, however ; a powerful understanding ; yet their thickness availed not to exclude the damps and cold of death ; and poor B., the gentle and eccentric scholar, passed to the better world, ere we were Sophs, sincerely mourned by all who knew him, and oh, so bitterly bewailed by that mother and sister, whose hope and stay and prop he was. Though "gentil he," to us that day he was an object of terror. How he did take me up in my pronunciation ! I had been fitted at a country school. How I envied those Boston boys, with their glib readiness ! Some of them, you recollect, acted the old fable of the tortoise and the hare.

The Latin Empire ended, and so the day. The different rooms were but the same spectacle, slightly varied ; like Meiggs's scrip, all bad, only differing in amount. We had managed to slip, scramble and stumble through—and, all assembled, we stood clustering in the broad walks and around the wide gates, before we separated for the night.

Most of us were to spend the night in Boston ; some lived there—others, from a distance, were stopping there, pending the decision of their fate, not venturing to invest in rooms and furniture, under the uncertainty which hung over their future. Some few adventurous spirits, I recollect, had taken rooms regardless of consequences ; and one said, "Come, fellows, let's go to my room," and, as he spoke, I think he spat tobacco juice ; it might have been preparatory liquorice, but I incline to the tobacco. He gave up his room immediately after the examination, and then he said the whole thing was "a d—d humbug." Was it?

How suddenly familiar we all grew ; all speaking at once—each telling his experience—prodigal in our assurances one to another, each of the other's success—mutually imbibing comfort from the joint stock confidence. Had we all been correct, we should have had a very large class. We didn't though. Somehow, we must have been mistaken. Presently, the mass broke into small knots and groups. We, you and I, this time walked over to the shed, alongside the church, where old Sam was just backing out the carryall. In we jumped. Sam saw by our faces that we were all right. Smack went his whip, off jumped the old horse ; a few moments more and we were at home. At home, did I say? You were at home, and I——, well, the kindness of your father made it home, indeed, to me, the homeless one. The gate was closed, so Sam stopped. We would not wait for him to open it, but jumping out, sprang through the stile, tore along the graveled walk into the house, and there the cloth was laid for tea—that good old-fashioned tea. We did not eat nasty messes at restaurants then.

Brighter than the silver; warmer than the bubbling water of the steaming urn; heartier than the contents of the well-spread board; better than all, was our cheerful greeting. First, a kiss for mother—then a sly pinch for Nelly—then a manly handshake with father. I, too, caught the other hand, sideling round, as he said to me, "And you, too, master Tom, must remember that I take a father's interest in your success." God bless him, he did. Then came the thick question and answer, as, shouldering our satchels, we fought our battles over again. Then tea, then a quiet game of "Loto," then early to bed, for to-morrow ushered in another day of trial. The morrow dawned, and yet another morrow. Still we rode in the carryall, and fretted and sweated in our stone prison of University Hall. The night of the third day saw our examination at an end, and we, the crowd, were waiting in suspense; eager as lover for answer from his mistress; anxious as merchant desiring discount; longing as loafer for a full meal. We were waiting in the entry, at the same door which we had first entered on the first day. Alphabetically we went out on that first day, and alphabetically we went inon the last. We, oh vexation, were among the W's. One by one, in our fellows went; some timid, some swaggering, some blushing, and some with a stiff upper lip. Singly, they came out; some sneakingly, some boldly, some smiling, and some, alas, for blasted hopes of parents and friends! weeping. At length you, and as you came out, victory in your mien; in I went. *Minos, Radamanthus!* if the trembling shades before your stern and awful judgment seat suffer half the mingled emotion that swelled my heart nigh to bursting during that expectant moment, their fate is hard. Rotund forms of sage professors; chairs, tables, parchments, swam before my troubled vision; my name—some incoherent words—I was admitted. I was the last, and you, waiting for me, as I came rushing out, were nearly alone, save some few disconsolate, who were standing mopingly on the steps, gazing at those stone walls, as if they would make the mute granite a witness of their unjust sentence. Poor fellows! there was no new trial for them, safe after much toil and study. One of them I rejoiced over. I had not forgotten how he had asked me to do a sum for him in the mathematical room, and had kicked me under the desk, because I, innocently having the fear of B—— and his sharp eyes before me, had refused. He it was who, in the Latin room, translating English into Latin, had rendered "remind me" by "*pone me in mentem.*" The brute—served him right. Another, I pitied, for there was a sad look in his large, dark eyes, as if his sun of hope was setting there. He, however, soon joined our class, having been re-examined, and we learned that it was timidity only which had momentarily dimmed the luster of his acquirements.

Little time had we for thought of any kind, as, leaping through the college grounds, we surprised old Sam asleep in the carryall, and had it nearly backed out of the shed before the old fellow, rubbing his eyes, awoke to a realizing sense of his whereabouts. Then how his old mouth stretched, as he grinned his welcome and chuckled forth, "Gully, wish you joy, Master John, and you, too, Master Tom." I rather think we hummed it home, slightly verging on the fast crab order, though we were innocent of fast crabs, or "2·40's" then. Perhaps we didn't sing and shout, and yell, and make ourselves ridiculous in every possible way, until the old horse, even, turned his head around to see what the row was; perhaps we didn't carry the hall door by assault, and enter the house with sufficient noise for a troop of horse; perhaps we did not hug and kiss the family, collectively and separately, jointly and individually; perhaps we did not tumble on the sofas, knock over the chairs, and make ourselves generally disagreeable, until even your long-suffering mother was forced to say, "Now boys." Perhaps we did'nt; but I rather think we did. Indeed, I have a dim recollection of bringing up in the kitchen, kissing plump Margaret, the cook. If I did, what harm? I've had worse kissing since. We cooled down a little at tea-time, still our appetites were on the diminutive order, and our hearts filled the passage intended for our food.

How we sang, and danced, and romped that night, (the Moselys were there,) until, fairly tired out, we sat down to our fruit and cake. Then your father, filling each a glass, for you, Robert Mosely and I, said, "Your good health, young gentlemen." Didn't you grow about that time? The Moselys went—then a breathing pause, like a rest in a rapturous song. Then Nelly, handing each of us a bed candle, desired us to partake of a light supper; then up the stairs, laughing still singing, to bed.

The next sun shone on us "Freshmen." Ah, how fresh! Like young bears, all our troubles were to come; yet I would not hesitate at any sacrifice, could I again feel the same exultant self-satisfaction and supreme contempt for all the world beside that I experienced that morning.

You felt so too, I know; for as we walked down the main street together, our first appearance thereon in all the brilliancy of our new frock coats and t'other things to match, you repelled with dignity all attempts at familiarity, and remarked to me, confidentially, that "Jim Smith seemed to think that a man had nothing to do but listen to his vulgar nonsense." Do you remember? If so, I'll jog your memory again.

SONG OF A CHRYSALIS.

BY G.

WHEN blushing morn gives radiant day
  Its first and sweetest breath,
And gloomy night, in pale affright,
  Shrinks in the arms of death—
'T is then, when earth in perfum'd dew
  Lies bath'd, I'd first behold,
At morning's prime, my sunny clime,
  And spread my wings of gold.

When noon-day with its sultry heat,
  Drives to the shady grove
The gentle bird, whose song is heard,
  In softest notes of love—

'T is then I'd cease my giddy flight,
  With life and joy elate,
And pass the hours amid the flowers,
  In bliss with some gay mate.

When sunset with its glowing tints
  Throws giant shadows round,
And blossoms close, and flowers repose,
  With heads bent to the ground—
'T is then I'd bid adieu to life,
  To earth and radiant sky,
Before the might of one dark night
  Had told me all must die.

CALIFORNIA, IN 1852.

BY SHIRLEY.

LETTER FIFTEENTH.

RESIDENCE IN THE MINES.

FROM OUR LOG CABIN, Indian Bar, April 10, 1852.

I HAVE been haunted all day, my dear M., with an intense ambition to write you a letter, which shall be dreadfully commonplace and severely utilitarian in its style and contents. Not but that my epistles are *always* commonplace enough, (spirits of Montague and Sevigné, forgive me!) but. hitherto I have not really *tried* to make them so. Now, however, I *intend* to be stupidly prosy, with malice aforethought, and without one mitigating circumstance, except, perchance, it be the temptations of that above-mentioned ambitious little devil to palliate my crime.

You would certainly wonder, were you seated where I now am, how any one with a quarter of a soul, *could* manufacture herself into a bore, amid such surroundings as these. The air is as balmy as that of a midsummer's day in the sunniest valleys of New England. It is four o'clock in the evening, and I am sitting on a segar-box outside of our cabin. From this spot not a person is to be seen, except a man who is building a new wing to the "Humboldt." Not a human sound, but a slight noise made by the aforesaid individual, in tacking on a roof of blue drilling to the room which he is finishing, disturbs the stillness which fills this purest air. I confess that it is difficult to fix my eyes upon the dull paper, and my fingers upon the duller pen with which I am soiling it. Almost every other minute, I find myself stopping to listen to the ceaseless river-psalm, or to gaze up into the wondrous depths of the California Heaven; to watch the graceful movements of the pretty brown lizards, jerking up their impudent little heads above a moss-wrought log which lies before me, or to mark the dancing water-shadow on the canvas door of the bake-shop opposite; to follow with childish eyes the flight of a golden butterfly, curious to know if it will crown, with a capital of winged beauty, that column of Nature's carving, the pine stump rising at my feet, or whether it will flutter down (for it is dallying coquettishly around them both,) upon that slate-rock beyond, shining so darkly lustrous through a flood of yellow sunlight; or I lazily turn my head, wondering if I know the blue or red-shirted miner who is descending the precipitous hill behind me. In sooth, Molly, it is easy to be commonplace at all times, but I confess that, just at present, I find it difficult to be utilitary; the saucy lizards—the great, orange-dotted butterflies—the still, solemn cedars— the sailing smoke-wreath and the vaulted splendor above, are wooing me so winningly to higher things.

But, as I said before, I have an ambition that way, and I *will* succeed. You are such a good-natured little thing, dear, that I know you will meekly allow yourself to be victimized into reading the profound and prosy remarks which I shall make, in my efforts to initiate you into the mining polity of this place. Now you may rest assured that I shall assert nothing upon the subject which is not perfectly correct; for have I not earned a character for inquisitiveness, (and you know that does *not* happen to be one of my failings,) which I fear will cling to me through life, by my persevering questions to all the unhappy miners from whom I thought I could gain any information. Did I not martyrize myself into a human mule, by descending to the bottom of a dreadful pit, (suffering mortal terror all the time, lest it should cave in upon me,) actuated by a virtuous desire to see with my own two eyes the process of underground mining, thus enabling myself to be stupidly correct in all my statements thereupon? Did I not ruin a pair of silk velvet slippers, lame my ancles for a week, and draw a "browner horror" over my already sun-burnt face, in a wearisome walk miles away, to the head of the "ditch," as they call the prettiest little rivulet (though the work of men)—that I ever saw; yea, verily, this have I done for the express edification of yourself, and the rest of your curious tribe, to be rewarded, probably, by the impertinent remark,—"What *does* that little goose, 'Dame Shirley,' think that *I* care about such things?" But madam, in spite of your sneer, I shall proceed in my allotted task.

In the first place, then, as to the discovery of gold. In California, at least, it must be confessed, that in this particular, science appears to be completely at fault;—or, as an intelligent and well-educated miner remarked to us the other day, "I maintain that science is the blindest guide that one could have on a gold-finding expedition. Those men, who judge by the appearance of the soil, and depend upon geological calculations, are invariably disappointed, while the ignorant adventurer, who digs just for the sake of digging, is almost sure to be successful." I suppose that the above observation is quite correct, as all whom we have questioned upon the subject repeat, in substance, the same thing. Wherever Geology has said that gold *must* be, there, perversely enough, it lies not; and wherever her ladyship has declared that it could *not* be, there has it oftenest garnered up in miraculous profusion the yellow splendor of its virgin beauty. It is certainly very painful to a well-regulated mind to see the irreverent contempt, shown by this beautiful mineral, to the dictates of science; but what better can one expect from the "root of all evil?" As well as can be ascertained, the most lucky of the mining Columbuses, have been ignorant sailors; and foreigners, I fancy, are more successful than Americans.

Our countrymen are the most discontented of mortals. They are always longing for "big strikes." If a "claim" is paying them a steady income, by which, if they pleased, they could lay up more in a month, than they could accumulate in a year at home, still, they are dissatisfied, and, in most cases, will wander off in search of better "diggings." There are hundreds now pursuing this foolish course, who, if they had stopped where they first "camped," would now have been rich men. Sometimes, a company of these wanderers will find itself upon a bar, where a few pieces of the precious metal lie scattered upon the surface of the ground ; of course they immediately " prospect " it, which is accomplished, by " panning out " a few basinsful of the soil. If it " pays," they " claim " the spot, and build their shanties ; the news spreads that wonderful " diggings " have been discovered at such a place,—the monte-dealers, those worse than fiends, rush vulture-like upon the scene and erect 'a round tent, where, in gambling, drinking, swearing and fighting, the *many* reproduce Pandemonium in more than its original horror, while a *few* honestly and industriously commence digging for gold, and lo ! as if a fairy's wand had been waved above the bar, a full-grown mining town hath sprung into existence.

But first, let me explain to you the " claiming " system. As there are no State laws upon the subject, each mining community is permitted to make its own. Here, they have decided that no man may " claim " an area of more than forty feet square. This he " stakes off " and puts a notice upon it, to the effect that he " holds " it for mining purposes. If he does not choose to " work it " immediately, he is obliged to renew the notice every ten days ; for without this precaution, any other person has a right to " jump it," that is, to take it from him. There are many ways of evading the above law. For instance, an individual can " hold " as many " claims " as he pleases, if he keeps a man at work in each, for this workman represents the original owner. I am told, however, that the laborer, himself, can " jump " the " claim " of the very man who employs him, if he pleases so to do. This is seldom, if ever, done ; the person who is willing to be hired, generally prefers to receive the six dollars *per diem*, of which he is *sure* in any case, to running the risk of a " claim " not proving valuable. After all, the " holding of claims " by proxy is considered rather as a carrying out of the spirit of the law, than as an evasion of it. But there are many ways of *really* outwitting this rule, though I cannot stop now to relate them, which give rise to innumerable arbitrations, and nearly every Sunday, there is a " miners' meeting " connected with this subject.

Having got our gold mines discovered, and " claimed," I will try to give you a faint idea of how they " work " them. Here, in the mountains, the labor of excavation is extremely difficult, on account of the immense rocks which form a large portion of the soil. Of course, no man can " work out " a " claim " alone. For that reason, and also for the same that makes partnerships desirable, they congregate in companies of four or six, generally designating themselves by the name of the place from whence the majority of the members have emigrated ; as for example, the " Illinois," " Bunker Hill," " Bay State," etc., companies. In many places the surface-soil, or in mining-phrase, the " top dirt," " pays " when worked in a " Long Tom." This machine, (I have never been able to discover the derivation of its name,) is a trough, generally about twenty feet in length, and eight inches in depth, formed of wood, with the exception of six feet at one end, called the " riddle," (query, why riddle ?) which is made of sheet-iron, perforated with holes about the size of a large marble. Underneath this cullender-like portion of the " long-tom," is placed another trough, about ten feet long, the sides six inches perhaps in hight, which divided through the middle by a slender slat, is called the " riffle-box." It takes several persons to manage, properly, a " long-tom." Three or four men station themselves with spades, at the head of the machine, while at the foot of it, stands an individual armed " wid de shovel and de hoe." The spadesmen throw in large quantities of the precious dirt, which is washed down to the " riddle " by a stream of water leading into the " long-tom " through wooden gutters or " sluices." When the soil reaches the " riddle," it is kept constantly in motion by the man with the hoe. Of course, by this means, all the dirt and gold escapes through the perforations into the " riffle-box " below, one compartment of which is placed just beyond the " riddle." Most of the dirt washes over the sides of the " riffle-box," but the gold being so astonishingly heavy remains safely at the bottom of it. When the machine gets too full of stones to be worked easily, the man whose business it is to attend to them throws them out with his shovel, looking carefully among them as he does so for any pieces of gold, which may have been too large to pass through the holes of the " riddle." I am sorry to say that he generally loses his labor. At night they " pan out " the gold, which has been collected in the " riffle-box " during the day. Many of the miners decline washing the " top dirt " at all, but try to reach as quickly as possible the " bed-rock," where are found the richest deposits of gold. The river is supposed to have formerly flowed over this " bed-rock," in the " crevices " of which, it left, as it passed away, the largest portions of the so eargerly sought for ore. The group of mountains amidst which we are living is a spur of the Sierra Nevada ; and the " bed-rock," (which in this vicinity is of slate) is said to run through the entire range, lying, in distance varying from a few feet to eighty or ninety, beneath the surface of the soil. On Indian Bar, the " bed-rock " falls in almost perpendicular " benches," while at Rich Bar, the friction of the river has formed it into large, deep basins, in which the gold, instead of being found, as you would naturally suppose, in the bottom of it, lies for the most part, just below the rim. A good-natured individual bored *me*, and tired *himself*, in a hopeless attempt to make me comprehend that this was only a necessary consequence of the under-current of the water ; but with my usual stupidity upon such matters, I got but a vague idea from his scientific explanation, and certainly shall not mystify *you*, with my confused notions thereupon.

When a company wish to reach the bed rock as quickly as possible, they "sink a shaft," (which is nothing more nor less than digging a well,) until they "strike" it. They then commence "drifting coyote holes" (as they call them) in search of "crevices," which, as I told you before, often pay immensely. These "coyote holes" sometimes extend hundreds of feet into the side of the hill. Of course they are obliged to use lights in working them. They generally proceed, until the air is so impure as to extinguish the lights, when they return to the entrance of the excavation, and commence another, perhaps close to it. When they think that a "coyote hole" has been faithfully "worked," they "clean it up," which is done by scraping the surface of the "bed

rock" with a knife,—lest by chance they have overlooked a "crevice,"
—and they are often richly rewarded for this precaution.

Now I must tell you how those having "claims" on the hills procure
the water for washing them. The expense of raising it in any way
from the river, is too enormous to be thought of for a moment. In
most cases it is brought from ravines in the mountains. A company,
to which a friend of ours belongs, has dug a ditch about a foot in width
and depth, and more than three miles in length, which is fed in this
way. I wish that you could see this ditch. I never beheld a NATURAL
streamlet more exquisitely beautiful. It undulates over the mossy roots,
and the gray, old rocks, like a capricious snake, singing all the time a
low song with the "liquidest murmur," and one might almost fancy it
the airy and coquettish Undine herself. When it reaches the top of
the hill, the sparkling thing is divided into five or six branches, each
one of which supplies one, two, or three "long-toms." There is an
extra one, called the "waste-ditch," leading to the river, into which the
water is shut off at night and on Sundays. This "race" (another and
peculiar name for it) has already cost the company more than five
thousand dollars. They sell the water to others at the following rates :
Those that have the first use of it pay ten per cent. upon all the gold
that they take out. As the water runs off from their machine, (it
now goes by the elegant name of "tailings,") it is taken by a company
lower down ; and as it is not worth so much as when it was clear, the
latter pay but seven per cent. If any others wish the "tailings," now
still less valuable than at first, they pay four per cent. on all the gold
which they take out, be it much or little. The water companies are
constantly in trouble, and the arbitrations on that subject are very
frequent.

I think that I gave you a vague idea of "fluming" in a former
letter ; I will not, therefore, repeat it here, but will merely mention,
that the numerous "fluming" companies have already commenced their
extensive operations upon the river.

As to the "rockers," so often mentioned in story and in song, I have
not spoken of them since I commenced this letter. The truth is, that
I have seldom seen them used, though hundreds are lying ownerless
along the banks of the river. I suppose that other machines are better
adapted to mining operations in the mountains.

Gold mining is Nature's great lottery scheme. A man may work in
a claim for many months, and be poorer at the end of the time than
when he commenced ; or he may "take out" thousands in a few hours.
It is a mere matter of chance. A friend of ours, a young Spanish
surgeon from Guatemala, a person of intelligence and education, told
us that, after "working a claim" for six months, he had taken out but
six ounces.

It must be acknowledged, however, that if a person "work his
claim" himself, is economical and industrious, keeps his health, and is
satisfied with small gains, he is "bound" to make money. And yet, I
cannot help remarking, that almost all with whom we are acquainted
seem to have *lost*. Some have had their "claims" jumped ; many
holes which had been excavated, and prepared for working at a great

expense, caved in during the heavy rains of the fall and winter. Often after a company has spent an immense deal of time and money in "sinking a shaft," the water from the springs, (the greatest obstacle which the miner has to contend with in this vicinity) rushes in so fast, that it is impossible to work in them, or to contrive any machinery to keep it out, and for that reason only, men have been compelled to abandon places where they were at the very time "taking out" hundreds of dollars a day. If a fortunate or an unfortunate (which shall I call him?) *does* happen to make a "big strike," he is almost sure to fall into the hands of the professed gamblers, who soon relieve him of all care of it. They have not troubled the Bar much during the winter, but as the spring opens, they flock in like ominous birds of prey. Last week one left here, after a stay of four days, with over a thousand dollars of the hard-earned gold of the miners. But enough of these best-beloved of Beelzebub, so infinitely worse than the robber or murderer;—for surely it would be kinder to take a man's life, than to poison him with the fatal passion for gambling.

Perhaps you would like to know what class of men is most numerous in the mines. As well as I can judge, there are upon this river as many foreigners as Americans. The former, with a few exceptions, are extremely ignorant and degraded; though we have the pleasure of being acquainted with three or four Spaniards of the highest education and accomplishments. Of the Americans, the majority are of the better class of mechanics. Next to these, in number, are the sailors and the farmers. There are a few merchants and steamboat-clerks, three or four physicians, and one lawyer. We have no ministers, though fourteen miles from here there is a "Rancho," kept by a man of distinguished appearance, an accomplished monte-dealer and horse-jockey, who is *said* to have been—in the States—a preacher of the Gospel. I know not if this be true; but at any rate, such things are not uncommon in California.

I have spun this letter out until my head aches dreadfully. How tiresome it is to write *sensible* (?) things! But I have one comfort,—though my epistle may not be interesting, you will not deny, dear M., that I have achieved my ambition of making it both commonplace and utilatory.

TO MINNIE SPEAR.

BY SHORTFELLOW.

Oh what sorrow in the parting
  From the friends we love so well:
Who can hide the tear from starting,
  When they bid a last farewell.

Oft I thought I heard it spoken,
  Out upon the dark, blue sea,
But it came in accents broken,
  Not as whispered unto me.

In my midnight vigils keeping,
  Voices come that I know well,

Not in kindly accents greeting,
  But in echos of farewell.

When in foreign lands we travel,
  Death may hover round our way,
Who can Fate's decrees unravel,
  Who can say we'll live to-day.

That farewell may be forever,
  There is one alone can tell;
And from friends we may not ever
  Hear another fond farewell.

SOMEWHAT OF THE HISTORY AND GEOLOGY OF THE MINES.

—

BY AN OLD MINER.

—

The great staple of California is gold ; and although almost every village in the thirty-one States of our Union, is represented by some one of its numbers in the mines, and many a parent's heart is gladdened by letters from an absent son,—yet how few of these give correct, accurate and reliable information, concerning the auriferous regions of California ; their letters are mostly of a private nature, containing the expression of the heart's feelings, or the relation of personal adventures ; therefore, in what I shall say touching the above topics, I shall aim to be practical, and to give such information as will enable persons unacquainted with the subject, to gain some correct knowledge of the great mining interests of California.

There has been a great change in the whole system of mining, within the last year or two. At first, the rocker, quicksilver-machine and long-tom were used. The first required but one man, who dug and carried his dirt in buckets to the shore of the stream, dipped his water with an oyster-can tied to a stick, poured it over the dirt in the "hopper" with one hand, while he "rocked the cradle with the other." The second, was a sheet-iron hopper and trough beneath it, with partitions filled with quicksilver—all set upon rockers. It required one man to rock, one to put in the dirt as it was dug and brought in wheelbarrows, and another to remove the "tailings." Water was brought from an elevation in hose, made of canvas, then turned into a box perforated with holes, above the hopper, and by this means sprinkled over the dirt, washing the fine particles through—the coarse being drawn out of the open end. The "long-tom" was a trough of some twelve feet in length, with a sheet-iron screen at the lower end, that let the gold and fine dirt into a trough below, with cells and quicksilver to save the gold ; the coarse stones and gravel were shoveled out by one man, while the dirt was put in by another.

But these devices, which served their day, are mostly superseded by the "sluice," which is a continuous inclined trough with, here and there, cells in the bottom to save the gold. Water is turned in at the upper end, and the dirt shoveled in wherever convenient. What is termed hydraulic washing, is where the sluice is set at the bottom of a "drift hill," and water is conducted from an elevation in hose ending in a metallic nozzle,—the stream being directed against the embankment, and by its force cutting it down and carrying it off in the sluice. This is the cheapest mode of washing, as it saves all the labor of digging, wheeling, etc., but can only be used where water can be conducted from a hill, and where the dirt is soft.

In our early history, placer and river mining were of the most importance ; now, tunneling seems to take precedence. Gold is obtained in this way, by first sinking shafts to find the lead, and then tunneling in from the foot of the hill,—generally from some creek, ravine or river.

Placer mining, is carried on where gold is found mixed with dirt, sand and gravel, upon the surface of the earth, or near it. The gold taken out of these diggings is of every variety of shape, from fine dust up to lumps or nuggets, weighing many pounds. River mining, is where gold is found in the bed and banks of streams. This gold is generally in the form of scales. There are two opinions as to the formation of these scales : one, that they are partial chrystalizations,—the other, that the small pieces are flattened between stones rolled about by the action of water.

Tunnel mining occurs where gold is found in the beds of ancient streams, where the earth is of a volcanic nature, mixed with ashes and lava of extinct volcanos. I do not intend now to touch upon the subject of quartz mining.

The original location of gold is the primary rocks, quartz being the principal one. There is a main ledge of quartz extending the entire length of California, situated along the western slope of the mountains, with numerous inferior ones, generally running in the same direction, and frequently crossing each other. At these crossings gold is more abundant. They are of igneous origin, and what is termed, veins of injection ; they are later, in the geological epoch, than the granite, being injected into cracks and seams, formed in the older strata by volcanic action. The elements for ages have been acting as the stamps of quartz mills, crushing and wearing away these ledges of quartz, scattering the gold broadcast, but leaving it the richest in the vicinity of these broken ledges. Sometimes it is carried, by the continued action of rivers, to considerable distances.

There are but few of these ledges that cross the summits of the Sierra Nevada, and as a natural result, gold is less plenty upon their eastern slope.

Tunnel mining is prosecuted generally in the bed of extinct rivers, that existed many years ago, even before these old mountains were elevated. The proofs of the theory of ancient rivers, are : First— Their continuous course. Second—The well defined banks of each shore. Third—The water-worn pebbles and boulders that no cause but running water produces. Fourth—Bars and islands in the leads. These leads run under hills and mountains, are cut across and exposed by streams of the present day, broken and tossed about by volcanic action, yet in many places for miles and miles, their general course has been traced, and found well defined. That these old rivers existed before the mountains were elevated, is proved also by their general direction, which is in a northern and southern course, cutting the streams of the present day at right angles ; the latter universally running in an easterly and westerly direction, or from the mountains down to the valleys. Gold is usually accompanied by iron ore as a gangue ; low down, this is in the shape of black sand or metallic oxide ; higher up, it is generally specular oxide. Sulphuret of iron, or iron pyrites, is frequently found in tunnels collected around fragments of wood.

The prevailing stratum in the mines is granite ; but in a few places only I have observed pure granite, useful for building purposes.

There is little variety in the minerals found in the mines ; those that belong to one general class of primary rocks, as quartz, feldspar, mica, hornblende, talcose, slate, cornelian, epidate, galena, garnet, jasper, serpentine, silicia, etc., being the principal. It has frequently been stated that stone-coal exists in the mines, but this is untrue, as coal does not occur in primary strata.

Much money has been expended in boring artesian wells to procure water for mining purposes, but it is only thrown away, as a general thing, for these wells are only found in stratified rocks, or under continuous beds of impervious clay, where water percolates from elevations between the strata, and being tapped by the auger, rises to a level with its source.

The elevating of these mountains occurred some time in the tertiary period. There is ample proof of this in the existence of these old river beds, that run in a northerly and southerly direction, and could not so do, if the mountains had been elevated when they existed, for they would have run as the streams of the present day—from east to west.

That the mountains have been recently elevated, is proved by large trees, belonging to a late period, being frequently found in tunnels ;— one of oak, a part of which I have seen, was thirty-six feet in diameter, and one hundred feet below the surface.

There are also evidences of the "glacis aqueous" period sometimes observed ;—but of this another time, when I shall have some rare facts to communicate.

In an article of this kind, it would be impossible to go into all the proofs at length, nor would it interest the general reader ; but what observations I have made, are founded upon some five years' personal experience in the mines. If I have made the subject of the great mining interests of California (which will be great for ages to come) better understood, my only object is accomplished.

MY LOVE IS AN ANGEL.

BY JOSEPH A. NUNES.

My love, tho' an angel, comes not from above,
Nor comes she in heavenly guise:
But her heart is a fountain of heavenly love,
And her spirit's as gentle as that of a dove;
While the Graces might study from her how to move,
And Paradise beams through her eyes.

My love is an angel, yet does not wear wings,
Nor seems she encircled with light ;
But her voice is as sweet as a seraph's that sings,
And her presence the essence of happiness brings,
And affection around her in tenderness clings,
As a home that is heavenly bright.

I'd not, if I could, that my angel might be
A creature of heavenly birth ;
But couldst thou observe how her face lights with glee,
As she looks for the hour that is to bring me,
Thou'dst admit, though an infidel, harden'd, that we
Have our own little heaven——on earth.

EDITOR'S TABLE.

MUSICAL AND THEATRICAL.

MARCH 20 TO APRIL 23.—The leading histrionic incidents of the month have been the reopening of the American Theater, the appearance of two new stars at the Metropolitan, and the farewell concerts of Madam Bishop.

THE METROPOLITAN.—Miss Davenport's engagement at this theater closed on the 30th of March. Her "Camille" was a fine piece of acting, the last scene drawing tears from the eyes of her audiences.

Mr. and Mrs. Barney Williams took a farewell benefit at this house on the 25th of March, prior to their departure for the East.

Mrs. Estelle Potter followed Miss Davenport, performing an engagement of a week's duration, and appearing in the usual star characters. She seemed to have a good deal of feeling, but to be wanting in force. It is hardly proper for us, however, to give a decided opinion upon her claims to distinction, since, unfortunately, it was out of our power to witness her "Lucrezia Borgia," which, we understand, is by far her best part, and which drew forth praises from all who witnessed it.

The delineator of Yankee characters, Josh Silsbee, followed Mrs. Potter,—his engagement commencing on the 16th April. He has not succeeded in drawing very full houses, but will probably do better in the Interior. Of course, he is by far the best "Yankee" we have had in California. His representation of the character has nothing of the extravagant about it. It is not made up entirely of whittling a piece of pine, and uttering remarks with an extravagant twang, such as is no where to be met on the face of the earth. If he whittles, his attention is not entirely absorbed in this portion of his work; he uses his jackknife, as a true Yankee would, merely to take up the time, while his keen eye and ear are awake, nevertheless, to all that is going on around him. His Yankee is in some respects such as one might have met in the back towns of New England before the lace-work of railroads mixed up the population of that section of the Union, carrying the city into the country and the village to the town. The independence of the Yankee character appears prominently in his acting, but there is a sly, cool shrewdness, a bargain-driving element which, so far as we have seen, is not so prominently marked in his Yankee as we anticipated it would be. Of course, he is much restricted in this respect by the language set down for him in the plays he presents. We have not seen him on every evening, it is true, but if those plays which we have not witnessed are similar to those which we have, he has certainly manifested bad judgment in selecting parts properly and fully to represent the Yankee character. Any one who understands the peculiarities of the Connecticut or New Hampshire-man, knows full well that the last thing he will do in presence of a female is to utter a remark even slightly off propriety; for, as well as a shrewdness, there is an innate bashfulness about the Yankee when addressing one of the gentler sex of his land, however much he may wish and appear to conceal it. Silsbee is performing as our record closes.

THE AMERICAN.—Shortly after our last issue the Monplaisir and Italian Opera Troupes finding, as we learn, that on account of some internal difficulties the season would be disastrous to them, closed the American. The house was, however, reopened on the 9th of April by Dr. Spaulding with a stock company. This efficient manager has introduced a marked improvement in the disposition of the dress circle, and the theater is now the most airy, pleasant and sociable we have yet had in California.

The company is by far the best that has ever been combined here. Miss Laura Keene, Mr. Wheatleigh, Mrs. Judah, and Miss Julia Gould, Mrs. Thoman, Mr. W. M. Leman and Messrs. J. A. Smith and Kent, form the attractions. They are nightly producing Shakespearean and other celebrated comedies, farces, etc., and are gathering about them a large and increasing number of permanent patrons. In common with the daily press, we extend our congratulations to the enterprising manager on the fact that the ladies of our city are beginning to encourage him with their presence. Miss Keene and Mr. Wheatleigh, Miss Gould, Mrs. Judah, Mrs. Thoman and Mr. Kent, are nightly received with plaudits; in fact, all the leading artists are great favorites with the public.

GENERAL ITEMS.—Madame Bishop's concerts, intended as the last prior to her departure for Australia, were, we are sorry to say, a complete failure. At her farewell benefit, however, which occurred on the 17th April, there was a moderate house. The secret of this ill-success seems to be, as nearly as we can understand, the unpopularity and mismanagement of Mr. Bochsa.

Miss Davenport performed an engagement at Stockton after her benefit at the Metropolitan, and left for Sacramento on or about the 21st April.

Meanwhile, Mrs. Potter and Neafie were performing at Sacramento, Neafie having just closed an engagement at Marysville.

The Monplaisirs also gave several entertainments at Sacramento during the month now closed, and have left for a tour through the mines.

Mr. Edwin Booth, one of the most promising actors upon the boards, and Mr. Anderson, an old favorite, have returned from Australia. Mr. W. B. and Miss Caroline Chapman, with a small company, are traveling in the mines, presenting vaudevilles, *petite* comedies, etc.

The Union Theater (French) of this city has been opened on Sunday evenings for the amusement of the foreign population of San Francisco.

The Golden Era says: "The Chinese Opera Troupe has appeared at the Celestial Theater, Sacramento. The papers are divided on the merits of the *prima donnas, bassos,* etc., but unite in pronouncing the orchestral accompaniments absolutely infernal."

GOSSIP WITH READERS AND CORRESPONDENTS.

WE have occupied so much of the attention of our readers in the earlier pages of this number, that we really haven't the heart to make further demands upon their time here. We still doubt very much the propriety of republishing the long article that has already appeared in the September, October and November Numbers, and of laying open to the world the paper which is so evidently private in its intention. Had it not been that there appeared to be a demand for the former, (which is out of print,) and for the urgent request on the part of many (perhaps *too* kind) friends for the latter, the step, which at best is somewhat questionable, would not have been taken. We have endeavored to make amends, however, by contracting the usual extent of the editorial department from twenty-eight or thirty pages to six, and inserting about as many contributed prose articles and poems as has been our wont. The few pages allotted to the Gossip we shall also yield mostly to our contributors. - - - WE must, however, before turning our attention to the letters before us, give one "melancholy attempt" ourselves, which we heard a day or two since. Many of you will doubtless remember the style which obtained among ladies some years since, of gathering their hair together and piling it in a stationary mound on the upper portion of the head by the aid of sundry little steel instruments, unknown to all dejected and miserable bachelors,—that is to say, known only by common report. While this fashion was in vogue, an Orthodox clergyman of a certain village, regarding it as an abomination, was determined to use his influence against it and "preach it down." Accordingly, one Sabbath morning, he mounted the pulpit, and gave as his text, "Top-knot, come down!" There was a good deal of staring and bobbing of "top-knots," and, in short, the congregation were much "exercised" because the worthy pastor had preached from a text not to be found in the Scriptures. On Tuesday they called him up before a convocation of the saints, for the purpose of making a formal charge against him and dismissing him from his cure. The charge was made, and he was asked if he had aught to say in reply. He mildly remarked, that the text was to be found in *his* Bible, but that any Bible would do,—that if they would hand him one, he would point out its *locale* and read it to them. A Bible was given him, and he turned slowly to the place, and read, "And let that man who is upon the house——*top not come down!*" A vote of adjournment was immediately passed. - - - WE have received from the publishers of Graham's Magazine a copy of a very splendid steel engraving of the likenesses of the fourteen Presidents of the United States. The testimonial is intended by R. H. See & Co. as a present to each of the patrons of the monthly, and is certainly a most splendid affair. A copy is to be presented to all those who become subscribers for the present year, and we doubt not numberless of our community will enroll their names as recipients. - - - THERE is, after all, a touch of one kind of human nature in the following "Overheard conversation in a low drinking-house," which we receive from the hands of an esteemed contributor:

TOMMY.—"I hates yer, Bill, and ye *knows* I do."

BILL.—"Well, what do yer hate me for, Tommy?"

TOMMY—(indignantly.) "Why, I hates yer, because ye squints, ye does—and ye knows it."

BILL—(deprecatingly.) "Well, if I does squint, how can I help it?"

TOMMY—(more indignantly still.) "Help it! why it's yer confounded *ignorance!*"

- - - And in this, which comes from the same hand—the scene having actually occurred at Meyer's breakfast house in San Francisco:

> *SCENE—A German Coffee Saloon.—Enter an Englishman and a German.*
>
> GERMAN—(to waiter.) "Zwei coffee."
>
> ENGLISHMAN—(to German friend.) "Tell me, what do you mean by 'zwei coffee?'"
>
> GERMAN FRIEND—(a wag.) "'Zwei'—that means the best coffee."
>
> ENGLISHMAN.—"Oh, that's it. I often hear them ask for 'zwei coffee' here, but could not understand what it meant."
>
> *Next day—Same place—Enter Englishman, solus.*
>
> "Waiter, 'zwei coffee.'"
>
> Accordingly, two coffees are placed before him.
>
> ENGLISHMAN—(surprised.) "What's the meaning of this? I don't want two cups of coffee."
>
> WAITER.—"You ordered two, sir."
>
> ENGLISHMAN—(very indignantly.) I did nothing of the kind. D'ye think I'm crazy? I asked you for 'zwei coffee.'"
>
> WAITER.—"Well, haven't I brought you 'zwei coffee?'"
>
> *TABLEAUX—Proprietor who has stepped up to explain—waiter trying to suppress a laugh—Englishman just discovering he has been sold.*

- - - WE have received from Dougliss's Music Emporium a very sweet little song entitled "Love me, Darling—Love me." Aside from the excellence of the words and music, it has a double interest from the fact that it bears upon its title-page the name of a San Franciscan as its composer. The words are by Mrs. H. Marion Ward, and the music by Mr. J. R. Lawrie. - - - THE following is a little too good to remain uncopied. We cut it from *The Boston Journal:*

"THE CAIFORNIA WIDOW: A BALLAD.

—

> IF I were *pun-ished*
> For every *pun* I *shed,*
> I could not find a *puny shed*
> In which to hide my *pun-ish head.*
> H. J. FINN.

A widow bold was Betsey Brown,
　That chanced Tom Young to know, sir,—
She was in flesh a *little gross,*
　And he a *little grocer.*

Now Betsey rather fancied Tom,
　And Tom was wont to utter,
While selling 'firkin' and 'fresh lump,'
　He'd have no other *but her.*

So they were wed,—one *evening* 'twas,
　Her *mourning* laid aside,
She at the altar *altered* stood,
　A flaunting, dashing bride.

And Tom spoke out the marriage vow,
　That all his freedom fettered,
And thought now he had *won his Bet,*
　His lot in life he'd *bettered.*

Mistaken Young—for as a wife,
　Had he some *young Miss taken,*
Instead of this bold, widowed one,
　He had not been forsaken.

Awhile they happy lived, although
　She had a *teasing way*
Of getting what poor Tom had earned
　In *weighing teas* all day—

Which scarce in *purse,* than straight was spent
　Her *person* to apparel,
The while Tom *bottling up* his wrath,
　Though he such waste could *bear ill.*

It chanced, howe'er, one stormy night,
　　The rain was fiercely *pouring*,
While Tom sat *poring* o'er the news,
　　His spouse in arm-chair snoring—

The door-be'l rang—the night so *foul*,
　　No wonder, made one *pull it*
With savage force. . Tom started up
　　As though struck by a bullet.

The door *ajar*, an ugly *mug*
　　Appeared before his sight;
Thought Tom, you're in a *dripping* state
　　To *drop in* such a night.

Outspoke the stranger, 'That you've wed
　　A Betsey Brown, they dare hint,—
No heir I hope yet? No? then here's
　　To make myself *apparent*.'

Then strode he in where Betsey sat,
　　Despite all Tom's restraint;
She gave one look, then shrieked, and *swooned*,
　　'Twas real and no *feint*.

To *rub her* then each *took a hand*,
　　And there was great ado,—
One brought some water, one brought salts,
　　At last they *brought her to*.

'O John, my first, can this be you!'
　　Said she, 'that broke my napping,—
It cannot be your *spirit*, for
　　You entered without *rapping*.

'We heard you'd met an awful fate
　　On California's shore,—
A stage upset, you'd *broke your skull*—
　　And so we *gave you o'er*.'

Said John, 'No such *stage tragedy*
　　E'er happened to me yet;
A *placer full of ore* was all
　　The *awful* fate I met.

'And now returned, I claim my wife,
　　So Young, you gay deceiver,
As I put in a *prior* right
　　I think you'll have to *leave her*.'

And so he did, for at a scene
　　His nature weak revolted,
In fond embrace he saw them *locked*,
　　Then took his hat and *bolted*.

So it *turned out*, Tom Young 'turned in'
　　That night a single fellow,
While over a hot mug of punch
　　The new-joined *pair* got *mellow*.

Brown with his gold now makes a show,
　　As Californians must,
And Bet *holds high her head*, but then
　　He *keeps her in the* '*dust*.'

As for poor Tom, though once he thought
　　Him happy in Bet's arms,
Now finds his little grocer's shop
　　For him has *counter* charms."

‑ ‑ ‑ An esteemed friend, sojourner on Staten Island, sends us the following "Judy Spree." Slightly "Saxey," and reminds one of—

　　　　"Now the smiles grow thicker,
　　　　　　Wonder what they mean.
　　　　—Faith he's got the Knicker-
　　　　　　Bocker Magazine."

It is entitled—

"NEVER GO TO SEA.

YE uneasy striplings
  Who are ever longing
To sail upon the ocean,
  Take a timely warning.
Follow what you choose, lads,
  But listen unto me—
If you care for comfort,
  Never go to sea.

Hardly off the Hook,
  Land is in the distance;
Feel a queer sensation,
  Call out for assistance;
Sailor standing by
  With an eye of glee,
Tells you very kindly
  Never go sea.

Nibble pilot buscuit,
  Drink a little brandy,
Crawl upon the deck,
  Legs not very *hand*-y,

Take a dozen steps,
  Ship pitches on the lea;
If you 'd keep your footing,
  Never go to sea.

Jump upon your feet,
  Make a push for supper—
Steer hard for the cabin,
  But fetch up in the scupper;
Dashing o'er the bulwarks,
  Water's rather free—
If you'd miss a ducking
  Never go to sea.

Tell you what it is lads,
  A nautical existence
Like a sulky countenance,
  Is charming —— in the distance.
Take a trip to Sing Sing,
  Go upon a spree,
Patronize the diggings,
  But *never* go to sea."

Send another, please. - - - WE have received from the Legislative Halls of our State the following account of a scene that occurred there not long since: The expense and trouble, writes our correspondent, of taking the ayes and nays in Legislative bodies, is the cause of frequent remark; and when a member renders his name particularly conspicuous by calling the ayes and nays, his position becomes anything but an enviable one. Such a position has been attained by Mr. F——, a member of the present State Senate. A few days since, during the reading of the journal, it was found that on a certain motion, Messrs. —— —— and K—— demanded ayes and nays." Mr. K—— denied the "call," and wished his name erased. The blank had to be filled, but who would take the responsibility? There was the rub! Finally, and after some five minutes had been spent in "doing nothing," Senator F——, in his usual manner, rose and said, "Mr. Clerk, put 'em down to me." He took his seat amidst a perfect roar among the lookers-on. - - - THE following letter from a broker in Nevada to a brother broker in this city, has been placed in our hands for publication. Notice the slight touch of "the shop" in it here and there. We cut off the top and strike directly *in medias res*:

"NEVADA, Feb. 4th, 1855.

"*Dear* uncle Ned," says the facetious rogue, "why don't you tell a body what's going on in San Francisco, when you write? and why don't you "post me up," (*here*, not there.) Really, I've almost forgotten how Montgomery St. looks, or the Plaza, or the Exchange, or any other locality. As for Nevada, why it is one of the mountain towns you read of, and has a large population of industrious, honest, enterprising Sons of Tem——, of *Adam*, besides a large number of ——. It was discovered one morning early, and created great excitement among those who had no 'collaterals,' but was kept quiet, and the thing was *settled* that day; since then it has stood *very high*, as it is known to possess abundant resources, doing a large cash business and having a *very little paper* out. Its circulating medium is derived from the issues of the *Banks* of 'Big Deer Creek' and its 'Branches,' and those of the old and firmly established concern of QUARTZ & MILLS. Quartz was here some time before Mills, but the business was left to take care of itself, and of course produced nothing. *Quartz* is an old Californian, with abundant resources, but required Yankee ingenuity and enterprise to develop and bring it into profitable use; *Mills* is a *smashing*, energetic, go-ahead institution, but has been here only since 1850, is very attentive to business, whilst *Quartz* is all over: if there are heavy mining operations going on, you're sure to find '*Quartz*' leads. For a long time, Quartz & Mills did not operate profitably together, and it was supposed *Quartz* would compel *Mills* to suspend operations, but *Mills* stood *firm,* and is now abundantly able to *crush* 'Quartz.'

The principal commodity of this place, is '*rocks,*' a term you may use in a geological sense, or as a common- nickname for *oro,* and nine-tenths of the population are engaged in getting the raw material ready for the manufacturer; the '*rocks*' geological are granite 'boulders,' varying in size from that of a hole in the ground to a pile of saw-dust; and as the supply is so much greater than the demand, the market for them is *heavy;* in fact, there is no *movement* in them, except for immediate use. The '*rocks*' oro-ical, are of an entirely different kind, and are always in demand—this always being greater than the *supply;* and although transactions in this kind are on a comparatively *small scale,* the numbers engaged therein make the total amount very large.

After all, however, the expenses are so great, that now, 'Uncle Sam' is the only one who really coins money by the operation.

The manufacture of lumber is also an extensive branch of business here, timber being very plenty and of superior quality. This has been a very profitable trade, out of which many "piles" have been made; labor in this department is very cheap, as many work for *board* only. There are trees here of most incredible dimensions, many of which, will measure more than three hundred feet in circumference; but for a description of these, and other statistics relating to the lumber business, I must refer you to a work on this subject, by Judge Bryant, formerly "Alcalde" of San Francisco, entitled, 'What I *saw* in California.' I am told the Judge built the first saw-mill in the State, and made a *large pile* by it."

And here we stop. - - - A POOR woman called at the mint the other day and inquired for the proprietor. The inquiry afforded the clerks a good deal of amusement, but politely directing her to Washington, they informed her that if she would knock at the "White House" and ask for "Uncle Sam," she would probably see him. - - - THE following stanzas, from the "Faerie Queene," written more than two centuries and a-half ago, seem like a prophecy and will apply to the present time. They occur in the conversation between the Red Cross Knight and the "holy aged man" of the "House of Holinesse." The latter has been showing to his guest the glories of the New Jerusalem:

> "'Till now,' said then the Knight, 'I weened well,
>   That great Cleopolis, where I have beene,
> In which that fairest Fary Queene doth dwell,
>   The fairest citty was that might be seene;
>   And that bright towre, all built of christall clene,
>   Panthea seem'd the brightest thing that was;
> But now, by proofe all otherwise, I weene;
>   For this great citty that does far surpass,
> And this bright Angels Towre, quite dims that towre of glas.'
>
> 'More trew,' then said the holy aged man;
>   ' Yet is Cleopolis for earthly frame,
> The fairest peece that eie beholden can:
>   And well beseemes all Knights of noble name
>   That covett in th'immortall booke of fame
> To be eternized, that same to haunt,
>   And doen their service to that soveraign Dame
> That glory does to them for guerdon graunt;
>   For she is heavenly borne, and heaven may justly vaunt.'"

[Book First, Canto X, stanzas 58, 59.

By Cleopolis, the capital of Faerie Land, was meant London, and by making Victoria the Faerie Queene, the above lines lose much of their fiction, and become almost truth. Little did Spenser think that his brilliant fancy, of a "bright towre all built of christall clene," would have found such a complete realization as the "towre of glass" which now stands as a glittering diadem upon the hill of Sydenham.

THE PIONEER.

Vol. III.]　　　　JUNE, 1855.　　　　[No. 6.

A PAIR OF MYTHS:
BEING CHAPTER FIFTH OF AN UNPUBLISHED WORK.

BY CAXTON.

EIGHT days passed away unreckoned, and still I remained utterly unconscious of everything occurring around me. The morning of the ninth dawned, dragged heavily along, and noon approached, whilst I lay in the same comatose state. No alteration had taken place, except that a deeper and a sounder sleep seemed to have seized upon me ; a symptom hailed by my physician with joy, but regarded by my mother with increased alarm.

Suddenly, the incautious closing of my chamber door, as my eldest sister—Miss Lucy Stanly, then in her fifteenth year—entered the apartment, aroused me from slumber and oblivion.

Abed, at noon-day ! What did it betoken ? I endeavored to recall something of the past, but memory for a long time refused its aid, and I appeared as fatally and irremediably unconscious as ever. Gradually, however, my shattered mind recovered its faculties, and in less than an hour after my awakening I felt perfectly restored. No pain tormented me, and no torpor benumbed my faculties. I rapidly reviewed, mentally, the occurrences of the day before, *when*, as I imagined, the disaster had happened, and resolved at once to rise from my bed and prosecute my intended journey.

At this moment, my father entered the apartment, and observing that I was awake ventured to speak to me kindly and in a very low tone. I smiled at his uneasiness, and immediately relieved him from all apprehension, by conversing freely and intelligibly of the late catastrophe. His delight knew no bounds. He seized my hand a thousand times, and pressed it again and again to his lips. At length, remembering that my mother was ignorant of my complete restoration, he rushed from the room, in order to be the first to convey the welcome intelligence

My bed was soon surrounded by the whole family, chattering away, wild with joy, and imprinting scores of kisses on my lips, cheeks and forehead. The excitement proved too severe for me in my weak condition, and had not the timely arrival of the physician intervened to clear my chamber of every intruder, except mamma Betty, as we all called the nurse, these pages in all human probability would never have arrested the reader's eye. As it was, I suddenly grew very sick and faint ; everything around me assumed a deep green tinge, and I fell into a deathlike swoon.

Another morning's sun was shining cheerily in at my window, when consciousness again returned. The doctor was soon at my side, and instead of prescribing physic as a remedy, requested my sister to sit at my bedside, and read in a low tone any interesting little story she might select. He cautioned her not to mention, even in the most casual manner, *Mormonism*, *St. Louis*, or the *Moselle*, which order she most implicitly obeyed; nor could all my ingenuity extract a solitary remark in relation to either.

My sister was not very long in making a selection ; for supposing what delighted herself would not fail to amuse me, she brought in a manuscript, carefully folded, and proceeded at once to narrate its history. It was written by my father, as a sort of model or sampler for my brothers and sisters, which they were to imitate when *composition-day* came round, instead of "hammering away," as he called it, on moral essays and metaphysical commonplaces. It was styled,

THE KING OF THE NINE-PINS: A MYTH.

Heinrich Schwartz, or Black Hal, as he was wont to be called, was an old toper, but he was possessed of infinite good humor, and related a great many very queer stories, the truth of which no one that I ever heard of had the hardihood to doubt ; for Black Hal had an uncommon share of "Teutonic pluck" about him, and was at times very unceremonious in the display of it. But Hal had a weakness— it was not liquor, for that was his strength—which he never denied ; *Hal was too fond of Nine-Pins.* He had told me, in confidence, that "many a time and oft" he had rolled incessantly for weeks together. I think I heard him say that he once rolled for a month, day and night, without stopping a single moment to eat or to drink, or even to catch his breath.

I did not question his veracity at the time, but since, on reflection, the fact seems almost incredible ; and were it not that this sketch might accidentally fall in his way, I might be tempted to show philosophically that such a thing could not possibly be. And yet I have read of very long fasts in my day—that, for instance, of Captain Riley in the great Sahara, and others, which will readily occur to the reader. But I must not episodize, or I shall not reach my story.

Black Hal was sitting late one afternoon in a Nine-Pin Alley, in the little town of Kaatskill, in the State of New York—it is true, for he said so—when a tremendous thunder-storm invested his retreat. His companions, one by one, had left him, until, rising from his seat and gazing around, he discovered that he was alone. The alley-keeper, too, could nowhere be found, and the boys who were employed to set up the pins had disappeared with the rest. It was growing very late, and Hal had a long walk, and he thought it most prudent to get ready to start home. The lightning glared in at the door and windows most vividly, and the heavy thunder crashed and rumbled and roared louder than he had ever heard it before. The rain, too, now commenced to batter down tremendously, and just as night set in, Hal just got ready to set out. Hal first felt uneasy, next unhappy, and finally miserable. If he had but a boy to talk to! I'm afraid Hal began to grow scared. A verse that he learned in his boyhood, across the wide sea, came unasked into his mind. It always came there precisely at the time he did not desire its company. It ran thus:

> "Oh! for the might of dread Odin,
>   The powers upon him shed,
> For a sail in the good ship Skidbladnir,*
>   And a talk with Mimir's head!" †

This verse was repeated over and over again inaudibly; gradually, however, his voice became a little louder, and a little louder still, until finally poor Hal hallooed it vociferously forth so sonorously that it drowned the very thunder. He had repeated it just seventy-seven times, when suddenly a monstrous head was thrust in at the door, and demanded in a voice that sounded like the maelstrom, "What do *you* want with Odin?" "Oh! nothing, nothing in the world, I thank you, sir," politely responded poor Hal, shaking from head to foot. Here the head was followed by the shoulders, arms, body and legs of a giant at least forty feet high. Of course he came in on all fours, and approached in close proximity to Black Hal. Hal involuntarily retreated, as far as he could, reciting to himself the only prayer he remembered, "Now I lay me down to sleep," etc.

The giant did not appear desirous of pursuing Hal, *being afraid,*— so Hal said,—*that he would draw his knife on him.* But be the cause what it might, he seated himself at the head of the nine-pin alley, and shouted, "Stand up!" As he did so, the nine-pins at the other end arose and took their places.

"Now, sir," said he, turning again to Hal, "I'll bet you an ounce of your blood I can beat you rolling."

Hal trembled again, but meekly replied, "Please, sir, we don't bet *blood* now-a-days—we bet *money.*"

"Blood's my money," roared forth the giant; "Fee, fo, fum!" Hal tried in vain to hoist the window.

"Will you bet?"

"Yes, sir," said Hal; and he thought as 'twas only *an ounce,* he could spare that without much danger, and it might appease the monster's appetite.

"Roll first!" said the giant.

"Yes, sir!" replied Hal, as he seized what he supposed to be the largest and his favorite ball.

---

* The ship Skidbladnir was the property of Odin. He could sail in it on the most dangerous seas, and yet could fold it up and carry it in his pocket.

† Mimir's head was always the companion of Odin. When he desired to know what was transpiring in distant countries, he inquired of Mimir, and always received a correct reply.

"What are you doing with Mimir's head?" roared forth the monster.

"I beg your pardon, most humbly," began Hal, as he let the bloody head fall; "I did not mean any harm."

"Rumble, bang-whang!" bellowed the thunder.

Hal fell on his knees and recited most devoutly, "Now I lay me down," etc.

"Roll on! roll on! I say," and the giant seized poor Hal by the collar and set him on his feet.

He now selected a large ball, and poising it carefully in his hand, ran a few steps, and sent it whirling right in among the nine-pins; but what was his astonishment to behold them jump lightly aside, and permit the ball to pass in an avenue directly through the middle of the alley. Hal shuddered! The second and third ball met with no better success. Odin—for Hal said it was certainly he, as he had Mimir's head along—now grasped a ball and rolled it with all his might; but long before it reached the nine-pins, they had, every one of them, tumbled down, and lay sprawling on the alley.

"Two spares!" said the giant, as he grinned most gleefully at poor Hal. "Get up!" and up the pins all stood instantly. Taking another ball, he hurled it down the alley, and the same result followed. "Two more spares!" and Odin shook his gigantic sides with laughter.

"I give up the game," whined out Hal.

"Then you lose double," rejoined Odin.

Hal readily consented to pay two ounces, for he imagined, by yielding at once, he would so much the sooner get rid of his grim companion. As he said so, Odin pulled a pair of scales out of his coat pocket, made proportionably to his own size. He poised them upon a beam in the alley, and drew forth what he denominated two ounces, and put them in one scale. Each ounce was about the size of a twenty-eight pound weight, and was quite as heavy.

"Ha! ha! ha!! ha! ha! ha!!! ha! ha! ha!!!!" shouted the giant, as he grasped the gasping and terrified gambler. He soon rolled up his sleeves, and bound his arm with a pocket handkerchief. Next he drew forth a lancet as long as a sword, and drove the point into the biggest vein he could discover. Hal screamed and fainted! When he returned to consciousness, the sun was shining brightly in at the window, and the sweet rumbling of the balls assured him that he still lay where the giant left him. On rising to his feet he perceived that a large coagulum of blood had collected where his head rested all night, and that he could scarcely walk from the effects of his exhaustion. He returned immediately home and told his wife all that had occurred; and though, like some of the neighbors, she distrusted the tale, yet she never intimated her doubts to Black Hal himself. The alley-keeper assured me in a whisper, one day, that upon the very night fixed on by Hal for the adventure, he was beastly drunk, and had been engaged in a fight with one of his boon companions, who gave him a black eye and a bloody nose. But the alley-keeper was always jealous of Black Hal's superiority in story telling; besides he often drank too much himself, and I suspect he started the report he related to me in a fit of wounded pride, or drunken braggadocio. One thing is certain, he never venturned to repeat the story in the presence of Black Hal himself.

—

In spite of the attention I endeavored to bestow on the marvelous history of Black Hal and his grim companion, my mind occasionally wandered far away, and could only find repose in communing with her who I now discovered for the first time held in her own hands the thread of my destiny. Lucy was not blind to these fits of abstraction, and whenever they gained entire control of my attention, she would pause, lay down the manuscript, and threaten most seriously to discontinue the perusal, unless I proved a better listener. I ask no man's pardon for declaring that my sister was an excellent reader. Most brothers, perhaps, think the same of most sisters; but there *was* a charm in Lucy's accent and a distinctness in her enunciation I have never heard excelled. Owing to these qualities, as much, perhaps, as to the strangeness of the story, I became interested in the fate of the drunken gambler, and when Lucy concluded, I was ready to exclaim, "And pray where is Black Hal now?"

My thoughts took another direction, however, and I impatiently demanded whether or not the sample story had been imitated. A guilty blush assured me quite as satisfactorily as words could have done, that Miss Lucy had herself made an attempt, and I therefore insisted that as she had whetted and excited the appetite, it would be highly unfraternal—(particularly in my present very precarious condition)—that parenthesis settled the matter—to deny me the means of satisfying it.

"But you'll laugh at me," timidly whispered my sister.

"Of course I shall," said I, "if your catastrophe is half as melancholy as Black Hal's. But make haste, or I shall be off to St. Louis. But pray, inform me, what is the subject of your composition?"

"*The Origin of Marriage.*"

"I believe, on my soul," responded I, laughing outright, "you girls never think about anything else."

I provoked no reply, and the manuscript being unfolded, my sister thus attempted to elucidate

THE ORIGIN OF MARRIAGE.

Professor Williams having ceased his manipulations, my eyes involuntarily closed, and I became unconscious to everything occurring around me. There's truth in mesmerism, after all, thought I, and being in the clairvoyant state, I beheld a most beautiful comet at this moment emerging from the constellation Taurus, and describing a curve about the star Zeta, one of the Pleiades. Now for a trip through infinite space! and as this thought entered my brain, I grasped a hair in the tail of the comet as it whizzed by me.

I climbed up the glittering hair until I found myself seated very comfortably on the comet's back, and was beginning to enjoy my starlit ramble exceedingly, when I was suddenly aroused from my meditations by the song of a heavenly minstrel, who, wandering from star to star and system to system, sang the fate of other worlds and other beings to those who would listen to his strains and grant him the rites of hospitality. As I approached, his tones were suddenly changed, his voice lowered into a deeper key, and gazing intently at me, or at what evidenced my presence to his sight, thus began:

The flaming sword of the cherub, which had waved so frightfully above the gate of the garden of Eden, had disappeared; the angel himself was gone; and Adam, as he approached the spot, where so lately he had enjoyed the delights of Heaven, beheld with astonishment and regret, that Paradise and all its splendors had departed from the earth forever. Where the garden lately bloomed, he could discover only the dark and smouldering embers of a conflagration; a hard lava had incrusted itself along the golden walks, the birds were flown, the flowers withered, the fountains dried up, and desolation brooded over the scene.

"Ah!" sighed the Patriarch of men, "where are now the pleasures, which I once enjoyed along these peaceful avenues? Where are all those beautiful spirits, given by Heaven, to watch over and protect me? Each guardian angel has deserted me, and the rainbow glories of Paradise have flown. No more the sun shines out in undimmed splendor, for clouds array him in gloom; the earth, forgetful of her verdure and her flowers, produces thorns to wound, and frosts to chill me. The very air, once all balm and zephyrs, now howls around me, with the voice of the storm and the fury of the hurricane. No more the notes of peace and happiness greet my ears, but the harsh tones of strife and battle, resound on every side. Nature has kindled the flames of discord in her own bosom, and universal war has begun his reign!"

And then the father of mankind hid his face in the bosom of his companion, and wept the bitter tears of contrition and repentance.

"O, do not weep so bitterly, my Adam," exclaimed his companion. "True, we are miserable, but all is not yet lost; we have forfeited the smiles of Heaven, but we may yet regain our lost place in its affections. Let us learn from our misfortunes the anguish of guilt, but let us learn also the mercy of redemption. We may yet be happy."

"O, talk not of happiness now," interrupted Adam; "that Nymph who once waited at our side, attentive to the beck, has disappeared, and fled from the companionship of such guilty, fallen beings, as ourselves, forever."

"Not forever, Adam," kindly rejoined Eve; "she may yet be lurking among these groves, or lie hid behind yon hills."

"Then let us find her," quickly responded Adam; "you follow the sun, sweet Eve, to his resting-place, whilst I will trace these sparkling waters to their bourn. Let us ramble this whole creation o'er, and when we have found her, let us meet again on this very spot, and cling to her side, until the doom of Death shall overtake us."

And the eye of Adam, beamed with Hope, then kindled for the first time on earth in the bosom of man; and he bade Eve his first farewell, and started eastward in his search.

Eve turned her face to the west, and set out on her allotted journey.

The sun had shone a hundred times in midsummer splendor, and a hundred times had hid himself in the clouds of winter, and yet no human foot had trod the spot where the garden of Eden once bloomed. Adam had in vain traced the Euphrates to the sea, and climbed the Himalaya mountains. In vain had he endured the tropical heats on the Ganges, and the winter's cold in Siberia. He stood at last upon the borders of that narrow sea, which separates Asia from America, and casting a wistful glance to the far-off continent, exclaimed—"In yon land, so deeply blue in the distance, that it looks like Heaven, Happiness may have taken refuge; alas! I cannot pursue her there! I will return to Eden, and learn if Eve too has been unsuccessful."

And then he took one more look at the distant land, sighed his adieu, and set out on his return.

Poor Eve! First child of misery, first daughter of despair! Poor Eve, with the blue of Heaven in her eye, and the crimson of shame upon her lip! Poor Eve, arrayed in beauty, but hastening to decay, —she too, was unsuccessful.

Wandering in her westward way, the azure waters of the Mediterranean soon gleamed upon her sight; she stood at length upon the pebbly shore, and the glad waves, silent as death before, when they kissed her naked feet, commenced that song, still heard in their eternal roar. A mermaid seemed to rise from the waters at her feet and to imitate her every motion. Her long, dark tresses, her deep blue eyes, her rosy cheek, her sorrowful look, all were reflected in the mermaid before her.

"Sweet Spirit," said Eve, "can'st thou inform me, where the nymph Happiness lies concealed? she always stood beside us in the garden of Eden, but when we were driven from Paradise, we beheld her no more?" The lips of the mermaid moved, but Eve could hear no reply.

Ah! mother of mankind, the crystal waters of every sea, reflecting thy lovely image, still faithful to their trust, conceal a mermaid in their bosom for every daughter of beauty, who looks upon them!

Neither the orange groves of the Arno, nor the vineyards of France, neither the forests of Germania, nor the caves of Norway, concealed the sought-for nymph. Eve explored them all! Her track was imprinted in the sands of Sahara, by the banks of the Niger, on the rocks of Bengola, in the vales of Abyssinia,—but all in vain!

"O, Happiness, art thou indeed departed from our earth? how can we live without thee? Come Death," cried Eve, "come now, and take me where thou wilt; this world is a desert, for Happiness has left it desolate."

A gentle slumber soon overcame the wearied child of sorrow, and in her sleep a vision came to comfort her. She dreamed that she stood before an aged man, whose hoary locks attested that the snows of many winters had whitened them, and in whose glance she recognized the spirit of Wisdom.

"Aged Father," said Eve, "where is Happiness?" and then she burst into a flood of tears.

"Comfort thyself, Daughter," mildly answered the old man; "Happiness yet dwells on earth, but she is no longer visible. A temple is built for her in every mortal's bosom, but she never ascends her throne until welcomed there by the child of Honor and Love."

The morning sun aroused Eve from her slumber, but did not dispel the memory of her dream. "I will return to Eden, and there await until the child of Honor and Love shall enthrone in my bosom the lost nymph Happiness;" and saying this, she turned her face to the eastward, and thinking of Adam and her vision, journeyed joyfully along.

The sun of Spring had opened the flowers and clothed the woods in verdure,—had freed the streams from their icy fetters and inspired the warbling world with harmony, when two forlorn and wearied travelers approached the banks of the river Pison—that river which had flowed through the garden of Eden, when the first sunshine broke upon the world. A hundred years had rolled away, and the echo of no human voice had resounded through the deserted groves. At length, the dusky figures emerge from the overshadowing shrubbery, and raised their eyes into each other's faces. One bound! one cry! and they weep for joy, in each other's arms.

Adam related his sad and melancholy story, and then Eve soon finished hers. But no sooner had she told her dream, than Adam, straining her to his bosom, exclaimed—

"There is no mystery here, my Eve; If Happiness on earth be indeed the child of Honor and Love, it must be in Matrimony alone! What else now left us on earth, can lay claim to the precious boon? approved by Heaven, and cherished by man, in the holy bands of Matrimony it must consist; and if this be all, we need seek no further; it is ours!"

They then knelt in prayer, and returned thanks to Heaven, that though the garden of Eden was a wild, and the nymph Happiness no longer an angel at their side, yet that her spirit was still present in every bosom, where the heart is linked to Honor and Love, by the sacred ties of Matrimony.

THE POET'S LIFE.

BY J. SWETT.

It is not true the poet lives
　Alone in fanciful *ideal*,
That love of poetry ever gives
　Distaste for plain, existing *real*.

It is not true the poet's heart
　Where gush the deepest springs of life,
Hath feebler power to act its part
　In daily scenes of toil and strife.

It is not true the poet's sky
　Is clouded by the mist of dreams,
That truthful nature to his eye,
　Less beautiful and simple seems.

Not in the strong and brawny arm
　Controlling might exists alone,—

There is a power that can disarm
　The battlements of brass and stone.

Who breathes in song the burning thought,
　Which quickens life in human mind,
A nobler deed of power hath wrought
　Than he who lords it o'er mankind.

There is an inner life in man,
　Too oft in slavish bondage cast,
A life which passion holds in ban,
　With iron fetters, strong and fast.

Who wakes the soul with spirit power,
　To break the fetters of the slave—
Holds over life a mightier power
　Than strength of muscle ever gave.

THE HALLS OF THE PAST.

BY *******

HE sat in the twilight, gazing into the fire. The flames flickered and lighted up his thoughtful and quiet face, and shone upon the tears which stole down his cheeks. The dear old man. He was sad and dreary; he felt that he was alone amidst a new generation; he felt that all the friends of his youth and manhood had passed away. The stars, serene and holy, looked down upon him, and he thought how long he had watched them in their quiet beauty alone. Sitting upon the shore of Time, hearing the swell of the mighty ocean, and seeing so many he loved depart across its waters, he felt almost as if he had been forgotten here. As sorrowful these thoughts came to him, he raised his eyes, and betwixt his tears he saw the tender-eyed Memory standing by his side. Lovingly she led him with her to the ivy-grown, mouldering Halls of the Past. How sad they seemed to him at first! How the long, sweeping arches echoed at the tread of his feet! How many visions and phantoms of long ago seemed to flit before his eyes! But it grew brighter soon, and the warm sunlight dispelled the illusions, and Memory pointed out to him, hanging on the wall, the life-pictures, which were to him the most precious possessions of his old age. How bright were the colors! how the figures stood out from the canvas!

See now, nestled among the hills, the simple cottage, overlooking scenes so dear to him. He was standing by the door; younger brothers and sisters played or wept around him, and his mother tearfully imprinted a kiss upon his forehead, for she well understood the dangers and hardships of the great world, for which he was leaving her. The first rosy glow of the spring morning lighted up the well-remembered hills and the valley, looked at its own beauty in the lake at his feet and shone upon the head of the young boy, as, full of promise and of joy, he left the scenes of his childhood to begin his battle of life. "Mother, sweet mother," the old man murmured, "you too are waiting for me there."———

Before the next picture, the old man stood entranced. The sun had risen higher now and shone beautifully and clearly through the leaves of the oak grove. Countless water lilies, children of the sunshine and the wave, rested queen-like near the shore, or hid their pink-white blossoms under their graceful leaves. Down the wood walked a youth and maiden, engaged in earnest conversation. They spoke of what life should be, and how love should lead them on, and smooth away life's trials, and transform the two into the image of the Perfect One. Nor should their love be confined to themselves alone, but widen to all around them, gladdening and brightening the hearts of others less happy than themselves. She spoke confidingly, for she knew that his heart was with her and that his manly strength would lead her on, when perhaps her heart would fail; and as he folded her to his bosom, he thanked the dear God who had granted him so much of happiness; —he, who felt so unworthy of it;—and the sunlight danced among the leaves and fluttered and slid down upon her golden hair, and in her eyes the deep blue heavens lay reflected, and the flowers rang their bells and lent an added fragrance to the air, and all nature seemed to be changed and glorified. "O Memory!" the old man cried, "thrice blessed Memory! Let me gaze forever upon her, as she walked home-ward through the oak-grove."————

How sad the face of Memory grew, as she pointed to the next scene, and drew aside the folds of the dark curtain, which hung before it. Noon, hot, scorching noon;—all freshness and life seemed to have vanished from the air, and only the dull, hot sun poured down his rays upon the earth, where not a leaf was seen, not a flower, not a sign of life. And did this hard, uncompromising face belong to the boy so full of promise,—to the youth so full of generous hopes, and was *this* the end of it all?

The old man gazed with streaming eyes. He remembered how, as wealth increased, his soul had seemed to die within him; he remem-bered how he had placed the Eternal Right lower than his own self-interest;—he saw the misery of the widow whom his avarice had left without a home;—he saw the stern, sad face of the man whose first trifling offense had passed unforgiven by him,—whom he had so cruelly wronged. He sank upon his knees before the dark picture, and hid his face in his hands with grief. "Blot out, O cruel Memory," he sobbed, "blot out this sad, sad picture from the walls!"————

Then Memory took him by the hand, and smiling, led him onward. He wiped away his tears as he gazed once more on that sunny, cheer-ful room. Yes, he was changed. Friends and fortune and beloved child had all been swept away from him, and an altered man he had risen from his bed of sickness. The warm glow of the autumn sun came in at his window betwixt the leaves of the flowering acacias, and filled the little chamber with fragrant light. Beside him, holding his hand, was his wife, grown older now, but wearing the same sweet, thoughtful look of her girlhood. The sad and subdued look which she had worn of late, had vanished. They spoke, as in their youth, of life's deep meaning; they spoke from their own experience of its cares, its fierce temptations and its joys. With bitterest tears of repentance, he had passed through the Valley of Humiliation, and had come at length to the golden Land of Peace. Mourning over the wasted years of his earlier manhood, he had resolved to make all the reparation in his power to wash away his guilt.

He had thanked God that his life was spared, that he might make atonement; and if in his face was no longer the rash confidence of his youth, you could trace there a deeper, holier resolve. Thinking on these things, he turned to his wife, who opened the book which lay on her lap and read these words to him—words which he had never for-gotten:—"Carry back with you into life this holy earnestness; for earnestness is what makes life eternity." "Yes, thou blessed wife," the old man murmured, "thou wert ever the angel at my side!" One could see by the next picture that he had kept his resolve.————

The sun had nearly sunk below the horizon, and the shadows were deepening. A few faint stars glimmered in the blue firmament, as through the snows of the cold winter twilight, the old man walked homeward as from the dwellings of the poor. He was alone now. She, who had been the idol of his youth, the darling of his manhood, had now, alas! become the most blessed memory of his age. Little children offered to the kind old man pet flowers, they had reared with so much care, and father and mother turned to bid a kindly, good evening to him, whose presence had always been a benediction to them. Was any generous, humane scheme to be set on foot, men knew to whom to go for assistance and advice. His was the heart and the hand always ready to enter into the joys and to relieve the sorrows of others. Nobly had he atoned for the sins of his manhood.

This was the last scene that Memory showed to him. He had come to the end of the corridor, and lovely in the roseate glow of the setting sun, stood the clear-browed figure of Hope. "O Hope," the old man cried, "beloved sister of the sweet, yet sad Memory, do not leave me again; be with me to the last." And smilingly the clear-browed Hope pointed to the skies. The old man's heart beat more quickly as he looked upon the beloved faces of those who had gone before him. Friends of his youth—friends of his manhood—mother, sister and beloved child—but before them all, in the radiance of her early youth, only grown more celestially fair, walked his wife. Through long vistas of oak trees, surrounded by starry hosts, with loving, outstretched arms she advanced to meet him. He sprang up—his old age had passed from him;—he was again the generous, noble youth; and the stars and the angels sang for joy as they witnessed the meeting of souls so dear to one another, of joy so pure and so intense.————

Yes, the old man was dead. Watched over by the tranquil stars, he sat there alone, with a smile of heavenly joy lighting up his countenance. They grieved to think they should no more hear his kindly voice, and mourned that he should have passed away *alone;* but they saw not the scenes he had passed through, nor the heavenly vision that had been with him at the last.

THE MIST OF THE MORNING.

BY JUSTINA.

Oh! fair is the mist when it rises to view,
O'er the lake in whose bosom its loveliness grew;
How softly it lingers as though loth to leave
The cool wave for bright Sol, who perchance may deceive.
But his beams still keep luring it upward and on—
Till far from its calm home the mist-wreath has gone.
It floats with the bright clouds of Heaven awhile,
Till they gather with dark frowns, to hide the sun's smile;
Then dissolved into tears it again seeks the earth
And sinks in the loved lake, where first it had birth.

Oh! there are some finely strung spirits of truth,—
Warm and bright as the sun, are the hopes of their youth;
But too gentle and pure for the storm-clouds of strife,
They fade like the mist in the morning of life;
Sick-hearted they turn from its turmoil to weep—
In the home of their childhood they lay them to sleep—
Till the light of the last morn shall ope the closed eye
To the unclouded glory of God in the sky—
Till the sound of the last trump shall wake the hushed heart,
To dwell in that glory never more to depart.

FACTS—NOT FICTION.

A TALE OF THE SOUTH-WEST.

BY MRS. S. A. DOWNER.

IT was one of the most oppressive mornings I had ever experienced, with that peculiar, muggy and unwholsome state of the atmosphere, that, had it been a few months later in the season, would have given rise to the expression, "real yellow fever weather." For a couple of hours it had rained, as it only can rain in New Orleans, in perfect torrents, flooding the streets, and rendering the crossings impassable while it lasted, or sinking a few inches, to be returned in vapor from the reeking pavements, as the sultry rays of the sun again broke forth with redoubled heat. The very air, as it entered through the glass doors, opening on the balcony, seemed laden with "Yellow Jack" and cholera. Lounging upon a sofa, too languid for any exertion— even to wave a fan required an effort—I began to count up the many months that must elapse, ere we could reasonably expect cool weather. This was early in April, and I quite shrank from the long rage of Summer, while the bare thought of mosquitos made me more nervous. I ran over in my mind the advantages and disadvantages of the various watering places that open on the Gulf of Mexico, and finally concluded that home was the best place after all;—decidedly the most comfortable place, if—one could only obtain a little fresh air. This was not to be expected, and I soon fell into a reverie, the subject of which was cooling streams, shaded by forest trees, and fanned by refreshing zephyrs ; or, of deep caverns by some lonely sea-side, where shelter from a tropical sun might at least be obtained. I had reached this point, and was profoundly sighing, "O for one breath of northern air!" when a young servant, who had been sent to the post-office, returned with letters, which he placed on the sofa-table beside me.

"A glass of water, Sam," and I took up the letters.

They were from beloved friends. The first was dated from Mississippi, and contained a cordial invitation for me to spend the Summer at the rural home of the writer. It was filled with glowing accounts of flowers then in bloom, of fruit just ripening,—to be followed by successive varieties,—and of the whole-soul welcome that awaited me if I would come. This was very gratifying. A sip of iced-water, and I opened another. The second was from Louisiana, on the opposite side of the river, and bore not only an invitation, but almost a command, to "pack up" and make them a visit. It said : "We are all here at the upper plantation, where we shall remain until May, when we leave for the north. In the meantime, do come up ; everything is looking so green and beautiful. The change will do you good and I have a great secret to impart. Of course it is quite useless to ask your good *mari* to accompany you, but I know he will not object to your coming without him. I shall therefore expect you on the next trip of the Magnolia, and will send the carriage to meet you at the landing."

"The very thing!" I exclaimed, "and it will be killing two birds with one stone!" Our '*mari*' did not object; *au contraire*, a superficial observer might have been led to suppose, from the alacrity with which any little deficiency pertaining to the toilet was obtained, and the solicitude exhibited in providing for all possible wants, that it was to be a mutual holiday—a trial of freedom extremely gratifying to at least one of the parties, but when the Saturday morning came, and I took possession of my commodious state-room, one had only to look in his honest face, as he placed me under the care of that prince of captains, the popular commander of the Magnolia, and read the expression of deep love, that welled up from a loyal heart, and filled his eyes to overflowing, to be satisfied that the advantage to be gained by another, was the sole consideration.

I had traveled so often with Captain T., and on that very boat, that it was with quite a home feeling, I seated myself at the door of my state-room, and glanced at the scenery as we passed up the coast. The river was high—almost even with the banks—affording a fine view of the rich sugar and cotton plantations, that stretched far back to the swamps, whose cypress trees, draperied with funereal moss, offered a strong contrast to the gay flower-gardens, beautiful shrubbery and the evergreen trees which surround the planter's mansion. These are spacious square buildings with rectangular roofs and a veranda partly enclosed with lattice-work, over which climbing plants cluster, to the exclusion of the sun. Hedges of rose and hawthorn, with groves of orange and lemon trees, spread on every side, extending almost to the levee's edge; while noble live-oaks with myrtle and China trees hide, with their thick foliage, the walks and arbors that environ these quiet abodes. It is pretty, but monotonous. Higher up fewer signs of cultivation appear, and after passing Bayou Sara, long intervals elapse before there are any signs of culture or settlement. The second day offered so little of interest, that it afforded sufficient time for my womanly curiosity to exercise itself in conjecturing the secret I was to learn.

That it was to be a wedding, I felt almost certain; but whose could it be? My friend was a widow—a widow for the second time, and of two years' standing—but no! it could not be her wedding. Widows do sometimes marry the third, or even the fourth time, but not she! it would have been almost sacrilege to doubt her constancy. There was a daughter, and a lovely girl she was; it must be she. To be sure, she had just left school, but what of that? it was not uncommon for school girls to marry, or for girls to marry and to go to school afterward. When I had got thus far, I ran over in my mind all the eligible matches my fancy could suggest, but not being able to settle it to my satisfaction, gave it up. Two days and a night brought us to the mouth of Lake St. Pierre, where I was landed and placed in the carriage by our ever courteous captain, after seeing my trunk well secured behind, and the troublesome bandbox on the vacant seat in front.

We rolled along the banks of the beautiful silver lake, just as the declining sun was sinking behind the thick hammocks of live oak on the opposite shore, where reposed large flocks of sheep, protected and kept together by a shepherd dog. The air was redolent with fragrance from the fresh opening blossoms of spring. A gentle breeze raised light curling ripples on the face of the stream, that sparkled and glowed with the rays of the setting sun. In its bosom vast shoals of mullet, with innumerable other fishes, rejoiced in their spring-day life secure from hook or net. Thirty years ago this was the favorite hunting ground of the Choctaw, and where is he now? West of the great Father of Waters he may find forests as deep, with lakes as clear; as warm a sun, as bright a sky; but will he ever again find a turf so green, or a spot so dear, as this on which his infant feet first trode? But we have no time to bestow on the red man or his wrongs, for an hour's drive through this beautiful region brings us to China Grove, the residence of my friends. It had become quite dark, but friendly voices greeted me on the portico, and loving hands drew me to the back dining-room, where the tea-table was spread, over which, bright lights gleamed, and where, conspicuous above all, stood a huge dish of strawberries, the first of the season.

And now, dear reader, to the inmates; for it is too dark and shady outside to attempt any description either of the house itself, or its surroundings. And first, let me introduce you to the mother of the family, and the mistress of this large plantation. Mrs. Morris is a lady of about forty-six years of age. She is tall and well made, of full proportions, with rather a dignified air, at the same time both graceful and gracious. Her complexion is rosy, her eyes are dark, her hair is nearly black, and so inclined to curl, it is with difficulty she can keep it smooth, parted over a rather low brow. She has a charming expression; her face beams with benevolence and affection, smiling on all around, and seeming as if it were her sole desire to make every one as good and happy as herself. She is dressed in mourning, for the recent loss of her oldest son, and this accounts for the impression of a chastened sorrow that her countenance wears when in repose. Emma, the only daughter, is sixteen, but looks to be a year older. She is quite as tall as her mother, with a slender and elegant figure, and finely chiseled features. Her delicate complexion is relieved by large, dark eyes, full of sensibility. She has a profusion of glossy hair of almost purple blackness—a rare tinge—and her cheek resembles more the leaf of the magnolia blossom, than the rose. She is very beautiful, her smile peculiarly so; with a quiet grace, gentle and self-possessed, but rather wanting in animation. Of the four boys, this could not be said; they were sprightly and good tempered, with much refinement of manner. Wallace, the oldest, was all animation and wide awake to all that was going on, from the heaviest business of the plantation, down to the braids of his sister's hair, which it was his especial delight to see dressed by the skillful hands of her maid. He was an ardent admirer of beauty, not so much of the beautiful, as of beauty; and "Now Clarise, fasten a white rose here," or, "Bring that band a little lower on the temple," could be heard in passing her dressing-room, where Wallace, standing in the doorway admiringly contemplated his beloved sister, who, book in hand, sate quite indifferent about the matter. Who blames the love of beauty—the admiration for grace of manner? Not we. The only mistake is to suppose that this beauty is a thing of form and coloring, merely. But we forget the tea-table, with its steaming black tea, delicious white biscuit, and well-buttered waffles, with the ripe strawberries, "smothered in cream," which Emma dispensed with a bountiful hand. Tea over, we withdrew to the well-lighted and elegantly furnished parlor, where began such a flood of questionings and answers, concerning mutual friends in the city and out of it, that the evening had nearly passed, before I could turn my attention to two other visitors I found there when I arrived.

The first was a niece of Mrs. Morris, from O., a young lady the same age as Emma, but how unlike! Catherine R., or " Cousin Kate," as the family called her, was a lively, airy creature, light and bounding as a fawn, with a wild, fanciful beauty in her bright, blue eyes, and in the play of her pretty features. Her riant mouth was a perfect Cupid's bow, and her sole occupation on this evening seemed to be that of making others laugh, whether they would or not. The other was a Mr. Selvyn of Washington, late from the Island of Cuba.

The son, Mrs. Morris had so recently lost, was the only child by her first marriage. During his stay at college in a northern State, were sown the seeds of a disease that developed itself with alarming rapidity, soon after his return to his southern home. After months of alternate hope and despair, he was ordered to make trial of the milder climate of Cuba. Mrs. Morris accompanied him, taking Emma with her from her boarding school in New Orleans. While on the Island they became acquainted with an American family of great respectability. The acquaintance was productive of mutual pleasure, the young people became almost inseparable, and the intimacy soon ripened into the warmest friendship. When Mrs. Morris was obliged to return home, Edward seemed to be improving. He was received into the family of Mr. Selvyn as a son and brother, for which their gratitude was only equaled by their hopes. Those hopes were soon to be destroyed. A few weeks brought word of his sudden demise, and they were but now recovering from the blow. This much I had known before, as also of the kindness extended to the poor invalid, who breathed his last under their hospitable roof. The present Mr. Selvyn who had passed many years in Europe, was the son of the friend in whose house Edward had died. He appeared to be about thirty-three years old and of middling hight, with a remarkably fine head. His black hair was soft and curling; his eyes, of deep blue, were full of feeling; his teeth like ivory. His countenance bore the stamp of intellect and mildness, his deportment was exceedingly refined and gentle, his manners were highly polished; while his conversation, replete with information, proved, that during the years spent by him abroad, he had been all eye, all ear, and all grasp. But not in one evening, reader, did I discover this; his attainments were not more conspicuous than his modesty.

"Is he *le futur*?" was my whispered inquiry of Emma, when I took leave for the night. She blushed " celestial, rosy, red," but made no attempt to reply.

Mrs. Morris accompanied me to my cool, airy chamber, where the neatly matted floor, windows draperied with thin, white muslin, and a snow-white bed, gave promise of luxurious rest, exceedingly grateful after the fatigues of travel. She carefully closed the door.

"You need not tell me," I exclaimed, "I have found it all out myself; and when is it to take place?"

"In two weeks; when we leave for Louisville."

"In two weeks!" I repeated; "why, you scarcely know him."

"That is true," she replied; "yet not exactly so, either. We are sometimes placed in such circumstances that the conventional rules of life are disregarded, and we become acquainted in less time than a fashionable code requires; circumstances that bind us in friendship forever with those who but an honr before were entire strangers."

I assented. "Mr. Selvyn had impressed me favorably, and if they were satisfied I had no reason to demur."

My exclamation, which seemed to imply a sense of unbecoming haste in the arrangement, appeared to have dissatisfied her, as with a certain stateliness of manner she proceeded.

"The engagement took place before we left Cuba, with the express understanding that a year or two should expire before their marriage. Had my son lived, we should have adhered to this determination; but ——." She applied her handkerchief to her eyes as she turned away for a moment. Recovering herself, she continued: "Mr. Selvyn pleads so strongly for an immediate marriage that I cannot resist. You are aware how perfectly unexceptionable the match is, in point of family, education and fortune. The latter consideration is of little moment. Emma's portion is large; more than enough; and Mr. Selvyn promised never to take her from me; so that instead of losing a daughter I shall gain a son. His moral character is of course beyond suspicion. Indeed, were I to look the world over, I could not find one with whom I should be better pleased."

There was nothing more to be said; yet, as I lay awake in my comfortable bed, I could not but contrast their ages, and surmise how so superior a man as Mr. Selvyn, with his cultivated tastes, could calmly contemplate the plodding and oftentimes revolting features of plantation life; or how confine himself to the limited circle that would surround him in their princely residence at O. My cogitations did not prevent me from enjoying a night of delicious sleep, from which I was awakened as the day broke by strains of melodious music. I opened a window, and there, on the topmost branch of a magnificent crapemyrtle, stood a mocking-bird caroling forth his song of love to the ears of his happy, listening maté.

I was soon dressed and on the gallery. A mist from the lake still hung over the grounds that were laid out in elegant walks and flowerbeds, with hedges of rose and althea. A long avenue, planted on each side with trees, whose interlacing branches formed into a perfect arcade, led down into the garden, whence Jerry, the old gardener, at that moment issued, bearing a bouquet of mammoth size, composed of every variety of tea rose, which grows here in the greatest magnificence.

"How d'e, uncle Jerry?" and I extended my hand.

"How d'e, missis? I's right glad to see you;" and the faithful fellow shook the hand warmly, in which he placed the bouquet.

"Is this for me? It is really superb!"

"Yes, missis. I knows how fond you is of flowers; sorry we've no figs ripe yet; but you'll stay till there is?"

"I shall stay two weeks, uncle Jerry."

"Two weeks! O, missis, you must stay all summer."

Old family servants feel as much bound as their owners to pay every polite attention to their master's guests; and the greeting from them is frequently fully as cordial; while such is southern hospitality, that were one to remain a whole year with a family, it is not improbable that when the time for departure arrived, the remark would be, "Just stay one year longer, or even six months, and they would not say one word; but to go now——!". To speed the parting guest is altogether unknown, or unpracticed, in this part of the country, the "welcome" extending indefinitely; but this, *par parenthése.*

I looked, and lingered long in the sylvan scene, now on the side gallery, and then on the front, where the sun was rolling the mist from the crystal lake, whose bright waves danced and sparkled, breaking into a thousand brilliant hues, as the water rippled and rose. I was soon joined by Emma, looking lovely as early morning, who greeted me with a kiss as she bade me a lively "*Bon jour.*" I inquired after the health of Mr. Selvyn. She smiled, and soon after spoke of her approaching marriage, but with a tranquility of manner that was quite alarming

"Do you love him, Emma?"

"I admire him greatly, and suppose I shall love him; but I am so very young that I scarcely yet know either life or myself. Besides," she continued, after a pause, "my education is still incomplete. I lost so much time from school during the long illness of my father, and since then of my brother, that I am very deficient, and feel how unsuitable a companion I shall be for a man like Mr. Selvyn."

The bell rang for breakfast. Emma seated herself near her mother, whom she aided in the most graceful manner during the simple repast, quite regardless of herself and attentive only to the wants of others. The time lost from books she had employed in assisting her mother in the discharge of the multifarious duties imposed upon a planter's wife, or in attendance in the sick-room, ministering to the wants of the sufferer; bearing with the weakness, or soothing the temper, disease had rendered querulous. While thus engaged, what she had lost in elementary knowledge she had gained in all the womanly attributes that adorn and sweeten home, and in those truly feminine attractions that should be the end of knowledge. Mr. Selvyn proposed that on their return in autumn she should commence a course of reading and resume some studies under his supervision. A glad assent to this had been given.

The two weeks which intervened between my arrival and the wedding day were very busy, indeed. There were so many finishing touches to be given to the wardrobes of each, so many directions concerning the business of the plantation, and so much to do and attend to in various ways, that it kept Mrs. Morris as busy as a bee. Kate and I lent a helping hand, as Emma was completely monopolized by Mr. Selvyn. I think I never saw a lover more delicate in his attentions. He was but little demonstrative, yet he listened to her lightest word, or with an eye beaming with affection, he watched her every movement.

"There is something about Mr. Selvyn that I do not like," remarked Kate, one morning, as she and I retired to the piazza, having felt ourselves somewhat *de trop* in the parlor. "Why can't he go out sometimes, and not remain there looking at Emma as though she were the only being in existence?"

"Why Kate! I consider him every way *comme il faut*; but he is in love; and you would not wish a lover to have eyes or ears for any other than his mistress?"

Her lips curled.

"Take care, Miss Kate! if ever your day comes, you will make a most exacting tyrant."

"Try me!" she retorted, with an arch smile, her countenance instantly recovering its good-humored expression. But really, Mr. Selvyn seems to possess very little energy; and there is a want of frankness about him that doesn't please me. Why don't he visit some of the gentlemen who have invited him? instead of which, he sits and watches Emma, as if he were jealous of her."

"How he watches us all, dear Kate, as if he feared we should talk treason to her;—but see! here are the horses, and yonder comes Mr. Laguerre; have you forgotten that we are engaged to ride with him, this morning? Let us go."

The wedding took place; and never was there a more beautiful bride. Brides are always beautiful, or should be, but in this instance we concede nothing to the character. Her dress was of India muslin, with deep flounces of costly lace. A diamond pin, of great value, fastened the berthe in front, and this, with the bridal wreath and a bouquet of rose-buds she held in her hand, was the only ornament she wore. As she entered, leaning on the arm of Mr. Selvyn, she turned a little pale, and then a little flushed, and at last had just the right quantity of bright, beautiful color. The relations and friends for miles around graced the wedding with their presence, each declaring that a handsomer couple had never been seen. Emma's self-possession was really remarkable, as she gracefully received their congratulations; and when the excitement had a little subsided, she stepped out on the gallery to the assembled negroes, each dressed in holiday array, (with a full holiday before them,) that they might behold her in her bridal attire. They were loud in their expressions of rapture, the more so, as Mr. Selvyn showered silver tokens with a liberal hand. Aunt Betsey, the cook, pronounced him a "ra-al gentleman;" to which her listeners responded, with the exception of the old nurse, who had had the care of each child from the moment of its birth. Mammy, alone, of all the sable crowd, seemed dissatisfied; as with a portentous shake of the head she declared, that "She didn't like such short courtships no how."

"Why Lor', Mammy, any one can see he's a gentleman."

"He oughter be a gentleman. Why not? and he oughter be a mighty good gentleman, too, to deserve Miss Emma."

A round of dinners was given to the bride, when the party separated. Kate returned home, I, to visit other friends, while the family pursued their route to the north. After placing the boys at school, Mrs. Morris, with Mr. Selvyn and Emma, visited every place of note, or fashionable resort. I received frequent letters from them, as also from other friends, at the same time sojourning at Newport and Saratoga. Emma's beauty and grace were the themes of general comment and admiration. She was indeed resplendently lovely. Renewed health gave a brighter glow to her cheek, while the diverse and gay scenes, in which they mingled, imparted to her spirits the animation they had heretofore required. They returned home in Autumn, and it was with a proud satisfaction, that Mr. Selvyn was presented to their old neighbors and friends at O.

How delightful they felt home to be, after the bustle and excitement of fashionable travel. Emma and Mr. Selvyn were now for the first time to enter upon the realities of married life, and their path seemed strewn with flowers. His unbounded devotion had awakened in the breast of Emma a profound and passionate sentiment of affection. She loved with all the depth of her nature, oftentimes trembling at the completeness of her bliss.

From her earliest infancy she had breathed only an atmosphere of kindness, while every luxury or wish that love could supply had been hers. Her being harmonized with the affluence that surrounded her, freed from the temptations that follow wealth, as others of a different nature attend want and misery. There are some rich, genial natures, which prosperity seems only to ripen and perfect, where gratitude leads to devotion and good works, freely imparting what has been so bountifully bestowed; and such a nature was Emma's. A sense of her own happiness made her considerate of the happiness of others; and often she asked herself the question, why it was that she should be so much more favored, than thousands equally deserving? Her inward consciousness was aroused, her perceptions of the high purposes of life were becoming clear. Wealth, with the advantages of leisure, opened before her a walk of more active beneficence for the future. She might not accomplish much, but that little she would undertake; and as she made this resolve, her bosom swelled with an emotion of indescribable joy and pleasure.

She had been standing on a balcony that overlooked an extensive lawn, covered with turf, smooth and green as velvet and dotted with magnificent trees that quite embowered the noble mansion. In front, in the middle of a flower-bed, a fountain threw high its silvery spray, which dropped into a marble basin, that was surrounded by fragrant flowers. Marble vases containing choice plants were ranged around, while Cape jessamines and the lemon-scented verbena filled the air with bloom and fragrance, as the setting sun shed over all a halo of beauty and splendor.　As the last rays departed, Emma re-entered the parlor and seating herself at the piano, rattled a lively piece of music.　She had a decided genius for music, partly inherited from her mother, who was an accomplished performer.　Her touch was brilliant and firm, and as her fingers flew over the keys, her flute-like voice burst out into an airy bird-like strain, that resembled a gush of gladness.　An hour or more passed, during which Mrs. Morris had joined her at the instrument, listening with intense delight, or mingling her own sweet voice with that of her happy child.　As lights were brought into the drawing-room, Emma turned from the piano.

"What on earth can keep Mr. Selvyn so late?"

"He has come, I fancy; there stands his horse."

Mrs. Morris had scarcely uttered this reply, when a stranger entered the open hall and inquired for Mrs. Selvyn.

He followed the servant into the apartment, and with an awkward attempt at a bow, said he had private business with that lady.

As soon as the waiter's back was turned, he advanced to where she had risen and was standing in wondering amazement.　He was of common appearance, the keeper of a cabaret in town, with a manner repulsively familiar, and in a sort of confidential tone, remarked, "If this is Mrs. Selvyn, I think ma'am you had better send and have Mr. Selvyn brought home."

"What do you mean?"

"No offense ma'am; but Mr. Selvyn has been drinking a little too much, and I thought you would like to know it."

She recoiled a few steps, with an air of complete bewilderment.

"There is some mistake, I am sure," said Mrs. Morris, coming forward; "you are mistaken in the person."

"No mistake, ma'am.　Mr. Selvyn has been at my house the greater part of the afternoon.　He had been drinking when he came, and I have taken the trouble to come over here and tell you out of pure kindness."

The "kindness," did not seem to be appreciated, as Mrs. Morris with some degree of hauteur in her tone, rejoined, "It cannot be Mr. *Albert* Selvyn,"—laying a strong emphasis on the Christian name.

"It is the son-in-law of the rich Mrs. Morris, any way.　At least I was told so, or I should not have troubled myself about him,"—replied the man with a sullen air.

"Mr. Selvyn left home this morning to call on Mr. Larue, at Richmond; he has returned, as I saw his horse a few moments since."

"Beg your pardon, ma'am.　*I* rode that horse here.　It was the horse that was first recognized; and Mr. Selvyn is now at my house, unable to get home."

His words carried conviction, and it was with a faltering voice Mrs. Morris remarked as she turned away, that she would send a servant with a note.

"Send a note! why, ma'am, he is *dead-drunk!*"

With a deep groan, Emma sank heavily upon a sofa.　She placed her hands before her eyes, as if to shut out some horrid vision.　Drunk! she had never in her life seen but one drunken man.　It was when she was a child, that a young servant rushed into the house, exclaiming, " O, mas'r ! Mr. Jones is whipping Aunt Betsey, just for nothing. Please do come, mas'r, he is cutting her up so!" Childlike, she had flown at the first word of "whipping Aunt Betsey," to the kitchen, where the overseer, with a countenance inflamed with drink and now distorted by passion, was applying the lash to the cook, who for some misdemeanor committed among her pots and kettles, had turned his pet dog out of her domains, and to insure her sense of his intrusion, bestowed on him a hearty kick, as his master happened to pass. The writhings of his victim, the horrid imprecations he uttered, with his disgusting appearance, terrified the child nearly out of her senses. She clung to her father for protection, as he, with righteous indignation, discharged him on the spot. She could never recall this scene without a shudder; even the mention of his name, excited her abhorrence; and as the transaction rose to her mind's eye in connection with Mr. Selvyn, she turned sick at heart, and fell back with a cry of anguish.

A servant entered in answer to the bell.

"Harrison," said Mrs. Morris, speaking in a hoarse voice, and articulating with difficulty, "tell Billy to put Mr. Selvyn's horse in the stable—to get up the carriage and accompany this man to his house in town, where Mr. Selvyn is——ill," she gasped out.

As the door closed behind them she sat down by Emma, whom she encircled in her arms. "My child, my poor child! what consolation can I offer you?" Emma's grief was speechless. She was too wretched even for tears, and she leant upon that faithful mother's breast with the trust and helplessness of a little child. An hour, which appeared an eternity, passed in unutterable agony, when Mrs. Morris, as if suddenly recollecting herself, started up and vehemently rang the bell.

The waiter appeared.

"Harrison, let the house be closed; and send all the servants to bed."

"*All*, of them missis? I'm not sleepy, and you'll want Mammy sure?"

"Not for the world!"

Recalled to a sense of the strangeness of her manner, by the astonishment depicted in his countenance, she added, in a soft tone, "Mammy is old, and must not be deprived of her rest; there is nothing very serious the matter, and Billy can attend to my wishes."

He bowed and withdrew.

Nothing very serious! how the attempt at concealment lowered her in her own eyes! With clasped hands she walked rapidly to and fro in the brilliantly-lighted and elegantly-furnished apartment. She saw nothing of the splendor that surrounded her; but one object was before her—the pallid face of her stricken child. How had this occurred? It was most strange and unaccountable. Mr. Selvyn, since their acquaintance, had been remarkable for his abstemiousness. Even claret wine, selected for its less stimulating properties, and used throughout the south as an accompaniment to the dinner-table, he had partaken of so sparingly as to draw from Emma the laughing remark that he drank it as though he were afraid of it.   It was altogether inexplicable, and how keep the occurrence from the knowledge of servants?   But, after all, might it not be a mistake?   It was not impossible.   She clung to this hope with the strength of despair, but alas ! the carriage returned in the silence of night, freighted with its burden of fallen manhood.   Her sensations were those of profound contempt, as she beheld him lifted from the carriage, and partly borne into the hall, where, reeling from one piece of furniture to another, he vainly endeavored to maintain an upright position.   His look was maudlin, as half recognizing the silent figure before him, he hickuped out, "Where am I?——am I?——

"You are drunk, sir," replied Mrs. Morris in a severe tone.   "Billy, take him to his room."

All the pride of her nature was aroused by the humiliating spectacle. Indignation, with a sense of betrayed trust, was the feeling that at first predominated.   Then came softer thoughts ;—thoughts of what he had been, of all that she had expected of him, and for the first time, hot, scalding tears ran down her cheek, as she exclaimed, "Oh, God ! I would rather have seen him in his coffin !"   No sleep visited the eyes of either mother or daughter that night, as weeping or locked in each others' arms, they could only reiterate the question—was this indeed true?   It was long before they could bring themselves to believe what had passed a reality, and then, what a fall was there ! The blow was absolutely stunning, and sent Emma to a sick bed?   It was late on the evening of the second day that Mr. Selvyn, pale and silent, made his appearance in the parlor.   Neither reproaches nor explanations took place ; a reserve rested on the whole party ; yet he constantly followed his wife and mother with beseeching eyes, as he paid those little attentions heretofore so graceful, and which had lent to his manner so great a charm.   As time wore on, he all at once became listless, depressed and uneasy.   He seemed equally restless, as incapable of exertion, and his wonted pursuits were abandoned.   Emma made no attempts to resume the studies this unfortunate occurrence had so rudely broken in upon.   Her confidence had received too great a shock easily to recover.   It was about a month after the above events, that all at once he was missing.   After several days of fruitless inquiries, and when their alarm was at its hight, they learned by mere accident that on the day he left home, he was seen on board the steamer which on that day left for New Orleans.   He had taken nothing with him, not even a change of clothing, and the motive for his journey was clouded in mystery.

When Mr. Selvyn left home it was merely to go on board the cotton-boat as she lay at the landing, to see what was going forward.   He had no particular business, other than to kill that time which now hung heavy on his hands.   Among the passengers from Memphis was a young man he had formerly known at Washington, who was a graduate of the same law-school.   This gentleman had been on a collecting tour throughout the south-west for houses in New York and Boston. Their acquaintance was joyfully renewed.   They took a glass of wine together ; old times and old friends were talked over and discussed ;

then another glass of wine, and another; until the last bell sounding with the cry of "All on board," he would have followed his friend to the end of the world, and did keep on with him to the city.

They took rooms at the St. Charles Hotel, and during the few days Mr. Bevis remained, had a gay time of it. After his departure, Mr. Selvyn ordered a supply of wine, with other liquors, to his room. A *douceur* secured the attendance of one of the waiters, who brought him his meals when desired, of which he sparingly partook, passing the time in drinking with a *goût* worthy a disciple of Epicurus, now resigning himself to the arms of Morpheus, again to rush into those of Bacchus, whose votary for the time he had become. The supply exhausted, the empty bottles were sent away; he was shaved and took a bath. Securing a passage he returned home after an absence of two weeks, very different in appearance from the elegant gentleman he had left it. His haggard looks and soiled linen did not escape the eye of the trim servant that admitted him, who hastened to announce his arrival to his mistress. Mrs. Morris and Emma felt that the time for silence was past. They schooled themselves to meet him, and together descended to the library. Emma, pale as marble and almost as cold, could only press that fond parent's hand in silence, for her heart was crushed, and her spring-day hopes, like the seared and withered leaves of winter, lay quivering at her feet.

Mr. Selvyn stood with his back to the door. As they entered he turned and attempted to take a hand of each. They were withdrawn. Tears of shame and penitence rained from his eyes as he threw himself at their feet.

"Rise, sir!" commanded Mrs. Morris. Her voice trembled, but her manner was firm; "rise up, Mr. Selvyn, and explain your conduct." He attempted to speak, but his quivering lips gave forth no sound.

"Oh! Mr. Selvyn, how could you so cruelly deceive us? You must have been addicted to such courses before we knew you. For I cannot suppose these derelictions the first, and have no reason to believe they will be the last. Your father, too, whom I respected so highly—I must speak plainly, Mr. Selvyn, in justice to my own :—your father, when he sanctioned the engagement, said you were all that the fondest parent could desire. If my suspicions be correct, he must have known his words were false."

"Spare my father, Mrs. Morris; he spoke what he believed to be the truth."

"Then you acknowledge that you are guilty?"

"Yes——No——I have erred, greatly erred, Mrs. Morris, but am not wholly criminal; for I have struggled against temptation. *How*, I have wrestled with the tempter, you can never know." He shuddered as he spoke—great drops of perspiration stood upon his brow and his lips were white as death.

"But Mr. Selvyn, when you sought my daughter's hand, you said nothing of this."

"To have done so would have been to destroy my hopes at once. Emma! Mrs. Morris! will you listen to me, while I go back to the time when I first left Cambridge and entered on my professional career in the City of Washington? Then it was that I became acquainted with some wild young men, attorneys like myself, who, obtaining few briefs, had only the more time to devote to pleasure. We became dissipated; and though perhaps the least so of any, I occasioned profound grief to my family. I promised reformation, again to cause them the most poignant sorrow. During some years, this was my state, when an excess laid me on a bed of sickness. Reason was for a time entirely dethroned. On recovering, my physician—it was the last visit he paid me—addressed me in an impressive manner. His warning words still ring in my ear. They were:—'Young man, if you return to your old courses you are lost! Mark me—body and mind will both be destroyed. I do not say this to alarm you unnecessarily. You possess a fine, nervous organization, that will not bear tampering with; and your only safety is in the total renunciation of stimulating drinks. For you, there is no middle course. You must either forswear the indulgence at once and forever, or make up your mind one day to become the inmate of a lunatic asylum.' I trembled while he spoke, and felt assured of the truth of what he said; but how break through the meshes which custom had drawn around me? He also spoke to my father, who soon found an opportunity of sending me abroad under the auspices of an old friend of my uncle's. This gentleman was of high character and great learning, and was besides, one of the best men I ever knew. He kindly consented, out of regard to my family, to be burdened with me, for I was a wretched burden even to myself. I will pass over months of misery, when the sight of a glass of liquor revived in me an appetite almost too difficult to control, and say nothing of the nervous depression into which I frequently sank, feeling that a fiend was ever at my elbow, urging the guilty cup and waiting to drag me down to unfathomable misery. Through the kind reasoning and tender forbearance of my invaluable friend, I at length recovered; and when he left me in Germany, I had but one engrossing passion—that was, self-improvement. My early love for art revived, and my indulgent parents supplied the means for my long residence in Europe. Soon after I joined my family in Cuba, whether it was the enervating effect of climate, or the absence of congenial employment I know not, but my old enemy returned, haunting me like a shadow. I was afraid of myself. I seemed beset by a demon that was constantly urging an indulgence that was to be my destruction. This was my state, when returning home from an excursion in the interior, I was introduced to yourself and family. The first glance at Emma decided my destiny. I felt that she was the angel, through whose purity and strength I should be enabled to triumph over the foe that had destroyed my peace. You blame me, Mrs. Morris, that I did not explain all this to you. I did intend one day, to unburden myself to my sweet wife——perhaps when the image of a little child should plead to the mother's heart for the weakness of its father. The events of the past two months have revived my despair —I was tempted and fell. Yet cast me not from you. Never again will you behold me in the condition, to which you were once the unwilling witness. Cast me not off without one more trial. I will absent myself for any term you dictate, only suffer me to hope that a victory over myself will be a restoration to your favor and love. O, Emma! my hopes of Heaven depend on your decision. Will you forgive me? Will you trust me?"

His face was bathed in tears as he made this candid confession, and plead with all the eloquence of deep passion. When was ever true eloquence without its influence? Not in this instance—they felt that he was sincere, and Mrs. Morris, placing her handkerchief to her eyes, turned away. Emma, whose gaze had never wandered, as she listened with suspended breath, cast on him the look of a pitying angel, and extended to him her hand. He received it reverently, covering it with kisses.

"Will I forgive you?—will I trust you?—ah, Mr. Selvyn, will I not? Depend not on a frail mortal like yourself, but put your trust in God. Pray to Him for strength to overcome this great temptation, and He will help you.

It was settled that Mr. Selvyn should pass the probation of a year, with his family. What good purpose this was to answer I could never rightly understand, but so it was. His letters reached them punctually. They were filled with repentance for the past, determination for the future, with wretchedness at the separation from his wife, for whom he expressed so much love and admiration, in which no complaints were mingled, that they touched them nearly ; and before the expiration of the year, he was invited to return.

He returned, looking both well and happy. There was now, no reserve between them, and manifesting a deep religious sentiment, he united himself to the church, to which Emma a few months previous had been admitted a member. Winter saw them again at the plantation, when Mr. Selvyn joined with heart and soul in all their plans for the improvement of their people. Never had he appeared to such advantage. His look was open and firm, his manner, assured and tranquil—and he became the light of their eyes to both Mrs. Morris and Emma. Christmas approached—a great time on plantations, where the Christmas holidays are religiously observed. Not always in a Christian-like manner, be it understood, but it is claimed by the negro, as his prescriptive right.

It was a lovely day. Mr. Selvyn was unusually joyous, and after assisting in the distribution of Christmas gifts to the scores of negroes who came in to receive them, he declared his intention of making a few calls on some of the neighboring planters. "Let me see," he said, enumerating the list—"there are —— and —— besides Mr. Baker. I saw him yesterday at your brother's, Mrs. Morris, and he appeared to feel really hurt at my not having yet returned his civility.

Mr. Baker lived with true southern hospitality. His house, his table, his servants, were all at the disposal of his friends, and never was he more pleased than when his house was well filled. Both Mr. and Mrs. Baker were rejoiced to see Mr. Selvyn. He was invited to remain and dine, which he declined doing. Being Christmas, he must join them in a glass of egg-nog. To this he politely responded that he made no use of stimulants, but the refreshment was ordered. It looked a harmless thing enough, as it filled the huge china bowl, above the top of which towered a pyramid of froth, as white and light as the driven snow.

"It is nothing more than custard, eggs and sugar, you know, with a slight dash of brandy," and Mr. Baker filled two glasses, one for himself, the other for Mr. Selvyn.

Again he would have declined, but Mrs. Baker, as she heaped on the top of each glass the proper amount of foam, declared that as she had made it herself, she should feel quite offended if he did not at least taste it.

"I would not willingly offend a lady." He bowed, smiled, and raised the fatal draught to his lips.

What was it as he did so, that sent a thrill through his frame and almost checked the beatings of his heart? He pronounced it "excellent," complimented her upon her *savoir faire*, and finished the glass.

Some other gentlemen coming in, he was induced before his departure to take a second glass, and he returned home in a state of intoxication. He was forgiven, and again he sinned. The shame of detection over, he seemed to have given himself over to the demon of drink. And now the disease, for disease it was, broke out in full force, and he implored for stimulus. Neither prayers, nor entreaties, could deter him from yielding to the insane craving that consumed him—the desire was beyond control. The full amount of wine and liquors the house contained was consumed, without satisfying in the least degree his craving thirst. Fearing that nothing short of personal restraint, would prevent him from seeking the indulgence, wherever it could be found, in great grief and perplexity, Mrs. Morris sent for her brother, Judge C., and besought his advice.

Judge C. was a man simply practical. He did not long deliberate. "If you wish to break him of the habit at once, send for a demijohn of brandy and let him drink his fill." "O, Liberty!" cried the unfortunate Madam Roland, "how many crimes are committed in thy name!" May we not with equal justice exclaim, O, Ignorance! of how much crime art thou the unconscious parent! In the pride of superior wisdom we speak of the Dark Ages as times that are past and gone. Alas, for our discernment! There needs but a glance at the state of society at large to comprehend the amount of ignorance that still exists. Ignorance of the natural laws, of man's inner self, of the best means for the advancement of fallen humanity, proves that in these days of boasted knowledge, "Let there be light!" is a crowning glory as devoutly to be wished as when the material world lay shrouded in impenetrable gloom. The brandy was sent for, a decanter placed before him, and though eagerly drained, afforded no satisfaction; a constantly recurring impulse urging him to drink till a stupor as of death arrested his hand. All solid food was now rejected; one insane cry constantly arose—"Give me drink!" Pardon me, gentle reader, if I draw a veil over the scenes that now followed. The house was closed; it was denied to visitors, and a gloom as of death hung over all. A suicide was being committed, without knowledge or power to avert the evil. And soon was it accomplished. In three weeks the gates were opened, and Mr. Selvyn, so capable of loving, so gentle and intelligent, so calculated in every way to adorn life, was placed in a drunkard's grave, over which bitterer tears were shed than manifold afflictions had yet called forth.

The above is a case of peculiar type, and is one to which many of my readers have doubtless seen a parallel. " I am not a Methusaleh," yet I can call to mind nearly a dozen similar instances, where the treatment pursued partook of the same degree of enlightenment, with results equally disastrous. Shall I speak of one who belonged to a family of three brothers, each of them distinguished for high, if not the highest talent? Two of them now occupy stations than which none higher on earth need be coveted. He, the eldest and most gifted, for upwards of fifty years exercised his gifts for the benefit of others, receiving as the reward, the respect to which a good man is entitled. Falling into ill-health, he was advised by his physician to take brandy as a tonic. He did so, and was benefitted. About this time he removed to the west to fill a station of public trust, carrying with him, if not the disease, the fatal habit the cure for that disease had engendered. Time passed on and he became the slave to a vice before which his fine mind sank, his character changed. Not all at once did he become a drunkard—no one becomes that despicable thing at once ; but by slow and sure degrees he fell, the wreck of his former self. For years his faithful wife resolutely endeavored to draw him from the brink of shame and despair. In vain. Heart-broken, she placed within his reach the means for his guilty indulgence, to try the effect. A terrible one, indeed ! She sank to the grave without one gleam of hope for that husband's future. He had fallen into a state of complete idiocy, with an unabated thirst for the fatal draught that had made him an object of deep commiseration to his friends and a burden upon two lovely and accomplished daughters.

I called on you to reflect, dear reader, and you have done so. I see by the thoughtful brow, and saddened countenance, that you are thinking of that wife and mother of many years' standing, before whom a barrel of rum was placed by her husband—and he a physician !—with permission to help herself, which she did—out of the world ; of that son just entering upon manhood, whose excesses had reduced him to a state of nervous exhaustion, for which he was allowanced a fearful amount of stimulus as his daily portion, until death ended the indulgence ; of one, a gray-haired sire was compelled to take from his family and place in a lunatic asylum ; who, just as confinement and judicious treatment were beginning to have a beneficial effect, was allowed by that fond, though weak parent, to be released from the wholesome restraint, and in consequence, before a month had passed, was picked up in a dying state from the sidewalk. Shall I go on? Ah, no ! the picture is too true—the reality too fearful—and what is the remedy?

We leave this question with others; let them look well to the answer.

THE MARINER.

BY SAMUEL WEBB.

Lo! in far distant lands,
There the pale future stands
Beckoning, with pallid hands,
　　Earth's sons and daughters:
While, from a better sphere,
Angels of hope appear
And in sweet accents clear,
　　Call o'er Time's waters.

Now on that ocean's verge,
Bathed by the glowing surge,—
At that low call emerge
　　Forms new created;
Ope they the wondering eye
On a strange earth and sky,
Born to suffer, born to die,
　　Mariners fated.

From childhood's sunny shore,
Out on the waters hoar,
Where Life's wild billows roar
　　In their strife madly,—
Launch on the solemn main,
Laden with Youth's bright train,
To Time's eternal strain,
　　Life's shallop, gladly:

Freighted with hopes and fears—
Sunny smiles and bitter tears,
Down the long line of years
　　Impatiently gazing;
Praying the hours to lend
Speed,—as the years descend
On to their mournful end,—
　　With young hopes blazing.

Know ye the light that beams
Bright, in thy childish dreams,
That in thy grasping seems,—
　　Outlies the living?
This side that glittering goal,
Death's gloomy waters roll
To the hope-cheated soul
　　Oblivion giving.

O, stay ye! think how dear
Are the joys blooming here—
Ah, youth ne'er drops a tear
　　O'er the years gliding!
Pursuing to man's estate,
As if that round of fate
Was but the golden gate
　　To joys abiding.

Spent like a summer beam—
Spent like a feverish dream—
Spent like a rain-wrought stream,
　　Dried up in an hour:
Gone while we watched its flight—
Gone—but the rest is night
Lit by the inverse light
　　Of faded flowers.

O! then, ye light of heart,
Ere ye from youth depart,
Pause—let the teardrop start—
　　Farewell forever!
Bend to the laboring oar—
Look to the Heaven before;
Ye shall return no more—
　　Never, oh never!

Then let Life's current stray
On its appointed way,
And for no future pray—
　　Pray for the present;

For if the present speeds,
Laden with faithful deeds,
Surely the future leads
　　On to the pleasant.

Look not to coming years—
Call not on buried years—
Why kindle smiles and tears
　　O'er time not ours?
Why to that goal, whose beams
Light to the land of dreams,
Urge ye the tide that seems
　　Freighted with flowers!

Ah! on Death's dusky bed,
Thus by the young heart led,
Mark ye the countless dead
　　Hope beguiled sleeping;
While a wan, trembling band
Stretch the entreating hand,
Back to Youth's faded land—
　　O'er the past weeping.

But tho' they weep and mourn,
From the long cherish'd torn,—
O'er the dim billows borne
　　Away they're going—
Now, pale as Winter's frost—
As the white sea-foam tost,
Sleep they—the living lost—
　　Unknown—unknowing.

But o'er the sleeping, bend
Hosts, that from Heaven descend,
And, like a cherish'd friend,
　　Call they the shrouded;
While, as Death's surges roll,
Loud shout the rescued soul
As to the unseen goal,
　　Mid scenes unclouded,—

Upward it takes its flight,
Thro' the rent bars of night,
Until in pure delight—
　　Gifted in vision—
Walks it the better land
With a redeemed band
Spirits blest, hand in hand,
　　Thro' fields elysian.

Thus to that gloomy coast,
Where reigns the kingly ghost,—
A vast, unnumbered host
　　Mournfully goeth—
And, upon every side,
Rolls the unfathomed tide—
From what it doth divide
　　Man little knoweth.

Then, that ye nothing dread,
As ye are onward led
To the reef of the dead,
　　Breaking Time's billow,—
Yield not the faith of youth—
Trust in the God of truth,
And not a shade of ruth
　　Shall cloud Death's pillow:

But the bright Cherubim
Shall sing thy funeral hymn,
Not 'neath earth's arches dim—
　　Dim and terrestrial;
But, turning every wire,
Sounding each golden lyre,
With the exalted choir,—
　　In halls Celestial.

PACIFIC SOUVENIRS.

BY J. N. APPLETON, LATE OF THE TEXAN NAVY.

NOTWITHSTANDING all that has been written, said and sung of those dream-lands of boyhood, the Islands of the Pacific, during the last century, and mauger the vivid pictures of Herman Melville, or the researches of Frederic Walpole, much, very much remains to be written, and there are yet to be found wide fields for the lover of enterprise and discovery among the coral rocks and fairy islets of Polynesia.

Twenty years ago, young in hope and years, with the whole world wearing in my future as bright hues as the lovely lands in which I wandered, I spent some time in various islands of the great Archipelago, and am not without hopes that a plain recital of my adventures, such as they were, may possess some little interest to the readers of *The Pioneer.* Should it be found so, the following pages will be succeeded monthly by others of a like nature, till my yarn shall be spun out.

It was in the year 1835 or '36, (I have forgotten the precise date,) I sailed from Honolulu in the hermaphrodite brig K———, or, as she was better known amongst the foreign residents of the town, the Waverley, bound to the Piscador Islands, in search of Capt. Dorcett and a boat's crew, who had been taken prisoners and detained by the natives of those islands a short time previous. The captain of the brig was a young man, named Cathcart—good-looking, with agreeable manners, a great admirer of the fair sex, and, like many other seafaring men, too apt to act rather from impulse and feeling than from good sense and reason. Our mate (I think his name was Joseph,) was a regular, down-east Yankee sailor—swore a little, drank a little, and chewed immensely ; a better seaman never trod a deck, nor one more obstinate, whether right or wrong, in maintaining an opinion. Our doctor was a German—every one at that time resident in Honolulu knew Dr. Icrear—a man full of infinite quirks and quiddities ; none could better tell a good story and keep the "table on a roar ;" few could sing a better song ; no man possessed a more open and friendly heart, and, as a climax to his virtues, he could play the fiddle to perfection. Rest his soul, we "shall not look upon his like again."

Your humble servant, *moi qui vous parle,* was made second mate, and, owing to my having had greater experience with South Sea natives than any other on board, coupled with the *bonhommie* of the captain and the friendship of the doctor, which I won in the early part of the voyage, there was a greater familiarity in our intercourse than second-deckers are generally favored with. After a pleasant passage we arrived at the Piscadors, a group of seven low islands, forming a lagoon. After a search of two days' duration we discovered a passage through the reef, and anchored some three hundred yards from the largest island, in four fathoms of water. As soon as our anchor dropped, the natives came down to the beach, waving a piece of tappa, and inviting us to come ashore, but did not seem inclined themselves to leave *terra firma.* The next day the captain took a whaleboat, and went as near to the beach as possible without grounding, but all inducements held out could not prevail upon the natives to come off to him, and he had determined not to trust himself on shore. As yet, we had seen very few natives, and those principally old men and boys—no women—and we judged, not incorrectly, that the young men kept out of sight for no good..

Two days passed in this way, the natives evidently determined not to trust themselves on board, and Capt. Cathcart equally resolved not to allow any of the crew to venture on shore. On the third day, towards evening, the mercurial doctor, tired of inaction, proposed that I should accompany him, and we would try what we could effect. I agreed, and we pulled off together. There were many natives on the beach, and when close to the shore I saw there were more young men than we had before seen, and among them one, who, by his dress and general appearance, was evidently of superior grade to any that had hitherto shown themselves. As usual, all our temptations of calico and beads were of no service in prevailing on them to venture near the boat; so with a piece of calico, and string of beads in my hand, I leapt on the beach and presented them to the young man I have mentioned. He seemed vastly delighted, and sent in return several baskets of cocoa nuts and tappa to the boat, and thus a communication was opened. I endeavored by signs to persuade him to go on board the brig; this he declined, but I gathered from his pointing to the setting sun, describing a half circle, and then pointing to the east, he wished to tell us he would visit us in the morning; and satisfied with what we had accomplished, we returned to the ship. At break of day the following morning, I was at the beach with the boat, nor had I long to wait; he came down, accompanied by four other young natives. They were evidently trying to dissuade him from his adventure, but he at last got into the boat. I ordered my men at once to shove off, but the natives got hold of and attempted to detain it; whereupon, with the butt-end of a spear he held in his hand, the chief laid two of them prostrate, and, in a minute afterwards, we were in deep water. It was well we made haste, for instantly there rushed down to the beach a large body of natives, all armed with spears and clubs, and headed by a venerable-looking old chief, who, with shouts and gestures, motioned us back. We, however, held on our way, and a few moments brought us alongside.

Our visitor, after his first surprise and strangeness wore off, made himself quite at home—sat down to breakfast, and seemed highly delighted with all he saw. After he had quite satisfied his curiosity, and had been presented with nearly everything that seemed to take his fancy, we put him ashore again, and such a jabbering was never heard since the days of Babel, as when he landed and began to show his presents.

There were many now as anxious to go aboard as had before been diffident; but our orders were strict not to bring any off unless accompanied by a chief; and, as the venerable-looking old fellow, who turned

out to be the principal chief and father of our visitor, declined honor-
ing us with his company, we returned alone. The next day, however,
he paid us a visit in a canoe of his own, the only one we had seen on
the island. This chief was the finest specimen of an old man I ever
saw. To judge by his appearance, he must have been at least eighty
years of age ; yet his frame was still straight and vigorous—his hair,
as yet only slightly thinned, was of the purest white, and hung down
over his shoulders, while his snowy beard reached to his waist. A
body-guard of six tall, well-formed men accompanied him, each armed
with a heavy club and long spear, and, with the exception of a narrow
strip of tappa round their waists, all perfectly naked. They remained
on board sometime, and, after partaking of a roast pig and receiving
some presents of iron, and other little matters, they returned on shore,
the doctor and myself accompanying them in a whale-boat. For the
first time, some few women came down to the beach, on our landing,
and really elegant specimens of South Sea women they were. They
wore a curiously-woven mat apron round their waist, which was their
only covering, though one or two of them had a very neat head-dress
of feathers twisted into their long, black hair, which was exceedingly
becoming.

The old chief was very eager for the doctor and myself to accompany him to the village, but we had been ordered not to leave the
beach, so could not comply with his requests. We now attempted to
make an acquaintance with the ladies, and soon discovered that love-
making, even when carried on by signs alone, is marvelously easy, when
the interested parties are both willing to understand. One dark-eyed
damsel seemed very anxious that I should accompany her to the village, while I was equally persuasive for her to go aboard the brig.
She, however, like many other maidens, was a little coquettish ; so,
after expending all our eloquence in vain, we put off without her.
However, when we were about half-way from the shore, she plunged
in and swam off after us. Of course, we at once turned the boat, and
picked her up. She very deliberately made her toilet, shook the water
out of her long hair, and with the merriest possible little laugh, sat
herself down in the stern-sheets by my side. Arrived at the brig, she
followed me up the ladder as if she had been used to climb a ship's side
all her life, and seemed determined to make herself at home. I shall
never forget her astonishment upon first seeing a mirror. She looked
at herself, then laughed, then laid it down and clapped her hands with
pleasure ; at last, she ran to the ship's side and held it up to those on
shore, as if they could look into it as well as herself.

After she had made herself extremely agreeable for some time, the
captain ordered me to have the boat manned and take her on shore ;
so off we went. But upon our arriving, and our pretty damsel displaying her presents, especially a looking-glass, to the other females, a
tremendous hubbub and chattering arose, and all, as with one impulse,
rushed into the boat. Thus it came about that I, who was sent ashore
with one girl, returned with fourteen others. I went down to the
cabin, wearing a very sheepish look, to make my report. After a brief

consultation, it was determined to let them remain for the present, as, by turning them ashore, we might possibly outrage the etiquette of the island and offend the natives, with whom we wished for the present, at any rate, to keep on good terms. It was one of those lovely nights only seen in the tropics; the full moon threw her soft light over the vast expanse of waters dotted by the green islands around, and then spreading, as far as the eye could reach, like a sheet of pure silver. All hands were on deck, singing, toying with the girls, and spinning yarns; at last the doctor bethought him of his fiddle, and then, to the great amusement of our lady visitors, the sailors danced reels and hornpipes till eight bells told the hour of midnight. Often have I thought since, had we left next morning, what a different opinion the natives would have had of us from that which they must now possess.

Early next morning a number of natives came off to the brig, and as we were pretty well satisfied that the population of the island was not sufficiently large to be dangerous, if we only used ordinary precaution, after breakfast the captain, doctor and myself, with two boats' crews well armed, landed and went up to the village. This consisted of twelve houses, made of cane, well lashed together with strips of bark. The chief's house was only distinguished from the others by having a palisade of stakes around it. Here we were received with apparent hospitality; fish, tarra, and a jelly made from arrowroot, were presented to us, and a dance got up for our especial gratification.

After the dance followed a sham fight between sixteen men, divided into two parties, separated only a few paces, and each man having a bundle of spears, which were darted at the opponents with great force and precision. But it was astonishing to witness the skill and dexterity with which these were caught or warded off. At last they seized their clubs and rushed upon each other, apparently with all the fury of a real engagement. Each combatant held his club by the middle, as an Irishman does his shillelah, and the strength and agility with which they were wielded all in a cluster together was formidable to look upon; yet such perfect masters of the weapon were they, that rarely was any one hit. When any one, however, did get a tap, it gave rise to shrieks of laughter from the women and boys standing around. All this time we did not feel particularly easy, as we were by no means certain that the sham fight was not preparatory to a real attack upon ourselves, so we drew up with our backs to one of the huts, and stood with muskets cocked, in case of treachery. But the precaution was needless; at a signal from the chief, every man threw down his spear and all ran off in different directions. We now began to wander round to see if we could find any trace of Dorcett or his companions, but for some time without success, until a Kanaka called our attention to a kippar tree in the rear of the chief's house, whereon were the names of Dorcett and three of his companions cut in the bark. We conjectured from this that they had not been killed, but where they were was the mystery. We could gain no other information, so returned on board at last to deliberate upon what further steps should be taken.

ODE TO IMAGINATION.

—

BY CHAS. E. HAVENS.

—

Come, stoled in orient state, as when the sun,
New risen, from the drapery of the East
Steps forth, and flames in splendor on the hills;
    While all the darkling vales are won
    With golden kisses, and the rills
Of music leap to light, the dewy morn
Laughing our petty griefs and ills to scorn.

Creative essence of the unseen mind!
Thy spiritual ray informs with light,
    Summoning day from night,
    When the twin orbs of sight
    Are suddenly struck blind.
Oh! come and chase the shadow from my soul,
    That broodeth long:
    Come harbingered by song!
And, while the mellowing tides of music roll
Their burden heavenward, lift thy front sublime
    Crowned with flickering tongues of fire,
Thy golden tresses streaming on the wind,
White-vested, as a bride in her attire,
And glorious in the splendor of thy prime,
Thronged round by shifting shapes, airy and undefined.

In what far-off, enchanted isle,
Sphered in a golden circle of the sea,
Whose shadowy verge is crowned for many a mile
    With thy reflected smile,
    Dwellest thou contentedly?
What breezes, steering from Sabæan shores,
With freight of incense, anchor at thy feet
    With all their honeyed stores?
What flowers bourgeon in thy dim retreat?

What time the sea upon thy island strands
Breaks in low thunder, and the argent moon
    Sheds silver on the sands,
And girdles all the waves with zones of light,
    Thou, through the night,
    Wanderest forth alone
    Over a bridge of light
    Moon thrown,
To yield us glimpses of thyself in dreams.
Or, doth the spirit doff its tent of clay
    When waxen slumber seals the eyes,
    Lured by thy flattering sway
Over the sleeping silver of the seas
To the charmed circle of thy mysteries?
    Through the shadowy hours
    Holding converse sweet,
      At thy feet
    In moon-loved bowers:
Delaying, until sunlight streaks the dawn;
Delaying, till the amber-dropping moon
    Dissolves the mist,
    And glistens all the dew,
And all the chilly mountain-tops are kissed
And warmed with amorous kisses through and through;
    Then hastes away
To reinform with life its house of clay.

No matter where may be thy dwelling-place;
It is enough to know that thou dost shine.
It is enough that we behold thy face
And bathe our spirits in thy light divine.
    But when, in some sudden hour,
Thou movest all the spiritual deep
    With thy expanse of power—
And opening up the heaven's starry floor,
Giveth, in shadowing luster far withdrawn,
    Glimpses of some diviner shore,
Transparent seas, and leagues of golden lawn,—
Then we, of earthly vision too confined
For such unusual presence, cry aloud,
"Oh! veil thee, lest thy splendor strike us blind."

CALIFORNIA, IN 1852.

BY SHIRLEY.

LETTER SIXTEENTH.

RESIDENCE IN THE MINES.

FROM OUR LOG CABIN, Indian Bar, May 1, 1852.

You have no idea, my good, little M., how reluctantly I have seated myself to write to you. The truth is, that my last tedious letter about mining and other tiresome things has completely exhausted my scribbling powers, and from that hour to this the epistolary spirit has never moved me forward. Whether on that important occasion, my small brain received a shock from which it will never recover, or whether it is pure, physical laziness, which influenced me, I know not; but this is certain, that no whipt school-boy ever crept to his hated task more unwillingly, than I to my writing desk on this beautiful morning. Perhaps my indisposition to soil paper in your behalf is caused by the bewildering scent of that great, glorious buoquet of flowers, which, gathered in the crisp mountain air, is throwing off cloud after cloud ("each cloud *faint* with the fragrance it bears,") of languid sweetness, filling the dark old room with incense, and making of it a temple of beauty; like those pure, angelic souls, which, irradiating a plain countenance, often render it more lovely than the chiseled finish of the most perfect features.

O, Molly! how I wish that I could send you this jar of flowers, containing, as it does, many which in New England are rare exotics Here, you will find in richest profusion the fine lady elegance of the syringa; there, glorious, white lilies, so pure and stately; the delicate yet robust beauty of the exquisite privet; irises of every hue and size; and, prettiest of all, a sweet, snow-tinted flower, looking like immense clusters of seed pearl, which the Spaniards call *libla*. But the marvel of the group, is an orange-colored blossom, of a most rare and singular fragrance, growing somewhat in the style of the flox; this, with some branches of pink bloom of incomparable sweetness, is entirely new to me. Since I have commenced writing, one of the Doctor's patients has brought me a bunch of wild roses. O! how vividly at the sight of them started up before me those wooded valleys of the Connecticut, with their wondrous depths of foliage, which for a few weeks in midsummer, are perhaps unsurpassed in beauty by any in the world. I have arranged the dear *home* blossoms with a handful of flowers which were given to me this morning by an unknown Spaniard. They are shaped like an anemone, of the opaque whiteness of the magnolia, with a large spot of glittering blackness at the bottom of each petal. But enough of our mountain earth stars; it would take me all day to describe their "infinite variety."

Nothing of importance has happened since I last wrote, except that the Kanaka wife of a man living at the Junction has made him the happy father of a son and heir. They say that she is quite a pretty little woman, only fifteen years old, and walked all the way from Sacramento to this place.

A few evenings ago, a Spaniard was stabbed by an American. It seems that the presumptuous foreigner had the impertinence, to ask very humbly and meekly that most noble representative of the stars and stripes, if the latter would pay him a few dollars which he had owed him for some time. His high mightiness, the Yankee, was not going to put up with any such impertinence, and the poor Spaniard received, for answer, several inches of cold steel in his breast, which inflicted a very dangerous wound. Nothing was done, and very little was said about this atrocious affair.

At Rich Bar they have passed a set of resolutions for the guidance of the inhabitants during the summer; one of which is to the effect that no foreigner shall work in the mines on that Bar. This has caused nearly all the Spaniards to immigrate upon Indian Bar, and several new houses for the sale of liquor etc., are building by these people. It seems to me that the above law is selfish, cruel and narrow-minded in the extreme.

When I came here, the Humboldt was the only public house on the Bar. Now there are the "Oriental," "Golden Gate," "Don Juan," and four or five others, the names of which I do not know. On Sundays, the swearing, drinking, gambling and fighting, which are carried on in some of these houses, are truly horrible.

It is extremely healthy, here; with the exception of two or three men who were drowned when the river was so high, I have not heard of a death for months.

Nothing worth wasting ink upon has occurred for some time, except the capture of two grizzly bear cubs by the immortal "Yank." He shot the mother, but she fell over the side of a steep hill, and he lost her. "Yank" intends to tame one of the cubs; the other he sold, I believe, for fifty dollars. They are certainly the funniest looking things that I ever saw, and the oddest possible pets.

By the way, we receive an echo from the outer world once a month, and the expressman never fails to bring three letters from my dear M. wherewith to gladden the heart of her sister, "Dame Shirley."

—

LETTER SEVENTEENTH.

May 25.

THE very day after I last wrote you, dear M., a troop of mules came on to the Bar, bringing us almost forgotten luxuries, in the form of potatos, onions and butter. A band of these animals is always a pretty sight, and you can imagine that the solemn fact of our having been destitute of the abovementioned edibles since the middle of February, did not detract from the pleasure with which we saw them winding cautiously down the hill, stepping daintily here and there with those absurd little feet of theirs, and appearing so extremely anxious for the safe conveyance of their loads. They belonged to a Spanish packer; were in excellent condition, sleek and fat as so many kittens, and of every possible color,—black, white, grey, sorrel, cream, brown, etc. Almost all of them had some bit of red, or blue, or yellow, about their trappings, which added not a little to the brilliancy of their appearance ; while the gay tinkle of the leader's bell, mingling with those shrill and peculiar exclamations, with which Spanish muleteers are in the habit of urging on their animals, made a not unpleasing medley of sounds. But the creameist part of the whole affair was— I must confess it, unromantic as it may seem—when the twenty-five or thirty pretty creatures were collected into the small space between our cabin and the Humboldt ; such a gathering together of ham and mackerel-fed bipeds—such a lavish display of gold dust—such troops of happy looking men, bending beneath the delicious weight of butter and potatos—and above all, *such* a smell of fried onions, as instantaneously rose upon the fragant California air, and ascended gratefully into the blue California Heaven, was, I think, never experienced before.

On the first of May a train had arrived at Rich Bar ; and on the morning of the day which I have been describing to you, one of our friends arose some three hours earlier than usual, went over to the aforesaid Bar, bought twenty-five pounds of potatos at forty cents a pound, and packed them home on his back. In less than two days afterwards, half a dozen cargoes had arrived, and the same vegetable was selling at a shilling a pound. The trains had been on the road several weeks, but the heavy showers, which had continued almost daily through the month of April, had retarded their arrival.

Last week I rode on horseback to a beautiful Bar called the Junction, so named from the fact that at that point the East Branch of the North Fork of Feather River unites itself with the main North Fork. The mule trail, which lies along the verge of a dreadful precipice, is three or four miles long, while the foot-path leading by the river is not more than two miles in length. The latter is impassable, on account of the log bridges having been swept away by the recent freshets. The other day two oxen lost their footing, and fell over the precipice ; and it is the general opinion that they were killed long before they reached the golden palace of the Plumerian Thetis. I was a little alarmed at first, for fear my horse would stumble, in which case I should have shared the fate of the unhappy beeves, but soon forgot all fear in the enchanting display of flowers which each opening in the shrubs displayed to me. "Earth's firmament" was starred with daphnes, irises and violets of every hue and size ; pale wood anemones, with but one faint sigh of fragrance as they expired, died by hundreds beneath my horse's tread ; and spotted tiger-lilies, with their stately heads all bedizened in orange and black, marshaled along the path like an army of gaily-clad warriors. But the flowers are not all of an Oriental character. Do you remember, Molly, dear, how you and I once quarreled when we were—oh ! such mites of children— about a sprig of syringa? The dear mother was obliged to interfere, and to make all right, she gave you a small brown bud of most penetrating fragrance, which she told you was much more valuable than the contested flower. I remember perfectly that she failed entirely in convincing *me* that the dark, somber flower was half as beautiful as my pretty, cream-tinted blossom ; and, if I mistake not, you were but poutingly satisfied with the substitute. Here, even if we retained, which I do not, our childish fascination for syringas, we should not need to quarrel about them, for they are as common as dandelions in a New England meadow, and dispense their peculiar perfume—which, by the way, always reminds me of Lubin's choicest scents—in almost sickening profusion. Besides the above-mentioned flowers, we saw wild roses, and buttercups, and flox, and privet, and whole acres of the "Wandlike lily." I have often heard it said, though I cannot vouch for the truth of the assertion, that it is only during the month of January that you cannot gather a bouquet in the mountains.

Just before one reaches the Junction, there is a beautiful grove of oaks, through which there leaps a gay little rivulet, celebrated for the grateful coolness of its waters. Of course, one is expected to propitiate this pretty Undine by drinking a draught of her glittering waters from a dirty tin cup, which some benevolent cold-water man has suspended from a tree near the spring. The bank leading down into the stream is so steep that people generally dismount and lead their animals across it. But F. declared that I was so light that the horse could easily carry me, and insisted upon my keeping the saddle. Of course, like a dutiful wife, I had nothing to do but to obey. So I grasped firmly the reins, shut my eyes, and committed myself to the Fates that take care of thistle seeds, and lo ! the next moment I found myself safely on the other side of the brook ; my pretty steed—six weeks ago he was an Indian pony running wild in the prairie—curveting about and arching his elegant neck, evidently immensely proud of the grace and ease with which he had conveyed his burden across the brook. In a few moments we alighted at the store, which is owned by some friends of F., whom we found looking like so many great daisies, in their new shirts of pink calico, which had been donned in honor of our expected arrival.

The Junction is the most beautiful of all the Bars. From the store, one can walk nearly a mile down the river quite easily. The path is bordered by a row of mingled oaks and firs—the former garlanded with misletoe, and the latter embroidered with that exquisitely beautiful moss which I tried to describe in one of my first letters.

The little Kanaka woman lives here. I went to see her. She is quite pretty—with large, lustrous eyes, and two great braids of hair, which made me think of black satin cables, they were so heavy and massive. She has good teeth, a sweet smile, and a skin not much darker than that of a French brunette. I never saw any creature so proud as she, almost a child herself, was of her baby. In jest, I asked her to give it to me, and really was almost alarmed at the vehement burst of tears with which she responded to my request. Her husband explained the cause of her distress. It is a superstition among her people that he who refuses to give another anything, no matter what—there are no exceptions which that other may ask for—will be overwhelmed with the most dreadful misfortunes. Her own parents had parted with her for the same reason. Her pretty, girlish face soon resumed its smiles when I told her that I was in jest, and, to console me for the disappointment which she thought I must feel at not obtaining her little brown treasure, she promised to give me the *next* one ! It is a Kanaka custom to make a present to the person calling upon them for the first time ; in accordance with which habit, I received a pair of dove-colored boots three sizes too large for me.

I should liked to have visited the Indian encampment, which lies a few miles from the Junction, but was too much fatigued to attempt it. The Indians often visit us, and as they seldom wear anything but a *very* tight and *very* short shirt, they have an appearance of being, as Charles Dickens would say, all legs. They usually sport some kind of a head-dress, if it is nothing more than a leather string, which they bind across their dusky brows in the style of the wreaths in Norma, or the gay ribbons garlanding the hair of the Roman youth in the play of Brutus. A friend of ours, who has visited their camp several times, has just given me a description of their mode of life. Their huts, ten or twelve in number, are formed of the bark of the pine— conically shaped, plastered with mud, and with a hole in the top, whence emerges the smoke, which rises from a fire built in the center of the apartment. These places are so low that it is quite impossible to stand upright in them, and are entered from a small hole in one side, on all fours. A large stone, sunk to its surface in the ground, which contains three or four pan-like hollows for the purpose of grinding acorns and nuts, is the only furniture which these huts contain. The women, with another stone, about a foot and a half in length, and a little larger than a man's wrist, pulverize the acorns to the finest possible powder, which they prepare for the table (?) in the following manner, viz :—Their cooking utensils consist of a kind of basket, woven of some particular species of reed, I should fancy, from the descriptions which I have had of them, and are so plaited as to be impervious to fluids. These they fill half full of water, which is made to boil by placing in it hot stones. The latter they drag from the fire with two sticks. When the water boils, they stir into it, until it is about as thick as hasty-pudding, the powdered acorns, delicately flavored with dried grasshoppers, and lo ! dinner is ready. Would you like to know how they eat ? They place the thumb and little finger together across the palm of the hand, and make of the other three fingers a spoon, with which they shovel into their capacious mouths this delicious compound.

There are about eighty Indians in all at this encampment, a very small portion of which number are women. A hostile tribe in the valley made a Sabine-like invasion upon the settlement, a few months since, and stole away all the young and fair *muchachas*, leaving them but a few old squaws. These poor, withered creatures, who are seldom seen far from the encampment, do all the drudgery. Their entire wardrobe consists of a fringe about two feet in length, which is formed of the branch or root—I cannot ascertain exactly which—of a peculiar species of shrub shreded into threads. This scanty costume they festoon several times about the person, fastening it just above the hips, and they generally appear in a startlingly unsophisticated state of almost entire nudity. They are very filthy in their habits ; and my informant said that if one of them should venture out into the rain, grass would grow on her neck and arms. The men, unhappy martyrs! are compelled to be a little more cleanly, from their custom of hunting and fishing, for the wind *will* blow off *some* of the dirt, and the water washes off more.

Their infants are fastened to a framework of light wood in the same manner as those of the North American Indians. When a squaw has anything to do, she very composedly sets this frame up against the side of the house, as a civilized housewife would an umbrella or broom.

Some of their modes of fishing are very curious. One is as follows: These primitive anglers will seek a quiet, deep spot in the river, where they know fish "most do congregate," and throw therein a large quantity of stones. This, of course, frightens the fish, which dive to the bottom of the stream, and Mr. Indian, plunging head-foremost into the water, beneath which he sometimes remains several minutes, will presently reappear, holding triumphantly in each hand one of the finny tribe, which he kills by giving it a single bite in the head or neck with his sharp, knife-like teeth.

Hardly a day passes during which there are not three or four of them on this Bar. They often come into the cabin, and I never order them away, as most others do, for their childish curiosity amuses me, and as yet they have not been troublesome. There is one beautiful little boy about eight years old, who generally accompanies them. We call him Wild Bird, for he is as shy as a partridge, and we have never yet been able to coax him into the cabin. He always wears a large, red shirt, which, trailing to his little bronzed feet, and the sleeves every other minute dropping down over his dusky models of hands, gives him a very odd appearance. One day Mrs. B., whom I was visiting at the time, coaxed Wild Bird into the house to see Charley, the hero of the champagne-basket cradle. The little fellow gazed at us with his large, startled eyes, without showing the least shadow of fear in his countenance; but his heart beat so violently that we could actually see the rise and fall of the old red shirt which covered its tremblings. Mrs. B. made our copper-colored cupidon a pretty suit of crimson calico. His protectors, half a dozen grim old Indians, (it was impossible to tell which was his father, they all made such a petted darling of him,) were compelled to array him in his new suit by main strength, he screaming dreadfully all the time. Indeed, so exhausted was he by his shrieks, that by the time he was fairly buttoned up in his crimson trappings, he sank on the ground in a deep sleep. The next day the barbarous little villain appeared trailing, as usual, his pet shirt after him at every step, while the dandy jacket and the trim baby trowsers had vanished we never knew whither.

The other morning an Indian appeared on the Bar robed from neck to heels in a large, white sheet, and you have no idea of the classic grace with which he had arranged the folds about his fine person. We at first thought him a woman, and he himself was in an ecstasy of glee at our mistake.

It is impossible to conceive of anything more light and airy than the step of these people. I shall never forget with what enchanted eyes I gazed upon one of them, gliding along the side of the hill opposite

Missouri Bar. One would fancy that nothing but a fly or a spirit could keep its footing on the rocks along which he stepped so stately, for they looked as perpendicular as a wall. My friend observed that no white man could have done it. This wild creature seemed to move as a cloud moves on a quiet day in summer, and as still and silently. It really made me solemn to gaze upon him, and the sight almost impressed me as something superhuman.

Viewed in the most favorable manner, these poor creatures are miserably brutish and degraded, having very little in common with the lofty and eloquent aborigines of the United States. It is said that their entire language contains but about twenty words. Like all Indians, they are passionately fond of gambling, and will exhibit as much anxiety at the losing or winning of a handful of beans as do their paler brothers when thousands are at stake. Methinks, from what I have seen of that most hateful vice, the *amount* lost or won has very little to do with the matter. But let me not speak of this most detestable of crimes. I have known such frightful consequences to ensue from its indulgence, that I dare not speak of it, lest I use language, as perhaps I have already done, unbecoming a woman's lips.

Hundreds of people have arrived upon our Bar within the last few days; drinking saloons are springing up in every direction; the fluming operations are rapidly progressing, and all looks favorably for a busy and prosperous summer to our industrious miners.

HOME PICTURES.

BY J. SWETT.

I REMEMBER the old farm-house,
   With dark, unpainted form,
Grown black by long exposure
   To wind, and rain, and storm;
The roof was grown with mosses,
   The frame-work huge and strong,
Like the ash tree standing near it,
   Where birds sang all day long.

I remember, I remember
   The tidy little bed
In the old, unfinished chamber,
   With the rafters overhead;
The patter of the rain-drops
   Was music to my ear
Which lulled me into pleasant dreams
   Unbroken by a fear.

I remember the old garden,
   When ripe fruit on the ground,
Like apples of Hesperides,
   Lay temptingly around;
The blue plums and red cherries,
   The pears and currants nice—
Ah! that humble little garden
   Was to me a paradise.

I remember the barn and swallows
   With white and glossy breasts,
That underneath projecting eaves
   In summer built their nests;
They twittered round their dwellings
   In ever joyous play,
And lived and loved each other
   In cottages of clay.

I remember, I remember
   The busy haying-time,
When I heard the mowers whetting
   Their scythes in merry chime;
I loved to spread the green grass
   And rake the new-made hay,
Or load the rattling hay-carts
   At close of summer day.

I remember fields of clover
   Like red-waved summer seas,
Where I listened to the music
   Of busy bumble-bees;
The dark green Indian cornfields,
   With silken tassels fair,
And slender cornstalks bristling
   Like lances, in the air.

I remember, I remember
   The steep and slippery hill
Where we coasted winter evenings,
   Though winds were keen and chill;
We shot like Indian arrows
   Upon the crusted snow,
Our toes and fingers freezing,
   But our hearts all in a glow.

I remember, and with sadness,
   The buoyant heart of youth,
With its ardent soul-aspirings
   For manliness and truth.
The memories of boyhood
   Come back with smiles and tears,
And I treasure up the pictures
   Of my home in early years.

THE OLD SCHOOL-HOUSE.

BY J. SWETT.

In this land of change, which has no past, where there is no exist-ence but in the present, where acquaintances—not friends—come and go, and are forgotten, it is very pleasant in the stillness of the night, when the wearied brain and strong will yield to the warm impulses of the soul, to commune with Memory, and call up old scenes, which, like old songs and familiar faces, grow dearer as they grow older. It is well for the man, whirled about in this turmoil of life, to rejuvenate himself at the pure fountain of childhood's simple pleasures, that he may not become harsh, cold and entirely unsympathizing. The brain may and must soon grow old, but let the heart keep fresh and youthful.

I expect to write nothing new; there are feelings common to all hearts, and best expressed in common words. The rare plant may delight the botanist, but to most is not the simple, every-day flower, that blooms around the door, by far the sweeter?

I look out at the window and see the stars gazing mildly into the silver mirror of the placid bay. I know the same stars are bending as brightly down over the granite hills of my New England home. I am there among the loved ones of early years, in whose presence the heart throbbed as it shall never throb again. My thoughts go back, back into the misty past, till they rest in the old school-house of my native village. There are times when childhood scenes come back with a vividness that is almost startling; when hill, and tree, and brook, and field, and pasture reappear, and the mind flashes and plays like the Aurora over the cloudless sky of boyish existence. Then how the warm feelings of the young heart come gushing up from the choked fountains of the soul! The singing of the birds, the rustle of the leaves, the murmur of the brook, fall not in strains of more exquisite music on the ear of childhood than their recollection on the breast of manhood.

I am a dreamer to-night, and among the thick-coming fancies is the picture of the well-remembered school-house. There it stands, perched on the summit of the "Great Hill." Our good forefathers always located the school-house on a hill-top, doubtless that the scholars might breathe a pure, moral atmosphere, and climb the hill of science from the power of association. Around it spreads the rocky pasture, where in sunny spring-days the blue-eyed violets smiled on the little knolls and hillocks, and eager hands of little bright-eyed girls plucked and pressed them to bosoms as pure and stainless as the flowers themselves. The interior of the house is in keeping with the exterior. Long rows of unpainted desks and benches bear striking evidences of the effect of sharp jackknives in the hands of whittling Yankee "shavers."

How we little urchins used to envy the wonderful skill of the "back-seat" boys in sinking and cutting curious "fly-boxes" in the thick plank of the desks! And how the big boys caught flies from the back windows, and cruelly imprisoned them in the dark cells! And how did one youth, more humane than the rest—he was a *wonderfu*

boy—make a little glass window for his captives to look through!
Welladay, such scenes are growing dim, hung as they are upon the
receding, vanishing corridors of memory.

Like all old New England school-houses, the master's platform was
in the middle of the room, the seats on each side rising one above
another, till the back ones were half way up the ceiling, and the heads
of "big boys" almost touched the plastering above. It is curious
that the descendants of Puritans should have adopted such a *theatrical*
style of arrangement. The legs of forty or fifty restless urchins, in
school-hours, were always dangling like so many pairs of pendulums
swinging away to kill time ; or like the legs of some monster centi-
pede crawling off with the desks upon its back. Opposite the entry
door was an old-fashioned, open fireplace, which the elder scholars used
to cram with huge logs on cold, winter mornings, till the fire went
roaring again up the chimney, glaring fiercely at the smaller boys on
the front seats, who, with their dripping boots, seemed a long row of
dissolving icicles. In summer we filled up the fireplace with spruce
and hemlock boughs, and, when the minister was to visit us, added
wreaths of evergreens and flowers. I cannot account for it, but I had
a holy horror of the minister. He told me once, when I was lying
half dead with a fever, that I was a very wicked boy. I was a mere
child, then, but I well recollect that I could not and did not believe
him. I was conscious that I loved and obeyed my father and mother,
and had always tried to do right. This was all the religion that my
childish mind could comprehend.

And then those early friendships! how sweet their memory! Who
cannot call to mind some one or more at the time when the soul was
just beginning to fathom its own depths, which revealed a glimpse of
the nobleness of manhood, or the loveliness of womanhood?———

We were a merry group as ever winked at the snap of a birchen
rod. How irksome was the confinement of the school-room! how
intolerably dull the dry drill of spelling-classes! and with what an
exulting shout did we rush from the door to engage in the exciting
game of ball! and then, again, what merry times we had coasting
down the long, steep hill in clear, frosty evenings of winter! and what
glorious times we had skating on the pond, where we swept away like
Arabian racers! And our mimic battles of snowballs, when each boy
felt himself a hero—how exciting they were! How we flocked into
the door at the rap of the master's ferule on the window, and piled
our mittens on the hearth, clustering like bees around the fire to warm
our aching fingers!———

You shared, dear Tom, those pleasures with me. These memories
of boyhood! they make me sad. Do they visit you around the camp-
fire still? When we toiled in the ravines, "drifted" in the hill-sides,
washed in the river-beds, "prospected" among the mountains, and
stretched our exhausted limbs on the cold ground at night, I know our
thoughts often, very often reverted to home and the bright visions of
youth. We did not dream then that we should meet in the wild glens
of the Gold Land. We did not dream that bitter struggles and bitterer disappointments could chill the enthusiasm of youth, and make
the life, once so joyous, hardly worth the keeping.

A CALIFORNIA LADY'S OPINION OF FANNY FERN.

BY A NEW CONTRIBUTOR.

RUTH HALL! Who has not read "Ruth Hall?" another "Fern Leaf from Fanny's Portfolio"—at first glance deceptive, notwithstanding its superficial showiness, effective in spite of its false luster, and charmingly fascinating with all its gaudiness and glitter.

Of course, every one believes that Fanny Fern is the heroine of the tale, and that all the other characters are her kith and kin ; and the work is seized with an avidity natural to eager and curious minds, for it aims to gratify a weakness of the world—curiosity about the private life of individuals whose minds are stamped with genius, or whose reputation places them in a position above the common herd.

And now for a word about this hero worship and hero hatred, so improperly directed by the public. Why should the world care about anything in extraordinarily gifted individuals, except what is really uncommon? What have we to do with their private lives, petty sins or family quarrels? Their sins they themselves must answer for; their private sufferings—if we cannot relieve them—should not be forced upon us. But no ; among one class, jealous of superiority, the distinguished are regarded as common targets at which to aim the sharp arrows from slanderous tongues ; while among another, consisting of worshippers of the high and beautiful, they are considered as above human reproach and as entirely devoid of human weaknesses. Howe'er it be, by common consent the slightest incident in the lives of "beings known to public fame" is "exceedingly interesting ;" and the very people that know not a line of the sublime Poet's effusions, that cannot appreciate a single original idea of some glorious Essayist, would "give the world" to know whether such really eat bread and butter like other people—whether they live upon an airy dream, or walk, talk or sleep in any peculiarly romantic manner; and should there be a rumor of a "Real Live Lion's" being in the neighborhood, what a staring of eyes —what appliances of lorgnettes there would be ! And then how like a book must he always talk ! What a bore it must be to be put forever upon one's good intellectual behavior, as though literary fame debarred one from any relaxation from mental gymnastics! We once witnessed an amusing illustration of the disappointment occasioned by the forgetfulness of a distinguished poetess of the lofty airs of her elevated nature. She met a friend in a public picture-gallery, on the occasion alluded to, and a crowd gathered about her, eager to catch a word of the sublime conversation ; but retired in disgust at hearing the divine oracle ask her friend where he procured those excellent sweet potatos she had eaten at his house a day or two before.

We do not intend this tirade upon hero worship for the truly appreciative, but for those false enthusiasts who gather autographs, portraits and anecdotes without an idea of the worth and character of the subjects of admiration ; those who rush forward to gaze with vulgar staring, for the mere gratification of idle curiosity, or to have the pleasure of making demigods of themselves by being "posted" upon the looks and actions of some of "God's chosen ones ;" those who are able to retail facts and fictions about celebrated authors, but have no knowledge of the grandeur of their original thoughts, or the merits of their works, which may, however, have been duly purchased and placed upon the shelves of the private, unread library, among the last new publications.

Some of the "big Lions," we grieve to say it, petted or fretted, teased or pleased by public opinion, which is equally capricious in laudation or complete annihilation of character and intellectual merit, are tempted to cater to this false hero worship, or pamper this morbid appetite.

And thus has Fanny Fern, with some knowledge of the weaknesses of the world, endeavored to attract particular attention to her powers, and presuming upon the ground that the heavenly gift of genius should exempt her from the usual trials of humanity, to draw forth sympathy for her supposed private sufferings, abuses and injuries. But while striving to do this, she has succeeded rather in exposing to the world her peculiar bitterness of heart, together with a variety of other faults to which the public in general and her admirers in particular were completely blind before the appearance of "Ruth Hall."

Oh, Fanny Fern, we grieve to learn that you possess so hard a heart, so malignant a spirit ! We have gloried in your genius, and trusted in your wonderful powers to awaken the wayward, through your brief life sketches, to a sense of wrong-doing. We have honored what we were deceived into believing your delicate and discriminating sense of right and wrong, and although we have detected gall mingled with the rich sap of your beautiful "Leaves," we have forgiven it, hoping that should there breathe a mortal possessed of the faults your sarcasm and satire so clearly and boldly arrayed, his eye might fall upon your grace-ful Leaves, his heart he touched with remorse, and with a tear of regret, and the burning blush of shame upon his cheek, he might re-solve, with a repentant prayer upon his lips, to "go and sin no more." Oh, Fanny Fern, you have perverted the good your covert hints of reform might have accomplished ! The eyrie to which you once soared is deserted, for by the indulgence of a petty, vindictive spirit of re-venge, you have fallen, never to rise again.

Right it may be to employ genius and the rules of art in caricaturing the sins and follies of humanity in a general way ; but what provoca-tion can there be so great that it should induce a woman to exaggerate and lay bare to the public gaze the sins and follies of father, mother, brother or sister ? If indeed it was the fate of Fanny Fern to belong to a family of monsters of cruelty and crime, was it not enough that her spirit, gentle as a dove's, had conceived and sent forth to the guilty gaze of the sinner the touching story of the heart's wrongs, so deli-cately unfolded in "The Widow's Trials," "The Wail of a Broken Heart," "Summer Days," or "The Young Wife's Afflictions"? But must these sketches be copied almost literally into "Ruth Hall," that the public shall know to whom they apply ? If true, they must already have left their impressions where it was intended they should be felt.

The wicked cause of little Daisy's loss, for instance, could scarcely read the recital of that death-scene and parent's agony, without a tear of repentance. The haggish, stony-hearted grandmother, who shook so roughly the innocent little Katy for stopping her ears that she might not listen to abuse heaped upon her angelic mother's head, could not be expected to pass many peaceful days or nights after perusing the account of the childish misery and mother's grief; and oh! could that vile man that feasted his friends upon the fat of the land, withstand that beseeching, imploring appeal of little Nettie's, "Please, mother, can I have a little more supper?"

Sure it is, if before the publication of "Ruth Hall," the public had suspected that Fanny Fern might be the victim of so many bitter heart-pangs, how much more would they have sympathized with her that she did not, in the Christian tenderness of her beautiful nature, directly draw down public opprobrium upon those who are near and who should be dear to her! The family circle has always been considered as sacred—its sorrows and joys, its errors and sins. The child even who has wept in secret over the shortcomings of its members, has until now ever been found ready to shield the erring parent or brother from the censure and scorn of the world—ever ready to palliate and excuse the grossest faults. How could we regard it in any other light than melancholy and reprehensible, if one of a family band—and that one a daughter and sister—should draw the veil and disclose the secrets of the domestic circle—should hold each thoughtless act of a brother or hasty speech of a mother in a false light—should exaggerate them and lure the easily prejudiced on to crush forever all of truth and holiness that might remain to redeem the wrong? If a father's sinful heart has not descended to the child, how could the undefiled nature of the latter brook to see his silver hairs going down to his grave in disgrace, pointed at with the finger of scorn and hatred? Such an act would be most unnatural, and a shocking evidence of a spirit not purified by suffering nor chastened by sorrow. And yet the hitherto much admired Fanny Fern, at the time when she would prove herself a bright example of Christian fortitude and patience, has violated the sanctity of the fireside and shown herself to be a lamentable example of malicious spite unprecedented in the literary annals of the world. The course of revengeful triumph which she has pursued, taints her name forever in the opinion of the noble-hearted women of our country. Is this example of hers worthy of a true mother? Can it be possible that one, who has taken upon herself the holy responsibility of rearing daughters to be brilliant ornaments of society and pure children of God, can thus influence their youthful minds by teachings of hatred and bitter revenge?

The course of Fanny Fern, even under the supposition that her lot may have been uncommonly and unnaturally hard, should be deprecated, and the corrupt principles of her example, even supposing her story to be true, should be denounced.

But what ought we to say—are there expressions severe enough to condemn her, should we find her book a tissue of slanderous fabrications? What are the inferences to be drawn from it? Its general aim seems to be the glorification of herself and the utter damnation of every one else connected with her either by the ties of kindred or the bond of acquaintanceship; and however much we may weep and smile by turns at the flashes of genius and play of wit and talent in the book, we cannot fail to note its inconsistencies, and tremble for the injurious effects of its circulation among the thoughtless and highly imaginative. Is it not barefaced effrontery in an authoress, to tell us, almost in so many words, that she is a saint immaculate, while at the same time he to whom she owed her being, every brother and sister, almost every acquaintance with whom she was at any time of her life brought into close contact, were destitute of all good? Whence, then, did she receive her remarkable traits of character? Can pure water spring from poisoned fountains? But nay, she goes further. As though this were not enough, she must assert that, while her husband was next to immaculate, *his* parents and friends, also, were equally bad with her own. Can it be that she is so foolish as to think for a moment that the public will believe this impossible condition of affairs— this wholesale iniquity everywhere except with herself, husband and children? We admit freely, that it is rarely that the utmost harmony exists in large families. Nor is it reasonable to consider the family of Fanny Fern as excepted from the general rule. But it is a little too much for us to be called upon to credit, that the father, the brother, and the acquaintances of such an earnest, high-minded, gentle, beautiful creature as Ruth Hall is represented to be, ever turned a totally deaf ear to her necessities, or seized every opportunity they could, without a single motive, to insult and crush her. It is a libel upon the denizens of the Athens of America—that city where talent always finds hosts of liberal friends rushing to its side and proud to render assistance—it is a libel upon Boston to assert that a delicate woman, endowed with the loveliest traits of character and with very wonderful mental powers, was left in neglect and hunger. We do not believe in the desertion of friends without a cause.

But even in our limited experience, we have met individuals who are ever dissatisfied and jealous; who are unreasonable in their demands; who are willingly self-martyrs, and whose oblique and unfortunate and disagreeable disposition it is to consider themselves the best abused in the world. If the father (whose circumstances are none of the best) does the little that is in his power—if the brother, whose pecuniary circumstances are equally unfortunate, may seem to be unreasonably neglectful, does it comport with the character of a meek, pure, gentle, beautiful daughter and sister, such as Ruth Hall is described, to come out and most venomously hold her nearest up to the scorn of the world. Now which are we to consider as the true character—that *described* in the book, the pure and faultless—or that to be *implied from* the book, the bitter, the sarcastic, the vain, the self-flattering, the over sensitive and exacting, the spirit that will, for the gratification of gnawing revenge, tear aside the sacred veil of the family circle? We cannot but regard "Ruth Hall" as a fiction sprung from a malignant heart, and intended by its artful mixture of fact, of exaggeration and untruth, to convey an erroneous general impression concerning the faults and shortcomings of those who are near, and who, notwithstanding all that may have *really* taken place, should be dear.   And we cannot but consider the book as sufficient to condemn Fanny Fern forever in the opinion of every true mother, sister and daughter.

Had the authoress remained in the high position she had gained through her first productions by a true and noble use of her powers, we should gladly have joined in her exultation and honest pride, and with enthusiasm have cried, "Brava, brava, Fanny Fern!" for to few have honor and praise been so soon awarded.   Few ladies can boast of receiving pecuniary remuneration for contributions to the press at the commencement of a literary career; and many a good writer has been grateful for a mere hearing, until reputation has been established.   But now we turn from "Fern Leaves" with abhorrence. The spirit that conceived the fiction, "Ruth Hall," has blasted them, and dry and perfumeless they remain forever.

HOME LYRICS: THE HILLS OF CONTRA COSTA.

BY CAXTON.

THE Hills of Contra Costa,
　How gloriously they rise,
Swelling proudly from the waters,
　Till they mingle with the skies!

Ofttimes whilst Winter hovers
　Over Yerba Buena's hight,
In morning's beams they glisten,
　Arrayed in spotless white.

Sometimes, in cloudy grandeur,
　They veil their summit's blue,
And black with boding tempests
　They frown upon the view:

At others, robed in emerald,
　Their garments flowing free,
They smile in peace, and beauty,
　As smiles a summer sea!

But most I love to view them,
　When the sun is in the west,
Whilst all his radiant glories
　Seem to settle on their breast.

He stains their peaks with crimson,
　And paints their rugged side
With the gay and transient blushes
　Of a young and blooming bride!

Or else with brush alluring,
　Streaks their jagged bosoms old
With a thousand seams of silver,
　And a thousand veins of gold!

Whilst peeping o'er their summits,
　Behold Diab'lo's eye
Flashing back the beams of sunset
　Like a diamond in the sky.

Ah, then I'd be an angel!
　That on the evening air
I might spread my snowy pinions
　And dye their plumage there!

NEWS SUMMARY.

MONTHLY SUMMARY OF EVENTS.

"With news the time's in labor and brings forth
Each minute some."

March 12. The semi-annual message of the Mayor, showing the condition of the affairs of the city, was presented to the Common Council. It stated the total amounts of warrants drawn upon the various department funds, from the 1st July, 1854, to the 1st March, 1855, to be $1,191,583 83. The actual expenses of the present City Government from October 1st to the date of its organization, to the 1st March, 1855, $360,273 00. The total amount of the liabilities of the city, exclusive of debts, contracted prior to May 1st, 1851, $1,959,238 45. The expenses for the remainder of the Fiscal Year were estimated at $266,567 92. The total amount of the receipts of the city from the 1st July, 1854, to the 1st March, 1855, were $1,343,433 18, and the disbursements during the same period, $1,401,-458 96, the above receipts being in such a form that only $501,088 50 were actually available, leaving a balance against the city of $842,344 58—to use the Mayor's own words, "a most unsatisfactory condition of affairs."

March 13. An adjourned meeting of the depositors and creditors of Wright's Bank was held, when the propositions made at the previous meeting were adopted. . . . News was received of the wreck of the Steamship Major Tompkins on the 10th February, at the mouth of Victoria Harbor. She was engaged in the Puget Sound trade.

March 14. The case of J. R. Robinson, charged with illegally disposing of the funds and assets of the Savings Bank, with intent to defraud his creditors, after a slight examination before the Recorder, was sent up to the Grand Jury. The bail of defendant was fixed at $4,000. . . . A suit was commenced in the Twelfth District Court against T. W. Park and F. Billings, on the complaint of A. A. Cohen, Receiver, that the former had extorted a fee of $10,000 from Adams & Co. on the evening previous to the suspension of that House. The matter caused a good deal of discussion, and led to the publication of several Cards upon the subject in the newspapers by the parties. . . . J. Hubert Sanders, a broker and lawyer, was arrested on a charge of forgery. He gave bonds in the sum of $10,000, and managed to make his escape from the city during the evening. He had manufactured or forged a number of mortgages, by which he had defrauded a number of Frenchmen of a large amount of money.

March 15. A Mr. Atkinson brought reports from the Kern River Mines declaring them to be a humbug. . . . The celebrated case of Hamilton Bowie, charged with malfeasance in office as City Treasurer, was brought to an end in the Court of Sessions, the jury bringing a verdict of "Not Guilty."

March 16. David B. Ackey, convicted of assault with a deadly weapon upon Judge McCabe, and sentenced to one year's imprisonment, was pardoned by the Governor. . . . The P. M. S. S. J. L. Stephens arrived and brought news that Messrs. Page & Bacon of St. Louis had resumed payment on the 15th February.

. . . The $8,000 stolen from Mr. Hagan, while on his passage to Sacramento in the steamer New World, were recovered by officer Gilchrist of that city. It was found stuffed away in a stove of a room in Sackett's building; the occupants, James McLane and C. T. Taylor, were arrested on suspicion.

March 17. St. Patrick's Day was celebrated by the Irishmen by a grand procession, a dinner and a ball. . . . In the case of Rodman Backus, convicted of manslaughter, the motion for a new trial was denied by Judge Lake, and the criminal was sentenced to pay a fine of $100 and suffer three years' imprisonment. A stay of execution was, however, granted. . . . News was received that the Bark America, with Meiggs and family, had arrived on the 12th Jan. at Talcahuana, and that the latter had taken up their residence in Concepcion. . . . Further accounts received from Kern River Mines declaring them not a humbug to those who chose to work.

March 18. The police expedition sent to capture Sanders, having proceeded as far as Monterey, returned without having been able to gain any intelligence of the fugitive. . . . A fruit vender named Antonio was stabbed by a newsboy on the corner of East and Jackson Streets.

March 19. Chas. D. Cushman was elected Assistant Alderman of the Sixth Ward.

March 22. Capt. T. B. Cropper, late commander of the Nicaragua Company's S. S. Cortes, died after a lingering illness of about three months. . . . Mr. Julius Levy, of the firm of St. Losky, Levy & Co., was arrested on charge of smuggling a quantity of cigars through the Custom House. . . . Mr. Cornwall, the Secretary of the Senate, was expelled, and Mr. Charles Dickinson elected in his place.

March 23. The remains of Capt. Cropper were attended to the grave with Masonic honors. . . . Two frame buildings on Sacramento Wharf, between Drum and East Streets, were precipitated into the Bay in consequence of the piles upon which they were erected having been destroyed by the worms.

March 26. The pavement on Kearny Street, between Clay and Washington, was completed.

March 28. The P. M. S. S. Golden Age arrived, bringing among the passengers Mr. W. H. Aspinwall, Senator Gwin and the Hon. M. S. Latham. She also brought news of the appointment of M. H. McAllister, Esq., to be U. S. Circuit Judge for Oregon and California; also of the confirmation by the U. S. Supreme Court of J. C. Fremont's celebrated claim to the Mariposas; also of that of A. A. Ritchie to the Suisun Rancho.

March 29. A letter purporting to be from Henry Meiggs, dated at Talcahuana, was published in the *Herald*. It denied the charges that had been made against him—threatened certain disclosures, and promised a return to San Francisco. . . . The House of Messrs. Page, Bacon & Co. resumed payment. . . . A man named Richard Yates committed suicide by shooting himself through the head with a pistol. The fatal act was supposed to have been caused by the news of domestic troubles at home. . . . The large jobbing house of Sherry, Janes & McCrea, failed for about $100,000. . . . A large meeting of the citizens was held at the Merchant's Exchange to express their feelings with regard to the Bill for the funding of the City Debt pending in the Legislature. A committee was appointed to draft resolutions. The general feeling was in favor of funding the debt at 5 per cent.

March 30. At an adjourned meeting of citizens at the Merchants' Exchange, the committee previously appointed reported a series of resolutions, the principal of which was, "That the legal and equitable indebtedness of the city should be funded at a rate of interest not exceeding eight per cent. per annum, and that the Legislature should appoint three commissioners of the highest character, whose duty should be to investigate all evidences submitted to them, and without whose approval no claim should be funded." This resolution, after being amended so as to read at five per cent. interest, was adopted. The question whether Street Assessment Warrants should be funded was put to vote and lost.

March 31. The Grand Jury, by their foreman, Lucien Herrman, Esq., for the February term, made their report to the Court of Sessions. They praised the general organization and discipline of the School Department, but advised the erection of other and suitable School Houses at the Mission, Rincon Point, and for Bush and Washington Street schools; also, an additional building for the accommodation of the colored population—recommended that the County Jail should be enlarged, and means taken for its proper ventilation and purification—suggested that Backus was given too much liberty for one confined on so serious a charge, in being allowed the freedom of the grounds within the inclosure—praised the condition of the City Prison, but censured the construction and arrangement of the out-houses, &c.,—questioned the right of Policemen to release any prisoner upon their own authority —directed attention to that class of nuisances called Sailor Boarding-Houses—presented W. H. Mathews, late City Tax Collector, for illegally and improperly collecting taxes; also, George Ensign, clerk of Street Commissioner, for receiving $100, to be used in influencing the vote of a certain Alderman in passing a Street bill—questioned the right of the City Controller to charge a commission for subdividing warrants issued on bills passed by the Common Council—hinted at the numerous reports about the malfeasance, corruption and dishonesty of the City officials, but declared that they were unable to arrive at results sufficiently clear to authorize them to frame indictments—lamented the present financial condition of the City, and lastly recommended, with a view to save expense, that the City and County offices be consolidated. In the matter of Adams & Co., Judge Lake suggested that there should be three Assignees elected, whose election should be dependent upon the majority of amounts, and appointed three referees to register the votes and amounts, and report accordingly. The Grand Jury indicted Charley Ah You, Chief of the Thung Shun Tung Company, for assembling parties of armed men for the purpose of disturbing the peace, and presented Aldermen Hyde, Van Bokkelen and Buckingham, and Assistant Aldermen Wilde, on a charge of malfeasance in office; they also indicted Assistant Alderman Merrill on a similar charge.

April 1. A man named Daniel O'Connor committed suicide—as supposed, on account of pecuniary embarrassment. . . . The whaling bark R. Adams arrived, after an absence of six months, bringing 6,000 gallons Sperm Oil, and 1,500 gallons Black Fish Oil.

April 2. The contract to take charge of the patients remaining in the State Marine Hospital, was awarded to Dr. Gibbons, at $5,000. . . . The second distribution of the California Art-Union took place at the Metropolitan Theater. The first prize was held by Mr. B. C. Horn, of the firm of B. C. & T. L. Horn, and drew an ingot valued at $5,000. The drawing was made by two little girls, and the whole affair was conducted to the satisfaction of every one. . . . J. T. Haus was declared elected Justice of the Peace for the Fifth Township. . . . The City election of Sacramento resulted in favor of the Know-Nothings, J. S. English being elected Mayor.

April 3. Madame Anna Bishop, assisted by a number of distinguished artists, gave the first of a series of musical performances at Musical Hall; it consisted of Haydn's celebrated Oratorio of the Creation.

April 4. Antoine Rosentiel, an old member of Col. Stevenson's regiment, who had for some time been suffering with consumption, suddenly fell dead on Bush Street.

April 5. The Supreme Court decided against the City in the case of the City *vs.* Kelsey Hazen, and, by such decision, declared that the sale of City Slip property in December, 1853, was null, because the ordinance authorizing it was not legally passed, it having received only four votes instead of five, the majority required by the Charter, and consequently, the title to the City Slip property not having passed by such sale, it still remained in the City. The effect of this decision was, that the entire Slip property was immediately covered by attachments, issued in favor of those who had claims against the City.

April 6. Good Friday: the Legislature adjourned out of respect to the day. The city papers on this and preceding days, contained various communications and statements, to the effect that the Zamorano documents, upon which the title of the City as a Pueblo chiefly rested, was a forgery, which caused much excitement in the community. . . . A great running match came off on the Sutter Race Course, near Sacramento, two mile heats, best three in five, for a stake of $10,000, and a purse of $1,000, between Attila and Wake-up-Jake, which was won by the latter.

April 7. The Special Committee appointed to investigate the charges of malfeasance against Assistant Aldermen Merrill and Wilde, reported a resolution requesting the accused to vacate their seats until the charges were fully investigated. . . . Mr. Ah The and Miss Sag Sung were united in the bonds of matrimony by Justice

O. Bailey. This is believed to have been the first civil Chinese marriage in California.
. . . The bill authorizing John A. Clark to sign the Records of San Francisco
County left unsigned by F. B. Russum, was passed by the Senate, and became a
law. . . . By a statement in the *Herald*, it appeared that the total amount of coinage of the U. S. Branch Mint at San Francisco for the period extending from April
3, 1854, to March 31, 1855, was—gold coinage, $7,615,307 00; silver, 45,400 00;
bars, $6,434,065 06; total $14,094,672 06. . . . The first number of the *Fireman's
Journal*, edited by Marcus D. Boruck, made its appearance.

April 9. In the Fourth District Court the bonds of the assignees of Adams &
Co. were fixed at $1,000,000, and of I. C. Woods, an insolvent debtor, at $250,000.

April 10. A desperate affray occurred among some "long-shore" men at a
sailor boarding-house on Jackson Street, in which a man named Ponsford received
several stabs which were thought mortal.

April 13. The P. M. S. S. Golden Gate arrived, bringing news that Congress
had authorized the transportation of the mails overland from Independence to San
Francisco by way of the Huerfano, Little Salt Lake and Stockton.

April 17. The claim of C. M. Weber to eleven square leagues of land in San
Joaquin County, called Campo Francia, and including the city of Stockton, was
confirmed by the U. S. Land Commissioners; also that of Joaquin Ysidra Castro
for San Pablo, four square miles in Contra Costa County.

April 18. A statement was published in the *Herald* that the notorious forger,
J. G. Hubert Sanders, left this city in the ship Elvira Harbeck, which sailed for
China *via* Honolulu.

April 20. An affray occurred on Clay Street between two Germans named
Albert Hoepkin and Rudolph Schandorf, in which the latter was mortally wounded.

April 21. In the U. S. District Court a warrant was issued for the apprehension
and recapture of a colored boy named George, the property of Jesse C. Cooper, of
Tennessee, who arrived in this country in 1849, under the Fugitive Slave Law.
. . . The Senate passed the Bill appropriating $100,000 for the construction of a
wagon road from Sacramento to the Eastern boundary of the State, by way of
Johnson's Cut-off.

April 23. A young man named Theodore Bahnsen, of the firm of Correa &
Bahnsen, committed suicide in Yerba Buena Cemetery. He was a native of
Denmark, arrived here in 1850, and was supposed to have been driven to the melancholy act by pecuniary embarrassment. . . . The San Francisco Blues and California Guards left in the Wilson G. Hunt on a pleasure excursion to Sacramento.

April 24. The body of Leslie Steen, whose mysterious disappearance on the
night of the 13th ult. gave rise to suspicions of foul play, was found floating in the
water under Pacific Street Wharf by a boatman named Palmer. A money-belt
containing about $3,000 was found secured around the body, and as no indications
were noted that warranted the supposition that the unfortunate man came to his
death by foul means, the Coroner's Jury returned a verdict of accidental drowning.
. . . Joaquin's head was seized by virtue of an attachment and taken to the Sheriff's office to satisfy a judgment for debt. . . . Six claims of José Y. Limantour to
tracts of land in various parts of the State, amounting in all to 119 square leagues
and 400 varas, were rejected by the U. S. Land Commissioners. . . . The Nicaragua S. S. Sierra Nevada, for San Juan del Sur left, carrying treasure to the value
of $317,937 50.

April 25. The clipper ship Neptune's Car arrived, 97 days from New York.

April 26. The Bill of Mr. Hawks to consolidate the Government of the City
and County of San Francisco, passed the Senate.

April 27. The new steamboat Surprise made a pleasure excursion to Vallejo
and Mare Island. . . . A man named Geo. Shropsline was arrested, charged with
obtaining a number of Adams & Co's Certificates from persons in Stockton on the
pretence that he could get them cashed at forty cents discount. . . . A son of
Capt. Harlowe, of the clipper ship Telegraph, fell from the mizzen-top and received
injuries which were supposed to be fatal.

April 28. Mr. Johnston's Bill providing a new charter for the City of San Francisco, passed the Senate, the section relating to the sale of city property being
stricken out. . . . The opera of "La Dame Blanche" was presented at the Metropolitan Theater, on which occasion a French Prima Donna, made her first appear-

ance. . . . A yacht-race came off between the Mischief, Eclipse and Flying Cloud, which was won by the latter. . . . A new propeller, named Martin White, intended for the coast trade, arrived in one hundred and thirty-eight days from Philadelphia.

May 1. The P. M. S. S. Sonora arrived, bringing news of the failure of the House of Page & Bacon, of St. Louis. Shortly after the receipt of this intelligence, attachments were issued against the House of Page, Bacon & Co. of this city to the amount of $98,769 46. . . . The P. M. S. S. Golden Gate left for Panama, carrying treasure to the value of $1,494,361 56. . . . An eclipse of the moon took place, commencing at 6 o'clock and 47 minutes, and ending at 47 minutes past 9 o'clock.

May 2. Shakespeare's comedy of "Much Ado About Nothing," was brought out at the Metropolitan, Mrs. Sinclair appearing as Beatrice, and Mr. Edwin Booth as Benedict. . . . In consequence of the disastrous news received from the East, a run was made upon the House of Messrs. Page, Bacon & Co. of this city. All the money at the time in its vaults, amounting to $317,000, was paid out to the depositors and those who had procured attachments. The House then confessed judgment for the sum of $400,000 in favor of the guarantors of time certificates issued after its first suspension, and its doors were closed. By a statement published in the *Herald*, it appeared that the total amount of the liabilities of the House was $620,169 58, and of attachments issued against it, $220,149 58, of which $93,947 70 were satisfied. . . . A preliminary meeting of gentlemen was held at the St. Nicholas Hotel for the purpose of organizing a Jockey Club.

May 3. The Opera of "I Lombardi" was to have been performed at the Metropolitan; but in consequence of a misunderstanding, the Italian Company refused to perform, and the comedy of "Much Ado About Nothing" was substituted in its place.

May 4. The Senate passed the Act to fund the Floating Debt of the city of San Francisco. . . . The brig Vesta left for Realejo, containing Col. Walker and fifty-six men, composing the Walker Nicaragua Expedition. . . . A fire broke out in a frame building situated on the east side of Montgomery, between Pine and Bush Streets, but was extinguished before it had caused much damage.

May 5. Mrs. James Stark took a benefit at the Metropolitan Theater, on which occasion "Richelieu" and "The Mountaineers" were performed. . . . The Senate passed "An Act to legalize the assessments of the City and County of San Francisco for the years 1854 and 1855."

May 6. The great Will case of Peralta *vs.* Peralta was decided by Judge Hester of the District Court of Santa Clara County. The effect of this decision is to set aside the Will of Peralta and give to his five daughters a *pro rata* proportion of the vast estate across the Bay, left to his four sons exclusively. . . . The annual German Spring Festival of *Mai Fest* commenced at Russ' Garden. . . . The Governor approved the Act to reincorporate the City of San Francisco. . . . The discussion of the Opera question between Mrs. Sinclair and Madame Thorn, called forth a statement from Mr. Blossom, treasurer of the Metropolitan, by which it appeared that the production of the operas by the Barili troupe had caused the management a loss of $9,977.

May 8. Both Houses of the Legislature adjourned. The amount of appropriations during the session had been $1,144,411 17. . . . A woman named Riley, who had been arrested for larceny, died at the Station House after giving birth to a child.

May 10. The sale of real estate for State and County Taxes, T. J. Poulterer, auctioneer, commenced before the City Hall.

May 11. The steamboat New World, while on her trip to Sacramento, and when about twenty-five miles from that place, was disabled by breaking her walking-beam, which fell, damaging the saloon, upper and cabin decks. She was towed into Sacramento by the Queen City. . . . A fire broke out in a tenement on Broadway, near Montgomery Street, which caused a damage to the building of about $300. . . . Several thousand dozens of shovels, purchased at an average price of $3 per dozen, were shipped on board the clipper ship Charmer, destined for the Crimea, to be used on the works of the railroad.

May 13. The schooner W. A. Tarlton arrived from the Gallapagos Islands, having on board 580 terrapins, the largest quantity ever brought to this port at one time. . . . Four prisoners, employed in the brickyard at Corte Madeira, broke away from their guard. Three managed to escape; the other was shot down. The former, however, afterwards returned and gave themselves up.

May 14. The Rousset Sisters reappeared at the Metropolitan after a long absence in the States, on which occasion Mr. Corby, a comic dancer of some little merit made his first appearance before a California audience. . . . The ship Sunny South cleared for China, having on board the dead bodies of seventy Chinamen.

May 15. The claim of J. A. Sutter to thirty-three square leagues of land, situated on the banks of the Sacramento, American and Feather Rivers, and including the City of Sacramento, was confirmed by the U. S. Land Commissioners. . . . The Board of Aldermen passed a resolution suspending Assistant Alderman J. Wilde from exercising the duties of his office, until the charges made against him are examined into and reported upon by the Grand Jury. . . . An appropriation of $130,000 was made for the Fire Department. . . . The steamboat Senator, when about four miles from the city, on her way to Sacramento, with a large quantity of freight and a number of passengers, was found to be leaking badly. She put back to the wharf; her passengers and freight were landed, and shortly afterwards she sunk.

May 16. The Senator was raised by means of a steam pump. She was found to have received but slight damage, and can soon be made to resume her place on the line. . . . The clipper ship Herald of the Morning arrived, after a passage of ninety-nine days and twelve hours. . . . The P. M. S. S. John L. Stephens arrived, bringing news of the loss of the steamer Golden Age, at the north-west point ot Ricaron Island, about 217 miles from Panama. The passengers and treasure were, however, all saved, many of the former returning on the Stephens to this port. . . . The P. M. S. S. Sonora left for Panama, carrying treasure to the value of $692,850, and the Nicaragua S. S. Uncle Sam for San Juan, with treasure to the value ot $523,472. . . . One hundred and fifty U. S. Dragoons arrived in the J. L. Stephens.

May 17. The election of delegates to the Democratic Nominating Convention took place. . . . In the case of Painter *vs.* Adams & Co., A. A. Cohen, Esq., Receiver of Adams & Co., was arrested for contempt, in refusing to inform the Superior Court regarding the assets and credits or other personal property belonging to Adams & Co. on the 23d February. He was afterwards discharged on a writ ot *habeas corpus* issued from the Fourth District Court.

May 18. A fire broke out in the large block of frame buildings bounded by Saaramento, Davis, Commercial and Front Streets, and consumed property to the value of $50,000.

May 21. By a statement of the County Treasurer, it appeared that the total amount of disbursements of the County for the period extending from June 30, 1855, to May 21, 1855, was $437,147 27, and of receipts, $377,103 47. . . . On this and the preceding days the Democratic Convention met to nominate candidates for the different municipal offices.

May 22. The U. S. Land Commissioners confirmed the claim of Gen. M. G. Vallejo to the place called Petaluma, containing fifteen square leagues; and to that called Soscol, containing eleven square leagues, including the city of Vallejo; also the claim of Joel S. Polack to the Island of Yerba Buena; also of Charles Covilland for part of eleven leagues first granted to John A. Sutter, located on the Feather River. . . . The Board of Supervisors passed an ordinance for the purchase at $24,000 of a fifty vara lot and brick building on Greenwich Street, near Jones, to be used as a Hospital for the Indigent Sick of the city and county.

May 23. The bark Yankee arrived from the Sandwich Islands, bringing news that Sanders, the notorious forger, had stopped at Honolulu on his way to China, per ship Elvira Harbeck. He had assumed the name of Albert, and did not make himself known to any of the Americans on the Island. . . . The Union Hotel property, corner of Merchant and Kearny streets, was sold under a sheriff's execution, and purchased by Abel Guy for $60,000.

May 24. A meeting of the holders of Page, Bacon & Co.'s Time Certificates was held in the Rotunda of the Merchants' Exchange. A report of the condition of the affairs of the House was made, and the meeting addressed by Messrs. Parrot, Naglee and others of the bondsmen, but nothing encouraging to the depositors was elicited.

EDITOR'S TABLE.

MUSICAL AND THEATRICAL.

FROM APRIL 23, TO MAY 27.—The month just closed has not been very prolific in theatrical events. Mr. Neafie has left for the transmontane States; Miss Davenport, Mrs. Estelle Potter and Madam Bishop, with Herr Mengis, have been performing at Sacramento, Stockton and Marysville, while the different towns and cities among the mountains have been visited by a number of traveling companies, prominent among which, were the small vaudeville troupe of Mr. William and Miss Caroline Chapman, Mr. Geo. Chapman's troupe, comprising, among others, the Monplaisirs and Thierry, the Stockton Dramatic Company, Lee & Marshall's Circus, Backus' Minstrels and the Robinson Family. Since our last, too, a new and very pretty little theater has been opened at Weaverville in the north.

At the American, the features of the month have been "Twelfth Night," "As you Like It," "The Comedy of Errors," "The Love Chase," and "Old Heads and Young Hearts." Dr. Spaulding is fast establishing for himself an enviable reputation as an energetic, liberal and successful caterer to the amusement of the public. "Twelfth Night" was well put upon the stage and had a very excellent run. Miss Keene appeared as Viola, Mr. Wheatleigh as Malvolio—so rendering his part as to give it prominence before the others,—Mr. Leman as Sir Toby Belch, Kent as Sir Andrew Ague Cheek, and Mrs. Judah as Maria. "As you Like It" was also well cast, and drew full houses. We are happy to learn that "Midsummer Night's Dream" is soon to be presented at this deservedly popular establishment.

At the Metropolitan, after the close of Mr. Silsbee's Engagement, Mr. Edwin Booth, who had then recently returned from Australia, made his appearance in the character of Richard III. We are very fearful that Mr. Booth devotes too little time to study. Mr. Stark has also appeared as Richelieu once during the month. Nothing further of note has occurred at this theater, except a short engagement of the Rousset Sisters, who presented "Sathaniel" and "La Sylphide" to the public, and were greeted with full and fashionable audiences. In our issue of a year ago last March, we spoke somewhat at length of the Roussets and Monplaisirs, instituting a comparison between the two troupes. It is therefore unnecessary for us to enter into an examination of their respective merits here, since our remarks would be but a repetition of what we have said before.

The Union Theater has undergone still another transformation and change of name, having recently become "The Italian Opera House." "I Lombardi" and

"Lucia" have been presented to good houses. We sincerely trust sufficient encouragement will be extended to the troupe to warrant the production of several operas never before presented in San Francisco.

GOSSIP WITH READERS AND CORRESPONDENTS.

A FRIEND informed us of an occurrence a day or two ago, which, as it is as characteristic of California as anything we have heard for a long time, we hold it meet that it should be set down here. It seems that some three years since, Mr. Moon—Mr. *John* Moon, "Professor," as he is styled on the bills, "Professor of Dexterity and Optical Deceptions, Fellow of the Mystic Lodge of .Arts, London," now one of the "Ethiopian Fakir Troupe" performing at the San Francisco Theater—was exhibiting his art at one of the mining towns of the Interior, to the great amusement or otherwise of the miners thereat and there-around collected. One of Professor Moon's most astonishing "experiments" consisted of holding a watch suspended from a short chain at arm's length, and allowing any one in the pit to pull pistol and "blaze away" at the word "Fire," whereupon the watch would most unconscionably disappear. An individual from "Pike County," who had attended several evenings and witnessed the "experiment," suspected, in the classic language of the times, that there was something of "shenanigan" in it. He thought the probability was that the individual in the pit, who fired the pistol, was invariably an accomplice dressed for the nonce in miner's clothes. And as a true, independent, self-reliant Californian, he thought he would assume the responsibility of testing and adjusting matters for his own satisfaction as well as for the good of the community generally. So on the next evening Mr. Pike was duly present, determined to be in advance in the shooting part of the performance of any other unknown miner. The "Professor" explained the experiment—the accomplice was of course in the pit ready with his pistol loaded with a blank cartridge—the "Fellow of the Mystic Lodge of Arts, London," held the watch out stepped to his position and gave the word "Fire." Pike was on the *qui vive*, pistol in hand and eyes upon his learned friend, the "Professor." As quick as thought he jerked up his pistol, and, at the word "Fire," blazed away, to the utter astonishment, doubtless, of his more tardy neighbor with the blank cartridge. The report had not more than sounded when the distinguished "Professor," "Fellow," etc., etc., etc., commenced a most extraordinary series of capers and shakings of the arm, accompanied by oaths and cries of pain. The audience, considering it all as a part of the performance, were "sufficiently amused," but Mr. Pike, having discovered that he had shot away two of the learned Professor's fingers and a half of his thumb, quietly left for the repose and seclusion of his cabin, voluntarily losing the rest of the performance. Now *could* that have happened anywhere else except in California? - - - THE *Fireman's Journal* is the name of a new aspirant for public patronage. It is issued weekly, and, as its name implies, is devoted to the interests of the firemen of our city and of the State generally. In typographical appearance it will compare favorably with any journal among our exchanges. It is edited with much ability by MR. MARCUS D. BORUCK, a gentleman long and favorably known as connected with the press of California. His sketches and interesting letters to the *Sacramento Union* were for many months a feature of that popular daily. We can only realize the great usefulness of the firemen by looking back to those diastrous days when men could do little else than stand and watch the devouring element, as it swept from one end of the city to the other, devastating the quiet home and the stately warehouse, and scattering the cherished hopes of thousands to the wind; and if there is a class among us who deserve to have their interests attended to and protected by means of a press devoted almost exclusively to them, it is that class which cannot but be regarded as the great Insurance Office of San Francisco. We congratulate the firemen upon this creditable acquisition to the ranks of the press of California. - - - "How often," writes an esteemed contributor, "have the wisest of us found ourselves, at times, in the same category with old Colonel Dyer, of Windham, Conn. He, good, honest soul, made no pretensions to wisdom, or to do more than plow and sow the same land and in the same manner that his father had done before him. Great was his surprise one day when a neighbor offered to purchase and pay the cash for a fifty acre lot that had been covered with a thick growth of white birch from time immemorial. The Colonel was well pleased to close the bargain, wondering what under the sun Mr. Brewster could want with that brushwood lot. Being a man of few words and fewer ideas, he kept his own counsel, well pleased to have so much less fencing to keep in repair around unproductive property. Some months after, the Colonel happened to be riding in the vicinity of his neighbor's purchase, when, to his amazement, he saw that the place had been cleared, plowed and sowed, and now presented as level and as fine a field of grain as any in the country. With a most lugubrious cast of countenance he shook his head emphatically a number of times, mournfully ejaculating, "If I hadn't I wouldn't." - - - It is quite certain that the following has never before appeared. It was brought to mind on reading in the "Editor's Drawer" of the March Number of *Harper's Magazine* two characteristic anecdotes of the great Dr. Mason, as he is there called; so termed, not only in contradistinction to several others of the same name, but as a merited title to one who stood pre-eminent in his time for pulpit eloquence, as well as for a degree of *brusquerie* of speech and manner that was at least spicy. Before the establishment of a Unitarian Society in this country, when the doctrine was little known and less understood, the Doctor was one day waited upon by a clergyman of that faith, bringing letters of introduction from friends in Boston. He was courteously received; and curiosity getting the better for the time of the Doctor's staunch orthodoxy, the new comer was invited to fill the pulpit of the latter on the ensuing Sabbath. Sitting at his side, the uncompromising Doctor listened—in silent rage, we may well imagine—to the new heresy. At the conclusion of the services, when the last words of the closing prayer were pronounced, he arose. His lofty stature looked taller than ever, and, stretching forth his hands in benediction, he invoked the blessing of the Triune God; "And now, to the Father, the Son, and the Holy Ghost, (speaking very slowly and distinctly,) three persons and one God, be ascribed all praise, majesty, and power. We implore that His blessing be amongst and remain with you always—and *blistered be the tongue that refuses assent.*" - - - DIFFERING somewhat is this, which relates to an eminent Divine of later date: On a visit home, during a college vacation, in company with several companions, he found himself one day in the presence of old Deacon Johnson, one of the pillars of Dr. Samuel Nott's church in the town of Franklin, Conn. After divers questions to the young men as to their future plans in life, the worthy Deacon turned to the bright and energetic youth: "What do *you* intend to do, William, when you get through college?" "I shall preach, sir," was the prompt reply. The Deacon, who was accustomed to look on the shady side of religion and to regard it as a Dead-Sea fruit of gloom and dulness, raised his eyes and brows in real or pretended astonishment, and lengthening the lower part of his face proportionably, slowly enunciated, "What! without grace?" "Oh, yes, sir; I shall preach, grace or no grace." That the Divine unction was not withheld, the life and writings of the Rev. Dr. Sprague fully attest, notwithstanding the incredulity of the aged Deacon. - - - "A FRIEND was just in," writes the "Old Man of the Mountains," "admiring a very pretty but small cabinet of minerals I have been collecting; and, speaking of these, reminds me that I must tell you a little mineral story that may answer, perhaps, in want of a better, for your 'Gossip.' A long time ago, when I was more easily struck with a pretty face or sympathizing heart than now, I was led far away from my Ohio home, in company with a lark of a friend, who is now preaching the Gospel at Shasta City. We visited the rural and beautiful little village of Governeur, N. Y.; I, in reality, to see a specimen made up of gelatin, fibrin, muscle, phosphate of lime, etc., with two diamond gems brighter than rubies, and incrusted with silks, satins, etc., etc., that I had met once upon a time. But, ostensibly, our business was to collect a cabinet of minerals. I had been told by a friend of a locality where I might prosecute my search, and with buggy and horse started away. I drove to the top of a hill, and was hammering off some most delicate specimens of mineral, when up came the owner, a smart Yankee, and said, 'What er yeou duin' here? Them's my stun; I want 'um to build stun fences.' There was a perfect mountain of the rock, but I told him if he would set a price, I would pay him for the little that I wanted. He ''lowed they were wuth twenty-five cents.' I put my hand in my pocket and found that, with the exception of a sixpence, I had nothing smaller than a five-dollar piece. I offered him the latter to change, but he had no change. I then offered the sixpence as the best I could do; he ''lowed ef the stuns wasn't wuth more'n that, he wouldn't take nothin'';—then stood a moment and said, 'Look a-here, stranger;' I looked up as his face lighted up with a suffusion of the keenest and brightest rays of intelligence, with a knowing air I could not but admire, 'you're a Doctor, and want them stuns to make pills on; and ef yeou don't pay fur 'um, I'll have the Cunstable after yer in tew hours,' and then left me. I procured what *pill materials* I wanted, and left, too, enjoying a most beautiful drive back to my hotel, amid the twilight of evening." - - - WHAT has become of John Phœnix? Whither has he betaken his genial face? It is many a day that his cordial shake of the hand has "been wanting to us." Ah, John, this will never do. There were several vacant pages awaiting thee in this number. But here is a page that thou shalt fill with one of thy ever welcome epistles. It was written weeks ago, but chide us not for the delay. There is a stack of the like at our left hand a foot high, patiently tarrying till their turn and space comes round. Hear John, and here John is:

"I find the following beautiful lines in an old copy of the *San Diego Herald*, and can but believe you will think them worthy of embalming in *The Pioneer*. They were written by a young gentleman named Harrison, connected with U. S. Coast Survey, and are all poetry, I'll "troth my plight" as C. E. H. would say. Don't you think so yourself? Yours Truly,

JOHN PHŒNIX.

EVENING.

BY MADENA.

THE lurid sun has shot his parting ray,
    And veiled his glories 'neath the western sea;
A mellow warmth yet lingers on the way,
    And twilight shadows tremble o'er the lea.

Now o'er the wave sweet star of evening beams—
And as the day grows dimmer on the sight—
Each lesser jewel through the azure gleams
And soft serenity pervades the night.

And now, from out the bosom of the lake,
Beneath the somber shadow of the oak,
A shrilly voice!—and answer from the brake!—
The distant pool gives back a sullen croak—

And then a chirrup—then a mimic scream—
And then a trilling unison of all—
And then a lull—as though it were a dream—
And then a burst so ringingly and full

Starts on the air, that every grassy blade
Seems to have turned its edge towards the sea,
And caught the zephyr, by its motion made
To tune its silence into minstrelsy!

To such an invocation, sweetly given,
An answer glimmers in the eastern sky,
Where the far hills obscure the verge of heaven,
A phantom twilight trembles fitfully.

Now steadily it comes, and brighter yet,
So chilly, pale, and of so pure a light!
Oh! who had seen it and could e'er forget
The moon's first coming on a Summer's night!

The silver segment, growing on the eye—
The swelling disk—and then the broad, round face,
Comes looming up in solemn majesty.
And now she's ours!—Not yet, for I can trace

The jagged outline of the lonely pine,
Whose leafless branches seem entangling
Their specter fingers in her light divine.
She struggles upward—*yet* the branches cling—

One effort more!—and now she's swinging free!—
Up for the zenith and the milky zone,
Through the blue depths of God's immensity,
Peerless and beautiful, she walks alone!

Yes, we do. ‑ ‑ ‑ COL. H., of Fort Yuma, a well-known Son of Temperance, casually strolled into the precincts of Barry & Patten, a few days since, in company with a friend who did'nt believe in moral suasion and doubted the constitutionality of the Maine Law. The friend, having been accommodated with a glass of lemonade—containing a little Jamacia, Martin, the agreeable Ganymede, turned to the Colonel with the polite inquiry, "And what can I do for you, Sir?" "I'll take a glass of water," replied the Colonel; which he accordingly did, and handing back the empty goblet, said, "Thank you; when you come to Fort Yuma, I'll return the favor in kind." "Ah, Colonel," rejoined Martin, "*Humor* appears to be your *forte* to-night." This wasn't bad, exactly—was it? ‑ ‑ ‑ OLD BARRY says, if the Pope should die, Nicholas would have a successor. Do you wonder why? Because there'd be another old Roman-off. ‑ ‑ ‑ UNDER the title of "Young America," the "City man" of our cotemporary of the *Sun*—who, by the way, has a habit of serving up to the readers of that sprightly little daily a feast of gracefully penned paragraphs—wrote as follows a short time since, viz:—

"'YOUNG AMERICA.'—We saw two young gentlemen in front of the 'What Cheer House,' yesterday, who attracted much notice. One of them, a youth of some '*five summers*,' was smoking a cigar with all the grace of a finished 'exquisite,' when another specimen of Juvenility, probably one year older, issued from a cigar shop with a cigar in *his* hand and swaggering up to the smoker, demanded a light, *a la Mose*, with a tone and gesture that the greatest admirer of Frank Chanfrau could not fail to applaud, had he seen it.

The 'smoker' replied to the demand, 'No *sir e-ee, I v-o-n-t;* der ye tink I'm *g-r-reen*, to spoil *my* Spanish wit your *common* cigar?' And then gracefully withdrawing his cigar, he brushed the ashes off the end of it, and carelessly referred his late colloquist to the keeper of the Bath House for a light, and thither he went and obtained what he wanted. Any cigar vender who would sell to or furnish such children with his wares, ought to be scouted out of the community."

Alas! that this should be scarcely an exaggerated specimen of the condition of affairs too generally prevailing among the juveniles of San Francisco. It may be well enough for California to give the man of twenty-five, in two or three years' time, the experience of the man of thirty elsewhere, and to crown the man of thirty with the knowledge of the man of forty; but is it not disgusting to see some of our "young gentlemen," thirteen, fourteen and fifteen years of age, treading our streets as though each stone were an egg, and playing the gallant so daintily, that one fears lest, should an idea approach within twenty feet of their heads, it would cause them to faint away? Oh how different from the boyhood we remember,—and by no means a score of years ago, either—the boyhood, as it were, of yester-day—the boyhood of kites, and trout-fishing—the boyhood of marbles and rambles in the woods—the boyhood when "One-ery, youry, ickery, *ann;* Phillisy, fallicy, Nicholas, *John,*" resounded at the street corners, whereat a half-dozen or ten youngsters were ranged in row, each awaiting his turn to be "out." Much as we love California we cannot but say, Alas for the scenes where boys were not men! By the way, we remember us of a pair of anecdotes illustrative of the hot-bed precocity of California children, which we had laid away in our Gossip box until a "convenient season" should occur: "Please sir, may I go out?" said a little fairy of five to the teacher of one of our city schools, the other day. "Why, you know it is against the rules to go out in the forenoon, unless you are sick; are you sick Carrie?" said the teacher. "No sir," said Carrie, throwing up her beautiful blue eyes with a languid look, "No sir, not exactly sick, but I *feel rather indisposed!*" ... "Alice," said little Mary the other day, "let us go to the boy's theater to-morrow!" "No," said Alice, "I can't go." "Why," persisted Mary, "why can't you?" "Because," said Alice, "I can't go without having a *contest with my Mother,* and I don't want to do that!" They are not much in themselves, but as they relate what actually happened, they are not without interest in the connection. - - - WAS there ever a more inane attempt at rivalry than Alexander Smith's last effort in a poem written to commemorate the Charge of the Six Hundred at Balaklava? What a contrast to Tennyson's immortal poem!—the one terse, Saxon and to the purpose,—the other long spun out and an evident struggle to carry off the palm; the one strong and original—the other imitative and weak; the one saying *all* in suggestive conciseness—the other striving to say *everything* and suggesting nothing except the better poem which it is endeavoring to excel; the one adding to its author's high fame,—the other detracting from the instable fame (that is to say, if we should not already begin to call it notoriety,) which its author is vainly endeavoring to sustain. Tennyson's poem has been republished again and again, but we cannot let another number pass without gathering it into our pages. O, we wish some one could read it to you as Judge T. did to us this afternoon:—

"Half a league, half a league,
Half a league onward,
All in the valley of Death
  Rode the six hundred.

Into the valley of Death
  Rode the six hundred;
For up came an order which
  Some one had blundered.
'Forward, the Light Brigade!
Take the guns,' Nolan said:
Into the valley of Death
  Rode the six hundred;

'Forward, the Light Brigade!'
No man was there dismayed,
Not though the soldier knew
  Some one had blundered:
Theirs not to make reply,
Theirs not to reason why,
Theirs but to do and die;
Into the valley of Death
  Rode the six hundred.

Cannon to right of them,
Cannon to left of them,
Cannon in front of them

Volleyed and thundered;
Stormed at with shot and shell,
Boldly they rode and well,
Into the jaws of Death,
Into the mouth of Hell
Rode the six hundred.

Flashed all their sabers bare
Flashed all at once in air,
Sab'ring the gunners there,
Charging an army, while
All the world wondered:
Plunged in the battery smoke,
With many a desperate stroke
The Russians' line they broke;
Then they rode back, but not,
Not the six hundred.

Cannon to right of them,
Cannon to left of them,
Cannon behind them
Volleyed and thundered;
Stormed at with shot and shell,
While horse and hero fell,
Those that had fought so well
Came from the jaws of Death,
Back from the mouth of Hell,
All that was left of them,
Left of six hundred.

When can their glory fade?
Oh, the wild charge they made!
All the world wondered.
Honor the charge they made!
Honor the Light Brigade,
Noble six hundred ! "

The man who took that up and cruelly rendered the refrain each time,

"Rode six or eight hundred,"

deserves to be put into the penitentiary. - - - A RICHER specimen of combined and condensed burlesque, sarcasm and humor—a more capital "hit," properly so speaking, than a contribution entitled "Important Literary Correspondence," which appeared in the *Town Talk* about three weeks since, we have not set eyes upon for a long time. A "right rare wag" was its author, and we inscribe his name side by side with that of "our John," the Phœnixian. Albeit the "Important Literary Correspondence" touched us nearly, thereat we could not help but "laugh consumedly," as Clark would say. If there is anything we do like, it is a good joke, neatly executed, even though it be at the expense of Number One. In lieu of a hat—the first and last one we ever wore having been incontinently kicked into the street some six years since—we respectfully hand over our cap to the author. We can forgive everything but the fact that he did n't let us have the first chance at publishing it. But *if* he 'll only send us something half as good for the next number, we will wipe out even that score chalked down against him. - - - WE must take this occasion to kill two birds with one stone by giving some of our friends at least a space for their kind contributions, and at the same time relieving our table of sundry papers that have been staring us in the face for two months back:—"Down on the old plantation," writes an esteemed friend, "a planter and his favorite slave Zip stood upon the piazza of the Mansion House, gazing at the weather. A furious storm of rain was raging, accompanied by thunder and lightning. 'Massa,' said Zip, 'had n't I better go drive in the cattle?' 'Oh no, they'll do well enough; the storm will soon be over, and a little rain wont hurt them any way.' 'But, Massa, dose fine horses under the trees; too bad to leab them out in the rain. I go dribe them in.' 'You need not trouble yourself, Zip; they are all right; we 'll trust them to Providence. But you 'd better come out of the rain yourself.' So saying, his master turned and went into the house. Zip, protesting against such a trustee, and extremely anxious for the fate of the horses, followed his example; but as soon as the storm was over he took a stroll around the farm to estimate the extent of the damages; and there, directly under the trees where they had been standing, he found both the horses dead: they had been struck by lightning. Half in triumph, half in dole, he ran back to the house and exclaimed, 'Dare, Massa, what I tell you?' 'What's the matter, Zip?' 'Did n't I tell you so?' 'Yes, but what's the matter?' 'Dare 's both de horses dead as stones—struck by lightnin'; *you* trust to Providence! you'd better 'a trusted old Zip!' . . . And if one is n't too many for you, here is another: On a dark and stormy night a noble ship, alone upon the trackless waters, was contending fearfully with the elements. The 'old man' had retired to his bunk, leaving strict orders that his slumbers should not be disturbed. The mate paced the quarter deck anxiously; the sky was overcast; the waves dashed mountains high; the wind howled through the cordage, and the vessel, under a heavy press of canvas, strained and labored terribly. He expected to see the topmasts carried away every moment. At last he ran to the companion-way and cried, 'Captain, it's blowing great guns; had n't I better strike the topmasts?' 'No,' answered the drowsy Captain, 'it wont amount to anything; the moon will soon come out and *scoof* everything away.' 'Ay, ay, sir,' and the Mate resumed his watch. Soon the sky cleared up, and the moon came out, but the wind did not abate; indeed, it blew more furiously than ever, and presently crash went every topmast by the board. The Mate ran to the cabin and met the Captain just as he. aroused by the noise, was emerging to see what was the matter. 'It is just as you said,' Captain, the moon *has* come out and *scoofed* away every topmast, and the ship's going to thunder.'"   - - -   IN the following sketchy letter we introduce to our readers a new and welcome correspondent who dwelleth somewhere among the "Hills of Contra Costa." The communication is very good, but it is evident enough our unknown friend can do still better:

GRIZZLY RANCH, Contra Costa County.

Sir:—For some couple of years past, it has been my lot to drop behind the world and into the quiet recesses of the Contra Costa Hills, where, may it please you, I cultivate potatos, pulse and pumpkins during the day—Punch, poetry and philosophy, during the night; the unprofitable results from the said potatos, pumpkins, etc., cause heavy drafts on the beforementioned philosophy, (which have hitherto been honored,) whilst the daily routine is so monstrously prosy, that the natural instinct for society pitches recklessly into poetry, as a tired traveler would into a rocking-chair; but punch, when formed on a proper basis, to wit; genu-*ine* Martel, combines both poetry and philosophy, and in spite of the depression of the Mining, Commercial and Agricultural interests, the rascality of Bankers and the confusion of monetary crises, it still occasionally puts a man, as it did Tom O'Shanter of jolly memory, "O'er all the ills of life victorious." Nevertheless, neither the simple but sordid labor of the agriculturist, the imperturbable calmness of the philosopher, the dreamy fancies of the poet, or the genial imaginings of the punch-bibber have succeeded in stifling the aspirations of an ambitious spirit. Sir, I am determined to be distinguished, and I am now fattening a bull-calf of magnificent proportions, and cultivating the dawning intelligence of a very "smart" pig; both I design for the next cattle show, where I trust that fame and a gold medal awaits me and my pig,—and that calf, pig and pumpkin grower will yet be the subject of a "remarkable" item in *The California Farmer* or *The County Advertiser.*

For me there appear two distinct roads to fame, viz:—the Cattle Show, or Literature—the *California Farmer* or the *Pioneer Magazine.* But here occurs the difficulty—if I go in for the calf and pig, adieu to Literature; and if for Literature, the sooner I make veal of my calf the better. So in the name of the Nine Spinsters of Parnassus, and those "Heathen Goddesses that wore no bodices, but ran stark naked through Greece long ago," let's "slay the fatted calf," or at least ignore its existence, and go pioneering for a while.

To reform and correct erroneous views on questions of absorbing interest to the Age, is the province of the wise and philanthropic. And to be most effective, the correction should be addressed to the fountain head of opinion, where thirsty souls, who are not gifted with bottled up ideas of their own, come to quaff notions of "things in general." Be it mine, Mr. Editor, to convince you, of the groundlessness of your contempt for spiritualism,—of the actual existence of that mysterious communion between dressed and undressed souls, and of the peculiar shrewdness and lucidity exhibited in the latter state.

This evening, happening to be looking over a volume of Berenger, I chanced upon "Le Chant du Cosaque." Apropos to the times, quoth I; I shall try if I can't translate this same song of the Cossack for *The Pioneer.* So getting ink and paper together, I managed to render the first stanza into English thus:—

> " Hark ! hark, my steed ! Come rouse thy speed, to the death paths let us forth.—
> Thou, the Cossack's pride and comrade tried, hark, the tempests of the North !
> Nor silver, nor gold, doth the Cossack hold, but this lance and sword of mine
> Shall win the spoil of city and soil, in the lands beyond the Rhine.
> Then proudly neigh, for our fierce hurrah ! on startled Europe rings,
> And trample down the Miter and Crown, and her peoples and her kings."

I had scarcely concluded this stanza, when a most novel sensation of awe crept over me, and I suddenly became aware that I was in communion with one from the spirit land. I summoned up courage, and straight made the inquiry, " Who and what art thou?" To which my visitor replied, " I'm the spirit of the Cossack of *the West.*" " The Cossack of the West," I rejoined, " Who is he?" " Why, they call him one of the illegitimate offspring of the Spirit of the Times, some do," said he, " And more call him Filibuster—and that sort of thing; but all's one; he's a reg'lar let-her-rip, go-a-head, he *is.*" Just then, recollecting the adjuration of Samuel to Saul, I threw as much solemnity as possible into my voice, and exclaimed—" Cossack, Fillibuster, *Buster,* or whatever thou art, what wantest thou with me?" " Well," returned he, " that's good for your size; you're a writing medium, and I want you to write that there verse jist over agin under my dictation, I'll give you the right version and the true Cossack i-*dee,*—what a precious fool that old Berenger was to go and put such fine language into the mouth of one of them miserable Cossacks of the *East,* that aint no freeman at all and that never had the benefit of common school edication; and you're no better, to be trying to put such stuff into English,— Now go ahead on the right track." Suddenly I felt my right hand and arm impelled by an uncontrollable impulse, and wrote as follows, which is a singularly free (though not very enlightened) rendering of the beforementioned " Chant du Cosaque : "—

> " Git up old hoss, and bear your boss, thro' the tracks of eternal smash,
> Sou'-west we go, and Mexico hears already our rifles crash.
> Not a cent have I, but by and by, I'll fill my pouch, as soon as
> We smoke and laugh *and our cocktails quaff in the Halls* of the Montezumas."

My pen stopped, and the pause that followed was soon broken by my spiritual visitor exclaiming vivaciously, " That's the Chat !" At this moment my mind reverted to another stanza and the process of reducing it to English meter had just commenced in my cranium, when the tormenting spirit again interrupted me with, " Hold hard there, will you? you're going at that cussed nonsense agin, can't you put it down in plain English, as a sensible Cossack ought to talk to his hoss? not inviting him into pillared porches and halls of art, as if the old hoss came all the way from Roosia to look at pictures and marbles and such stuff,—now go ahead agin with the right *Idee.*" And again as an unfortunate medium I wrote as follows:

> " G'in and make your stall, in some big-bug's hall, or the haunts of wealth and ease,
> Or some ancient shrine, of the Aztec line,—or, wherever you ——————."

I could stand it no longer, the style of expression and expletive that I was thus made the medium of conveying, was intolerable to ears polite; so throwing down my pen, throwing my chest out and my person generally back in my chair, I solemnly exclaimed in the deepest barytone I could muster, " Dry up," and immediately after I had the gratification of feeling that the presence and influence of the Cossack of the West had departed from me.

My nerves are shaken, my mind dazed, and my previous theories on spirit manifestation thrown into confusion by this unexpected and extraordinary development; I turned hopefully for renewed strength and inspiration, to my ancient friend *Martel,* (Brand of '47) but alas! he has dried up too. I cannot write any more, I stand up to retire to my couch, but human nature unhappily is weak, and between *two* spirits, (like Jeremy Diddler between two stools,) *I fall to the ground* and remain (till morning)

Thine at full length,
HARD KNOCKS.

N. B. If the editor accepts the foregoing contribution and desires further, he will please note to that effect.

Certainly, my dear sir. Send them along. We know you can do better next time. Only in future missives, *please* don't make any allusion to " spiritualism " again; for if *you* are not sick of the whole thing, there's one at the table that is heartily. - - - ONE of the most popular places of amusement in the city is Frank Wheeler's Gymnasium on Battery Street, near the Oriental. Go there any hour of the day and you shall find a number of intelligent, congenial companions gathered, not only for the re-invigoration of weakened systems, but for hearty, generous rivalry. One month at this institution, and the debilitated will find himself "throwing physic to the dogs." One may admit in casual conversation the beneficial influence of the gymnasium,—in fact, every one must admit it; but no one can have a realizing sense of it without personal experience. The terms are reasonable, the proprietor most obliging and gentlemanly, and we take pleasure in recommending the establishment to our readers. - - - Two months since we published an anecdote in our gossip, in which the name of Blossom was given to the character. We need scarcely say that the individual alluded to was by no means the gentlemanly treasurer of the Metropolitan. It is furthest from our intention to insert anything in these pages which can in any way be construed into a personality. There are certainly influences enough already in California continually tending to mar the amenities of life, to preclude the necessity of our erecting *The Pioneer* into another means to the same end. - - - A DAY or two since we heard a pair of anecdotes of an individual, whom we shall call Tompkins, residing in Charleston, S. C., broadly illustrating the ridiculous position in which what Cicero calls "new men," sometimes unwittingly place themselves. Tompkins was superlatively ignorant; but somehow he had managed, through a run of excellent luck, to amass several hundred thousand dollars. He became of course one of the leading citizens of the place, and was always anxious to see his name in the papers and to be prominent in every public movement. His ignorance did not fail to furnish a constant source of fun to some of the wags of the city, notwithstanding his immense wealth. On the occasion of the death of Calhoun, a meeting of the citizens was called to decide upon the proper means of publicly expressing their sense of bereavement. The matter in discussion for the moment was the style in which the hall, where the eulogy was to be delivered, should be decorated. A proposition was made that the bust of Calhoun be placed upon the platform. After a somewhat lengthy debate, a wag at Tompkins' side suggested to the latter that it was outrageous to do the thing shabbily—that there ought to be some little liberality manifested by the citizens of Charleston. Whereupon Tompkins, prompted by his friend, sprung to his feet and shouted out, "Mr. President; it does not comport with the dignity and enlightenment of this city, the home of the venerated dead, to manifest any illiberality whatever in this affair; I therefore move you, sir, that we have a *full length bust* of Calhoun upon the stage." Tompkins was astounded at the quick responding roar of laughter, and took his seat gesticulating to his neighbors, and urging nevertheless that the thing ought to be done. At the close of the meeting another wag beset the poor fellow, who, urged by the former, arose once more and moved that "the meeting do now adjourn *sine qua non.*" The President, who by the way was a bit of a wag, too, soberly remarked, "Gentlemen, it is moved by Mr. Tompkins that this meeting do now adjourn *sine qua non.*" The vote was put and carried unanimously, amid shouts of laughter and the blank amazement of the millionaire. - - - WE were unexpectedly gladdened a week or so since by a visit from our epistolary friend and co-laborer of the *Sierra Citizen,* Mr. Calvin B. McDonald, and a right genial companion did we find in him; modest and retiring at the first meeting, but, on closer acquaintance, opening up and displaying all the rich qualities of a mind and character with which nature has been by no means a niggard. His stay was short, but it has left a memory lingering in our heart. How natural is the desire to see with one's own eyes the man who has charmed us with his thought. Such a desire felt we to behold the rare spirit who rests quietly in the mountains, abiding his time. Nor were we a whit disappointed. Mr. McDonald is one of the most charming writers in California, and he has given the little hebdomadal, over which he presides, a most enviable position among the papers of the Interior. - - - As many of our readers are doubtless aware, it is the custom for planters at the South to purchase clothing for their slaves by the wholesale; and as, of course, they have not the opportunity to examine closely each article, they are sometimes swindled by a few bad ones being thrown in among the good. An acquaintance of ours tells us that, on one occasion, he had laid in a box of shoes, and distributed the most of them among the negroes. A few days afterwards "old Bob," a favorite servant, found that the shoes that had fallen to his lot were bursting out. So, going to his master, he said, "Massa, where you buy dose shoes?" "I bought them in New Orleans, Bob," responded our friend. "Well, where did de New Orleans people buy 'em?" "They bought them from the people up North—they bought them from the Yankees." "Well, where do de Yankees get 'em?" persisted the negro? "The Yankees?—why they pick them off of trees, Bob." "W-w-well," responded the darkey, holding up his shoes, "I reck'n de Yankee did n't pick dese pair soon enough, massa; I reck'n he waited till—till—*till dey was a little too ripe.*" - - - With this number closes the third volume of our existence. We are not of those who parade our private affairs before the gaze of the public. We have never closed one volume or commenced another with a flourish of trumpets. But it is perhaps time that our friends, who have been kind enough to express some little anxiety for the success of our enterprise, should receive at least an assurance one way or the other from us. It is due to them to say, that at the end of each volume we have found our prospects materially brightened. The increase of our circulation has been steady and healthy. And, so far as our foundation is laid, we can assure them it is solid. When the magazine was first started, it was considered by all connected with it as an experiment, merely. But in the fourth month of its existence, although we found our anticipations that we might be prematurely in the field realized, yet such was the encouragement extended to us, that we determined to bear *The Pioneer* through its darker days, confident that light would in the course of time break upon us. We may safely say we have not been disappointed. Our circulation has more than doubled within the last year; and, although we have received no remuneration, as yet, for the capital expended, *The Pioneer* is safely afloat, and may be regarded as a permanent portion of the press of California.

[END OF VOL. III.]